Italy
FOR
DUMMIES®
3RD EDITION

by Bruce Murphy and
Alessandra de Rosa

WILEY

Wiley Publishing, Inc.

Italy For Dummies,® 3rd Edition
Published by
Wiley Publishing, Inc.
111 River St.
Hoboken, NJ 07030-5774
www.wiley.com

WILEY

About the Authors

Bruce Murphy has lived and worked in New York City, Boston, Chicago, Dublin, Rome, and Sicily. His work has appeared in magazines ranging from *Cruising World* to *Critical Inquiry*. In addition to guidebooks, he has published fiction, poetry, and criticism, most recently the *Encyclopedia of Murder and Mystery* (St. Martin's Press).

Alessandra de Rosa was born in Rome and has lived and worked in Rome, Paris, and New York City. She did her first cross-Europe trip at age 2, from Rome to London by car. She has continued in that line ever since, exploring three out of five continents so far. Her beloved Italy remains her preferred destination and where she lives part of the year.

Dedication

To our editor, Lorraine Festa, who has been absolutely wonderful at helping us make this book the way it is. To Alexis Lipsitz Flippin, who was absolutely wonderful as an editor of the previous edition and who has been of great support throughout. To Bruce's parents, who have been exploring Italy with our books, providing us with an invaluable test. To Alessandra's parents and family, who have welcomed us in their homes and helped us in many ways. And finally, to our 2-year-old son, who has traveled with us and been very patient while we were writing away at our computers instead of reading and playing with him.

Publisher's Acknowledgments

We're proud of this book; please send us your comments through our Dummies online registration form located at www.dummies.com/register/.

Some of the people who helped bring this book to market include the following:

Editorial

Editors: Jennifer Connolly, Lorraine Festa

Copy Editor: Jennifer Connolly

Cartographer: Roberta Stockwell

Editorial Manager: Michelle Hacker

Editorial Supervisor: Carmen Krikorian

Editorial Assistant: Nadine Bell

Senior Photo Editor: Richard Fox

Front Cover Photo: © Dave Bartruff Photography

Back Cover Photo: © Daryl Benson/ Masterfile

Cartoons: Rich Tennant, www.the5thwave.com

Composition

Project Coordinator: Erin Smith

Layout and Graphics: Lauren Goddard, Denny Hager, Joyce Haughey, Melanee Prendergast, Heather Ryan, Julie Trippetti

Proofreaders: David Faust, Leeann Harney, Jessica Kramer, Carl William Pierce, TECHBOOKS Production Services

Indexer: TECHBOOKS Production Services

Publishing and Editorial for Consumer Dummies

Diane Graves Steele, Vice President and Publisher, Consumer Dummies

Joyce Pepple, Acquisitions Director, Consumer Dummies

Kristin A. Cocks, Product Development Director, Consumer Dummies

Michael Spring, Vice President and Publisher, Travel

Brice Gosnell, Associate Publisher, Travel

Kelly Regan, Editorial Director, Travel

Publishing for Technology Dummies

Andy Cummings, Vice President and Publisher, Dummies Technology/General User

Composition Services

Gerry Fahey, Vice President of Production Services

Debbie Stailey, Director of Composition Services

Contents at a Glance

Introduction 1

Part 1: Introducing Italy 7
Chapter 1: Discovering the Best of Italy 9
Chapter 2: Digging Deeper into Italy 14
Chapter 3: Deciding Where and When to Go 26
Chapter 4: Following an Itinerary: Five Great Options 38

Part 11: Planning Your Trip to Italy 45
Chapter 5: Managing Your Money 47
Chapter 6: Getting to Italy 62
Chapter 7: Getting Around Italy 71
Chapter 8: Booking Your Accommodations 79
Chapter 9: Catering to Special Travel Needs
    or Interests 87
Chapter 10: Taking Care of the Remaining Details 92

Part 111: The Eternal City: Rome 103
Chapter 11: Settling into Rome 105
Chapter 12: Exploring Rome 142
Chapter 13: Going Beyond Rome: Two Day Trips 179

Part 1V: Florence and the Best of Tuscany
and Umbria 187
Chapter 14: Florence 189
Chapter 15: Northern Tuscany and the Cinque Terre 238
Chapter 16: Southern Tuscany 272
Chapter 17: Umbria 306

Part V: Venice and the Best
of the Pianura Padana 329
Chapter 18: Venice 331
Chapter 19: Padua, Verona, and Milan 380

Part VI: Naples, Pompeii, and
the Amalfi Coast 413
Chapter 20: Naples 415
Chapter 21: Going Beyond Naples: Three Day Trips 438
Chapter 22: The Amalfi Coast 451

Part VII: Sicily 461

Chapter 23: Palermo 463
Chapter 24: Taormina and the Rest of Sicily 487

Part VIII: The Part of Tens 509

Chapter 25: *Non Capisco:* The Top Ten Expressions
You Need to Know 511
Chapter 26: Ten Great Italian Artists 514

Appendix: Quick Concierge 518

Index 529

Maps at a Glance

Rome Orientation 110
Rome Accommodations and Dining 122
Rome Attractions 144
The Roman Forum and Imperial Forums 151
The Vatican 161
The Vatican Museums 164
Rome and Environs 181
Florence Orientation 193
Florence Accommodations and Dining 200
Florence Attractions 216
The Uffizi Gallery 222
Tuscany and Umbria 240
Lucca 242
Pisa 252
The Cinque Terre 263
The Chianti 275
Siena 284
San Gimignano 301
Perugia 309
Assisi 317
Spoleto 323
Venice Orientation 337
Venice Accommodations and Dining 344
Venice Attractions 360
Piazza San Marco 365
St. Mark's Basilica 368
The Pianura Padana and Milan 381
Padua 384
Verona 393
Milan 402
The Gulf of Naples and Salerno 417
Naples 419
Herculaneum 443
Pompeii 444
Capri 448
The Amalfi Coast 452
Palermo 466
Taormina 489
Agrigento and the Valley of the Temples 508

Table of Contents

Introduction 1

About This Book 1
Conventions Used in This Book 2
Foolish Assumptions 3
How This Book Is Organized 4
   Part I: Introducing Italy 4
   Part II: Planning Your Trip to Italy 4
   Part III: The Eternal City: Rome 4
   Part IV: Florence and the Best of Tuscany
     and Umbria 4
   Part V: Venice and the Best of the Pianura
     Padana 5
   Part VI: Naples, Pompeii, and the
     Amalfi Coast 5
   Part VII: Sicily 5
   Part VIII: The Part of Tens 5
   Quick Concierge 5
Icons Used in This Book 5
Where to Go from Here 6

Part 1: Introducing Italy 7

Chapter 1: Discovering the Best of Italy 9

The Best Museums 9
The Best Churches 10
The Best Ruins 10
The Best Hotels 11
The Best Restaurants 12
The Most Indescribable Experiences 12
The Best Traditional Italian Souvenirs 13

Chapter 2: Digging Deeper into Italy 14

History 101: The Main Events 14
Architecture: From Ruins to Rococo 18
A Taste of Italy: Eating Locally 20
   Tasting Tuscany 21
   Roaming Roman restaurants 22
   Noshing in Naples 22
   Savoring Sicily 22
   Visiting Venetian eateries 23

Background Check: Recommended
Books and Movies 24
True stories 24
Works of fiction 24
The moving image 25

Chapter 3: Deciding Where and When to Go 26

Going Everywhere You Want to Be 26
Roaming Rome 27
Exploring Florence and the best of
Tuscany and Umbria 27
Viewing Venice and the Pianura Padana 28
Visiting Naples, Pompeii, and the
Amalfi Coast 28
Seeing Sicily 29
Scheduling Your Time 29
Revealing the Secrets of the Seasons 30
Spring 31
Summer 32
Fall 32
Winter 33
Perusing a Calendar of Events 33
January 33
February 34
March/April 34
May 35
June 35
July 36
August 36
September 36
October 37
November 37
December 37

Chapter 4: Following an Itinerary: Five Great Options 38

Seeing Italy's Highlights in One Week 38
Touring the Best of Italy in Two Weeks 39
Discovering Italy with Kids 41
Unearthing Italy's Ancient History 42
Drawing from the Art Buff's Tour 42

Part II: Planning Your Trip to Italy 45

Chapter 5: Managing Your Money 47

Planning Your Budget 47
  Transportation 49
  Lodging 50
  Dining 51
  Sightseeing 52
  Shopping 53
  Nightlife 53
Tips on Tipping 53
Cutting Costs — But Not the Fun 54
Handling Money 56
  Making sense of the euro 56
  The euro look 57
  Using ATMs and carrying cash 58
  Charging ahead with credit cards 59
  Toting traveler's checks 59
Taking Taxes into Account 60
Dealing with a Lost or Stolen Wallet 60

Chapter 6: Getting to Italy 62

Flying to Italy 62
  Finding out which airlines fly there 63
  Getting the best deal on your airfare 64
  Cutting ticket costs by using consolidators 64
  Booking your flight online 65
Arriving by Other Means 66
Joining an Escorted Tour 67
  Choosing an escorted tour 67
  Finding an escorted tour to Italy 68
Choosing a Package Tour 69

Chapter 7: Getting Around Italy 71

By Plane 71
By Train 72
By Bus 73
By Ferry 73
By Car 74
  Knowing the rules of the road 74
  Preparing yourself for driving in Italy 75

Chapter 8: Booking Your Accommodations 79

Getting to Know Your Options 79
Finding the Best Room at the Best Rate 82
Finding the best rate 82
Surfing the Web for hotel deals 83
Reserving the best room 85
Finding Alternative Housing,
from Camps to Villas 85

Chapter 9: Catering to Special Travel Needs or Interests 87

Traveling with the Brood: Advice for Families 87
Opting for child care 87
Getting some family-travel advice 88
Making Age Work for You: Tips for Seniors 88
Accessing Italy: Advice for Travelers
with Disabilities 89
Following the Rainbow: Resources for Gay
and Lesbian Travelers 90
Making the Grade: Advice for Student Travels 91

Chapter 10: Taking Care of the Remaining Details 92

Getting a Passport 92
Applying for a U.S. passport 92
Applying for other passports 93
Playing It Safe with Travel and Medical Insurance ...94
Staying Healthy When You Travel 96
Staying Connected by Cellphone or E-mail 97
Using a cellphone outside the U.S. 97
Accessing the Internet away from home 98
Keeping Up with Airline Security 100

Part III: The Eternal City: Rome 103

Chapter 11: Settling into Rome 105

Getting There 105
By air 105
By train 108
By car 108
Orienting Yourself in Rome 109
Introducing the neighborhoods 112
Finding information after you arrive 115
Getting Around Rome 116
By metro (subway) 116
By bus (autobus) 117

On foot 117

By tram 117

By taxi 118

By motor scooter *(motorino)* 119

Staying in Style 119

The top hotels 120

Runner-up accommodations 129

Dining Out 130

Fast Facts: Rome 139

Chapter 12: Exploring Rome 142

Discovering the Top Attractions 143

Finding More Cool Things to See and Do 165

Seeing Rome by Guided Tour 168

Bus tours 168

Walking tours 169

Boat tours 169

Air tours 170

Suggested 1-, 2-, and 3-Day Itineraries 170

Rome in 1 day 170

Rome in 2 days 171

Rome in 3 days 171

Shopping the Local Stores 171

Best shopping areas 172

What to look for and where to find it 172

Living It Up After Dark 175

The performing arts 175

Cafes 176

Jazz and other live music 177

Bars and pubs 177

Dance clubs 178

Gay and lesbian bars 178

Chapter 13: Going Beyond Rome: Two Day Trips 179

Tivoli and Its Trio of Villas 179

Getting there 179

Taking a tour 180

Seeing the sights 180

Dining locally 182

Ostia Antica: Rome's Ancient Seaport 183

Getting there 184

Taking a tour 184

Seeing the sights 184

Dining locally 185

Part IV: Florence and the Best of Tuscany and Umbria 187

Chapter 14: Florence 189

Getting There 190
   By air 190
   By train 191
   By car 191
Orienting Yourself in Florence 192
   Introducing the neighborhoods 192
   Finding information after you arrive 195
Getting Around Florence 195
   On foot 195
   By bus 196
Staying in Style 196
   The top hotels 197
   Runner-up hotels 205
Dining Out 205
Exploring Florence 212
   Discovering the top sights 213
   Finding more cool things to see and do 227
   Seeing Florence by guided tour 228
   Following 1-, 2-, and 3 days itineraries 229
Shopping the Local Stores 230
   Best shopping areas 232
   What to look for and where to find it 232
Living It Up After Dark 233
   The performing arts 234
   Bars and pubs 234
   Discos 235
   Gay and lesbian bars 235
Fast Facts: Florence 235

Chapter 15: Northern Tuscany and the Cinque Terre 238

Lucca 238
   Getting there 239
   Getting around 239
   Spending the night 243
   Dining locally 244
   Exploring Lucca 245
Fast Facts: Lucca 249

Pisa 250
    Getting there 250
    Getting around 251
    Spending the night 251
    Dining locally 254
    Exploring Pisa 256
Fast Facts: Pisa 261
The Cinque Terre 261
    Getting there 262
    Getting around 263
    Spending the night 264
    Dining locally 266
    Exploring the Cinque Terre 268
Fast Facts: The Cinque Terre 271

Chapter 16: Southern Tuscany 272

The Chianti 273
    Getting there 273
    Getting around 273
    Spending the night 274
    Dining locally 277
    Exploring the Chianti 279
Fast Facts: The Chianti 282
Siena 283
    Getting there 283
    Getting around 286
    Spending the night 286
    Dining locally 288
    Exploring Siena 291
    Shopping the local stores 296
Fast Facts: Siena 297
San Gimignano 298
    Getting there 298
    Getting around 299
    Spending the night 299
    Dining locally 300
    Exploring San Gimignano 302
Fast Facts: San Gimignano 304

Chapter 17: Umbria 306

Perugia 307
    Getting there 307
    Getting around 308
    Spending the night 308

Dining locally 309
Exploring Perugia 311
Fast Facts: Perugia 313
Assisi 314
Getting there 314
Getting around 315
Spending the night 315
Dining locally 316
Exploring Assisi 318
Fast Facts: Assisi 321
Spoleto 321
Getting there 322
Getting around 322
Spending the night 322
Dining locally 324
Exploring Spoleto 326
Fast Facts: Spoleto 327

Part V: Venice and the Best of the Pianura Padana 329

Chapter 18: Venice 331

Getting There 332
By air 332
By train 333
By ship 333
By car 334
Orienting Yourself in Venice 334
Introducing the neighborhoods 334
Finding information after you arrive 336
Getting Around Venice 338
On foot 338
By vaporetto 339
By gondola and traghetto 339
By water taxi 340
Staying in Style 341
The top hotels 342
Runner-up accommodations 349
Dining Out 350
Exploring Venice 357
The top attractions 359
More cool things to see and do 370
Guided tours 373
Suggested 1-, 2-, and 3-day itineraries 373

Shopping the Local Stores 374
    Best shopping areas 374
    What to look for and where to find it 375
Living It Up After Dark 376
    The performing arts 377
    Bars and pubs 377
    Cafes 377
Fast Facts: Venice 378

Chapter 19: Padua, Verona, and Milan 380

Padua: Home of Giotto's Fabulous Frescoes 380
    Getting there 382
    Spending the night 382
    Dining locally 383
    Exploring Padua 386
Fast Facts: Padua 390
Verona: City of Juliet and Romeo 391
    Getting there 391
    Spending the night 392
    Dining locally 394
    Exploring Verona 395
Fast Facts: Verona 399
Milan: Italy's Business and Fashion Center 400
    Getting there 400
    Getting around 401
    Spending the night 401
    Dining locally 404
    Exploring Milan 405
    Shopping the local stores 409
    Living it up after dark 409
Fast Facts: Milan 410

Part VI: Naples, Pompeii, and the Amalfi Coast 413

Chapter 20: Naples 415

Getting There 415
    By train 416
    By plane 416
    By ferry 416
    By car 416
Orienting Yourself in Naples 416
    Introducing the neighborhoods 418
    Finding information after you arrive 420

Getting Around Naples 420
   On foot 420
   By subway, bus, funicular, and tram 421
   By taxi 421
Staying in Style 422
Dining Out 424
Exploring Naples 427
   The top attractions 427
   More cool things to see and do 431
   Guided tours 432
   Suggested 1-, 2-, and 3-day itineraries 432
Shopping the Local Stores 433
Living It Up After Dark 434
Fast Facts: Naples 435

Chapter 21: Going Beyond Naples: Three Day Trips 438

Mount Vesuvius 438
   Getting there 439
   Taking a tour 439
   Seeing the sights 440
Pompeii and Herculaneum 440
   Getting there 440
   Taking a tour 441
   Seeing the sights 441
   Dining locally 445
Capri and the Blue Grotto 445
   Getting there 445
   Taking a tour 446
   Seeing the sights 446
   Dining locally 449
   Spending the night 450

Chapter 22: The Amalfi Coast 451

Getting There 451
   By hired car 451
   By bus 452
   By ferry 452
Spending the Night 453
Dining Locally 454
Exploring the Amalfi Coast 456
   The top attractions 456
   More cool things to see and do 458
Fast Facts: The Amalfi Coast 459

Part VII: Sicily *461*

Chapter 23: Palermo **463**

Getting There 464
  By ferry 464
  By air 464
  By train 465
Orienting Yourself in Palermo 465
  Introducing the neighborhoods 465
  Finding information after you arrive 467
  On foot 468
  By bus 468
  By taxi 469
Staying in Style 469
  The top hotels 469
  Runner-up accommodations 471
Dining Out 471
Exploring Palermo 473
  The top attractions 474
  More cool things to see and do 480
  Guided tours 481
Suggested 1-, 2-, and 3-day Itineraries 482
  Palermo in 1 day 482
  Palermo in 2 days 482
  Palermo in 3 days 483
Shopping the Local Stores 483
Living It Up After Dark 484
  The performing arts 484
  Discos, bars, and pubs 484
Fast Facts: Palermo 485

Chapter 24: Taormina and the Rest of Sicily 487

Taormina 488
  Getting there 488
  Spending the night 490
  Dining locally 492
  Exploring Taormina 493
  More cool things to see and do 495
Fast Facts: Taormina 496
Syracuse 496
  Getting there 497
  Spending the night 498
  Dining locally 498
  Exploring Syracuse 499

Fast Facts: Syracuse 502
Agrigento and the Valley of the Temples 503
   Getting there 503
   Taking a tour 504
   Spending the night 504
   Dining locally 505
   Exploring Agrigento 506

Part VIII: The Part of Tens 509

Chapter 25: *Non Capisco:* The Top Ten Expressions You Need to Know 511
   Per Favore 511
   Grazie 511
   Permesso 512
   Scusi 512
   Buon Giorno and Buona Sera 512
   Arrivederci 512
   Dov'è 513
   Quanto Costa? 513
   Che Cos'è? 513
   Non Capisco 513

Chapter 26: Ten Great Italian Artists 514
   Giotto 514
   Donatello 514
   Giovanni Bellini 515
   Leonardo da Vinci 515
   Michelangelo 515
   Rafael 516
   Titian 516
   Tintoretto 516
   Gian Lorenzo Bernini 516
   Caravaggio 517

Appendix: Quick Concierge 518
   Fast Facts..518
   Toll-Free Numbers and Web Sites 522
   Where to Get More Information 525
      Visitor information 525
      Other sources of information 526

Index 529

Introduction

*I*taly is one of the most enticing travel destinations in the world. A trip to Italy sometimes feels like traveling through a museum, and sometimes like living in a dream. What other country has three cities as captivating and culturally important, and yet so utterly different, as Rome, Florence, and Venice? The "problem" with visiting Italy is also its major appeal: It's totally saturated with things to see and do (and eat and drink, too).

Italy has seen big changes in recent years, from the celebration of the Papal Jubilee in 2000 to the economic integration of all of the European Union under the euro, the unit of currency that replaced the old *lire*. With many of its monuments refurbished and museums and attractions revamped, it is now more tourist-friendly than ever. Yet it can still be bewildering. Italy's proud individualism — from the regional level down to the town and the neighborhood — has been a source of endless variety and, historically, sometimes comical confusion (books of "Italian hours" were published in earlier centuries because *time* itself varied from place to place). A language barrier remains, of course — unless you know Italian — though a few key words and phrases will go a long way. (We list some of them throughout this book and especially in Chapter 25.) You'll find the Italian people warm and welcoming and ready to help ease you into *la dolce vita*.

About This Book

With a history stretching from the dawn of time through the Roman Empire, the Middle Ages, the Renaissance, and up to the new Europe, Italy offers too much to see in one visit, unless your visit is a long one, and we mean *really* long. Whether you're a first-timer or making a repeat visit to see sights you missed the first go-round, *Italy For Dummies*, 3rd Edition, is designed to give you all the information you need to help you make savvy, informed decisions about your trip.

Some people spend more time planning their trip than they do taking it. We know your time is valuable, and Italy has too much to see to waste a lot of time sorting out the endless details. So here we happily do the work for you, to help ease you painlessly into a memorable Italian vacation. Unlike some travel guides that read more like a phonebook-style directory listing everything and anything, this book cuts to the chase. We've done the legwork for you, offering our expertise and not-so-humble opinions to help you make the right choices for your trip. This book is a reference work as well as a guidebook — a place where you can quickly look up information as you travel and that you can refer to again and again.

Conventions Used in This Book

The structure of this book is nonlinear: You can open it at any point and delve into the subject at hand. We use icons to guide you toward particular kinds of tips and advice (see "Icons Used in This Book," later in this chapter).

We list hotels, restaurants, and sights alphabetically within each city or regional destination. Exact prices are attached to every listing in this book, as well as our frank evaluation. Prices are given in euro, with the U.S. dollar conversion; the exchange rate used is 1€ = $1.15. Although we give you definite prices, establishments sometimes change prices without notice. Also, there have been cases where a price went *down* but because of exchange fluctuations, the cost went up. (See sidebar for more on euro exchange rates.)

We use this series of abbreviations for credit cards in our hotel and restaurant reviews:

AE: American Express

DC: Diners Club

MC: MasterCard

V: Visa

Note that Discover is not listed. The Discover Card is unknown in Italy, so it's a good idea to carry one or more of the big three — American Express, Visa, MasterCard.

We use a dollar-sign system to alert you to the prices of restaurants listed in the book. Here are the price categories:

$	Up to 35€ ($40)
$$	36€–50€ ($41–$58)
$$$	51€–65€ ($59–$75)
$$$$	66€ and up ($76 and up)

Those prices reflect a per-person charge for a meal consisting of a pasta or appetizer, a main course (called *secondi* or entrée in Italy), a side dish (*contorno*), and dessert. It does not include beverages. Within the listing info, though, we give you the price range of just the main course, listed as *secondi*.

Follow the bouncing euro

Only a few years ago, the euro was worth about 90¢. Now it has bounced back strongly, and it costs $1.15 to buy a euro. That's a 25-cent swing, which can make a huge difference. The 100€ per night hotel that seemed like a bargain at $90 a couple years ago now costs $115 (if you can still find it; for more about price changes and increases, see Chapter 5). Obviously it will help to keep an eye on the euro while you are planning for your trip.

Hotels are rated similarly. The price categories are listed below. See Chapter 8 for a detailed chart telling you exactly what to expect in each category.

$	Up to 130€ ($150)
$$	131€–230€ ($151–$265)
$$$	231€–330€ ($266–$380)
$$$$	331€–500€ ($381–$575)
$$$$$	More than 500€ (Over $575)

Another thing you will find attached to each listing is contact information. Web sites are listed whenever possible. As for telephone numbers, don't be surprised if you see ☎ 0743-220-320 just near ☎ 055-290-832. The number of digits in Italian phone numbers is not standardized as it is in the United States. Area codes can have 2, 3, or 4 numbers; the rest of the number could have as few as 4 or as many as 7 digits.

For those hotels, restaurants, and attractions that are plotted on a map, a page reference is provided in the listing information. If a hotel, restaurant, or attraction is outside the city limits or in an out-of-the-way area, it may not be mapped.

Foolish Assumptions

We've made some assumptions about you and what your needs may be as a traveler. Here's what we assume:

- ✔ You may be wondering whether to take a trip to Italy and how to plan for it. You may be a first-time visitor to Italy.

- ✔ Perhaps you're an experienced traveler, but don't have a ton of time to plan your trip or to spend in Italy after you get there. You want expert advice on how to maximize your time and enjoy a hassle-free trip.

> ✔ You're not looking for a book that provides every bit of information available about Italy. Instead, you're looking for a book that focuses on the places that will give you the best experience in Italy.

If you fit any of these criteria, then *Italy For Dummies*, 3rd Edition, provides the information.

How This Book Is Organized

The book has eight parts plus an appendix. Each can be read independently if you want to zero in on a particular area or issue.

Part 1: Introducing Italy

The first part is all about Italy — its history, culture, people, architecture, and cuisine. It begins with our rundown of the best of Italy and includes climatic information, a calendar of special events (Chapter 3), and sample itineraries (Chapter 4).

Part II: Planning Your Trip to Italy

Part II is intended to guide you through trip planning, whether you make the travel arrangements yourself or work through an agent. As you know, some of the best deals to be had are found on the Internet, and we include Web sites throughout the section (and indeed, the whole book). First comes budgeting, with tips on where to save money — and where not to. Escorted or package tours can offer savings, or at the very least convenience. We also address the special concerns of families, seniors, students, and gays and lesbians.

Part III: The Eternal City: Rome

Rome may be eternal but it's far from dead. The capital of Italy, it is as contemporary as it is ancient, a living ruin still under construction. This section provides a tour of this wonderful maze of ancient and modern treasures, and includes side trips off the beaten track to Tivoli and its villas and the ancient seaport of Ostia Antica.

Part IV: Florence and the Best of Tuscany and Umbria

Florence may be the center of Tuscany and its still brilliant Renaissance heritage, but all of Tuscany is dotted with historic and picturesque towns, including Lucca, Pisa, Siena, and San Gimignano. Though now at peace, their jealous competition (and even war) in centuries past led to the development of unique local cultures that still exist. Neighboring Umbria has its share of dramatic hill towns, such as Assisi, Spoleto, and Perugia. And cities are not the only attraction: the Chianti has attracted sightseers and painters for centuries.

Part V: Venice and the Best of the Pianura Padana

It's not hard to see why Venice was called "La Serenissima," with its mysterious and lovely villa-crowded islands seeming to float upon the water. Venice isn't going to disappear anytime soon, though it may sink your budget, so we give you lots of tips on where to stay and where to eat affordably. In the surrounding region of the Pianura Padana are beautiful Verona and Padua, and a bit further afield the business and fashion center of Milan, also home to amazing art.

Part VI: Naples, Pompeii, and the Amalfi Coast

This corner of Italy is packed with diversity and contrast. Naples is as frenetic and fascinating as ever, a hive of activity as well as a treasure trove of history and art. Pompeii and Herculaneum are also marvelous, though for opposite reasons — their preservation as dead cities buried by Mount Vesuvius. The Amalfi Coast and Capri have their share of history but the major attraction is breathtaking natural beauty.

Part VII: Sicily

A stone's throw from Africa and hundreds of miles from the Alps, the island of Sicily seems at once most intensely "Italian" and strangely different. Goethe captured its mystery when he called Sicily the "key to everything." In no place is the presence of the past as ghostly as the Greek temples and ruins of Agrigento, Syracuse, and Taormina. And nowhere is the mix of cultures more dazzling than in the region's capital, Palermo.

Part VIII: The Part of Tens

The Part of Tens allows us to squeeze in some extra stuff — Italian expressions worth knowing and our favorite Italian artists — that doesn't really fit in elsewhere in the book.

Quick Concierge

This A-to-Z directory gives you the facts you need to know, such as how the telephone system works and what to expect at Customs. We also provide a list of toll-free telephone numbers and Web sites for airlines, hotels, and car-rental agencies serving Italy, and tell you where to go for more information.

Icons Used in This Book

As you have already seen, we use icons throughout this book as signposts and flags for facts and information of a particular nature or interest. Following are the five types of icons:

This icon highlights money-saving tips and/or great deals.

This icon highlights the best the destination has to offer in all categories — hotels, restaurants, attractions, activities, shopping, and nightlife.

 This icon gives you a heads up on annoying or potentially dangerous situations such as tourist traps, unsafe neighborhoods, rip-offs, and other things to beware of.

 This icon highlights attractions, hotels, restaurants, or activities that are particularly hospitable to children or people traveling with kids. When the icon is used in conjunction with a restaurant listing, it means that high chairs and *mezza porzione* (half portions) are available. When it's used with a hotel listing, it means that the hotel can add a crib or an extra bed or two to your room (or the hotel has triples and quads available). It also means that the hotel might offer baby-sitting and/or amenities suitable for children, such as a garden, swimming pool, or play area.

 This icon points out useful advice on things to do and ways to schedule your time.

Where to Go from Here

Now you can dig in wherever you want. The next chapter highlights the best of Italy, from museums to hotels to intangibles (experiences you might not want to miss). If you already have an itinerary in mind you can jump ahead to the ins and outs of finding a flight and making a budget; or you can browse through city destinations you might want to visit. And if you've already visited Italy once or a score of times, you are sure to find something here you *haven't* seen.

Part I
Introducing Italy

The 5th Wave   By Rich Tennant

Magnifico!

Molto bello!

"I insisted they learn some Italian. I couldn't stand the idea of standing in front of the Trevi Fountain and hearing, 'gosh', 'wow', and 'far out'."

In this part . . .

This is where we get you excited about your trip before you go and satisfy your curiosity about this Italian world you have decided to discover. We will help you decide when and exactly where to go. We tell you what sort of weather to expect, where you are likely to have to deal with tourist hordes and where, instead, you can relax in relative solitude off the beaten path. In this part, we sort through your options, showing the advantages and drawbacks of each choice and mentioning special considerations.

In Chapter 1, we highlight the best of Italy. In Chapter 2, we give you more information about Italy's history and culture, including Italy's regional cuisine and local wines. In Chapter 3, we describe the best seasons in which to travel and also give you a calendar of the most important festivals and events. If you don't want to plan your own trip, you can follow one of the five itineraries we provide in Chapter 4.

Chapter 1

Discovering the Best of Italy

In This Chapter

▶ From museums to ruins

▶ From churches to tchotckes

▶ From hotels to dining

*P*eople visit Italy for all sorts of reasons. Art lovers flock to its great museums, the faithful make pilgrimages to the Vatican, gourmands devour its glorious cuisines. In *Italy For Dummies,* 3rd Edition, we give you our vision of the best Italy has to offer. Here's a taste of what's ahead:

The Best Museums

✔ The **Vatican Museums (Musei Vaticani)** in Rome tops our list. Not only do they include dozens of rooms dedicated to painting and sculpture, but this is home to the **Sistine Chapel (Cappella Sistina),** decorated with Michaelangelo's frescoes — the most famous artwork in all of Italy, and, after the **Mona Lisa,** probably the most famous single artwork in the world. Don't forget your binoculars. See Chapter 12.

✔ The smaller **Galleria Borghese (Borghese Gallery),** known especially for its Caravaggio paintings and Bernini sculptures, is also in Rome. It boasts an incredible number of treasures. See Chapter 12.

✔ Florence's **Uffizi Gallery (Galleria degli Uffizi)** is a required stop on any Italian intinerary for its breathtaking pageant of Renaissance art. Only between the covers of a book could you find so many Italian masterpieces in one place. See Chapter 14.

✔ The **Gallerie dell'Accademia (Academy Galleries)** in Venice houses the greatest collection of Venetian painting in the world, from the incandescent paintings of Bellini to monumental works by Tintoretto and Veronese. See Chapter 18.

✔ The **Brera Gallery (Pinacoteca Nazionale di Brera)** is the principal painting gallery in northern Italy outside of Venice (though it
includes works by Tintoretto and other Venetians), and is housed
in a beautiful palace of the seventeenth century. See Chapter 19.

✔ The recently renovated **Museo e Gallerie Nazionali di
Capodimonte (National Museum and Gallery of Capodimonte)**
houses its huge painting collection in an enormous palace high
above Naples and surrounded by a beautiful park. See Chapter 20.

✔ The **National Archaeological Museum (Museo Archeologico
Nazionale)**, also in Naples, is Italy's foremost museum of the art of
antiquity. Some treasures of Pompeii, removed from the buried city
for safekeeping, can also be seen here. See Chapter 20.

The Best Churches

✔ **St. Peter's Basilica** in Rome is only the most famous church in a
country filled with magnificent churches. Its majestic collonade and
soaring dome create a symbol of Rome as well as of the Catholic
Church; inside are art treasures that include Michaelangelo's *Pietà*.
See Chapter 12.

✔ The **Duomo** in Florence, with Brunelleschi's red-tiled dome soaring
over it, is second in size only to the Vatican among Italian churches.
This architectural masterpiece also is known for its artworks, bell
tower, and the famous doors of the nearby baptistry. See Chapter 14.

✔ Venice's **Basilica di San Marco** is as dreamlike and magical as the
rest of the city. Decorated inside with 3,717 sq. m (40,000 sq. ft.)
of gilded mosaics, it contains a host of marvels and has been the
focus of the piazza that bears its name since the 11th century. See
Chapter 18.

✔ The **Duomo** of Milan may look like a whimsical construction, with
its 135 towers (it resembles a sandcastle), but it actually took half a
millenium to build. A fabulous example of Italian Gothic architecture.
See Chapter 19.

✔ The **Duomo di Monreale,** located in a small town in the hills above
Palermo, is a 12th-century Romanesque church whose austere exterior makes the 5,111 sq. m (55,000 sq. ft.) of Byzantine mosaics even
more awe-inspiring. See Chapter 23.

The Best Ruins

✔ **Rome** is a city of ruins, from the majestic and austere **Colosseum
(Colosseo)** where the Romans watched "sports" (as in, fights to
the death), to the **Roman Forum (Foro Romano)** and the **Imperial
Forums (Fori Imperiali)** with their remains of temples, public

buildings, and triumphal arches. The **Castel Sant'Angelo** is a multi-use building: it actually started out as a mausoleum for the Emperor Hadrian and was later incorporated into the city's defenses. Archaeology in Rome continues today and literally uncovers something new every day. See Chapter 12.

✔ The **Villa Adriana** near Tivoli, outside Rome, is more than just a "villa." It is a huge complex of buildings, gardens, reflecting pools, and theaters built by the Emperor Hadrian in the second century A.D. The villa was situated in the mountains above Rome where Hadrian and a few hundred friends could get away from it all, and it remains an atmospheric retreat. See Chapter 13.

✔ The **Valley of the Temples** at Agrigento in Sicily is the most dramatic archaeological site in Italy. A series of majestic temples dominated this city founded in the 6th century B.C. The ruins stand on their own in a dramatic, unspoiled landscape overlooking the city, and include one of the largest temples of antiquity, the **Temple of Jove or Zeus,** which was over 30m (110 ft.) tall. See Chapter 24.

The Best Hotels

✔ If you can afford it, the **Gritti Palace** in Venice will give you the experience of a lifetime, carrying you back to the Venitian grandeur of the 17th century. See Chapter 18.

✔ The **Loggiato dei Serviti** is set in what is arguably Florence's most beautiful square. When you lie in your canopied bed in your beautifully appointed room in this 16th-century monastery, you are transported to the time of the Renaissance. See Chapter 14.

✔ The **Albergo Santa Chiara** in Rome, is one of the oldest hotels in Rome and our favorite. The beauty of the palace and the quality of the service make it a great value. See Chapter 11.

✔ The **Palazzo Dragoni** in Spoleto may be the closest you'll ever come to living like a Renaissance king. Situated in a beautiful 15th-century *palazzo* that sits atop the remains of 10th-century houses, the Dragoni has beautifully (and tastefully) decorated rooms filled with antiques and elegant, spacious common rooms. See Chapter 17.

✔ The **Hotel Luna Convento** in Amalfi takes its name from the 12th-century convent in which the hotel is housed. The monastic accomodations have been upgraded to elegance and comfort, and the spectacular views over the cliffs are truly uplifting. See Chapter 22.

✔ The **Grand Hotel Villa Igea** is not only a place to stay but an attraction: Located outside Palermo, the villa is a masterwork of Sicilian art nouveau architect Ernesto Basile (he even designed furnishings for the villa). See Chapter 23.

The Best Restaurants

✔ For fantastic views over the Eternal City, with wonderful food to match, try **La Pergola**. This elegant restaurant will be one of your most romantic experiences in Rome. See Chapter 11.

✔ For a truly Roman experience — Alessandra, a Rome native, ought to know — nothing is better than the historical restaurant in Monte Testaccio, **Checchino**. See Chapter 11.

✔ Don't miss **Cibreo** if you're visiting Florence. The restaurant's creative chef puts a unique spin on the best of Tuscan cuisine. See Chapter 14.

✔ Everything at **Tartufo** in Spoleto features truffles — and they're the best you'll find. See Chapter 17.

✔ Provided you can stomach the check, **Cipriani** in Venice — inside the hotel of the same name — is a must: The Cipriani family are the ones who gave us the Harry Bar and this is their flagship. Not only the food is extraordinary, but so is the service and the location. See Chapter 18.

✔ If you're a fan of risotto, visit **Casa Fontana** in Milan. The restaurant is a bit out of the way, but where else are you going to find 23 varieties of risotto on the menu every day? See Chapter 19.

✔ For the best view over the Bay of Naples, and the best local food to accompany it, go to **La Cantinella.** You will fall in love all over again. See Chapter 20.

✔ The **San Pietro** in Positano — inside the hotel by the same name — is one of the best, and most beautiful places, to dine on this beautiful stretch of coast. See Chapter 22.

The Most Indescribable Experiences

✔ The **Pantheon** is the most perfectly preserved building of ancient Rome. Built in 27 B.C., it was spared the looting that befell other Roman structures because it was turned into a Christian church. It doesn't feel like a church, however. From its soaring dome (with a round opening through which you see the Roman sky) to its marble pavement, it is a stunning, airy space in which you literally walk through antiquity. See Chapter 12.

✔ Siena's **Palio delle Contrade** is more than a horse race: It's a grudge match between the city's neighborhoods that's been going on for hundreds of years. Wonderfully, it's still carried out with all the pomp, ceremony, and costumes of Renaissance Siena. The race (quite dangerous) is held in the main square of the town — filled with dirt for the occasion. Imagine the Kentucky Derby being held in Times Square. See Chapter 16.

✔ Taking a **gondola ride** through Venice may be expensive and "touristy," but — especially at dusk — it is an almost mystical experience (follow our advice about finding a reputable gondolier). The water shimmering with reflections, the imposing and yet whimsical Venetian architecture, the stillness and the sheer unbelievability of it all, must be experienced. See Chapter 18.

✔ Walking the streets of **Pompeii** is an awe-inspiring experience. Buried beneath volcanic ash by the eruption of Mount Vesuvius in 79 A.D., Pompeii is a flourishing Roman town caught in amber. Even corpses were turned into human statues. See Chapter 21.

✔ The **Teatro Greco-Romano (Greco-Roman Theater)** at Taormina in Sicily would be special enough as the best-preserved antique theater in Italy, where plays were staged starting in third century B.C. But to see a play performed there today is truly amazing. See Chapter 24.

The Best Traditional Italian Souvenirs

✔ Select a set of **carved figurines** for the *presepio* (creche) in Naples for someone who will appreciate them. See Chapter 20.

✔ Make a gift of a beautiful *cammeo* **jewel,** the finely carved stones that have been the pride of Torre del Greco (near Naples) since antiquity. See Chapter 20.

✔ Check out the colorful **porcelain** — dinnerware, pitchers, tiles, vases — in Vietri, on the Costiera Amalfitana; once you see what's on the shelves you will become addicted. See Chapter 22. Palermo porcelain is also colorful but totally different in style. In Sicily, check out the shops carrying the earthware made in Caltagirone, Santo Stefano, and Sciacca. See Chapter 23.

✔ The beautiful, extensive selection of **marbled paper goods** at Giulio Giannini & Figlio in Florence are worth checking out; they make perfect gifts and come in many price levels. See Chapter 14. You can also find a large selection of marbleized paper at Piazzesi in Venice. See Chapter 18.

✔ Invest in some **Murano glass** art work or find smaller blown glass items that make perfect gifts. If the item is authentic Murano glass, even the most inexpensive item will appreciate in value. See Chapter 18.

✔ And of course, take your pick of **fashion accessories** — scarves, leather gloves, handbags, wallets, watches, sunglasses — from the many local designers in Rome, Milan, Naples, Capri, Positano, and Florence. See Chapters 12, 14, 19, 20, 21, and 22.

Chapter 2

Digging Deeper into Italy

● ●

In This Chapter

▶ Understanding Italy, past and present

▶ Exploring 2,500 years of great architecture

▶ Savoring Italy's culture and cuisine

▶ Looking for more to see and read about Italy

● ●

The Italian peninsula has been a magnet for visitors for millennia. Under the Roman Empire, all roads really did lead to Rome, which was the cosmopolitan heart of the Roman civilization. Rome later became a pilgrimage site after the city was made the Holy See (the official papal seat). In the 15th century, artists and scholars of the northern Renaissance were drawn to the country's burgeoning centers of art and learning, which disseminated a new way of thinking — humanism — to the rest of Europe. Then, just a mere 200 to 300 years ago, what we would call modern tourism began.

In the 19th century, Americans made taking the Grand Tour — the classic, months-long European tour enjoyed by the rich and satirized by Mark Twain in *The Innocents Abroad* — a rite of passage for the well-heeled. Anyone who has seen a Merchant Ivory film (*A Room with a View,* for one) knows that Italy was among the most popular stops along the Grand Tour. Italy is still a giant cultural and religious pilgrimage site. It retains an almost mythical status in the minds of many for its fantastic range of natural and cultural attractions. One of the things that accounts for the country's amazing diversity is that modern Italy is such a recent invention: unification was only completed in 1870, and local customs, culture, and cuisine still follow more ancient traditions and distinctions that date back centuries. Selecting your destinations from among these riches is a delicious challenge.

History 101: The Main Events

If Mesopotamia is the cradle of civilization, Italy is the cradle of Western culture. Greek civilization preceded Rome, of course, but the Roman Empire borrowed heavily from it — and from every other culture that it absorbed. The principles of Roman civilization and the Renaissance are the bedrock of modern Western values and institutions. Summarizing

Italy's history in anything less than a book-length study is impossible, but the more background you have, the richer the experience of traveling in Italy will be.

Around 1000 B.C., Italy began developing into the vital cultural center it would become for the following 3,000 years. The **Etruscans** had already developed a sophisticated culture in Tuscany and Umbria when Rome was still a collection of shepherd's huts. Other peoples in Italy included the Italics, divided into several subgroups or tribes such as the Villanova tribe that settled in the region of Rome, and the Celts (or Gauls) who dominated the north. Where the Etruscans came from is still a mystery (probably Asia Minor), but they were famed for their seafaring, gold and metal work, and trading. As they expanded southward, the Etruscan effect on Rome was huge — they gave it its name, for one thing, but they also drained the swamps, built sewers, and introduced writing. Weakened by their struggles with the Greeks who were colonizing southern Italy, the Etruscans lost their power over Rome near the beginning of the fifth century B.C.

The **Roman Republic** was founded in 509 B.C., when the last of Rome's kings was overthrown. The republic was headed by two consuls and the senate, all controlled by the upper or *patrician* (aristocratic) class. The *plebeians* (working class) later obtained their own council and were represented by tribunes. It took hundreds of years for Rome to gain control over the Italian peninsula; it suffered many reverses, including the destruction of the city by the Gauls in 390 B.C.

Gradually Roman military supremacy was established. The Romans have been called the "Prussians of the ancient world" for their militarism, and they first showed their might in decades of bloody war against the city of Carthage, whose empire spread across North Africa and into Spain. Known as the Punic Wars, these conflicts began in 264 B.C. It took the Carthagian general Hannibal six months to make his famous march over the Alps to attack the Romans in 218 B.C., which marked the start of the Second Punic War. His army inflicted crushing defeats on the Roman armies, but eventually the Punic Wars ended with the Romans literally erasing Carthage from the map in 146 B.C. The door was then open for Rome to spread its influence across the Mediterranean. It ruled its provinces through governors and allowed subject countries to retain local government and customs — though betrayal of Rome was brutally avenged. The republic became fantastically rich, and Hellenic and Eastern art, wealth, and cultural influences flowed into Rome.

The end of the Roman Republic and the beginning of the **Roman Empire** arrived largely through the antagonism of two great generals, **Pompey** and **Julius Caesar,** who became a tyrant after his defeat of Pompey. Following Caesar's murder on the Ides of March in 44 B.C., civil war ensued and was won by Caesar's grandnephew and adopted son, Octavian, who became the first emperor, **Caesar Augustus.** His regime turned Rome into a glowing marble city the likes of which the world had never seen, but he was followed by a string of mostly debauched and even insane rulers: **Tiberius, Caligula, Claudius** (a partial exception, even though his third wife, Nero's mother, was also his niece), and **Nero.**

Roman empire at a glance

1500 B.C.	Bronze age peoples settle the site of Rome.
c.509 B.C.	Last of the Roman kings is overthrown, and the Republic is born.
264 B.C.	Punic Wars with Carthage begins.
216 B.C.	In the worst defeat in Roman history, more than 50,000 Romans fall at the battle of Cannae against Hannibal's smaller force.
146 B.C.	Carthage is destroyed and all human habitation of the site is forbidden.
44 B.C.	Julius Caesar assassinated.
31 B.C.	Octavian (Augustus) defeats Mark Antony and Cleopatra at the battle of Actium. Reigns as emperor for the next 40 years.
27 B.C.– A.D.180	The famous Pax Romana ("Roman peace"), observed from the ascension of Augustus to the death of Marcus Aurelius. There is plenty of war during the "pax," but Rome brings the whole Mediterannean world under its administrative control.
27 B.C.	Marcus Agrippa, friend of Augustus, builds Pantheon.
A.D. 64	Great fire of Rome, blamed by history on Nero (and by Nero, on Christians)
A.D. 69	Due to power struggle after Nero's death, Rome has four emperors in one year.
A.D. 79	Pompeii and Herculaneum destroyed.
A.D. 80	Colosseum completed.
A.D. 98	Ascension of Trajan, first of the so-called "good" emperors.
A.D. 148	Rome celebrates its 900th anniversary.
A.D. 161	Reign of the humanistic Marcus Aurelius begins.
A.D. 395	Emperor Constantine builds Constantinople. Empire splits into eastern and western factions.
A.D. 441	The Romans get behind in their payments to Attila the Hun, who begins his attacks on the empire. Other barbarian invasions follow.
A.D. 476	Western emperor Julius Nepos is executed and the German warrior Odoacer is proclaimed king, effectively ending the Roman empire.

At its height, the empire extended from the Caspian Sea to Scotland. However, a chaotic period beleaguered by war, plague, barbarian invasions, and inflation spelled the beginning of the bitter end. As **Emperor Constantine** converted to Christianity and founded Constantinople in A.D. 330, Rome's wealth shifted east. The western empire crumbled under barbarian pressure: The **Goths** sacked Rome in A.D. 410; the Huns came next under **Attila,** and were followed by the **Vandals** of North Africa. In A.D. 476, the German chief Odoacer deposed the western Roman emperor, in effect signaling the end of the once invincible Roman Empire.

Independent local governments developed along the peninsula, while Rome became the seat of the Catholic church and the popes ruled central Italy. The French king **Charlemagne** tried to revive the western empire in A.D. 800 when the pope crowned him emperor but instead founded the forerunner of the **Holy Roman Empire.** This historical oddity profoundly affected Italy's history during the Middle Ages and Renaissance. The German emperor was elected by the German princes, but only the pope could crown him Holy Roman Emperor. For the next 1,000 years, Italian politics were defined by the struggle among the Holy Roman Emperor (who was German), the Pope, Spain, and France (aspiring to the imperial crown). During the height of the Renaissance, city-states like Florence and Siena sought the help of these powerful large states in their local wars, thus inviting foreign intervention in Italy.

In the 13th century, Italy was the crossroads of the Mediterranean; a banking and commercial culture was based on the great seafaring empires of **Venice** and **Genoa** and powerful **Florence.** Even **Amalfi** and **Pisa** had trading empires. The **Renaissance** was above all the rediscovery of classical learning and culture, which in turn led to an explosion of creativity, art, and exploration. The new philosophy of *humanism* promoted the dignity and goodness of the human individual and developing secularism, in contrast with the Middle Ages' emphasis on human sinfulness and doctrinal orthodoxy. Only in the south and in Sicily, where the **Normans** (Viking descendants) founded a kingdom in the 11th century, did medieval feudalism take root. Later, the Spanish rulers used feudalism for their own political aims and induced it to hang on — one of the causes of north-south cultural and economic disparities that still persist.

The etiquette of standing in line

Italian rules for lining up at museums take some getting used to. You may think that people are packed together, trying to push their way through, but each person is more or less aware of who was there first. Even if the mass of people doesn't look like a line, it's sort of structured like one. Be ready to slightly modify your posture so the person behind you knows that *you* know when it's your turn, and you know that they know that you know, and so on. (Remember, body language is important in Italy!)

The treaty of 1559 that acknowledged Spanish claims in Italy was the start of a 250-year decline. The mercantile empires and the city-states waned, and between them the Spanish and the Popes imposed a reactionary and stultifying rule that was only relieved with the arrival of **Napoleon** and revolutionary ideas. Although the end of the Napoleonic era brought back reactionary regimes, nothing could stop the *Risorgimento* ("resurgence") movement, which envisioned a unified Italy. Secret societies like the *Carbonari* were born. The radical Giuseppe **Mazzini** favored an Italian republic, but unification eventually came about by the creation of a liberal state formed around the house of Savoy, rulers of Piedmont and Sardinia. The revolutionary Giuseppe **Garibaldi** threw his weight and military genius behind the liberal plan. After Garibaldi conquered the Kingdom of the Two Sicilies, Umbria and Marche were annexed to Sardinia and the Kingdom of Italy was proclaimed in 1861. Veneto was obtained in 1866 and Rome finally wrested from Papal-French control in 1870, thus completing the unification.

Between 1870 and World War I, Italy saw massive emigration to the United States and Argentina. The country was tempted by territorial promises to join the Allies in 1915 (mainly in order to get Venice back from the Austrians), and 650,000 Italians lost their lives. After **World War I,** discontent and economic depression helped **Mussolini** rise to power. Mussolini's imperialist adventures abroad were matched by repression at home, and his alliance with the Nazis was disastrous. Italians turned against him in 1943 and then continued in **World War II** on the Allied side while suffering under German occupation.

Italy rebuilt after the war and became a modern democratic state. Today, unemployment is a persistent problem, and many Italians — even those educated in such professions as law, academics, and architecture — work for free for years just to get a foot on the employment ladder. **Corruption** has also been a nagging problem, but in the 1990s, a series of scandals and dramatic trials of key Mafia leaders led to a major housecleaning and the proclamation of the "new Italy." Still, Italy is famous for its numerous changes of government in the postwar period; its current prime minister, Silvio Berlusconi, was reelected after being ousted in 1994 during corruption investigations. The ramifications of the ongoing **European unification** are yet to be seen. Italy has received massive influxes of immigrants and refugees in recent years, and the long-term effects of demographic changes are another great unknown.

Architecture: From Ruins to Rococo

Italy offers a compendium of architectural styles — Roman and Greek, Romanesque, medieval, Gothic, Renaissance, baroque, and rococo. With its foot as far south as Africa and its head in the Alps, the peninsula has been a corridor for influences passing back and forth. This is perhaps most obvious in Sicily, with its mixture of Arab, Norman, and other influences, but almost any church (especially one like Milan's **Duomo,** which took 500 years to build) will show traces of more than one style.

Sicily's temples at **Segesta** and **Agrigento** (the famous "valley of temples") are examples of the architecture brought to Italy from Greece by colonists. These temples date from the fifth and sixth centuries B.C. and display the **Doric** style (most easily spotted in the simple rectilinear capitals at the tops of columns). Roman architecture absorbed this early style as well as later Greek developments, such as the **Ionic** capital (like a scroll) and the **Corinthian** (the most ornate capital, decorated with a profusion of leaves). The **Colosseum** in Rome demonstrates all three styles or "orders."

Of the country's Christian-era churches, the earliest to be found are in the **Romanesque** style, which as its name suggests drew inspiration from Roman architecture, and particularly the use of the arch. These churches have thick walls and massive piers that support the superstructure of the building. While some people find the Romanesque stolid and gloomy, it can have an appealing simplicity (especially in comparison with some later gaudy developments in church architecture). **Spoleto** has several Romanesque churches, including its beautiful **Duomo.**

Unlike the Romanesque, the **Gothic** style is known for its soaring towers and the flying buttresses that support the building — Paris's Notre Dame cathedral is the most famous example. But Gothic developed in a different way in Italy. Not surprisingly, while Milan's famous **Duomo** in the north most closely resembles the French style, further south there are many variations on the theme. Rome's only card-carrying Gothic church, **Santa Maria Sopra Minerva,** is a less obvious version of the style, much restored (and, alas, mutilated) over the centuries.

The architecture of **Tuscany** and **Umbria** is famous for its alternating striations of colored marble; not only black and white, but also pink and green. This characteristic element can be found in churches considered Gothic, as in the **Duomo** of **Siena,** but also in **Renaissance** masterpieces like the **Duomo** of **Florence,** capped by the magnificent dome designed by Brunelleschi. The Renaissance style stressed proportion and balance, and avoided some of the higgledy-piggledy accretions that occurred in Gothic churches built over hundreds of years. The classical orders were also employed, with the Doric in the first story of the building, the Ionic in the middle, and the Corinthian at the top. Michelangelo's **Palazzo Farnese** in Rome is a classic example of the Renaissance style, as is his dome of **St. Peter's Basilica.**

But again, nothing is ever that simple. The sweeping colonnade in front of St. Peter's, designed by Bernini, is considered **baroque.** If baroque was an elaboration of the Renaissance style, then **rococo** was overkill — the addition of all sorts of baubles and flourishes to the underlying structure. Perhaps the best word to describe rococo is "busy." With its twisting columns and encrusting of gold, Bernini's **baldacchino** (a baldaquin or canopy) inside St. Peter's shows the baroque starting to get out of hand

The variety of Italy's architecture from region to region is amazing. But there are two places in Italy that simply can't be categorized. At opposite ends of the country, they both, however, show a deep Eastern influence. **Venice** has a style all its own, including its gem, the delicate and almost mystical **Venetian Gothic St. Mark's Basilica (Basilica di San Marco).** The onion domes and the ornate decoration reflect a Byzantine influence; its exotic materials, including porphyry, gold, and jewels, came from across the Venetian empire. **Sicily,** too, has its own style, which reflects Norman influence as well as eastern art and crafts imported during the period when the island was ruled by Arabs (from their conquest in 831 until their defeat by the Normans Robert Guiscard and Robert I in 1072). The **Cappella Palatina (Palatine Chapel)** within the **Palazzo Normanni** is an astounding synthesis of Byzantine mosaics, Islamic art, and an intricate ceiling that is a masterpiece of Arab woodcarving. Later, the island developed its own version of baroque, the **Sicilian Barocco,** a captivating and ornate style that is found in many cities in Sicily and contrasts with the stark beauty of Norman architecture in Palermo.

A Taste of Italy: Eating Locally

Italian cuisine is really many different styles of cooking that vary from region to region. Of course, you'll find spaghetti, penne, tagliatelle, and innumerable other varieties of fresh pasta *everywhere* in Italy — prepared with *vongole* (clams) in the south, *cinghiale* (wild boar sauce) in Tuscany, sardines in Sicily, and an abundance of seafood in Venice. You can also find fresh filled pasta, such as tortellini, ravioli, and lasagne — the richest pasta specialties of all. For Italians, fresh filled pasta is reserved for special days, but as a visitor you can indulge any day you choose. Meals are divided between *primi*, *secondi*, and *contorni* (first courses, second courses, and side dishes), with *antipasti* (appetizers, literally "before pasta") first and *dolci* (sweets) for dessert.

Following is a brief discussion of the various cuisines you'll encounter while eating your way through Italy. No matter where you travel in Italy, however, you can expect sublime olive oils and herbed vinegars; delicious fresh fruits and vegetables like grapes, figs, and tomatoes; locally made cheeses such as mozzarella, including the famous *mozzarella di bufala* (buffalo mozzarella) and *parmigiano reggiano* (the original Parmesan cheese), which makes the commercial stuff taste like sawdust; and cured meats, such as the incomparable *prosciutto di Parma* air-cured ham.

Be adventurous, and try the local specialties when you can. But wherever you are, don't miss the local gelato (rich, creamy ice cream), *granita* (frozen coffee or lemon ice and, in Sicily, almond ice), creamy *zabaglione* (made with sugar, egg yolks, and Marsala wine), or *tiramisù* (layers of mascarpone cheese and espresso-soaked ladyfingers).

Tasting Tuscany

Much as they hate to admit it, a lot of Italians from other regions will tell you that the best food is in **Tuscany**. (We don't have to tell you what Tuscans themselves say.) Poised between the north, where the food is heavier and rich with butter and animal fats, and the south, where the flavors (dominated by tomato sauces) tend to be sharper, Tuscan cuisine may be the perfect balance of the two. Many of the traditional dishes are farm country recipes based around plenty of fresh vegetables and game, though others were refined for the Florentine sovereigns.

Tuscan's primi specialties include *crostini* (toasted bread with savory toppings), *affettati* (traditional cold cuts), *ribollita* (cabbage, bread, and vegetables in a thick soup), and *pappardelle al sugo di lepre* (large fettuccine with hare sauce). *Coniglio* (rabbit), cinghiale, and a variety of meats grilled or fried are common for secondi, and *fagioli all'uccelletto* (white Tuscan beans in a light tomato sauce) are a traditional contorno. Typical desserts are *cantucci col vin santo* (hazelnut biscotti with a strong sweet wine) or *zuccotto* (a dome-shaped sponge cake filled with chocolate mousse, cream, dried fruits, and nuts).

Within a region, you will also find local specialties. For example, in **Pisa**, seafood supplements the Tuscan specialties. Typical is *baccala* (codfish), prepared in various ways but often with chickpeas. **Lucca**'s specialty is its *olio di oliva delle Colline Lucchesi* (extra-virgin olive oil), one of the best olive oils in the world. **Sienese** cuisine shares many of the specialties of Florentine cooking, but also has local favorites like *pici* (hand-rolled spaghetti), usually prepared with bread crumbs and tomato sauce, and *pappa col pomodoro* (a soup of tomatoes and bread). Among the cold cuts are *finocchiona,* a fennel-flavored salami famous all over Italy.

Nearby **Umbria** has a cuisine similar to that of Tuscany, with one major difference: **truffles**. These come in white and black varieties; the former, which has a milder flavor, is the most coveted. Further afield, the cuisine of the **Cinque Terre** is typical Ligurian, highlighted by lots of fresh fish. Pesto sauce, now famous around the world, originated in the Cinque Terre. Another Ligurian specialty is *zuppa di pesce,* a savory, brothy fish stew. In the north, the most typical dish of **Milanese** cuisine is *risotto,* Italian rice seasoned and slowly cooked and served with grated *Parmigiano Reggiano* (Parmesan cheese).

The Tuscan/Florentine specialty to order if you love meat is *bistecca alla fiorentina* (and if you like meat only once in a while, make this one of those times). This specialty is a two-pound-plus steak. The real *fiorentina* comes from the Chianina cow, a breed raised only in the Tuscan countryside and blessed with especially delectable meat.

Thirsty? Chianti is perhaps the best-known Tuscan red, and is often served as table wine *(vino della casa)* — even on tap, from huge casks — in Tuscan restaurants. If you want to splurge, Vino Nobile di

Montepulciano or Brunello di Montalcino are among Italy's greatest wines. For a white wine, try Vernaccia di San Gimignano, and for a dessert wine, the famous *vin santo*.

Roaming Roman restaurants

Some Italian gourmands maintain that there isn't a really good restaurant in **Rome** — and we think that's unfair. While landmark upscale restaurants are few, you can find hundreds of excellent trattorie and *osterie* — small joints, simple (if not basic) in decor, offering typical Roman cuisine, and *pizzerie* — serving pizza and little else. Some of the best food in Rome is served only in mom-and-pop places that may not have a sign but serve real homemade cuisine. If you poke around *il centro* (the center) or just try some of our picks, you can find your own favorite hangout.

Roman specialties include: *pasta all'amatriciana* (a tomato-and-bacon sauce with pecorino cheese), *pasta all'arrabbiata* (tomato and lots of hot red pepper), the famous Thursday specialty *gnocchi* (potato dumplings usually in a tomato-based sauce), and *cannelloni* (pasta tubes filled with meat or fish and baked). Delicious *abbacchio* (young lamb) is prepared *alla cacciatora* ("hunter's style," with sautéed herbs and wine) or *scotta-dito* (literally "finger burning" small grilled cutlets). Another justly famous secondo is *saltimbocca alla romana* (literally "jump in your mouth" — veal or beef stuffed with ham and sage and sautéed in a Marsala sauce). For the more adventurous, there is *trippa alla romana* (tripe Roman style).

The best-known wines of Rome come from the nearby Castelli Romani (hill towns to the east of the city), and the white varieties, like Frascati, are especially good — very dry and treacherously refreshing.

Noshing in Naples

Naples is famous for **pizza** — the Neapolitans invented it, and are still the masters (it helps that they have better mozzarella than anywhere else). But the city has more to offer than just pizza, including lots of seafood dishes, like *pasta alle cozze* (pasta with mussels). And if you have a sweet tooth, try Naples's specialty: the *sfogliatella,* a fragrant, crisp, crusty triangular pocket filled with sweet ricotta. They're the perfect accompaniment to a Neapolitan coffee — another area of acknowledged supremacy. The *babá* is another pastry, a soft brioche soaked in rum and sugar syrup and often filled with cream.

Naples is famous for the *Lachrymae Christi* (tears of Christ), a wine made from grapes grown on the slopes of Mount Vesuvius, hence produced only in small quantities.

Savoring Sicily

When it comes to cooking (as in so many other things), **Sicily** is in a class by itself. Here you'll find the most unique combinations — like Italian-looking pasta with pistachio nuts and North African spices. The Sicilians perfected multiculturalism centuries ago. And because Sicily is an island, its cuisine is highlighted by tastes from the sea. Typical dishes are *pasta con le sarde* (pasta with shredded fresh sardines), *caponata* (cubed eggplant with other vegetables, spiced and sautéed), *tonno con aglio e menta* (fresh tuna with garlic and mint), and fish dishes with *finocchietto* (small fresh fennel). If you want only a sandwich, go for *focacce,* the typical Palermo sandwich. It can be filled with anything, from the excellent *caciocavallo* (typical cheese) to fried spleen — yes, spleen, plus a little lung to round things out. (It's definitely an acquired taste — we tried it and liked it okay — especially if you're very hungry.) Less adventurous "fast food" includes *arancini* (deep-fried flavored rice balls) and *panelle* (chickpea fritters). Sicilians really excel at desserts and pastries. *Cassata* is a fabulous creation: ricotta mixed with sugar and candied fruit, which is covered with a layer of cake and finally almond paste. Some people say that gelato was even invented in Palermo.

Sicilian wines tend to be red and strong. There is a large variety, and you might be familiar with the Corvo di Salaparuta, which is quite good. Nero d'Avola is one of the best.

Visiting Venetian eateries

Fish and shellfish served on rice, pasta, or *polenta* (cooked corn meal) are the staples of **Venetian** cuisine. Typical dishes are *risi e bisi* (rice and peas), *risotto* (creamy rice cooked with fish or vegetables), *bigoli in salsa* (whole-wheat spaghetti with anchovy-and-onion sauce), *sarde in saor* (sardines in a sauce of vinegar, onions, and pine nuts), *baccalà mantegato* (creamed cod fish served cold), and the famous *fegato alla veneziana* (liver sautéed with onions and wine). Pastry shops have a variety of local cakes and the famous *Bussolai* and *S e' Buranei* — O- and S-shaped cookies, respectively, originally from the small island of Burano.

In the area around Venice, the best local wines are Amarone and Valpolicella, earthy reds that can take the chill out of the damp weather in winter. If you prefer it white, there are the Cartizze and the excellent Prosecco — a fizzy wine produced with a different method than champagne, and to some, yielding a better result.

The etiquette of drinking

Don't expect to order a martini before dinner. In restaurants, but more particularly in trattorie, *osterie,* and *pizzerie,* you probably won't find a full bar, because Italians simply don't drink liquor before dinner. And unless they're in a pub, Italians don't drink alcohol at all without eating something. You're likely to find liquor in larger, more touristy restaurants, where you can ask for a scotch and water and won't be rewarded with a perplexed stare. Elsewhere, follow the "when in Rome" rule: Start with wine and have a *grappa* (a clear brandy) or an *amaro* (a 60- to 80-proof bitter drink, made with herbs) *after* your meal.

Background Check: Recommended Books and Movies

The number of books and films about Italy is staggering. Whether you want to bone up on history or be entertained by sights of the Eternal City, here are a few surefire favorites.

True stories

↙ **Johann Wolfgang von Goethe** was the first great modern literary visitor to Italy, and his wonderful *Italian Journey* (1816; reprinted by Penguin Books, 1992) recounts his travel there.

↙ American novelist **Henry James** lived most of his life in Europe. Some of his essays on art and culture are collected in *Italian Hours* (1907; reprinted by Penguin Books, 1995) — the pieces on Venice are particularly good.

↙ **D. H. Lawrence** wrote several books about Italy, including *The Sea and Sardinia* (1921) and *Etruscan Places* (1927); a selected edition, *D.H. Lawrence and Italy,* has been published by Penguin (1997).

↙ If you read 25 pages a day, it'll take you only about four months to get through **Edward Gibbon's** *History of the Decline and Fall of the Roman Empire* (begun in 1776), a monument of English prose. (You can find a less monumental Penguin abridged version [1983] in paperback.)

↙ **Robert Graves** wrote two novels — *I, Claudius* (1934; reprinted by Vintage Books, 1989) and its sequel, *Claudius the God* (1934; reprinted Penguin Books, 1989) — about the best of Augustus's Claudian successors.

↙ Italian **Giorgio Vasari** was a painter, architect, and (literally) Renaissance man. His *Lives of the Most Eminent Painters and Sculptors* (1550; expanded 1568) has been criticized for inaccuracy, but is full of interesting information about the great painters of the Renaissance. The Oxford edition (1998) is one of the many abridgements in translation of this huge work.

↙ **Benvenuto Cellini's** famous *Autobiography* (published 1728; translation reprinted Penguin 1999), presented a vivid picture of Cellini's time in Renaissance Florence.

Works of fiction

↙ **Ignazio Silone** was an important socialist writer who had to go into exile during Mussolini's reign. *Bread and Wine* (*Pane e vino,* 1937; translated by New American Library, 1988) is a vivid novel set during the Fascist period — a modern classic.

✔ **Giuseppe Lampedusa** (actually Giuseppe Tomasi, prince of Lampedusa), wrote a single masterpiece, *The Leopard* (*Il Gattopardo*; 1958; translasted by Pantheon, 1991), about the effect on a noble Sicilian family of Garibaldi's invasion and the war of unification.

✔ **Alberto Moravia**, one of the great Italian writers of the 20th century, wrote many novels and short stories, but none as famous as *The Conformist* (*Il Conformista*, 1951; translated by Steerforth Press, 1999), a study of the fascist personality.

✔ Sicilian novelist **Leonardo Sciascia** wrote works that subtly peel apart layer by layer the Mafia culture. Among the best of his works is *The Day of the Owl* (*Il Giorno della Civetta*, 1961; translated by New York Review of Books, 2003).

✔ **Alessandro Manzoni's** *I Promessi Sposi* (*The Betrothed*, 1825–27; translated by Penguin, 1984), considered one of the greatest works of fiction in any language, is a sweeping romantic novel set in 17th-century Italy.

The moving image

The neorealist film director **Luchino Visconti** made an epic movie of Lampedusa's *The Leopard*. *The Earth Trembles* (*Terra Trema*, 1948) also by Visconti, is a version of Verga's *I Malavoglia*. **Bernardo Bertolucci** made a haunting and chilling classic out of Moravia's *The Conformist* in 1970.

Over the last dozen years or so, Italy has been the subject or the setting of several hit films. It all began with *A Room with a View* (1985), based on E.M. Forster's novel and containing beautiful scenes of Florence. *Enchanted April* (1992) is a sometimes schmaltzy but irresistible movie about a group of Londoners leaving the drizzle and fog of home for a sunny Italian villa. *The Postman* (*Il Postino,* 1994) became an instant cult classic, and concerns the encounter of the ordinary man of the title with the extraordinary personality of the poet Pablo Neruda, living in exile in Italy. The Oscar-winner *Life is Beautiful* (1997), by Italy's current leading comic actor, Roberto Benigni, is set during World War II and moves from Tuscany to a German concentration camp. *Mediterraneo* (1991) was also set during World War II, a comedy dealing with what happens when a group of Italian soldiers are sent to garrison a lovely Greek island. Somewhat stereotypically, their Italian love of life wins out over their mission. At the opposite end of the spectrum is Nanni Moretti's *The Son's Room* (2001), about the death of a child — a film so powerful that it is perhaps the only movie ever to be given an R rating for being so *sad.*

We have to mention one of the great oldies, *Roman Holiday* (1953), the Gregory Peck/Audrey Hepburn romance that is said to have caused a surge in tourism to Rome. Another hugely popular film of the same era is *Spartacus* (1960), the Oscar-winning Kirk Douglas movie about a slave revolt in ancient Rome (we can't vouch for its historical accuracy). It was a precursor to Russell Crowe's *Gladiator* (2000), which also gives a visceral feel for the brutality of the empire at its worst.

Chapter 3

Deciding Where and When to Go

In This Chapter

▶ Exploring Italy's regions
▶ Knowing the right time to visit
▶ Scanning a calendar of the best festivals and events

*I*taly has always been a maze of attractions and distractions, cuisines, and subcultures, but its charms have been enhanced in recent years: The Papal Jubilee in 2000 spurred a wave of renovation for long-neglected sights like the soot-blackened **Palazzo Farnese** in Rome, and the **Scrovegni Chapel** frescoes in Padua. Also, many hotels and restaurants got facelifts, too, but perhaps more important, the tourist industry and the art and cultural management have started thinking in a modern way that makes things easier for international tourists: longer opening hours, Web sites, information hot lines, cumulative tickets, air-conditioning, navette services, and so on. In addition, the euro is easier to deal with for visitors used to dollars or pounds — no more 3,500-lire ice cream cones or shoes costing a cool quarter-million lire. The European unification has made the overall European economy stronger. The standardization of the monetary system helps business, which, in turn, benefits you, the traveler.

Thankfully, however, beneath the surface the same proud traditions live on. In a country where you couldn't count the political parties even on both hands and feet, diversity is not in danger. Centuries-old patterns are what give Italy its unique flavors, voices, and places.

Going Everywhere You Want to Be

Every region of Italy offers eye-popping sights as well as places to spend quiet hours. The overview below will help you begin to narrow down your destinations, whether this is your first trip to Italy or your fifth. You may also want to visit smaller centers within striking distance of the main cities (see "Scheduling Your Time" later in this chapter).

Roaming Rome

Rome is still the capital of Italy, as it was in ancient times. As the site of the Holy See, it was central to European culture for many centuries after the end of the Roman Empire. Hence its unparalleled saturation with world-famous sights: the **Colosseum (Colosseo),** the **Roman Forum (Foro Romano)** and **Imperial Forums (Fori Imperiali),** St. Peter's **Basilica (Basilica di San Pietro)** and the **Vatican Museums (Musei Vaticani),** and the **Pantheon,** to name a few. Even sights underground, like the **Catacombs,** and new archaeological sites are continually being opened, such as the **Domus Aurea,** the "golden house" of Nero.

You know the expression "When in Rome, do as the Romans do"; well, one of the things Romans do is to get out of Rome. For example, you can explore the Castelli Romani (the hill towns at the east of Rome), where it's pleasurably cool in summer and the food and wine are superb. You can also immerse yourself in ancient times at the ruins of Rome's seaport, **Ostia Antica,** or at **Hadrian's Villa** in Tivoli, where you can also visit the cool fountain gardens of the Renaissance **Villa d'Este** and enjoy a nice meal.

As a major modern city, Rome also offers a varied and exciting nightlife, a huge selection of restaurants, plentiful comfortable hotels, and world-famous shops. But it has some endemic big-city problems as well. The traffic in Rome is as eternal as the Eternal City itself: Buses and metros are crowded at rush hour, and the streets are filled with pedestrians and motorbikes jostling for space. See Part III for coverage of Rome.

Exploring Florence and the best of Tuscany and Umbria

Tuscany is currently *the* destination for Americans, who, like many travelers around the world, are attracted to the lush Italian countryside (where most people would love to own a villa). **Florence,** with its beautiful **Duomo (cathedral)** and museums overflowing with art treasures — the **Uffizi Gallery (Galleria degli Uffizi)** foremost among them — is the regional capital as well as one of the finest cultural cities in the world. Other top destinations in Tuscany include **Pisa,** with its **Leaning Tower** (Galileo Galilei made his experiments with gravity here, a few centuries back); **Siena** (where the exciting **Palio delle Contrade** horse race occurs twice a year); **San Gimignano,** with its soaring medieval towers; and **Lucca,** a medieval and Renaissance jewel. The **Chianti,** a sub-region of Tuscany, is renowned for its beautiful hill towns and delicious food and wine. A little farther afield, and actually in the neighboring region of Liguria, are five ancient fishing/farming villages nestled along a stretch of coast that rivals the more famous **Amalfi Coast** in steepness and natural beauty: the **Cinque Terre.**

To the south and west of Tuscany is the smaller region of **Umbria.** Its attractions include **Perugia,** a city known for its medieval architecture and culinary traditions; **Assisi,** with the famous frescoes by Giotto celebrating the life of St. Francis; and **Spoleto,** acclaimed for its music-and-arts festival as well as its medieval architecture and imposing fortress.

Although you may not find the climate of Tuscany and Umbria ideal (it's baking hot in summer and chilly and damp in winter), its main attractions are hardly a secret, drawing crowds of tourists from all over the planet. However, most people prefer to give up almost anything else in Italy before they cut this region from their itinerary. See Part IV for more about Tuscany and Umbria.

Viewing Venice and the Pianura Padana

Many artists and writers have been utterly smitten by **La Serenissima (the Serene Republic),** as Venice called itself when it was an independent state. No place promotes dreaming like **Venice.** In a country lush with one-of-a-kind sights, Venice is truly in a class by itself. Along with Rome and Tuscany, it rounds out the top three destinations in Italy. Its most glorious cultural attractions are the **Doge's Palace (Palazzo Ducale), St. Mark's Basilica (Basilica di San Marco)** and **St. Mark's Square (Piazza San Marco)** and the **Academy Gallery (Gallerie dell'Accademia).**

Although summer humidity, crowds, and the stench of the canals in hot weather can be a bit much, Venice is always captivating. If you're planning an especially romantic vacation, Venice is a must.

The region surrounding Venice, the **Pianura Padana,** is not to be ignored. **Verona** is a delightfully romantic town where (supposedly) Romeo and Juliet lived out their tragic affair. Speaking of tragedy, you can also see an opera in the Roman amphitheater in Verona. Nearby **Padua,** a charming Renaissance university town, features Giotto's most celebrated frescoes in the **Chapel of the Scrovegni (Cappella degli Scrovegni)** and is the perfect start for a captivating river cruise toward Venice. See Part V for our coverage of Venice and the Pianura Padana.

Visiting Naples, Pompeii, and the Amalfi Coast

Naples seems more Italian than the rest of Italy, if such a thing is possible. It's an intense city, perhaps too much so for some people. The city's somewhat sorry reputation has improved markedly in recent years, thanks to a steady program of renovations, and the city is full of often overlooked art and cultural treasures. The **National Archaeological Museum (Museo Archeologico Nazionale)** is the richest in Italy and the city's many churches and museums hold important Renaissance art.

The **Amalfi Coast** is a scenic area with beautiful seaside resorts, such as Positano and Amalfi, nestled along plunging cliffs. Closer to Naples, **Herculaneum** and **Pompeii,** Roman cities wiped out by Vesuvius in A.D. 79, are among the country's most important archaeological attractions. And, of course, there's **Mount Vesuvius** itself, an eerie presence towering over the city.

Off the coast of Naples is one of the most famous islands in Italy: **Capri,** a green hill that rises steeply from the sea and has been a trendy resort since the days when Tiberius and Caligula sought "amusement" there. See Part VI for Naples and environs.

Seeing Sicily

The farther south you go, the more intense Italy becomes. **Sicily's** rugged beauty, bountiful waters, and rich soils have been fought over for millennia. The region's reputation as headquarters of the Mafia and its bloody vendettas used to scare people away, but a government crackdown has spawned a Sicilian renaissance, and even though getting there takes extra time, it's worth the trip. You won't find such an exciting and pleasing mix of sights, cultures, and flavors anywhere else in Italy. Early Greek settlers left behind the magnificent temples in **Agrigento,** in the appropriately named **Valley of the Temples,** and in Segesta. The Normans (a name that comes from Norsemen) created a uniquely beautiful style of art in the capital city of **Palermo** and throughout the island. You can also admire the splendors of the Sicilian baroque and Liberty (Art Nouveau) styles in Palermo. Snow-capped **Mount Etna** dominates the island and in particular the fashionable city of **Taormina,** which is home to both well-preserved ancient sites and a modern resort. Down the coast is **Syracuse,** with its dark and fascinating history — the early part of which is still visible in the excavations of the **Archaeological Zone** and on the island of **Ortigia.** See Part VII for coverage of Sicily.

Scheduling Your Time

A quick glance at the map will show that the enticing attractions discussed in the previous section are spread out over a peninsula over 700 miles long. (Put another way, would you combine Montréal and Washington, D.C. in the same vacation?) How is it possible to get everywhere? Practically speaking, it isn't.

In Chapter 7, we discuss different ways of getting around Italy. If you can afford to fly everywhere, you could conceivably get to **Venice, Florence, Rome, Naples,** and **Sicily** in a fairly short trip. Otherwise, you will need to choose a base and make some decisions.

Driving in the major cities and finding a place to park can be a major pain. Public transportation is highly developed, however, and you don't need a car anyway. If you happen to arrive in a big city by car, either return it to the rental agency (because you won't need it anymore) or garage it if you want to use it again when you leave. For example, you can pick up a car at Pisa's airport, drive through Tuscany's hill towns for several days, and then continue on to Florence, and get rid of the car as soon as you arrive. See Chapter 7 for more on driving around Italy.

An important feature of **Rome** is its central location, which makes it easy to use as a base for a visit either farther south to Naples and the Amalfi Coast (Sicily is a bit of a stretch) or north into Tuscany and Umbria (Venice is a bit of a stretch). Of course, the city itself is an inexhaustible source of things to do.

Tuscany is a central location, and starting from there will allow you still to visit Rome but you will be that much closer to Venice (or the Cinque Terre, or Milan). However, it will make Naples a real hike (traveling on the ground) and put Sicily out of reach (except by air, of course). But with **Florence, Pisa,** and **Lucca,** and the **Cinque Terre** and **Spoleto** and **Assisi** not too far away, it's easy to see why Tuscany can be a base for the duration of your vacation.

Venice is a long way north and east — next stop Trieste, and then Slovenia — making sites in northern Italy accessible. Tuscany is not too far, though Rome is at least a five-hour train ride. The great thing about having Venice as a base, however, is that you're in Venice; a lot of tourists spend one or at most two days there, and never get into the back streets where you don't have to shout to be heard over the clicking of cameras. A big downside is that Venice is generally very expensive.

Naples is the jumping-off point for exploring some of southern Italy's most popular sites. If you like ancient art and natural beauty, it could make a good starting place. Naples — not to mention **Sicily** — is not a place that most first-time visitors would choose to begin their tour. But if you have seen the top sites in Tuscany and Rome already, Naples, as the gateway to the south, could be the start of a beautiful friendship.

People may hate us for saying this, but generally, the further south you go, the less dependable the train service is and the longer the delays. Don't build an itinerary with lots of close shaves.

Revealing the Secrets of the Seasons

Italy has a warm, dry climate with well-defined seasons. Thanks to a relatively mild climate, there isn't really a tourist season per se — Italy is a year-round destination. But because the peninsula is over 1,100km (700 miles) long and mountainous, the weather can vary greatly between north and south and between the coast and inland areas.

You know your limits, so if you find waiting in line for two hours in the hot sun to get into the Vatican Museums unendurable, don't come to Italy in July or August. Make sure that you check the average temperatures we list in Table 3-1.

Table 3-1		Average Temperatures and Precipitation in Selected Cities										
	Jan	Feb	Mar	Apr	May	June	July	Aug	Sept	Oct	Nov	Dec
Rome												
High (°C/°F)	12/53	13/55	15/59	18/65	23/73	27/81	30/87	30/87	27/80	22/71	16/61	13/55
Low (°C/°F)	3/37	4/38	5/41	8/46	11/52	14/58	17/63	18/64	15/59	11/51	7/44	4/39
Rainfall (cm/in.)	10.3/4	9.8/4	6.8/3	6.5/3	4.8/3	3.4/1	2.3/1	3.3/1	6.8/3	9.4/4	13/5	11.1/4
Venice												
High (°C/°F)	6/42	8/47	12/54	16/61	21/70	25/77	28/82	27/81	24/74	18/65	12/53	7/44
Low (°C/°F)	-1/30	1/33	4/39	8/46	12/54	16/61	18/64	17/63	14/58	9/49	4/40	0/32
Rainfall (cm/in.)	5.8/2	5.4/2	5.7/2	6.4/3	6.9/3	7.6/3	6.3/2	8.3/3	6.6/3	6.9/3	8.7/3	5.4/2
Palermo												
High (°C/°F)	15/59	15/59	16/61	18/65	22/71	25/77	28/83	29/84	27/80	23/73	19/67	16/61
Low (°C/°F)	10/50	10/50	11/52	13/55	16/61	20/67	23/73	24/74	22/71	18/64	14/58	12/53
Rainfall (cm/in.)	7.2/3	6.5/3	6.0/2	4.4/2	2.6/1	1.2/0	0.5/0	1.3/1	4.2/2	9.8/4	9.4/4	8.0 /3

The advice to travel in Italy at other times than the summer seems to be taken by more and more people, because the well-defined off season in winter is disappearing. More and more tourists are taking advantage of the off season's lower prices, often better and more attentive service, and fewer crowds at the prime attractions. Following are what we consider to be the pros and cons for traveling in each season.

Spring

In our opinion, the period between April and June is one of the best times to visit Italy. Here's why:

✔ Temperatures are moderate and the weather is mild.

✔ Limited rainfall allows you to get out and really enjoy the outdoor activities.

But keep in mind:

- ✔ Everybody knows this is a great season, so rooms book up in advance. Make your reservations as early as possible, particularly for such major destinations as Florence, Rome, and Venice.

- ✔ Herds of Catholic pilgrims and large — and *very* noisy — school groups from around Europe descend on Italy (particularly Rome and Florence) around Easter. We recommend visiting the smaller towns at this time.

- ✔ Labor Day is May 1 and all workers have a day off. Everything shuts down, even public transportation.

Summer

There are reasons for the throngs of tourists in the summertime:

- ✔ The weather is beautiful throughout most of Italy.

- ✔ You can get discount rates in Sicily. Be forwarned, though: After June, this is sunstroke territory.

- ✔ Discount rates can be had in all the large cities, which tend to be deserted.

On the other hand:

- ✔ Airfares are their highest.

- ✔ You can expect long lines for major attractions.

- ✔ The heat can make things quite uncomfortable — Italy is still mostly non–air-conditioned country.

- ✔ The seaside resorts, which can provide a respite from the heat, are mobbed with Italian tourists.

- ✔ Many city shops and restaurants close — particularly in August, most definitely on August 15, the Italian holiday of Ferragosto.

Fall

Next to spring, fall is our favorite time to travel to Italy. Here's why:

- ✔ The weather is still fairly mild and pleasant.

- ✔ Many potential tourists are busy with back-to-school preparations, making crowds relatively sparse.

On the other hand:

- ✔ You have to watch for the rain, which typically falls from October through December. It's at its heaviest in November.

Winter

More and more vacationers are reaping the benefits of traveling to Italy in the winter. Its reputation as the "off season" is fast disappearing.

- ✔ The relatively mild weather and little rain keep the country pleasant for touring.

- ✔ You can enjoy the mid-winter lull in February, when the crowds are at their lowest.

- ✔ Airfares and many hotel rates are at their lowest.

But keep in mind:

- ✔ You may have fewer lodging choices in some areas because of seasonal closures — most hotels and restaurants in Italy take a winter break of about two to three weeks.

- ✔ It can get cold and quite foggy in the northern regions.

Perusing a Calendar of Events

Italy has many festivals worth planning a holiday around. Some are famous, like Venice's Carnevale (Mardi Gras) or Siena's Palio, but all are unique. To enjoy these events you may have to cope with less than-perfect weather and no doubt an onslaught of fellow revelers. Alternatively, you can use the following calendar to *avoid* big events and their attendant crowds. Either way, a rundown of Italy's primary festivals and events — plus a few unusual choices — lets you know what to expect.

Most Christian holidays — not just Christmas and Easter, but saint's days and **Tutti Santi (All Saints' Day** — November 1), are marked throughout the country by some kind of celebration and often processions and special foods.

January

Celebrate the new year in Florence with the annual boat race, the **Regata sull'Arno (Regatta on the Arno; ☎ 055-23320).** January 1.

Throughout the country the religious holiday **Epifania (Feast of the Epiphany)** is very important for children, because they receive their Christmas gifts on this day, not on December 25. On the days preceding Epiphany, open-air fairs selling children's toys and gifts are held in most towns. Full of carts and stands selling gifts and sweets, the fair on Rome's Piazza Navona stays open till dawn on feast day. January 6.

February

Everywhere in Italy, **Carnevale** swallows up the week before Ash Wednesday, culminating on Fat Tuesday or *Martedi Grasso*. You can best observe this former pagan rite of the coming of spring in Venice, where people dress up in spectacular costumes and participate in masked balls and a variety of events (music, concerts, fireworks, and so on) organized by the city. Contact the Venetian Tourist Office, A.P.T. Venezia, Castello 4421, 30100 Venezia (☎ **041-529-8711;** Fax: 041-523-0399) for a calendar of events. Every town in Italy celebrates Carnevale to one degree or another — at least by making *frappe,* thin slices of crunchy fried dough with powdered sugar, and *castagnole,* deep-fried balls of dough, often filled with custard. The famous parade of floats in Viareggio in Tuscany culminates celebrations that last a whole month (☎ **0584-47-503**). In Rome, you can find concerts and organized events, as well as lots of people parading around the city (particularly along Via Veneto) in costume on Fat Tuesday evening. Call the tourist office at ☎ **06-4889-991**, or check www.comune.roma.it for details. One week prior to Ash Wednesday.

March/April

On the high holy day of **Venerdì Santo (Good Friday),** the Catholic rite of the procession of the stations of the cross *(Via Crucis)* is presented in many Italian towns as a reenactment with costumes. In Rome, the procession takes place at night, led by the Pope, between the Colosseum and Palatine Hill. Other spectacular processions are the ones in Assisi and in several towns in Sicily. Friday before Easter Sunday.

In Rome, the Pope gives his traditional **Benedizione Pasquale (Easter Benediction)** in Piazza San Pietro. Easter Sunday, between the end of March and mid-April.

In Florence, folks celebrate Easter with a bang, otherwise known as **Scoppio del Carro (Explosion of the Cart;** ☎ **055-290-832).** During morning Mass, a cart laden with fireworks covered with flowers and led by white oxen is blown up by a mechanical dove containing a fuse, which slides down a wire from the Duomo and ignites the cart. Easter Sunday.

During the **Mostra delle Azalee (Exhibition of Azaleas)** exhibition, more than 3,000 azalea plants are exhibited on the Spanish Steps in Rome to celebrate the beginning of spring. Concerts are held in Trinità dei Monti at the head of the steps. Call ☎ **06-4889-991** for more information. One week in mid-April, weather dependent.

In Venice, the religious holiday **Festa di San Marco (Festival of St. Mark)** is marked by a procession to St. Mark's Basilica in honor of the city's patron saint. Also, the Venetian men mark the day by giving women a red rose. April 25.

May

Assisi's pagan celebration of spring, called **Calendimaggio** (☎ 075-812-534 or www.umbria2000.it), includes singing, dancing, medieval costumes, and competitions. First weekend after May 1.

Rome's **Concorso Ippico Internazionale (International Horse Show)** attracts the best riders and mounts from all over to Villa Borghese's beautiful Piazza di Siena. You can buy ticket at the gate. For details, contact the ticket agent of the Piazza di Siena ☎ 06-638-3818 or visit www.piazzadisiena.com. Near the end of May.

Italy's oldest and most prestigious music festival — **Maggio Musicale Fiorentino (Florentine Musical May)** — is held in Florence. This concert and dance series includes famous performers and world premiers. Tickets range from 11€ to 85€ ($13–$98). Call ☎ 0935-564-767 for information; tickets are available online at www.maggiofiorentino.com. May into June.

Each year by turns in Venice, Amalfi, Genoa, or Pisa, the **Regata delle Grandi Repubbliche Marinare (Regatta of the Great Maritime Republics)** is a rowing competition between the great medieval maritime Republics. For details, call the tourist office of Pisa at ☎ 050-560-464, Venice at ☎ 041-529-8711, or Amalfi at ☎ 089-871-107. Second or third weekend in May.

Rowers train year-round for **Vogalonga** (☎ 041-529-8711), a "long row" and major competition in Venice. Second half of May.

June

The **Festival di Spoleto (Spoleto Festival),** now in its fourth decade, includes concerts, opera, dance, and theater. Contact the Associazione Spoleto Festival for info (☎ 0743-220-320; Fax: 0743-220-321; www.spoletofestival.it). Tickets are available online. Throughout June.

The **Arena di Verona (Verona Amphitheater)** festival features opera performed in Verona's well-preserved Roman arena. For details, call ☎ 045-800-5151 or check the Web at www.arena.it. June through September.

In honor of the feast of San Giovanni, patron saint of Florence, Florentines hold a tournament of rough-and-tumble Renaissance soccer, the **Gioco di Calcio Storico Fiorentino** (☎ 055-290-832). With 27 players per side, it's part sport, part free-for-all. Fireworks are set off on the Arno River at night. June 16, 24, and 30.

The **Estate Romana (Roman Summer)** is a program of concerts, theater, special exhibits, and other events throughout Rome. Performances held inside Roman ruins are particularly dramatic. For details, call ☎ 06-4889-991 or visit www.comune.roma.it. Mid- to late June through August.

One of the premier art expositions in the world, the **Biennale di Venezia (Venice Biennial)** takes place in odd-numbered years in the Giardini, Venezia's public park and exhibition center. Call ☎ 041-521-8846 or visit www.labiennale.org. June through October.

July

The **Palio delle Contrade of July 2nd** is first of Siena's two *palios* and one of Italy's most famous spectacles. Horses and riders wearing the colors of their Sienese neighborhoods ride around Piazza del Campo in a wild, dangerous race. The event is preceded by much fanfare and pageantry lasting for days. Call ☎ 0577-280-551 or visit www.terresiena.it. June 29 through July 3.

In Palermo, the **Festa di Santa Rosalia (Festival of St. Rosalia)** celebrates the anniversary of the rediscovery of the saint's remains in 1624. A religious procession with a decorated triumphal carriage carrying an orchestra parades through the city, and a candlelight procession ascends the mountain overlooking the harbor. July 11 through July 15.

Umbria Jazz is one of Europe's top jazz events, held in Perugia. Contact the Associazone Umbria Jazz for more info (☎ 075-572-8685; Fax: 075-572-8697; www.umbriajazz.com). Mid- to late July.

The **Festa del Redentore (Feast of the Redeemer)** includes boating and fireworks in Venice's lagoon to mark the lifting of the plague in 1571. Third Saturday and Sunday of July.

August

The pagan holiday of **Ferragosto** is acknowledged nationwide and celebrates the culmination of the summer. Italians vacation on the seashore and in the mountains. Most businesses are closed, so check your destination in advance to know what will be open. August 15.

Siena's second *palio,* **Palio delle Contrade of August 16th,** is held between the finalists of the previous *palio* in July. The program is the same as the one in July, except that the number of participating *contrade* is smaller — but the celebrations are as grand as ever. Call ☎ 0577-280-551 or visit www.terresiena.it. August 13 through August 17.

September

Held at the Palazzo del Cinema on the Lido, the **Venice International Film Festival** (☎ 041-521-8861; www.labiennale.org) is one of the top film festivals in the world. Despite the proliferation of bigwigs and wannabes, you can actually get tickets to screenings. Book early for hotel reservations. First two weeks of September.

In Venice, the **Regata Storica (Historic Regatta)** is a rowing event held in the Grand Canal. You need tickets to see it. Call ☎ **041-529-8711.** First Sunday of September.

The **Settembre Lucchese** (☎ **0583-473-129;** www.in-lucca.it) opera festival celebrates the memory of Puccini in his hometown of Lucca with live performances. Throughout September.

October

The **Festa di San Francesco d'Assisi (Feast of St. Francis of Assisi),** a celebration for the patron saint of Italy, is observed in various towns and cities, notably Rome and Assisi, with processions, special masses, and other religious events. October 4.

November

In Venice, the **Presentation of Mary in the Temple** is a religious holiday that's celebrated with a procession that crosses the city, including a bridge made of boats strung across the Grand Canal at La Salute. November 21.

December

For Rome's **Crèche Exhibit** more than 50 nativity scenes are displayed in the Villa Giulia, and many others are on view in churches around the city. Particularly nice are the ones in the Basilica di Santa Maria Maggiore, Santa Maria d'Aracoeli (see Chapter 12), Santa Maria del Popolo (Piazza del Popolo 12; ☎ **06-361-0487**), and Chiesa del Gesù (Piazza del Gesù, off Via del Plebiscito; ☎ **06-679-5131**). The three weeks before Christmas.

On Christmas Day, the pope gives a special **Christmas Blessing** to Rome and the world from St. Peter's Square at noon. December 25.

Italians love **New Year's Eve,** and partying reaches its climax at midnight when the country explodes — literally — with fireworks. There are organized displays in some towns and cities, but everybody gets into the act, shooting fireworks from every window and roof of the country. By tradition, fireworks are accompanied by the symbolic throwing away of something old to mark the end of the old year. Some people get carried away, so watch out for falling UFOs if you take a stroll in major cities shortly after midnight! December 31.

Chapter 4

Following an Itinerary: Five Great Options

● ●

In This Chapter

▶ Touring Italy for one or two weeks
▶ Visiting Italy with your kids
▶ Discovering two special-interest itineraries

● ●

*I*taly offers an endless array of things to see, do, and taste — but, alas, few of us have the time to do it all. But even if you want to cram as much of Italy into your trip as possible, you still have some tough choices on your hands. This chapter gives some sample itineraries that won't break your budget or your back. Two special-interest tours — for ancient-history or art buffs — are also outlined.

Seeing Italy's Highlights in One Week

In one week you can only take in the highlights of Italy, and there won't be much time to linger anywhere. But if all you have is one week — grab it! Think of it as a crash course in Italian life and culture.

Fly into Rome and get settled in your hotel, which will need to be fairly central (see Chapter 11) given the amount of ground you'll want to cover. On Day One, from Termini train station take the three-hour **ATAC bus tour** to get a general city orientation. The bus makes slightly extended stops at **St. Peter's (San Pietro)** and the **Colosseum.** Following the tour, enjoy a leisurely stroll and dinner in the funky medieval neighborhood of **Trastevere,** on the south side of the river Tiber, and call it a day; you'll need to rest up for Day Two.

On both Day Two and Day Three, see one major and two minor sights of your choice (check out Chapter 12 for detailed information). Major sights include the **Vatican Museums/Sistine Chapel, Roman Forum/Imperial Forums/Palatine Hill,** and **Borghese Gallery (Galleria Borghese).** Minor

attractions (in terms of time commitment, not importance) include the
Spanish Steps and **Piazza di Spagna, Trevi Fountain,** the **Pantheon,** and
Piazza Navona. You can work in other *piazze* (squares) at night using
our restaurant choices in Chapter 11.

On Day Four, take an early train (leaving no later than 8 or 9 a.m.) to
Florence (see Chapter 14 for hotel, restaurant, and attraction reviews),
where you will arrive about two hours later. Check into your hotel, and
then head for the **Duomo, Giotto's Bell Tower,** the **Baptistry,** and the
Duomo Museum (Museo dell'Opera del Duomo). Have dinner in one of
our recommended restaurants.

On Day Five, get up early and get to the **Uffizi Gallery (Galleria degli
Uffizi)** — of course, you've reserved tickets in advance so you won't
have to stand in line for hours. In the afternoon, go to the **Accademia
Gallery (Galleria dell'Accademia)** — reserve tickets here — to see
Michelangelo's *David* and other works if you have time. Take a pre-dinner
stroll on the **Ponte Vecchio.** Don't forget to see the **Palazzo Vecchio**
(from the outside only) and **Piazza della Signoria** on the way back.

On Day Six, take an early two-and-a-half-hour train ride to **Venice** (covered in Chapter 18), and check into your hotel. Then get out onto **Grand
Canal** by catching vaporetto no. 1 for a slow cruise down the canal; note
the *palazzi* (palaces) lining the canal and the **Rialto Bridge** as you pass
under it. Get off to explore **St. Mark's Square (Piazza San Marco)** and
St. Mark's Basilica (Basilica di San Marco). In the afternoon, go to the
Accademia Galleries (Gallerie dell'Accademia) for a tour of several
hundred years of Venetian art.

On the morning of Day Seven, visit **Santa Maria Gloriosa dei Frari** and
the nearby **Scuola di San Rocco.** After lunch, see the **Doge's Palace** and
the **Bridge of Sighs.** You can then either head back to Rome by train that
night (about five hours) and fly out the next day, or spend your last night
in Venice and fly home from there the next morning. If you don't have
that extra day, use the afternoon and evening of Day Six to walk around
the city (you may even want to skip the visit to the Accademia Galleries
altogether), and just skip Day Seven.

Touring the Best of Italy in Two Weeks

We recommend that you still begin your tour in Rome, spending Day
One acclimating yourself through a general tour; days Two and Three
are taken up with major sights and the minor ones you can fit in (see
"Seeing Italy's Highlights in One Week," above, for details). On Day Four
in Rome, you can also take a side trip to Tivoli and see the **Hadrian's
Villa** and **Villa d'Este,** or go to **Ostia Antica** to see the ruins of Rome's
ancient seaport (see Chapter 13).

Early on Day Five, take the two-and-a-half-hour train ride from Rome to Naples, and check your luggage at the station. Transfer to the train to **Pompeii** (a 45-minute trip), and visit the archeological park in the late morning and early afternoon (see Chapter 21). Returning to Naples, spend the rest of the afternoon strolling the waterfront and historic neighborhood nearby, seeing the **Castle of the Egg (Castel dell'Ovo), Riviera di Chiaia, New Castle (Castel Nuovo),** and **Palazzo Reale** (see Chapter 20). Get back to the train station for your luggage and take a taxi to the Molo Angioino, where you will catch the Tirrenia overnight ferry for Sicily (see Chapter 23). Check into your cabin and enjoy the cruise (if you wake up at the right time in the night, you may catch a glimpse of Stromboli, an active volcano of the Eolian Islands, spewing fireworks into the evening sky).

You'll arrive in Palermo the next morning. Spend the morning of Day Six seeing Palermo's **Palazzo Reale, Palatine Chapel (Cappella Palatina),** and **Duomo.** After lunch, take the bus to the **Duomo di Monreale** and the **Cloister,** where you can see some of the world's most incredible mosaics (see Chapter 23 for more details). Return to Palermo for a family-style Sicilian dinner.

On the morning of Day Seven, take a train to **Agrigento** and the **Valley of the Temples (Valle dei Templi),** a breathtaking panorama containing some of the finest Greek ruins in existence. If you drive to Agrigento rather than take the train, you can also make a quick detour to see the Doric temple in **Segesta** as well. You can then come back to spend the night in your hotel in Palermo.

On Day Eight, fly directly from Palermo to Florence on an early flight. (Alternatively, but only during the summer, you can catch the fast SNAV morning ferry back to Naples — a four-hour trip — and enjoy the rest of the day visiting what you missed in Naples on Day Five. Spend the night there and catch a very early train to Florence on the morning of Day Nine — about a five-hour trip. In that case, you'll have one less half-day each in Florence and Venice.) Spend Days Eight and Nine visiting Florence; be sure to reserve tickets for the **Uffizi** gallery and the **Accademia** so that you waste minimal time standing in line (see Chapter 14 and "Seeing Italy's Highlights in One Week," above, for more details).

On Day Ten, explore **Siena** and/or other hill towns of Tuscany. See Chapter 16 for tour companies, or rent a car to give yourself optimum flexibility.

On Day Eleven, take an early train to Venice (or an early-afternoon train if you arrived in Florence on Day Nine) and spend Days Eleven and Twelve exploring this magical city (see Chapter 18 and the one-week itinerary earlier in this chapter for details).

On Day Thirteen, journey beyond the city center to visit some of the other islands: **Murano, Torcello,** and the **Lido.** On Day Fourteen, take a last stroll around **St. Mark's Square**, and take an afternoon flight home.

Discovering Italy with Kids

Italy offers many attractions and sights that kids will enjoy. One of the big issues, however, is how much cultural sightseeing (particularly museums) your children can take. In general, we think that Rome and Venice are better destinations than Florence for families with children, mainly because many of their major attractions are outdoor experiences and appeal to children of all ages. In Florence, on the other hand, most of the major attractions are actually museums or churches.

Don't rule out the museums just because you have kids. If you have a child under 18 months, for example, most museums have benches where you can rest or nurse (Italians are pretty tolerant; if you get any funny looks, it'll probably be from other tourists). If you have a rambunctious toddler, you can take turns visiting the museum alone.

If you have a week in Italy, plan to spend Days One, Two, and Three in Rome. Bring your kids to the **Roman Forum,** the **Mercati Traianei,** the **Colosseum,** and the **Palatine Hill;** take a bike tour of the **Appian Way** and visit the **Catacombs** (they don't really feel like a cemetery at all). If you have time left, take a boat ride down the Tiber or go to a museum: They will enjoy the **Museo Nazionale delle Paste Alimentari** (the noodle museum) and the wonderful Egyptian section of the **Musei Vaticani** (see Chapter 12). If there's any extra time in Rome, your kids can definitely burn off some energy at the Roman Forum, **Imperial Forums,** and Palatine Hill; the **Villa Borghese;** the **Spanish Steps;** and the **Piazza di Spagna** (see Chapters 11 and 12). Rome is a bustling modern city that offers kids much of the stuff they like to do at home.

For Days Four and Five, you can visit either Naples and the Amalfi Coast, or Tuscany and the Cinque Terre, depending on your inclinations. From Rome, take the train to Naples. They will love taking a side trip to **Pompeii,** and you can also visit the volcano that destroyed it, **Vesuvius,** and gaze into the crater. On your second day you can show your kids the **Amalfi Coast;** in addition to seeing its breathtaking vistas, you can take a break to play on the beach and enjoy the warm Mediterranean (see Chapter 22).

Alternatively, you can rent a car in Rome and visit Tuscany: See the **Chianti** countryside, including beautiful **Siena** (they'll love the **Palio** if you are there for it); or take a train to **Pisa** to see the Leaning Tower; or visit the **Cinque Terre** (literally, "five towns"), which offer beautiful scenery and lots of walking, hiking, and swimming.

Whichever of these destinations you choose, stay there overnight and then take the train to **Venice,** where you will spend the rest of your vacation. In Venice, the kids will love **Canal Grande, St. Mark's Square, boat rides** on the *vaporetto* transportation system, the **Secret Itineraries** guided tour of **Palazzo Ducale,** and all the islands in the **lagoon,** as well as the **Museo Storico Navale.** The **Rolling Venice** program, highlighting a more lively look at the city, is designed especially for teenagers (see Chapter 18 for more details).

Unearthing Italy's Ancient History

If archeology and ancient history and culture are your thing, the focus of your visit should be central and southern Italy — Rome, Naples, and Sicily, where the main intersection of Etruscan, Greek, Carthaginian, Roman, Norman, and Arab influences took place. You will skip the Renaissance cities of Florence and Venice.

To begin this weeklong itinerary of ancient historical sights, fly into Rome. On Day One, see the **Roman Forum, Imperial Forums,** and **Palatine Hill.** Day Two is devoted to the very rich **Roman National Museum (Museo Nazionale Romano)** in the **Palazzo Massimo** and the **Palazzo Altemps** for Greek and Roman sculpture; in the afternoon visit the **Etruscan Museum (Museo Etrusco di Villa Giulia).** On Day Three, travel by train to Tivoli's **Villa Adriana** or to **Ostia Antica,** Rome's ancient seaport (see Chapters 12 and 13).

On Day Four, take a very early train to **Naples,** where you will stay for one night. On the day you arrive, see the **National Archaeological Museum (Museo Archeologico Nazionale),** where many of the frescoes and other treasures from Pompeii are on display, alongside a rich collection of Greek and Roman art. On Day Five visit **Pompeii** itself, and if you rise very early you can try to squeeze in a visit to **Herculaneum** as well. You can then take the night ferry to **Sicily** on the evening of Day Five (see Chapter 23) — you will arrive on the morning of Day Six.

If you want, spend part of Day Six in Palermo, visiting the **Palazzo Reale** with its **Palatine Chapel (Cappella Palatina),** and the **Duomo di Monreale** with its **Cloister;** otherwise, rent a car and head directly for **Agrigento,** for its **Valle dei Templi** (see Chapters 23 and 24). Spend the night in **Agrigento**, and start very early the next day for **Syracuse.**

On Day Seven, in Syracuse, visit the **Zona Archeologica** with its spectacular ruins and then stroll around the harbor and the island of **Ortigia.** Leave the next morning for **Taormina,** site of a beautifully preserved Greek/Roman theater hanging over an azure sea in the shadow of **Etna,** a magnificent setting for your last night in Italy. Fly back home on Day Eight, either from nearby Catania airport or from Palermo.

Drawing from the Art Buff's Tour

If art is what draws you to Italy, you'll probably want to focus on the Renaissance. Your key destinations will be Rome, Florence, Naples, Venice, and Palermo. Of course, that is far too much if you only have a week. In that case, you have to make the difficult decision of what to skip: Sicilian Baroque is unique and very interesting, but Sicily is far away. On the other hand, you could squeeze in Palermo if you take the time to visit the rich collection of the **National Museum and Gallery of the Capodimonte (Museo e Gallerie Nazionali di Capodimonte)** in Naples.

For a one-week tour, we suggest you follow the "Seeing Italy's Highlights in One Week" itinerary (earlier in this chapter), with some changes. When you arrive, skip the bus tour and the ancient Roman attractions, going instead to the **Galleria Borghese** (having reserved a ticket in advance). This is a small museum packed with masterpieces; it should be doable on Day One. On Day Two, visit the **Vatican Museums/Sistine Chapel (Musei Vaticani/Cappella Sistina)** and also take in the **Caravaggios** in some of the churches, such as **San Luigi dei Francesi.** On Day Three, visit the **Palazzo Barberini** and leave the afternoon open for one of the many changing exhibitions that are always going on in Rome. Leave early on Day Four for Florence, where you will want to devote the rest of the day to the **Uffizi.** On Day Five, you can give a brief look at the **Duomo** and then spend an hour or two at the **Palazzo Pitti.** You will not want to miss the **Accademia Gallery (Galleria dell'Accademia)** — reserve tickets here — to see Michelangelo's *David.* Try to squeeze in the **Basilica di San Lorenzo** and the **Medici Chapels (Cappelle Medicee)** as well. On Day Six, take the train to Venice. Of course you will want to see **St. Mark's Square (Piazza San Marco)** and **St. Mark's Basilica (Basilica di San Marco),** but these visits must be fairly brief to leave sufficient time for the **Accademia Galleries (Gallerie dell'Accademia).** On Day Seven, visit **Santa Maria Gloriosa dei Frari** and the nearby **Scuola di San Rocco.** If there is time, see the **Doge's Palace,** or make time in the afternoon to go to the **Peggy Guggenheim Collection.**

If you have two weeks, follow the "Touring the Best of Italy in Two Weeks" itinerary above, with the following changes: Use your extra day in Rome to visit the **Villa d'Este** in Tivoli (see Chapter 13). Otherwise, spend your extra time in **Naples,** a town well worth three days. Allow a whole day to visit (and digest) the enormous **National Museum and Gallery of the Capodimonte (Museo e Gallerie Nazionali di Capodimonte).** With the rest of your time you can take in the art in the churches of **Sant'Anna dei Lombardi, Santa Chiara,** and the **Certosa di San Martino.** See the **Teatro San Carlo** and the **Galleria Umberto I** (see Chapter 20). When you head to Sicily, skip Agrigento in favor of more time in Palermo in order to make room for a visit to the **Palazzo Abbatellis,** which contains, among other things, the famous *Madonna* by Antonello da Messina, and for a visit to the **Teatro Massimo** (see Chapter 23). Head for Florence by air and spend your extra time seeing the paintings by Fra Angelico in the **St. Mark's Museum (Museo San Marco)** and the Masaccio in the church of **Santa Maria del Carmine** (see Chapter 14). On the way to Venice, stop in **Padua** (see Chapter 19) to see Giotto's masterpiece, the **Scrovegni Chapel (Cappella degli Scrovegni);** alternatively, you can stop in **Perugia** (see Chapter 17), to visit the **Galleria Nazionale dell'Umbria (National Gallery of Umbria).** In Venice, use your extra day to visit some of the other churches, such as **Santa Maria della Salute,** filled with masterpieces by Tintoretto, Tiziano, and other Venetian masters.

Part II
Planning Your Trip to Italy

The 5th Wave   By Rich Tennant

"And how shall I book your flight to Italy – First Class, Coach, or Medieval?"

In this part . . .

In this part, we get down to the nuts and bolts of organizing your trip. We even suggest smart choices that will help you reduce the cost and enjoy your trip even more. Plus, we give tips for travelers with special interests and needs.

Chapter 5 discusses money; we deal with budget-related questions, and list some tips for pinching a euro here and there without sacrificing, as well as the best ways to handle your money. Chapter 6 concerns the various ways of getting to Italy, and Chapter 7 gives you information about getting around Italy after you arrive. Chapter 8 covers hotel options and booking your room. In Chapter 9, we offer some advice for a variety of special situations, including traveling with children. Chapter 10 takes care of the details that travelers too often leave to the last minute, such as getting a passport, thinking about medical and travel insurance, and making reservations for special events.

Chapter 5

Managing Your Money

. . . .

In This Chapter

▶ Devising a realistic budget

▶ Determining traveling, lodging, and dining expenses

▶ Remembering the extras: shopping and entertainment

▶ Tipping, Italian-style

▶ Saving money

. . . .

*W*hen it comes to planning a vacation budget, you usually deal with two different numbers: what you'd *like* to spend and what you *can* spend. But if you trim here and there on the incidentals and splurge just on the things that really matter to you, you can still design a terrific vacation without breaking the bank. In this chapter, we give you some pointers on being realistic and keeping track of all the costs that you'll have to bear in mind.

Planning Your Budget

Budgeting your vacation dollars isn't hard, it's the choices that hurt — and the mistakes. We figure there are six major elements that eat up your vacation budget: transportation, lodging, dining, sightseeing, shopping, and nightlife. How well you plan certain elements in advance can make or break your budget.

Consider transportation for example: If you wait until mid-June to reserve a flight to Italy for July, you'll be lucky to pay $1,000 — if you can find a seat at all. Book ahead and you might save a couple hundred bucks that you could put towards a shopping splurge.

Lodging is another big-ticket item. You can save on lodging and get the cost down around $120 a night if you are willing to forego amenities and put up with a certain amount of inconvenience (less central location, shared bath, and so on). How elastic your budget is will depend on how flexible you are. If you book all your hotels in advance, you'll know that piece of the budget before you leave, too.

A pocketful of change

In many of Italy's churches, fragile paintings are kept in semi-obscurity, but you will often find a light box nearby. When you insert a coin or two, a light pops on to illuminate a painting, fresco, or sculpture for a limited amount of time. Therefore, carrying a pocketful of coins is always a good idea.

In Italy, dining is a great place to save money because the food is so good. Pizza is cheap, and so is a bowl of pasta, though it may be the best you ever tasted. Armed with a corkscrew and a plastic fork, you can assemble a fine picnic lunch from the supermarket using ingredients you won't even find at your local gourmet shop.

The following sections provide more tips and consideration as you plan your budget. Tables 5-1 and 5-2 give you a sampling of costs that you may encounter on your trip. Oh yes, and don't forget taxes — we cover that in "Taking Taxes into Account," later in this chapter.

Table 5-1	What Things Cost in Rome
A metro or city bus ride	1€ ($1.15)
Can of soda	1€–1.50€ ($1.15–$1.75)
Pay-phone call	0.10€ (15¢)
Movie ticket	3 €–6€ ($3.50–$7)
Caffè lungo (American-style espresso)	0.65€ (75¢)
Cappuccino (or something similar)	.80€ ($.90)
Ticket to the Galleria Borghese	7.50€ ($8.50) res. incl.
Gasoline	1.15€ ($1.32) per liter = 4.35€ ($5) per gallon
Average hotel room	175€ ($200)
Liter of house wine in a restaurant	5€ ($5.75)
Individual pizza in a pizzeria	8€–12€ ($9–$14)
First-class letter to U.S. (or any overseas country)	0.80€ (90¢)

Table 5-2	What Things Cost in Greve in Chianti
A subway or city bus ride	0.65€ (75¢)
Can of soda	1€ (1.15¢)
Pay-phone call	0.10€ (15¢)
Caffè lungo (American-style espresso)	0.65€ (75¢)
Cappuccino (or something similar)	0.80€ (90¢)
Gasoline	1.15€ ($1.32) per liter = 4.33€ ($5) per gallon
Average hotel room	115€ ($132.25)i
Liter of house wine in a restaurant	4€ ($4.60)
Individual pizza in a pizzeria	6€–10.00€ ($6.90–$11.50)
First-class letter to U.S. (or any overseas country)	0.80€ (90¢)

Transportation

Airfare is one of the biggest components of your budget. Keeping it low gives you a sort of cushion for the rest of your expenses. The actual cost depends on the time that you travel (but booking in advance helps, too). In high season, you're lucky to find a round-trip ticket for less than about $850; other times, though, you may find tickets for half that much or even less. Make sure that you check out our money-saving tips before you buy an airline ticket (see Chapter 6).

In-country travel is an expense that can vary widely. If you visit Italy for a week and focus on the major sights in Rome and Florence, you're only talking about one round-trip ticket between the two cities on top of your airfare.

Transportation within Italy offers many more choices. In some tourist destinations you either *shouldn't* rent a car (New York City or Paris) or absolutely *must* rent one (the American West or Scotland). In Italy, however, the answer is less clear-cut. Because the country's train and bus systems are highly developed and because gasoline (*benzina* to Italians) is so expensive (about $5 per gallon), you don't save much money by driving. Renting a car is also likely to be more expensive than you're used to back home — see Chapter 7 for more on rentals. (Other issues may keep you from driving abroad as well, such as high speeds and hair-raising curves.)

Without a car, you don't have the hassle of trying to find parking and paying for it. If you arrive in Venice, Florence, or Rome with a car, you have to keep it garaged during your entire stay. Venice has no roads at all (except watery ones), Florence is small and bans cars from the historic center, and Rome has too many roads and drivers for you to want to deal with (and also bans nonresidents from driving in the *centro*). There's also a fatigue factor. Think how much better you'll feel after looking out the window at the countryside instead of the cars speeding by you.

The only time you may want to have a car in Italy is when you have the time to see more than just the highlights, and when you're planning to visit smaller towns and countryside areas.

Keep in mind that you'll probably be picking up and returning your car in a major city, but in most cities, rental agencies have locations on the edge of town, making exiting and entering fairly simple.

Lodging

Accommodations in Italy probably aren't much like the hotel or motel in your hometown. For one thing, your lodging in Italy may be in a building that went up when your hometown was still a big empty spot on the map. And originally, the building may have been a princely *palazzo,* a grand townhouse, or a spartan monastery. We list many renovated hotels in this book, but keep in mind that space is at a premium in Italy. For a detailed discussion of what you can expect in Italy's hotel rooms, see Chapter 8.

Hotel bathrooms in Italy are often tiny, and it's easy to see why. Buildings are much older than in the United States, and private bathrooms were added to preexisting rooms, creating sometimes funky results. Be aware that in many smaller hotels, rooms still exist with a shared bath down the hall and just a sink (or nothing) in the room itself. If you absolutely want a nice, *private* bathroom, be willing to fork over extra euro for a more expensive hotel. On the other hand, you can save a lot of money if you don't mind smaller private facilities or even going down the hall for a shower. Keep in mind that hotel rates vary from region to region and from city to city: Florence and Venice are pricier than Rome, but Naples, and even more so Sicily, are cheaper. Figure that 150€ ($170) buys you a decent double room with private bath anywhere (though a much better room in the south than in the north), but 230€ ($265) buys you a nice room all over the country. From 350€ ($400) and up, you're buying a luxury room. Of course, the amount that these estimates represent in dollars constantly varies according to the current currency exchange rates.

 You can save money if you renounce the breakfast that your hotel serves, unless it's included with your room rate. Breakfast is worth paying for only at the more expensive hotels ($$$ and above), where you find a buffet with a variety of foods, usually including eggs, sausage, cheese, cold cuts, yogurt, fruit, and cereal. This kind of breakfast may run about 15€ ($17), so you have to decide if what you get is worth the money.

In all the hotel reviews in this guide, we supply the *rack rates,* which in Italy is the highest rate the hotel can charge you (at the peak of high season and when the hotel is completely full). You should be able to do better than that in most cases. See Chapter 8 for a table indicating what the $ symbols ($–$$$$$) mean.

Dining

As in any destination, you can spend a lot or a little when it comes to dining in Italy. For example, less-formal restaurants (called *pizzerie,* trattorie, *osterie,* and *rosticcerie*) often offer the best combination of quality and price. You can generally count on all of these having traditional fare served in simple surroundings. *Pizzerie* (obviously) specialize in pizza; trattorie and *osterie* are casual, family-run restaurants serving full, hearty meals at relatively inexpensive prices; and *rosticcerie* are cafeterias with pre-prepared hot dishes and roasting chickens in the window. Of course, you can find some famous *ristorantes* (restaurants) that are elegant and pricey and serve fantastic food, but the equation *high price=good food* is not at all a certain bet in Italy.

To confuse the issue even further, the names for the different eateries are not as descriptive as they once were. Many high-priced joints take the name trattoria for its homey, feel-good vibe, and smaller places anoint themselves as *ristorantes* to try to class up the place. When in doubt, always go for the simpler option. Chances are you'll get homemade cooking for only a few dollars.

Although things are changing, *pranzo* (lunch) used to be the big meal in Italy, where the lunch "hour" was more like one-and-a-half to two hours. Lunch prices may also be cheaper, so in most cities two people can eat a nice lunch with a half-liter of wine for about 30€ to 40€ ($35–$46) if they don't eat in a touristy piazza or a glitzy restaurant. Dinner in the same type of place will be 45€ ($52) and up for two.

Most restaurants impose a basic **table-and-bread charge,** called *pane e coperto,* of about 2€ to 4€ ($2.30–$4.60), and you'll probably like to drink mineral water (fizzy or not, it's much cheaper than in the United States). On the other hand, service is usually included (look for the words *servizio incluso* on the menu) unless otherwise noted. If it's not, leave a 10 to 15 percent tip on the table if service was satisfactory.

Just as with the hotels, we use a dollar-sign system to alert you to the prices of restaurants. See the Introduction for a table indicating what the $ symbols ($–$$$$). These prices reflect a per-person charge for a meal consisting of a pasta or appetizer, a main course *(secondi),* a side dish (called a *contorno* in Italy), and dessert. It does not include wine or alcoholic drinks, the prices of which can vary widely. Within the listing information we give you the price range of just the main course, listed as *secondi.*

More and more Italian restaurants are adding a side dish to the entrée. It used to be that if you ordered grilled salmon as your main course, that's what you got — just grilled salmon. Now you may find a side dish such as a vegetable sharing the plate.

 On a tight budget? Try our splurge-and-save approach to dining: If we really want to try a particular expensive restaurant, we make up for the extra outlay by eating a lunch or dinner of fresh bread, locally cured prosciutto, regional cheeses, raw or cooked vegetables, and local wine or mineral water, all of which can be found at Italy's great markets and *rosticcerie*. A picnic lunch is also a great way to visit some of the outdoor sights.

Sightseeing

Museums and other attractions charge anywhere from 2€ to 9€ ($2.30–$10.35) for admission. Most churches are free (avoid visiting during services unless you're attending the service, however). Frankly, sightseeing isn't an area where you can save a lot of money, and you'll probably be sorry if you try. On the other hand, entrance fees for most attractions aren't that expensive to begin with (with some notable exceptions), so your budget won't be stretched to its limits by daily sightseeing expenditures.

 In the specific destination chapters, we note whenever you can find special combination discount tickets and special discount cards. (In Venice, for instance, people under 30 can receive a discount for shopping, accommodations, and sightseeing with the Rolling Venice pass.)

Beware that many special discounts are available based on reciprocity between countries. Therefore, many discounts — senior and children discounts especially — aren't available to Americans but are available to British and other residents of European Union (EU) countries.

 Because of the long lines at times of great tourist influx, many major museums in Italy have started offering advance ticketing. You can now make reservations before you leave home, thus bypassing waits of up to three hours. The list of museums for which you can make reservations includes Rome's **Galleria Borghese** (see Chapter 12) and Florence's **Uffizi Gallery** and **Accademia Gallery** (see Chapter 14).

Don't sit to sip

Be aware that any time you sit down in a *caffè* or bar in Italy, things cost more. Coffee at an outside table in Piazza del Popolo or Piazza San Marco, for example, may cost the same as lunch anywhere else. Most Italians stand at the bar while they have a coffee or a beer.

Shopping

Shopping is the one expenditure that is totally within your control: You can spend hundreds on a full-length leather coat for yourself or for a friend, or you can skip shopping completely. Throughout this book, we give you our recommendations for the best shops and items that each city offers.

Italy is famous for its artwork, design, and crafts — art glass, pottery, leather, gold, and lace, among many other fine wares. Italian fashion isn't half-bad either — Versace, Dolce & Gabbana, and Armani are a few of the world-famous Italian firms.

Depending on exchange rates, you may actually save by buying Italian goods in Italy. More important, though, it gives you a chance to buy things that simply aren't available, or not in such variety, back home. Use your trip as a chance to pick up that special something you have an irresistible craving for — maybe a Murano chandelier, a pair of leather boots, or a Gucci handbag (you might find a nice used Ferrari).

Nightlife

Visiting the opera, going out for a drink, listening to music in a jazz club, and dancing the night away are all extra pleasures that make your time in Italy that much more memorable. You can spend big bucks in this department, or you can cut your costs by enjoying those serendipitous little things that are free or nearly so, such as people-watching on a beautiful floodlit piazza or ordering a coffee or drink in a classic *caffè* and soaking in the atmosphere.

If you want to attend a performance of an ancient Greek tragedy or a Verdi opera, we give you the best options for getting tickets at each venue and tips for saving money at the same time. Nightclubs in Italy are about as expensive as anywhere else, but you may be able to avoid a cover charge by sitting or standing at the bar rather than taking a table, or by arriving before a certain hour. If you happen to be in Italy during a public holiday or festival, you may enjoy abundant free entertainment, much of it in the streets.

Tips on Tipping

Tipping isn't a big extra in Italy the way it is in some destinations. Because waiters are better paid and employers can't wriggle out of paying them a wage by assuming they'll get tips, gratuities aren't a large part of their income. Leaving a few euro as a token of appreciation is always a polite gesture, though. If, on the other hand, you eat in the restaurants of big glitzy hotels in major cities, keep in mind that such places may expect you to fork over the usual American 15 to 20 percent. Check for the words *servizio incluso* (service included) on the menu; if they aren't there, expect to pay a full gratuity.

You do have to tip bellhops who carry your bags, and you should give cab drivers a small tip as a token of appreciation, much like you would waiters.

Cutting Costs — But Not the Fun

Don't feel like taking out a second mortgage on your house so you can afford a vacation to Italy? Well, start thinking like an Italian. Italians have relatively less disposable income than Americans; the closer you mirror the way they live and travel, the cheaper your trip will be — and the closer you get to the Italians themselves. Staying in a huge hotel designed for foreign tourists with all the fixings will cost you a lot as will the luxury of renting a big car. Tack on a few five-star restaurant experiences and your budget flies out the window. Instead, try to live for a week without your own private bathroom. Make big, healthy sandwiches from the delicious stuff you bought in a market. Pass on the postcards, trinkets, and other things that you pick up just to say that you've been to Italy — you might even save enough for a splurge here and there.

But remember that sometimes paying more makes sense. For example, if you're facing sightseeing overload and are dead tired, you may not want to take an hour-long bus ride to the other side of town to your hotel. Take a cab instead. And why not grab a bite to eat in the slightly expensive cafe near where you are rather than deal with crossing town to an extra-cheap restaurant? Plus, there are areas where you shouldn't make cuts: not seeing Florence's Uffizi, Venice's Accademia, Rome's Vatican Museums and Sistine Chapel, or some other major sights, just because they cost more, would be a tragedy. We'd rather skip lunch and take the opportunity to go to one of these must-sees twice. Who knows when you'll be back that way again?

Throughout this book, you can find Bargain Alert icons that highlight money-saving tips and/or great deals. Here are some additional cost-cutting strategies:

- ✔ **Go off season.** If you can travel at nonpeak times (usually winter, with the exception of the Christmas/New Year's holidays), you can find airfares and hotel prices as much as 20 percent less than during peak months.

- ✔ **Travel during off-peak days of the week.** Airfares vary depending not only on the time of the year but also on the day of the week. In Italy, weekend rates are often cheaper than weekday rates. When you inquire about airfares, ask if you can obtain a cheaper rate by flying on a different day.

- ✔ **Surf the Web.** Airlines often have special Internet-only rates that are appreciably cheaper than rates quoted over the phone. Also, you can find good hotel packages online.

✔ **Try a package tour.** For popular destinations like Italy, you can book airfare, hotel, ground transportation, and even some sightseeing by making just one call to a travel agent or packager, and you may pay a lot less than if you tried to put the trip together yourself. But always work out the prices that you'd pay if you arranged the pieces of your trip yourself, just to double check. See the section on package tours in Chapter 6 for specific suggestions.

✔ **Pack light.** Packing light enables you to carry your own bags and not worry about finding a porter (don't forget to tip yourself). Likewise, you can take a bus or a train rather than a cab from the airport if you pack light, saving you a few more euro.

✔ **Reserve a room with a refrigerator and coffeemaker.** You don't have to slave over a hot stove to cut a few costs; several motels have minifridges and coffeemakers. Buying supplies for breakfast will save you money — and probably calories.

✔ **Always ask for discount rates.** Membership in AAA, frequent-flier plans, trade unions, AARP, or other groups may qualify you for discounts on plane tickets, hotel rooms, or even meals. Ask about everything — you may be pleasantly surprised with the answer you receive.

✔ **Get out of the center of town.** In many places, you may find that staying in hotels just outside the city center or across the river aren't quite as convenient but are a great bargain. You may only need to do a little more walking or take a short commute. See the chapter on each destination for hotel information. On the other hand, if you pick a hotel out of the way, you'll waste precious time in transportation and you may well ruin your trip. The key is always to have a short commute to the attractions you want to visit.

✔ **Ask if your kids can stay in your room with you.** Many hotels won't charge you the additional-person rate if your extra person is pint-sized and related to you. You can save much more if you don't take two rooms, even if you have to pay some extra for a rollaway bed.

✔ **Try expensive restaurants at lunch instead of dinner.** At most top restaurants, prices at lunch are usually considerably less than those at dinner, and the menu often offers many of the same specialties.

✔ **Have a picnic.** You can put together some delicious and inexpensive meals at an Italian grocery store, and then enjoy your feast in a garden or park.

✔ **Use public transportation.** In Italy, moving from one destination to another by train is cheap and easy. (The map on the inside front cover can get you started — it includes Italy's train system.) Using the local bus system in large cities like Venice and Rome is a little more complicated, but it's also a great way to visit the city.

✔ **Don't rent a gas guzzler.** Renting a smaller car is cheaper, and you save on gas to boot. Unless you're traveling with kids and need lots of space, don't go beyond the economy size. For more on car rentals, see Chapter 7.

✔ **Walk a lot.** A good pair of walking shoes can save you money in taxis and other local transportation. Remember that the historic center of most cities and towns is pretty small, so you can actually walk almost anywhere you need to go. You'll save money, get your exercise for the day, and get to know the city more intimately.

✔ **Skip the souvenirs.** Your photographs and your memories could be the best mementos of your trip. If you're concerned about money, you can do without the T-shirts, key chains, salt-and-pepper shakers, and other trinkets.

Handling Money

You're the best judge of how much cash you feel comfortable carrying or what alternative form of currency is your favorite. That's not going to change much on your vacation. True, you'll probably be moving around more and incurring more expenses than you generally do (unless you happen to eat out every meal when you're at home), and you may let your mind slip into vacation gear and not be as vigilant about your safety as when you're in work mode. But, those factors aside, the only type of payment that won't be quite as available to you away from home is your personal checkbook.

Making sense of the euro

Italy's currency, the **euro** (the plural is also *euro* and it's abbreviated as € in this guide), was introduced in January 2002 in Italy and in 11 other European countries. You can use the same currency in Austria, Belgium, Finland, France, Germany, Greece, Ireland, Italy, Luxembourg, the Netherlands, Portugal, and Spain.

The transformation to euro has made things much easier for Americans, because 1 euro exchanges in a range nearer $1 (the exchange rate used in this book is 1€ = $1.15; we round off all dollar values above $5). Many Web sites present the latest exchange rates, but one of the best is www. ex-rates.com, where you can get up-to-date (and historical) comparisons between the euro and your currency, whether it is the U.S. or Canadian dollar, the British pound, or something else.

Note that in the word "euro," Italians pronounce both vowels, so it's *ay-ur-oh*, not *yurr-oh*.

All did not go smoothly with the transition to the euro from the old *lire,* however. In many cases, Italian businesses, museums, and other attractions set their prices in euro as an *exact* equivalent to former prices in liras. The result was a lot of funny looking prices like 14.03€, 18.61€, and so on — and a lot of annoyed Italians searching through fistfuls of change. As they became more comfortable with the new currency, businesses started rounding up their prices. At first this caused a wild increase in prices, but the Italian Government stepped in and demanded that price increases be justifiable. Now, after a couple of years, the situation is much more under control. It is true that a number of prices have increased, but you also usually get more.

For example, some museum admissions have increased, but the opening hours have also been extended, to be more in line with opening hours in the rest of Europe and the world. In other cases, prices have *decreased*, because they have been rounded off to the lower whole euro amount. In Rome, the Palazzo Altemps admission went from 5.16€ to 5€.

Similarly, some hotel prices have gone up considerably, but more and more hotels are now offering a level of amenities comparable to American hotels.

Of course, from the American standpoint, Italian prices have increased, and quite a lot. This is due to the loss of value suffered by the dollar on international currency markets. For example, although that admission to Palazzo Altemps we just mentioned went down from 5.16€ to 5€, in dollars the price went up from $4.70 to $6, because at press time the dollar can buy fewer euro than two years ago. By the time you read this, the two currencies may be closer to parity, but then again maybe not. It's all the more important, then, to plan ahead and get the best deals you can.

The euro look

Paper bills come in 5€, 10€, 20€, 50€, 100€, 200€, and 500€ denominations. All bills are brightly colored and have a different shade for each denomination. In addition, the higher the value, the larger the physical size of the bill. A 50€ bill is bigger than a dollar bill, and even the smaller denominations are taller than U.S. dollars; if you have a bunch, you'll find stuffing them in your wallet a bit difficult. Remember that shops are always short of change, and breaking those large bills to buy a soft drink is sometimes difficult. Think ahead and try to have enough 10€ bills with you as you travel in Italy.

Coins come in 2€ and 1€ (both thin and brass-colored); 50-cent, 20-cent, and 10-cent (all brass colored); and 5-cent, 2-cent and 1-cent (all copper-colored) denominations.

For more information and pictures of the currency, check online at the official Web site of the **European Union** (http://europa.eu.int/euro) or at the site of the **European Central Bank** (www.euro.ecb.int).

Don't be surprised to see different country names on euro bills and coins: One face is the European side, common to each of the 12 participating countries, and the reverse face is the national side, where each country has printed its own design. All are valid and accepted in each of the countries.

You can exchange money at the airport, at banks, and at exchange bureaus, which usually display multilingual signs ("Change/Cambio/Wechsel"). Rates may vary to some degree. For example, some bureaus advertise "no fee," but then give you a lower rate so you come out the same anyway. Arriving with a small supply of euro, at least enough to pay for a cab to your hotel, is a good idea.

Nowadays, you don't even need to go to your bank to buy euro: You can get foreign currencies delivered to your door before you leave. The **OANDA** Web site, www.oanda.com, provides everything you ever wanted to know about currency (including the euro's most recent value against your own country's currency). The minimum purchase is $200 and the maximum is $1,500; shipping is free if you buy over $500, and you'll probably want to pay by debit card. (If you pay by credit card, you're charged as you would be for a cash advance, with the consequent fees.)

Using ATMs and carrying cash

The easiest and best way to get cash away from home is from an ATM (automated teller machine). The **Cirrus** network (☎ 800-424-7787; www.mastercard.com) is the most common international network in Italy. **PLUS** (☎ 800-843-7587; www.visa.com) exists in Italy but is less common. The Banca Nationale del Lavoro (BNL) is one bank that does offer PLUS in its ATMs; you can find BNL branches all over Italy, but not in every small town.

Before departing for Italy, make sure that you check the daily withdrawal limit for your ATM card and ask whether you need a new personal identification number, or PIN. (You need a four-digit PIN for Europe, so if you currently have a six-digit PIN, you must get a new one.)

Not all ATM keypads in Italy display letters as well as numbers. Some have only numbers. Therefore, if your PIN is "SPOT" or "HIMOM," you need to know how it translates into numbers (check this before you leave home!).

Look at the back of your bank card to see which network you're on, then call or check online for ATM locations at your destination. Be sure you know your four-digit PIN before you leave home and be sure to find out your daily withdrawal limit before you depart. Also keep in mind that many banks impose a fee every time your card is used at a different bank's ATM, and that fee can be higher for international transactions (up to $5 or more) than for domestic ones (where they're rarely more than $1.50). On top of this, the bank from which you withdraw cash may charge its own fee. To compare banks' ATM fees within the U.S., use www.bankrate.com. For international withdrawal fees, ask your bank.

In major cities, ATMs are never far away, so you can walk around with 100€ ($115) in your wallet and you should be set to dine and pay your museum admissions (but not your hotel bill). Before going off on a driving tour of the countryside, however, such as in Sicily or Chianti, make sure that you have a good stock of cash in your wallet; banks and ATMs are rarer outside the big cities.

If you have linked checking and savings accounts and you're in the habit of moving relatively small amounts of money from savings to checking as you need it, beware: Italian ATMs won't show you the transfer-between-accounts option, and they won't allow you to withdraw money directly from your savings account. If your checking account runs dry, you must call or write your bank to move money from savings to checking. (We did so, and our bank charged us $30. Ouch!)

Charging ahead with credit cards

Credit cards are a safe way to carry money: They also provide a convenient record of all your expenses, and they generally offer relatively good exchange rates. You can also withdraw cash advances from your credit cards at banks or ATMs, provided you know your PIN. If you've forgotten yours, or didn't even know you had one, call the number on the back of your credit card and ask the bank to send it to you. It usually takes 5 to 7 business days, though some banks will provide the number over the phone if you tell them your mother's maiden name or some other personal information.

Keep in mind that when you use your credit card abroad, most banks assess a 2 percent fee above the 1 percent fee charged by Visa or MasterCard or American Express for currency conversion on credit charges. But credit cards still may be the smart way to go when you factor in things like exorbitant ATM fees and higher traveler's check exchange rates (and service fees).

Some credit card companies recommend that you notify them of any impending trip abroad so that they don't become suspicious when the card is used numerous times in a foreign destination and block your charges. Even if you don't call your credit card company in advance, you can always call the card's toll-free emergency number if a charge is refused — a good reason to carry the phone number with you. But perhaps the most important lesson here is to carry more than one card with you on your trip; a card might not work for any number of reasons, so having a backup is the smart way to go.

Toting traveler's checks

These days, traveler's checks are less necessary because most cities have 24-hour ATMs that allow you to withdraw small amounts of cash as needed. However, keep in mind that you will likely be charged an ATM withdrawal fee if the bank is not your own (in Italy, it won't be), so if you're withdrawing money every day, you might be better off with traveler's checks — provided that you don't mind showing identification every time you want to cash one.

You can get traveler's checks at almost any bank. **American Express** offers denominations of $20, $50, $100, $500, and (for cardholders only) $1,000. You'll pay a service charge ranging from 1 to 4 percent. You can also get American Express traveler's checks over the phone by calling ☎ **800-221-7282;** Amex gold and platinum cardholders who use this number are exempt from the 1 percent fee.

Visa offers traveler's checks at Citibank locations nationwide, as well as at several other banks. The service charge ranges between 1.5 and 2 percent; checks come in denominations of $20, $50, $100, $500, and $1,000. Call ☎ **800-732-1322** for information. AAA members can obtain Visa checks without a fee at most AAA offices or by calling ☎ **866-339-3378.** **MasterCard** also offers traveler's checks. Call ☎ **800-223-9920** for a location near you.

If you choose to carry traveler's checks, be sure to keep a record of their serial numbers separate from your checks in the event that they are stolen or lost. You'll get a refund faster if you know the numbers.

Taking Taxes into Account

You may feel like you're "getting away from it all" on your vacation, but there's one fact of life that can't be escaped, alas: taxes.

Italy's **value-added tax** (known as the IVA) is a steep 19 percent, but you can get a refund for purchases costing more than 155€ ($178). The value-added tax is included in all the prices that you're quoted. Stores displaying a "Tax Free" insignia can give you an invoice that you can cash at the airport's Customs office as you leave Italy. Otherwise, you have to take the invoice from the store, have it stamped at the airport by Customs, and then mail it back to the store, which will then send you a check or credit your charge account.

Dealing with a Lost or Stolen Wallet

Being on vacation is a blissful time of distraction and discovery. Unfortunately, this makes a tourist a ripe target for pickpockets. In Italy violent crime is rare; most of the wallets are lost to pickpockets, not muggers.

If you discover your wallet has been lost or stolen, contact all of your credit card companies right away. You'll also want to file a report at the nearest police precinct. Your credit card company or insurer may require a police report number or record of the loss. Most credit card companies have an emergency toll-free number to call if your card is lost or stolen; they may be able to wire you a cash advance immediately or deliver an emergency credit card in a day or two. Call the following emergency numbers in the United States:

> ✔ **American Express** ☎ **800-221-7282** (for cardholders and traveler's check holders)
>
> ✔ **MasterCard** ☎ **800-307-7309** or 636-722-7111
>
> ✔ **Visa** ☎ **800-847-2911** or 410-581-9994

For other credit cards, call the toll-free number directory at
☎ **800-555-1212.**

If you need emergency cash over the weekend when all banks and American Express offices are closed, you can have money wired to you via **Western Union** (☎ **800-325-6000;** www.westernunion.com).

Identity theft or fraud are potential complications of losing your wallet, especially if you've lost your driver's license along with your cash and credit cards. Notify the major credit-reporting bureaus immediately; placing a fraud alert on your records may protect you against liability for criminal activity. The three major U.S. credit-reporting agencies are **Equifax** (☎ **800-766-0008;** www.equifax.com), **Experian** (☎ **888-397-3742;** www.experian.com), and **TransUnion** (☎ **800-680-7289;** www.transunion.com). Finally, if you've lost all forms of photo ID call your airline and explain the situation; they might allow you to board the plane if you have a copy of your passport or birth certificate and a copy of the police report you've filed.

Watch your purse, wallet, briefcase, or backpack in any public place. And when walking on the streets, keep your purse on the side away from traffic, so a thief on a motor scooter can't speed by and grab it from you.

Chapter 6

Getting to Italy

. . . .

In This Chapter

▶ Checking out major airlines
▶ Finding alternate ways to Italy
▶ Sorting out package tours and escorted tours

. . . .

*I*f you live near a major city, getting to Italy may be even easier than reaching another destination in your own country — but it won't be cheaper. Airfares to Italy are significantly higher than those from the U.S. to England, for example, and a round-trip ticket during peak times can run between $800 and $1,000. Of course, with the cutthroat competition among airlines, you may be able to lock in a much better deal — especially if you book well in advance and have a flexible itinerary. This chapter outlines all the ways and means you have to make getting to Italy a snap.

Flying to Italy

Rome and Milan are the only two Italian cities to which you can fly non-stop from North America; for Florence, Venice, Naples, or Sicily, you will have to switch to a connecting flight. Fly into Milan if you're focusing on northern Italy; choose Rome if you're focusing on the south.

Because Italy is long and skinny in shape, flying into one airport and leaving from the other makes sense, especially if you have only a week or ten days to travel and you want to see sights in both northern and southern Italy. If, for example, you landed in Milan, you could take a train to Venice, then pick up a car and drive down through Tuscany, loop around the near south taking in Rome and some other sites, and then fly out of Rome. For the right price, this plan may save you hundreds of miles of driving or sitting on the train just to retrace your steps to the airport where you entered.

Finding out which airlines fly there

Alitalia, the Italian national airline, offers flights from most major city in the world to every destination in Italy by way of Rome or Milan (☎ **800-223-5730** in the U.S., 800-361-8336 in Canada, 020-7602-7111 in London or 0990-448-259 in the rest of the U.K., 1300-653-747 or 1300-653-757 in Australia, toll-free 1478-65-643 or 06-65643 in Italy; www.alitalia.it). Alitalia also offers daily flights to all European capitals. Direct daily flights are scheduled from a number of U.S. cities as well as Toronto and Montréal. Likewise, Alitalia offers direct service between Sydney and Italy, but not every day. **British Airways** (☎ **800-247-9297**; www.ba.com) has lots of flights to Italy from many cities in North America, though you will be routed through London.

Also **American Airlines** (☎ **800-433-7300**; www.aa.com), **Delta** (☎ **800-241-4141;** www.delta.com), **United** (☎ **800-538-2929;** www.united.com), **US Airways** (☎ **800-428-4322;** www.usairways.com), **Continental** (☎ **800-525-0280;** www.continental.com), and **Northwest/KLM Airlines** (☎ **800-447-4747;** www.nwa.com) all usually offer direct nonstop flights to Rome or Milan from the United States, at least during peak season.

From Britain, your best bet is **British Airways** (☎ **0845-773-3377** in the U.K.; www.britishairways.com), though smaller charter companies also offer flights. **Alitalia** (☎ **020-8745-8200;** www.alitalia.it) is another possibility. Innovative options include **Ryanair** (☎ **0871-246-0000;** www.ryanair.com) and **EasyJet** (www.easyjet.com), which fit the old no-frills or discount airline slot.

From Australia and New Zealand, once again there is **Alitalia** (☎ **02-9922-1555;** www.alitalia.it). **Cathay Pacific** (☎ **1-300-361-060** in Australia, 0800-800-454 in New Zealand; www.cathaypacific.com) offers three flights a week to Rome from Melbourne and Sydney, connecting through Hong Kong. The airline also offers two flights from Perth and Cairns, connecting through Hong Kong, and one flight from Brisbane connecting through Hong Kong. Auckland is also served thrice weekly, also with a connection through Hong Kong. Another option is **Qantas** (☎ **13-13-13;** www.qantas.com), which offers some direct flights — daily from Melbourne to Rome and several days a week from Sydney. **Air New Zealand** (☎ **0800-737-000;** www.airnz.com) doesn't fly directly to Italy. You have to change in another European city to a national carrier.

On any day of the week, you can get a connecting flight through a major European capital, where you switch to the national carrier — for example, connecting through London with British Airways or through Paris with Air France. European airlines include **British Airways** (☎ **800-247-297;** www.britishairways.com), **Air France** (☎ **800-237-2747;** www.airfrance.com), **KLM** (☎ **800-374-7747;** www.klm.nl), and **Lufthansa** (☎ **800-645-3880;** www.lufthansa-usa.com).

All European carriers will make you stop over in their own country before you fly on to Italy. In order to encourage travelers to choose a non-direct alternative, round-trip rates are often handsomely discounted, and direct connections sometimes involve no more than an hour or two of layover. By connecting in major European hubs, you may be able to avoid Milan and Rome by flying into Italy's secondary airports, such as Venice, Turin, or Genoa. If you plan to travel on one of the European carriers, you may also want to consider combining a stop of a few days in a major European city en route to Italy.

Getting the best deal on your airfare

Competition among the major U.S. airlines is unlike that of any other industry. Every airline offers virtually the same product (basically, a coach seat is a coach seat is a . . .), yet prices can vary by hundreds of dollars.

 Business travelers who need the flexibility to buy their tickets at the last minute and change their itineraries at a moment's notice — and who want to get home before the weekend — pay (or at least their companies pay) the premium rate, known as the *full fare*. But if you can book your ticket far in advance, stay over Saturday night, and are willing to travel midweek (Tues, Wed, or Thurs), you can qualify for the least expensive price — usually a fraction of the full fare. For example, a flight from New York to Rome on two days' notice is a gruesome $3,000. But make it a seven-day advance purchase ticket, and the price immediately drops to $1,100. Make it 14-day advance purchase and it drops further, and so on.

The airlines also periodically hold sales, in which they lower the prices on their most popular routes. These fares have advance purchase requirements and date-of-travel restrictions, but you can't beat the prices. As you plan your vacation, keep your eyes open for these sales, which tend to take place in seasons of low travel volume — for Italy, that means the dead of winter. You almost never see a sale for travel from around mid-May through the peak summer vacation months of July and August and into September for Italy; you also pay top dollar at Thanksgiving and Christmas, when many people fly, regardless of the fare they have to pay.

Cutting ticket costs by using consolidators

Consolidators, also known as *bucket shops,* are great sources for international tickets, although they usually can't beat the Internet on fares within North America. Start by looking in Sunday newspaper travel sections; U.S. travelers should focus on the *New York Times, Los Angeles Times,* and *Miami Herald.* For less-developed destinations, small travel agents who cater to immigrant communities in large cities often have the best deals.

 Bucket shop tickets are usually nonrefundable or rigged with stiff cancellation penalties, often as high as 50 to 75 percent of the ticket price, and some put you on charter airlines with questionable safety records.

Several reliable consolidators are worldwide and available on the Net. **STA Travel** (☎ 800-781-4040; www.statravel.com), the world's leader in student travel, offers good fares for travelers of all ages. **ELTExpress** (☎ 800-TRAV-800; www.flights.com) started in Europe and has excellent fares worldwide. Flights.com also has "local" Web sites in 12 countries. FlyCheap, an industry leader, has become **Lowestfare.com** (www.lowestfare.com), and is owned by Priceline (see later in this chapter). **Air Tickets Direct** (☎ 800-778-3447; www.airticketsdirect.com) is based in Montréal and leverages the currently weak Canadian dollar for low fares. **The TravelHub** (☎ 888-AIR-FARE; www.travelhub.com) represents nearly 1,000 travel agencies, many of whom offer consolidator and discount fares.

Booking your flight online

The "big three" online travel agencies, **Expedia** (www.expedia.com), **Travelocity** (www.travelocity.com), and **Orbitz** (www.orbitz.com) sell most of the air tickets bought on the Internet. (Canadian travelers should try www.expedia.ca and www.travelocity.ca; U.K. residents can go for expedia.co.uk and opodo.co.uk.) Each has different business deals with the airlines and may offer different fares on the same flights, so shopping around is wise. Expedia and Travelocity will also send you an **e-mail notification** when a cheap fare becomes available to your favorite destination. Of the smaller travel agency Web sites, **SideStep** (www.sidestep.com) receives good reviews from users. It's a browser add-on that purports to "search 140 sites at once," but in reality only beats competitors' fares as often as other sites do.

Great **last-minute deals** are available through free weekly e-mail services provided directly by the airlines. Most of these deals are announced on Tuesday or Wednesday and must be purchased online. Most are only valid for travel that weekend, but some can be booked weeks or months in advance. Sign up for weekly e-mail alerts at airline Web sites or check mega-sites that compile comprehensive lists of last-minute specials, such as **Smarter Living** (smarterliving.com). For last-minute trips, www.site59.com in the U.S. and www.lastminute.com in Europe often have better deals than the major-label sites.

If you're willing to give up some control over your flight details, use an *opaque fare service* like **Priceline** (www.priceline.com) or **Hotwire** (www.hotwire.com). Both offer rock-bottom prices in exchange for travel on a "mystery airline" at a mysterious time of day, often with a mysterious change of planes en route. The mystery airlines are all major, well-known carriers — and the possibility of being sent hither and yon before you arrive in Italy is remote. But your chances of getting a 6 a.m. or 11 p.m. flight are pretty high. For example, Hotwire has a "no red eye" check-off, but be aware that they think that a 6 a.m. flight for which you have to be at the airport two hours in advance (it's hardly worth putting on your jammies, is it?) is *not* a red eye. Hotwire tells you flight prices before you buy; Priceline usually has better deals than Hotwire, but you have to play their "name our price" game — and with each try, you have to change something besides your bid, which is to prevent people from making endless iterations starting at 20 bucks. If you have fixed travel dates, better make a realistic bid to start or you'll have to change them or look elsewhere. In order to cover all the bases, Priceline has created/purchased **Lowestfare.com** (www.lowestfare.com), in which you don't have bid for seats.

Keep in mind that European national airlines (Alitalia, Lufthansa, Air France, and so on) may cost more, but they also seem to have more legroom and better service. This may be an important consideration, given that the flight from New York to Rome is about eight hours compared with five hours to London.

For Italy, the high season is long and getting longer, and snagging low fares is increasingly difficult; at certain times, you may be lucky just to get on any plane heading for Italy. But fear not: You don't have to pay top dollar for your airline seat. Here are some tips on scoring the best airfare:

- ✔ **Book in advance and be flexible.** Passengers who can book their ticket long in advance, who can stay over Saturday night, or who are willing to travel on a Tuesday, Wednesday, or Thursday after 7 p.m., for example, will pay a fraction of the full fare. If your schedule is flexible, say so — ask if you can secure a cheaper fare by staying an extra day, by flying midweek, or by flying at less-trafficked hours. Buying in advance makes a big difference as well: If you can book your airfare more than 21 days in advance, you may be able to snag supersaver seats.

- ✔ **Shop around for specials — and keep shopping.** Remember that if you already hold a ticket when a sale breaks, exchanging your ticket, which usually incurs a $100 to $150 charge, may pay off. Keep in mind that the lowest-priced fares are often nonrefundable, require advance purchase of one to three weeks and a certain length of stay, and carry penalties for changing dates of travel.

- ✔ **Join frequent-flier clubs.** Accruing miles on one program is best, so you can rack up free flights and achieve elite status faster. But opening as many accounts as possible makes sense, no matter how seldom you fly a particular airline. It's free, and you get the best choice of seats, faster response to phone inquiries, and prompter service if your luggage is stolen, if your flight is canceled or delayed, or if you want to change your seat.

Arriving by Other Means

You may be adding Italy to a larger European vacation, or perhaps you live in Britain or Ireland (if you are in Britain and are tempted to drive your own car to Italy, don't — we once drove from Brittany to Rome and it was *long* and exhausting). It will be cheaper for you to fly to Italy and rent a car there — or not. So you may be looking for other ways to get to Italy. If so, check out our list below of alternate ways to get to Italy:

✔ **Train:** Paris is connected to Italy by high-speed TGV trains to Torino-Novara-Milan. From Paris, you can also take the famous Palatino, the overnight train to Rome. You can also catch overnight trains from Germany (Hanover, Düsseldorf, Köln, Bonn, and Frankfurt). For more on taking the train in Italy, see Chapter 7.

✔ **Ferry:** Several ferry companies service Genoa from both France and Greece. Naples-based **Grimaldi Ferries** (☎ 081-496-444; www.grimaldi-ferries.com) offers service to and from Salerno to Palermo (Sicily), Malta, and Valencia (Spain).

✔ **Bus: Eurolines** (☎ 0990-143-219; www.eurolines.com) is the leading operator of scheduled coach services across Europe, and services to Italy depart from London's Victoria Coach Station. Its comprehensive network services Turin, Milan, Bologna, Florence, and Rome — plus summer routes to Verona, Vicenza, Padua, and Venice.

Joining an Escorted Tour

You may be one of the many people who love escorted tours: The tour company takes care of all the details; they tell you what to expect at each leg of your journey; you know your costs up front; and you don't get many surprises. Fans of escorted tours know that they can take you to the maximum number of sights in the minimum amount of time with the least amount of hassle. We give you some tips in this section on how to choose the escorted tour that best fits your vacation needs.

Choosing an escorted tour

If you decide to take an escorted tour, we strongly recommend buying travel insurance, especially if the tour operator asks to you pay up front. It's wise to buy travel insurance through an independent agency. (More about the ins and outs of travel insurance in Chapter 10.)

Wine, antiques, and hunting for mushrooms: Specialty tours on the Internet

You can find tours in Italy centered around just about anything — antiques, archaeology, art history, cooking, cycling, gay life, nudism, religion, walking, wineries, and more — at **InfoHub Specialty Travel Guide** (www.infohub.com). Two other good resource sites for specialty tours and travels are the **Specialty Travel Index** (www.specialtytravel.com), which offers a comprehensive selection of Italian tours from ballooning to mushroom hunting to river cruises, and **Shaw Guides** (www.shawguides.com), with links to a substantial volume of trips to Italy, from archaeological programs to falconry trips to tours for opera fans.

When choosing an escorted tour, along with finding out whether you have to put down a deposit and when final payment is due, ask a few simple questions before you buy:

- ✔ **What is the cancellation policy?** Can they cancel the trip if they don't get enough people? How late can you cancel if you are unable to go? Do you get a refund if you cancel? If they cancel?

- ✔ **How jam-packed is the schedule?** Do tour organizers try to fit 25 hours into a 24-hour day, or is there ample time for relaxing and/or shopping? If getting up at 7 a.m. every day and not returning to your hotel until 6 or 7 p.m. at night sounds like a grind, certain escorted tours may not be for you.

- ✔ **How big is the group?** The smaller the group, the less time you spend waiting for people to get on and off the bus. Tour operators may be evasive about this, because they may not know the exact size of the group until everybody has made reservations, but they should be able to give you a rough estimate.

- ✔ **Is there a minimum group size?** Some tours have a minimum group size, and may cancel the tour if they don't book enough people. If a quota exists, find out what it is and how close they are to reaching it.

- ✔ **What is included?** Don't assume anything. You may have to pay to get yourself to and from the airport. A box lunch may be included in an excursion but drinks may be extra. How much flexibility do you have? Can you opt out of certain activities, or does the bus leave once a day, with no exceptions? Are all your meals planned in advance? Can you choose your entree at dinner, or does everybody get the same chicken cutlet?

Finding an escorted tour to Italy

Some companies specialize in escorted Italian tours. Here's a brief list (prices quoted below include airfare except as noted; remember that packages and prices change all the time):

- ✔ **Italiatour** (☎ **800-845-3365** or 212-675-2183; www.italiatour.com) is associated with Alitalia and offers a variety of tours and native expertise. It is also the only tour operator with a desk right at the airport (at Fiumicino, in Rome). Some of their tours offer very competitive prices: In the late spring season, you can get a five-night Rome and Florence package for $1,199 including airfare. *Hint:* from their Internet home base, follow the link to the site for your country, where the packages are listed, such as italiatourusa.com and italiatour.co.uk. If you are in Canada, you will go through their partner, cittours-canada.com.

- ✔ **Perillo Tours,** 577 Chestnut Ridge Rd., Woodcliff Lake, NJ 07675-9988 (☎ **800-431-1515** or 201-307-1234; www.perillotours.com), has been in business for more than half a century. Its itineraries range from 8 to 15 days and are very diverse. Their 11-day "Tuscany and the Riviera" tour runs $3,739. Optional excursions are offered (at an extra charge) to allow you to customize your tour somewhat. Perillo tries to cover all the bases, and even has a package to help you get married in Italy.

✔ **Central Holidays** (☎ 800-935-5000; www.centralholidays.com) offers fully escorted tours in addition to their packages. Several levels of tours — and levels of "escort" — are offered. Their "Grand Tour" of Italy, lasting 19 days, takes you from the Alps to Syracuse. The pricetag varies from $4,999 in April to $5,299 in the summer months.

✔ For luxurious tours of Italy, you can also try **Abercrombie & Kent,** 1520 Kensington Rd., Oak Brook, IL 60523 (☎ **800-554-7016;** www.abercrombiekent.com; London address: Sloan Square House, Holbein Place, London SW1W 8NS; ☎ **020-7730-9600**). Their ten-day, "Highlights of Italy" tour focusing on the big three (Rome, Florence, and Venice) costs $3,945 *excluding* airfare.

✔ Some Italian tour companies focus on one specific region. For an in-depth tour of Sicily, for example, consider **Compagnia Siciliana Turismo (CST),** Via E. Amari 124, 90139 Palermo (☎ **091-582-294;** Fax: 091-582-218; web.tin.it/cst), which offers a number of organized tours of Sicily, lasting from a few days to two weeks. **Authentic Sicily,** 300 W. 23rd St., Suite 8G, New York, NY 10011 (☎ **877-SICILY-1;** www.authenticsicily.com) takes small groups on tours of "authentic" Sicily, promising a family-style environment and a relaxed pace. A typical eight-day tour is $2,300 *excluding* airfare.

Choosing a Package Tour

For lots of destinations, package tours can be a smart way to go. In many cases, a package tour that includes airfare, hotel, and transportation to and from the airport costs less than the hotel alone on a tour you book yourself. That's because packages are sold in bulk to tour operators, who resell them to the public.

Package tours can vary widely. Some offer a better class of hotels than others; others provide the same hotels for lower prices. Some book flights on scheduled airlines; others sell charters. In some packages, your choice of accommodations and travel days may be limited. Some let you choose between escorted vacations and independent vacations; others allow you to add on just a few excursions or escorted day trips (also at discounted prices) without booking an entirely escorted tour.

To find package tours, check out the travel section of your local Sunday newspaper or the ads in the back of travel magazines such as *Travel & Leisure, National Geographic Traveler,* and *Condé Nast Traveler.* **Liberty Travel** (call ☎ **888-271-1584** to find the store nearest you; www.libertytravel.com) is one of the biggest packagers in the Northeast, and usually has a full-page ad in Sunday papers.

Another good source of package deals is the airlines themselves. Most major airlines offer air/land packages, including **American Airlines Vacations** (☎ 800-321-2121; www.aavacations.com), **Delta Vacations** (☎ 800-221-6666; www.deltavacations.com), **Continental Airlines Vacations** (☎ 800-301-3800; www.coolvacations.com), and **United Vacations** (☎ 888-854-3899; www.unitedvacations.com). Several big **online travel agencies** — Expedia, Travelocity, Orbitz, Site59, and Lastminute.com — also do a brisk business in packages. If you're unsure about the pedigree of a smaller packager, check with the Better Business Bureau in the city where the company is based, or go online at www.bbb.org. If a packager won't tell you where it's based, don't fly with them.

Remember that the **escorted tour** operators discussed earlier also offer packages. For example, **Central Holidays** (www.centralholidays.com) has a seven-day "Tuscany at Leisure" package offering airfare, accommodations in a four-star hotel, and a car for about $1,500 to $1,800 per person depending on the season.

Other recommended packagers include **Kemwell** (☎ **800-678-0678;** www.kemwell.com) and **Italiatour** (☎ **800-845-3365** or 212-675-2183; www.italiatour.com), which offers interesting packages and specializes in tours for independent travelers, who take a car or train between destinations for which Italiatour books accommodations at a discounted rate.

If you search for a package on the Internet at an airline Web site, be prepared to spend a long time playing around with the variables. A dozen or more outbound and return flight options may pop up, each of which will affect the price. Your selected departure city matters, too. At the **American Airlines Vacations** site, we came up with a whopping $5,822 for a five-day air/hotel package to Florence in July, flying from Boston. Change the departure airport to New York's JFK and the price for the same trip plummets to $2,081. This is not unique to American; with any of these airline sites, you will need to do a lot of fiddling to get the best price. And always look for the specials and last-minute deals they are running first.

Chapter 7

Getting Around Italy

● ●

In This Chapter

▶ Flying to and fro
▶ Traveling on land

● ●

*A*fter you arrive in Italy — at either the Rome or Milan airport —
chances are you're going to want to explore the country a little
more. In this chapter, we give you the information you need to travel
throughout Italy and tips for choosing the type of transportation that
best suits your plans. We also give you a comparison of travel times
between major destinations using different modes of transportation.

By Plane

Although the most expensive travel option, air travel lets you see the
most sights, from Venice to Syracuse. **Alitalia,** the national airline of Italy
(☎ **800-223-5730** in the U.S., 800-361-8336 in Canada, 020-7602-7111 in
London, 0990-448-259 in the rest of the U.K., 1300-653-747 or 1300-653-757 in
Australia, and toll-free 1478-65643 or 06-65643 in Italy; www.alitalia.it
or www.alitaliausa.com), offers flights to every destination in the
country.

You can also get around via regional airlines. **Air Sicilia** (☎ 06-6501-
71046) flies to Sicily from other Italian cities and sometimes offers better
rates than Alitalia. Other private airlines include **Air One** (☎ 06-488-8069
outside Italy; 199-20-70-80 in Italy; www.air-one.it) and **Meridiana**
(☎ 0789-52-682; www.meridiana.it).

When traveling on domestic flights in Italy, you can receive a 30 percent
fare reduction if you take a flight that departs at night.

Table 7-1 provides the travel times between major Italian cities using different modes of transportation.

Table 7-1	Travel Times between the Major Cities			
Cities	*Distance*	*Air Travel Time*	*Train Travel Time*	*Driving Time*
Florence to Milan	298km/185 miles	55 min.	2½ hrs.	3½ hrs.
Florence to Venice min.	281km/174 miles	2 hrs., 5 min.	4 hrs.	3 hrs., 15
Milan to Venice	267km/166 miles	50 min.	3½ hrs.	3 hrs., 10 min.
Rome to Florence	277km/172 miles	1 hr., 10 min.	2½ hrs.	3 hrs., 20 min.
Rome to Milan	572km/355 miles	1 hr., 5 min.	5 hrs.	6½ hrs.
Rome to Naples	219km/136 miles	50 min.	2½ hrs.	2½ hrs.
Rome to Venice	528km/327 miles	1 hr., 5 min.	5 hrs., 15 min.	6 hrs.
Venice to Naples	747km/463 miles	1 hr., 45 min.	7 hrs., 45 min.	8½ hrs.

By Train

Train travel in Italy is convenient and affordable. The express trains are fast and comfortable, and they service practically everywhere. It might be slower that flying, but it is cheaper and you depart and arrive right from the center of town, not a distant airport. To check how well your chosen destinations are served by rail, see the map on the inside front cover of this guide.

One train-travel option is buying a pass from the **Rail Europe Group** (☎ 877-257-2887 in the U.S. and 800-361-RAIL in Canada; www.rail europe.com). The Rail Europe Group offers several options, based on how many days you want to travel. The **Trenitalia Pass** allows you unlimited travel in Italy for four days for $191; for ten days, the pass costs $315. What does that all mean? Obviously, you are better off the more ground you want to cover. If your four legs are Rome-Florence, Florence-Venice, Venice-Naples, and Naples-Rome, you are getting a lot of miles for your buck (consider that a single unreserved round-trip Amtrak fare from Boston to Washington, D.C. costs, as of this writing, about $200).

Another option is buying a kilometric ticket directly from the **FS (Ferrovia dello Stato;** www.ferroviedellostato.it), Italy's national rail company. With a kilometric ticket you purchase a distance in kilometers, which may be used for as many as four passengers. Several amounts are available; for example, you can buy 3,000km (1,860 miles) for 115€ ($132), and use as many kilometers as you want at a time. Shorter distances are available, too. You save about 15 percent over what you'd spend buying individual tickets. Each time you travel, go to the train-station window and have the pass validated; the teller will write down how many kilometers you have left. You can also ask the teller to write down all your stops (for example, "Roma to Venezia, via Firenze") so you don't have to go to the ticket booth at your through-stops. However, after the ticket is validated for a trip, you must complete the trip within four days. Surcharges apply to the express Eurostar trains, and in the high travel season, you have to reserve your seat (at a slight extra charge).

Kilometric tickets and rail passes are sold at all train stations. You can also buy rail passes before you leave the United States through a travel agent or Rail Europe (see the contact information earlier in this section). The official U.S. representative of the Italian national rail company is **CIT Tours,** 15 W. 44th St., Suite 104, New York, NY 10036 (☎ **800-845-3365;** http://cit-tours.com). You can also find FS rail info or buy tickets online at www.ferroviedellostato.it.

By Bus

In Italy, you can get virtually anywhere by public transportation and quite easily. If you are up to it and have the time, you don't really need to rent a car even to reach destinations in the middle of nowhere. Where the train system stops, the bus system takes over, and gets you even into the small-est hamlets in the countryside, with at least a few runs per day. The largest towns and cities are connected so well, with buses and trains leaving every few minutes, that *not* using public transportation becomes foolish unless you have special reasons to have a car. In this book, we list bus compa-nies for each destination where taking a bus makes sense. You won't see too many tourists on buses, which is good if you want to get a feeling for what life is really like in Italy and meet local people. It's not like the U.S. or England, where you could sit there in a clown suit and everyone would be too "polite" to speak to you. Italians will ask you who you are, where you're from, and where you're going. And if you invest just a few hours familiarizing yourself with Italian (through *Italian For Dummies,* for example), you might be able to give some interesting answers.

Be sure to check schedules in advance because they change frequently. Tickets must be bought at the bus station; drivers don't have cash to make change. Do not plan to use the bus, though, to hit several small towns in a day — the bus schedules usually won't allow for it. The system is meant not for tourists, but for people who need to commute between the small town where they live and the larger towns of the area. To see five little countryside villages in a day requires a car.

By Ferry

The only ferries you're likely to use in Italy are the ferries to Capri (see Chapter 21) and Sicily (see Chapter 23) from Naples, and the ferry to Capri from Positano (see Chapter 22); ferries to Sicily take cars. For more information, see the relevant chapters.

If you want to bring your car on a ferry, you must make a reservation well in advance — especially during the high season. Taking your car on a ferry also means that you'll have to pay more, sometimes a lot more. In some cases, you may save money renting your car on arrival rather than taking it on a ferry.

By Car

In order to drive in Italy, you need to get an International Driver's License before leaving the United States. Any branch of the **American Automobile Association (AAA)** (☎ **800-222-1134** in the U.S. or 613-247-0117 in Canada; www.aaa.com) issues International Driver's Licenses. You have to fill out the AAA application form and provide a 2-x-2-inch photograph of yourself, a photocopy of your U.S. driver's license, and $10. Don't forget to bring your U.S. license with you in Italy, though, because the International license is valid only in combination with your regular license. An alternative to the International Driver's License is to take an Italian translation of your U.S. license (prepared by AAA or another organization) to an office of the **Automobile Club d'Italia** (☎ **06-4477** for 24-hour information and assistance) in Italy to receive a special driving permit.

If you're planning to drive, make sure that you have a good road map. The best maps are published by the Automobile Club d'Italia and the Italian Touring Club and are widely available in bookstores and at newsstands in Italy. A lot of highway building is going on in Italy, so maps change often.

Knowing the rules of the road

You need to know two very important rules when driving in Italy: 1) Drive defensively, and 2) always be ready to get out of the way.

It's a myth that Italians drive badly, or at least worse than anyone else. They drive fast but are usually skilled drivers. For one thing, you won't see (as we have in the United States) someone driving along a highway reading a newspaper or putting on makeup. (If you tried that in Italy, you'd be killed.) Italians love to drive; however, there's a reason why the Ferrari, the Maserati, and the Lamborghini are Italian cars — Italians love to drive fast. If you're going 90kmph (56 mph) and passing a car going 80kmph (50 mph), someone may zoom up behind you going 140kmph (87 mph) and flashing his lights (a perfect time to apply Rule 2). People do, however, follow the rules of the road, even (or perhaps especially) at 160kmph (100 mph).

Road signs in Italy for the *autostrada* (limited access, national or international toll road) are white on green; signs for local roads are white on blue. A white-on-blue sign saying "SS119" means that you're on the *strada statale* (state road) number 119.

A puzzling sign placed close to the ground is the white arrow on a blue circle; it points you to the lane that you should enter or the correct way around an obstacle, a traffic island, and so forth. Another important sign is No Parking — a blue-and-red circle with a diagonal stripe pointing to the side of the street where you can't park. If the sign shows two stripes (an X), you can't park on either side of the street. *Senso Unico* means a one-way street, and the white-on-red stop sign is obvious. Another useful sign to know is *Stazione* or *Stazione FS* (or only *FS*), indicating the direction of the local train station (the sign may also include the name of the station).

Keep your eyes peeled for exits (each marked *Uscita*). They're often indicated on the highway far in advance, and then right on top of the ramp — not a few hundred yards in advance, where it's helpful.

The following three rules are rigidly obeyed on the highway in Italy:

Rule 1: Pass only on the left.

Rule 2: Never stay in the passing lane unless you're going faster than everybody else (in our experience, someone is *always* going faster than you are). Just pull out, pass, and get back in the slow lane right away.

Rule 3: When you're entering on a highway and you have a sign to yield, you *do* have to yield, which may mean stopping and waiting for the merging lane to be available. Do not assume people will move over; they won't. They know they have the right of way over you and take it for granted that you'll wait your turn. The same is true of any merging intersection between a minor and a major road, and when you come out of a gas station or rest area. At regular intersections, the person on the right *always* has the right of way unless otherwise indicated; in traffic circles, the cars already in the circle have priority over those trying to enter.

Preparing yourself for driving in Italy

Driving in Italy can be nerve-racking, especially if at the same time you are trying to decipher road signs and find your hotel. The bottom line is that unless you really mean to get off the beaten track, don't rent a car. If you are going to spend a week exploring the big three cities — Rome, Florence, and Venice — traveling by train is faster, cheaper, and more pleasant. Because even smaller cities like Siena, Perugia, and Assisi are served by trains, only a real countryside hegira justifies a car. If you aren't in shape or have mobility difficulties, however, a car of course makes sense.

Here's a good compromise: Plan your itinerary so that you can either spend a few days in a city, and then pick up your car when you're ready to leave (not at the airport upon your arrival), or plan your rural driving first, and then dump your car as soon as you get to the city where you'll spend the most time. That way you'll get to do some countryside exploring but won't be saddled with a car for your whole trip.

If you do choose to rent a car, just reviewing the rules of the road (see the section above, "Knowing the rules of the road") may not be enough. Use this section to prepare yourself for what driving in Italy can be like before you make a rental reservation.

Naples is in a class by itself — even other Italians won't drive there. Consider that on our first visit, in one block we saw a motorcyclist riding a wheelie the length of the street and a tiny car that drove up on the sidewalk and around the signal pole to avoid a red light! If you arrive in Naples by car, find a garage or parking space fast, and then walk or take the bus.

If you're used to highways that run in straight lines and city streets that follow neat grids, prepare yourself for twisting roads and plunging cliffs, paved ancient Roman roads, city streets with kidney-shattering cobblestones, big broad piazze without lines indicating lanes, and streets only as wide as one Italian car. More and more cities are blocking off the center to car traffic, except for locals who live there. In Italian cities, you also find swarms of *motorini* (mopeds). If you're first at a stoplight, a swarm of 15 can easily surround you by the time the light changes. Look out for them, because they certainly aren't looking out for you.

In Italy, driving a car is often more expensive than traveling by train or bus, because tolls are high and gas is very expensive (about 4.5€/$5 per gallon). Driving from Rome to Florence and back, for example, can cost you two tanks of gas (70€/$80 plus) and another 9€ to 17€ ($10–$20) in tolls depending on how much of the *autostrada* you use. Add parking on top of that.

If you do rent a car, remember that Italian cars are small, and are designed for Italian roads; even the big ones are never larger than an American midsize and the trunk has half the capacity of American cars. Keep your luggage to a minimum; you don't want to drive around and park with your extra suitcase sitting in the back seat — a sure way to have your car broken into.

Keep in mind that gas stations often close for lunch and shut down all day on Sunday (except along the *autostrada*), so don't let your gas gauge get too low, especially if you're cruising the rural countryside.

If you plan on doing a lot of countryside touring, you may choose to rent a car after all. If you don't know how to drive a car with a manual transmission, consider learning how before leaving for Italy. Most Italian cars are standard shift. The country is very mountainous, and a car with an automatic shift is often a pain, costs more to rent, and the agency may run out of them. Standard shift cars also get better gas mileage, especially crawling up and down steep grades.

Getting the best deal on a car rental

Car rental rates vary even more than airline fares. The price depends on the size of the car, the length of time you keep it, where and when you pick it up and drop it off, where you take it, and a host of other factors. Asking a few key questions may save you hundreds of dollars.

- ✔ Weekend rates may be lower than weekday rates. If you're keeping the car five or more days, a weekly rate may be cheaper than the daily rate. Ask if the rate is the same for pickup Friday morning as it is Thursday night.

- ✔ Some companies may assess a drop-off charge if you don't return the car to the same rental location; others don't.

- ✔ Check whether the rate is cheaper if you pick up the car at a location in town rather than at the airport.

- ✔ Find out whether age is an issue. Many car rental companies add on a fee for drivers under 25, while some (especially in Italy) don't rent to them at all.

- ✔ If you see an advertised price in your local newspaper, be sure to ask for that specific rate; otherwise you may be charged the standard (higher) rate. Don't forget to mention membership in AAA, AARP, and trade unions. These memberships usually entitle you to discounts ranging from 5 to 30 percent.

- ✔ Check your frequent-flier accounts. Not only are your favorite (or at least most-used) airlines likely to have sent you discount coupons, but most car rentals add at least 500 miles to your account.

- ✔ As with other aspects of planning your trip, use the Internet to comparison shop. You can check rates at most of the major agencies' Web sites. Plus, all the major travel sites — **Travelocity** (www.travelocity.com), **Expedia** (www.expedia.com), **Orbitz** (www.orbitz.com), and **Smarter Living** (www.smarterliving.com), for example — have search engines that can dig up discounted car-rental rates. **Yahoo!** allows you to look up rental prices for any size car at more than a dozen companies in hundreds of cities. It will even make your reservation for you. Point your browser to http://travel.yahoo.com/travel and choose "Car" from the options.

In addition to the standard rental prices, other optional charges apply to most car rentals (and some not-so-optional charges, such as taxes). The *Collision Damage Waiver* (CDW), which requires you to pay for damage to the car in a collision, is covered by many credit card companies. Check with your credit card company before you go so you can avoid paying this hefty fee (as much as $20 a day).

The car rental companies also offer additional *liability insurance* (if you harm others in an accident), *personal accident insurance* (if you harm yourself or your passengers), and *personal effects insurance* (if your luggage is stolen from your car). Your insurance policy on your car at home probably covers most of these unlikely occurrences. However, if your own insurance doesn't cover you for rentals or if you don't have auto insurance, definitely consider the additional coverage (ask your car rental agent for more information). Unless you're toting around the Hope diamond, and you don't want to leave that in your car trunk anyway, you can probably skip the personal effects insurance, but driving around without liability or personal accident coverage is never a good idea. Even if you're a good driver, other people may not be, and liability claims can be complicated.

Some companies also offer *refueling packages,* in which you pay for your initial full tank of gas up front, and can return the car with an empty gas tank. The prices can be competitive with local gas prices, but you don't get credit for any gas remaining in the tank. If you reject this option, you pay only for the gas you use, but you have to return the car with a full tank or face high per-gallon (or in this case, per-liter) charges for any shortfall.

In Italy, most rental companies will require that you pay for theft protection insurance, because car theft is unfortunately common in Italy. Although many credit cards cover you for damage to a rental car, check with your company to see if your card's benefit extends outside the United States.

Rental agencies serving Italy

The best known car-rental companies operating in Italy are **AutoEurope** (☎ 800-223-5555; www.autoeurope.com), **Avis** (☎ 800-331-1084; www. avis.com), **Europcar** (☎ 800-014-410 toll-free in Italy; www.europcar. it), **Europe by Car** (☎ 800-223-1516; www.europebycar.com), **Hertz** (☎ 800-654-3001; www.hertz.com), **Kemwel** (☎ 800-678-0678; www. kemwel.com), and **National/Maggiore** (☎ 800-227-7368; www.maggiore. it/eng/Master_Eng.htm).

Chapter 8

Booking Your Accommodations

. . . .

In This Chapter

▶ Discovering your hotel options
▶ Booking a room and a great rate
▶ Avoiding getting stuck without a place to sleep

. . . .

ravelers have journeyed to Italy for the past 3,000 years (at least), and more than a few inns can claim several centuries of service. This history creates an enormous variety in Italy's hotels, from romantic 15th-century hostels and 17th-century *palazzi* with frescoes to simple 19th-century farmhouses and modern luxury hotels. This chapter gives important tips on choosing among what may be an unfamiliar variety of choices.

Getting to Know Your Options

Hotels in Italy often don't resemble hotels in the United States. In most American hotels, you'll find spacious, air-conditioned rooms, big bathrooms with tub/shower combos, beds that come in a variety of sizes (mostly large to extra large), and amenities galore — even in the most basic rooms. In Italy, the buildings that house guest accommodations are sometimes centuries old; there often isn't room to fit all the modern amenities. The average hotel room is smallish, with a relatively tiny bathroom with shower only, with twins beds that can be pushed together to create a double. Here are the major in-room differences you'll find in Italy:

> ✔ **Beds.** The majority of hotels in Italy have only one kind of bed — a large twin. In a double room, you usually find two separate twin beds. If you ask for a double bed, the host or hostess puts together the two twins into a *matrimoniale* (large bed), making the bed up tight with sheets. You may think this practice is unusual, but you'll discover that it's not uncomfortable. On the good side, most hotels in Italy, and certainly all the ones in our listings, are proud of the quality of their bedding, providing good mattresses with a medium degree of firmness.

✔ **Bathrooms.** Thanks to increased pressure to meet international standards, bathrooms have been shoehorned into rooms so that most of them *technically* have a private bath. The result is that prices have jumped accordingly. Historic buildings, however, just don't have the space for a big bathroom or even a tub. Therefore, it's not at all unusual for the shower to be a wall fixture over part of the tiled floor, with a curtain around it (not a door) and the drain below it. (Prepare yourself for wet floors.) Renovating buildings that are protected as historic sites can be difficult.

✔ **Air-conditioning.** As part of the recent push to standardize and upgrade lodging, air-conditioning is now more the rule than the exception.

✔ **TVs.** Regular TVs are standard, but these simple TVs don't offer English-language programs. For English-language programming, you need satellite TV, which is available only in the higher-end hotels. Then again, you didn't go to Italy to watch TV, did you?

✔ **Telephones.** All rooms usually have telephones; only in smaller villages or very simple accommodations will you not have a phone in your room.

✔ **Smoking vs. nonsmoking rooms.** In Italy, don't count on getting a nonsmoking room; most hotels have few such rooms, though changes are underway. Fortunately, because rooms usually have hard floors instead of carpeting and it's a common practice to wash curtains often, even a regular room is less likely to smell of old tobacco.

If you must have American-style amenities, you will have to opt for a deluxe hotel (often operated by a chain, and either housed in modern buildings or more spacious villas and *palazzi*). If you can adapt to simpler accommodations, you can choose a more modest *albergo* (hotel) or *pensione* (a small, family-run hotel offering basic rooms and services). In the countryside, you can opt to stay in a farmhouse, apartment, or bedroom on a working Italian farm as part of a nationwide program known as *agriturismo* (wine-producing estates make up a large part of these), or at a villa-resort (usually a patrician country residence transformed into a hotel and featuring swimming pools, spas, and beautiful gardens).

Throughout this guide, we include recently built hotels that provide modern amenities (including bathrooms) at good prices. Some of these newer accommodations are a little outside the city center or away from fashionable neighborhoods — in hill towns (Spoleto, Perugia, and so on), they may be at the foot of the hill rather than up in the old city. But face it: You may not want old-world charm every night; sometimes reading a book in a decent-sized tub or crashing early and comfortably is more important.

When you make a hotel reservation back home, you probably don't ask about the flooring. In Italy, you will usually find tile or marble floors, so bring slippers to get around the room and go to the bathroom in the cooler months if you don't want to get cold feet!

In this book, we list our favorite hotels, using cleanliness, comfort, and the most amenities at the best prices as essential criteria. Each listing includes a key indicating the cost of the hotel with a number of dollar signs that correspond to the following amounts.

Table 8-1 below explains the price scale used in this book, and what you can expect to get for your money in each category.

Table 8-1	Key to Hotel Dollar Signs	
Dollar Sign(s)	*Price Range*	*What to Expect*
$	Up to 130€ ($150)	No frills but dignified, with small rooms, some but not all with private baths. Could indicate a shared bath for some properties, but we'll always spell that out for you.
$$	131€–230€ ($151–$265)	All guest rooms have private bathrooms and air conditioning. Bathrooms tend to be small, especially at the bottom end of the scale, and furnishings rather plain, especially in more expensive destinations.
$$$	231€–330€ ($265–$380)	Now you get a bathroom that's really a room, not a corner; rooms are more spacious and have a number of amenities; they might even be luxurious in less expensive towns and villages. Usually, a nice buffet breakfast is included.
$$$$	331€–500€ ($381–$575)	These are luxurious hotels, sometimes owned by international interests; they offer standard luxury amenities plus special touches, ranging from antique furnishings and fine fabrics to lavish bathrooms, free parking (a luxury in Italy), pools, gyms, and sometimes spas. Usually, an American-style breakfast is included.
$$$$$	More than 500€ ($575 and up)	If the previous category is baroque, this is rococo; you will find amenities up to the highest international standards, luxurious accommodations, lots of space, and attentive professional staff. The hotel is in a new or very historic building. You're staying not only in luxury, but in style — perhaps in a former *palazzo* or castle.

Finding the Best Room at the Best Rate

Getting the room you want at the right price is the name of the game.
Following are some tips on reserving your room and cutting your costs.

Finding the best rate

The *rack rate* is the maximum rate a hotel charges for a room. The rack
rate is the rate you get if you walked in off the street at the peak of high
season and asked for a room for the night when the hotel is almost full.
You see this rate printed on the fire/emergency exit diagrams posted on
the back of guest room doors. We quote the rack rate for each of our
hotel listings throughout this book.

Hotels are happy to charge you the rack rate, but you don't always have
to pay it. Perhaps the best way to avoid paying the rack rate is surprisingly simple: Ask for a cheaper or discounted rate. You may be pleasantly
surprised. The price offered for a room may often be lower than the rack
rate, because that refers to high season and full hotel occupancy, whereas
you may have scheduled your trip during a slightly less mobbed time.

In all but the smallest accommodations, the rate you pay for a room
depends on many factors — chief among them being how you make your
reservation. A travel agent may be able to negotiate a better price with
certain hotels than you can get by yourself. (That's because the hotel
often gives the agent a discount in exchange for steering his or her business toward that hotel.)

Reserving a room through the hotel's toll-free number may also result in
a lower rate than calling the hotel directly. In Italy, this will help you if
you are reserving a room in a hotel that is part of an international chain.

Going direct — Italian hotel Web sites

To look at Italian hotels online and even make reservations, we recommend the following sites, most of which have English versions:

www.giroscopio.com www.italyhotelink.co

www.initaly.com www.itwg.com

www.italyguide.com www.venere.it

www.italyhotel.com www.wel.it

More and more, hotels are offering their own Web sites, and we note these sites in the
city listings. If you know some Italian, you can also go to the Web site of the Italian Web
server Tiscali (www.tiscali.it), click on "Viaggi" (travels, vacations), and follow
the link to "Hotels."

Room rates change with the seasons as occupancy rates rise and fall. But even within a given season, room prices are subject to change without notice, so the rates quoted in this book may be different from the actual rate you receive when you make your reservation. Hotels in the United States give discounts for members of AAA, AARP, frequent-flyer programs, or other corporate rewards programs. But in Italy, it's unlikely that a frequent-flier number for an airline that doesn't even fly to Italy, or membership in an organization they've never heard of, is going to help. It's more likely you will find good deals on the Internet (see later in this chapter). The best way your airline can help you is probably through a package deal, when you buy your accommodation along with your ticket (see Chapter 6).

When reserving, you might want to ask for a corner room. They're usually quieter, and have more windows and light than standard rooms, and they don't always cost more. (On the other hand, in some buildings 500 or more years old, corner rooms may not be the most spacious.)

The prevalence of old buildings raises another issue: renovations. When you make your reservation, ask if the hotel is renovating. If it is, request a room that's already been renovated or, failing that, a room away from the renovation work. If the hotel is on a busy street, request a room away from the street. If a hotel has a garden or courtyard, ask if rooms that overlook it are available. Likewise, inquire about the location of restaurants, bars, and discos in the hotel — and if noise or smoke bothers you, ask for a room as far away from them as possible.

And finally, remember that if you aren't happy with your room when you arrive, you can talk to the front desk about moving to another one.

Surfing the Web for hotel deals

Shopping online for hotels is generally done one of two ways: by booking through the hotel's own Web site or through an independent booking agency (or a fare-service agency like Priceline). These Internet hotel agencies have multiplied in mind-boggling numbers of late, competing for the business of millions of consumers surfing for accommodations around the world. This competitiveness can be a boon to consumers who have the patience and time to shop and compare the online sites for good deals — but shop they must, for prices can vary considerably from site to site. And keep in mind that hotels at the top of a site's listing may be there for no other reason than that they paid money to get the placement.

Of the "big three" sites, **Expedia** (www.expedia.com) offers a long list of special deals and "virtual tours" or photos of available rooms so you can see what you're paying for (a feature that helps counter the claims that the best rooms are often held back from bargain booking Web sites). **Travelocity** (www.travelocity.com) posts unvarnished customer reviews and ranks its properties according to the AAA rating system.

Also reliable are **Hotels.com** and **Quikbook.com**. An excellent free program, **TravelAxe** (www.travelaxe.net), can help you search multiple
hotel sites at once, even ones you may never have heard of — and conve-
niently lists the total price of the room, including the taxes and service
charges. Another booking site, **Travelweb** (www.travelweb.com), is
partly owned by the hotels it represents (including the Hilton, Hyatt, and
Starwood chains) and is therefore plugged directly into the hotels' reservations systems — unlike independent online agencies, which have to
fax or e-mail reservation requests to the hotel, a good portion of which
get misplaced in the shuffle. More than once, travelers have arrived at
the hotel, only to be told that they have no reservation. To be fair, many
of the major sites are undergoing improvements in service and ease of
use, and Expedia will soon be able to plug directly into the reservations
systems of many hotel chains — none of which can be bad news for consumers. In the meantime, it's a good idea to **get a confirmation number**
and **make a printout** of any online booking transaction.

In the opaque Web site category, **Priceline** (www.priceline.com) and
Hotwire (www.hotwire.com) are even better for hotels than for airfares;
with both, you're allowed to pick the neighborhood and quality level
of your hotel before offering up your money. Priceline's hotel product,
which covers Europe, is much better at getting five-star lodging for three-
star prices than at finding anything at the bottom of the scale. On the
down side, many hotels stick Priceline guests in their least desirable
rooms. Be sure to go to the BiddingforTravel Web site (www.bidding
fortravel.com) before bidding on a hotel room on Priceline; it features
a fairly up-to-date list of hotels that Priceline uses in major cities. For
both Priceline and Hotwire, you pay upfront, and the fee is nonrefundable. *Note:* Some hotels do not provide loyalty program credits or points
or other frequent-stay amenities when you book a room through opaque
online services.

A few other sites worth checking are:

- ✔ **All Hotels on the Web** (www.all-hotels.com): Although the name
  is something of a misnomer, the site does have tens of thousands of
  listings throughout the world. In Italy, it covers Rome and Venice.
  Bear in mind that each hotel has paid a small fee ($25 and up) to be
  listed, so it's less an objective list and more like a book of online
  brochures.

- ✔ **hoteldiscount!com** (www.180096hotel.com): This site lists bargain
  room rates at hotels in mamy of the cities discussed in this book,
  including the three biggies (Rome, Florence, Venice). The toll-free
  number is ☎ **800-364-0801**; call if you want more options than
  those that are listed online.

- ✔ **InnSite** (www.innsite.com): InnSite has B&B listings in many
  Italian cities and towns (though for smaller towns there may only
  be one). Prices can vary widely: one B&B in Florence has four
  rooms, ranging from 45€ to 120€ ($51–$138). But the site allows
  you to see pictures of the rooms and check prices and availability.

This extensive directory of B&Bs includes listings only if the proprietor submitted one (it's free to get an inn listed). The descriptions are written by the innkeepers and many listings link to the inn's own Web sites.

Reserving the best room

If you're traveling during high season (Easter to the end of summer, though in August large cities tend to be slightly less crowded because of the heat), reserve your hotel rooms as soon as you've finalized your itinerary and know definitely where you're going. The longer you wait, the fewer choices you'll have. In the city and regional chapters in this book, we note those highly sought-after hotels where you should make reservations months in advance. Reserving your rooms as far as possible in advance for stays in Venice and Florence is an especially good idea; Rome is much larger and has many more hotels, but if you have your eye on a particular place, jump on it as soon as you can.

Making reservations can get complicated when you buy an E-fare or other last-minute bargain ticket. This cost-effective approach leaves you with relatively little time to get organized and make reservations, so you may end up booking into a large chain hotel that has lots of rooms or a more expensive hotel with vacancies. (In our opinion, the higher cost for accommodations is worth it. If the money evens out, we'd rather spend more on the place we stay than on our plane tickets.)

After you've reserved your rooms in whichever cities you plan to visit, remember to request faxed confirmations from the hotels, and then make sure that you bring these with you to Italy. If you check into a hotel that suddenly says they have no record of your reservation — mistakes occur everywhere — you can produce your faxed confirmation.

If you don't reserve your accommodations before leaving home, remember that in the train station(s) of each major city you can find a hotel desk whose staff will call around town and find you a room, if one is available. (In the high season, there's always the risk that rooms aren't available.) Sometimes this service is free and sometimes you have to pay a small fee.

Even if you don't sign up with a tour or a package, you may want to investigate their offerings to see which hotels they feature. Some packages offer a better class of hotels than others. Some offer the same hotels for lower prices than their competitors. Some offer no flexibility on hotel selections at all.

Finding Alternative Housing, from Camps to Villas

Italy offers several other accommodations options, ranging from camping under the stars to staying at a luxurious spa. If you plan to stay in one place for a week or more, you can also rent an apartment. Another option is to stay at one of the many convents and other religious houses that rent out rooms (they allow couples — the rooms aren't monastic cells). However, in this book we don't list religious houses that accept guests because they usually have curfews (10 to 11 p.m., sometimes even earlier), and we don't think that you want to deal with a curfew, especially if your trip is relatively short.

Likewise, campsites are usually located outside the cities and aren't convenient. If you have a car and camping gear, contact the **Federazione Italiana Campeggiatori,** Via Vittorio Emanuele 11, 50041 Calenzano (☎ **055-882-391;** Fax: 055-882-5918; www.federcampeggio.it), or ask at the accommodations desk in the city train stations for prices and directions to nearby campsites.

If you want to rent an apartment, consult an organization that specializes in such arrangements. Here are a few:

✔ **Hideaways International,** 767 Islington St., Portsmouth, NH 03801 (☎ **800-843-4433;** www.hideaways.com)

✔ **At Home Abroad,** 405 E. 56th St., Suite 6H, New York, NY 10022 (☎ **212-421-9165;** Fax: 212-533-0095; http://hometown.aol.com/athomabrod)

✔ **Rentals in Italy,** 700 East Main St., Ventura, , CA 93001 (☎ **800-726-"6702** or 805-641-1650; Fax: 805-641-1630; www.rentvillas.com)

To rent something really ritzy, like a *palazzo* or a castle, try **Abitare la Storia,** Località L'Amorosa, 53048 Sinalunga, Siena (☎ **0577-679-683;** Fax: 0577-632-160; www.abitarelastoria.it).

Another option — a favorite with Italians is *agriturismo* (staying on a working farm or former farm somewhere in the countryside). *Agriturismo* (agricultural tourism) is particularly popular in Tuscany. Contact **Italy Farm Holidays,** 547 Martling Ave., Tarrytown, NY 10591 (☎ **914-631-7880;** Fax: 914-631-8831; www.italyfarmholdays.com) for information on some of the farms that offer this type of accommodation. Your lodging usually includes breakfast and at least one other meal (your choice of dinner or lunch), most likely prepared and produced on the farm or by other local small farms.

At the **Vacation Rentals by Owner** Web site (www.vrbo.com), you can see hundreds of listings of homes for rent. Each listing contains pictures, prices, and descriptions of the area where the house or apartment is located. Usually you deal directly with the owner, and so you may save considerably over the rates that would be charged for the same property by a broker (listings are in English).

Chapter 9

Catering to Special Travel Needs or Interests

. . . .

In This Chapter

▶ Traveling with kids
▶ Making the most of senior advantages
▶ Rising to the challenge — disabled travelers
▶ Answering travel questions for gay and lesbian travelers and students

. . . .

*E*very traveler is a special traveler, but bringing kids along on your trip to Italy or trying to find or arrange for wheelchair accessibility, all require extra care and thought. Seniors may be interested in special programs and activities; gays and lesbians may wonder how friendly and welcoming Italy will be. All these issues are considered in this chapter.

Traveling with the Brood: Advice for Families

Italy has a very family-oriented culture, which makes it much easier to travel here with your kids. In fact, Italians love children, and you'll find that people will often talk to or inquire about your child(ren). Italian society is quite traditional, however; Italians, in general, believe that children should be well behaved (act politely like little adults in museums and other public places), and they aren't worried that disciplining their children will give the kids a complex. Tantrums, whining, and other outbursts are frowned upon.

Opting for child care

Child care in Italy is also handled in a traditional way. Members of the extended family — grandparents and other relatives — often help care for children during the day if both their parents work. Having one parent (usually the mother) stay home taking care of the kids is also more common in Italy than in the United States. As a result, Italy doesn't have a major infrastructure of day care and child care (see the Appendix for more about baby-sitting). In fact, finding a hotel with day-care service can be difficult. However, many hotels can arrange for a sitter from a baby-sitting service, and in a few small family-run places, a daughter or son may pitch in and watch your kids. You can find standard day-care service only at the bigger and more expensive hotels in the big urban areas. Thus, if you have a very small child, you may find that you wind up paying more for lodging simply because you need the amenities of the higher-priced hotels.

Kids can have a great time in Italy; it helps if you talk to them before-hand about special things in store for them. Involve your children in planning for the trip. Go over the list of sights and activities in the cities and areas that you plan to visit, particularly noting those labeled with the Kid Friendly icon in this book. Let your kids make their own list of things they want to do. Older children can research Italy on the Internet (see the Appendix for a list of Web sites worth checking out).

Getting some family-travel advice

If you have enough trouble getting your kids out of the house in the morning, dragging them thousands of miles away may seem like an insurmountable challenge. But family travel can be immensely rewarding, giving you new ways of seeing the world through smaller pairs of eyes.

Familyhostel (☎ 800-733-9753; www.learn.unh.edu/familyhostel) takes the whole family, including kids ages 8 to 15, on moderately priced domestic and international learning vacations. Lectures, field trips, and sightseeing are guided by a team of academics.

You can find good family-oriented vacation advice on the Internet from sites like **Family Travel Forum** (www.familytravelforum.com), a comprehensive site that offers customized trip planning; **Family Travel Network** (www.familytravelnetwork.com), an award-winning site that offers travel features, deals, and tips; **Traveling Internationally with Your Kids** (www.travelwithyourkids.com), a comprehensive site that offers customized trip planning; and **Family Travel Files** (www.thefamily travelfiles.com), which offers an online magazine and a directory of off-the-beaten-path tours and tour operators for families.

How to Take Great Trips with Your Kids (The Harvard Common Press) is full of good general advice that can apply to travel anywhere. *Family Travel Times*, another good resource, is published six times a year (☎ 888-822-4FTT or 212-477-5524; www.familytraveltimes.com) and includes a weekly call-in service for subscribers. Subscriptions are $39 per year for quarterly editions.

Making Age Work for You: Tips for Seniors

In general, Italy accords older people a great deal of respect, probably because of the continued existence of the extended family as well as the nature of the Italian language (polite forms of address are to be used when speaking with someone older than yourself). Therefore, you're unlikely to encounter ageism.

Members of **AARP** (formerly known as the American Association of Retired Persons), 601 E St. NW, Washington, DC 20049 (☎ **888-687-2277** or 202-434-2277; www.aarp.org), get discounts on hotels, airfares, and car rentals. AARP offers members a wide range of benefits, including *AARP: The Magazine* and a monthly newsletter. Anyone over 50 can join.

Being a senior entitles you to some terrific travel bargains. Many reliable agencies and organizations target the 50-plus market. **Elderhostel** (☎ **877-426-8056;** www.elderhostel.org) arranges study programs for those aged 55 and over (and a spouse or companion of any age) in the United States and in more than 80 countries around the world. Most courses last five to seven days in the United States (two to four weeks abroad), and many include airfare, accommodations in university dormitories or modest inns, meals, and tuition. **ElderTreks** (☎ **800-741-7956;** www.eldertreks.com) offers small-group tours to off-the-beaten-path or adventure-travel locations, restricted to travelers 50 and older.

Recommended publications offering travel resources and discounts for seniors include: the quarterly magazine *Travel 50 & Beyond* (www.travel50andbeyond.com); *Travel Unlimited: Uncommon Adventures for the Mature Traveler* (Avalon); *101 Tips for Mature Travelers,* available from Grand Circle Travel (☎ **800-221-2610** or 617-350-7500; www.gct.com); *The 50+ Traveler's Guidebook* (St. Martin's Press); and *Unbelievably Good Deals and Great Adventures That You Absolutely Can't Get Unless You're Over 50* (McGraw-Hill).

 Senior discounts on admission at theaters, museums, and public transportation are subject to reciprocity between countries. Because the United States hasn't signed the bilateral agreement (you discount us and we'll discount you), Americans aren't eligible for senior discounts in Italy. (The same rule applies to the under-17 discount.) All discounts apply if you're a citizen of a European Union country.

Accessing Italy: Advice for Travelers with Disabilities

Most disabilities shouldn't stop anybody from traveling, and more options and resources are available than ever before.

However, Italy isn't as advanced as some other countries in its accessibility. Part of the problem is the age of the housing stock and the difficulty of retrofitting medieval buildings with elevators or ramps. Some of the major buildings and institutions have been converted; others have not. Calling ahead is always best, especially because, although special entrances may exist for the disabled, you may need to be met there by an attendant. Italy is working to make its treasures more accessible, but it's a slow process. Public transportation reserves spaces for the disabled, but getting in and out of the train or bus can prove difficult, even impossible, if you're in a wheelchair.

You can avoid some of these problems by joining a tour that caters specifically to your needs. Many travel agencies offer customized tours and itineraries for travelers with disabilities. **Flying Wheels Travel** (☎ 507-451-5005; www.flyingwheelstravel.com) offers escorted tours and cruises that emphasize sports and private tours in minivans with lifts. **Access-Able Travel Source** (☎ 303-232-2979; www.access-able.com) offers extensive access information and advice for traveling around the world with disabilities. **Accessible Journeys** (☎ 800-846-4537 or 610-521-0339; www.disabilitytravel.com) caters to wheelchair travelers and their families and friends.

Avis Rent a Car's "Avis Access" program offers such services as a dedicated 24-hour toll-free number (☎ 888-879-4273) for customers with special travel needs; special car features such as swivel seats, spinner knobs, and hand controls; and accessible bus service.

Organizations that offer assistance to disabled travelers include the **Moss Rehab Hospital** (www.mossresourcenet.org), which provides a library of accessible-travel resources online, and **SATH,** the **Society for Accessible Travel and Hospitality** (☎ 212-447-7284; www.sath.org; annual membership fees: $45 adults, $30 seniors and students), which offers a wealth of travel resources for all types of disabilities and informed recommendations on destinations, access guides, travel agents, tour operators, vehicle rentals, and companion services. The **American Foundation for the Blind** (☎ 800-232-5463; www.afb.org) provides information on traveling with Seeing Eye dogs.

For more information specifically targeted to travelers with disabilities, the community Web site **iCan** (www.icanonline.net/channels/travel/index.cfm) has destination guides and several regular columns on accessible travel. Also check out the quarterly magazine **Emerging Horizons** ($14.95 per year, $19.95 outside the U.S.; www.emerginghorizons.com); **Twin Peaks Press** (☎ 360-694-2462; http://disabilitybookshop.virtualave.net/blist84.htm), offering travel-related books for travelers with special needs; and *Open World Magazine,* published by SATH (see above; subscription: $13 per year, $21 outside the U.S.).

Following the Rainbow: Resources for Gay and Lesbian Travelers

Italy is a fairly tolerant country, and violent displays of intolerance such as gay bashing are extremely unusual. However, as in the United States, there is an active gay and lesbian movement that is trying to raise public consciousness about prejudice and discrimination.

All major towns and cities have an active gay life, especially Florence, Rome, and Milan, which considers itself the gay capital of Italy and is the headquarters of **ARCI–Gay/ARCI-Lesbica** (www.arcigay.it), the country's leading gay organization with branches throughout Italy. Their Web site has an English version. The Tuscany branch can be found at www.gaytoscana.it; for Rome visit www.arcigay.it/roma. ARCI-Gay has offices in **Siena** (☎ **0577-288-977;** www.gaysiena.it) and **Pisa** (☎ **050-555-618**).

Capri is the gay resort of Italy, rivaled only by the gay beaches of Venice and Taormina. The first-ever World Pride event was held in Rome in July 2000, to coincide with the Jubilee celebrations.

The International Gay & Lesbian Travel Association (IGLTA) (☎ **800-448-8550** or 954-776-2626; www.iglta.org) is the trade association for the gay and lesbian travel industry, and offers an online directory of gay- and lesbian-friendly travel businesses; go to their Web site and click on "Members."

Making the Grade: Advice for Student Travels

If you're a student planning a trip to Italy, get an **International Student Identity Card (ISIC),** which offers substantial savings on rail passes, plane tickets, and entrance fees. It also provides you with basic health and life insurance and a 24-hour help line. The card is available for $22 from **STA Travel** (☎ **800-781-4040,** and if you're not in North America there's probably a local number in your country; www.statravel.com), the biggest student travel agency in the world. If you're no longer a student but are still under 26, you can get a **International Youth Travel Card (IYTC)** for the same price from the same people, which entitles you to some discounts (but not on museum admissions). (*Note:* In 2002, STA Travel bought competitors **Council Travel** and **USIT Campus** after they went bankrupt. It's still operating some offices under the Council name, but it's owned by STA.)

Travel CUTS (☎ **800-667-2887** or 416-614-2887; www.travelcuts.com) offers similar services for both Canadians and U.S. residents. Irish students should turn to **USIT** (☎ **01-602-1600;** www.usitnow.ie).

Chapter 10

Taking Care of the Remaining Details

. . . .

In This Chapter

▶ Getting your documents in order

▶ Purchasing insurance — or not

▶ Making sure you stay healthy while traveling

▶ Keeping connected when you travel

▶ Understanding airline security measures

. . . .

*E*ven if you have a destination, an itinerary, and a ticket in hand, you aren't going anywhere until you get a passport. You also need to figure out whether to get traveler's insurance, and how you want to stay in touch with the folks back home. In this chapter, we help you tie up all the loose ends.

Getting a Passport

A valid passport is the only legal form of identification accepted around the world. You can't cross an international border without it. Getting a passport is easy, but the process takes some time. For an up-to-date country-by-country listing of passport requirements around the world, visit the "Foreign Entry Requirement" Web page of the U.S. State Department at `http://travel.state.gov/foreignentryreqs.html`.

Applying for a U.S. passport

If you're applying for a first-time passport, follow these steps:

1. Complete a **passport application** in person at a U.S. passport office; a federal, state, or probate court; or a major post office. To find your regional passport office, either check the U.S. State Department Web site, `http://travel.state.gov`, or call the National Passport Information Center (☎ **202-647-0518**).

2. Present a **certified birth certificate** as proof of citizenship. (Bringing along your driver's license, state or military ID, or social security card is also a good idea.)

3. Submit **two identical passport-size photos,** measuring 2-x-2-inches in size. You often find businesses that take these photos near a passport office. *Note:* You can't use a strip from a photo-vending machine because the pictures aren't identical.

4. Pay a **fee.** For people 16 and over, a passport is valid for ten years and costs $85. For those 15 and under, a passport is valid for five years and costs $70.

 Allow plenty of time before your trip to apply for a passport; processing normally takes three weeks but can take longer during busy periods (especially spring).

If you have a passport in your current name that was issued within the past 15 years (and you were over age 16 when it was issued), you can renew the passport by mail for $55. Whether you're applying in person or by mail, you can download passport applications from the U.S. State Department Web site at http://travel.state.gov. For general information, call the **National Passport Agency** (☎ **202-647-0518**). To find your regional passport office, either check the U.S. State Department Web site or call the **National Passport Information Center** toll-free number (☎ **877-487-2778**) for automated information.

 Losing your passport may be worse than losing your money. Why? Because a passport shows (and proves to authorities) that you are you. Safeguard your passport in an inconspicuous, inaccessible place like a money belt. Always carry a photocopy of your passport with you and keep it in a separate pocket or purse. If you lose your passport, visit the nearest consulate of your native country as soon as possible for a replacement.

Applying for other passports

Australians can visit a local post office or passport office, call the **Australia Passport Information Service** (☎ **131-232** toll-free from Australia), or log on to www.passports.gov.au for details on how and where to apply.

Canadians can pick up applications at passport offices throughout Canada, at post offices, or from the central **Passport Office, Department of Foreign Affairs and International Trade,** Ottawa, ON K1A 0G3 (☎ **800-567-6868;** www.ppt.gc.ca). Applications must be accompanied by two identical passport-sized photographs and proof of Canadian citizenship. Processing takes five to ten days if you apply in person, or about three weeks by mail.

New Zealanders can pick up a passport application at any New Zealand Passports Office or download it from their Web site. Contact the **Passports Office** at ☎ **0800/225-050** in New Zealand or 04-474-8100, or log on to www.passports.govt.nz for more information.

United Kingdom residents can pick up applications for a standard ten-year passport (five-year passport for children under 16) at passport offices, major post offices, or a travel agency. For information, contact the **United Kingdom Passport Service** (☎ **0870-521-0410;** www.ukpa.gov.uk).

 When you get your passport photos taken, ask for six to eight total photos if you're planning to also apply for an International Driving Permit and an international student or teacher ID, which may entitle you to discounts at museums. Take the extra photos with you. You may need one for random reasons on the road, and if — heaven forbid — you ever lose your passport, you can use them for a replacement request.

Playing It Safe with Travel and Medical Insurance

Three kinds of travel insurance are available: trip-cancellation insurance, medical insurance, and lost luggage insurance. The cost of travel insurance varies widely, but expect to pay between 5 and 8 percent of the vacation itself. Here is our advice on all three:

✓ **Trip-cancellation insurance** helps you get your money back if you have to back out of a trip or go home early, or if your travel supplier goes bankrupt. Allowed reasons for cancellation can range from sickness to natural disasters to the State Department declaring your destination unsafe for travel. (Insurers usually won't cover vague fears, though, as many travelers discovered who tried to cancel their trips in October 2001 because they were wary of flying.)

A good resource is **"Travel Guard Alerts,"** a list of companies considered high-risk by Travel Guard International (www.travelinsured.com). Protect yourself further by paying for the insurance with a credit card — by law, consumers can get their money back on goods and services not received if they report the loss within 60 days after the charge is listed on their credit card statement.

Note: Many tour operators, particularly those offering trips to remote or high-risk areas, include insurance in the cost of the trip or can arrange insurance policies through a partnering provider, a convenient and often cost-effective way for the traveler to obtain insurance. Make sure the tour company is a reputable one, however: Some experts suggest you avoid buying insurance from the tour or cruise company you're traveling with, saying it's better to buy from a "third party" insurer than to put all your money in one place.

✔ For domestic travel, buying **medical insurance** for your trip doesn't make sense for most travelers. Most existing health policies cover you if you get sick away from home — but check before you go, particularly if you're insured by an HMO.

For travel overseas, most health plans (including Medicare and Medicaid) do not provide coverage, and the ones that do often require you to pay for services up front and reimburse you only after you return home. Even if your plan does cover overseas treatment, most out-of-country hospitals make you pay your bills up front, and send you a refund only after you've returned home and filed the necessary paperwork with your insurance company. As a safety net, you may want to buy travel medical insurance, particularly if you're traveling to a remote or high-risk area where emergency evacuation is a possible scenario. If you require additional medical insurance, try **MEDEX Assistance** (☎ **410-453-6300**; www.medexassist.com) or **Travel Assistance International** (☎ **800-821-2828**; www.travel assistance.com; for general information on services, call the company's Worldwide Assistance Services, Inc., at ☎ **800-777-8710**).

✔ **Lost-luggage insurance** is not necessary for most travelers. On domestic flights, checked baggage is covered up to $2,500 per ticketed passenger. On international flights (including U.S. portions of international trips), baggage coverage is limited to approximately $9.07 per pound, up to approximately $635 per checked bag. If you plan to check items more valuable than the standard liability, see if your valuables are covered by your homeowner's policy, get baggage insurance as part of your comprehensive travel-insurance package or buy Travel Guard's "BagTrak" product. Don't buy insurance at the airport, as it's usually overpriced. Be sure to take any valuables or irreplaceable items with you in your carry-on luggage, as many valuables (including books, money, and electronics) aren't covered by airline policies.

If your luggage is lost, immediately file a lost-luggage claim at the airport, detailing the luggage contents. For most airlines, you must report delayed, damaged, or lost baggage within four hours of arrival. The airlines are required to deliver luggage, once found, directly to your house or destination free of charge.

For more information, contact one of the following recommended insurers: **Access America** (☎ 866-807-3982; www.accessamerica.com); **Travel Guard International** (☎ 800-826-4919; www.travelguard.com); **Travel Insured International** (☎ 800-243-3174; www.travelinsured.com); and **Travelex Insurance Services** (☎ 888-457-4602; www.travelex-insurance.com).

Staying Healthy When You Travel

For domestic trips, most reliable health-care plans provide coverage if you get sick away from home. For travel abroad, you may have to pay all medical costs up front and be reimbursed later. For information on purchasing additional medical insurance for your trip, see the previous section.

Talk to your doctor before leaving on a trip if you have a serious and/or chronic illness. For conditions such as epilepsy, diabetes, or heart problems, wear a **MedicAlert identification tag** (☎ **888-633-4298;** www.medicalert.org), which immediately alerts doctors to your condition and gives them access to your records through Medic Alert's 24-hour hotline. Contact the **International Association for Medical Assistance to Travelers (IAMAT)** (☎ **716-754-4883** or, in Canada, 416-652-0137; www.iamat.org) for tips on travel and health concerns in the countries you're visiting, and lists of local, English-speaking doctors. The United States **Centers for Disease Control and Prevention** (☎ **800-311-3435;** www.cdc.gov) provides up-to-date information on health hazards by region or country and offers tips on food safety.

If you do get sick in Italy, ask the concierge at your hotel to recommend a local doctor — even his or her own doctor, if necessary. If you can't locate a doctor, try contacting your embassy or consulate — they maintain lists of English-speaking doctors. For an emergency dial ☎ **113** for the police or ☎ **112** for the *Carabinieri* (army police corps): They can call an ambulance or help you in many ways. If your situation is life-threatening, go to the *pronto soccorso* (emergency department) at the local hospital.

Under the Italian national health-care system, you're eligible only for free *emergency* care. If you're admitted to a hospital as an in-patient, even from an accident and an emergency department, you're required to pay (unless you're a resident of the European Economic Area). You're also required to pay for follow-up care. For the names, addresses, and phone numbers of hospitals offering 24-hour emergency care, see the "Fast Facts" section at the end of each destination chapter.

Avoiding "economy-class syndrome"

Deep vein thrombosis, or as it's know in the world of flying, "economy-class syndrome," is a blood clot that develops in a deep vein. It's a potentially deadly condition that can be caused by sitting in cramped conditions — such as an airplane cabin — for too long. During a flight (especially a long-haul flight), get up, walk around, and stretch your legs every 60 to 90 minutes to keep your blood flowing. Other preventative measures include frequent flexing of the legs while sitting, drinking lots of water, and avoiding alcohol and sleeping pills.

Staying Connected by Cellphone or E-mail

If you're from England, you're lucky: Your phone already works in Italy. If you're from another continent, things are a little complicated.

Using a cellphone outside the U.S.

The three letters that define much of the world's **wireless capabilities** are GSM (Global System for Mobiles), a big, seamless network that makes for easy cross-border cellphone use throughout Europe and dozens of other countries worldwide. In the U.S., T-Mobile, AT&T Wireless, and Cingular use this quasi-universal system; in Canada, Microcell and some Rogers customers are GSM; and all Europeans and most Australians use GSM.

If your cellphone is on a GSM system, and you have a world-capable multiband phone such as many Sony Ericsson, Motorola, or Samsung models, you can make and receive calls across civilized areas on much of the globe. Just call your wireless operator and ask for "international roaming" to be activated on your account. Unfortunately, per-minute charges can be high — usually $1 to $1.50 in Western Europe.

That's why it's important to buy an "unlocked" world phone from the get-go. Many cellphone operators sell "locked" phones that restrict you from using any other removable computer memory phone chip (called a **SIM card**) card other than the ones they supply. Having an unlocked phone allows you to install a cheap, prepaid SIM card (found at a local retailer) in your destination country. (Show your phone to the salesperson; not all phones work on all networks.) You'll get a local phone number — and much, much lower calling rates. Getting an already locked phone unlocked can be a complicated process, but it can be done; just call your cellular operator and say you'll be going abroad for several months and want to use the phone with a local provider.

For many, **renting** a phone is a good idea. While you can rent a phone from any number of overseas sites, including kiosks at airports and at car-rental agencies, we suggest renting the phone before you leave home. That way you can give loved ones and business associates your new number, make sure the phone works, and take the phone wherever you go — especially helpful for overseas trips through several countries, where local phone-rental agencies often bill in local currency and may not let you take the phone to another country.

Phone rental isn't cheap. You'll usually pay $40 to $50 per week, plus airtime fees of at least a dollar a minute. If you're traveling to Europe, though, local rental companies often offer free incoming calls within their home country, which can save you big bucks. The bottom line: Shop around.

Two good wireless rental companies are **InTouch USA** (☎ **800-872-7626**; www.intouchglobal.com) and **RoadPost** (☎ **888-290-1606** or 905-272-5665; www.roadpost.com). Give them your itinerary, and they'll tell you what wireless products you need. InTouch will also, for free, advise you on whether your existing phone will work overseas; simply call ☎ **703-222-7161** between 9am and 4pm Eastern standard time, or go to http://intouchglobal.com/travel.htm.

In Italy, you don't have to look for a place to rent a phone; you can make the phone come to you. **Rentacell** (☎ **877-736-8355** in the U.S.; 39-02-8633-7799 in Italy; www.rentacell.com) will deliver a phone to you anywhere for free. You can also pick it up in the U.S. before you leave. Incoming calls are free. **Easyline** (☎ **800-010-600** in Italy) also delivers phones for free.

Accessing the Internet away from home

Travelers have any number of ways to check their e-mail and access the Internet on the road. Of course, using your own laptop — or even a PDA (personal digital assistant) or electronic organizer with a modem — gives you the most flexibility. But even if you don't have a computer, you can still access your e-mail and even your office computer from cybercafes.

It's hard nowadays to find a city that *doesn't* have a few cybercafes. Although there's no definitive directory for cybercafes — these are independent businesses, after all — two places to start looking are at www.cybercaptive.com and www.cybercafe.com.

One of the leading global Internet cafe companies is **Easy Everything** (www.easyeverything.com). It currently has franchises in Milan, Florence and two in Rome, but the company is rapidly expanding, and by the time you read this there may well be more — check the Web site for other locations. But they will have trouble catching the **Internet Train** (www.internettrain.it), which not only has multiple sites in the big cities like Rome, Florence, and Milan, but also serves second-tier cities like Verona, and even smaller towns like Greve in Chianti and Agrigento.

Aside from formal cybercafes, most **youth hostels** nowadays have at least one computer you can get to the Internet on. And most **public libraries** across the world offer Internet access free or for a small charge. More and more **hotels** are adding "Internet points" to their amenities. Sometimes this service is free, or you may have to pay a small fee. Check with your hotel about the option. **Hotel business centers** should be avoided, however, unless you're willing to pay exorbitant rates.

Most major airports now have **Internet kiosks** scattered throughout their gates. These kiosks, which you'll also see in shopping malls, hotel lobbies, and tourist information offices around the world, give you basic Web access for a per-minute fee that's usually higher than cybercafe prices. The kiosks' clunkiness and high price mean they should be avoided whenever possible.

To retrieve your e-mail, ask your **Internet Service Provider (ISP)** if it has a Web-based interface tied to your existing e-mail account. If your ISP doesn't have such an interface, you can use the free **mail2web** service (www.mail2web.com) to view and reply to your home e-mail. For more flexibility, you may want to open a free, Web-based e-mail account with **Yahoo! Mail** (http://mail.yahoo.com). (Microsoft's Hotmail is another popular option, but Hotmail has severe spam problems.) Your home ISP may be able to forward your e-mail to the Web-based account automatically.

If you need to access files on your office computer, look into a service called **GoToMyPC** (www.gotomypc.com). The service provides a Web-based interface for you to access and manipulate a distant PC from anywhere — even a cybercafe — provided your "target" PC is on and has an always-on connection to the Internet (such as with Road Runner cable). The service offers top-quality security, but if you're worried about hackers, use your own laptop rather than a cybercafe computer to access the GoToMyPC system.

If you are bringing your own computer, the buzzword in computer access to familiarize yourself with is **Wi-fi** (wireless fidelity), and more and more hotels, cafes, and retailers are signing on as wireless "hotspots" from where you can get high-speed connection without cable wires, networking hardware, or a phone line. You can get Wi-fi connection one of several ways. Many laptops sold in the last year have built-in Wi-fi capability (an 802.11b wireless Ethernet connection). Mac owners have their own networking technology, Apple AirPort. For those with older computers, an 802.11b/**Wi-fi card** (around $50) can be plugged into your laptop. You sign up for wireless access service much as you do cellphone service, through a plan offered by one of several commercial companies that have made wireless service available in airports, hotel lobbies, and coffee shops, primarily in the U.S. (followed by the U.K. and Japan). **T-Mobile Hotspot** (www.t-mobile.com/hotspot) serves up wireless connections at more than 1,000 Starbucks coffee shops nationwide. **Boingo** (www.boingo.com) and **Wayport** (www.wayport.com) have set up networks in airports and high-class hotel lobbies. IPass providers also give you access to a few hundred wireless hotel lobby setups. Best of all, you don't need to be staying at the Four Seasons to use the hotel's network; just set yourself up on a nice couch in the lobby. The companies' pricing policies can be byzantine, with a variety of monthly, per-connection, and per-minute plans, but in general you pay around $30 a month for limited access — and as more and more companies jump on the wireless bandwagon, prices are likely to get even more competitive.

There are also places that provide **free wireless networks** in cities around the world. To locate these free hotspots, go to www.personal telco.net/index.cgi/WirelessCommunities.

If Wi-fi is not available at your destination, most business-class hotels throughout the world offer dataports for laptop modems, and a few thousand hotels in the U.S. and Europe now offer free high-speed Internet access using an Ethernet network cable. You can bring your own cables, but most hotels rent them for around $10. **Call your hotel in advance** to see what your options are.

In addition, major Internet Service Providers (ISPs) have **local access numbers** around the world, allowing you to go online by simply placing a local call. Check your ISP's Web site or call its toll-free number and ask how you can use your current account away from home, and how much it will cost. If you're traveling outside the reach of your ISP, the **iPass** network has dial-up numbers in most of the world's countries. You'll have to sign up with an iPass provider, who will then tell you how to set up your computer for your destination(s). For a list of iPass providers, go to www.ipass.com and click on "Individual Purchase." One solid provider is **i2roam** (www.i2roam.com; ☎ **866-811-6209** or 920-235-0475).

Wherever you go, bring a **connection kit** of the right power and phone adapters, a spare phone cord, and a spare Ethernet network cable — or find out whether your hotel supplies them to guests.

If getting your e-mail is really important to you and you're not bringing your own computer, once you have your itinerary set, go to the Web sites of the Internet cafes and find out the locations *before* you leave home. It'll be one less detail to deal with.

Keeping Up with Airline Security

With the federalization of airport security, security procedures at U.S. airports are more stable and consistent than ever. Generally, you'll be fine if you arrive at the airport **one hour** before a domestic flight and **two hours** before an international flight; if you show up late, tell an airline employee and she'll probably whisk you to the front of the line.

Bring a **current, government-issued photo ID** such as a driver's license or passport. Keep your ID at the ready to show at check-in, the security checkpoint, and sometimes even the gate. (Children under 18 do not need government-issued photo IDs for domestic flights, but they do for international flights to most countries.)

In 2003, the Transportation Security Administration (TSA) phased out **gate check-in** at all U.S. airports. And **E-tickets** have made paper tickets nearly obsolete. Passengers with E-tickets can beat the ticket-counter lines by using airport **electronic kiosks** or even **online check-in** from your home computer. Online check-in involves logging on to your airlines' Web site, accessing your reservation, and printing out your boarding pass — and the airline may even offer you bonus miles to do so! If you're using a kiosk at the airport, bring the credit card you used to book the ticket or your frequent-flier card. Print out your boarding pass from the kiosk and simply proceed to the security checkpoint with your pass and a photo ID. If you're checking bags or looking to snag an exit-row seat, you will be able to do so using most airline kiosks. Even the smaller airlines are employing the kiosk system, but always call your airline to make sure these alternatives are available. **Curbside check-in** is also a good way to avoid lines, although a few airlines still ban curbside check-in; call before you go.

Security checkpoint lines are getting shorter than they were during 2001 and 2002, but some doozies remain. If you have trouble standing for long periods of time, tell an airline employee; the airline will provide a wheelchair. Speed up security by **not wearing metal objects** such as big belt buckles. If you've got metallic body parts, a note from your doctor can prevent a long chat with the security screeners. Keep in mind that only **ticketed passengers** are allowed past security, except for folks escorting disabled passengers or children.

Federalization has stabilized **what you can carry on** and **what you can't.** The general rule is that sharp things are out, nail clippers are okay, and food and beverages must be passed through the X-ray machine — but that security screeners can't make you drink from your coffee cup. Bring food in your carry-on rather than checking it, as explosive-detection machines used on checked luggage have been known to mistake food (especially chocolate, for some reason) for bombs. Travelers in the U.S. are allowed one carry-on bag, plus a "personal item" such as a purse, briefcase, or laptop bag. Carry-on hoarders can stuff all sorts of things into a laptop bag; as long as it has a laptop in it, it's still considered a personal item. The TSA has issued a list of restricted items; check its Web site (www.tsa.gov/public/index.jsp) for details.

Airport screeners may decide that your checked luggage needs to be searched by hand. Travel Sentry certified locks (available at luggage and travel shops, at Brookstone stores or online at www.brookstone.com) are approved by the TSA and can be opened by inspectors with a special code or key. If you use something other than TSA-approved locks, your lock will be cut off your suitcase if a hand-search is required.

Part III
The Eternal City: Rome

The 5th Wave   By Rich Tennant

ATTENZIONE!

"It says, children are forbidden from running, touching objects, or appearing bored during the tour."

In this part . . .

Rome is not only Italy's largest city, but it's also the hub from which you'll probably do most of your traveling. The treasures of Rome stretch from pre-Republic ruins to Bernini's baroque marvels to the stylish, convulsive Rome depicted by Fellini in his famous movies. Though modern, today's sprawling city still breathes to the rhythm of its history and is set in a beautiful countryside, where affluent Romans have been building palaces and villas since . . . well, the Romans.

Chapter 11 provides everything you need to know to get to Rome, get oriented in the city, find a comfortable place to stay, and order a delicious Italian meal. Included are rundowns of the best hotels, plus some runner-up choices, and the best restaurants. In Chapter 12, we describe the major sites and activities (not only how to see the Colosseum and the Vatican Museums but also where to shop and where to go for fun after dark). Chapter 13 takes you into Rome's countryside.

Chapter 11

Settling into Rome

In This Chapter

▶ Arriving in Rome
▶ Getting to know your way around the city
▶ Finding a room in Rome
▶ Appreciating Roman cuisine
▶ Information at your fingertips

The seven hills of Rome (Roma) have been continuously inhabited for the past 3,000 years or so. As early as 700 B.C. it was the meeting place of Etruscan, Italic, and Sabine culture. Not long after, Greek settlers added an indispensable element to the melting pot that gave birth to the Roman Empire, which laid the foundation for a cosmopolitan European culture. The collapse of Rome took centuries, during which it (perhaps ironically) nurtured the civilization that would follow it — Christian medieval Europe, with the Roman curia its heart.

It's not surprising then that nowhere else will you find such a cultural density and layering of periods and styles. For instance, Rome has 913 churches, many lavishly decorated with masterpieces. The Papal Jubilee in 2000 brought about much-needed renovations, as well as efforts to make the center of the city less congested and polluted. These changes have made a big difference, and tourists pour into the city in ever-increasing numbers.

Getting There

Getting to Rome is fairly straightforward: It has two airports, is a major train hub, and highways — many of them paved-over Roman roads — arrive from all directions.

By air

Rome's main airport, Leonardo da Vinci in **Fiumicino,** is also the largest of the two intercontinental airports in Italy (the other is in Milan). Charter flights and some of the smaller European companies arrive in the smaller airport of **Ciampino.**

Getting oriented at Fiumicino/Leonardo da Vinci

Officially called Leonardo da Vinci, everybody refers to this airport as Fiumicino (☎ 06-659-51; www.adr.it), after the nearby town. The airport is relatively small and very well organized, with three terminals connected by a long corridor: Terminal A handles domestic travel, Terminal B handles domestic and Schengen European Community flights (that is, flights internal to the countries of the European Community who have signed a special agreement to wave custom controls), and Terminal C manages all other international flights and is your likely point of entry. Terminal C is connected to a newer set of gates by a cool monorail. ATMs and a *cambio* (change) office are located just outside customs in the international arrivals area, but all terminals have ATMs.

If you are using traveler's checks, you may want to stand in line at the *cambio* office — its rates are usually the best in town.

On your way out to ground transportation, you'll find a very good **tourist information desk** (☎ 06-6595-6074), providing information on Rome at one end, and on the rest of Italy at the other. Nearby is a help desk for **last-minute hotel reservations** — the service, however, doesn't cover all hotels in Rome. Public transportation, including taxis and car rental shuttle buses, is just outside along the sidewalk; the train station is on the second floor of the international terminal.

Navigating your way through passport control and customs

After landing and on your way to get your luggage, you will have to line up at the passport-control gates — one for European Union citizens and one for everyone else. Outside the passport check, you proceed to the baggage-claim area and then through customs. Items for personal use enter duty-free. When you leave customs, you're in the main concourse. While at the airport, you may notice the high level of security: Don't be concerned if you see police officers with submachine guns walking around — due to recent world events, it's now routine conduct.

Be aware that the security forces at Fiumicino have terrorists in mind, not common thieves: Watch your belongings like a hawk and don't leave anything precious in your check-in luggage.

Getting from the Fiumicino airport to your hotel

Fiumicino lies about 30km (18 miles) from Rome and is well connected by highway, train, shuttle train, and bus.

The easiest way to get to your hotel, of course, is by taking a **taxi:** The line forms on the curb just outside the terminals and is marked by a sign; taxis are white and have a meter. For three adult passengers — sometimes they'll accept four — expect to pay about 40€ ($46) for the 50-minute ride (well over an hour at rush hours), plus a luggage fee of

1€ ($1.15) per item for *everything* that goes in the trunk, so keep your purse or any small bags with you inside the car. Expect a night surcharge (10 p.m.–6 a.m.) of 2.60€ ($3) and a Sunday and holiday surcharge of 1€ ($1.15), and a luggage supplement of 1€ ($1.15) for each bag put in the trunk.

Beware of gypsy cab drivers who approach you as you exit the arrival gate. They don't have meters and often charge you more than the regulated cab rates.

It's also simple to take the **train** into Rome. If you have a lot of luggage you can hire help at the baggage claim area for 2€ ($2.30) per item; they'll take your bags to the train. The railroad terminal is connected to the air terminal through a corridor on the second floor, just outside arrivals. The **Leonardo Express,** a 35-minute shuttle ride to **Termini** (Rome's central rail station), runs daily every 30 minutes from 6:37 a.m. to 11:37 p.m. and costs 9.50€ ($11). The local commuter train arrives at one of the other railroad stations in Rome. It takes about 40 minutes, depending on your stop, and runs every 15 minutes Monday through Saturday and every 30 minutes on Sunday for about 5€ ($5.75). Get off at **Roma Ostiense** if your hotel is in the area of the Aventino, the Colosseum, St. Peter's (San Pietro), or the Centro; or get off at **Roma Tiburtina,** if your hotel is in the Porta Pia or Villa Borghese area. At the railroad station, you can catch a taxi or take the metro or a city bus to your final destination. Taxi stands are immediately outside the stations; beyond them are the ranks of buses, with signs indicating their numbers and routes. Tickets for both train and shuttle are sold at the ticket booth in the terminal.

If you're planning to use public transportation in Rome, consider buying a day-pass ticket or a tourist three-day ticket (see "Getting around Rome," later in this chapter) at the tobacconist in the railroad terminal — you will have it all ready for later use. *Definitely* do so if you are planning to use the commuter train from the airport to Rome, because the ride is included in either of those passes (only for the regular train, though, not for the Leonardo Express).

As a final choice, you could take a **bus shuttle** into Rome but they are usually less convenient. **Terravision** (☎ 06-7949-4572; www.terravision. it) runs a shuttle to Termini station and to Tiburtina station, with stops to a few major hotels for 9€ ($10) and 5€ ($5.75) for children aged 2 to 12.

Arriving at Ciampino

A number of international charter flights and some minor European companies arrive at **Ciampino** (☎ 06-794-941 or 06-7934-0297), 16km (10 miles) from the center of Rome. This airport has few structures or services; it's almost like an American civil aviation airport.

The easiest way to get to town from Ciampino is by taking a **taxi**. Expect to pay about 35€ ($40): Your ride will take about 45 minutes. You can also take a **bus; Terravision** (☎ 06-7949-4572. www.terravision.it) runs a shuttle service in concert with Ryanair flights, and **Schiaffini** runs a shuttle coinciding with easyJet flights. Both take you to Termini station for 8€ ($9.20); tickets are sold at the Hotel Royal Santina or at the Hotel Stromboli on Via Marsala, just across from Termini train station.

By train

Rome is a major railroad hub offering service to every domestic and international destination. Italy's train service is excellent: cheap, reliable, and frequent; **Trenitalia** is the Italian railroad company (☎ 892-021; www.trenitalia.it). Six rail stations are located in the center of Rome, but the central and largest is **Termini** (☎ 800-431-784); the second most important, is **Tiburtina.** Trains usually stop at one or the other.

The recently renovated Termini station has virtually every service you could want, from ATMs to bathrooms to a supermarket on the lower level. On the ground level are the platforms *(binari),* a pharmacy, news-stands, information booths, and the large entrance hall, where you will find the ticket windows and ticket vending machines, plus a large book-store. Public toilets and luggage check are at either end of the platform area. The lower level has a complete mall, with services ranging from cosmetics to shoe repair.

Termini is the major public transportation hub of the city, with many bus lines starting and ending in the large square in front of the station (Piazza dei Cinquecento), and with the two Roman subway lines cross-ing underneath (see "Getting Around Rome," later in this chapter). A taxi line awaits just outside the station near the metro sign on the right. For some mysterious reason, the line forms at the end farthest from the exit of the train station, so you have to walk a bit. Take your cab from the line of taxis (taxis are white, with a checkered line on the side in yellow and black).

Although they've virtually disappeared, a few gypsy cabbies hang around the station and will approach you on your walk from the train to the taxi line. Reject their offers, be firm, and get in line for a regulation ride.

By car

Rome is the big transportation hub of Italy (all roads really do lead there). As a result, even Italians dread driving to Rome — not only because of the intricate network of roads, but also thanks to constant traffic, the aggressive driving style (for Romans it's survival; they'd never get home otherwise), and the impossibility of parking. If you are planning to rent a car, we recommend that you do so from the Fiumicino airport, before or after your visit to Rome. You do not need a car during your stay in Rome.

Even if you follow our advice, having a good map and precise driving directions is still imperative because the network of highways converging into Rome gets very complicated. You will want to use the circular highway that runs around the outer limits of Rome, indicated **G.R.A. (Gran Raccordo Anulare),** also known as just the *Raccordo.* All the highways empty onto the G.R.A. while some of them (in particular the *consular roads* [state roads originally built by ancient Roman consuls]) cross it and lead into town. Before approaching Rome, make sure you know which of these roads you want to take; note that they bear names, not numbers. Note that the signs on the G.R.A. don't mention all the exits, but just the next few. Therefore, you have to know which exit comes next when you enter the G.R.A. in order to get on going in the right direction.

Orienting Yourself in Rome

Rome spreads out like a starfish. From the older central body springs arms of newer urban development that have logically formed along the consular roads. The central body corresponds to Rome's medieval perimeter and to the ancient Roman center — the medieval city walls were built on top of the Roman walls, and are still up at various points. Interestingly, Rome didn't spread beyond its walls until the end of the 19th century. The city has therefore occupied pretty much the same area for about three millennia, and consecutive layers of urban development have created a confused layout of streets, with tiny medieval roads crossed by larger and more recent avenues. The central body is still the heart of the city today and the part that you'll most want to visit.

Rome is divided by the river **Tevere,** which meanders north–south; about a third of the city's central part lies on its western bank and the rest on its eastern bank. On the western bank is the **Vatican,** the tiny city-state that heads the Catholic religion, with the Pope as both a religious and administrative leader; its major feature is the basilica of **San Pietro.** North of the Vatican is the largish area called **Prati,** crossed by the busy **Via Cola di Rienzo.** Also on the western bank are **Trastevere,** and **Testaccio.** On the eastern bank of the Tevere, the *centro* covers the whole area within the city walls down to the Tiber. It is the political, cultural, commercial, and tourist heart of the city. At the north end is **Termini** — Rome's main train station and major public transportation hub. Branching out of Termini and the connected Piazza della Repubblica are three major downhill avenues: **Via Cavour** going to the **Colosseum, Via Nazionale** going to **Piazza Venezia** (with the **Campidoglio** and the **Altare della Patria** [Victor Emmanuel Memorial]), and **Via Barberini,** going to **Via Veneto** and **Via del Tritone.** From Piazza Venezia, the major avenue **Via del Corso** brings you to **Piazza del Popolo, Via del Plebiscito** to **Corso Vittorio Emanuele II** and the river Tiber. **Via dei Fori Imperiali** brings you to the **Colosseum.**

Rome Orientation

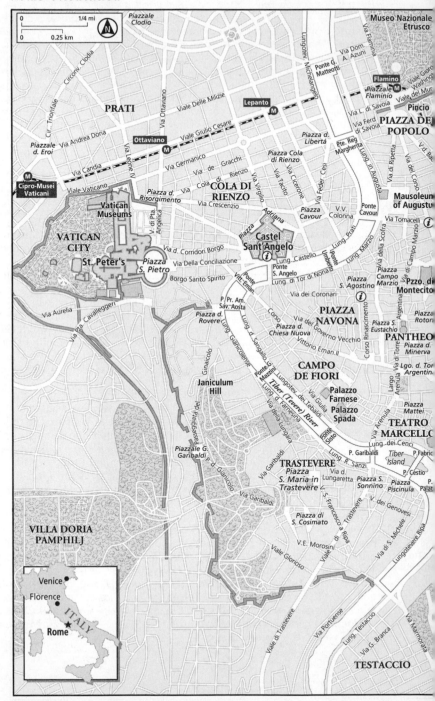

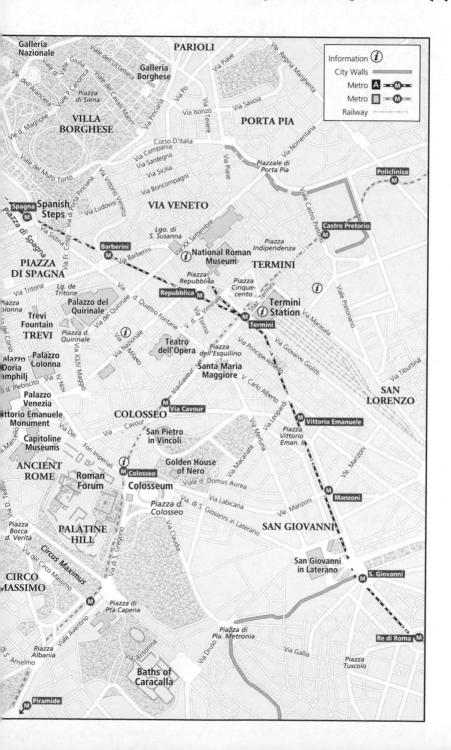

Introducing the neighborhoods

Historic Rome is divided into districts that are named after the original seven hills on which the city was built 3,000 years ago, but people usually refer to either much larger neighborhoods — such as the *centro* — or to much smaller areas around a monument or other landmark. All the neighborhoods here are safe — but you must be on your guard for the ubiquitous pickpockets — and all are desirable places to stay with lively nightlife, restaurants, and cafes. The *centro* is especially desirable because most of the attractions are within easy reach. Of course, everyone knows that so you will sometimes encounter a huge press of people, including locals and tourists — but you'd be hard-pressed to find a place that's more romantic.

Campo de' Fiori

In the southern area of the *centro,* this authentic neighborhood is mostly residential, but is made very lively by the market square and the connected commercial strip of **Via dei Giubbonari.** You'll find plenty of restaurants and an active nightlife. Among the attractions is the beautiful **Palazzo Farnese.**

Circo Massimo

Located to the south of the Colosseum and at the southern edge of the *centro,* the area around Circo Massimo — an oblong Roman theater once used for chariot races (but today not much more than a dirt track for jogging) — was already a residential neighborhood at the time of the ancient Romans. In those days, however, plebians resided in what has now become a rather patrician area, the **Aventino** hill. Graced by the **Terme di Caracalla** to the east, and the **Pyramid of Caius Cestius** to the west, you will find quiet, but few restaurants and hotels.

Cola di Rienzo

This "new" residential neighborhood on the western bank of the Tiber is in the hearth of **Prati** — parts of it were still fields *(prati)* at the end of the 19th century. It stretches between **St. Peter's Basilica** and **Castel Sant' Angelo.** Reflecting its late-19th century origin, streets are wide and straight and lined with trees. The area is pleasant and close to the *centro;* it has a relatively active if subdued nightlife, with restaurants and jazz clubs and an important shopping area along **Via Cola di Rienzo.**

Colosseo

In the eastern part of the *centro,* this old neighborhood sloping up along Via Cavour is still very authentic and residential. Although not elegant, it is experiencing a new life with many trendy restaurants, small hotels, and bars. Downhill from here you find the most illustrious monuments of ancient Rome, including the **Palatino,** the **Roman Forum,** the **Campidoglio,** and the **Colosseum** itself.

Pantheon

At the hearth of the *centro* on the southwestern side of the **Corso,** this is a lively neighborhood with some elegant Renaissance buildings, including the beautiful ones housing the government and the two chambers of the Italian Parliament — **Parlamento** and **Senato.** You'll find many hotels (catering to the many tourists) and many restaurants (catering to the Italians who work nearby). In spite of the crowds, though, it is probably one of the most romantic neighborhoods *and* it's the location of our favorite monument in Rome: the **Pantheon.**

Parioli

Beyond the city walls to the north, on a hill overlooking the heart of Rome, this residential neighborhood is among the most elegant in the city. The **Villa Borghese** park fills the air with fragrance and provides a beautiful (and more important, shady) place for a quiet stroll. Though the prices match the area's exclusivity, this is a great place to be — just a short walk away from many attractions, yet far from the madding crowd. There are a few neighborhood restaurants and some hotels.

Piazza del Popolo

At the north edge of the *centro,* around one of the most beautiful squares of Rome, this lively neighborhood has a lot of new trendy restaurants and bars in the area extending along the west of the **Corso.**

Piazza di Spagna

In the *centro,* on the east side of the **Corso,** this used to be a residential neighborhood, but has been almost completely taken over by the fashion and the tourist industries. It is the best shopping neighborhood in Rome, home to all the great names of Italian couture, plus a lot of nice other shops. It also has many hotels, including the city's best. The shopping street get a bit deserted at night.

Piazza Navona

On the west of the *centro,* and still residential and very romantic, this small neighborhood is livened by Rome's most beautiful square. Some nice restaurants and bars can be found along **Via del Governo Vecchio** and some of the best antiques shops are along **Via dei Coronari.**

Porta Pia

Pia Gate (Porta Pia) opens at the northeast of Rome's city walls onto **Via Nomentana,** one of the oldest of the consular roads. This traditional Roman residential area is not as upscale as the Parioli, but it's an interesting mix of beautiful villas from the 18th and 19th centuries, elegant buildings, and middle-class dwellings. Very close to both Stazione Termini and Via Veneto, it is also very well connected by public transportation and has many restaurants, cafes, and pubs that are popular with the locals. It's an excellent choice for quieter accommodations that are still quite central to the big attractions and have moderate prices.

San Giovanni

Extending between the **Basilica of San Giovanni** and the **Colosseum**, this is still a residential and very Roman neighborhood, with a few hotels and some nice neighborhood restaurants.

San Lorenzo

This old neighborhood just outside the city walls to the northeast, was a relatively poor residential area, but the development of the University of Rome nearby brought it to a new life. It has a lively restaurant and bar scene, which attracts all ages, and a few hotels.

San Pietro

On the western bank of the river Tiber, this area is mainly occupied by the walled city of the **Vatican** (seat of the *Holy See* and site of the Vatican Museums and the Sistine Chapel). It is dominated, of course, by the grandiose **St. Peter's Basilica (Basilica di San Pietro).** Flanking the basilica are two small, ancient residential neighborhoods that are quite picturesque.

Teatro Marcello

This area covers what is still commonly referred to as the Ghetto, the old Jewish neighborhood. It is among the most authentic of the neighborhoods in the *centro,* and still residential. Some nice restaurants are tucked away in its small streets.

Termini

Located at the *front* of Rome's main train station, at the northeast of the *centro,* this is not a particularly romantic neighborhood, but very convenient and with many moderately priced hotels. Note that the area behind Termini (along the tracks) and around Piazza Vittorio is instead a bit seedy.

Testaccio

This flatter neighborhood of narrow streets, located on the western bank of the Tiber, is famous for its restaurants, jazz, and nightlife. It is otherwise a quiet residential neighborhood, livened by the open-air food market and still very authentic.

Trastevere

Located on the western bank of the Tiber at the foot of the **Gianicolo** hill, this neighborhood is just across the river from the Aventino and the Colosseum areas. Literally meaning "on the other side of the Tiber," this was the traditional (and rather seedy) residence of poorer artisans and workers from Roman times. Its character was preserved during the Middle Ages and the Renaissance and to some extent up to the last century. In recent times, though, it has become an artsy neighborhood, famous for its restaurants and nightlife and popular with younger and not-so-young Romans and visitors.

Trevi

At the heart of the *centro* on the east side of the **Corso,** this neighborhood slopes up the Quirinale hill with the magnificent Renaissance Presidential residence as its centerpiece. Aside from the tourist hubbub around its famous fountain, it's a relatively unspoiled neighborhood.

Via Veneto

At the north of the *centro,* this is a very elegant neighborhood with some of the best hotels in Rome. It is very quiet at night and has fewer restaurants and nightspots than other area neighborhoods. Whatever activity there is exists along the avenue itself.

Finding information after you arrive

The main tourist information office is at Via Parigi 5, off Piazza della Repubblica, just north of Stazione Termini (☎ **06-3600-4399;** www. romaturismo.it). Open Monday through Saturday from 9 a.m. to 7 p.m., the office offers plenty of literature on Rome and on side trips from the city, plus a free map and a monthly calendar of events. You will also find a tourist information desk at the international arrivals in the Fiumicino Airport (☎ **06-6595-6074;** open daily 8:15 a.m.–7:00 p.m.) and several information kiosks around the city near major attractions. The staffs at the kiosks are usually less overwhelmed and more available than the staff in the main tourist office; they offer free city maps, a calendar of events, and much more. Open daily 9 a.m. to 6 p.m., the kiosks are at the following addresses:

- ✔ **Castel Sant'Angelo,** Piazza Pia, to the east of the Castel Sant'Angelo (☎ **06-6880-9707;** Metro: Ottaviano–San Pietro)

- ✔ **Largo Goldoni,** off Via del Corso (☎ **06-6813-6061;** Metro: Piazza di Spagna)

- ✔ **Piazza delle Cinque Lune,** just north of Piazza Navona (☎ **06-6880-9240;** Minibus: 116)

- ✔ **Piazza Tempio della Pace,** off Via dei Fori Imperiali, just across from the entrance (☎ **06-6992-4307;** Metro: Colosseo)

- ✔ **Santa Maria Maggiore,** Via dell'Olmata, on the southeastern side of the church (☎ **06-4788-0294;** Metro: Termini)

- ✔ **Termini,** Piazza dei Cinquecento, in front of the railroad station (☎ **06-4782-5194;** Metro: Termini)

- ✔ **Trastevere,** Piazza Sonnino (☎ **06-5833-3457;** Tram: 8)

- ✔ **Via Nazionale,** across from the Palazzo delle Esposizioni (☎ **06-4782-4525;** Bus: 64)

The **Holy See,** being a separate state, maintains its own tourist office. It is located in Piazza San Pietro (☎ **06-6988-4466;** open Mon–Sat 8:30 a.m.– 6 p.m.), just left of the entrance to the Basilica di San Pietro. The office has information on the Vatican and its tourist attractions and religious events. You may also make reservations for a visit to the Vatican gardens or fill out the form to participate in a papal audience, but making a reservation to do so before you leave home may be better (see "How to attend a papal audience," in Chapter 12).

Getting Around Rome

Rome's historical hills are no myth: They are real — and sometimes steep. The one myth is that there are only seven of them. Rome may look flat on a map but it's very hilly — you'll soon understand why locals use mopeds (or cars, unfortunately) and public transportation, and why you'll see so few bicycles around.

Remember also that the city is thousands of years old, so much of it isn't designed for any mode of conveyance other than old-fashioned foot power. But what is wonderful on foot would be a nightmare by car. There are times, however, when you'll welcome public transportation. Taxis, for example, are great at night when crossing large sections of city.

Rome is generally very safe, especially in the center, and you can follow general big-city precautions. The most common form of crime is pickpocketing, which is practiced extensively at crowded locations such as on buses and at markets. Roving gangs of Gypsy children are now less common than they once were; they virtually surround you, creating distraction and confusion, while some Artful Dodger picks your pocket. Hold tight to your wallet and purse, and brush your way past with a stern "no." In addition, don't walk on the edge of the sidewalk near the curb — thieves on motor scooters sometimes yank bags or purses from people's shoulders.

To enjoy Rome's delightful labyrinth, you'll need a good map. Making your way around Rome without a map is very difficult; the free tourist-office map is okay, but the free bus and metro map you can get (when available) at the ATAC information stand in front of the Termini station is better. None of them, however, report all the tiny streets in the historic center of Rome. We recommend that you buy a detailed city maps available at any newsstand and many bookstores; choose one with a *stradario*, an alphabetical street directory.

By metro (subway)

Although Rome has only two metro lines, it is the best way to get around; it doesn't suffer from the terrible city traffic and routes stay the same, unlike the city bus system, which is under constant reorganization. **Line A** and **Line B,** cross each other at the Termini station — which is also the head of many bus lines. Metro A runs near San Pietro, passing Piazza di Spagna and the Palazzo Barberini (Via Veneto) on one side and San Giovanni on the other. Take Line B to get to the Colosseum. The metro runs Sunday through Friday from 5:30 a.m. to 11:30 p.m. and Saturday from 5:30 a.m. to 12:30 a.m.

 The Colosseum, Circus Maximus, and Cavour stops on line B don't offer full elevator/lift service and aren't disabled-accessible. (For tips for travelers with disabilities, see Chapter 9.)

By bus (autobus)

The ATAC bus system is large and under continuous improvement. However, Rome's ancient layout resists any real modernization, so things don't always go smoothly: Buses are very crowded at rush hours, and traffic jams are endemic. Still, buses remain an excellent resource because they go absolutely everywhere in Rome, especially the diminutive electric buses that are the only vehicles allowed in the tiny narrow streets of the historical heart of the city. These electric buses are the ones you will be using most often: **116, 117,** and **119** in the *centro* and **115** in Trastevere. Of the large number of regular bus lines that service Rome — and many of them overlap in the center of town — the bus you're most likely to use is **64,** which runs from Termini train station to San Pietro, crossing the *centro.* Most buses run daily from 5:30 a.m. to 12:30 a.m., but some stop at 8.30 p.m. A few night lines are marked with an *N* for *notturno* (night); they usually run every hour, leaving the ends of the line on the hour.

 When you arrive in Rome, one of the first things you should do is pick up an updated bus map from the bus information booth outside the Termini station in Piazza dei Cinquecento or from the tourist information office inside the station. Routes we mention in this book may have changed. How important is it to get a current map? We were once on a bus when the *driver* asked the passengers what the route was, so you may have to live with a little confusion. When in Rome . . .

On foot

Exploring on foot is our favorite, because you see the most; streets curve, merge, narrow to almost shoulder-width, change names, and meander among beautiful old buildings. Remember to wear very comfortable shoes, and be ready to switch to another form of transportation — usually all handy — when you get tired.

By tram

Rome still has a few tram lines which belong to the same system as the buses. They aren't as spectacular as the cable cars in San Francisco, but they're fun to ride; also, trams have a separate lane, so they're less frequently stopped by traffic. The routes are long, however, and you may have an extended — though scenic — ride. A line we like a lot is the **3,** which passes by the Basilica di San Giovanni and the Colosseum. Another one that you are likely to use is number **8** to Trastevere. Trams are indicated on the free ATAC bus map by a green line.

By taxi

Taxi rates are reasonable in Rome, but taking a taxi can be expensive during those busy times of day when you're stuck in traffic. They're a great resource for getting to your hotel from the train station and traveling around at night after the buses and metro stop running, as well as for getting to some areas that are poorly served by public transport, such as the Gianicolo. A taxi is always the best option if you have a lot of luggage, but if you don't and it's rush hour, take the bus.

Taxi fare starts at 2.35€ ($2.70), and then the meter adds .80€ (90¢) for every kilometer (.62 mile) if you are moving at least 20kmph (12mph); if you are stuck in traffic, the meter racks up a charge of .10€ (12¢) every 19 seconds. Don't forget the night surcharge (10 p.m.–6 a.m.) of 2.60€ ($3), the Sunday and holiday surcharge of 1€ ($1.15), or the luggage supplement of 1€ ($1.15) for each bag put in the trunk.

Hailing a taxi on the street isn't really done, and isn't easy, particularly at night. Taxis don't cruise the streets as in most U.S. cities, but return to taxi stands and wait for a call. You'll find many taxi stands around Rome, especially in the *centro* near major landmarks, including **Piazza Barberini** (at the foot of Via Veneto), **Piazza San Silvestro**, and **Piazza SS. Apostoli** (both not far from the Trevi Fountain). You can identify taxi stands by a smallish telephone on a pole marked "TAXI." But if you're starting from a place with a phone — a hotel, restaurant, and so on it's easiest to ask the staff to call a taxi for you. For a **24-hour radio taxi,** call ☎ 06-88-177, 06-66-45, or 06-49-94.

Getting a ticket to ride

ATAC (☎ 800-431-784 or 06-4695-2027; www.atac.roma.it), Rome's transport authority, runs all metro, trams, and buses in the city, so that your ticket is valid for all public transportation in Rome. You need to buy tickets **before boarding** any mode of transportation, and you must **stamp** them upon boarding, or they aren't valid (on subway and trains the stamping machines — little yellow boxes — are at the entrance gates, on busses and trams they are on board). A regular *biglietto* (ticket) for the bus/metro is valid for 75 minutes and costs 1€ ($1.15). Within the 75 minutes of validity, you can take as many buses and trams as you want, but you can take only one subway ride. If you're still on the bus when you approach the expiration of the 75 minutes of validity, stamp your ticket again at its other end; this will show that you boarded the bus during the period of validity of your ticket and not after it expired, so you'll be in the clear if a ticket inspector boards the bus. You can also get a daily pass called **BIG** and costing 4€ ($.4.60) and a 3-day ticket called **BTI** for 11€ ($13); both passes give you unlimited rides on bus, metro, and trains (2nd-class travel) within Rome's urban area. You can buy tickets at most bars, tobacconist shops (signed *tabacchi* or by a white *T* on a black background), and newsstands. Tickets and passes are also sold at the ticket booths in the metro, at the ATAC bus information booth in front of Stazione Termini (near Platform C), and from machines at many locations — machines usually take only exact change.

By motor scooter (motorino)

Most Romans travel around via moped, or so it seems when you're on a street corner waiting for the signal to turn green. If you want to try this combination sport/mode of transportation yourself, the best spot to rent a *motorino* is **Treno e Scooter (TeS)** just outside Stazione Termini by the taxi stand and metro entrance (☎ **06-4890-5823**). TeS gives you a 10 percent discount if you've traveled by train that day. The scooters are very good quality and the prices (for example, 52€/$59 for the weekend) include insurance, taxes, and a free map. To get there, take the metro to Termini.

Rent a Scooter Borgo, Via delle Grazie 2, just off Via di Porta Angelica, on the right side of the Vatican (☎ **06-687-7239;** Metro: Ottaviano) and **New Scooter,** Via Quattro Novembre 96/a, just up from Piazza Venezia (☎ **06-679-0300;** Bus: 64), are also good options.

Riding a scooter can be quite dangerous in Rome's most busy areas. Accidents are increasingly common. It is a great way to travel on Sundays and holidays, however, when traffic is light and fewer buses are out, or to explore quiet neighborhoods.

Staying in Style

Rome accommodations vary from the very basic to the supremely elegant. Still, in high tourist season you may find it difficult to find the type of lodging you prefer. If you come to town without a reservation at all, you will be lucky to find a decent room, period.

Many hotels have been recently refurbished and several new ones have opened, but prices have risen sharply in recent years. A weak dollar and poor exchange rate haven't helped. Rome is a capital city, and capital cities the world over are expensive. The best way to get a deal is to plan in advance; see Chapter 8 for money-saving tips on booking your accommodations.

Good hotels in the bottom price category are few and far between, because the top rate in high season is rarely under $130. A hotel whose *top* rack rate is $100 is not usually a place where you would want to stay. You are better off trying to get a discount on a hotel on the next step up. Also, many of our hotels offer Internet specials, which can offer savings of 25 percent or more. See the table in Chapter 8 for a description of what the $ symbols mean.

Following are our picks for the best places to stay, followed by some acceptable alternatives if you have trouble booking a room. Unless otherwise specified, all rooms in the hotels we recommend come with private bathrooms. Note that many of the hotels in historical areas are housed in ancient buildings and have relatively few rooms, so reserve well in advance.

If you arrive without a room reservation (something we advise against), remember that there's a hotel desk at the airport and that Enjoy Rome (see "Finding information after you arrive," earlier in the chapter) offers a free room-finding service.

The top hotels

 ### Albergo Cesàri Hotel
$$ Pantheon

The Cesàri has been a hotel since 1787 (they still have their original license from Pope Pius VI), and has been run by the same family since 1899. The Cesàri was recently renovated and is variably furnished; some rooms are more modern, while others have beautiful hardwood reproduction beds and armoirs. Tiled baths and bathtubs are a plus. You can't beat the location: The hotel lies between the Pantheon and the Corso, and the Trevi Fountain is not far away either. Most of the guest rooms have been soundproofed, because this is a highly congested tourist area. For families or small groups, inquire about the triple and quad rooms.

See map p. 122. Via di Pietra 89a. ☎ *06-674-9701. Fax: 06-674-97030.* www.albergo cesari.it. *Bus: 60 or 116 to Via di Pietra, just south of Piazza Colonna on the Corso. Free parking nearby. Rack rates: 200€ ($230) double. AE, DC, MC, V.*

Albergo del Sole al Pantheon
$$$$ Pantheon

This claims to be Rome's oldest hotel (since 1467), but that's not why you should stay here. True to its name, the Albergo is right across from the Pantheon and has some rooms with spectacular views — which, luckily, don't include the McDonald's downstairs (though sometimes the odor of grease fills the beautiful square). The original coffered ceilings are handpainted, and the confusing layout is typical of medieval Rome, with a warren of rooms and stairways and different levels. The guest rooms are individually (and usually tastefully) decorated; in a building of this age, don't expect them to be large, however. Some of the furnishings appear to be antiques, while other pieces are quite modern. Suites offer baths with hydromassage. Check the Web site for specials, which can mean considerable savings.

See map p. 122. Piazza della Rotonda 63. ☎ *06-678-0441. Fax: 06-6994-0689.* www.hotel solealpantheon.com. *Bus: 116 to Pantheon or 64 to Largo Argentina, then walk north. Rack rates: 350€ ($403) double. Rates include buffet breakfast. AE, DC, MC, V.*

 ### Albergo Santa Chiara
$$$ Pantheon

This is one of Rome's oldest hotels, operated since 1838 by the Corteggiani family, and a great value. Just behind the Pantheon and a few steps from Piazza della Minerva, it's functional and comfortable. From the beautiful entry hall, with its statuary and porphyry columns, to the skylit breakfast room, the Santa Chiara offers a feeling of elegance. The guest rooms are furnished in modern or reproduction style, with carpeting or wood floors. Some are in the attic storey and have sloping ceilings, sometimes beamed. The beds are generally large by Italian standards.

See map p. 122. Via Santa Chiara 21. ☎ **06-687-2979.** *Fax: 06-687-3144.* www.albergo santachiara.com. *Bus: 116 to Pantheon or 64 or 70 to Largo Argentina, then walk north. Rack rates: 233€ ($268) double. Rates include breakfast. AE, DC, MC, V.*

Aldrovandi Palace Hotel
$$$$ Parioli

Opened in 1981, the Aldrovandi Palace is housed in an elegant villa facing the park of the Villa Borghese. Although pricey, the hotel offers many extras that you wouldn't expect to find in Rome: a large free parking area, pool, private park, gym and health club, and restaurant. It's extremely quiet at night — a rare advantage in Rome. All the guest rooms are very spacious (the smallest are about 21 sq. m/225 sq. ft.), and are decorated with modern Italian furnishings and carpeting. The beds are queen- or king size. A number of rooms are disabled-accessible. Don't forget to ask about special offers the hotel may running, which may bring the steep prices down a bit.

Via Ulisse Aldrovandi 15 (behind the Villa Borghese). ☎ **06-322-3993.** *Fax: 06-322-1435.* www.aldrovandi.com. *Tram: 19 or 30 to Via Ulisse Aldrovandi. Free parking. Rack rates: 475€ ($546) double. AE, DC, MC, V.*

Casa Kolbe
$ Teatro Marcello

Near the Jewish Ghetto, steps from the major classical sites — the Capitoline Hill, Palatine Hill, Roman Forum, and Colosseum — this is an old-fashioned hotel in a former convent; it offers room-and-board combinations if you want. The guest rooms are clean but sometimes a little worn and the furnishings simple. For the price, however, you can't beat it. This is a peaceful area, and the quietest rooms overlook the small inner garden. Many tour groups book here, so reserve in advance. A number of rooms are disabled-accessible.

See map p. 122. Via San Teodoro 44. ☎ **06-679-4974.** *Fax: 06-6994-1550. Bus: 60 or 81 to Bocca della Verità, and then walk east to Via San Teodoro. Rack rates: 86€ ($99) double. AE, DC, MC, V.*

Casa Valdese
$ Cola di Rienzo

The name "Valdese" refers to a Swiss religious sect; this is a simple, small hotel on the Vatican side of the river, it is near the shopping district of Cola di Rienzo and the Castel Sant' Angelo. Just across the river is the *centro,* and with the subway close by you are a short ride from major destinations. The rooms are not large but they are clean, servicable, and the price is very reasonable for Rome.

See map p. 122. Via A. Farnese 18. ☎ **06-321-8222.** *Fax: 06-321-1843. Metro: Lepanto. Walk toward the river and take your first right; walk one and a half blocks on Via Farnese. Rack rates: 116€ ($133) double. AE, V.*

Rome Accommodations and Dining

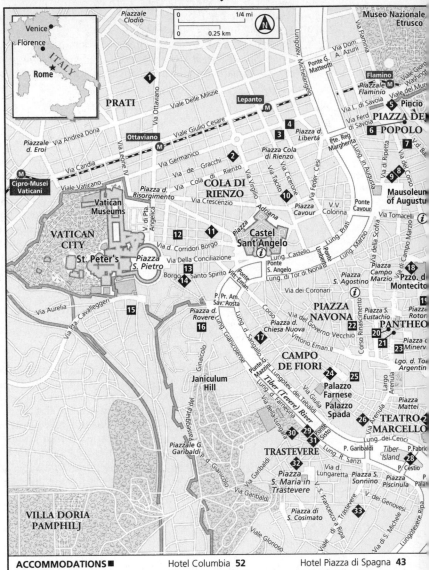

ACCOMMODATIONS ■

Albergo Cesàri Hotel **19**
Albergo del Senato **20**
Albergo del Sole al Pantheon **21**
Albergo Santa Chiara **23**
Casa Kolbe **53**
Casa Valdese **4**
Hotel Art **7**
Hotel Barberini **50**
Hotel Barocco **49**
Hotel Celio **58**

Hotel Columbia **52**
Hotel Columbus **13**
Hotel de Russie **6**
Hotel Emmaus **15**
Hotel Farnese **3**
Hotel Grifo **55**
Hotel Homs **44**
Hotel La Rovere **16**
Hotel Laurentia **53**
Hotel Navona **22**
Hotel Parlamento **45**

Hotel Piazza di Spagna **43**
Hotel Ranieri **39**
Hotel Santa Prassede **54**
Hotel Scalinata di Spagna **42**
Hotel Turner **37**
Hotel Venezia **51**
Hotel Villa del Parco **36**
Rose Garden Palace **41**
Sant'Anna **12**
Teatro di Pompeo **25**

Information (i)
City Walls
Metro A
Metro B
Railway

Galleria Nazionale
PARIOLI 34
Galleria Borghese 35
Via Regina Margherita
Via Piave
VILLA BORGHESE
Piazza di Siena
Viale P. Canonica
Via Pinciana
Via Po
Via Isonzo
Via Savoia
PORTA PIA 36
Via Nomentana
Corso D'Italia
Via Campania
Via Sardegna
Via Sicilia 40
Via Boncompagni
Piazzale di Porta Pia 38
Piazza di Porta Pia
Policlinico M
41
Spagna M Spanish Steps
Piazza di Spagna
VIA VENETO 39
Castro Pretorio M
42
44 PIAZZA DI SPAGNA 49
Barberini M
Via Barberini
Lgo. di S. Susanna
Via XX Settembre
National Roman Museum (i)
Piazza Indipendenza
TERMINI 51
Castro Pretorio
Via Tritone
Lg. de Tritone
50
Palazzo del Quirinale
Repubblica M
Piazza Repubblica
Piazza Cinquecento
52
Termini Station (i)
Via Marsala
46
47 Trevi Fountain
48 TREVI
Piazza d. Quirinale (i)
Via Nazionale
Via del Quirinale
Via Quattro Fontane
Via Vimi...
Via Torino
Termini M
Via Principe Amedeo
Via Giovanni Giolitti
Viale Pretoriano
Palazzo Colonna
Palazzo Doria Pamphilj
Palazzo Venezia
Via IV Nov.
Via XXIV Maggio
Teatro dell'Opera
Piazza dell'Esquilino
Santa Maria Maggiore 54
V. Carlo Alberto
53 SAN LORENZO
Via Tiburtina
Vittorio Emanuele Monument
Capitoline Museums
ANCIENT ROME
55 Via Cavour M
COLOSSEO
San Pietro in Vincoli
Piazza Vittorio Eman. II
Vittorio Emanuele M
59
Via Manzoni
Roman Forum 57
(i) 56
Colosseo M
Golden House of Nero
Colosseum
Viale d. Domus Aurea
Via Labicana
Manzoni M
Piazza d. Colosseo 58
PALATINE HILL
Piazza Bocca d. Verità
Via di S. Giovanni in Laterano
SAN GIOVANNI
San Giovanni in Laterano
S. Giovanni M
CIRCO MASSIMO
Circus Maximus

DINING ◆

Arcangelo **10**
Bolognese **5**
Bric **24**
Cesarina **40**
Checco er Carettiere **30**
Da Benito e Gilberto **11**
Da Giggetto **27**
Da Maciste al Salario, Pizza, Vino e Cucina **34**
Dante Taberna de' Gracchi **2**
Ferrara **29**
Gelateria alla Scala **32**
Gelateria Trevi **46**
Giolitti **18**
Gusto **9**
Hostaria Nerone **56**
Il Drappo **17**
La Taverna Trevi da Tarquinio **46**
La Veranda **14**
Osterie Ponte Sisto **31**
Palazzo del Freddo di G. Fassi **1, 59**
Pica **26**
Pizzeria Ivo **33**
Presidente **47**
Quirino **48**
Sora Lella **28**
Yogobar **35, 38**

Hotel Art
$$$$ Piazza di Spagna

This new hotel, located in one of the most desirable areas of Rome, is not just modern; it's postmodern. Each floor is color coordinated with the details of the rooms (down to the stationery and pens). The furniture, much of it of fine hardwoods, is in a contemporary international style. Hotel Art has much the feel of the boutique hotels you find in all the great cities of the world. The crystal staircase of the entry hall and the columned bar, both striking, illustrate the artistic "eclecticism" on which the hotel prides itself. The accent is on comfort, service, and of course, style.

See map p. 122. Via Margutta 56. ☎ *06-328-711. Fax: 06-3600-3995.* www.hotelart. it. *Tram: 19 or 30 to Via Ulisse Aldrovandi. Free parking. Rack rates: 490€ ($564) double. AE, DC, MC, V.*

Hotel Barocco
$$$ Via Veneto

Right off Piazza Barberini, this charming small hotel has a fantastic location on one of the quieter streets behind Via Veneto, slightly removed from the noise and yet still near major attractions. Its guest rooms are tastefully furnished in dark woods and fine fabrics, and have marble bathrooms. The beds in the suites are particularly large. The refined ambience is pleasant without being stuffy.

See map p. 122. Via della Purificazione 4. ☎ *06-487-2001. Fax: 06-485-994.* www.hotel barocco.com. *Metro: Line A to Barberini, and then walk up Via della Purificazione, on the west side of the piazza. Rack rates: 295€–325€ ($339–$374) double. Rates include breakfast. AE, MC, V.*

Hotel Celio
$$$ San Giovanni

Still radiant from a recent overhaul, this jewel is housed in an 1870 building. The classical details, mosaic floors, frescoed ceilings, *trompe l'oeil* paintings, and fine furniture combine to create a classic old-world feeling. Each room has a reproduction fresco in ancient Roman style. No expense has been spared — even on the hallways, which are elegantly decorated as well. The bathrooms are nicely tiled and the fixtures are brand new but in classic style. Some even have a Jacuzzi. The roof garden affords a view of the nearby Colosseum.

See map p. 122. Via dei SS. Quatro 35/c. ☎ *06-7049-5333. Fax: 06-709-6377.* www.hotel celio.com. *Metro: to Colosseo. Free parking. Rack rates: 290€–310€ ($334–$357) double. Rates include continental buffet breakfast. AE, DC, MC, V.*

Hotel Columbia
$$ Termini

Renovated in 1997, this hotel dates back to 1900 and is still family run. The Murano chandeliers are nice touches in otherwise simple, modern guest rooms. The décor is easy on the eye, with bright white bedspreads and beamed ceilings in some rooms. There's a nice rooftop garden with a bar. The Hotel Venezia (later in this section) is under the same management.

*See map p. 122. Via Viminale 15. ☎ **06-474-4289**. Fax: 06-474-0209.* www.hotel columbia.com. *Metro: Line A to Repubblica, and then walk toward Stazione Termini. Rack rates: 205€ ($236) double. Rates include breakfast. AE, DC, MC, V.*

Hotel Columbus
$$$ San Pietro

Only steps from St. Peter's Basilica, this spacious hotel occupies the Palazzo della Rovere, built in the late 1400s by Cardinal Domenico della Rovere, and surrounds a garden courtyard. Charles VIII is one of the many notables who have occupied it at one time or another. The public spaces preserve the feeling of a dignified aristocrat's palace. Some of the frescoes were done by Pinturicchio. The rooms are somewhat austere but comfortable; they are also large (some of them almost cavernous). **La Veranda** restaurant (reviewed later in this chapter) offers refined Roman and Italian cuisine and tables in the garden in the summer. The hotel is disabled-accessible.

*See map p. 122. Via della Conciliazione 33. ☎ **06-686-5435**. Fax: 06-686-4874.* www. hotelcolumbus.net. *Bus: 64 to last stop, and then walk south to Via della Conciliazione and turn left. Free parking. Rack rates: 320€ ($368) double. Rates include breakfast. AE, DC, MC, V.*

Hotel de Russie
$$$$$ Piazza di Spagna

Since it opened in 2000, this hotel has become a chic place to stay in Rome — Bill and Chelsea stayed there when they were in town. In a palazzo just by the Piazza del Popolo, furnished in elegant, contemporary Italian style, with every detail coordinated in an overall impression of elegance. The beds, like the rooms, are commodious. The interior courtyard and terraced gardens are beautiful, and there is a spa with sauna and health club; there's even a swimming pool. Its restaurant, Le Jardin du Russie, gets rave reviews and boasts a world-class chef.

*See map p. 122. Via del Babuino 9. ☎ **06-32-8881**. Fax: 06-3288-8888.* www.hotel derussie.it. *Metro: Line A to Flaminio. Cross Piazza del Popolo. Rack rates: 640€–800€ ($760–$920). AE, DC, MC, V.*

Hotel Farnese
$$$ Cola di Rienzo

Tucked between the Castel Sant'Angelo and Piazza del Popolo in a quiet neighborhood, this hospitable hotel occupies a 1906 patrician palazzo which has been completely renovated. Quiet and off the tourist path, it is elegantly decorated, with an Art Deco feeling. The guest rooms are spacious, and the bathrooms are particularly nice, with new modern fixtures and marble and tile. The Farnese is steps from one of Rome's best shopping streets — Via Cola di Rienzo — and within walking distance of the Vatican and the medieval center. The hotel also has a roof garden.

See map p. 122. Via A. Farnese 30. ☎ *06-321-2553. Fax: 06-321-5129.* www.hotel-farnese.com. *Metro: Line A to Lepanto, and then walk northeast on Via degli Scipioni to Via A. Farnese. Free parking. Rack rates: 258€ ($297) double. AE, MC, V.*

Hotel Grifo
$$ Colosseo

With large, bright rooms with white walls and modern wood furniture, the Hotel Grifo offers simplicity, value, and a central location. The tiled bathrooms are smallish but functional (some have tubs). The hotel also has a roof garden.

See map p. 122. Via del Boschetto 144. ☎ *06-487-1395. Fax: 06-474-2323.* www.hotelgrifo.com. *Metro: Line B to Cavour, turn right on Via Panisperna and walk one block. Rack rates: 150€ ($173) double. Rates include buffet breakfast. AE, MC, V.*

Hotel Laurentia
$$ San Lorenzo

This new hotel located near the university in an area of restaurants and student hangouts, offers reasonable prices and easy accessibility by public transportation to the city center. The rooms are large with blonde wood furnishings and new, comfortable beds. The three rooms on the top floor have access to a large terrace with views over Rome and the nearby countryside.

See map p. 122. Largo degli Osci 63. ☎ *06-445-0218. Fax: 06-445-3821.* www.hotellaurentia.com. *Bus: 492 or 71 to Via Tiburtina. Rack rates: 145€ ($167) double. Rates include breakfast. AE, DC, MC, V.*

Hotel Navona
$ Piazza Navona

This family-run hotel is just off Piazza Navona, and the location is its great attraction (that, and the price). It recently changed its name from "pensione," signifying that it now has private baths for all its rooms. The furnishing is functional, with an effort to accent the rooms with coordinated curtains and other details. Some rooms have coffered ceilings. Nearby is the Residenza Zanardelli, owned by the same family, which has plusher accommodations for more money. Air-conditioning is available on request and for an extra fee, but the high ceilings keep the house cool even on the hottest days.

See map p. 122. Via dei Sediari 8. ☎ *06-686-4203. Fax: 06-6880-3802.* www.hotel navona.com. *Bus: 70, 81, or 116 to Via dei Sediari, which is east of the southern tip of Piazza Navona, just off Corso Rinascimento. Parking: 15€ ($17). Rack rates: 120€ ($138) double. No credit cards.*

Hotel Parlamento
$$ Pantheon

Located right in the center, this hotel is housed in a 15th-century building but offers modern accommodations at a great price (off-season prices can be half the rack rate). Rooms are spacious with tiled floors, large beds, and comfortable bathrooms, some of them with tubs. The only drawback is that air-conditioning is an extra charge of 12€ ($14) per day.

See map p. 122. Via delle Convertite 5, just off Piazza San Silvestro. ☎ *and Fax: 06-6992-1000.* www.hotelparlamento.it. *Bus: 492 or 116 to Piazza San Silvestro. Rack rates: 158€ ($181) double. Rates include breakfast. MC, V.*

Hotel Piazza di Spagna
$$$ Piazza di Spagna

This hotel is not only a stone's throw from Piazza di Spagna, but it was completely renovated just a few years ago. It has been a family-run hotel for three generations. The guest rooms are small but comfortable, decorated in a simple style that is vaguely Spanish. All have minibars; a few have Jacuzzis and/or private terraces. A popular hotel, noted for its cleanliness, atmosphere, and prime location, it books up fast — make your reservations well in advance.

See map p. 122. Via Mario de' Fiori 61. ☎ *06-679-6412. Fax: 06-679-0654.* www.hotel piazzadispagna.it. *Metro: Line A to Spagna, and then walk a block southeast to Via Mario de' Fiori. Rack rates: 240€–270€ ($276–$311) double. Rates include buffet breakfast. AE, DC, MC, V.*

Hotel Santa Prassede
$$ Centro/Termini

This recently renovated hotel features spacious rooms with large beds. The furnishings are modern and some of the rooms have wood floors. It may not have "old world" charm, but it's a great value for spacious accommodations with everything clean and new, all in the heart of Rome. Many fine restaurants and local eateries can be found on nearby Via Panisperna.

See map p. 122. Via di Santa Precede 25. ☎ *06-481-4850. Fax: 06-474-6859.* www. hotelsantaprassede.it. *Metro: Termini, walk down Via Cavour past Santa Maria Maggiore; take the first street on your left. Parking: 13€ ($15). Rack rates: 135€ ($155). MC, V.*

Hotel Scalinata di Spagna
$$$–$$$$ **Piazza di Spagna**

This is a charming hotel located just above the Spanish Steps. The guest rooms are not huge but are cheery and nicely appointed; some may have exposed beams or a private small terrace. It feels more like a country inn on a hill — the view from the roof garden is spectacular — than a hotel in the congested *centro*.

See map p. 122. Piazza Trinità dei Monti 17. ☎ *06-679-3006. Fax: 06-6994-0598.* www.hotelscalinata.com. *Metro: Line A to Spagna, and then walk up the Spanish Steps. Rack rates: 320€–350€ ($368–$403) double. Rates include buffet breakfast. AE, MC, V.*

Hotel Villa del Parco
$$ **Porta Pia**

This family-run hotel is housed in one of the elegant villas on Via Nomentana and is surrounded by a garden. Although outside the historic center, it's situated in a zone of beautiful 19th-century villas, parks, and quiet tree-lined streets. The Nomentana is a major thoroughfare and is well-served by public transportation. The rooms are above average in size and the bathrooms are large and modern. Each room is brightly (but tastefully) decorated, each one different from the others; the furnishings giving a quaint, country feeling. A recent renovation included the installation of an elevator.

See map p. 122. Via Nomentana 110. ☎ *06-4423-7773. Fax: 06-4423-7572.* www.hotels-venice.com/villaparco.html. *Bus: 60 or 62 to third stop after Porta Pia on Via Nomentana. Free parking. Rack rates: 205€ ($236). Rates include breakfast. AE, DC, MC, V.*

Rose Garden Palace
$$$–$$$$ **Via Veneto**

In the exclusive area around Via Veneto, this is a new hotel housed in an Art Nouveau building from the beginning of the 20th century. The eponymous rose garden is a lovely place for a private stroll. There's more than charm, however; the amenities are top notch. The marble bathrooms have both shower and bathtub, the rooms themselves are large, and the entire hotel is furnished with very modern, sleek décor. A new health club and even a swimming pool are on site.

See map p. 122. Via Bonconpagni 19. ☎ *06-421-741. Fax: 06-481-5608.* www.rosegardenpalace.com. *Bus: 116 to Via Boncompagni, walk north one block. Free parking. Rack rates: 300€–438€ ($345–$504). Rates include American buffet breakfast. AE, MC, V.*

Sant'Anna
$$ **San Pietro**

In a charming and authentic neighborhood near the Vatican, this hotel is in a 16th-century building that surrounds a courtyard. The rooms are larger than average and have modern furnishings, carpeting, and marble bathrooms. The Sant'Anna has a brightly decorated breakfast room, offers wheelchair access, and allows pets.

See map p. 122. Via Borgo Pio 134. ☎ *06-6880-1602. Fax: 06-6830-8717.* www.hotel santanna.com. *Bus: 64 to the next-to-last stop, and then walk north to Borgo Pio. Free parking. Rack rates: 210€ ($242) double. Rates include buffet breakfast. AE, MC, V.*

Teatro di Pompeo
$$ Campo de' Fiori

The name of this hotel comes from a 55 B.C. Roman theater that lies beneath the hotel — some of it can still be seen in the breakfast room. The rest of the building is from the 15th century, as revealed by the beamed ceilings in some of the rooms. The rooms are spacious for this ancient area of Rome, and the white plaster walls and simple furnishings give it an old-fashioned charm. The hotel is small, so reserve your room early.

See map p. 122. Largo del Pallaro 8. ☎ *06-6830-0170. Fax: 06-6880-5531. E-mail:* hotel.teatrodipompeo@tiscalinet.it. *Bus: 64 to Sant'Andrea della Valle, then walk east on Via dei Chiavari and turn right. Rack rates: 190€ ($219) double. Rates include breakfast. AE, DC, MC, V.*

Runner-up accommodations

Albergo del Senato

$$$ **Pantheon** A good-value hotel near the Pantheon, the spacious rooms are beautifully furnished. The marble baths are huge (for Rome) and nicely appointed. The terrace has a spectacular view. *See map p. 122. Piazza della Rotonda 73.* ☎ *06-678-4343. Fax: 06-699-40297.* www.albergodelsenato.it.

Hotel Barberini

$$$$ **Via Veneto** This hotel is expensive but beautiful, with elegant reproduction furniture and luxurious baths. It's located just off Via Veneto near the Fontana di Trevi. *See map p. 122. Via Rasella 3.* ☎ *06-481-4993. Fax: 06-481-5211.* www.hotelbarberini.com.

Hotel Emmaus

$$ **San Pietro** This recently renovated hotel is only a hundred yards from the Basilica di San Pietro. All the guest rooms have modern furnishings and some afford views over St. Peter's dome. *See map p. 122. Via delle Fornaci 25.* ☎ *06-635-658. Fax: 06-635-658.* www.hotelemmaus.com.

Hotel Homs

$$$ **Piazza di Spagna** Only a short walk from the Spanish Steps, the Hotel Homs offers nice amenities and reasonably large guest rooms (some of them disabled-accessible) with contemporary furniture, as well as a roof terrace where you can have breakfast. *See map p. 122. Via della Vite 71.* ☎ *06-679-2976. Fax: 06-678-0482.*

Hotel La Rovere

$$ San Pietro   Set on the lower slope of the Gianicolo on a quaint side street, the Rovere is close to Trastevere and the Vatican. It's quiet, with comfortable rooms, some of them with beamed ceilings. A buffet breakfast is included in the price. *See map p. 122. Vicolo Sant'Onofrio 4–5.* ☎ **06-6880-6739.** *Fax: 06-6880-7062.* www.hotellarovere.com.

Hotel Ranieri

$$ Termini   This hotel is within walking distance of Via Veneto and was renovated in the last ten years. The guest rooms offer modern baths and air-conditioning. *See map p. 122. Via XX Settembre 43.* ☎ **06-4201-4531.** *Fax: 06-4201-4543.* www.hotel.ranieri.com.

Hotel Turner

$$ Porta Pia   With large rooms and elegant, almost gaudy furnishings, Hotel Turner is a good value, located on the Nomentana — outside the center, but closely connected by transportation. *See map p. 122. Via Nomentana 27, by Porta Pia.* ☎ **06-4425-0077.** *Fax: 06-4425-0165.* www.hotelturner.com.

Hotel Venezia

$$ Termini   In a residential district near the university, this hotel boasts relatively large guest rooms appointed with Murano chandeliers. *See map p. 122. Via Varese 18.* ☎ **06-445-7101.** *Fax: 06-495-7687.* www.hotelvenezia.com.

Dining Out

Italian gourmands have long maintained that there isn't a really good restaurant in Rome — but they can't say that any longer. Rome still has hundreds of good little trattorie, *osterie,* and *pizzerie* (see Chapter 2 for more on Roman specialties and cuisine), but new trends are sweeping the dining scene, and lots of middle- and upper-end quality restaurants have opened. Partly, it's because Romans are going out more, both for lunch and dinner — supply and demand has done the rest.

One of the most interesting trends is what Romans are calling *"crudi"* — sashimi, Italian style. Italians have always eaten *carpaccio* (thinly sliced raw beef served with oil and Parmesan cheese) or fish made in the *ceviche* style (prepared with lemon juice, which in effect "cooks" the fish), but the trend toward raw fish is completely new.

The best (and most convenient) areas to eat are still *il centro* (the center) between the Corso and the river Tiber, and Trastevere. The area around Campo de' Fiori continues to be a hot spot where new restaurants are constantly cropping up. However, good restaurants are popping up all over the place, including in outlying neighborhoods and industrial areas.

Thanks to Rome's dining boom, it gets easier and easier to find nice restaurants, but harder and harder to find cheap ones. Even the pizzerias seem to have raised their prices considerably. Therefore, having a sandwich standing up in a *bar* or other cheap eats for lunch becomes ever-more useful — you can save your lunch money for dinner.

 In fine weather, a nice (and inexpensive) option is to make a sandwich and have a picnic in Villa Borghese or on the Gianicolo (see Chapter 12). An excellent place to buy farm-fresh food for your picnic is the **Fattoria la Parrina** (Largo Toniolo 3, between Piazza Navona and the Pantheon; ☎ 06-6830-0111), which offers wonderful cheese, wine, and veggies.

Al Regno di Re Ferdinando II
$$$ Testaccio   NEAPOLITAN

In one of the historic cellars of Monte Testaccio — the hill formed by discarded pottery shards under Nero — this restaurant offers excellent Neapolitan food. The choice of fresh pasta is superb and the *Sfizietto del Re* (a huge portion of linguine with a mountain of shellfish from the nearby Tirrenian Sea) delights any palate and leaves an everlasting memory after you finish — *if* you can finish. The other seafood dishes are excellent as well. This restaurant also makes pizza — the Neapolitan specialty — but the pasta is much better. If you visit in the summer, bring a jacket — the place isn't air-conditioned, but the cellar maintains an icy temperature inside.

Via di Monte Testaccio 39. ☎ *06-578-3725. Reservations recommended. Metro: Line B to Piramide, but taking a cab is best. Secondi: 15€–30€ ($17–$36). AE, DC, MC, V. Open: Lunch Tues–Sat; dinner Mon–Sat.*

Arcangelo
$$ Cola di Rienzo   ROMAN/INNOVATIVE ITALIAN/FISH

The chefs at this new restaurant are among those who've taken to the trend of enlivening Italian cuisine with new combinations that grandma didn't make. Here the experiments are subtle and delicious — though they keep your options open with the more traditional offerings on the menu. The *maccheroni all'amatriciana* (pasta in a spicy tomato and bacon sauce) are excellent, but so are the less usual *spaghetti aglio olio e mazzancolle* (spaghetti with garlic, olive oil, and local crayfish), the *tonno arrosto con melanzane* (baked tuna with eggplants), and the *anatra in salsa di frutta secca* (duck in dried fruit sauce).

See map p. 122. Via G.G. Belli, 59/61, off Via Cicerone, 1 block from Piazza Cavour. ☎ *06-321-0992. Reservations recommended. Bus: 30, 70, 81. Secondi: 13€–21€ ($15–$24). AE, DC, V. Open: Lunch and dinner Mon–Sat. Closed Aug.*

Bolognese
$$ Piazza del Popolo ITALIAN

Elegant and hip, this restaurant serves well prepared food at moderate prices in a nicely appointed dining room or on the outdoor terrace. Even Romans admit Bologna has produced some good dishes, like the *lasagna* prepared so well here; the *tagliatelle alla Bolognese* (home made pasta with tomato and meat sauce) and the *fritto di verdure e agnello* (tempura of vegetables and lamb bits) are mouth-watering. End with something from the unusually large selection of delicious desserts.

See map p. 122. Piazza del Popolo 1/2. ☎ 06-361-1426. Reservations recommended. Bus: 117, 119. Secondi: 14€–23€ ($16–$26). AE, DC, MC, V. Open: Lunch daily, dinner Tues–Sun. Closed Aug.

Bric
$$ Campo de' Fiori LATIUM/FRENCH/MEDITERRANEAN

In this pleasant, informal restaurant, you can relax with some wine and cheese selected from an extensive list — of both Italian and international provenance — or have a more substantial meal from the inventive and somewhat "fusion" menu. Try the *charlotte di carciofi con guanciale croccante e pecorino* (*charlotte* of artichokes, bacon, and pecorino cheese), or the *abacchio alla parmigiana* (lamb in Parmesan sauce). Bric is a great stop in the trendy but authentic area of Campo de' Fiori, a perfect setting for dinner.

See map p. 122. Via del Pellegrino 51, off Campo de' Fiori. ☎ 06-687-9533. Reservations recommended. Bus: 116 to Campo de' Fiori. Secondi: 9€–19€ ($10–$22). DC, MC, V. Open: Dinner Tues–Sun. Closed 10 days in Aug.

Cesarina
$$$ Via Veneto ROMAN/BOLOGNESE

Offering a nice selection of specialties from Rome and Bologna, this restaurant is an excellent choice in the residential area north of Via Veneto, away from the crowds. The food is wonderful and perfectly prepared. Go for the tasting menu of homemade pastas and/or the choice of meat dishes. The *bollito misto* (variety of boiled meats) is delicious.

See map p. 122. Via Piemonte 109. ☎ 06-488-0828. Reservations recommended. Metro: Line A to Barberini. Bus: 56 or 58 to Via Piemonte (the fourth street off Via Boncompagni coming from Via Veneto). Secondi: 15€–28€ ($17–$32). AE, DC, MC, V. Open: Lunch and dinner Mon–Sat.

Checchino dal 1887
$$ Testaccio ROMAN

An elegant restaurant but with a lively atmosphere, Checcino is one of several restaurants housed in the Monte Testaccio (hill of broken pottery — the Roman pottery dump). It serves real Roman specialties such as *lingua con salsa verde* (tongue in a green sauce of garlic, parsley, and olive oil) and *penne con broccoletti strascinati al pecorino romano* (short pasta with sauteed broccoli rabe with pecorino cheese), and the classic *coda alla vaccinara* (oxtail with pinoli nuts and raisins).

Via di Monte Testaccio 30. ☎ *06-574-3816.* www.checcino-dal-1887.com. *Reservations recommended. Metro: Line B to Piramide, but taking a cab is best. Secondi: 14€–25€ ($16–$29). AE, DC, V. Open: Lunch and dinner Tues–Sat; closed Aug and Dec 24–Jan 1.*

Checco er Carettiere
$$ **Trastevere   ROMAN**

This traditional trattoria is still faithful to the old Italian cuisinary values of fresh ingredients and professional service. They even prepare the fish for you at your table. The *bombolotti all'amatriciana* (pasta in spicy tomato sauce with bacon) are excellent, and so are the *abbacchi scottadito* (grilled lamb chops), and the *coda alla vaccinara* (oxtail stew). Homemade desserts round out the program nicely.

See map p. 122. Via Benedetta, 10 near Piazza Trilussa. ☎ *06-580-0985.* www.checco ercarettiere.it. *Reservations recommended. Bus: 23, 115 to Piazza Trilussa. Secondi: 13€–18€ ($15–$21). AE, DC, MC, V. Open: Lunch daily, dinner Mon–Sat.*

Da Benito e Gilberto
$$ **San Pietro   FISH**

Don't expect a written menu and a lot of time to make up your mind. In this informal restaurant you'll have to listen to the daily offerings and recommendations of your waiter and go for it. Don't worry, you won't regret it: The quality of the ingredients and the preparation of the food are outstanding. The *pasta e fagioli con frutti di mare* (bean and seafood soup) is better than Alessandra's — and she can make a mean one, the *tagliolini alla pescatora* (homemade pasta with seafood) superb and the *fritto di paranza* (fried small fish) delicious. Also excellent is the grilled daily catch.

See map p. 122. Via del Falco 19, at Borgo Pio. ☎ *06-686-7769.* www.dabenitoe gilberto.it. *Reservation required several days in advance. Bus: 23 and 81 to Via S. Porcari. Secondi: 11€–18€ ($13–$21). AE, MC, V. Open: Dinner Tues–Sat. Closed Aug.*

Da Giggetto
$$ **Teatro Marcello   JEWISH ROMAN**

This famous restaurant has for decades been the destination of Romans who want to taste some of the specialties of Jewish Roman cuisine. Some Romans say Giggetto is a little past its prime, but we think it's still a good place to sample such typical specialties as *carciofi alla giudia* (crispy fried artichokes), as well as traditional Roman dishes such as *fettuccine all'amatriciana* (pasta with a tomato-and-bacon sauce) and *saltimbocca alla romana* (sauteed veal with ham and sage).

See map p. 122. Via del Portico d'Ottavia 21. ☎ *06-686-1105. Reservations recommended. Bus: 63, 23, then walk north behind the synagogue. Secondi: 12€–18€ ($14–$21). AE, DC, MC, V. Open: Lunch Tues–Sun; dinner Tues–Sat; closed two weeks in Aug.*

Looking for a gelato break?

Italian ice cream (gelato) is among the best in the world. It comes in a variety of flavors, divided between fruits and creams. In addition to *limone* (lemon), *arancio* (orange), and other fruits, you can choose from specialties such as *mora* (blackberry) and *frutti di bosco* (mixed berries). The best cream flavors are *zabaglione* (a rum-and-egg combo, like eggnog), *bacio* (hazelnut chocolate), and *stracciatella* (vanilla with chocolate chips).

The oldest gelato parlor in Rome is **Giolitti,** Via Uffici del Vicario 40 (☎ 06-699-1243; Minibus: 116), which offers a huge selection of flavors — the fruit and chocolate flavors are usually excellent. The second oldest is the **Palazzo del Freddo di G. Fassi,** with two locations: one on Viale Angelico off San Pietro (Metro: Line A to Ottaviano), and the main store on Via Principe Eugenio 65–67 (☎ 06-446-4740; Metro: Line A to Piazza Vittorio). (We think that the main store is much better.) In Trastevere, try the **Gelateria alla Scala,** Via della Scala 5 (☎ 06-581-3174; Tram: 8), for excellent homemade ice cream. Off Campo de' Fiori, go to **Pica,** Via della Seggiola 12 (☎ 06-6880-3275; Tram: 8), which prepares one of the best ice creams in Rome. Near the Fontana di Trevi, don't miss the **Gelateria Trevi,** Via del Lavatore 84–85 (☎ 06-679-2060; Bus: 116 or 492).

A new passion in Rome is frozen yogurt, made with real fresh yogurt and fruit. You can find some of Rome's best at **Yogobar,** with several locations, including Viale Regina Margherita 83b, just north of Via Nomentana (☎ 06-855-1374; Bus: 63 or tram 30), and Via Lucania 23–27, off Via Boncompagni, east of Via Veneto (☎ 06-4288-3001; Minibus: 116).

Da Maciste al Salario, Pizza, Vino e Cucina
$ Villa Borghese   ROMAN/PIZZA

A great place to go for lunch before or after your visit to the Galleria Borghese, this large basement eatery gets really busy with locals from nearby offices and shops. The food is simple but excellent, and the pizza is one of the best Roman-style pizzas around — thin and crispy and seasoned to perfection. Lunch is served cafeteria style: Walk up to the counter and choose from the buffet. Get there early because the best choices disappear fast, and definitely take the side bread dish with a few pieces of pizza *bianca* (focaccia). At dinner they offer a large choice of great antipasti, hearty primi, and pizza.

See map p. 122. Via Salaria 179/a, at Via Metauro. ☎ 06-884-8267. Reservations required for dinner. Bus: 63 to Via Salaria; or exit Galleria Borghese in the rear and take Via Pinciana, bearing right on Via Giovannelli to Salaria. Secondi: 6.50€–12€ ($7.50–$12). AE, DC, MC, V. Open: Lunch Mon–Sat; dinner Tues–Sun.

Dante Taberna de' Gracchi
$ San Pietro   ROMAN

This classic Roman restaurant comprises several small (and air-conditioned) dining rooms. Among the specialties are *spaghetti alla vongole* (spaghetti with clams), *scaloppine al vino bianco* (veal cutlets sauteed in white wine), and a daily soup with choice of various *sfizi fritti* (fried "tidbits").

See map p. 122. Via dei Gracchi 266, between Via M. Colonna and Via Etzio. ☎ *06-321-3126.* www.tabernadeigracchi.com. *Reservations required. Metro: Line A to Lepanto, walk on Via Colonna for three blocks and turn right. Secondi: 12€–16€ ($14–$18). AE, DC, MC, V. Open: Lunch Tues–Sat, dinner Mon–Sat. Closed Christmas and 3 weeks in Aug.*

Enoteca Capranica
$$$ Pantheon   WINERY/ITALIAN

This elegant historical *enoteca* is housed in the beautiful Palazzo Capranica. It offers a wonderful wine list with hundreds of Italian and foreign labels, accompanied by creative cuisine, including such flavorful forays into the unusual as *crudo di spigola di mare agli agrumi con finocchio selvatico* (raw sea bass with citrus fruits and wild fennel) and *paccheri di Gragnano con asparagi, cipollotti e pecorino di fossa* (homemade pasta with asparagus, small onions, and specially aged pecorino cheese). They also have two tasting menus and an extensive choice of cheese.

See map p. 122. Piazza Capranica 99/100. ☎ *06-6994-0992.* www.enoteca capranica.it. *Reservations recommended. Bus: 117, 119. Secondi: 21€–32€ ($24–$37). AE, DC, MC, V. Open: Dinner daily.*

Ferrara
$$$ Trastevere   ITALIAN/INNOVATIVE

A seasonal menu with many interesting flavors served in warm and picturesque surroundings is what has made this restaurant a favorite in spite of steepish prices. If it's on offer, we recommend the *brandade di baccala con uova di quaglia e fiori di zucca* (salted cod concoction with quail eggs and zucchini flowers), or the *minestra di primavera con legumi e quenelle di ricotta di bufala* (bean-and-vegetable soup with buffalo ricotta "quenelles," which are sort of like sausages). But leave room for white chocolate mousse with *fragoline di Nemi* (local strawberries).

See map p. 122. Piazza Trilussa 41, at Ponte Sisto. ☎ *06-5833-3920. Reservations recommended. Bus: 23 or 115 to Piazza Trilussa. Secondi: 16€–28€ ($18–$32). DC, V. Open: Dinner daily.*

Gusto
$$ Piazza del Popolo   ITALIAN/INTERNATIONAL

If an establishment can be all things to all people, this is it: a restaurant, an *enoteca*, a pizzeria, a wine bar, a cigar club — and a kitchenware store. The pastas are tasty — if it's on the menu, try the *carbonara di maccheroncini con fave* (carbonara with homemade pasta and favas). The *trancio di tonno alla cajun con finocchi e olio di agrumi* (Cajun tuna steak with fennel and citrus oil) is delicious. As for the pizzas, we loved the *cicoria e funghi* (with dandelion greens and mushrooms). The menu also features items like couscous, wok-prepared Asian dishes, and continental choices. Popular with workers during the day and young people at night, the restaurant keeps late hours: lunch till 3 p.m., and dinner until midnight. The wine bar in back offers a large choice of drinks, whiskies, and *grappas* (Italian brandy). A great brunch buffet is served on Saturdays and Sundays.

See map p. 122. Piazza Augusto Imperatore 9.☎ 06-322-6273. www.gusto.it. *Reservations recommended for dinner. Bus: 117 or 119 from Piazza del Popolo to Via della Frezza/Piazza Augusto Imperatore. Secondi: 11€–21€ ($13–$24). AE, MC, DC, V. Open: Lunch and dinner daily.*

Hostaria L'Archeologia
$$ Appian Way ROMAN

This old hostaria is decorated like a country tavern, with beamed ceilings and rustic decorations — the kind of place Romans like to visit on a week-end outing. If you're visiting the nearby catacombs, of course, it's very convenient. The hearty Roman fare includes *vitello alla massenzio* (veal with mushrooms, artichokes, and olives), *tagliatelle al ragu di scorfano* (homemade pasta with tomato sauce and rockfish), grilled meats, and homemade gnocchi on Thursday — the traditional day for making this Roman potato dumpling dish.

Via Appia Antica 139. ☎ 06-488-0828. www.larcheologia.it. *Reservations recommended on weekends. Bus: 218 to Appia Antica. Secondi: 12€–21€ ($14–$24). AE, DC, MC, V. Open: Lunch and dinner Wed–Mon.*

Hostaria Nerone
$ Colosseum ITALIAN

This old family hostaria lies near the ruins of Nero's palace — but you don't need the budget of an emperor to enjoy the great view from the terrace (or the good food). We like it especially for the heartier Roman specialties, like *osso buco* (stewed veal shank) and even *trippa alla Romana* (tripe, with a light tomato sauce), an acquired taste.

See map p. 122. Via Terme di Tito 96, off Via Niccola Salvia. ☎ 06-481-7952. Reservations necessary Sat only. Metro: Colosseo; walk toward Colosseum for 1 block and turn left. Secondi: 9€–14€ ($10–$16). AE, MC, V. Open: Lunch and dinner Mon–Sat.

Il Drappo
$ Campo de' Fiori SARDINIAN

The subdued atmosphere of Drappo is a perfect setting for excellent food at moderate prices. The *malloreddus con vongole pomodorini e basilico* (typical homemade pasta with clams, cherry tomatoes, and basil) and the *fettuccine con fiori di zucca* (homemade pasta with zucchini flowers) are wonderful combinations of flavors. Other typical dishes are *maialino al mirto* (suckling pig) and *anatra alle mele* (duck with apples).

See map p. 122. Vicolo del Malpasso 9, off Via Giulia. ☎ 06-687-7365. www.ildrappo.it. *Reservations recommended. Bus: 116, 117 to Lungotevere Sangallo. Secondi: 11€–16€ ($13–$18). AE, DC, MC, V. Open: Lunch and dinner Mon–Sat. Closed four weeks Aug/Sept.*

La Pergola
$$$$ Monte Mario ITALIAN CONTEMPORARY

No doubt about it, this restaurant, located inside the Rome Cavalieri Hilton on the Monte Mario (a steep hill overlooking Prati), is a hike. There's also no doubt that it's one of the best restaurants in Italy. The site is breathtaking, with the whole panorama of Rome laid out at your feet. Chef Heinz Beck, a master of Italian cuisine, is known for concocting unexpected combinations, such as *tortellini verdi con vongole e calamaretti* (green tortellini with clams and squid) and *triglia su ragout di carciofi* (red mullet served over a ragout of artichokes). The tasting menu is a great way to sample several inventions at once (there's even a tasting menu of seven different desserts). Finding your way here by public transportation would be laborious; take a taxi.

Via A. Cadlolo 101, up the Monte Mario hill. ☎ *06-3509-2152.* www.cavalieri-hilton.it. *Reservations necessary. Bus: no; take a taxi. Secondi: 36€–54€ ($41–$62). AE, DC, MC, V. Open: Dinner Tues–Sat.*

La Taverna Trevi da Tarquinio
$ Fontana di Trevi ABBRUZZESE/ROMAN

Opening into a courtyard-size square shared with Il Chianti, the Taverna is a great spot to dine outdoors in nice weather. Given its location, you'd expect one of those touristy prix-fixe places, but Romans love the center as much as visitors, and this restaurant has so far maintained its standards. The food is good traditional Abbruzzese and Roman, with a variety of delicious homemade pastas, *abbacchio* (lamb roast), and a choice of grilled meats.

See map p. 122. Via del Lavatore 82. ☎ *06-679-2470. Reservations recommended. Bus: 116 to Via del Tritone, and then turn right on Via Poli, pass in front of the Fontana di Trevi, and turn right on Via del Lavatore. Secondi: 11€–17€ ($13–$20). MC, V. Open: Lunch and dinner Mon–Sat.*

La Veranda
$$$ San Pietro INNOVATIVE ITALIAN

This restaurant is in the Palazzo della Rovere, which also houses the Hotel Columbus (see "Staying in Style," earlier in this chapter). When the weather's fine, you can eat in one of Rome's nicest garden courtyards. But the draw is not just location, it's the interesting and even surprising cuisine. In addition to *piatti della storia* (dishes made from recipes from Renaissance Rome), La Veranda has branched out into experiments like *ravioli al rosmarino e cavalfiore con ragout di tonno* (ravioli with rosemary and cauliflower with a tuna ragout). Even more adventurous is the dessert *millefoglie con melanzane al ciccolato* — a Napoleon with eggplant and chocolate — which works, strangely enough.

See map p. 122. Borgo Santo Spirito 73. ☎ *06-687-2973.* www.hotelcolumbus.net. *Reservations recommended on weekends. Bus: 62 to San Pietro, and then turn right on Borgo Santo Spirito. Secondi: 16€–28€ ($18–$32), including (side dish). AE, MC, V. Open: Daily lunch and dinner.*

Osteria Ponte Sisto
$ Trastevere   ROMAN

Offering traditional Roman fare, this famous *osteria* has been a longstanding destination for locals and tourists alike. Try the delicious *risotto al gorgonzola* (Italian rice cooked with Gorgonzola cheese) or, if you dare, some truly Roman specialties such as *trippa alla romana* (tripe in a light tomato sauce) or beef roasted on a charcoal grill.

See map p. 122. Via Ponte Sisto 80, off Piazza Trilussa. ☎ *06-588-3411. Reservations recommended. Bus: 23 or 115 to Piazza Trilussa. Secondi: 9€–16€ ($10–$18). AE, MC, V. Open: Lunch and dinner Thurs–Tues; closed Aug.*

Pizzeria Ivo
$ Trastevere   PIZZA

One of Rome's most established *pizzerie*, Ivo is as popular with locals as it is with visitors. Luckily, the place is big! Here you can enjoy an entire range of pizzeria appetizers, pizzas, crostini, and calzones. All the pizzas are good, but we love the seasonal one with *fiori di zucca* (zucchini flowers) and the *capricciosa* (prosciutto, carciofini, and olives).

See map p. 122. Via di San Francesco a Ripa 158. ☎ *06-581-7082. Reservations not necessary. Tram: 8 to Via di San Francesco a Ripa (on the right off Viale Trastevere). Secondi: 8€–12€ ($9.20–$14). DC, MC, V. Open: Lunch and dinner Wed–Mon.*

Presidente
$$$ Trevi   FISH

Looking rather nondescript from the outside — if anything, a bit touristy — this restaurant is a hidden pearl where you can taste excellent fish dishes accompanied by one of many fine wines. The tasting menus are definitely recommended and include raw and cooked fish. A wonderful pasta dish is the *fettuccine con calamaretti bottarga e pomodori* (homemade pasta with squid, fish roe, and tomatoes).

See map p. 122. Via in Arcione 95, off Piazza Fontana di Trevi. ☎ *06-679-7342. Reservations recommended. Bus: 116 117, 119 to Largo del Tritone; walk one block toward underpass and turn right. Secondi: 15€–28€ ($17–$32). MC, V. Open: Dinner Tues–Sun.*

Quirino
$$ Trevi   ROMAN

A traditional Roman restaurant with some Sicilian influence, Quirino's focus is on seafood, for example *fritto di paranza* (mixed deep-fried small fish and calamari). The seafood also gets worked into their homemade pasta dishes, like *spaghetti alle vongole* (spaghetti with clams).

See map p. 122. Via delle Muratte 84, off Via del Corso. ☎ *06-679-4108. Reservations recommended. Bus: 116, 117, 119 to Via del Corso. Secondi: 11€–18€ ($13–$21). AE, MC, V. Open: Lunch and dinner Mon–Sat. Closed 3 weeks in Aug.*

Sora Lella

$$ Trastevere ROMAN

This family-run restaurant was already a Roman institution, but with the recent renovations — both in the dining room and on the menu — it has won new admirers. Beside the solid traditional menu, the gnocchi are superb and there are many innovative dishes, such as the delicious *polpettine al vino* (small meat balls in a wine sauce). Tasting menus and a vegetarian menu are available, and the traditional Roman *contorni* such as *cicoria* (dandelion greens), or *carciofi* (artichokes), are exceptional.

See map p. 122. Via di Ponte Quattro Capi 16, on Isola Tiberina, in the river between the center and Trastevere. ☎ 06-686-1601. Reservations recommended. Bus: 23, 63, and 115 to Isola Tiburina. Secondi: 14€–20€ ($16–$23). AE, DC, V. Open: Lunch and dinner Mon–Sat. Closed in Aug.

Fast Facts: Rome

Area Code

The city code for Rome is **06**.

American Express

The office is at Piazza di Spagna 38 (☎ 06-676-41; Metro: Linc A to Spagna), open Monday through Friday 9:00 a.m. to 5:30 p.m. and Saturday 9:00 a.m. to 12:30 p.m.

ATMs

They're available everywhere in the center and near hotels. Most banks are linked to the Cirrus network, so if you need the Plus network, look for a BNL (Banca Nazionale del Lavoro) ATM.

Currency Exchange

A very good exchange bureau is located at the airport and another is inside Stazione Termini (the main train station). Otherwise, you can find change offices *(cambio)* scattered all around town and concentrated in the *centro*.

Also, you can find automatic exchange machines that operate 24 hours a day outside many banks and at the airport.

Doctors and Dentists

- Contact your embassy or consulate (see list below) to get a list of English-speaking doctors or dentists.

Embassies and Consulates

Rome is the capital of Italy and therefore the seat of all the embassies and consulates. United States: Via Vittorio Veneto 119a (☎ 06-46-741; Metro: Line A to Barberini; Minibus: 116); Canada: Via Zara 30 (☎ 06-445-981; Bus: 60 or 62 to Via Nomentana); United Kingdom: Via XX Settembre 80a (☎ 06-482-5441 or 06-4220-0001; Bus: 60, 62, or 490 to Porta Pia); Ireland: Piazza Campitelli 3 (☎ 06-697-9121; Bus: 81 to Via del Teatro di Marcello); Australia: Via Alessandria 215 (☎ 06-852-721; Tram: 19 or 3 to Viale Regina Margherita); New Zealand: Via Zara 28 (☎ 06-440-2928; Bus: 60 or 62 to Via Nomentana).

Emergencies

Ambulance, ☎ **118**; Police, ☎ **113**; *Carabinieri* (other police force), ☎ **112**; Fire, ☎ **115**; First Aid ☎ **06-5820-1030** (night and holidays) other times ☎ 06-683-7299.

Hospitals

All large hospitals in Rome have a 24-hour *Pronto Soccorso* (first-aid) service. The main hospitals are the Santo Spirito on Lungo-tevere in Sassia 1 (☎ 06-68-351; Bus: 62 or 64) and the Fatebenefratelli on the Isola Tiberina (☎ 06-68-371; Bus: 23; Tram: 8), both in the *centro*.

Information

See "Finding information after you arrive," earlier in this chapter.

Internet Access

The ever-expanding Easy Everything has a big Internet access point at Piazza Barberini 2/16 (open 24 hours/7 days a week with 350 computers) . The Internet Train has several locations, including Via Pastini 125, near the Pantheon; Via delle Fornaci 3, near San Pietro; Via Merry del Val 20, in Trastevere; and Via in Arcione 103 by Fontana di Trevi.

Maps

You can buy maps at newsstands and kiosks around Rome. Get a map with a *stradario* (street directory); one of the best, albeight a bit bulky is *Tutto Città,* which costs about 8€ ($9.20) and is a largish booklet with full street directory.

Newspapers and Magazines

All the newspaper kiosks in the *centro* offer the European issues of *Time, The Economist,* and the *Financial Times,* and the kiosk on Via Veneto, off Piazza Barberini across from the U.S. Embassy has a particularly large choice. For information on restaurants and nightlife, you can buy the magazine *Time Out Rome*, or pick up for free the very well done monthly *the happening city* at one of the tourist information kiosks. *Roma C'è,* which has a section in English and comes out on Thursdays, and *Wanted In Rome,* an all-English publication, are also available at newsstands.

Pharmacies

Pharmacies are open Monday through Friday from 8:30 a.m to 7:30 p.m. They operate in rotation on evenings and Saturdays and Sundays, so that there is an open pharmacy in each neighborhood. To find out which is open, call ☎ 06-228-941. Or you can go to one of the all-night pharmacies, such as the one near Termini at Piazza della Repubblica (☎ 06-488-0410) or in Prati at Via Cola di Rienzo 213 (☎ 06-324-4476), or Piazza Barberini 49 (☎ 06-487-1195).

Police

There are two police forces in Italy; call either one. For the Polizia, call ☎ **113**; for the Carabinieri, call ☎ **112.**

Post Office

Rome's central post office is in Piazza San Silvestro 19 (off Via del Tritone and the Corso). It's open Monday to Friday, 9 a.m. to 6 p.m. and Saturday from 9 a.m. to 2 p.m. The Vatican has its own post office in Piazza San Pietro, under the colonnades.

Restrooms

Some public toilets are scattered around town, but not many. You can find one outside the Colosseum across the road toward Via Labicana, and a convenient one is halfway up the steps from Piazza del Popolo to the Pincio, on the left side. Facing San Pietro, you can find toilets under the colonnade on the right. Your best bet may be to go to a nice-looking cafe (though you have to buy something, like a cup of coffee).

Safety

Rome is a very safe city except for pickpockets. Pickpockets concentrate in tourist areas, on public transportation, and around crowded open-air markets like the Porta Portese. One area that gets somewhat seedy at night is behind the main rail station Termini.

Smoking

Smoking is allowed in cafes and restaurants and is very common, but an increasing number of restaurants are setting non-smoking areas.

Taxes

See Chapter 5 for information on IVA (Value Added Tax).

Taxis

If you need a taxi, call ☎ 06-88-177, 06-66-45, 06-49-94, 06-55-51, or 06-65-45.

Transit/Tourist Assistance

The tourist information hotline at ☎ 06-3600-4399 will provide you with information in four languages including English from 9 a.m. to 7 p.m. The local public transportation authority is ATAC (☎ 800-431-784 or 06-4695-2027; www.atac.roma.it). For railroad information call Trenitalia (☎ 892-021 daily 7 a.m.–9 p.m. within Italy; www.trenitalia.it).

Weather Updates

For forecasts, your best bet is to look at the news on TV (there's no phone number to get weather forecasts). On the Web, check out http://meteo. tiscalinet.it.

Chapter 12

Exploring Rome

- -

In This Chapter

▶ Experiencing Rome's great attractions
▶ Checking out other fun things to see and do
▶ Going through Rome by guided tour
▶ Choosing from itineraries
▶ Finding Rome's hot shopping spots
▶ Discovering Roman nightlife

- -

The Eternal City has lived through thousands of years of history, but Rome is no lifeless museum of the past. A couple million people live and work in this place designed for chariots instead of cabs, with city buses and hordes of *motorini* (mopeds and motor bikes) buzzing around ancient sights. They walk on ruins from the days of Caesar, turn along the same alleyways trod by masters of the Renaissance, and thrill to the same lighted fountains that were reflected in the eyes of Fellini's beautiful debauchers.

Rome also contains a state — the **Vatican,** the official seat of the Catholic faith; its vast complex of museums, apartments, chapels, and gardens filled with masterpieces and riches. Rome wasn't built in a day, or even a millennium, so don't think you can *see* it all in a day: Set aside several days to do the city right.

 If you are already planning to visit the Colosseum and the Roman National Museums in Palazzo Altemps and Palazzo Massimo, you might want to give yourself a chance to visit seven other archeological sites for just one euro more than the price of the combined admission for those attractions. The seven-day **Roma Archeologia Card** costs 20€ ($23) and gives you access to the four admission-charging sites of the **Roman National Museum** — Palazzo Altemps, Palazzo Massimo, Terme di Diocleziano, and Cripta Balbi — plus the Colosseum, the Palatino, the Baths of Caracalla, and the Tomb of Cecilia Metella and the Villa of the Quintili on the Via Appia. The card can be purchased directly at any of the sites (except for Tomb of Cecilia Metella and the Villa of the Quintili) or at the main Visitor Center of the Tourist Board of Rome (APT), at Via Parigi 5.

The **Museum Card** is also a seven-day pass which gives you access to the four paying sites of the Roman National Museum (noted above) for 9€ ($10). It is sold at each of the four branches of the Roman National Museum. The card is good for just one visit to each of the sights. Another special offer is the 9.90€ ($11) ticket for the **Musei Capitolini;** it's good seven days.

 The Vatican Museums are free the last Sunday of every month — and everyone knows it. Be prepared for huge mobs — or pay your way at another time.

 For a service fee of 1.50€ ($1.75), you can make reservations in advance for many Roman attractions — and even buy your tickets online — by contacting the ticket broker **Pierreci** (☎ **06-3996-7700;** www.pierreci. it). You will receive a voucher by e-mail and be able to pick up your tickets at a special desk directly at the attraction entrance. For phone service, Pierreci's hours are Monday through Saturday 9 a.m. to 1:30 p.m. and 2:30 to 5 p.m. (Greenwich mean time, plus 2 hours).

Discovering the Top Attractions

To accommodate its hordes of tourists, the city of Rome continues to expand opening hours for museums and other attractions, especially during holidays and the summer months. Check with a local tourist office for changes that might occur during your visit. See "Finding information after you arrive," in Chapter 11 for locations.

 Remember that, as a rule, ticket booths close 30 minutes to one hour before the stated closing time.

 To fully appreciate the Roman Forum, the Colosseum, and other ruins, pick up a copy of the small book *Rome Past and Present* (Vision Publications), sold in bookstores or at stands near the Forum. Its plastic overleafs show you how Rome looked 2,000 years ago.

 ### Basilica di San Giovanni in Laterano
San Giovanni

This church, and *not* St. Peter's Basilica, is the cathedral of the diocese of Rome. Built in A.D. 13 by Constantine, it suffered many indignities, including being sacked by the *Vandals* (a barbarian tribe whose name has given us the word *vandalism*), burned, and then damaged in an 896 earthquake. The basilica was restored and rebuilt at various times by different architects. The facade, designed and executed by Alessandro Galilei in 1735, is crowned by **15 giant statues** (7m/22-ft. tall) representing Christ, St. John the Baptist, John the Evangelist, and other Doctors of the Church; you can see them from many parts of Rome. Outside is an **Egyptian obelisk,** the tallest in Rome (32m/105 feet), consecrated in the fourth century as a symbol of Christianity's victory over pagan cults.

Rome Attractions

Basilica di San Giovanni in Laterano **33**
Basilica di Santa Maria Maggiore **23**
Basilica di San Pietro **5**
Campo de' Fiori **11**
Cappella Sistina **4**
Capitoline Museums **27**
Castel Sant'Angelo **6**

Cimitero dei Cappuccini **17**
Colosseum (Colosseo) **30**
Domus Aurea **29**
Foro Romano **28**
Galleria Borghese **13**
Galleria Doria Pamphili **24**
Gianicolo **12**
Mercati Traianei and Foro di Traiano **25**
Musei Vaticani **3**
Museo Nazionale Etrusco di
   Villa Giulia **1**
Museo Nazionale delle Paste
   Alimentari **22**
Palatine Hill (Palatino) **31**
Palazzo Altemps **7**
Palazzo Barberini **18**
Palazzo Massimo alle Terme **20**
Pantheon **9**
Piazza del Popolo **2**
Piazza del Quirinale **22**
Piazza di Spagna **16**
Piazza Navona **8**
Santa Maria d'Aracoeli **26**
Santa Maria in Cosmedin **32**
Santa Maria sopra Minerva **10**
Terme di Caracalla **34**
Terme di Diocleziano and Aula
   Ottagonale **19**
Trevi Fountain (Fontana di Trevi) **21**
Villa Borghese **15**
Villa Torlonia **14**

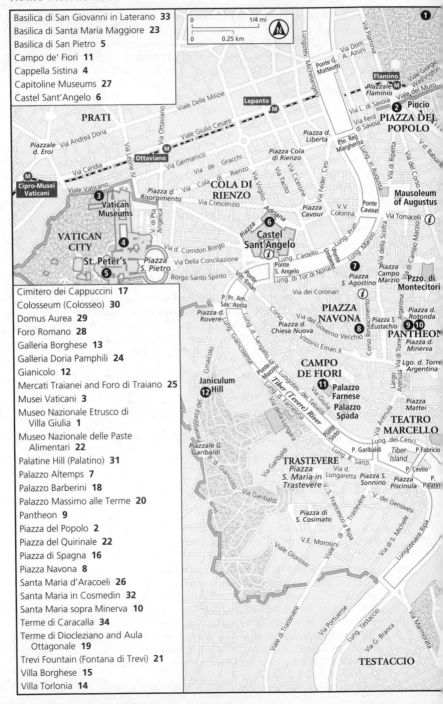

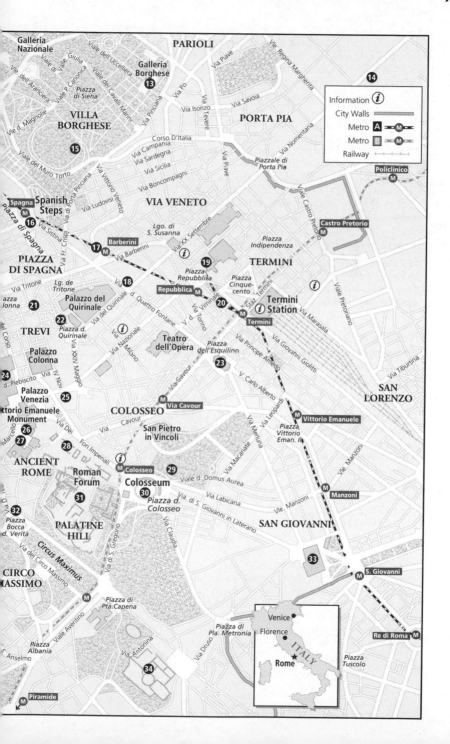

The interior of the basilica as you see it today was redesigned by Borromini in the 17th century. The **papal altar** — under a beautiful 14th-century *baldacchino* (canopy) — conserves an important relic: the wooden altar on which Peter and the other paleo-Christian popes after him are said to have celebrated mass in ancient Rome's catacombs. In the left transept is the altar of the **Santissimo Sacramento,** decorated with four giant gilded bronze columns that are the only remains of the original basilica. Under the *baldacchino* of this altar is another important relic, said to be the table of Christ's Last Supper. The apse was redone during the 19th century, and its mosaics are copies of the original medieval mosaics. However, the fresco fragment depicting Pope Boniface VIII, who declared the first Papal Jubilee in 1300, is from the 13th century. The **Baptistry** was built by Constantine in the fourth century, making it the first of the Western world. (The walls are still original, although the interior was restored several times and the present form was designed by Borromini.) The 13th-century cloister was designed by Vassalletto and is a showcase for remains and art from the older basilica, including paleo-Christian inscriptions.

See map p. 144. Piazza di San Giovanni in Laterano. ☎ *06-6988-6433. Metro: Line A to San Giovanni. Bus: 81, 85, 850, or minibus 117. Tram: 3. Open: Basilica and cloister daily 7 a.m.–6 p.m. (in summer to 6:45 p.m.); Baptistry daily 9 a.m.–1 p.m. Admission: Basilica free; cloister 2.07€ ($1.86).*

Basilica di San Pietro (St. Peter's Basilica)

See "The Vatican," later in this chapter.

Basilica di Santa Maria Maggiore
Termini

This church's history stretches back 1,600 years, and though it's undergone many changes over the centuries, Santa Maria Maggiore remains one of the city's four great basilicas. Ordered constructed by Pope Sisto III, it was built as a sanctuary for Mary (mother of Jesus) and was originally referred to as Santa Maria della Neve (St. Mary of the Snow) because its outline was drawn in the snow that had miraculously fallen in the summer of A.D. 352. The current baroque facade was designed by Ferdinando Fuga, who sandwiched it between two palaces that had been built in the meantime (one in the 17th and the other in the 18th century). The walls, though, are original, as are the mosaics of the apse and side walls. Although restored, the floors are the original 12th-century Cosmatesco-style, and the 15th-century coffered wooden ceiling is richly decorated with gold (said to be the first gold brought back from the New World and donated by the Spanish queen). One of the church's main attractions is in the loggia: the **13th-century mosaics** preserved from the old facade. Look carefully to the right side of the altar for the **tomb of Gian Lorenzo Bernini,** Italy's most important baroque sculptor/architect. In the crypt are relics of what is said to be pieces of Jesus's crib.

See map p. 144. Piazza di Santa Maria Maggiore. ☎ *06-488-1094. Metro: Line A or B to Termini, and then walk south on Via Cavour. Bus: 70. Open: Daily 7 a.m.–7 p.m. Admission: Free.*

Campo de' Fiori
Campo de' Fiori

Surrounded by cafes, restaurants, and bars, the lovely square of Campo de' Fiori boasts many attractions. Its **fruit-and-vegetable market** is one of the city's best and certainly one of the liveliest. Though popular with working people as a lunch spot, the campo is even more popular with young people (both Romans and foreigners) at night. The **central statue of the hooded Giordano Bruno** hints at the more sinister parts of the campo's history — it was the site of executions in the Middle Ages and the Renaissance, and Bruno was burned at the stake here in 1600. Bruno was a philosopher who championed the ideas of early scientists like Copernicus and maintained such heretical ideas as his theory that the earth revolved around the sun. Nearby is the delightful **Piazza Farnese,** dominated by the **Palazzo Farnese** (currently the seat of the French Embassy), surely one of Rome's most dramatic buildings, designed by Sangallo and Michelangelo. The cleaning completed in 1999 turned its somber gray color into a startling pale yellow. It can be visited on selected Sundays; call the French Embassy at ☎ **0668-6011.**

See map p. 144. Off Via dei Giubbonari, near Largo Argentina. Bus: 116.

Capitoline Museums (Musei Capitolini)
Teatro Marcello

On the Capitoline Hill (Capitolino), the **Capitoline Museums** open onto the beautiful **Piazza del Campidoglio,** designed by Michelangelo. The oldest public collections in the world, the museums hold a treasury of ancient sculpture and an important collection of European paintings from the 17th and 18th centuries. The first masterpiece you see stands in the middle of the square, the famous **equestrian statue of Marcus Aurelius** (this is a copy; the original second-century bronze is inside for protection). The statue was saved only because early Christians thought it was the first Christian emperor Constantine. In the **Capitoline Museum (Museo Capitolino)** (housed in the Palazzo Nuovo), the other famous sculptures are the *Dying Gaul,* a Roman copy of a Greek original, and two statues of female warriors known as *The Amazons* (under restoration at press time) that were originally in Hadrian's Villa.

Across from the Palazzo Nuovo is the **Palazzo dei Conservatori Museum.** You may have already seen photos of the huge head, hands, foot, kneecap, and other dismembered pieces of an ancient 40-foot **statue of Constantine II** that stands in the courtyard and of the famous *Lupa Capitolina,* the wolf suckling Romulus and Remus, a fifth-century-B.C. bronze. Another famous work is the bronze of a **boy removing a thorn from his foot**. These artworks are ones that will likely appeal to children (especially in the fresh air of the courtyard). On the top floor is the **Capitoline Picture Gallery (Pinacoteca Capitolina).** The paintings in the Pinacoteca are amazing, including Caravaggio's *Fortune Teller* and *John the Baptist,* Titian's *Baptism of Christ*, and works by Veronese, Rubens, and others.

Between the Palazzo Nuovo and the Palazzo dei Conservatori, closing Piazza del Campidoglio to the south, is the **Senatorial Palace (Palazzo Senatorio).** This palace was used for administrative purposes until recently, when it was included in the Capitoline Museums to provide additional expository space and show the results of the recent excavations under it. It was built in the Middle Ages over the **Tabularium,** an imposing Roman building that housed the public archives of the Republic in Roman times. The Tabularium was built of massive stone blocks with Doric columns in the facade. You can clearly see its remains from the Forum (3 of the original 11 arcades remain). It's now part of the museum complex, and its admission is included in the ticket.

When the Palazzo Nuovo was recently restored, the Greek and Roman sculpture collection was permanently moved to a new site, the **Centrale Montemartini.** The first electrical plant built in Rome (1912), it was transformed into a multimedia center in 1990 and is a beautiful setting for the art collection. It contains 400 sculptures that were formerly housed in the Capitoline museums. Among the most important pieces are a beautiful **giant mosaic with hunting scenes** (20 x 40 feet) from an imperial Roman residence.

See map p. 144. Piazza del Campidoglio 1. ☎ *06-6710-2475.* www.museicapitolini. org. *Bus: minibus 117 to Campidoglio (on the right around the monument to Vittorio Emmanuele II). Open: Tues–Sun 9 a.m.–8 p.m. Admission: 6.20€ ($7.10) for Museo Capitolino; 1.60€ ($1.85) extra for special exhibits.*

Extension of Museo Capitolino at the Centrale Montemartini. Via Ostiense 106. ☎ *06-574-8038.* www.centralemontemartini.org. *Metro: Line B to Pyramide; walk down Via Ostiense. Bus: 23 to Via Ostiense. Tram: 3 to Piazza di Porta San Paolo (Stazione Ostiense, Piramide). Open: Tues–Sun 9:30 a.m–7 p.m. Admission: 4.20€ ($4.85); integrated ticket for museum, Tabularium and Montemartini 8.26€ ($7.50).*

Castel Sant'Angelo
San Pietro

This "castle" is a perfect example of Roman reuse: it began as a mausoleum to house the remains of Emperor Hadrian and other important Romans, later became a fortress, and is now a museum. It may have been incorporated into the city's defenses as early as 403 and was attacked by the Goths (one of the barbarian tribes who pillaged Rome in its decline) in 537. Later, the popes used it as a fortress and hideout and connected it to the Vatican palace with an elevated corridor, which you can still see near Borgo Pio stretching between St. Peter's and the castle. Castel Sant'Angelo houses a museum of arms and armor; you can also visit the papal apartments from the Renaissance, as well as the horrible cells in which prisoners were kept (among them sculptor Benvenuto Cellini).

See map p. 144. Lungotevere Castello 50. ☎ *06-681-9111. Bus: 62 or 64 to Lungotevere Vaticano, and then walk north along the river. Open: Tues–Sun 9 a.m.–8 p.m. Admission: 5€ ($5.75) adults, children 17 and under and adults 60 and over free.*

Catacombe di San Callisto
Via Appia

There are several places to visit catacombs in Rome (including the catacombs of St. Sebastian at Via Appia Antica 136; ☎ **06-785-0350,** and those of Ste. Domitilla, Via delle Sette Chiese 282; ☎ **06-511-0342**; www. catacombe.domitilla.it), But the catacombs of St. Callisto are among the most impressive, with 20km (12½ miles) of tunnels and galleries underground and organized on several levels. (It's cold down there at 18m/ 60 ft., so bring a sweater.) The catacombs began as quarries outside ancient Rome where travertine marble and the dirt used in cement were dug. Early Christians, however, hid out, held mass, and buried their dead in the catacombs. The Catacombs of St. Callixtus (Callixtus III was an early pope, elected in 217) have four levels, including a crypt of several early popes and the tomb where St. Cecilia's remains were found. Some of the original paintings and decoration are still intact and show that Christian symbolism — doves, anchors, and fish — was already developed.

Via Appia Antica 110. ☎ *06-5130-1580.* www.catacombe.roma.it. *Metro/Bus: Line A to Colli Albani (on Sun to Arco di Travertino), and then bus 660 to Via Appia Antica. Open: Thurs–Tues 8:30 a.m. to noon and 2:30–5 p.m. (in summer to 5:30 p.m.; closed in Feb). Admission: 5€ ($5.75).*

Colosseum (Colosseo or Anfiteatro Flavio)
Colosseo

The Colosseum, along with St. Peter's Basilica, is Rome's most recognizable monument. However, the "Colosseum" isn't its official name. Begun under the Flavian emperor Vespasian, it was named the Amphiteatrum Flavium and finished in A.D. 80. The nickname came from the colossal statue of Nero that once stood nearby — it was part of the grounds of Nero's Domus Aurea (see the following listing). Estimates show that the Colosseum could accommodate as many as 50,000 spectators. The entertainment included fights between gladiators, battles with wild animals, and naval battles where the arena was flooded. In the labyrinth of chambers beneath the original wooden floor of the Colosseum, deadly weapons, vicious beasts, and unfortunate human participants were prepared for the mortal combats. (Contrary to popular belief, it is now thought that Christians were never fed to lions here.) The Colosseum was damaged by fires and earthquakes and eventually abandoned; it was then used as a marble quarry for the monuments of Christian Rome, until Pope Benedict XV consecrated it in the 18th century. Next to the Colosseum is the **Arch of Constantine,** built in 315 to commemorate the emperor's victory over the pagan Maxentius in 312. Pieces from other monuments were reused, so Constantine's monument includes carvings honoring Marcus Aurelius, Trajan, and Hadrian.

In the summer of 2000, for the first time in centuries, the Colosseum was brought to life again with performances under the aegis of the Estate Romana (see Chapter 2 and "Nightlife," later in this chapter); now it also houses special exhibitions.

See map p. 144. Via dei Fori Imperiali. ☎ *06-3996-7700. Metro: Line B to Colosseo. Bus: minibus 117.* www.pierreci.it. *Open: Daily 9 a.m.–1 hour before sunset. Admission: 8€ ($9.20) plus 2€ ($2.30) for exhibitions. Ticket price includes admission to the Palatine Hill.*

Domus Aurea (Nero's Golden House)
Colosseo

The Domus Aurea (Golden House) was the brainchild of the infamous emperor Nero. Although it once covered more than 200 acres, after the decline of Rome, this grandiose structure fell into ruin and disappeared from history. It was stumbled upon in the 18th century when Romans digging in the "hill" across from the Colosseum found caves that turned out to be ceilings of ancient rooms decorated with Roman frescoes. Only since 2000, however, have tourists been allowed to visit these cavernous spaces, some of which still have traces of the elegant interior paintings that decorated Roman villas. Often done in red tones, they tend to show mythological scenes surrounded by fine traceries and flourishes, of which you can see some fragments here.

See map p. 144. Via della Domus Aurea, off Via dei Fori Imperiali. ☎ *06-3996-7700 (reservations necessary, by phone or* www.pierreci.it*). Metro: Line B to Colosseo. Bus: minibus 117; Tram: 3. Open: Daily 9 a.m.–7 p.m. Admission: 5€ ($5.75), 1.50€ ($1.70) for advance reservation.*

Foro Romano (Roman Forum)
Colosseo

Rome has many forums. The original, the **Roman Forum,** lies in the valley between the Palatine and Capitoline hills (Palatino and Capitolino), on either side of the **Via Sacra** ("sacred way"), which still runs through it. This area was the heart of Rome for more than a thousand years, and a stone discovered under the Forum in 1899 bears an inscription from the time of the Roman kings (sixth century B.C.). The Forum has many ruins (some, like the sanctuary of the sewer goddess Venus Cloaca, are just a mark on the ground) as well as a few standing buildings. The most important is the square **Curia,** on the spot where the Senate once met. Although much of what you see is a restored structure from 1937, inside the third-century marble-inlay floor is still visible. The **Temple of Antoninus and Faustina** (Antoninus Pius succeeded Hadrian in 138) was later turned into a church and given a baroque facade (Chiesa di San Lorenzo in Miranda). Near the Curia is the **Arch of Septimius Severus,** built in 203 to commemorate his victories. The arch mentioned his two sons, Caracalla and Geta, but after Caracalla murdered Geta, Geta's name was removed. At the other end of the Forum is the **Arch of Titus.** Titus reigned as emperor from 79 to 81.

The Roman Forum and Imperial Forums

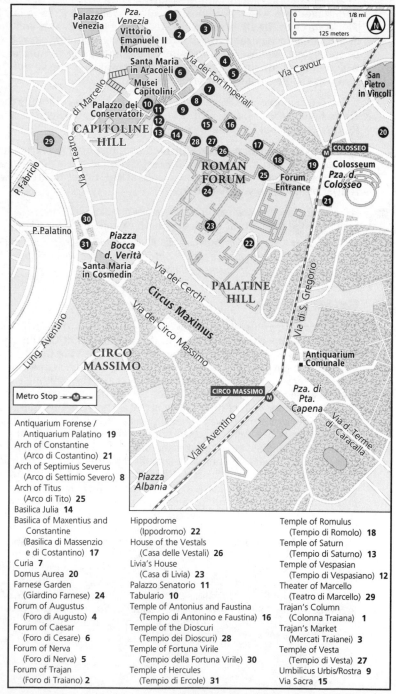

Antiquarium Forense /
  Antiquarium Palatino **19**
Arch of Constantine
  (Arco di Costantino) **21**
Arch of Septimius Severus
  (Arco di Settimio Severo) **8**
Arch of Titus
  (Arco di Tito) **25**
Basilica Julia **14**
Basilica of Maxentius and
  Constantine
  (Basilica di Massenzio
  e di Costantino) **17**
Curia **7**
Domus Aurea **20**
Farnese Garden
  (Giardino Farnese) **24**
Forum of Augustus
  (Foro di Augusto) **4**
Forum of Caesar
  (Foro di Cesare) **6**
Forum of Nerva
  (Foro di Nerva) **5**
Forum of Trajan
  (Foro di Traiano) **2**

Hippodrome
  (Ippodromo) **22**
House of the Vestals
  (Casa delle Vestali) **26**
Livia's House
  (Casa di Livia) **23**
Palazzo Senatorio **11**
Tabulario **10**
Temple of Antonius and Faustina
  (Tempio di Antonino e Faustina) **16**
Temple of the Dioscuri
  (Tempio dei Dioscuri) **28**
Temple of Fortuna Virile
  (Tempio della Fortuna Virile) **30**
Temple of Hercules
  (Tempio di Ercole) **31**

Temple of Romulus
  (Tempio di Romolo) **18**
Temple of Saturn
  (Tempio di Saturno) **13**
Temple of Vespasian
  (Tempio di Vespasiano) **12**
Theater of Marcello
  (Teatro di Marcello) **29**
Trajan's Column
  (Colonna Traiana) **1**
Trajan's Market
  (Mercati Traianei) **3**
Temple of Vesta
  (Tempio di Vesta) **27**
Umbilicus Urbis/Rostra **9**
Via Sacra **15**

Nearby is the hulking form of the fourth-century **Basilica of Constantine and Maxentius,** which occupies the site of what was Rome's law courts. The **Temple of the Dioscuri,** dedicated to the twins Castor and Pollux, is immediately recognizable for its three remaining columns joined by a piece of architrave. Against the Capitoline Hill you see the **Temple of Saturn**, which housed the first treasury of Rome. It was also the site of the feast that was the pagan ancestor of Christmas.

If you buy a map of the Forum when you enter, you can identify the some-times faint traces of a host of other structures (also see the map "The Roman Forum and Imperial Forums," on p. 144).

Note: The **Antiquarium Forense,** which contains materials from the exca-vations of the Forum, was closed for restoration at press time. No date has been set for the re-opening, but check at the ticket booth or with the tourist office when you visit there.

As with any archaeological site, things often make much more sense if you take a guided tour. Ask at the ticket booth or call ahead for a reservation.

See map p. 144. Via dei Fori Imperiali. ☎ *06-3996-7700. Metro: Line B to Colosseo, cross the street to the entrance to the right of the Colosseo. Bus: Minibus 117. Open: Daily 9 a.m.–1 hour before sunset. Admission: Free.*

Galleria Borghese
Parioli

The Galleria Borghese is housed in the building that Cardinal Scipione Borghese created for his art collection inside the Villa Borghese (now a large public park; see "Finding More Cool Things to See and Do," later in this chapter). Closed for restoration for 13 years, the building and site are now an attraction in themselves, while the art inside is probably the most stunning smaller collection on view in Italy. The structure can accommo-date only so many people, so reservations are required for admission and your visit must be limited to two hours. (The large number of true mas-terpieces will make you long for a second visit.) The ground floor focuses on sculpture, including Canova's sensual reclining *Paulina Borghese as Venus Victrix* (Paulina was Napoleon's sister) and breathtaking marble carvings by the young Gian Lorenzo Bernini. His *David*, captured in the middle of a slingshot wind-up, is full of charmingly boyish concentration; *Apollo and Daphne* freezes in marble the moment when Daphne turns into a laurel tree, her fingers bursting into leaves and bark enveloping her legs. In the *Rape of Proserpine,* a sculpture he executed in collaboration with his father, the god's fingers seem actually to press into her marble flesh. The extensive painting collection contains many masterpieces: Caravaggio's haunting self-portrait as *Bacchus* and his *St. Jerome Writing,* Antonello da Messina's subtle and mysterious *Portrait of a Man,* a young Raphael's *Deposition,* and Tiziano's *Sacred and Profane Love.* Andrea del Sarto, Coreggio, Lucas Cranach, Bronzino, Lorenzo Lotto, and many other artists are also represented.

See map p. 144. Piazzale Scipione Borghese 5. ☎ 06-841-7645. Reservations required: Call ☎ 06-328-101 or visit www.ticketeria.it. *Bus: 52, 53, or 910 to Via Pinciana behind the villa, 490 to Viale San Paolo del Brasile inside the park or minibus 116 to the Galleria Borghese. Metro: Line A to Spagna; take the Villa Borghese exit and walk up Viale del Museo Borghese. Open: Tues–Sun 9 a.m.–7 p.m. Admission: 6.50€ ($7.50) plus 2€ ($2.30) booking fee.*

Museo Nazionale Etrusco di Villa Giulia (National Etruscan Museum of Villa Julia)
Parioli

This papal villa built by the most prominent architects of the 16th century houses the world's most important Etruscan collection. Originally from Asia Minor, the Etruscans were a mysterious people who dominated Tuscany and Lazio, including Rome, up to the fifth century B.C. Many of the objects in this museum came from Cerveteri, an important Etruscan site northwest of Rome. One of the most spectacular objects is the **bride and bridegroom sarcophagus** from the sixth century B.C., upon which two enigmatic figures recline. You can also see a fairly well-preserved **chariot** and impressive sculptures. Some of the most amazing works are the tiniest: The Etruscans made **intricate decorative objects** from woven gold. (Their goldsmithing techniques remain a mystery today.) In the summer, the garden is the site of musical events (see "Nightlife," later in this chapter).

See map p. 144. Piazzale di Villa Giulia 9. ☎ 06-322-6571. www.ticketeria.it. *Tram: 3 or 19 to last stop, and then walk down Viale delle Belle Arti to Piazzale di Villa Giulia or 225 to Via di Villa Giulia. Open: Tues–Sun 8:30 a.m.–7:30 p.m. Admission: 4€ ($4.60).*

Musei Vaticani and Capella Sistina (The Vatican Museums and Sistine Chapel)
See "The Vatican," later in this chapter.

Palatine Hill (Palatino)
Colosseo

If you find the ruins in the Roman Forum confusing, you'll find those on the **Palatino** behind it sometimes incomprehensible. Huge blocks of brick surrounded by trees and greenery testify mutely to what was once an enormous residential complex of patrician houses and imperial palaces, built under the grandiose ambitions of the emperors. The throne room of the **Domus Flavia** was approximately 30m (100 ft.) wide by 39.3m (131 ft.) long. Although Augustus began the development of the Palatine residences, they were vastly expanded under Domitian, a notoriously cruel emperor.

The Palatino is also where the first Roman developments started and where Romulus drew the original square for the foundation of Rome. Excavations in the area found remains that date back to the eighth century B.C. **Livia's**

House (Casa di Livia) is one of the best-preserved homes. During the Middle Ages, the site was transformed into a fortress, and during the Renaissance it again became the residence of the aristocracy, who built large villas (the **Horti Palatini,** built by the Farnese on top of the palaces of Tiberius and Caligula, for example). From the hill, you can look down behind to the **Circus Maximus (Circo Massimo),** where a quarter-million Romans once watched chariot races. Unfortunately, the structures flanking the arena were plundered for their stone, as happened with many Roman buildings.

Also interesting to visit is the **Museo Palatino (Palatine Museum),** inside an ex-convent. The Museo Palatino showcases art from the archeological excavations of the Palatino, including frescoes and sculptures.

See map p. 144. Palatino: Via di San Gregorio 30; ☎ *06-3996-7700, or Piazza Santa Maria Nova 53* ☎ *06-699-0110. Metro: Line B to Colosseo, cross the street to the entrance to the right of the Colosseo. Bus: minibus 117. Open: 9 a.m. to 1 hour before sunset. Admission: 8€ ($9.20) for Palatino, Palatine Museum, and Colosseo.*

Palazzo Altemps
Piazza Navona

Behind Piazza Navona, the Palazzo Altemps was begun sometime before 1477; continued by the cardinal of Volterra, Francesco Soderini, from 1511 to 1523; and finished by Marco Sittico Altemps, who enlarged it at the end of the 1500s. The palace was restored in such a way that you can see the layers of medieval, Renaissance, and later decoration. Inside is the **Ludovisi Collection,** one of the world's most famous private art collections, particularly strong in Greek and Roman sculpture, as well as Egyptian works.

The most important piece from the Ludovisi Collection is the **Trono Ludovisi,** a throne thought to be the work of a fifth-century-B.C. Greek sculptor brought to Rome from Calabria. One side depicts Aphrodite Urania rising from the waves, another shows a female figure offering incense, and another side features a naked female playing a flute. The remarkable **statue of a soldier** apparently committing suicide with a sword was commissioned by Julius Caesar and placed in his gardens to commemorate his victories in Gaul. The *Ares Ludovisi,* a statue restored by Bernini in 1622, is believed by art historians to be a Roman copy of an earlier Greek work and shows a warrior (possibly Achilles) at rest. The colossal **head of *Hera*** (also known as Juno) is one of the best-known Greek sculptures; Goethe wrote of it as his "first love" in Rome and said it was like "a canto of Homer." It has been identified as an idealized portrait of Antonia Augusta, mother of Emperor Claudius.

See map p. 144. Piazza Sant'Apollinare 44. ☎ *06-3996-7700. Bus: minibus 116 to Via dei Coronari, walk northeast away from Piazza Navona. Open: Tues–Sun 9 a.m.–7.45 p.m. Admission: 5€ ($5.75).*

Palazzo Barberini and Galleria Nazionale d'Arte Antica
Via Veneto

Finished in 1633, the Palazzo Barberini is a magnificent example of a baroque Roman palace. Bernini decorated the rococo apartments in which the gallery is now housed, and they're certainly luxurious. Also preserved in the Palazzo Barberini is the wedding chamber of Princess Cornelia Costanza Barberini and Prince Giulio Cesare Colonna di Sciarra, exactly as it was centuries ago. Although the structure itself is an attraction, the collection of paintings that make up the Galleria Nazionale d'Arte Antica is most impressive, including Caravaggio's *Narcissus,* Tiziano's *Venus and Adonis,* and Raphael's *La Fornarina,* a loving informal portrait of the bakery girl who was his mistress (and the model for his Madonnas). Other artists represented are the great Sienese painters Il Sodoma and Simone Martini, and Filippo Lippi. The galleria's **decorative-arts collection** contains not only Italian pieces but also fine imported objects, including some from Japan. In addition to the regular collections, the gallery frequently houses special exhibits.

See map p. 144. Via delle Quattro Fontane 13. ☎ *06-482-4184. Metro: Line A to Barberini. Bus: 62 or minibus 116 to Quattro Fontane. Open: Tues–Sun 9 a.m.–7 p.m. Admission: 5€ ($5.75).*

Palazzo Massimo alle Terme
Termini

A branch of the National Roman Museum, this palace houses a rich sculpture collection. The museum was founded in 1889, and pieces of ancient art and sculpture have been added over the years from excavations in Rome's environs.

Among the works in the **Museo Nazionale,** which is housed in the Palazzo Massimo, are a **satyr pouring wine,** a Roman copy of the original by Greek sculptor Praxiteles; the *Daughter of Niobe from the Gardens of Sallust;* and an *Apollo* copied from a sculpture by Phidias, one of the greatest Greek sculptors. These few examples are only highlights — the museum's collection includes literally hundreds of statues, including an interesting series showing how the style of representation changed under various emperors, and even discussing the family resemblances of the Claudians, Flavians, and other dynasties. It is a very instructive museum as well as an impressive one. The basement of the museum contains a **rare Roman mummy,** as well as an huge and fascinating **numismatic display** containing coins from ancient times through the 19th century based on a collection that once belonged to the king of Italy. It explains, among other things, the economy of ancient Rome and of Renaissance Italy. Audioguides are available and are free for the first three hours.

See map p. 144. Largo di Villa Peretti 1. ☎ *06-3996-7700. Metro: Line A, B to Termini; Bus: 64 or 70. Open: Tues–Sun 9 a.m.–7:45 p.m. Admission: 6€ ($6.90).*

Pantheon
Pantheon

Rome's best-preserved monument of antiquity, the imposing Pantheon was built by Marcus Agrippa in 27 B.C. (though later rebuilt by Hadrian) as a temple for all the gods (from the ancient Greek "pan-theon," meaning "all Gods"). It was eventually saved from destruction by being transformed into a Christian church. The adjective that all descriptions of the Pantheon should contain is *perfect:* The building is exactly 42.6m (142-ft.) wide and 42.6m (142-ft.) tall. The portico is supported by huge granite columns, all but three of which are original, and the bronze doors weigh 20 tons each. Inside, the empty niches surrounding the space once contained marble statues of Roman gods. Animals were once sacrificed beneath the beautiful **coffered dome** with a 5.4m (18-ft.) hole *(oculus)* in the middle through which light (and sometimes rain) streams. An architectural marvel, this dome inspired Michelangelo when he was designing the dome of St. Peter's, though he made the basilica's dome .6m (2 feet) smaller. Buried here are the painter Raphael and two kings of Italy. Crowds always congregate in the square in front, **Piazza della Rotonda** (Piazza del Pantheon for Romans). The square contains a Giacomo della Porta fountain and many cafes — though the eyesore of a McDonald's and the attendant greasy smell make the place less attractive.

See map p. 144. Piazza della Rotonda. ☎ 06-6830-0230. Bus: minibus 116 to Piazza della Rotonda. Open: Mon–Sat 8:30 a.m.–7:30 p.m., Sun 9 a.m.–6 p.m. Admission: Free.

Piazza del Popolo
Piazza del Popolo

The "piazza of the people" really lives up to its name: Romans like to meet here to talk, have a drink, hang out, and people-watch. You can do the same, though be warned that the two cafes fronting the piazza gouge you unmercifully if you sit at an outdoor table (or even an indoor one) instead of taking your coffee at the counter like a Roman. **Santa Maria del Popolo** (☎ 06-361-0836) stands by the gate leading out to busy **Piazzale Flaminio** (where you can catch lots of buses). Founded in 1099, the church contains magnificent Caravaggios as well as a Pinturicchio. The brace of baroque churches directly across the square is the work of Carlo Rainaldi, Bernini, and Carlo Fontana. In the center is an **Egyptian obelisk,** one of Rome's most ancient objects, dating from 1200 B.C. It came from Heliopolis, where Ramses II set it up, and was brought during Augustus's reign (it stood in the Circo Massimo until one of the popes, in their nearly endless reshuffling and meddling with monuments, moved it here). When you leave the piazza, head up the steps into the trees on the east side. This path leads to the Pincio, the park overlooking the square, which is one of the best places to see the sun set over Rome.

See map p. 144. Intersection of Via del Babuino, Via del Corso, and Via de Ripetta. Metro: Line A to Flaminio. Bus: 490 to Piazzale Flaminio; Minibus 117 or 119 to Piazza del Popolo; Tram: 225 to Piazzale Flaminio.

Piazza del Quirinale and Palazzo del Quirinale
Trevi

Now the home of Italy's president, the Palazzo del Quirinale was the residence of the king up until the end of World War II, and earlier in history, the pope lived here — or rather hid, in the case of Pius VII, who locked himself in after excommunicating Napoleon (soldiers broke in and carted him off to Fontainebleau for the duration of the Napoleonic era). The royal family of Savoy substituted some gaudy and second-rate 19th-century art for earlier decoration, but the palace is still impressive and has some spectacular rooms. The **fountain (the Fontana di Monte Cavallo)** has two giant statues of Castor and Pollux, the founders of Rome. The **Egyptian obelisk** adorning the square was taken from the Mausoleum of Augustus by Pius VI in 1793. For this attraction, you need to bring your passport so you can prove who you are. You may also get to see the changing of the guard.

See map p. 144. End of Via XX Settembre. ☎ *06-4699-3125.* www.quirinale.it. *Metro: Line A to Barberini. Bus: Minibus 116 or 117 to Via del Quirinale. No telephone. Open: Sun 9 a.m.–1 p.m.*

Piazza di Spagna and the Spanish Steps (Scalinata di Spagna)
Piazza di Spagna

The Piazza di Spagna and the Spanish Steps (Scalinata di Spagna) rising from the piazza are the meeting place of Rome. In spring, the steps are decorated with colorful azaleas, but in any season the square is atmospheric — though you can hardly see it when it's covered with wall-to-wall tourists, lovers, backpackers, Roman youth, and so on. The atmosphere is festive and convivial, though. The piazza's name comes from the 16th century, when the Spanish ambassador made his residence here. In those days, the piazza was far less hospitable. (People passing through the piazza at night sometimes disappeared. Because it was technically Spanish territory, the unwary could be pressed-ganged into the Spanish army.) The area's most famous resident was English poet John Keats, who lived and died in the house to the right of the steps, which is now the **Keats–Shelley House** (☎ **06-678-4235;** open daily 9 a.m. to 1 p.m. and 2 to 5:30 p.m.; admission 5.16€/$4.70). The real name of the steps isn't the Spanish Steps but the Scalinata della Trinità del Monte, because they lead to the **Trinità del Monte church,** whose towers loom above. At the foot of the steps, the **boat-shaped fountain** by Pietro Bernini, father of Gian Lorenzo, is one of the most famous in Rome.

See map p. 144. Via del Babuino and Via dei Condotti. Metro: Line A to Spagna. Bus: Minibus 117 or 119 to Piazza di Spagna.

Piazza Navona
Piazza Navona

One of Rome's most beautiful piazze and also one of its most popular hangouts, Piazza Navona was built on the ruins of the **Stadium of Diocletian,** where chariot races were held (note the oval track form). In medieval times, the popes flooded the square for mock naval battles. Besides the twin-towered facade of the 17th-century **Santa Agnes,** the piazza boasts several baroque masterpieces, the greatest being Bernini's **Fountain of the Four Rivers (Fontana dei Quattro Fiumi),** with massive figures representing the Nile, Danube, della Plata, and Ganges — the figure with the shrouded head is the Nile, because its source was unknown at the time. The **obelisk** is Roman, from Domitian's time. At the piazza's south end is the **Fountain of the Moor (Fontana del Moro),** also by Bernini; the **Fountain of Neptune (Fontana di Neptuno),** which balances that of the Moor, is a 19th-century addition.

On the east side of the square is the famous **Palazzo Braschi,** which opened its doors in May 2002 after 15 years of closure and an $8-million restoration. It houses the **Museo di Roma,** covering the cultural, social, and artistic life of the city from the Middle Ages to the first half of the 20th century. Interesting temporary exhibitions, such as the 2004 exhibition of travel photos by master photographers of the 19th century, are often on display as well. The *palazzo* is also an attraction in itself, a baroque palace with a grand staircase (☎ **06-8207-7304;** www.museodiroma.commune.roma.it; Open: Tues–Sun 9 a.m.–7 p.m; Admission: 6.20€/$7.15).

See map p. 144. Just off Corso Rinascimento. Bus: 70 or 116 to Piazza Navona.

Santa Maria d'Aracoeli
Teatro Marcello

Next to Piazza del Campidoglio (just by the Capitoline Museums), Santa Maria d'Aracoeli dates from 1250 and is reached by an impressive high flight of steps (you can't miss them as you approach the Campidoglio). It stands on the site of an ancient Roman temple. The exterior of the church is austere but is punctuated by two rose windows, and inside are a number of interesting works of art. The floor is an excellent example of **Cosmati marblework** (the Cosmati were Roman stoneworkers of the Middle Ages). The **Cappella Bufalini** is decorated with Pinturicchio masterpieces, frescoes depicting scenes from the life of St. Bernardino of Siena and St. Francis receiving the stigmata.

See map p. 144. Piazza d'Aracoeli. ☎ 06-679-8155. Bus: minibus 117 to Campidoglio; then walk to the right around the Vittorio Emanuele II Monument. Open: Daily 7 a.m.–noon and 4–7 p.m. Admission: Free.

Santa Maria in Cosmedin and Bocca della Verità
Circo Massimo

Although this orthodox church is very pretty inside and outside — it's one of the few Roman churches to have escaped baroque "restoration" — the real attraction is the famous **Bocca della Verità (Mouth of Truth),** a Roman marble relief of a head with an open mouth that sits against the wall under the porch outside the church. The round marble piece used to be a manhole cover, but legend has it that if you put your hand inside the mouth while lying, it will bite off your hand. (Remember the scene with Gregory Peck and Audrey Hepburn from *Roman Holiday?*) Kids get a kick out of putting their hands in the mouth. The church opens on **Piazza Bocca della Verità,** one of the nicest squares in town — at its best during off hours — with two small Roman temples still standing, believed to be a temple of Vesta and a temple of Castor and Pollux.

See map p. 144. Piazza Bocca della Verità. ☎ *06-678-1419. Bus: 81. Open: Daily 7 a.m.–6:30 p.m. Admission: Free.*

Santa Maria sopra Minerva
Pantheon

The construction of this church started in the eighth century on the foundation of an ancient temple to Minerva (goddess of wisdom), but the present structure dates from 1280. This is the only Gothic church in Rome (though you wouldn't know it from the facade, due to a 17th-century revision — one of many). The treasures inside include Michelangelo's **Cristo Portacroce** in the sanctuary, as well as frescoes by Filippino Lippi. Under the altar are the **relics of St. Catherine of Siena.** The church also houses the **tomb of the painter Fra Angelico.** On the square in front of the church is the much-photographed Bernini **elephant sculpture** that serves as the base for a sixth-century-B.C. Egyptian obelisk.

See map p. 144. Piazza della Minerva. ☎ *06-679-3926. Bus: 62 or 64 to Largo Argentina, or minibus 116 to Piazza della Minerva. Open: Daily 7 a.m.–noon and 4– 7 p.m. Admission: Free.*

Terme di Diocleziano e Aula Ottagonale (Diocletian Baths and Octagonal Hall)
Termini

This grandiose Roman bath complex has only recently re-opened to the public after extensive restoration. Today it once again houses two branches of the Roman National Museum. The **Aula Ottagonale**, which is part of the original baths but now has a separate entrance, is a beautiful example of ancient Roman architecture and the site for a collection of sculptures coming from several of the bath complexes in Rome; the **Terme di Diocleziano** hold a very rich epigraphy collection. Also in the Terme is the collection of proto-historical material relative to the site before Roman times. Many of the objects in the National Roman Museum originally came from the Terme, parts of which were later used to build **Santa Maria degli Angeli**, the church that stands on Piazza della Repubblica (☎ 06-488-0812).

See map p. 144. Terme di Diocleziano: Via G. Romita 8. ☎ *06-488-0530. Metro: Line A to Repubblica; Bus: 60, 62, or minibus 116T to Piazza della Repubblica. Baths: Viale E. de Nicola 78. Hall: Via G. Romita 8.* ☎ *06-3996-7700. Metro: Line B to Repubblica. Baths open: Tues–Sun 9 a.m.–7:45 p.m. Admission: 5€ ($5.75); Hall open: Tues–Sat 9 a.m.–2 p.m. and Sun 9 a.m.–1 p.m. Admission: Free.*

Trevi Fountain (Fontana di Trevi)
Trevi

The massive Trevi Fountain, fronting its own little piazza, became one of the sights of Rome following the opening of the film *Three Coins in the Fountain*. Today it seems that many of the thousands who clog the space in front of it don't take the time to *really* look at it — instead, they throw coins in it, have their pictures taken in front of it, and go away. You'll be lucky if you have a tranquil moment to actually appreciate the artwork (only possible late at night or early in the morning). The fountain was begun by Bernini and Pietro da Cortona, but there was a 100-year lapse in the works and the fountain wasn't completed until 1751 by Nicola Salvi. The central figure is Neptune, who guides a chariot pulled by plunging sea horses. *Tritons* (mythological sea-dwellers) guide the horses, and the surrounding scene is one of wild nature and bare stone.

Of course, you have to toss a coin in the Trevi. To do it properly (Romans are superstitious), hold the coin in your right hand, turn your back to the fountain, and toss the coin over your left shoulder. According to tradition, the spirit of the fountain will then see to it that you return to Rome one day.

See map p. 144. Piazza di Trevi. Bus: 62 or minibus 116 or 119 to Via del Tritone, then walk right on Via Poli.

The Vatican
San Pietro

In 1929, the Lateran Treaty between Pope Pius XI and the Italian government recognized the independent state of the Holy See, with its physical seat in Vatican City (St. Peter's Basilica and adjacent buildings). Politically independent from Italy, the Vatican is the world's second-smallest sovereign state, with its own administration, post office, and tourist office. The Vatican comprises St. Peter's Basilica, the Vatican Museums, and the Vatican Gardens, all reviewed below.

Making the **tourist office** (☎ **06-6988-4466;** open Mon–Sat 8.30 a.m.–7 p.m.) the first stop on your visit is a good idea — it's just to the left of the entrance to St. Peter's. In the tourist office, you can get a plan of the basilica — very useful given the sheer size of the thing — and make a reservation for a tour of the Vatican Gardens. You can also find the **Vatican Post Office** — nice stamps and reliable service — and public restrooms.

Consider that at the Vatican, even the men wear ankle-length gowns, and the most popular color is black. Bare shoulders, halter tops, tank tops, shorts, and skirts above the knee will *definitely* result in your being turned away from the basilica. This is, after all, the center of a world religion, and not just a tourist extravaganza.

The entrance to the Vatican is through one of the world's greatest public spaces — Bernini's **St. Peter's Square (Piazza San Pietro).** As you stand in the huge piazza (no cars allowed), you're in the arms of an ellipse partly

The Vatican

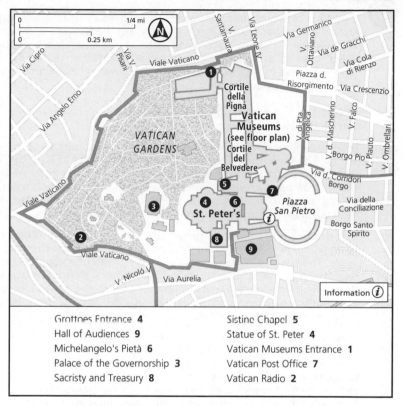

Grottoes Entrance **4**	Sistine Chapel **5**
Hall of Audiences **9**	Statue of St. Peter **4**
Michelangelo's Pietà **6**	Vatican Museums Entrance **1**
Palace of the Governorship **3**	Vatican Post Office **7**
Sacristy and Treasury **8**	Vatican Radio **2**

enclosed by a majestic Doric-pillared colonnade, atop which stand statues of some 140 saints. Straight ahead is the facade of **St. Peter's Basilica (Basilica di San Pietro)** (the statues represent Saints Peter and Paul, Peter carrying the Keys to the Kingdom), and to the right, above the colonnade, are the dark-brown buildings of the **papal apartments** and the **Vatican Museum (Musei Vaticani).** In the center of the square is an **Egyptian obelisk,** brought from the ancient city of Heliopolis on the Nile delta. Flanking it are two 17th-century **fountains** — the one on the right by Carlo Maderno, who designed the facade of St. Peter's, was placed here by Bernini himself; the other is by Carlo Fontana. The piazza is particularly magical at night during the Christmas season, when a *presepio* (Nativity scene) and a large tree take center stage.

Beneath the basilica are **grottoes,** extending under the central nave of the church. You can visit them and wander among the tombs of popes. In addition to the papal tombs, **paleo-Christian tombs** and **architectural fragments of the original basilica** have been found here.

To visit **Michelangelo's dome** and marvel at the astounding view, you have to climb some 491 steps. Make sure that you're ready and willing to climb, however, because after you've started up you're not allowed to turn around and go back down. If you want to take the elevator as far as it goes, it'll save you 171 steps. You have to make a reservation when you buy your ticket to go up in the dome (you'll pay an additional 1€/$1.15). On busy days, you have to wait in line because the elevator can't accommodate all the people who want to use it.

Basilica di San Pietro (St. Peter's Basilica)
San Pietro

In 324, Emperor Constantine commissioned a sanctuary to be built on the site of St. Peter's tomb. The first Apostle was thought to have been buried here under a simple stone, and excavation and studies commissioned by the Vatican have produced additional proof that the tomb is indeed St. Peter's. You can find the tomb in the present basilica's central nave, under the magnificent altar by Bernini.

The original basilica stood for about 1,000 years. After a millenium of remodeling, pillaging, sacking, and rebuilding, it was on the verge of collapse. The basilica you see today, mostly High Renaissance and baroque, began with the renovation begun in 1503 following designs by Sangallo and Bramante. Michelangelo was appointed to finish the magnificent dome in 1547 but wasn't able to do so; he died in 1564, and his disciple Giacomo della Porta completed the job.

The inside of the basilica is almost too huge to take in; walking from one end to the other is a workout, and the opulence will overpower you. On the right as you enter is Michelangelo's exquisite *Pietà,* created when the master was in his early 20s. (Because of an act of vandalism in the 1970s, the statue is kept behind reinforced glass.) Dominating the nave is Bernini's 29m (96-ft.) tall *baldacchino,* supported by richly decorated twisting columns. Completed in 1633, it was criticized for being excessive and because the bronze was supposedly taken from the Pantheon. It

How to attend a papal audience

One of the reasons Catholics come to Rome is to attend a *papal audience,* during which the pope addresses a crowd of people gathered in the Vatican (but of course, you don't have to be Catholic). To attend a papal audience (Wednesdays only; entrance between 10 and 10:30 a.m.) you must get free tickets from the **Prefecture of the Papal Household** (☎ **06-6988-3114**) at the bronze door under Piazza di San Pietro's right-hand colonnade (Mon–Sat 9 a.m.–1 p.m.). To get tickets in advance, write to the Prefecture of the Papal Household, 00120 Città del Vaticano, indicating your language, the dates of your visit, the number of people in your party, and (if possible) the hotel in Rome to which the office should send your tickets the afternoon before the audience.

stands over the papal altar, which in turn stands over the **tomb of St. Peter.** A **bronze statue of St. Peter** (probably by Arnolfo di Cambio — 13th century) marks the tomb; and its right foot has been worn away by the thousands of pilgrims kissing it in the traditional devotional gesture to salute the pope. By the apse, above an altar, is the **bronze throne** sculpted by Bernini to house the remains of what is, according to legend, the chair of St. Peter.

See map p. 144. Piazza San Pietro, ☎ *06-6988-4466. Bus: 62 or 64 to Via della Conciliazione. Metro: Line A to Ottaviano/San Pietro; then walk down Viale Angelico to the Vatican wall. Open: Winter daily 7 a.m.–6 p.m., summer daily 7 a.m.–7 p.m.; Grottoes daily 8 a.m.–5 p.m.; Dome winter daily 8 a.m.–4:45 p.m., summer daily 8 a.m.– 5:45 p.m.; Admission: Basilica free; Dome 4€ ($4.60), with elevator 5€ ($5.75).*

Musei Vaticani and Capella Sistina (The Vatican Museums and Sistine Chapel)
San Pietro

This enormous complex of museums could swallow up your entire vacation with tons of Egyptian, Etruscan, Greek, Roman, paleo-Christian, and Renaissance art. You will find four museums: the **Gregorian Egyptian Museum** — a fantastic collection of Egyptian artifacts; the **Gregorian Etruscan Museum** — a beautiful collection of Etruscan art and jewelry; the **Ethnological Missionary Museum** — a large collection of artifacts from every continent, including superb African, Asian, and Australian art; and the **Pinacoteca (picture gallery).** The most famous of the Vatican museums, the Pinacoteca contains works by medieval and Renaissance masters. In room 9 is Leonardo da Vinci's *St. Jerome,* which has been pieced back together — one piece had ended up as a stool seat in a shoemaker's shop, the other as a table top in an antiques shop. In room 2 is Giotto's luminous *Stefaneschi Triptych,* and in room 8, Raphael's *Transfiguration.* Other highlights include works by Beato Angelico, Perugino, Bernini, and Caravaggio (a single but great painting, the *Deposition from the Cross*).

Also part of the Museums are the **Stanze di Raffaello (Raphael's Rooms)** — in fact the private apartments of Pope Julius II, which were frescoed by the artist. The largest of the four rooms is the room of **Constantine,** painted between 1517 and 1524, which illustrates key moments in the life of the first Christian emperor, including his triumph over Maxentius and his vision of the cross. Along the way you'll come across the **Appartamento Borgia (Borgia Apartments),** designed for Pope Alexander VI (the infamous Borgia pope), and the **Cappella di Nicola V (Chapel of Nicholas V),** with floor-to-ceiling frescoes by Fra Angelico.

But, of course, it is the **Cappella Sistina (Sistine Chapel),** Michelangelo's masterpiece, that is the crowning glory of the museums. Years after their restoration, conflict continues over whether too much paint was removed, flattening the figures. On the other hand, the brilliant color has been restored. Whether you like the colors of the drapery or not, Michelangelo's modeling of the human form is incredible. The *Creation of Adam* and the

The Vatican Museums

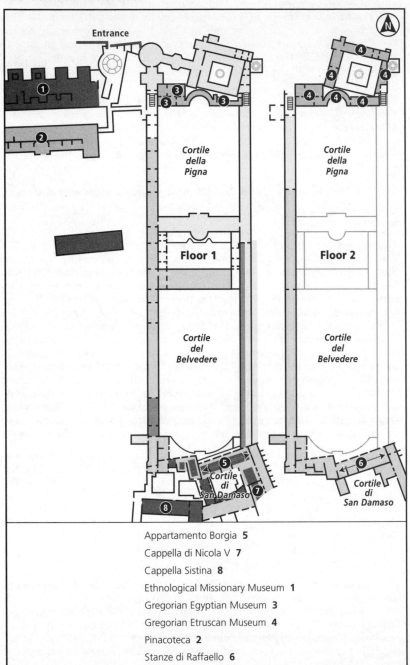

Appartamento Borgia **5**

Cappella di Nicola V **7**

Cappella Sistina **8**

Ethnological Missionary Museum **1**

Gregorian Egyptian Museum **3**

Gregorian Etruscan Museum **4**

Pinacoteca **2**

Stanze di Raffaello **6**

temptation and fall of Adam and Eve are the most famous scenes. Michelangelo also painted a terrifying and powerful *Last Judgment* on the end wall.

 Binoculars or even a hand mirror will help you appreciate the Sistine ceiling better; your neck tires long before you can take it all in. Just think how poor Michelangelo must have felt while painting it flat on his back atop a tower of scaffolding.

 It is impossible to visit the whole place in one sitting. If you don't want to take a guided tour, you can follow one of the **four color-coded itineraries** (A, B, C, or D), taking you to the highlights of the museums. They range from 1½ to 5 hours and all end at the Sistine Chapel. We recommend that you pick and choose according to your personal taste: you might be an Ancient Egypt maven and be only marginally interested in paintings, or vice versa care most about African and Asian art and the frescoed appartments. Whatever you do, we recommend the audio guide (rental: 5.50€/ $6.33) to avoid the "Stendahl syndrome" of sensory overload. The guide discusses over 300 artworks; select what you want to hear by pressing in a work's label number.

People often think that the Vatican is made up of only the basilica and its neighboring buildings, but the grounds behind the main structures are actually quite large. Although you can't visit most of the Vatican (you need a special permit to enter the Vatican grounds), guided tours take small numbers of visitors to admire the beautiful **Vatican Gardens (Giardini Vatlcanl).** If you'd like to take the tour, sign up at the ticket office of the Vatican Museums.

See map p. 144. Viale Vaticano, walk around the walls of the Vatican to the right of the basilica. ☎ *06-6988-4947.* www.vatican.va. *Open: Museums Mon–Fri 8:45 a.m.– 4:45 p.m., Sat 8:45 a.m.–1:45 p.m., mid-Mar–Oct; Mon–Sat 8:45 a.m.–1:45 p.m., Nov–mid- Mar. Closed Catholic holy days. No admission about 85 minutes before closing time. Admission: 12€ ($14) adults, 8€ ($9.20) children; free last Sun of the month.*

Finding More Cool Things to See and Do

If you've covered all of Rome's musts — and there are plenty — here are a few more of our favorite attractions.

✔ The **Galleria Doria Pamphili** (Piazza del Collegio Romano 1/A; ☎ **06-679-7323** or 06-7707-2842; www.doriapamphilj.it; Bus: minibus 117 or 119 to Piazza San Marcello on the Corso or 116 to Piazza del Collegio Romano) is the place to come if you want to know what it was like to live in an 18th-century Roman palace. The Doria Pamphili family traces its history back to Admiral Andrea Doria. The *palazzo's* richly decorated apartments are filled with tapestries, beautiful furnishings, and artworks. The gallery has paintings by Filippo Lippi, Raphael, Caravaggio, Tiziano, and others. Velázquez's portrait of Pope Innocent X is a true masterpiece. The gallery is open Friday through Wednesday from 10 a.m. to 5 p.m. It is also open selected evenings for classical music concerts, which you can combine with a visit to the galleries. Admission is 8€ ($9.20); if you visit the **Galleria Borghese** up to five days prior to your visit to the Doria Pamphili, present your ticket stub for a reduced ticket price of 5.70€ ($6.55).

✔ The **Gianicolo (Janiculum Hill)**, overlooking Trastevere, is one of the two best places to see the panorama of Rome, the other being the **Pincio** (see the entry for Piazza del Popolo, earlier in this chapter). You can take the 870 bus to the top of the hill (though the best idea is taking a cab up and walking down, rather than waiting for the bus and possibly missing the sunset). On the hill is a monument to Giuseppe Garibaldi, perhaps the most beloved figure of the 19th-century Italian struggle for self-determination, and a little farther down is a unique equestrian statue of his wife, Anita.

✔ The **Museo Nazionale delle Paste Alimentari** (Piazza Scanderbeg 117; ☎ 06-699-1119; www.pastainmuseum.com; Bus: 116 or 117 to Piazza del Quirinale; Admission: 7.75€/$8.90) is a unique museum covering 800 years of the most renowned Italian contribution to cuisine (besides pizza). Everything having to do with the production of pasta, from the ancient and traditional to the modern, is covered. The museum is open daily from 9:30 a.m. to 5:30 p.m.

✔ The **Casina delle Civette (Cottage of the Owls)** (Villa Torlonia, Via Nomentana 70; ☎ 06-820-7304; www.zetema.it; Admission: 2.60€/$3) is an Art Nouveau jewel, with whimsical architecture and beautiful stained-glass windows, located in the park of the Villa Torlonia; it now houses the museum of Art Nouveau glassworks. The Torlonia were — and are — an important Roman family (no less than princes they). Back in the 19th century, they allowed their artistic son to build this cottage as a bachelor apartment; years later they donated it, and the entire villa and the surrounding park, to the city. Also in the park are the main residence and the beautiful conservatory (both in ruins but plans are in process to restore the conservatory) and the **Casino dei Principi (Cottage of the Princes)** (additional admission: 2.60€/$3), an elegant outbuilding which was the residence of Mussolini when he was in power and which was recently restored. Some of the collected artworks of the Torlonia family are preserved here. The beautiful grounds of the Villa Torlonia are a popular place for Romans to exercise, meet, and relax. You can make a reservation for a guided tour of the Casina delle Civette, which we recommend. All buildings are open to visitors Tuesday through Sunday, from 9 a.m. to 7 p.m. in the summer, and 9 a.m. to 5 p.m. in winter.

✔ Just above Piazza del Popolo and extending north beyond the city walls is the **Villa Borghese,** one of Rome's most beautiful parks. It's famous for the Galleria Borghese (see earlier in this chapter) and the **Pincio,** the terrace above Piazza del Popolo offering a beautiful view over Rome — particularly striking at sunset. Inside the park is also the **Piazza di Siena,** a picturesque oval track surrounded by tall pines, used for horse races and particularly for the **Concorso Ippico Internazionale di Roma** (Rome's international horse-jumping event), held in May (see Chapter 3). This park is perfect for a family picnic, especially in summer, when its beautiful Roman pines offer relief from the heat.

✔ On the **Appian Way (Via Appia Antica),** you can walk over an original section of what was the first and most important Roman consular road — called the **Regina Viarum (Queen of Roads).** Started in 312 B.C., the road was a main link to Capua but eventually was extended all the way to Brindisi. It was on this road that St. Peter, in flight from Rome, had his vision of Jesus (a church stands where Peter asked, *"Domine quo vadis?"* or "Lord, where are you going?") and turned back toward his martyrdom. The street was paved with large, flat basalt stones and lined with villas, tombs, and monuments. The whole area is now a park (☎ 06-513-0682; www.parcoappiaantica.org), which you can visit via the hop-on-hop-off **archeobus** (see "Seeing Rome by Guided Tour," later in this chapter) or by bicycle — you can rent a bike at the park info point **Cartiera Latina** (via Appia Antica 42) or at the **Bar Caffe dell'Appia Antica** (Via Appia Antica 175). Among the archeological remains, one of the most important is the **Tomba di Cecilia Metella,** a first-century B.C. mausoleum of a patrician gentlewoman (☎ 06-3996-7700; open Tues–Sun 9 a.m. to one hour before sunset; admission is 2€/$2.30). Recently opened is the **Villa dei Quinitili,** which was the largest private villa in the Roman suburbs. It was the property of two consuls in 151 A.D. For centuries it was a mine of statuary for treasure hunters; much of it is now in many of the great museums of the world. For its sheer size, the site is quite impressive. (Via Appia Nuova 1092; ☎ 06-3996-7700; open Tues–Sun 9 a.m. to one hour before sunset; admission is 4€/$4.60, included in the **Archeologia card** discussed earlier in this chapter). Also on the Via Appia you will find two sets of Catacombs (see Catacombe of San Callisto earlier in this chapter).

✔ A wonderful way to experience Rome is sailing down the Tiber. You can book an excursion or use the regular boat service offered by **Compagnia di Navigazione Ponte San Angelo** (☎ 06-678-9361 for info and reservations; info@battellidiroma.it). Service runs operate between **Ponte Duca d'Aosta** and **Ponte Marconi.** Boats have 50 seats and leave every hour from 8 a.m to 1 p.m. and 4 to 7 p.m.; check for the latest schedule because they change often. You can catch a boat at one of the intermediary stops at the following bridges: **Risorgimento, Cavour, Sant'Angelo, Sisto, Isola Tiberina,** and **Ripa Grande.** A single fare is only 1€ ($1.15) and you can get a daily pass for 2.30€ ($2.65).

✔ The **Cimitero dei Cappuccini/Chiesa dell'Immacolata Concezione** (Via Veneto 27, not far from the U.S. Embassy; ☎ 06-487-1185; Metro: Line A to Barberini; Bus: 62 or minibus 116 or 119 to Largo Tritone) is a fascinating if ghoulish sight: a Capuchin monk used the bones of 4,000 of his brothers to create a monument that reminds us — literally — that "in the midst of life, we are in the midst of death." The ceilings and walls are decorated with skeletal bits (for example, rows of spinal vertebrae trace the vaults). Note: This might be a "kid-friendly" sight if you've got a teenage boy, but it would disturb and frighten smaller children. The monument was closed at press time for restoration; no date for re-opening has been planned.

Seeing Rome by Guided Tour

The French writer Stendhal once wrote, "As soon as you enter Rome, get in a carriage and ask to be brought to the Coliseum [sic] or to St. Peter's. If you try to get there on foot, you will never arrive: Too many marvelous things will stop you along the way."

Taking a bus tour of this complicated city when you first arrive is an excellent idea. Doing so helps you get the general feeling of the place and gives you an idea of what you'd like to see in depth. After you decide what you want to see in more detail, you can take a walking tour of the area or areas that interest you most and do the rest by yourself.

Bus tours

If you like a hop-on-hop-off formula, here are the three best options:

✔ Rome's public transportation authority, **ATAC,** gives the best bus tours of Rome (☎ **06-4695-2252** daily 8:30 a.m.–8 p.m. for reservations and info; www.trambus.com/servizituristici.htm); you can't beat the price or the options. The tourist line 110 "open" decker buses leave from Piazza dei Cinquecento in front of Stazione Termini every 20 minutes; you can stay on the bus for the whole itinerary (the tour lasts about 2 hours) or hop on and off along the way at one of ten stops. Tickets cost 13€ ($15) per person, children under 6 ride free. The buses are new and the tour guides professionals. It's a great way to see many of the major sights of Rome. You can buy tickets at the ATAC bus information booth in front of Stazione Termini, or on the bus (in which case you need the exact fare in cash).

✔ Also run by ATAC, the **Archeobus** tour (☎ **06-4695-2343** daily 8:30 a.m.–8 p.m. for reservations and info; www.trambus.com/servizituristici.htm) is another hop-on-hop-off itinerary (if you decide to stay on board, the whole tour takes 1 hr., 45 min.) taking in 15 historic sites of ancient Rome. The small 15-seat electric buses leave every hour from Piazza dei Cinquecento (in front of Termini train station) between 9:45 a.m. and 4:45 p.m.; tickets cost 7.75€ ($8.90).

✔ **Stop 'n Go/C.S.R.** (Via Ezio 12; ☎ **06-4782-6379;** www.romecitytours.com) offers nine departures daily for 12€ ($14) per person. The tour starts in Piazza dei Cinquecento (in front of Stazione

Termini) at the corner of Via Massimo d'Azeglio and makes 14 stops; you can get on or off at your leisure. (You can buy the ticket directly on the bus; try to have exact change, but it's not required.) If you'd prefer to spend more time at the sights, Stop 'n Go offers two- and three-day tickets for 18€ ($21) and 24€ ($28), respectively.

Should you prefer a more traditional bus tour instead, several formulas are available. Tours usually depart around 9 a.m., 3 p.m., and 8 p.m. — with possible pick up from your hotel included — and cost about 28€ ($32) for a three-hour tour. Here are the three best operators: **Appian Line** (Piazza dell'Esquilino 6; ☎ 06-48-7861; www.appianline.it); **Green Line** (Via Farini 5/A; ☎ 06-483-787; www.greenlinetours.com); and **Vastours** (Via Piemonte 34; ☎ 06-481-4309; www.vastours.it). For a guided tour of the **Vatican Museums** and the **Vatican Gardens**, you can reserve at the "guided tour" windows of the Vatican Museums; call ☎ **06-6988-4466,** or fax a request to **06-6988-5100**.

Walking tours

Enjoy Rome (Via Varese 39, three blocks north off the side of Stazione Termini; ☎ **06-445-1843;** www.enjoyrome.com; Metro: Termini) offers a variety of three-hour walking tours, including a night tour that takes you through the *centro* and its sights, and a tour of Trastevere and the Jewish Ghetto. All tours cost 21€ ($24) adults and 15€ ($18) for those under 26, including the cost of the tour and admission to sights. The office is open Monday through Friday from 8:30 a.m. to 2 p.m. and 3:30 to 6.30 p.m. and Saturday from 8:30 a.m. to 2:00 p.m. Enjoy Rome also organizes a bike tour, with English-speaking guides. Reserve at least 2 weeks in advance, and you can arrange special-interest tours such as "Fascist Rome: The Urban Planning of Mussolini," and "Caravaggio in Rome" (prices quoted upon request).

For **Scala Reale** (Via Varese 52; ☎ **888-467-1986** or 06-4470-0898; Metro: Termini), American architect Tom Rankin organizes small-group walking tours with an architectural twist for as little as 20€ ($23) per person. Discounts are available for groups of four; children under 12 are free.

Boat tours

The **Compagnia di Navigazione Ponte San Angelo** (☎ **06-678-9361**; E-mail: info@battellidiroma.it) runs a regular boat service on the Tiber (see "Finding More Cool Things to See and Do," earlier in this chapter). Additional tours include a morning cruise down to the Tiber mouth — with a 2-hour stop to **Ostia Antica,** for 10€ ($12) one way and 11€ ($13) round trip; and a **candlelight dinner cruise** in the city for 43€ ($50) per person.

Società Tourvisa (☎ **06-448-741**;. www.tourvisaitalia.com) organizes 3-hour weekend dinner cruises from March to December for 45€ ($52) per person; boats leave from the pier at Ponte Umberto I, off Piazza Cavour at 8:30 p.m.

Air tours

Through **Cityfly** (☎ **06-88-333;** www.cityfly.com), you can take an aerial tour of the Eternal City for 70€ ($81), children under 10 get a 30 percent discount. The views are breathtaking. The only drawback is that the tour leaves from the Aeroporto dell'Urbe, on Via Salaria 825, just north of Rome (40 minutes by taxi, or take the urban train — fare included in your ATAC pass if you got one — from Tiburtina station. Head in the direction of Monterotondo/Mentana and get off at the Salaria Urbe stop).

Suggested 1-, 2-, and 3-Day Itineraries

So much to see, so little time. In the following three itineraries we make recommendations on how best to spend your time in Rome.

Rome in 1 day

It's a tall order to try to see the Eternal City in what amounts to the blink of an eye. You can get a sense of the flavor, however, by starting with the **ATAC bus tour** (see earlier in this chapter); at least you will see the **Colosseum**, the **Trevi Fountain, St. Peter's Basilica,** and some of the other top sights. This tour will leave you hungry for more — and hungry, period. But if you started early, you still have time to take in the **Pantheon** and nearby **Piazza di Spagna and Spanish Steps** — sights that the ATAC tour buses can't get near — before lunch. Afterward, head for **Bolognese** (see Chapter 11), an outstanding restaurant on the beautiful **Piazza del Popolo** just down the Via del Babuino, a street lined with high-fashion and antiques stores (see "Shopping the Local Stores," later in this chapter). After lunch, you can drop into **Santa Maria del Popolo** to see the magnificent paintings by Caravaggio, then climb the steps to the Pincio, where the panorama of Rome spreads out at your feet (see earlier in this chapter under "Piazza del Popolo"). Then stroll through the nearby **Villa Borghese** — it's a beautiful walk to the **Galleria Borghese** (you will need to reserve in advance), where you will find one of the most stunning assemblages of masterpieces in Italy. Afterward, you can still visit the **Foro Romano (Roman Forum)** because it's open until an hour before sunset. Then you can do what the Romans do — stroll through center, window shop, stop for a coffee (see "Cafes" later in this chapter), and people watch. Later, have dinner in **Trastevere** to get a sense of that neighborhood; at **Checco er Carettiere**, you can enjoy Roman specialties in the atmosphere of a traditional trattoria. If you have time (or if you're a night owl), see the Colosseum lit up at night as a final, indelible memory of Rome.

Rome in 2 days

If you have two days in Rome, you can spend time absorbing sights rather than just seeing them and moving on. You also don't have to make as many painful choices. You can begin with **day 1** as in the "Rome in 1 Day" itinerary earlier in this chapter, getting a feel for the city with a bus tour, lunch at **Piazza del Popolo**, and a visit to the **Galleria Borghese** and the **Roman Forum**. But don't stay up too late after dinner in Trastevere, because on the morning of **day 2** you need to be at the **Vatican Museums** bright and early. You should budget least 3 hours, and preferably more, to savor its mind-boggling array of artworks (chief among them, of course, the **Sistine Chapel**). You'll be famished afterward; luckily, the charming traditional tavern **Dante Taberna de' Gracchi** is not far away; even closer is the inventive **La Veranda** (see Chapter 11). Afterward, you can take a bus back across the river to the center of Rome. But after a morning at the museum, you may want to spend at least part of your afternoon outside; in that case, you can walk down the **Via Cola di Rienzo** and do some window shopping on your way to the center. You can extend your outdoor time by clambering around the ruins on the **Palatine Hill** (a little further on is the **Domus Aurea**, the remains of Nero's grandiose palace, which you can visit if you still have time). Afterward, you can hop on the metro at the **Colosseum** and take it a couple stops to **Testaccio**, and treat yourself to a lavish meal at **Checcino dal 1887** or **Al Regno di Re Ferdinando II**, two fine restaurants that occupy caverns dug out of the Monte Testaccio (see Chapter 11 for more on these restaurants). If you're up for it, you can stop in at **Aldebaran**, one of Testaccio's musical venues (see "Living it Up After Dark," later in this chapter).

Rome in 3 Days

After following the itinerary "Rome in 2 Days," start your third day with a visit to the **Palazzo Altemps**, seeing its great works of ancient Roman sculpture and also getting a feeling for life in a Renaissance Roman palace. You can relax afterward with a stroll through nearby **Piazza Navona** (don't forget to look at what special exhibits are on at the **Museo di Roma**) and an espresso at **Antico Caffè della Pace** (see "Cafes," later in this chapter). Crossing Corso Vittorio Emanuele II, you come to one of the most atmospheric squares in Rome, the **Campo de' Fiori**. Eat lunch at the nearby **Bric** (see Chapter 11), where you can savor imaginative versions of Mediterranean cuisine. Afterward, head to the **Museii Capitolini** for a look at one of Rome's great collections of antiquities; alternatively, if your taste tends more toward Renaissance art, you can visit the **Palazzo Barberini**. For your third and final dinner in Rome, try something different: **Da Giggetto**, in the old Jewish quarter of the city.

Shopping the Local Stores

A lot of people say Rome isn't good for shopping, at least not compared to Florence and Milan. That may be true, but it doesn't mean there's nothing to buy in Rome, or that you won't find bargains. True bargain hunters always find bargains, or at least have a good time looking.

In terms of crafts, Rome isn't as rich as it was in ages past. Alas, very few workshops still practice traditional arts. On the other hand, Rome is the capital of the country, so you can find basically everything — including specialties here from places that you may not have time to visit.

Shopping hours are generally 9:00 or 9:30 a.m. (later for boutiques) to about 1:00 or 1:30 p.m., and then from 3:30 or 4:00 to 7:30 p.m. Many shops close Monday mornings, and most are closed all day Sunday. In the *centro,* however, many shops now stay open at lunchtime and on Sunday.

Best shopping areas

The best shopping area is in the heart of the *centro,* the streets of medieval and Renaissance Rome between Piazza del Popolo and Piazza Venezia. Now with restricted car circulation, **Via del Corso** (also known as just the Corso) is the area's heart, lined with shops selling everything from clothing to shoes to CDs. On the east side of Piazza di Spagna lie the most elegant streets — like **Via Frattina** and **Via dei Condotti** — with designer boutiques and all the big names of Italian fashion (Bulgari, Ferragamo, Valentino, Armani, and so on), and prices so high you might get a nosebleed. But you'll also find small shops specializing in items ranging from stylish Italian housewares to antiques. On the west side of the Corso are intricate medieval streets hiding a variety of elegant and original boutiques and some of the oldest establishments in Rome. Here you can find even more variety of goods, from old prints to exclusive fashions, from books to antique furniture.

Another good shopping area is **Via Cola di Rienzo** and **Via Ottaviano** on the San Pietro side of the Tevere. It doesn't boast the luxury shops of Via dei Condotti, but you can find the big names of Italian fashion, and you might actually find something affordable. This area is also excellent for shoes, with many shops of every level of price and style.

Via Nazionale off Piazza della Repubblica near Stazione Termini and running almost to Piazza Venezia is a less elegant zone where real people shop. It has attracted some big names (perhaps fleeing the ridiculous rents of the tourist center) but is still frequented more by Italians than tourists. Known especially for leather goods, this may be the best place to find that jacket you want.

What to look for and where to find it

If you're after a particular item, here are the places to find it.

Antiques

Antiques are one area where Rome *is* the place to go. **Via dei Coronari**, in the *centro,* literally offers one shop after another on both sides of the street. Whether it's furniture, glass, lamps, or paintings, you'll find it here. And even if you aren't planning on lugging home an armoire or a trestle table from a convent home, the street is something of a museum where you could (theoretically) buy the exhibits. **Via Giulia, Via del Babuino,** and **Via Margutta** nearby have some even pricier shops. For more casual shopping, try **Via del Pellegrino.**

Artworks

If you had a euro for every picture that's been drawn of the Forum over the years, you could buy your own villa. Rome has been a magnet for artists for centuries, and views of the city's ancient and baroque monuments are endlessly reproduced. For high-quality prints, two well-known shops are **Nardecchia** (Piazza Navona 25; ☎ 06-686-9318; Bus: minibus 116) and **Alinari** (Via Alibert 16/a; ☎ 06-679-2923; Metro: Line A to Spagna). On the upscale Via del Babuino, at number 180, is **Fava** (☎ 06-361-0807; Metro: Line A to Spagna), specializing in Neapolitan scenes. **Antiquarius** (Corso Rinascimento 63; ☎ 06-688-02941; Bus: minibus 116) is a nice shop across from the Palazzo Madama. At these shops, you find higher-quality — and somewhat more reliable — articles than at the nearby **antiquarian book and print market** on Piazza Fontanella Borghese (Bus: 81 or minibus 117 or 119 to the Corso at Via Tomacelli). The market, however, is a great place to browse if you know your stuff; otherwise, *caveat emptor* (let the buyer beware), to use a Roman (or at least Latin) phrase.

Books and magazines

The **English Bookshop** (Via di Ripetta 248; ☎ 06-320-3301; Bus: minibus 117 or 119 to Piazza del Popolo) stocks a wide variety of books — you guessed it — in English. The **Libreria Babele** (Via dei Banchi Vecchi 116; ☎ 06-687-6628; Bus: minibus 116 to Via dei Banchi) is Rome's most central gay/lesbian bookstore. In addition, many of the larger newsstands in the *centro* have English-language newspapers and magazines as well as bestsellers in fiction and perhaps some classics.

Clothing

For clothing, the best strategy is to shop in the *centro* or in the area of **Via Ottaviano** and **Via Cola di Rienzo** (Vatican/San Pietro). For women's fashion, the hot area is around **Piazza di Spagna** (logically — this area includes the highest concentration of tourists), but don't expect bargains unless you hit a sale. You can find **Fendi** (Via Borgognona 39; ☎ 06-696-661), **Valentino** (Via dei Condotti 13; ☎ 06-673-9420), **Gucci** (Via Condotti 8; ☎ 06-679-3888), **Armani** (Via dei Condotti 77; ☎ 06-699-1460), and **Emporio Armani** (Via del Babuino 140; ☎ 06-3600-2197) nearby. For men's clothes, the specialists are **Battistoni** (Via dei Condotti 61/a; ☎ 06-697-611) and **Testa** (Via Frattina 104, ☎ 06-679-1294). You can find all the shops that we mention in this paragraph a short walk away from the Spanish Steps (Metro: Line A to Spagna).

Big Italian designer labels often turn up at U.S. discount stores. Why not check out a smaller Roman store that you will never see on the other side of the Atlantic? An elegant men's store, **Davide Cenci** (Via Campo Marzio 1–7; ☎ 06-699-0681; Bus: minibus 116 to Pantheon), is popular with locals. Just a stone's throw away is **Tombolini** (Via della Maddalena 31/38; ☎ 06-6920-0342), which carries handsome clothes and shoes for women and men, with an emphasis on classic rather than chic.

Crafts

Local Roman crafts do survive here and there, for example, in the medieval area around **Piazza Navona.** Here you can find *vimini* (basketry) on **Via dei Sediari,** ironwork on **Via degli Orsini,** and even reproductions of Roman and Pompeian mosaics.

Leather clothing and accessories

Although Florence is more the place for **leather clothing,** you can find some nice stores on Rome's **Via Nazionale.** For leather accessories, the two best areas are **Via dei Condotti** in the *centro* and **Via Cola di Rienzo** in the Vatican area. For leather bags and wallets (if money isn't an issue), go either to **Bottega Veneta** (Piazza San Lorenzo in Lucina 9; ☎ 06-6821-0024; Bus: 81 or minibus 116 to Piazza San Lorenzo), famous for its beautiful woven designs, or to **Prada** (Via dei Condotti 88/90; ☎ 06-679-0897; Metro: Line A to Spagna), both off the Corso. Excellent leather gloves can also be found around **Piazza di Spagna.**

Shoes

For shoes, the two best areas are **Via dei Condotti** in the *centro* and **Via Cola di Rienzo,** near the Vatican. Among the top names are **Dominici** (Via del Corso 14; ☎ 06-361-0591), **Ferragamo** (Via dei Condotti 73–74; ☎ 06-679-8402), and **Ferragamo Uomo** (Via dei Condotti 75; ☎ 06-678-1130). However, if you really want to make your friends green with envy, have a pair of shoes custom-made by **Listo** (Via della Croce 76; ☎ 06-678-4567). These shops are all a short walk from the Spanish Steps (Metro: Line A to Spagna). Another cluster of shoe shops with varying prices (and quality) can be found in the winding streets near the Pantheon.

Stationery

Paper in various forms — colored, marbled, deckle-edged — is an Italian specialty, and can be found all over Rome. For especially refined stationery and paper, go to **Pineider,** founded in 1774 (two locations: Via Fontanella Borghese 22; ☎ 06-687-8369; Bus: minibus 117 or 119 to the Corso at Via Tomacelli and Via dei Due Macelli 68; ☎ 06-679-5884; Bus: minibus 116, 117, or 119 to Via Due Macelli).

Wine

Rome has many a fine *enoteca* (wine shop). If you want to buy wine to take home, go to the granddaddy of Roman wine stores, **Trimani** (Via Goito 20; ☎ 06-446-9661; www.trimani.com; Bus: 60 or 62), a family business since 1821 with literally thousands of bottles. It's lodged in the old residential neighborhood behind the Terme di Diocleziano. Rome's most special source of intoxicants is **Ai Monasteri** (Corso Rinascimento 72; ☎ 06-6880-2783; Bus: minibus 116), off the east side of Piazza Navona. Here you can find the liqueurs, elixirs, and other alcoholic concoctions that Italian monks have been making since the Middle Ages.

Living It Up After Dark

Romans love to stroll about their beloved city by night on what they call a *passeggiata*. All the major monuments are illuminated, and the ancient Roman ruins join the Renaissance and baroque buildings to create a magical tableau. Don't miss a tour of the Roman piazze by night. Sample Rome's wonderful ice cream (gelato — see the sidebar in Chapter 11) or sit on the outdoor terrace of a famous cafe and watch the pageant as you sip an espresso or a glass of Chianti.

The performing arts

From June through September, Roman nights come alive with **Roman Summer (the Estate Romana),** a series of musical, theatrical, and other cultural events. You can find details on the Web at www.comune.roma. it or call ☎ **06-6880-9505** Monday through Saturday from 10 a.m. to 5 p.m. Events include important concerts with performances by the **Accademia Nazionale di Santa Cecilia**, one of Italy's premier musical associations, and the **summer edition of the opera** at the monumental Olympic Stadium (Stadio Olimpico), across the Tevere from Piazza Mazzini.

The performing arts scene in Rome has really developed in recent years. Not least is the use of ancient Rome itself as the ultimate stage. During the summer of 2000, the **Colosseum** opened its doors to the public again after 15 centuries with a performance of Sophocles's *Oedipus*. In the summer of 2004, the **Teatro dell'Opera di Roma** (see later in this chapter) performed works by Verdi in the dramatic **Baths of Caracalla (Terme di Caracalla).** You can also check out a summer season of theater at the **Teatro Romano** at Ostia Antica (see Chapter 13).

Another recent development — almost ten years in the making — is the completion of the new home of **Accademia Nazionale di Santa Cecilia** (Parco della Musica, Viale Coubertin 34; ☎ **8024-2051** or ☎ 808-2058 [box office]; www.santacecilia.it; Metro to Flaminio, then tram 2), probably the largest addition to the Roman cultural and architectural landscape in decades. In February 2003 they moved from the San Pietro district to the **Parco della Musica**, a daring, modernistic complex designed by the famous architect Renzo Piano. Located 2km (1¼ miles) from **Piazza del Popolo**, the entire site takes up 55,000 sq. m (13.6 acres). It has three concert halls as well as other structures, including "La Cavea," a 3,000-seat outdoor concert space reminiscent of a classical amphitheater. The Parco della Musica is designed not only for classical music, but pop and contemporary, as well as theater. Restaurants, stores, lecture halls, and a host of other activities and services are also on the site. During the construction of the center, as often happens in Rome, ancient ruins were found, and there is now a permanent exhibition of the Roman villa that was uncovered.

Rome is famous for theater. Of course, if you don't understand Italian you won't get much out of it — but if you do, you'll be delighted by the number of performances, from classical to contemporary. Opera is a notable exception, because you may already know the story and the same operas are performed everywhere. Performances run from January to June at the newly restored **Teatro dell'Opera** (Piazza Beniamino Gigli 1, just off Via Nazionale; ☎ **06-481-60** or ☎ 06-4816-0255 [box office]; www. opera.roma.it; Metro: Line A to Repubblica; Bus: minibus 116 to Via A. Depretis). In the summer, the theater performs among the ruins of the **Baths of Caracalla.** To hear Verdi's *Requiem* played at night amid those massive crumbling structures is a truly remarkable musical experience.

The **Rome Opera Ballet** performs classical and modern ballet at the Teatro dell'Opera (see above for contact information). The **Teatro Olimpico** (Piazza Gentile da Fabriano; ☎ 06-326-5991; www.teatro olimpico.it; Tram: 225 from Piazzale Flaminio) hosts musical performances of all kinds, and it's also the venue of the **Filarmonica di Roma.**

Cafes

Rome boasts many famous old cafes that have never lost their glamour. Very pleasant, if a little expensive, the **Antico Caffè della Pace** (Via della Pace 3–7; ☎ 06-686-1216; Bus: minibus 116 to Piazza Navona) is one of the most popular cafes in the city. Another is the beautifully furnished **Caffè Greco** (Via Condotti 84; ☎ 06-679-1700; Metro: Line A to Spagna); among its customers were famous writers like Stendhal, Goethe, and Keats. The **Caffè Sant'Eustachio** (Piazza Sant'Eustachio 82; ☎ 06-6880-2048; Bus: minibus 116) is a traditional Italian bar that has been serving Rome's best espresso since 1938, made with water carried into the city on an ancient aqueduct.

Also famous is the **Caffè Rosati** (Piazza del Popolo 4–5; ☎ 06-322-5859; Bus: minibus 117 or 119), which retains its 1920s Art Nouveau decor. **Tre Scalini** (Piazza Navona 30; ☎ 06-687-9148; Bus: minibus 116) is a perfect spot for a drink or an ice cream (they're famous for *tartufo* — ice cream coated with bittersweet chocolate, cherries, and whipped cream). And if you're a coffee drinker, you haven't lived until you've tried the *granita di caffè* (a concoction of frozen espresso and thick cream) at the **Tazza d'Oro,** just by the Pantheon (☎ 06-678-9792; Bus: minibus 116 to Pantheon).

Jazz and other live music

Romans love jazz, and the city is home to many jazz venues. Among the most famous: **Alexanderplatz** (Via Ostia 9, just off the Musei Vaticani; ☎ 06-3974-2171; Metro: Line A to Ottaviano/San Pietro; Bus: 23 to Via Leone IV), where reservations are recommended; it costs 6 € ($6.90) to get in. **Big Mama** (Vicolo San Francesco a Ripa 18 in Trastevere; ☎ 06-581-2551; www.bigmama.it; Metro: Piramide; Tram: 8) attracts both small and big names in jazz and blues, and is somewhat more expensive, depending on how bright the star is. For an eclectic mix of music, try

Fonclea (Via Crescenzio 82/a behind Castel Sant'Angelo; ☎ **06-689-6302**; Bus: 23 to Via Crescenzio); the emphasis is on jazz, but you never know what you're going to hear.

In addition to jazz and contemporary music, you might hear traditional Italian songs at **Arciliuto** (Piazza Montevecchio 5; ☎ **06-687-9419**; Bus: 62 or 64 to Corso Vittorio Emanuele), located in the maze of streets behind Piazza Navona. Unfortunately, it's closed most of the summer.

Bars and pubs

On Campo de' Fiori you can find a full range of nightspots. The exceedingly popular but old-fashioned wine bar called **Vineria** at building no. 15 (no phone) still holds its own amid the nightly crowds swarming this trendy piazza. There's a crowded **Taverna del Campo** snack stop with *crostini, panini,* and beer next door at no. 16 (☎ **06-687-4402**), and a few more doors down you can find the often jammed **Drunken Ship** at nos. 20–21 (☎ **06-6830-0535**), an American style bar with a DJ. To get to these hot spots, take bus 62 or 64 to Corso Vittorio Emanuele at Largo San Pantaleo or minibus 116 to Campo de' Fiori.

For something calmer, you can try the bar at **Gusto** (see Chapter 11), which has an intimate romantic atmosphere. Or stop at the **wine bar attached to Trimani** (see the "What to look for and where to find it" section in this chapter), the famous wine seller.

The Italian craze for Irish pubs hit Rome very hard. These are among the nicest ones: **Mad Jack** (Via Arenula 20, off Largo Argentina; ☎ **06-6880-8223**; Tram: 8) is the place for Guinness and a choice of light food. It also features live music on Wednesday and Thursday. The **Abbey Theatre Irish Pub** (Via del Governo Vecchio 51–53, near Piazza Navona; ☎ **06-686-1341**; Bus: 62 or 64 to Corso Vittorio Emanuele II) is in the oldest part of town and features an authentic decor and souvenirs from the famous theater. The **Albert** (Via del Traforo 132, off Via del Tritone, before the tunnel; ☎ **06-481-8795**; Bus: minibus 116, 117, or 119 to Largo del Tritone) provides a real English atmosphere and beer, with everything from the furnishings to the drinks imported from England.

Dance clubs

You can hear a mixture of live and recorded music at **Alpheus** (Via del Commercio 36, near Via Ostiense; ☎ **06-574-7826**; Bus: 23, but best to take a cab). Several rooms offer different kinds of music, from jazz to Latin to straight-ahead rock, so if you don't want to dance there are actually comfortable places to sit and have a drink. The cover hovers around 10€ ($12), depending on the day.

Alien (Via Velletri 13–19; ☎ **06-841-2212**; www.aliendisco.it; Bus: 490 to Piazza Fiume) continues to work at its reputation as Rome's clubbiest club — with mirrors, strobe lights, and a New York–style atmosphere. It's not cheap to get in — an 18€ ($21) cover includes one drink — but that doesn't seem to matter to the frenetic 20-something crowd. Not to be outdone in the club-as-phenom category is **Gilda** (Via Mario de Fiori 97; ☎ 06-679-7396; www.gildadiscoclub.it; Metro: Line A to Spagna), which caters to an older crowd and plays classic rock as well as some newer stuff. The cover charge is comparable at 20€ ($23).

In **Testaccio,** clubs come and go, but the neighborhood remains one of the preeminent Roman hot spots. **Club Picasso** (Via Monte Testaccio 63; ☎ 06-574-2975; Metro: B to Piramide) has blasting music — from rock to blues — for most of the night.

Gay and lesbian bars

The hottest gay club in Rome is **Alibi** (Via di Monte Testaccio 40–44; ☎ 06-574-3448; www.alibionline.it; Bus: 23 or tram 3 to Via Marmorata, and then walk down Via Galbani — taking a cab is best), with a rotating schedule of DJs and a great summer roof garden. The cover is 6€ to 10€ ($6.90–$12). The gay disco **Angelo Azzurro** (Via Cardinale Merry del Val 13 in Trastevere; ☎ 06-580-0472; Tram: 8 to Viale Trastevere at Piazza Mastai) welcomes all ages and offers an eclectic mix of music. Admission is free, and Friday night welcomes ladies only.

The leading lesbian club is **New Joli Coeur** (Via Sirte 5; ☎ 06-8621-5827; Bus: 56 or 88 to Piazza Sant'Emerenziana), is for women-only on Saturday nights, but all are welcome at other times. The weekend cover charge is about 10€ ($12).

Chapter 13

Going Beyond Rome: Two Day Trips

In This Chapter
▶ Visiting the fountains of Tivoli
▶ Traveling back in time to Ostia Antica

*L*azio, the region surrounding Rome, is rich in beautiful and interesting sites that you can easily reach from the capital. If you have the time, you can stay a couple extra days in Rome and branch out from there for some enjoyable day trips.

Tivoli and Its Trio of Villas

Tivoli, a small town on a hill 32km (20 miles) northeast of Rome, is the single best day trip from Rome in the summertime. Tivoli enjoys a cooler climate during the hot months of summer and has been a traditional getaway for the wealthy and famous since ancient Roman times. Its three famous villas — one ancient Roman, one baroque, and one romantic — reveal Rome's architectural history as it played out over almost 2,000 years.

Getting there

Trains leave Rome's Stazione Tiburtina for Tivoli about every hour. The ticket costs 2.50€ ($2.90) for the 40-minute trip. The Tivoli train station is a little outside the town center, and, although the walk is not too long, it is completely uninteresting, since it crosses the new part of town. You can as easily take a taxi — available just outside the train station — to get to your destination; the fare to the center of town is about 4€ ($4.60). You will definitely need a taxi to visit Villa Adriana (see later in this chapter) since it is out of town.

Buses are also a good way to get to Tivoli. The bus company **Linee Laziali** (☎ 077-411-137) offers frequent service from Ponte Mammolo in Rome. You can also take **Metro Line B** to the last stop, Rebibbia (a 15-minute trip); at the bus terminal outside the Rebibbia metro station switch to a

COTRAL (☎ 0774-720-096) bus for Tivoli. Buses depart about every 20 minutes for the 30-minute trip, and tickets cost $6€ ($6.90). ***Beware:*** Buses operate less frequently on Saturday and quite infrequent on Sunday. If you want to travel by bus on a Sunday, check the schedule in advance to ensure that you'll have a bus at a convenient time for your return.

A **short drive** from the capital — only 31km (20 miles) — Tivoli lies at the end of a very busy consular road, Via Tiburtina, running northeast of Rome east of the Via Nomentana. Tivoli is like a suburb of Rome, and many people commute to and from the city daily, so traffic at peak hours can be horrible. And of course, once you get there, parking is at a premium and can be quite costly.

Taking a tour

If you sign up with a tour from Rome, you can avoid the hassle of driving and the trouble of dealing with transportation in a foreign language. A reliable agency that organizes excursions to Tivoli is **Argiletum Tour Operator** (Via Madonna dei Monti 49, off Via Cavour; ☎ 06-4782-5706; www.argiletumtour.com). They run a four-hour tour leaving Tuesday through Sunday — in the afternoon in summer and in the morning in winter — for 49€ ($56); price includes admission to Villa Adriana and Villa d'Este (Villa Gregoriana was closed at press time) and pick up from centrally located hotels.

Seeing the sights

The **tourist office in Tivoli** is in the central square of Largo Garibaldi (☎ 0774-334-522); summer hours are Monday through Saturday 9 a.m. to 6 p.m. and Sunday 9 a.m. to 2 p.m. (in winter it closes one hour earlier).

Visiting the three villas shouldn't make you forget to have a look at the town of Tivoli itself. The highlights are the 2nd-century B.C. **Tempio della Sibilla,** on the Roman Acropolis (on the other side of the Aniene River); the 12th-century churches of **San Silvestro** (southwest of the Villa d'Este) and **Santa Maria Maggiore;** and the 1461 **Rocca Pia,** Pope Pius II's castle, which was turned into a prison after 1870.

Villa Adriana

Hadrian, one of Rome's "good" emperors, had this villa built between A.D 118 and 138 as his holiday home. He spent the last three years of his life here. The villa, placed on the site of a Roman villa from Republican times, is magnificent, though it has lost its marbles, so to speak — many of its sculptures are now conserved in Roman museums. Much of the marble once covering the structures has gone, because the estate was used as a "quarry" during the Renaissance, as were many other Roman buildings, like the Colosseum. Here, Hadrian wanted to be surrounded by the architectural marvels he'd seen during his trips across the Empire: On the 300

Rome and Environs

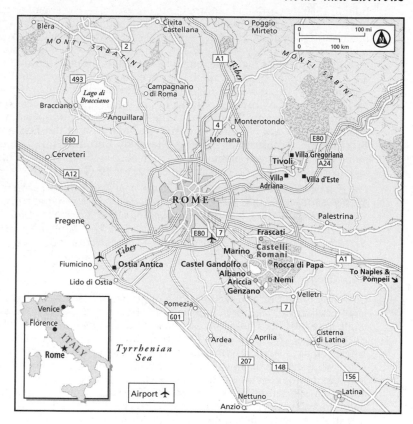

acres of this self-contained world for his vast royal entourage, he constructed replicas of famous buildings of antiquity, such as the **Canopus** (the Egyptian round canal ringed with statues) and the **Lyceum** (the school of Aristotle), as well as temples and theaters, monumental thermal baths, fountains and gardens, and a library. Although most of the monuments are today in ruins, the effect is still impressive. For a glimpse of what the villa looked like in its heyday, see the reconstruction at the entrance. Like any ruin in Italy, the villa gets very hot at midday during summer, so the best time to visit is early in the morning or late in the afternoon.

Via di Villa Adriana, 5km (3½ miles) from the center of Tivoli. ☎ 0774-530-203. Bus: 4 and 4X from Largo Garibaldi (the main square of Tivoli) to Villa Adriana. Admission: 6.50€ ($7.50). Open: Daily Nov–Jan 9 a.m.–5 p.m.; Feb 9 a.m.–6 p.m.; Mar and Oct 9 a.m.–6:30 p.m.; Apr and Sept 9 a.m.–7 p.m.; May–Aug 9 a.m.–7:30 p.m. Ticket booth closes 1½ hours before close.

Villa d'Este

Built in 1550 by Cardinal Ippolito d'Este of Ferrara — the son of notorious Lucrezia Borgia and Alfonso I d'Este — this villa would be just another beautiful 16th-century villa if it were not for its gardens. Designed by architect Pirro Ligorio, they are graced by a complex system of fountains — a true masterpiece of hydraulic engineering. Using an underground spring and the natural slope of the land, Ligorio managed to have naturally feeding fountains, two of which are sonorous. The work is really magnificent and is enhanced by the sculptural work of the fountains themselves: the **Fontana dell'Organo (Fountain of the Organ)** by Claude Veanard, the **Fontana del'Ovato (Ovato Fountain)** by Ligorio, and the **Fontana del Bicchierone (Fountain of the Big Glass)** by Bernini. The gardens are incredibly refreshing in summer and a perfect spot to be at midday on your visit to Tivoli. You can pick up an audioguide for 4€ ($4.60) at the entrance.

Piazza Trento, just west of Largo Garibaldi, the main square in the center of Tivoli. ☎ *199-766-166 in Italy and 0424-600-460 from abroad.* www.villadestetivoli. info. *Admission: 6.50€ ($7.50). Open: Daily Oct 8:30 a.m.–6:30 p.m.; Nov–Jan 8:30 a.m.– 5 p.m.; Feb 8:30 a.m.–5:30 p.m.; Mar 8:30–6:15 p.m.; Apr 8:30–7:30 p.m.; May–last Sat in Sept 8:30 a.m.–7:45 p.m. Ticket booth shuts down 1 hour before closing.*

Villa Gregoriana

Currently closed for renovation, Villa Gregoriana, the newest of the three famous villas of Tivoli, was built in the 19th century — but it isn't a villa at all. In reality, it's a beautiful garden built to enhance the natural beauty of the gorges of the Aniene — the river that meets the Tiber in Rome, where it makes some scenic waterfalls and disappears underground for a short while (creating the grottoes of Nettuno and Sirene). Pope Gregory XVI had a path carved all the way down to the bottom of the ravine to allow him to admire the 90m (300-ft.) waterfall, grottoes, and ponds. The deep slopes are covered with vegetation and mighty trees, making it a magical spot, especially in summer.

Largo San Angelo, just north of Largo Garibaldi, the main square in the center of Tivoli. ☎ *0774-334-522. At press time, the villa was closed for restoration, and no dates were set for its reopening; contact the local tourist office after you arrive.*

Dining locally

Tivoli has a number of trattorie and restaurants that are Sunday favorites for Romans on outings. The food is typically Roman, with such specialties as *cannelloni saltimbocca, abbacchio,* and *trippa alla Romana* (see Chapter 2 for more details on Roman cuisine).

Albergo Ristorante Adriano
$$$ **Villa Adriana ROMAN**

Countryside elegance describes this tree-surrounded villa offering well-prepared Roman specialties. Everything is homemade, from the delicious pastas — try the *cannelloni* or the excellent *fettuccine* — to the desserts.

And if you decide to stay overnight, you can rent one of the few guest rooms at 120€ ($138) per double.

Via di Villa Adriana 194, near the ticket booth to Villa Adriana. ☎ *0774-382-235. Reservation not necessary. Bus: 4 and 4X to Villa Adriana. Secondi: 10€–18€ ($12–$21). AE, DC, MC, V. Open: Lunch daily; dinner Mon–Sat.*

Antica Hostaria de' Carrettieri
$$ Villa Gregoriana   ROMAN/SARDINIAN

The food is excellent in this old-fashioned restaurant, and intriguing, as the menu places Sardinian specialties side by side with dishes true to the strictest Roman tradition — that's because the chef is originally from Sardinia. The *rigatoni all'amatriciana* (pasta in a spicy tomato and bacon sauce) were excellent, and so were the *gnocchetti in salsa di formaggio piccante* (little potato dumplings with a spicy cheese sauce) and the *tortino ai porri* (leek quiche).

Via D. Giuliani 55. ☎ *0774-330-159. Reservations recommended on weekends. Secondi: 8€–15€ ($9.20–$17). AE, DC, MC, V. Open: Lunch and dinner Thurs–Tues; closed 2 weeks in Aug.*

Le Cinque Statue
$$ Villa Gregoriana   ROMAN

Decorated with marble statues — the five statues in the restaurant's name — this reliable family-run restaurant offers typical Roman cuisine, such as *rigatoni all'amatriciana* (pasta in a spicy tomato and bacon sauce) and *agnello alla scottadito* (grilled lamb cutlets), which you can enjoy with a choice of local wines, mostly from the nearby Castelli region.

Via Quintilio Varo 8, just off the entrance to the Villa Gregoriana. ☎ *0774-335-366. Reservations recommended on weekends. Bus: Near the last stop of the COTRAL bus from Rome. Secondi: 9€–14€ ($10–$16). AE, DC, MC, V. Open: Lunch and dinner Sat–Thurs; closed the second 2 weeks in Aug.*

Ostia Antica: Rome's Ancient Seaport

Southwest of Rome, toward the sea, is **Ostia Antica,** the archeological site of ancient Rome's commercial harbor. Its ruins are particularly attractive early in the morning or at sunset, when many Romans like to come for an evening *passeggiata* (stroll). It's popular also on weekends for picnics, but most popular are the shows — music and theater — held in the Roman theater, the **Teatro Romano,** in July.

The ancient city of Ostia served as a shipyard, a gathering place for the fleet, and a distribution center for ancient Rome. Founded in the fourth century B.C. as a military colony for the defense of the river Tevere, Ostia flourished for about eight centuries before being progressively abandoned as a result of the silting up of the river and the spread of malaria in the region (no longer a concern, thankfully).

Keep in mind that the ruins are incredibly hot in summer. They're spread across a flat plain, and shade is hard to come by. If you don't like heat, come early, end your visit just before lunch, and head elsewhere to eat.

Getting there

Ostia Antica is about 28km (16 miles) from Rome. It's linked by **train** from Stazione Ostiense (take Metro Line B to the Piramide stop and follow the signs for Ostia to your platform), with trains departing every half-hour and costing about 1€ ($1.15) for the 25-minute trip. You can easily reach the site on foot from the train station, which is across the street. However, we find that the best way is to get there by boat, as the ancient Romans would have done (see "Taking a tour," below).

Taking a tour

To take a regular guided tour of the sights, check out **Stop 'n Go/C.S.R.** (Via Ezio 12; ☎ **06-321-7054;** e-mail: csr@gisec.it). It organizes half-day tours of Ostia Antica leaving Tuesday through Sunday at 9:30 a.m. from the Stop 'n Go Terminal of Via Giolitti in Rome (on the side of Termini train station) for 12€ ($14).

For a more unusual option, the **Compagnia di Navigazione Ponte San Angelo** (☎ **06-678-9361** for reservations; e-mail: info@battellidiroma.it) will take you on a morning cruise down to the Tiber mouth — with a 2-hour stop to **Ostia Antica,** for 10€ ($12) one way; 11€ ($13) round trip; and 35€ ($40) round trip plus buffet lunch during your return. Boats leave the Marconi bridge at 9:15 a.m. Tuesday throug Sunday and you can get there by subway or taking the regular boat service from one of the more central stops in town (see "Finding more cool things to see and do," in Chapter 12).

Seeing the sights

Ostia Antica includes a small village, quite cute but really small, and the major site of the archaeological area, which is what people come here to visit.

Area Archeologica di Ostia Antica
Ostia Antica

The archaeological site covers the impressive excavations of the ancient town of Ostia. The main streets of the town have been unearthed, as have some of the principal monuments. After entering the site, on the right you'll find **Via delle Corporazioni,** leading to the **Roman Theater (Teatro Romano).** Noting the mosaics indicating the nature of each of the businesses once housed along this street is interesting. The theater is still in use today for performances of works by modern and ancient authors during July as part of the **Estate Romana** (you can find details on the Web at www.comune.roma.it or by calling ☎ **06-6880-9505;** Mon–Sat 10 a.m.–5 p.m.).

Returning to the main street and continuing ahead, you'll find on your left the **Forum** and behind it the **Terme (thermal baths).** There are two temples on the left, and the **Capitolinum** on the right. The site also includes many interesting houses and buildings. The tourist office in Rome has a relatively good map of the park. Remember to bring a picnic; you'll enjoy dining under a tree among the ruins. Allow a minimum of three hours for the visit, more if you visit the museum. The **Museum** — conserving all the material found during the excavations of the site — just opened its doors after a restoration that lasted several years. The entrance to the museum is within the excavations and admission is included; it observes the same hours as the site as a whole.

Viale dei Romagnoli 717, off Via Ostiense ☎ *06-5635-8099.* www.itnw.roma.it/ ostia/scavi. *Admission: 4€ ($4.60). Open: Summer Tues–Sun 9 a.m.–6 p.m.; winter Tues–Sun 8:30 a.m.–4 p.m.*

Dining locally

The surroundings of the archeological area hold only a small restaurant and a bar in the village of Ostia Antica. You can do much better in the nearby town of Ostia, where there are some excellent restaurants overlooking the sea — or do as many Romans do and bring a picnic lunch.

Capannina
$$$ Ostia   FISH

Very popular with the locals — and Romans who come here on weekends — this is a typical seaside fish restaurant, offering a great variety of excellent fish dishes and more. The menu depends on the market, but you'll usually find the *insalata di mare e di polpo* (cold octopus, squid, and fish salad), the *rigatoni ai gamberi rossi* (pasta with large shrimp sauce), and a choice of the now fashionable *crudi* (raw fish).

Lungomare A. Vespucci 156. ☎ *06-5647-0143.* www.lacapannina.it. *Reservation recommended on weekends. Secondi: 12€–21€ ($14–$24). AE, DC, MC, V. Open: Summer, lunch and dinner daily; winter, lunch and dinner Tues–Sun. Closed 3 weeks in Nov.*

Vecchia Pineta
$$$ Ostia   FISH

This classic restaurant might appear a bit serious in its decor, but its cuisine is the best in Ostia. Try the perfect *risotto alla pescatora* (seafood risotto) or the *spaghetti alle vongole veraci* (spaghetti with clams), followed with one of the daily specials prepared grilled, baked or *in guazzetto* (light herb and tomato broth), as you choose.

Piazza dell'Aquilone 4, on the Lungomare. ☎ *06-5647-0282.* lavecchiapineta@ libero.it. *Reservation recommended on weekends. Secondi: 12€–22€ ($14–$25). AE, DC, MC, V. Open: Summer, lunch and dinner daily; winter, lunch daily, dinner Mon and Wed–Sat.*

Part IV
Florence and the Best of Tuscany and Umbria

The 5th Wave   By Rich Tennant

I know <u>how</u> to ask for directions to a McDonalds in Italian, I'm just afraid to.

In this part . . .

Tuscany is the most visited region in Italy, and for a great reason: The concentration of attractions here — sights, scenery, food, and wine — is beyond imagination. Practically every hill town offers something interesting to visit. (This is true of all of Italy, but you'll find so many more hills in Tuscany!) Tuscany has a proud tradition and a unique character and flavor, including the regional delicacies that each part of Italy seems to offer. Umbria is a less-toured region, but it's also famous for its cuisine and the art of its towns. Perugia, a city on a hill (of course) with a rich artistic patrimony, is Umbria's capital.

In the following chapters, we give you the top of the top, the not-to-be-missed things to see and do in these regions. Chapter 14 is dedicated to the beautiful city of Florence. Chapter 15 covers the northern Tuscan towns of Lucca and Pisa and detours to the Italian Riviera for a glimpse of the Cinque Terre (five fishing villages). In Chapter 16 we take you to southern Tuscany and explore the Chianti region and the towns of Siena and San Gimignano. Chapter 17 covers the highlights of Umbria, including the cities of Assisi, Perugia, and Spoleto.

Chapter 14

Florence

In This Chapter

▶ Finding your way to and around Florence
▶ Discovering the best neighborhoods, hotels, and restaurants
▶ Exploring the magnificent sights of Florence
▶ Getting the scoop on the best shopping areas and nightlife attractions

• •

Along with Venice and Rome, Florence is the top destination for Americans in Italy. What's so special about it? Well, Florence maintains its compact medieval scale and Renaissance core, and at the same time feels like a real place. But that's only part of it. Florence holds one of the world's most incredible repositories of art and architecture, home to such treasures as the paintings by Botticelli and Leonardo in the Galleria degli Uffizi, Michelangelo's *David* in the Galleria dell'Accademia, Brunelleschi's dome crowning the Duomo (Santa Maria del Fiore), Giotto's Campanile (bell tower), Ghiberti's "Gates of Paradise" on the Baptistry (Battistero di San Giovanni), and the Ponte Vecchio over the Arno River.

Florence thrived from its ninth-century-B.C. beginnings, but in medieval times — when it grew to be a great banking center, dominating the European credit market — the city truly reached its apogee. Florence's riches enabled the flourishing of the arts: Dante was born here in 1265, and so was the painter Cimabue (Giotto's teacher). The Renaissance blossomed in the 1300s, despite a flood, the Black Plague, and political upheaval. The 15th century brought the rule of Lorenzo the Magnificent, head of the powerful Medici clan, and then a brief restoration of the Republic. In this, Florence's greatest period, the artists Leonardo, Michelangelo, and Raphael were producing amazing works. In 1537, the Medici family returned to power in the person of Cosimo I.

Florence has remained a center of intellectual life into the modern period; in fact, it was the capital of Italy from 1865 to 1870. By that time, it had become one of the paramount stops on the Grand Tour (the cultural trip that educated people took through Europe in the 18th and 19th centuries), and its past had been transformed into its most important asset. Tourism has exploded in recent years — this relatively small town is crammed with six million visitors annually. But not to worry: In the following sections, we tell you how to maneuver the city with ease and confidence.

Getting There

Located in the region of Tuscany, Florence is easy to reach by air, train, or car.

By air

Florence is served by its own airport, the **Aeroporto Amerigo Vespucci,** but is also accessible from Pisa's nearby **Aeroporto Galileo Galilei** (see Chapter 15). There are no direct flights from the United States to Florence, but connecting flights are available from a number of European cities.

Getting oriented at the airport

Both airports are easy to get around, though the Florence airport is smaller and a bit older, whereas the Pisa airport is newer and very well organized. ATMs, currency exchange booths, and tourist information desks can be found at either airport.

Navigating your way through passport control and customs

Passport control is usually divided into two checkpoints, one for European Union citizens and one for everybody else. Some flights internal to the European Union countries are not subject to passport control; in those cases, you go directly to customs, where, again, you'll find two gates: one for those who have something to declare (beyond allowance), and one for those who don't. You probably will be going through the "nothing to declare" gate, under the watchful eye of a customs official: this is where there might be random checks. If you are singled out, you'll have to step to a table and open your luggage for a check.

Getting from Aeroporto Amerigo Vespucci/Peretola to your hotel

The **Aeroporto Amerigo Vespucci** (☎ 055-306-1300; www.safnet.it), is generally called the **Aeroporto di Peretola,** which is the name of the small town where it's located. The airport is only 4km (2½ miles) outside of Florence and all public transportation is just outside Arrivals, on your right.

The easiest way to get from the airport to your hotel is by taking a **taxi,** which will take about 15 minutes and cost about 20€ ($23). The ATAF/SITA **airport shuttle buses** (SITA ☎ 800-373-760; ATAF ☎ 800-424-500) run every 20 minutes between 5:30 a.m. and 8:30 p.m. and hourly later on, and arrives at the Florence's SITA bus terminal, just behind the central rail station of Santa Maria Novella. The trip takes about 25 minutes and costs 4€ ($4.60); you can purchase tickets at the airport Bar-Cafe or from the driver. You can also get into Florence by regular **city bus** (number 62; .80€/90¢), which takes about half an hour and also arrives at Santa Maria Novella.

Getting from Aeroporto Galileo Galilei to your hotel

Pisa's **Aeroporto Galileo Galilei** (☎ 050-849-111; www.pisa-airport.com) is 80km (50 miles) from Florence. You can take a special shuttle train from the airport's own train station directly to Florence's Santa Maria Novella rail station; it makes ten runs a day, costs about 4.95€ ($5.70), and takes about an hour.

Leaving Florence, you can check your bags for your flight directly at the **rail station of Santa Maria Novella** (look for the sign "Air Terminal"; ☎ 055-216-073) to avoid lugging them to the airport yourself (see section "By train," below, for information on how to get to your hotel from the rail station).

By train

By far the best way to get to Florence from other destinations in Italy, trains are frequent from all major Italian cities. One train arrives about every hour from both Rome and Venice. The trip takes about two hours from Rome and three from Venice, depending on the kind of train (intercity or the faster Eurostar). You'll arrive at Florence's station Santa Maria Novella, often abbreviated **SMN Firenze** (☎ 055-288-765), from which you can get to almost anywhere in the city via a taxi, a bus, or on foot. Public transportation is just outside the station. Some trains stop at other stations on Florence's outskirts, but don't get off there; you'll be able to access the hotels we recommend later in this chapter by debarking at SMN.

At Santa Maria Novella, you can leave luggage at the office at the head of Track 16. The station's tourist office (see "Finding information after you arrive," later in this chapter) mainly arranges hotel rooms but also distributes some information, such as the free city map; this is where you can pick up your reserved tickets for the Uffizi or the Accademia (see the tip under "Exploring Florence," later in this chapter).

By car

Florence is at the intersection of several major highways, so it's easy to get there from any direction. After you're inside the city, however, your car will become a huge pain. The city is closed to cars except for those of Florence residents; and the historic center — the part you're interested in — is closed to all vehicles except city buses. If you already have a hotel reservation, you're allowed to drive to your hotel and unload, but then you have to find a place to stow your car — and city parking lots are expensive (your hotel may have one; check when you book). Rates near the center are about 1€ to 3€ (90¢–$2.70) per hour.

If you're planning a driving tour of smaller towns in Tuscany, schedule it before or after your stay in Florence; that way, you can either dump off the car when you arrive or pick it up when you're ready to leave. You'll spare yourself plenty of headaches.

Orienting Yourself in Florence

Florence has much expanded in recent times, but the new areas have little of historic interest. Like other Italian cities, Florence developed beyond its medieval perimeter only toward the end of the 19th century, and most of its attractions are within that perimeter. The old part of town is quite small and has a relatively simple layout, bisected by the river Arno. The top attractions are mostly clustered on the north side of the river, around **Piazza della Repubblica** and along the north/south axis made by **Via dei Calzaiuoli** and **Via Ricasoli**, in the **centro storico.** Four bridges allow you to cross the Arno from the *centro storico,* but chances are that you'll use only two of them: the famous **Ponte Vecchio,** the most central, and **Ponte Santa Trinità,** the next westward bridge. Both lead you to **Oltrarno,** the part of the historic district that lies on the other side of the Arno. North of the *centro storico* is the **railroad station Santa Maria Novella** and **Fortezza da Basso,** a fortress and armory now transformed into an exposition hall. West is a residential area, and in the hill to the north of town lies Fiesole, once a separate town, and today, basically a neighborhood of Florence.

Introducing the neighborhoods

Here we give you the layout of the historic districts of Florence, the part that interests you as a tourist. Most of the historic part lies on the north side of the Arno. This area is packed with monuments and museums. We don't want you to neglect the other bank of the river, however, so we describe the major attractions in that neighborhood as well.

Centro storico (the historic district)

This is the heart of Medieval Florence. Packed with monuments and museums, it's where you'll find the best of the best in terms of attractions. At the northwest edge of this rough square is the church of **Santa Maria Novella;** at the northeast edge is the **Accademia,** near **Piazza San Marco;** at the southeast edge is the church of **Santa Croce;** in the middle are the **Duomo** and, further south, **Piazza della Signoria.** Completely closed to traffic — public buses and electric *navettes* (shuttle buses) excluded — it is a tourist heaven, with many exciting restaurants and most of the best hotels. Of course, locals come here all the time, to shop in the elegant commercial district along **Via dei Tornabuoni,** to work in the business area by Piazza della Repubblica and Via Roma, and to dine in the many fine restaurants; but few live here. The choice is yours: Stay here and you'll be right in the center of it all, with everything at your fingertips — hotel, restaurants, attractions, even shopping — but very little of the other Florence, the Italian Florence. Distances within the *centro storico* are not huge, but for ease of navigation we subdivided this neighborhood by five of its famous landmarks: **Centro storico/Duomo** and **Centro storico/Signoria** at the heart of it; **Centro storico/Santa Maria Novella, Centro storico/Santa Croce,** and **Centro storico/Accademia** around its boundaries.

Florence Orientation

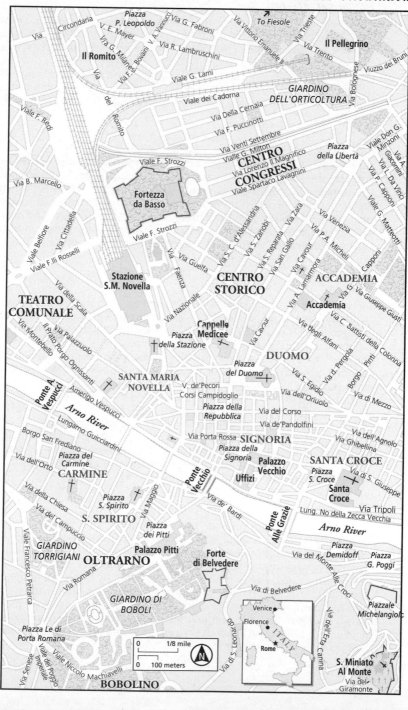

Teatro Comunale

Stretching around the theater that houses the Maggio Fiorentino Festival (see "More cool things to see and do," later in this chapter), this residential area just west of Santa Maria Novella is a very pleasant place to stay. Although not completely closed to traffic, it is part of medieval walled Florence and a quiet and historical neighborhood. Hotels are cheaper than in *centro storico,* because they are not right by the Duomo or the Uffizi, but these attractions are only a short walk away. We definitely recommend it.

Centro Congressi

On the east side of the rail station Santa Maria Novella and of the Fortezza da Basso, this area caters mostly to businesspeople attending the commercial expositions that are held in the fortress. Being walking distance from the *centro storico,* though, makes it attractive to tourists, plus you get cheaper rates and more real-life surroundings. The downside to staying here is that it is outside of the pedestrian zone, and cars can circulate here. We think it's a good compromise: hotel's standards are high but prices are contained.

Oltrarno (Across the Arno)

Included within the walls of Florence "only" in 1173, the south side of the Arno was and still is a quiet — and in certain areas, elegant — residential area. This is where the rulers of Florence decided to build their last palace, the **Pitti Palace.** The number of attractions here is limited, yet the magic of the medieval city is still present, with the great advantage of reduced crowds and the **Ponte Vecchio** only steps away. Many restaurants have been opening in the streets near the river, and the whole area is starting to take on some of the characteristics of Trastevere in Rome — especially the old popular neighborhood of San Frediano to the west. You'll find fewer hotels here than in other areas of town, but this is a much more civilized Florence. Again, distances are not great, but we split this neighborhood in two, around the two most famous squares — Piazza Santo Spirito, and Piazza del Carmine: **Oltrarno/Santo Spirito** and **Oltrarno/Carmine**.

Fiesole

The one other "neighborhood" you may want to visit outside the center is actually a separate small town 4.5km (3 miles) away — **Fiesole** (see "More cool things to see and do," later in this chapter) — from which you can get marvelous views of Florence and the surrounding hills. Plus, the *centro storico* is only 10 to 20 minutes away by bus, depending on the traffic. Fiesole is particularly pleasant in the summer, when it offers cooler air and a welcome break from the stuffy city. Fiesole is a preferred outing for Florentines on summer nights and is an excellent place to stay if you want to be away from the crowds (see the hotel and restaurant listings later in this chapter).

Finding information after you arrive

The following three offices offer additional tourist info and maps.

- ✔ **APT office at Via Cavour 1r** (☎ **055-290-832** or 055-290-833), about three blocks north of the Duomo; open Monday through Saturday 8:30 a.m. to 6:30 p.m. and Sunday 8:30 a.m. to 1:30 p.m.

- ✔ **Tourist office at Piazza Stazione 4/a** (☎ **055-212-245**) in the SMN train station; open Monday through Saturday 9 a.m. to 7 p.m. and Sunday 8:30 a.m. to 2:00 p.m.

- ✔ **Tourist office at Borgo Santa Croce 29r** (☎ **055-234-0444**), just behind Piazza Santa Croce, east of the Uffizi and not far from the river; open Monday through Saturday 9 a.m. to 7 p.m., Sunday 8:30 a.m. to 2:00 p.m.

Getting Around Florence

Florence's city center has long been closed to automobiles except those belonging to the residents, and the **centro storico** is free from all traffic except city buses — no cars, no taxis, and no mopeds or motor bikes (the ubiquitous and very noisy *motorini*). Although some still protest — taxi drivers in particular — we think it was a great decision, because it made the city much more pleasant for visitors (for everybody, in fact) and easier to visit.

The free **tourist office map** is completely adequate for most visitors, especially if you combine it with the free bus map you can get from ATAF (see later in this section), but if you're an ambitious explorer and don't feel satisfied, you can pick up a **cartina** (map) at a newsstand for about 6€ ($6.90). Choose one with **stradario** (street directory).

Florence has its own peculiar way of marking street addresses: Restaurants, agencies, and shops have numbers of their own, separate from the residential and hotel building numbers. Business numbers have the letter *r* appended to the number (for *rosso* or "red") and are painted in red, while residential numbers are painted in black or blue. For example, the address of one branch of the tourist office, Via Cavour 1r, refers to business no. 1 on Via Cavour, whereas the address Via Cavour 1 is the private building with the entrance no. 1. Such seemingly similar addresses can be many doors away from one another.

On foot

The best way to get around Florence is on foot. The walk from the Duomo at one end of the major historic district to the Palazzo Pitti in Oltrarno at the other takes only about 30 minutes at a leisurely pace; you'd also pass most of the major sights in town. As compact as any medieval city, Florence has a dense concentration of attractions, so you can basically walk from one sight to another.

By bus

The electric *navettes* (minibuses, identified by letters [A,B,C...]) within the **centro storico** do come in handy when your feet ache after a long day at the Uffizi or shopping on Via Tornabuoni. Also, we find the bus particularly useful to move back and forth between the Palazzo Pitti/Giardino di Boboli and the center of town on the other side of the river Arno.

Florence's bus system is well organized and easy to use. You can get a **bus map** at the ATAF ticket and information booth outside the SMN train station (Via Valfonda) — in fact, that's the only place where you can get one. Each bus stop has a name that's neatly written on the post at the stop and is reported on the map. When there's more than one stop by the same name (for example, on the same street), a number is added. This will help you figure out where you are and check your progress on the map as you ride.

You can buy a **biglietto (ticket)** for the bus at most bars, tobacconist shops (signed *tabacchi* or by a white *T* on a black background), and newsstands; it is valid for one hour and costs 1€ ($1.15). If you think you are going to use the buses a lot, ATAF offers several money-saving options. The **Carta Agile,** for example, is an electronic 12-ticket card sold for the price of 10 tickets (10€/$11.50), or 25 tickets for the price of 20 (20€/$23). The Carta Agile can be used by more than one person, you just pass it in front of the magnetic eye of the machine in the bus as many times as you have passengers in your group (if you want to know how much money you have left on the card, press the button marked "info" on the machine and swipe your card in front of it; the display will tell you). **Day-passes,** on the other hand, may not be shared. They allow unlimited rides and are sold in various denominations: the **24-hour pass** is 4.50€ ($5.20); the **two-day pass** is 7.60€ ($8.70); the **three-day pass** is 9.60€ ($11); and so on. Tickets are also sold at the bus information booth outside the Santa Maria Novella rail station. Within the hour of validity, you can take as many buses as you want. Remember that you need to stamp the ticket at your first ride using the machine inside the bus; without the stamp, the ticket isn't valid. After hours (9 p.m.–6 a.m.), you can buy a ticket on the bus, but the charge is double and you can buy only a regular one-hour ticket.

Always have a ticket when boarding the bus and be sure to properly stamp it; some people may tell you that no one ever checks, but they're wrong. Within five minutes of boarding our first bus in Florence, a rider was nabbed by the ticket inspector — a scene we saw repeated several times. And, come on, why try to wriggle out of a bargain 1€ ($1.15) ride?

Staying in Style

Because Florence is such a major tourist and business destination, hotels are plentiful and varied. Sometimes they are more expensive that they need to be. Below are some of the best in each price category.

If you arrive in Florence without a room reservation (something we advise against), remember that the **tourist office in Stazione Santa Maria Novella** offers a room-finding service. If you arrive by car, stop at the office in the **Area di Servizio AGIP Peretola** (rest area) on Highway A11 (☎ **055-421-1800**) or in the office at the **Area di Servizio Chianti Est** on Highway A1 (☎ **055-621-349**). Both maintain hotel databases and can tell you if rooms are available in town and can even make reservations if you like.

 For more recommendations on booking a room — and saving money in the process — see Chapter 8.

The top hotels

Alessandra
$$ Centro storico/Signoria

Steps from the Ponte Vecchio and the Uffizi, this *pensione* offers simple guest rooms at moderate prices. The whole hotel has been renovated and guest rooms are air-conditioned and quite large — but not all of them have private bathrooms.

See map p. 200. Borgo Santi Apostoli 17, just steps from Ponte Vecchio. ☎ *055-283-438. Fax: 055-210-619.* www.hotelalessandra.com. *Bus: B. Parking: 18€ ($21). Rack rates: 145€ ($167) double. Rates include breakfast. AE, MC, V.*

Bellettini
$$ Centro storico/Duomo

Just west of the Duomo, this 14th-century *palazzo* has been a guesthouse for the past 300 years. The old-fashioned Bellettini offers simple, clean guest rooms — some with fantastic views — and one of the best breakfasts in town for the price, with a buffet that includes ham and fresh fruit. The owners, two sisters, are very friendly and helpful — many of their guests keep coming back, so you'll have to reserve in advance. Some of the rooms share a bath, so be sure to ask when you reserve.

See map p. 200. Via de' Conti 7, steps from the Duomo. ☎ *055-213-561. Fax: 055-283-551.* www.hotelbellettini.com. *Bus: 1, 6, 11 to Martelli, take Via de' Cerretani and turn right on Via de' Conti. Parking: 18€ ($21). Rack rates: 140€ ($161) double. Rates include buffet breakfast. AE, DC, MC, V.*

Bigallo
$$ Centro storico/Duomo

This pleasant and centrally located hotel offers elegant and bright guest rooms with parquet floors, pastel-colored walls, and fine fabrics in warm colors. Bathrooms are new (some with Jacuzzis) and many rooms afford romantic views over the Duomo. Because of its location, though, it might be a little noisy sometimes in the evening, especially in summer; the moderate price may compensate for that.

See map p. 200. Vicolo degli Adimari 2, off Via Calzaiuoli. ☎ *and Fax: **055-216-086**.* www.hotelbigallo.it. *Bus: 1, 6, 11, to Martelli; walk south between the Baptistry and the Duomo to Vicolo degli Adimari. Parking: 16€ ($18). Rack rates: 186€ ($214) double. Rates include breakfast. DC, MC, V.*

Boboli
$ Oltrarno/Santo Spirito

A short walk from the Ponte Vecchio, this simple, modern hotel is a nice value in a residential part of town that's full of much pricier choices. Guest rooms are simply furnished but with careful pleasant details, and bathrooms are really tiny, but all extremely clean and well cared for. The Boboli is a good choice if you want to be in a quiet area yet near the major sights; it's good for families as well, as it has some triple rooms and a couple of quads.

See map p. 200. Via Romana 63, just south of the Palazzo Pitti. ☎ ***055-229-8645** or 055-233-6518. Fax: 055-233-7169.* www.hotelboboli.com. *Bus: 11, 36, 37 to Serragli 05; walk south on Via dei Serragli, turn left on Via Serumido, and left again on Via Romana. Parking: 11€ ($13). Rack rates: 130€ ($150) double. Rates include breakfast. AE, DC, MC, V.*

Casa del Lago
$$ Teatro Comunale

This family-run hotel offers beautiful views over the Arno from most of its guest rooms, which are bright and good sized. The furniture is simple — modern light wood or veneer, but comfortable. The hotel also has an Internet point free for its guests. Consider that it is only a ten-minute walk from Ponte Vecchio, you can't hope for better at the price. Note that a few of the rooms share a private bath. The hotel is accessible to people with disabilities.

See map p. 200. Lungarno A. Vespucci 58, at Via Garibaldi. ☎ ***055-216-141**. Fax: 055-214-149.* www.hotelcasadellago.com. *Bus:A, B. Parking: 18€ ($21). Rack rates: 145€ ($167) double. Rates include breakfast. AE, DC, MC, V.*

Croce di Malta
$$$ Centro storico/Santa MariaNovella

This elegant hotel offers nicely appointed large guest rooms — furnished with modern but classic hand-crafted furniture — a garden with a small swimming pool, and a roof terrace where you can have breakfast or a drink and enjoy the lovely view. Venetian plaster in warm tones on the walls and quality carpeting give each room an individual ambience; many of the upper-floor guest rooms have small balconies. The hotel is accessible for people with disabilities and the staff is extremely helpful.

See map p. 200. Via della Scala 7, at Piazza Santa Maria Novella. ☎ ***055-261-1870**. Fax: 055-287-121.* www.crocedimalta.it. *Bus: A, 11, 36, 37. Parking: 18€ ($21). Rack rates: 297€ ($342) double. AE, DC, MC, V.*

Desirée
$ Centro Congressi

This Liberty-style (Italian Art Nouveau) hotel boasts stained glass windows by Polloni, rare and beautiful floral-decorated floors, and nicely appointed rooms with painted wood furniture or iron bedsteads. Some of the rooms offer romantic views over the dome of San Lorenzo.

See map p. 200. Via Fiume 20, off Via Nazionale, near the train Station. ☎ *055-238-2382. Fax: 055-291-439.* www.desireehotel.com. *Bus: 4, 12, 25. Parking: 20€ ($23). Rack rates: 123€ ($141) double. AE, DC, MC, V.*

Grand Hotel Cavour
$$ Centro storico/Duomo

Grand public spaces with marble floors welcome you to this centrally located hotel. The beautifully appointed guest rooms are of a good size, with fine furniture, rich carpeting, and fabrics in modern but classic style. Bathrooms are new. The hotel's roof garden, where you'll find the restaurant and breakfast buffet, affords beautiful views. The rooms overlooking the street are a bit noisy in spite of the double-paned windows. The hotel is accessible to people with disabilities.

See map p. 200. Via del Proconsolo 3, at Via del Corso. ☎ *055-266-2701. Fax: 055-218-955.* www.albergocavour.it. *Bus: A. Parking: 18€ ($21). Rack rates: 232€ ($267) double. Rates include buffet breakfast. AE, DC, MC, V.*

Grand Hotel Villa Medici
$$$$$ Teatro Comunale

We think this is the best of the luxury hotels in Florence: housed in a beautiful 18th-century *palazzo* with a large garden *and* a swimming pool, and right in the center of town. The large guest rooms are individually decorated, each with taste and elegance. Rooms on the higher floors have panoramic views over the city and all have beautiful bathrooms. The buffet breakfast is American style, but will cost you an additional 30€ ($35).

See map p. 200. Via il Prato 42, at Via Rucellai and Via Palestro. ☎ *800-273-226 or 055-238-1331; Fax: 055-238-1336.* www.villamedicihotel.com. *Bus: D, 1. Free parking. Rack rates: 540€–nd650€ ($621–$748) double. AE, DC, MC, V.*

Hotel Casci
$$ Centro storico/Accademia

Occupying a 15th-century *palazzo* once owned by the musician Gioacchino Rossini, the Hotel Casci offers comfortable guest rooms, simply but pleasantly furnished. Bathrooms are small, but the hotel location is excellent, and the buffet breakfast is served in a room decorated with original frescoes.

See map p. 200. Via Cavour 13, off Piazza San Marco. ☎ *055-211-686. Fax: 055-239-6461.* www.hotelcasci.com. *Bus: 1, 6, 7, 10, 11. Parking: 18€ ($21). Rack rates: 150€ ($173) double. Rates include buffet breakfast. AE, DC, MC, V.*

Florence Accommodations and Dining

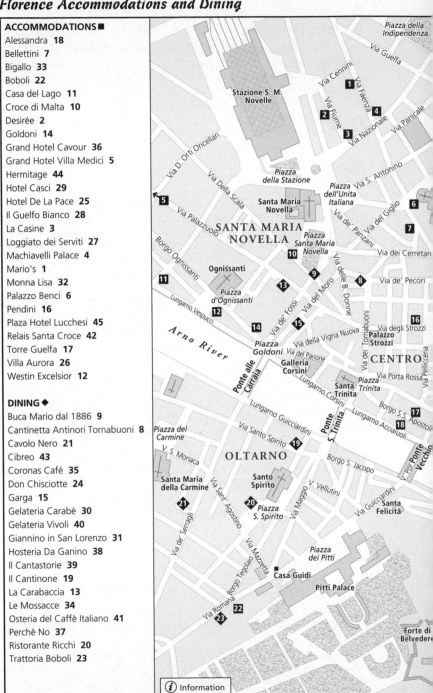

ACCOMMODATIONS ■
Alessandra **18**
Bellettini **7**
Bigallo **33**
Boboli **22**
Casa del Lago **11**
Croce di Malta **10**
Desirée **2**
Goldoni **14**
Grand Hotel Cavour **36**
Grand Hotel Villa Medici **5**
Hermitage **44**
Hotel Casci **29**
Hotel De La Pace **25**
Il Guelfo Bianco **28**
La Casine **3**
Loggiato dei Serviti **27**
Machiavelli Palace **4**
Mario's **1**
Monna Lisa **32**
Palazzo Benci **6**
Pendini **16**
Plaza Hotel Lucchesi **45**
Relais Santa Croce **42**
Torre Guelfa **17**
Villa Aurora **26**
Westin Excelsior **12**

DINING ◆
Buca Mario dal 1886 **9**
Cantinetta Antinori Tornabuoni **8**
Cavolo Nero **21**
Cibreo **43**
Coronas Café **35**
Don Chisciotte **24**
Garga **15**
Gelateria Carabè **30**
Gelateria Vivoli **40**
Giannino in San Lorenzo **31**
Hosteria Da Ganino **38**
Il Cantastorie **39**
Il Cantinone **19**
La Carabaccia **13**
Le Mossacce **34**
Osteria del Caffè Italiano **41**
Perchè No **37**
Ristorante Ricchi **20**
Trattoria Boboli **23**

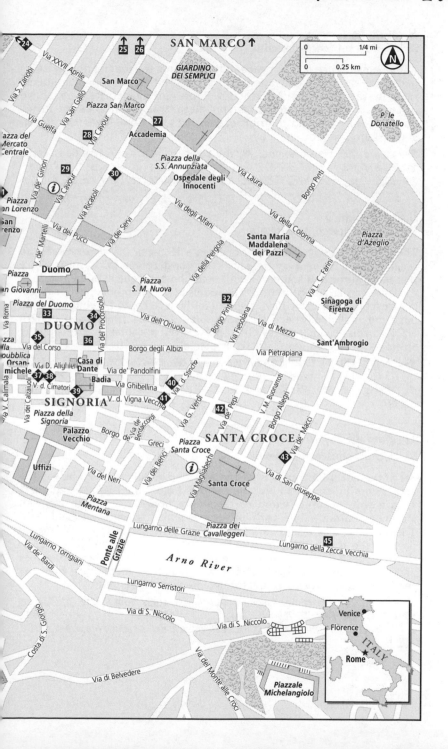

SAN MARCO ↑

24

25 26

GIARDINO
DEI SEMPLICI

Via XXVII Aprile

San Marco

Piazza San Marco

Via S. Zanobi

Via Guelfa

Via San Gallo

27 Accademia

28

Via Cavour

azza del
Mercato
Centrale

29 (i)

30

Via de' Ginori

Via Cavour

Via Ricasoli

Piazza della
S.S. Annunziata

Ospedale degli
Innocenti

Via Laura

Via degli Alfani

Via della Colonna

Piazza
an Lorenzo

San
enzo

V. de' Martelli

Via dei Pucci

Via dei Servi

Via della Pergola

Santa Maria
Maddalena
dei Pazzi

Piazza
d'Azeglio

Piazza
an Giovanni

Piazza del Duomo

Duomo

33

DUOMO

34

Piazza
S. M. Nuova

Via dell'Oriuolo

Via del Procónsolo

32

Sinagoga di
Firenze

azza
la
oubblica

Orsan-
michele

35 Via del Corso

36

Borgo degli Albizi

Via Pietrapiana

Sant'Ambrogio

Via Fiesolana

Via di Mezzo

Via D. Alighieri

Casa di
Dante

Via de' Pandolfini

37 38 Badia

V. d. Cimatori

39

Via Ghibellina

40

V. d. Stinche

SIGNORIA

V. d. Vigna Vecchia

41

Piazza della
Signoria

Palazzo
Vecchio

Uffizi

Borgo de'

Via de' Bentaccordi

42

Via G. Verdi

Via de' Pepi

V.M. Buonarroti

Borgo Allegri

Via de' Macci

SANTA CROCE

43

Greci

Piazza
Santa Croce

Via de' Benci

Via del Neri

(i)

Santa Croce

Via di San Giuseppe

Piazza
Mentana

Via Magliabechi

Piazza dei
Cavalleggeri

Lungarno delle Grazie

45

Ponte alle
Grazie

Lungarno della Zecca Vecchia

Lungarno Torrigiani

Via de' Bardi

Arno River

Lungarno Serristori

Via di S. Niccolo

Costa di S. Giorgio

Via di S. Niccolo

Venice

Florence

ITALY

Rome

Via di Belvedere

Via del Monte alle Croci

Piazzale
Michelangiolo

0   1/4 mi
0   0.25 km
N

P. le
Donatello

Via L. C. Farini

Borgo Pinti

Hotel De La Pace
$$ Centro storico/Accademia

Aptly named (*pace* means peace in Italian), this welcoming hotel exudes feelings of quiet and relaxation. The good-sized guests rooms are decorated in warm tones, with terracotta floors and fine fabrics; many have balconies. Furnishings are modern but elegant and bathrooms are attractive with white tiles and colorful accents and tubs. Complimentary pickup at the station on request.

See map p. 200. Via Lamarmora 28, at Via Venezia, north of Piazza San Marco. ☎ *055-577-343. Fax: 055-577-576.* www.hoteldelapace.it. *Bus: 1, 7. Parking: 20€ ($23). Rack rates: 195€ ($224) double. Rates include breakfast. AE, DC, MC, V.*

Il Guelfo Bianco
$$ Centro storico/Accademia

This recently renovated hotel occupies a 15th-century *palazzo* and its neighboring 17th-century *palazzo*. The guest rooms in the former are pleasantly furnished and come with beautiful bathrooms; many overlook the inner garden and courtyard. The rooms in the other building boast ceiling frescoes, and some have painted and carved wood ceilings. All are large and individually decorated with some antique furniture and modern art. And you need not worry about noise, even in rooms overlooking the street — the new windows are triple-paned!

See map p. 200. Via Cavour 57r, at Via Guelfa. ☎ *055-288-330. Fax: 055-295-203.* www.ilguelfo bianco.it. *Bus: 1, 6 to Cavour 02 or 1, 6, 7, 10, 11 to San Marco 01. Parking: 21€ ($24). Rack rates: 235€ ($270) double. Rates include breakfast. AE, DC, MC, V.*

Loggiato dei Serviti
$$ Centro storico/Accademia

Set in the beautiful square near the Accademia Gallery — some say the most beautiful square in Florence — this hotel offers good-sized guest rooms, with beautiful wood or terracotta floors, decorated in a rich Florentine baroque style, with fine drapes and most with canopied beds. The hotel occupies a landmark 16th-century building designed by Antonio da Sangallo il Vecchio (the Elder) to match the twin buildings of the Ospedale degli Innocenti across the square. It was originally a monastery and was trasformed into a hostel only early in the 20th century. Recently renovated, it was restored to its simple Renaissance beauty.

See map p. 200. Piazza Santissima Annunziata 3, steps from Piazza San Marco. ☎ *055-289-592. Fax: 055-289-595.* www.loggiatodeiservitihotel.it. *Bus: C. Parking: 20€ ($23). Rack rates: 205€ ($236) double. Rates include breakfast. AE, DC, MC, V.*

Machiavelli Palace
$$ Centro Congressi

Housed in an early 18th-century palace that was once a convent, this hotel boasts frescoes and coffered ceilings; its guest rooms are very nice, with pastel-colored walls and furnished with elegant drapes and bedsteads. A full buffet with cold cuts and cheese is served in the frescoed refectory of the old convent. Rooms overlooking the street are somwhat noisy, though.

See map p. 200. Via Nazionale 10, at Via Faenza. ☎ *055-216-622. Fax: 055-214-106.* www.hotelmachiavelli.it. *Bus: 12, 35. Parking: 20€ ($23). Rack rates: 218€ ($251) double. Rates include buffet breakfast. AE, DC, MC, V.*

Monna Lisa
$$$$ Centro storico/Santa Croce

The Monna Lisa yearns to be a private collector's home and indeed you'll feel like a guest in someone's home. The guest rooms of this beautiful 14th-century *palazzo*, once home to the Neri family, vary in style and size. The antique furnishings, original coffered ceilings, inner garden and patio, modern bathrooms (some with Jacuzzis), and important artworks make this hotel very desirable. The hotel is accessible for people with disabilities.

See map p. 200. Borgo Pinti 27, off Via dell'Oriuolo. ☎ *055-247-9751. Fax: 055-247-9755.* www.monnalisa.it. *Bus: A, 14, or 23 to Salvemini. Parking: 12€ ($14). Rack rates: 350€ ($403) double. Rates include breakfast. AE, DC, MC, V.*

Palazzo Benci
$$ Centro storico

Recently opened west of the Duomo, this hotel occupies a lovingly restored 16th-century *palazzo*, the residence of the Renaissance Benci family. The guest rooms are simple but tasteful; many rooms open onto the delightful inner garden courtyard. The common spaces are absolutely gorgeous, with richly stuccoed walls, and the breakfast room boasts coffered wooden ceilings.

See map p. 200. Piazza Madonna degli Aldobrandini 3, off Via del Giglio, behind San Lorenzo. ☎ *055-213-848. Fax: 055-288-308. E-mail:* palazzobenci@iol.it. *Bus: 1, 6, 11 to Martelli; walk west on Via dei Gori, then across Piazza San Lorenzo and around the church on Corso Tonelli into Piazza Madonna degli Aldobrandini. Rack rates: 192€ ($221) double. Rates include breakfast. AE, DC, V.*

Pendini
$$ Centro storico

Minutes from Via dei Calzaiuoli and the top sights, the old-fashioned Pendini is just off busy Piazza della Repubblica. This family-style *pensione* dates from the 19th century, when Florence was briefly the capital of Italy. It underwent renovations during the 1990s and offers insulated guest rooms with double-paned windows and new bathrooms.

See map p. 200. Via Strozzi 2, off Piazza della Repubblica. ☎ *055-211-170. Fax: 055-281-807. E-mail:* pendini@dada.it. *Bus: A. Parking: 21€ ($24). Rack rates: 150€ ($173) double. Rates include breakfast. AE, DC, MC, V.*

Plaza Hotel Lucchesi
$$$$ Centro storico/Santa Croce

Some of the spacious and bright guest rooms in this historical hotel have private balconies and all afford romantic views over the river or over Santa Croce. Bathrooms are modern and the comfortable furniture ensures a warm and welcoming feeling. The hotel opened in 1860 at the eastern edge of the historic district and was completely renovated in 2001, with good taste and attention to details.

See map p. 200. Lungarno della Zecca Vecchia 38, seast of Santa Croce. ☎ *055-26-236. Fax: 055-248-0921.* www.plazalucchesi.it. *Bus: B. Parking 20€ ($23). Rack rates: 387€ ($445) double. Rates include breakfast. AE, DC, MC, V.*

Relais Santa Croce
$$$$$ Centro storico/Santa Croce

This small luxury hotel in the heart of the *centro storico* is destined to become one of the best in Florence. Just opened at press time, it offers the comfort level of the other luxury hotels, but with a warm atmosphere and real style — no dusty old elegance nor arrogant trendiness here. Originally built for Marquis Baldinucci, treasurer to the pope, the 18th-century Ciofi-Jacometti palace combines antique furnishings and period architectural details — the original frescos are magnificent — with Italian contemporary design. Precious fabrics, elegant wood panels, and marble baths — all with separate shower and tub — perfectly complete the picture.

See map p. 200. Via Ghibellina 87, at Via de' Pepi. ☎ *055-234-2230. Fax: 055-234-1195.* www.relaissantacroce.it. *Bus: A. Parking: 20€ ($23). Rack rates: 750€ ($863) double. Rates include breakfast. AE, DC, MC, V.*

Villa Aurora
$$$ Fiesole

In Fiesole's central square, just near the terminus of the city bus from Florence, this hotel is elegant and comfortable, if a bit pretentious — but they have their reasons: After all, this is where the VIPs of the 19th century would stay (Queen Victoria, Queen Margherita di Savoia, Queen Emma of Holland, among others). The guest rooms in back enjoy the gorgeous view over Florence, while the ones on the side overlook the garden. Some rooms have balconies, and some rooms have Jacuzzis. The old-world feeling doesn't extend to the rooms, however, where the fixtures and furniture are modern.

See map p. 200. Piazza Mino 39. ☎ *055-59-363. Fax: 055-59-587.* www.logicad.net/ aurora. *Bus: 7 to last stop. Free parking. Rack rates: 300€ ($345) double. AE, DC, MC, V.*

Runner-up hotels

Goldoni

$$ **Teatro Comunale** This historic hotel — Mozart was a guest at the inn of his time — offers large rooms with tiled floors and Florentine baroque-syle furnishings. The buffet breakfast is a plus. *See map p. 200. Via Borgo Ognissanti 8.* ☎ *055-284-080. Fax: 055-239-6983.* www.hotelgoldoni.com.

Hermitage

$$$ **Centro storico** This hotel is right off the Ponte Vecchio, nearer to the Uffizi, and has been recently renovated; many of the guest rooms have beautiful views over the river and all have antique furniture and premium bathrooms. The very pleasant rooftop garden-terrace is a real plus. *See map p. 200. Vicolo Marzio 1.* ☎ *055-287-216. Fax: 055-212-208.* www.hermitage hotel.com.

Le Cascine

$$ **Centro Congressi** Guests rooms in this very nice hotel have a warm atmosphere, with quality wall plaster, terracotta floors, carpeting, classic furniture, and ironwork bedsteads. *See map p. 200. Largo Fratelli Alinari 15, off Via Nazionale.* ☎ *055-211-066. Fax: 055-210-769.* www.hotellecascine.it.

Mario's

$$ **Centro Congressi** Recently renovated, this hotel offers bright, pleasant, medium-size guest rooms with pastel-colored walls and wood-beamed ceilings. *See map p. 200. Via Faenza 89.* ☎ *055-218-801. Fax: 055-212-039.* www.hotelmarios.com.

Torre Guelfa

$$$ **Centro storico/Signoria** Near the Ponte Vecchio and the Uffizi, the Torre Guelfa offers pleasant and richly decorated guest rooms, good service, and a breathtaking view from its 13th-century tower. *See map p. 200. Borgo Santi Apostoli 8.* ☎ *055-239-6338. Fax: 055-239-8577.* www.hotel torreguelfa.com.

The Westin Excelsior

$$$$$ **Centro storico** The best luxury hotel in the centro storico, with an outstanding Florentine baroque decor, including beautiful stained glass windows, rich wood-carved and painted ceilings, and marble columns. Check the Web site for Internet specials. *See map p. 200. Piazza Ognissanti 3;* ☎ *888-625-5144 in the U.S. and Canada, or 055-27-151. Fax: 055-210-278.* www. westin.com/excelsiorflorence.

Dining Out

The best dining in Florence is in the area between Santa Croce and Signoria in *centro storico,* and west of Piazza Santo Spirito in Oltrarno, around Piazza del Carmine — the popular area of San Frediano. As you'd expect some of the restaurants in *centro storico* are tourist traps.

French? I don't think so!

Tuscans love to remind people that many typical French dishes are largely descended from Tuscan specialties imported to France by the gourmet queen Caterina de' Medici in the 16th century. Not trusting Northern barbarians to cook food to her liking, she brought her own cooks with her when she married Henri II of France. For example, French crêpes are derived from Florentine *crespelle,* and *omelette* is nothing else but *frittata.*

Strong on soups — *ribollita* (bread, vegetable, and bean soup), and *pappa al pomodoro* (tomato and bread soup) are the most famous — and grilled meats, Florentine cuisine is also famous for the *fagioli all'uccelletto* (white Tuscan beans in a light tomato sauce), and the *pappardelle al sugo di lepre* (homemade pasta with hare sauce), among others. See Chapter 2 for a more in-depth description of Tuscan and Florentine food.

Buca Mario dal 1886
$$$ Centro storico/Santa MariaNovella   FLORENTINE

This historic restaurant, serving very good traditional Tuscan cuisine in a friendly atmosphere, is housed in a cellar ("buca" in Florentine), with vaulted and whitewashed dining rooms decorated with dark wood paneling — the decor is original. Buca Mario prides itself in being a repository of Tuscan culinary tradition, and indeed everything is well prepared, although it doesn't come cheap. We liked the classic *ribollita,* and the *ossobuco alla fiorentina con fagioli all'uccelletto* (sliced veal shank with beans), as well as the *coniglio fritto* (fried rabbit), a Tuscan delicacy!

See map p. 200. Piazza degli Ottaviani 16r, just south of Santa Maria Novella. ☎ *055-214-179.* www.bucamario.it. *Reservations recommended. Bus: A, 36, or 37 to Piazza Santa Maria Novella. Secondi: 18€–28€ ($21–$32). AE, MC, V. Open: Lunch Fri–Tues; dinner Thurs–Tues; closed 4 weeks in Aug.*

Cantinetta Antinori Tornabuoni
$$$ Centro storico/Santa MariaNovella   FLORENTINE/ITALIAN

Typical Tuscan dishes and many specialties from the Antinori farms are served in the restaurant to accompany the wine. Antinori is the family name of the oldest and one of the best producers of wine in Italy. The *cantinetta* (small wine cellar) occupies the 15th-century *palazzo* of this noble family and serves as their winery in town. You can stay at the counter and sample the various vintages, or sit and have a full meal. The *pappa al pomodoro,* was delicious, and so was the *risotto agli scampi* (with prawns).

See map p. 200. Piazza Antinori 3r, off the north end of Via de' Tornabuoni. ☎ *055-292-234. Reservations recommended. Bus: A, 6, 11, 36, or 37 to Piazza Antinori. Secondi: 14€–25€ ($16–$29). AE, DC, MC, V. Open: Lunch and dinner Mon–Fri. Closed 1 week at Christmas and 1 week in Aug.*

Cavolo Nero
$$ Oltrarno/Piazza del Carmine FLORENTINE

Cavolo Nero serves great food, prepared with enthusiasm and creativity, in a free interpretation of Florentine tradition. The name of the restaurant refers to the black cabbage (similar to kale) that is typical of Tuscan cooking. The menu, which changes monthly, isn't very extensive, but its offerings are delicious. On one of our visits we enjoyed the homemade *gnocchi con broccoli e finocchietto selvatico* (potato dumplings with broccoli and wild fennel), and the *filetto di spigola arrostito fasciato con melanzana su fonduta di peperone giallo* (bass filet rolled in eggplant strips served over a yellow pepper puree).

See map p. 200. Via d'Ardiglione 22, off Via de' Serragli. ☎ **055-294-744.** www. cavolonero.it. *Reservations recommended. Bus: D, 11, 36, or 37 to Via de' Serragli. Secondi: 10€–16€ ($12–$18). AE, DC, MC, V. Open: Dinner Mon–Sat. Closed 3 weeks in Aug.*

Cibreo
$–$$$ Centro storico/Santa Croce FLORENTINE

Renowned chef-owner Fabio Picchi changes his menu daily, depending on the market and his imagination. The backbone of the menu is historical Tuscan, with some recipes that go back to the Renaissance, but are presented with modern interpretation. One hallmark is that you won't find pasta of any kind, but there are soufflès, roasted and stuffed birds, polenta, and more. The *pomodoro in gelatina* (tomato aspic) is a well-known specialty of this restaurant, and the *piccione farcito di mostarda di frutta* (pigeon stuffed with a traditional fruit preparation) is well worth trying if it is on the menu. Their many vegetable soups are always delicious. The small trattoria next door serves a smaller selection of dishes at lower prices, but they don't accept reservations and you have to get there early (by 1 p.m. for lunch and by 8 p.m. for dinner).

See map p. 200. Restaurant: Via Andrea del Verrocchio 8r/ trattoria: Via de'Macci 122r. ☎ **055-234-1100.** *Email:* cibreo.fi@tin.it. *Reservations required for the restaurant; not accepted for the trattoria. Bus: A to Borgo la Croce or Agnolo 04 stop; walk south on Via de' Macci from Piazza Sant'Ambrogio (outdoor vegetable market). Secondi: 14€ ($16) at trattoria and 35€ ($40) at restaurant. AE, DC, MC, V. Open: Trattoria, Tues–Sat lunch and dinner; restaurant, Tues–Sat dinner. Closed end-July through early Sept and first week in Jan.*

Don Chisciotte
$$ Centro Congressi FLORENTINE/SEAFOOD

This small restaurant is justly known for its flavorful and imaginative fish dishes, served in a friendly and informal atmosphere. Just north of the main tourist area, the restaurant gets quite busy, especially on weekends. The dining room is on the second floor of a typical *palazzo*. We liked the *tagliatelle con scampi e asparagi* (fresh pasta with asparagus and prawns) and the *tagliata di tonno con misticanza e crema di cipolle* (tuna steak with cooked greens and cream of onions).

Via C. Ridolfi 4r, just off Fortezza da Basso, the fortress east of the SMN train station. ☎ *055-475-430. Reservations recommended. Best by taxi. Secondi: 15€–21€ ($17–$24). AE, DC, MC, V. Open: Lunch Tues–Sat; dinner Mon–Sat.*

Enoteca Ristorante Mario
$$ Fiesole   TUSCAN

On Fiesole's main square, this restaurant offers a choice of excellent wines to accompany the nicely prepared Tuscan specialties. You'll find dishes that are typical of various parts of Tuscany, and the service is very good. You can start with *crostini* or *affettati misti* (assorted cured meats) and follow with *pappardelle al sugo di lepre* (homemade pasta with hare sauce) and a wild boar stew or some delicious grilled vegetables. The restaurant occupies two floors, and the decor is stylish, with wooden ceiling beams and a small art gallery on the walls.

See map p. 200. Piazza Mino 9r, the main square in Fiesole, the restaurant is on the northwest side. ☎ *055-59-143. Reservations recommended on Sat. Bus: 7 to last stop in Fiesole. Secondi: 15€–21€ ($17–$24). AE, MC, V. Open: Lunch and dinner Tues–Sun.*

Garga
$$$ Centro storico/Santa MariaNovella   TUSCAN/CREATIVE

The ebullient personality of the chef-owner, Garga, has overflowed onto the walls, which he has personally decorated with his own frescoes. The extravagant atmosphere pairs perfectly with his extravagant interpretation of Tuscan fundamentals. Elegant yet laid back, this restaurant isn't cheap. Try the famous *taglierini alla Magnifico* (fresh homemade angel-hair pasta with a mint-cream sauce flavored with lemon and orange rind and Parmesan cheese).

See map p. 200. Via del Moro 50r. ☎ *055-239-8898.* www.fol.it. *Reservations required. Bus: A to Via del Moro. Secondi: 21€–23€ ($24–$26). AE, DC, MC, V. Open: Dinner Tues–Sun.*

Giannino in San Lorenzo
$$ Centro storico/Duomo   FLORENTINE

Serving roasted meats since 1920, this restaurant prides itself on its *fiorentina* (grilled porterhouse steak of local beef), and justifiably so. Under the vaulted ceilings of a 17th-century shopping gallery, you can relax and have excellent Tuscan food at moderate prices, attentively served. This is an informal restaurant where you can enjoy your *crostini* (toasted bread with savory toppings) *ribollita, maiale* (pork) served in a variety of ways, and famous *salsicce toscane alla griglia con cannellini* (grilled local sausages with Tuscan white beans). And for the wine, you can visit the wine steward in the wine cellar to help you make your selection.

See map p. 200. Via Borgo San Lorenzo 35/37r. ☎ *055-212-206.* www.gianninoin
florence.com. *Reservations recommended Fri–Sat. Bus: 1, 6, 7, 10, 11 to Duomo.
Secondi: 8.50€–18€ ($9.80–$21). AE, MC, V. Open: Lunch and dinner daily.*

Hosteria Da Ganino
$$ **Centro storico/Signoria FLORENTINE**

At this cozy, centrally located small trattoria, you'll find ubiquitous
Florentine specialties like *bistecca alla fiorentina* and *tagliatelle con tartufi*
(homemade pasta with truffle sauce), served on paper tablecloths over
polished stone tables. If prices are a bit high for this simple setting, the
food is nicely prepared and served by an attentive staff; welcome the offer-
ing of *mortadella* before you order.

See map p. 200. Piazza dei Cimatori 4r. ☎ *055-214-125. Reservations recommended.
Bus: A to Condotta or Cimatori; Via dei Cimatori is 2 short blocks north of Piazza della
Signoria. Secondi: 9€–18€ ($10–$21). AE, DC, MC, V. Open: Lunch and dinner
Mon–Sat.*

Il Cantastorie
$ **Centro storico/Signoria TUSCAN**

With a good singer performing every night, excellent wine, and hearty
food, Il Cantastorie is always a lively spot. Defining itself as a bit of Tuscan
countryside in the heart of Florence, this pleasant trattoria is decorated in
the Tuscan tradition of terracotta floors, wooden tables, and paneling; the
vaulted ceilings and white tablecloths add to the warm atmosphere. You'll
find all the typical Tuscan specialties and some of the best Chianti you've
ever had. *Ribollita, salsiccia e bietola* (pork sausages and green chard),
crostoni (larger version of *crostini*), *filetto di maiale al finocchio* (pork filet
in fennel sauce), Tuscan cold cuts and *sottoli* (vegetables preserved in
herbs and olive oil), and homemade desserts are some of the choices you
may find on a menu that changes daily. The same management runs Il
Cantinone (reviewed below).

Fixings for a garden picnic

For a cheap but delicious meal that'll give your wallet a rest and let you do as the locals
do, drop by an *alimentari* (grocery shop) for the fixings for a picnic. You can buy some
delicious Tuscan bread, local ham and cheese, fruit, mineral water, or wine. Stop by
Consorzio Agrario Pane and Co., Piazza San Firenze 5r, at the corner of Via Condotta
(☎ **055-213-063;** Bus: A to Condotta), where you'll find excellent *cinghiale* salami and
a choice of local cheeses and cured pork delicacies, plus water, wine, and all the rest.
You can also get a nice fruit tart or some *paste* (cream puffs and other small sweet
pastries). The best place to have a picnic is in Fiesole or in the Boboli Gardens (see
"The top sights," later in this chapter).

See map p. 200. Via della Condotta 7/9r, just east of Piazza della Signoria.
☎ *055-239-6804. Reservations recommended on Sat. Bus: A to Ghibellina. Secondi: 8€–16€ ($9.20–$18). MC, V. Open: Lunch and dinner Wed–Mon.*

Il Cantinone
$$ Oltrarno/Santo Spirito   FLORENTINE

Il Cantinone combines a convivial atmosphere and good traditional Florentine cuisine in this setting of low arched ceilings and long wooden tables for this *enoteca del Chianti Classico* (winery specializing in Chianti Classico, the heart of the DOCG [that's denomination controlled and guaranteed] Chianti). To accompany the excellent wine, try some of the excellent soups — *ribollita, pappa al pomodoro, pasta e fagioli* (pasta and beans) — or the *salsicce* (grilled pork sausages). A particularly interesting offering is the prix-fixe menu *degustazione,* a meal for two including a different wine with each serving.

See map p. 200. Via Santo Spirito 6R. ☎ *055-218-898. Reservations recommended on Sat. Bus: 11, 36, or 37 to Sauro or Frescobaldi; walk south to Via Santo Spirito, a block south of the river, off Ponte Santa Trinita and Ponte alla Carraia. Secondi: 8€–18€ ($9.20–$21). MC, V. Open: Lunch and dinner Tues–Sun.*

Looking for a gelato break?

Ice cream is certainly one of the best treats in Italy, and Florence is famous for its gelato. Of a different school from the Venetian, the Roman, or the Sicilian gelati, Florentine ice cream was invented — as were many other Tuscan gastronomic specialties — to gratify the palates of the Medicis. Alas — to our taste at least (one of us is from Rome, you know) — the Medici family had a very big sweet tooth, judging from the result: Florentine ice cream is extremely sweet. The flavors are basically the same that you'll find all over Italy, with all kind of nuts, such as *pistacchio* (pistachio) and *nocciola* (filbert), fruits such as *limone* (lemon) and *pera* (pear), and creams such as chocolate and vanilla based.

Try the celebrated **Gelateria Vivoli** (Via Isola delle Stinche 7r, between the Bargello and Santa Croce; ☎ 055-292-334; Bus: A to Piazza Santa Croce), which is truly a marvel for its zillions of flavors. There are many other *gelaterie* in town, such as **Coronas Café** (Via Calzaiuoli 72r; ☎ 055-239-6139; Bus: A to Orsanmichele) for good *produzione propria* (homemade) ice cream, and **Perchè No** (Via dei Tavolini 19r, just off Via Calzaiuoli; ☎ 055-239-8969; Bus: A to Orsanmichele), one of the oldest Florentine *gelaterie*. And if you can't go to Sicily on this trip, try the **Gelateria Carabè** (Via Ricasoli 60r, near the Accademia; ☎ 055-289-476; Bus: C, 6, to Santissima [SS] Annunziata) for a typical Sicilian gelato or granita; the owner has the ingredients — lemons, almonds, pistachios — shipped from Sicily, and his ice cream has been rated among the best in Italy.

La Carabaccia
$$ Centro storico/Santa MariaNovella   FLORENTINE

The name of this restaurant refers both to a traditional working boat that once plied the Arno and to *zuppa carabaccia,* a hearty onion soup favored by the Medicis during the Renaissance. The menu features daily choices of pasta, fresh vegetables, and fish according to what caught the chef's eye in the market, plus a variety of delicious homemade breads.

See map p. 200. Via Palazzuolo 190r. ☎ *055-213-203. Reservations recommended on Sat. Bus: A to Moro; turn left from Via del Moro into Via Palazzuolo, west of Via de' Tornabuoni. Secondi: 9.50€–21€ ($11–$24). AE, MC, V. Open: Lunch Tues–Sat; dinner Mon–Sat; closed 2 weeks in Aug.*

Le Mossacce
$ Centro storico/Duomo   FLORENTINE

This small and cheap historic *osteria* offers home-style Florentine food. Listen up to the daily offerings from the waiter — there is a written menu, but they don't like to waste the time — and make your pick among the choice of Tuscan specialties like *crespelle* (eggy crepes, served lasagne-style or rolled, filled with ham or ricotta and spinach, cheese, and tomato sauce) and *ribollita* as well as *spaghetti alle vongole* (spaghetti with clams), and lasagne. Among the secondi, try the *involtini* (rolled and filled veal scaloppina cooked in tomato sauce).

See map p. 200. Via del Proconsolo 55r, near the Duomo. ☎ *055-294-361. Reservations recommended. Bus: 14 or 23 to Proconsolo. Secondi: 7€–15€ ($8.05–$17). AE, MC, V. Open: Lunch and dinner Mon–Fri.*

Osteria del Caffè Italiano
$$ Centro storico/Santa Croce   FLORENTINE

This is our favorite place in Florence: serving genuine Tuscan food all day long till late at night, with a great choice of some of the best Tuscan wines by the glass. No wonder — thanks to the imaginative owners, this *osteria* is the urban antenna of Tuscany's ten best vineyards, which send a choice of their finest products here regularly. Featuring both a more formal dining room and a tavern, this place allows you to choose between a complete meal or light fare; specially priced lunches are also available (in either room). *Ribollita, farinata al cavolo nero* (thick black cabbage soup), *bollito misto* (mixed boiled meats), *cinghiale in salmì* (wild boar stew), *bistecca alla fiorentina,* and a great choice of *affettati misti* (Tuscan cold cuts) will more than satisfy.

See map p. 200. Via Isola delle Stinche 11–13r. ☎ *055-289-020.* www.caffeitaliano. it. *Reservations recommended on Sat. Bus: A or 14 to Piazza Santa Croce. Secondi: 9€–19€ ($10–$22). AE, DC, MC, V. Open: From lunch to after-theater dinner Tues–Sun.*

Ristorante Ricchi
$$$ Oltrarno/Santo Spirito   TUSCAN/FISH

A glass of prosecco and a little something to eat while you order welcome you at this friendly fish restaurant. Recently renovated, the whitewashed walls, wood beamed ceilings, soft lighting, and tasteful furnishings are a perfect complement to the very well-prepared food. The menu changes daily and includes only fish dishes. We loved their version of fried zucchini flowers with crabmeat, also excellent were the *carpaccio di branzino*, the *riso nero* (squid ink risotto), and the grilled fish. The cafe next door also serves light fare in the evening.

See map p. 200. Piazza Santo Spirito 8/9r. ☎ ***055-215-864.*** www.caffericchi.it. *Reservations recommended. Bus: D, 11, 36, 37 to Piazza Santo Spirito. Secondi: 18€–24€ ($16–$21). AE, DC, MC, V. Open: Dinner Mon–Sat. Free parking for patrons on Via del Presto di San Martino (on the east side of the church of Santo Spirito).*

Trattoria Boboli
$ Oltrarno/Pitti   FLORENTINE

Near the Palazzo Pitti and the entrance to Boboli Gardens, this is a real mom-and-pop operation where you'll find all the specialties of Tuscan cuisine and a lot of warmth. The dining room is small, but the food is good. The menu changes but they make a good *ribollita* and *pappa al pomodoro*, as well as an excellent *ossobuco* (sliced veal shank).

See map p. 200. Via Romana 42r. ☎ ***055-233-6401.*** *Reservations recommended. Bus: D, 6, 11, 36, 37 to Via Romana. Secondi: 8€–16€ ($9.20–$18). AE, MC, V. Open: Lunch and dinner Thurs–Tues.*

Exploring Florence

Florence is known as the birthplace of the Renaissance, as well as its heart. This city is the hometown of many of the greatest artists who ever lived. At every turn, you'll see beautiful paintings, legendary statues, and magnificent buildings. Take a look at the top sights we recommend and be sure to give yourself enough time to admire the ones that interest you the most.

When planning your trip to Florence take into account that all the top museums are closed on Monday, and a number of attractions are closed in the afternoon (We list hours of operation in the reviews below). It is also important to know that the last week of May is the *Settimana della Cultura,* a statewide event during which admission to all the major museums is free — hence, no reservations are taken and the whole thing becomes a zoo, with thousands of school groups roaming around. If you can, schedule your visit to major destinations at a different time — we promise, it is worth paying your admission.

If you want to visit the Uffizi and the Accademia Galleries, **reserve your tickets in advance** — consider it a must, it can save you three hours of waiting in line. You can make reservations by calling ☎ **055-294-883** (Mon–Fri 8:30 a.m.–6:30 p.m., Sat 8:30 a.m.–12:30 p.m.) or faxing your request to 055-264-406 *before* leaving home. You can actually reserve for each of the Florentine State museums — Galleria degli Uffizi, Galleria dell'Accademia, Museums and Galleries of Palazzo Pitti, Cappelle Medicee, Museo San Marco, Museo Nazionale del Bargello, Museo Archeologico, and Museo delle Pietre Dure — but you probably need to reserve tickets only for the Uffizi and Accademia. Here's how it works: You make an appointment for a certain day and time, pay by credit card (or international bank draft if you don't have a credit card), and pick up your tickets at the tourist office in the Santa Maria Novella train station. You can also make your reservations once in Florence at the information booth inside the Uffizi, where you can also buy or pick up your tickets. There is a reservation fee of 3€ ($3.45) per ticket.

During special exhibitions, expect the regular admission price to be higher by 2€ to 5€ ($2.30–$5.75), depending on the museum and on the exhibit.

Since opening times change often, another good idea is to stop by one of the tourist information booths (see "Finding information after you arrive," earlier in this chapter) and pick up the flier listing the current opening and closing times of museums and monuments.

Discovering the top sights

Basilica di San Lorenzo
Centro storico/Duomo

San Lorenzo, founded in the fourth century, was the parish church of the powerful Medici family, some of whom are buried in the **Medici Chapels** (see later in this section). While the outside of the facade remained unfinished, its internal side was done by Michelangelo, and the rest of the interior is a showcase of Brunelleschi's artistic skills. The **Sagrestia Vecchia (Old Sacristy)** is a masterpiece of Renaissance architecture, designed by Brunelleschi and then decorated by Donatello, who executed the cherubs all around the cupola; also note the bronze pulpits from 1460 and the terracotta bust of San Lorenzo — also attributed to Donatello, but maybe by Desiderio da Settignano. At the left of the Sacristy's entrance is a the monument for Giovanni and Piero de' Medici, a masterpiece by Verrocchio. Michelangelo also designed the 1524 **Biblioteca Laurenziana (Laurentian Library)**, where a few of the Medicis' fabulous manuscripts are displayed and which you can reach via an elaborate stone staircase from the nice cloister on the left of the basilica facade.

See map p. 216. Piazza San Lorenzo, off Borgo San Lorenzo ☎ 055-216-634. Bus: 1, 6, 7, 10, 11 to Martelli 02. Admission: 2.50€ ($2.90). Open: Mon–Sat 10 a.m.–5 p.m.

Basilica di Santa Croce, Cappella Pazzi, and Museo dell'Opera di Santa Croce
Centro storico/Santa Croce

Santa Croce, the world's largest Franciscan church, is significant both for its architecture and for what (and whom) it contains. The basilica was begun in 1294 by Arnolfo di Cambio, the first architect of the Duomo, and is a magnificent example of Italian gothic. It boasts some Giotto frescoes, although they are not the most well preserved of his works. Within the convent compound you can also visit the 15th-century **Cappella Pazzi,** a wonderful example of early Renaissance architecture by Brunelleschi, and the Museo dell'Opera di Santa Croce which houses several art pieces taken from the church itself and the cloisters. The most noteworthy piece is a large sculpure of San Lodovico da Tolosa by Donatello from 1423, originally meant for the Orsanmichele church. Cimabue's famous *Crucifixion* is also on display, although the restoration was not able to redeem the great damages caused by the flood in 1966. In the church you'll also find the final resting places of many notable Renaissance figures — over 270 tombstones pave the floor, and monumental tombs house luminaries like Michelangelo, Galileo, Rossini, and Machiavelli. Note that Dante's tomb is really just a *cenotaph* (an empty tomb): He died in exile in Ravenna and was buried there.

See map p. 216. Piazza Santa Croce. ☎ *055-246-6105. Bus: C. Admission: 4€ ($4.60) includes admission to the Museo dell'Opera di Santa Croce. Open: Mon–Sat 9:30 a.m.–5:30 p.m., Sun and holidays 1–5:30 p.m.*

Basilica di Santa Maria Novella and Museo di Santa Maria Novella
Centro storico/Santa MariaNovella

This splendid example of Italian Gothic was built as a Dominican church between 1246 and 1360; it is decorated with frescoes by such great artists as Domenico Ghirlandaio and Filippino Lippi, but the star of the show is the *Trinità* by Masaccio, newly restored for the 600th centenary of his birth in 2001. The other star is Giotto's *Crucifix,* finally back to grace the main nave after a lengthy restoration. Adjoining the church is the entry to the museum, which occupies what was originally the cloisters annexed to the church. From here, you can access the **Green Cloister (Chiostro Verde),** named for the beautiful coloration of its frescoes (some by Paolo Uccello), and the **Cappellone degli Spagnoli,** named for Cosimo de' Medici's wife, Eleonora of Toledo (who permitted her fellow Spaniards to be buried here), and frescoed by Andrea di Buonaito between 1367 and 1369. The frescoes depict scenes from the lives of Christ and St. Peter, but the *Trionfo di San Tommaso* and the *Trionfo dei Domenicani* (the triumphs of St. Thomas and the Dominicans, respectively) are especially beautiful.

See map p. 216. Piazza Santa Maria Novella. ☎ *055-215-918. Bus: 6, 11, 36, 37, A. Admission: Basilica 2.50€ ($2.90); Museum 1.40€ ($1.60). Open: Basilica Mon–Thurs and Sat, 9:30 a.m.–5 p.m., Fri, Sun, and holidays, 1–5 p.m.; Museum Mon–Sat 9 a.m.–5 p.m., Sun and holidays 9 a.m.–2 p.m.*

Battistero di San Giovanni (Baptistry of St. John)
Centro storico/Duomo

Part of the tricolored marble trio on Piazza del Duomo (see also Duomo and Campanile di Giotto, in this section), the octagonal Baptistry is a beautiful example of the Florentine Romanesque style from the 11th and 12th centuries. It was likely built on the site of a Roman palace. The Baptistry's marvels are the exterior doors: The beautiful bronze reliefs adorning the north and east doors were the life's work of Lorenzo Ghiberti. He began the north doors in 1401 when he was 20 and finished them more than two decades later — one of the most important pieces of Renaissance sculpture, they depict Isaac's sacrifice with marvelous detail. However, the east doors, completed shortly before the artist's death, are the real stars, known as the **Gates of Paradise** (when he saw them, Michelangelo supposedly said, "These doors are fit to stand at the gates of Paradise"); the ten panels show stunning scenes from the Old Testament. The panels presently in place are copies, because the originals have been moved to the **Museo dell'Opera del Duomo** (see later in this section). The south doors were created by Andrea Pisano in the mid-14th century and show a more static Gothic style than Ghiberti's revolutionary work.

See map p. 216. Piazza San Giovanni (or Duomo) ☎ *055-230-2885. Bus: 1, 6, 7, 10, 11, A. Admission: 3€ ($3.45). Open: Mon–Sat noon–7 p.m., Sun 8:30 a.m.–2 p.m.*

Campanile di Giotto (Giotto's Bell Tower)
Centro storico/Duomo

You may ask, "Wasn't Giotto a painter and not an architect?" Yes, but shortly before the end of his life he designed this beautiful, soaring bell tower banded with pink, green, and white marble, from which you have excellent views of the city and especially of the Duomo next door. Giotto had completed only the first two levels by his death in 1337, and the replacement architect had to correct the mistakes Giotto had made — such as not making the walls thick enough to support the structure. Some of the artworks that originally graced the tower — by Donatello, Francesco Talenti, Luca della Robbia, and Andrea Pisano — are now housed in the **Museo dell'Opera del Duomo** (see later in this section), and copies take their place.

Note that there are 414 steps up to the top of this 84m (276-ft.) tower, and the last entrance is 20 minutes before closing.

See map p. 216. Piazza Duomo. ☎ *055-230-2885. Bus: A, 1, 6, 7, 10, 11. Admission: 6€ ($6.90). Open: Daily 8:30 a.m.–7:30 p.m.*

Cappelle Medicee (Medici Chapels)
Centro storico/Duomo

The octagonal **Chapel of the Princes (Cappella dei Principi)** is a gaudy baroque affair, decorated with marble and semiprecious stones and containing monumental tombs of Medici grand dukes. By contrast, the **New**

Florence Attractions

Basilica di San Lorenzo **7**
Basilica di Santa Croce, Cappella Pazzi, and Museo dell'Opera di Santa Croce **18**
Basilica and Museo di Santa Maria Novella **1**
Battistero di San Giovanni **8**
Campanile di Giotto (Giotto's Bell Tower) **11**
Chiesa and Museo di San Marco **4**
Duomo (Basilica di Santa Maria del Fiore) **9**
Galleria dell'Accademia (Accademia Gallery) **5**
Galleria degli Uffizi (Uffizi Gallery) **17**
Museo della Casa Buonarroti **14**
Museo dell'Opera del Duomo **10**
Museo Nazionale del Bargello **13**
Orsanmichele **12**
Palazzo Medici-Riccardi **6**
Palazzo Pitti and the Boboli Gardens (Giardino di Boboli) **3**
Palazzo Vecchio **16**
Piazza della Signoria **15**
Ponte Vecchio **2**

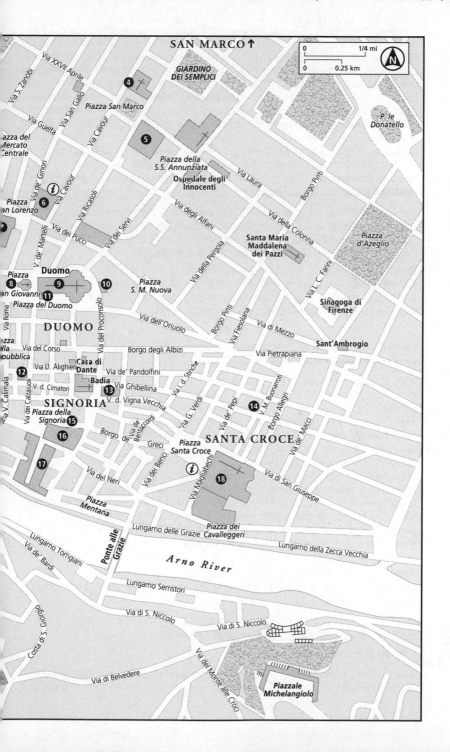

Sacristy (Sagrestia Nuova), begun by Michelangelo and finished by the artist/author Vasari, is somber and impressive. The design reflects some of the elements of the Old Sacristy inside San Lorenzo (see earlier in this section), but with bold innovations so that it became one of the founding works of the Mannerist style. Michelangelo's funerary sculptures are brilliant: the **Monumento a Lorenzo Duca d'Urbino** represents the seated duke flanked by *Aurora* (Dawn) and *Crepuscolo* (Dusk); the **Monumento a Giuliano Duca di Nemours** (the son of Lorenzo the Magnificent) is shown rising, with the figures of *Giorno* (Day) and *Notte* (Night) at his sides. In front of the sacristy's altar is Michelangelo's *Madonna and Child;* Lorenzo the Magnificent is buried under this sculpture. Because Michelangelo didn't live to complete his plan (he died in 1564), Lorenzo got a far less magnificent tomb than some of the lesser Medicis.

To the left of the altar is a small subterranean chamber containing some drawings attributed to Michelangelo; you can see them by making an appointment when you enter. The place is more a tribute to Michelangelo than to the people who bankrolled the Renaissance.

Piazza Madonna degli Aldobrandini, behind the church of San Lorenzo. ☎ *055-238-8602. Bus: 1, 6 to Martelli 02. Admission: 6€ ($6.90). Open: Tues–Sat 8:15 a.m.– 4:50 p.m., Sun and holidays 8:15 a.m.–4:45 p.m., closed second and fourth Sun of each month and open second and fourth Mon of each month.*

Chiesa and Museo di San Marco
Centro storico/Accademia

This Dominican monastery is a stop on the Grand Tour of Florence's art treasures because of the incomparable Fra' Beato Angelico, whose vividly painted, exceptionally human works are early Renaissance masterpieces. The dormitory contains his famous *Annunciation,* and the part of the structure that's now a museum contains panel paintings and altar pieces, including the *Crucifixion.* Another notable work is Ghirlandaio's *Last Supper.* The church itself is decorated with works by Fra Bartolomeo and other artists. Another former resident — actually the prior — of the monastery was the passionate reformer Girolamo Savonarola. His sermons against worldly corruption brought him into conflict with Pope Alexander VI (who had four illegitimate children, including Cesare and Lucrezia Borgia). Excommunicated and betrayed by the Florentines who at one time supported him, he was executed on Piazza della Signoria in 1498.

See map p. 216. Piazza San Marco 1. ☎ *055-238-8608. Bus: C, 1, 6, 7, 10, 11, . Admission: 6€ ($6.90). Open: Tues–Fri 8:15 a.m.–1:50 p.m., Sat 8:15 a.m.–6:50 p.m.; open second and fourth Sun 8:15 a.m.–7 p.m. and first, third, and fifth Mon 8:15 a.m.–1:50 p.m.*

Duomo (Basilica di Santa Maria del Fiore)
Centro storico/Duomo

The Duomo, surmounted by Filippo Brunelleschi's famous red-tiled dome, is the symbol of Florence. The largest in the world at the time it was built, the dome is 45m (150-ft.) wide and 104m (300-ft.) high from the drum — where previous builders had left off, unsure of how to complete the building — to the distinctive lantern at the top of the cupola. Brunelleschi's ingenious solution was constructing the dome of two layers enclosing a space inside, and having each layer become progressively thinner toward the top, thus reducing the weight. You can climb 463 spiraling steps to the top inside the space between the layers (the last ascent is 40 minutes before closing). The dome was finished in 1436, but other architects fiddled with it through the ages, and the facade was redone in neo-Gothic style hundreds of years later. As a whole, the Duomo is more impressive on the outside than on the inside, its alternating bands of white, green, and pink marble echoing the patterns on the Baptistry and Campanile. Inside are Paolo Uccello frescoes from the 1430s and 1440s, including his memorial to Sir John Hawkwood, an English mercenary hired by the Florentines (they promised him a statue but gave him a fresco of a statue instead). Restored in 1996, the frescoes inside the dome were begun by Giorgio Vasari and finished by Frederico Zuccari in 1579. The **New Sacristy** is where Lorenzo de' Medici hid out after he and his brother (who was murdered) were ambushed during Mass by some of their rivals in one of Florence's endless power struggles; its bronze doors are the work of Luca della Robbia.

Under the Duomo are the remains of **Santa Reparata,** the former Duomo, torn down in 1375 to build the new cathedral. Excavations, begun in 1966, uncovered a rich trove of material dating back over centuries, including walls of Roman houses and Roman ceramic, glass, and metalwork, as well as paleo-Christian and medieval objects (Brunelleschi's tombstone was also discovered here).

See map p. 216. Piazza Duomo. ☎ 055-230-2885. Bus: A, 1, 6, 7, 10, 11 . Admission: Cathedral free; cupola 6€ ($6.90). Open: Mon–Wed and Fri 10 a.m.–5 p.m., Thurs and first Sat of each month 10 a.m.–3:30 p.m.; other Sat 10 a.m.–4:45 p.m., Sun and holidays 1:30–4:45 p.m. Cupola: Mon–Fri 8:30 a.m.–7 p.m., Sat 8:30 a.m.–5:40 p.m., except first Sat of month, 8:30 a.m.–4 p.m.

Galleria degli Uffizi (Uffizi Gallery)
Centro storico

Occupying a Renaissance *palazzo* built by Vasari to house the administrative offices (*uffizi* means "offices") of the Tuscan Duchy, the gallery houses a mind-blowing collection of work. Here you pictorially experience the birth of the Renaissance, seeing how the changing ideas about the nature of humanity (the new humanism) were translated into visual form. Medieval artists weren't bad painters — their work reflected a holistically Christian viewpoint, with no concept of "nature" as something separate from the divine; the new humanism changes all this. You can witness the change if you start your visit with Cimabue's great *Crucifixion,* still inspired by the flat forms and ritualized expressions of Byzantine art. Follow with the work of his student Giotto, where the human figure begins to take on greater and greater realism. The work of Sandro Botticelli — with his ***Birth of Venus*** (the goddess emerging from the waves on a shell) and *Primavera* (an ambiguous allegory of spring) — show how the revival of classical (pagan) myth opened a new range of expression and subject. Across from Botticelli's *Venus,* don't miss the spectacular **triptych** of Hugo van der Goes, whose humanism emerges in the intensity of expression and powerful realism of his poor peasants (also look for the fanciful monster lurking in the right panel). Piero della Francesca's famous **diptych** with full-profile portraits of Federico da Montefeltro and his wife was painted in the third quarter of the 15th century; note how he brings his subjects to life, with luminosity and incredible detail, warts and all. You can then delight in the full explosion of the Renaissance, with Masaccio's *Madonna and Child with St. Anne,* Leonardo's *Adoration of the Magi* and *Annunciation,* several **Raphaels,** Michelangelo's *Holy Family,* Caravaggio's *Bacchus* . . . there's so much at the Uffizi that you should really come twice to absorb it all.

See map p. 216. Piazzale degli Uffizi 6, just off Piazza della Signoria. ☎ *055-238-8651 or 055-294-883 for reservations. Bus: B. Admission: 6.50€ ($7.50); reservation additional 3€ ($3.45). Open: Tues–Sun 8:15 a.m.–6:50 p.m.; Sat June15–Sept 15 8:15 a.m.–10 p.m.*

Remember to reserve your tickets for the Uffizi and the Accademia (for details, see the beginning of this section).

Galleria dell'Accademia (Accademia Gallery)
Centro storico/Accademia

The Accademia's undisputed star is Michelangelo's *David,* set on a pedestal at the heart of the museum. Lines to see him are usually huge, so make a reservation if you are keen to go in. We think it might be a better use of your time to visit the Museo del Bargello, a much richer sculpture collection (see later in this section). That is not to say that *David* isn't worth your time; it is a superb piece of art. Michelangelo was just 29 when he took a 5.1m (17-ft.) column of white Carrara marble abandoned by another sculptor and produced the masculine perfection of *Il Gigante (The Giant),* as *David* is nicknamed. The statue stands beneath a rotunda built expressly for it in 1873, when it was moved here from Piazza della Signoria (a copy stands in its place on the square). In 1991, *David* was attacked by a lunatic with a hammer, so you have to view him through a reinforced-glass shield (like the *Pietà* in Rome). The gallery's other remarkable Florentine works include, among its paintings: Perugino's *Assumption* and *Descent from the Cross* (the latter done in collaboration with Filippino Lippi); *The Virgin of the Sea,* thought to have been painted by Botticelli; and Pontormo's *Venus and Cupid. David* isn't the only Michelangelo sculpture here — his *St. Matthew* and his interesting series of *Slaves* (which are either unfinished or were poetically left partly escaped from the original hunks of stone) also illustrate the master's remarkable skills.

See map p. 216. Via Ricasoli 60, at Via Guelfa. ☎ *055-238-8609 or 055-294-883 for reservations. Bus: 1, 6, 7, 10, 11 to Via Guelfa then walk 1 block east; C to Piazza San Marco, then walk 1 block south. Admission: 6.50€ ($7.50). Open: Tues–Sun 8:15 a.m.–6:50 p.m.*

Museo dell'Opera del Duomo
Centro storico/Duomo

This museum is where you'll need to go to see the original Renaissance works, such as Ghiberti's breathtaking bronze **Gates of Paradise panels** for the Baptistry, that were removed from their settings to avoid damage from pollution or hammer-wielding maniacs. The museum also contains works that once graced Giotto's Campanile, like Donatello's highly realistic **sculpture of Habbakuk;** his *Maddalena (Mary Magdalen),* in polychromed wood, is perhaps equally striking for its tortured expression. Michelangelo is represented with a *Pietà;* Luca della Robbia's **cantoria** (choir loft) faces a similar work by Donatello, offering an example of the diversity of Renaissance styles.

See map p. 216. Piazza Duomo 9, behind the Duomo. ☎ *055-230-2885. Bus: 1, 6, 7, 10, 11, A. Admission: 6€ ($6.90). Open: Mon–Sat 9 a.m.–7:30 p.m., Sun and holidays 9 a.m.–1:40 p.m.*

Museo Nazionale del Bargello
Centro storico/Signoria

The Palazzo del Capitano del Popolo, a building dating back to 1255, is the oldest seat of Florence's government and was the official residence of the Podestà (governor) till 1502 when it became the seat of the Justice and Police Council. Hence the name *bargello,* which means "cop," and it was used to refer to the chief of police. The prisons here were used until the 19th century and it was only in 1886 that the Bargello was transformed into the sculpture museum of Florence. Now the Bargello is a treasury of Renaissance sculpture, including two *Davids* (one in marble, the other in bronze) by Donatello and several works by Michelangelo, including another *David* (it may also be Apollo), a **bust of Brutus,** and the *Bacco ebbro* he executed when he was only 22. You'll also find the bust of Cosimo I by Benvenuto Cellini, whose *Autobiography* offers a fascinating look at Florence during the Renaissance and is well worth reading. You can also compare two bronze panels of the *Sacrifice of Isaac,* one by Brunelleschi and one by Ghiberti, which were submitted in the famous contest to see who'd get to do the Baptistry doors (see "Battistero di San Giovanni," earlier in this section). The Bargello also has impressive collections of Islamic art, majolica, and terracotta works by the della Robbia family.

See map p. 216. Via del Proconsolo 4, between Via Ghibellina and Via della Vigna Vecchia. ☎ *055-238-8606 or 055-294-883 for reservations. Bus: A. Admission: 4€ ($4.60). Open: Tues–Sun 8:15 a.m.–1:50 p.m.*

Orsanmichele
Centro storico/Signoria

Born as a granary and warehouse, this building was transformad into a church in the 14th century, when it was the site of a miracle — an image of the Madonna supposedly appeared there. The new church was decorated

The Uffizi Gallery

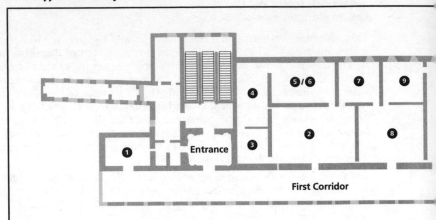

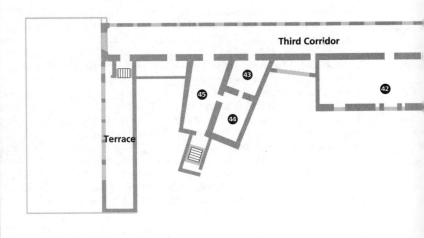

1	Archaeological Room	**15**	Leonardo da Vinci
2	Giotto & 13th-Century Paintings	**16**	Geographic Maps
3	Sienese Paintings (14th Century)	**17**	Ermafrodito
4	Florentine Paintings (14th Century)	**18**	The Tribune
5/6	International Gothic	**19**	Perugino & Signorelli
7	Early Renaissance	**20**	Dürer & German Artists
8	Filippo Lippi	**21**	Giovanni Bellini & Giorgione
9	Antonio del Pollaiolo	**22**	Flemish & German Paintings
10/14	Botticelli & Ghirlandaio	**23**	Mantegna & Correggio

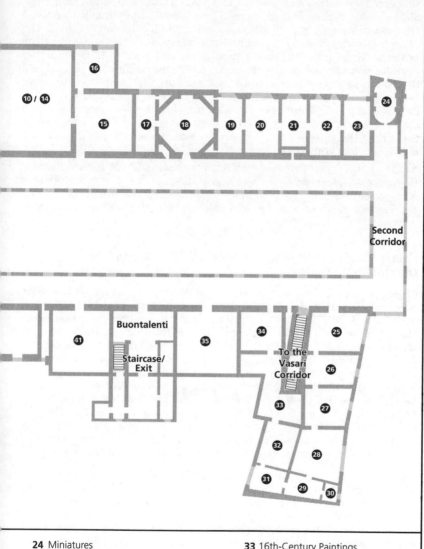

24 Miniatures
25 Michelangelo & Florentine Artists
26 Raphael & Andrea del Sarto
27 Pontormo & Rosso Fiorentino
28 Tiziano & Sebastiano del Piombo
29 Parmigianino & Dosso Dossi
30 Emilian Paintings
31 Veronese
32 Tintoretto

33 16th-Century Paintings
34 Lombard School
35 Barocci
41 Rubens & Flemish Paintings
42 Niobe
43 Caravaggio
44 Rembrandt
45 18th-Century Paintings

with original artwork from the best artists of the time, including Donatello, Ghiberti, Verrocchio, and others. Inside, you'll find vaulted Gothic arches, 500-year-old frescoes, and an encrusted 14th-century tabernacle by Andrea Orcagna protecting a 1348 *Madonna and Child* by Bernardo Daddi. The church is connected by a second-floor walkway to the *palazzo* of the powerful wool (in Italian "*lana*") merchants guild, built in 1308. From that corridor you can access the museum; you'll enter either the second and third floors of Orsanmichele, which holds the original sculptures that have been replaced with copies. All of the sculptures outside are scheduled to be replaced with copies to be protected from further weather damage, and displayed in the museum, but the process has not been completed yet. At press time, the museum was temporarily closed; ask at the tourist office if it is open when you arrive.

See map p. 216. Via Arte della Lana, off Via Orsanmichele. ☎ *055-284-944. Bus: A to Orsanmichele. Admission: Free. Open: At press time it is closed for restorations but is scheduled to re-open at the following hours: Mon–Fri 9 a.m. to noon and 4–6 p.m., Sat, Sun, and holidays 9 a.m.–1 p.m. and 4–6 p.m.; closed the first and last Mon of each month.*

Palazzo Pitti and the Giardino di Boboli (Boboli Gardens)
Oltrarno/Santo Spirito

Begun in 1458 by the textile merchant/banker Luca Pitti, this golden *palazzo* was finished by the Medicis in 1549 (they tripled its size and added the Boboli Gardens). It houses a superb painting collection in the **Galleria Palatina (Palatine Gallery).** Some of the greatest works are a collection of Raphaels, including his *Madonna of the Chair* and the famous *La Fornarina* (modeled on the features of his Roman mistress). It also has what is perhaps the largest single collection of works by moody psychological painter Andrea del Sarto; and several famous portraits by Titian, Veronese, and Tintoretto. Well worth a visit are the **Royal Apartments (Appartamenti Reali),** where three dynasties have resided (Medici, Lorena, and finally Savoy), now adorned with furnishings and rich decorations from Renaissance to Rinascimento. Note that in February and March the Royal apartments are visible only by reservation.

On the first floor and the mezzanine of the *palazzo* is the **Museo degli Argenti (Silver Museum)** — a collection of objects in precious metals, ivory, and crystal (notable are the semiprecious stone vases of Lorenzo de' Medici and the cameos and carved precious stones of the Medici collection). Beautiful also are the frescoes and decorations of the rooms and halls housing the collection. Also worth visiting is the **Galleria d'Arte Moderna (Modern Art Gallery),** with a collection of Italian paintings from the 1800s and early 1900s, including some famous paintings of the movement of the Macchiaioli (the Italian counterpart to the French Impressionists; notably the paintings of Giovanni Fattori and Telemaco Signorini). The *palazzo* also houses the **Galleria del Costume** (historical clothing collection).

Behind the palace is one of the most grandiose examples of an Italian garden, the **Boboli Gardens.** This expanse of 45,000 sq. m (11.1 acres) of gardens was designed in the 16th century and expanded in the 18th and 19th centuries.

Among the highlights are several fountains and sculptures, such as the 17th-century **Fontana del Carciofo (Artichoke Fountain)** and the **Piazzale dell'Isolotto** off the Viottolone (large lane) lined with laurels, cypresses, and pines and punctuated by statues. On the *piazzale* (a small piazza) is the beautiful **Fontana dell'Oceano (Ocean Fountain).** Beautiful also the **Palazzina della Meridiana,** an 18th-century neoclassical pavilion. In the elegant **Casino del Cavaliere** — built in the 17th century as a retreat for the Granduca and dominating the whole park from the top of the hill — is the **Museo delle Porcellane (Porcelain Museum),** a collection of precious porcelain by great European makers, including Sèvres, Chantilly, and Meissen, as they were used at the tables of the three reigning families that resided in the palace.

See map p. 216. Piazza de' Pitti, just steps from the Ponte Vecchio. ☎ *055-238-8614 or 055-294-883 for reservations. Bus: D. Admission: Galleria Palatina and Appartamenti Reali 6.50€ ($7.50); Galleria d'Arte Moderna 5€ ($5.75) admission includes Galleria del Costume; Giardino di Boboli 4€ ($4.60), admission includes Museo delle Porcellane and Museo degli Argenti. Cumulative ticket for the all of the above 10.50€ ($12). Open: Galleria Palatina and Apartamenti Reali Tues–Sun 8:15 a.m.–6:50 p.m. Feb–Mar Appartamenti Reali open only by reservation. Galleria d'Arte Moderna and Galleria del Costume Tues–Sat 8:15 a.m.–1:50 p.m also open second and fourth Mon and first, third, and fifth Sun of each month. Museo degli Argenti and Museo delle Porcellane Nov–Feb Tues–Sat 8:15 a.m.–4:30 p.m., Mar 8:15 a.m.–5:30 p.m., Apr–May and Sept–Oct 8:15 a.m.–6:30 p.m., June–Aug 8:15 a.m.–7:30 p.m., open second and fourth Mon and first, third, and fifth Sun of each month. Giardino di Boboli daily 8:15 a.m. to one hour before sunset, closed first and last Mon each month.*

Palazzo Vecchio
Centro storico/Signoria

The Palazzo Vecchio (Old Palace) looks either like a fortress disguised as a palace or a palace trying to be a fort. It's actually a little bit of both, built as the town hall from 1299 to 1302. Cosimo de' Medici (that's Giambologna's equestrian statue of him in the middle of the piazza; see "Piazza della Signoria," below) and his family made changes to the *palazzo* in the mid-16th century. The highlight of the interior is the **Hall of the 500 (Sala dei Cinquecento),** where the 500-man council met when Florence was still a republic and before the Medicis' despotic rule. The frescoes by Vasari and others are nothing to write home about, yet those planned by Michelangelo but never painted would've been; note Michelangelo's *Genius of Victory* statue. Bronzino's **paintings in the private chapel of Eleanora di Toledo** (wife of Cosimo), Donatello's *Judith and Holofernes,* and Ghirlandaio's fresco of *St. Zenobius Enthroned* are other notable works. Some of the collections are open only at certain times (mainly in summer), such as the collection of musical instruments. In summer, you can view the city from the balustrade and hope for a breath of wind.

See map p. 216. Piazza della Signoria, behind the Uffizi. ☎ *055-276-8465. Bus: B. Admission: 6€ ($6.90). Open: Fri–Wed 9 a.m.–7 p.m., Thurs 9 a.m.–2 p.m.*

Piazza della Signoria
Centro storico/Signoria

Florence's most famous square was built in the 13th and 14th centuries. Signoria is the name of the political system that governed the city at the time — the Medicis were the *signori* (lords) — and this was the political heart of Florence. A beautiful example of medieval architecture, the L-shaped square is flanked by the **Palazzo Vecchio** (see listing, above) on the east side and the famous **Loggia della Signoria** on the south. The loggia is also called the Loggia dei Lanzi (after the *Lanzichenecchi,* soldiers who camped there in the 16th century) or the Loggia dell'Orcagna (after a belief it was built by Andrea di Cione, who was known as Orcagna). In fact, this Gothic structure was built from 1376 to 1382 by Benci Cione and Simone Talenti for political ceremonies. Later it was used as a sculpture workshop and is still used as a showplace for statues. The most famous piece here is Giambologna's ***Ratto delle Sabine (Rape of the Sabines),*** an essay in three-dimensional Mannerism; also by Giambologna are the **bronze of Duke Cosimo de' Medici on horseback** and *Hercules with Nessus the Centaur.* Also here is Benvenuto Cellini's famous *Perseus* holding up the severed head of Medusa (the original was moved to the Uffizi in 1996 and replaced with a copy, but the original was replaced here in late 2000).

The **Fountain of Neptune (Fontana del Nettuno)**, at the corner of the Palazzo Vecchio, was built by the architect Ammannati in 1575 and criticized by many, including Michelangelo; Florentines used to mock it as Il Biancone ("big whitey"). The small disk in the ground near the fountain marks the spot where the famous Dominican monk Savonarola was executed. His efforts to purify the Florentines and rid the church of corruption (he directed the burning of jewels, books, riches, and art pieces judged too "pagan" on pyres erected in Piazza della Signoria) gave him increased political power but also led to his excommunication from the church. He was condemned as a heretic and burned on the square in 1498.

The *David* that you can see in the square is a copy of the original statue by Michelangelo, which was moved to the Accademia in the 19th century. The statue flanking it is *Ercole* **(Heracles)** by Baccio Bandinelli.

See map p. 216. Off Via dei Calzaiuoli. Bus: B.

Ponte Vecchio
Centro storico

The Ponte Vecchio (Old Bridge) is the only remaining original of Florence's many lovely medieval bridges spanning the Arno — the Germans blew the rest of them up during their retreat from Italy near the end of the World War II (they've since been rebuilt). This symbol of the city of Florence offers beautiful views and thrives with shops selling leather goods, jewelry, and other commodities. If you look up, you'll see the famous **Vasari Corridor (Corridoio Vasariano)**. The bridge was built in 1345, but after the completion of the Palazzo Pitti in the 16th century, Cosimo de' Medici commissioned Vasari to build an aboveground "tunnel" running along the Ponte Vecchio rooftops linking the Uffizi with the Pitti. The corridor was richly decorated with art, and you can visit it from the Uffizi at certain times.

See map p. 216. At the end of Via Por Santa Maria. Bus: B.

Santo Spirito
Oltrarno/Santo Spirito

Behind its 18th-century facade you'll find an architectural jewel designed by Filippo Brunelleschi. The church was built between 1444 and 1488 and is divided in three naves separated by elegant arches; the sacristy was designed by Sangallo. Among the paintings inside is a beautiful *Madonna col Bambino e santi* by Filippino Lippi. The handsome bell tower on the left of the facade was designed by Baccio d'Agnolo and dates from 1503.

Piazza Santo Spirito. ☎ *055-210-030. Admission: Free. Open: Mon–Tues and Thurs–Fri 10 a.m.–noon and 4–5:30 p.m., Wed 10 a.m.–noon, Sat–Sun 4–5:30 p.m.*

Finding more cool things to see and do

After you've exhausted all the "musts" on your list, here are a few more worthwhile sights and activities:

✔ The **Museo della Casa Buonarroti** (Via Ghibellina 70; ☎ 055-241-752; Bus: A. Admission. 6.50€/$7.50. Open: Wed–Mon 9:30 a.m.–2 p.m.) may never have had Michelangelo as a tenant, but he and his heirs did own it. His grand-nephew got the homage going early by turning the house into a museum. Some of the holdings are very interesting; they include some of the master's earliest works, such as the *Madonna of the Steps,* which he did when only in his mid-teens.

✔ The **Palazzo Medici Riccardi** (Via Cavour 3; ☎ 055-276-0340; Bus: 1, 6, 7, 10, 11. Open: Thurs–Tues 9 a.m.–7 p.m. Admission: 4€/$4.60) is where Cosimo de' Medici and his family lived before they took over the Palazzo Vecchio. It was built by Michelozzo in 1444 and has a less-heavy feeling than later *palazzi,* such as the Pitti. Benozzo Gozzoli, a student of Fra Angelico's, decorated the chapel — **Cappella dei Magi** — with marvelous frescoes. The *palazzo* gives a good idea of what upper-class Florentine life was like during the Renaissance.

✔ If you are in Florence from the end of April to June, you will have to work hard to miss the **Maggio Musicale Fiorentino** (see "Living it Up After Dark," later in this chapter). Around this celebrated music festival, the city organizes a variety of other events, including special exhibits in museums, street performances, musical events in bars, pubs, and boutiques, and even a golf tournament! A prize is awarded for the best shop window decorations following the Maggio Fiorentino theme. Keep your eyes open and ask your hotel and the tourist office about specific events; a special brochure is published and distributed for the occasion.

✔ The little town of **Fiesole,** just 4.5km (3 miles) north of Florence, makes a wonderful excursion. Probably one of the nicest bus rides you'll ever take is the one through the green fields and past the villas lining the route to this hill town (take the no. 7 from SMN train station or Piazza San Marco and get off at the last stop). Fiesole existed well before Florence — it started as an Etruscan settlement in the sixth century B.C. and retains the character of a small town and its independence as a municipality. In the summer the town hosts music, theater, and other cultural events, making it a great place to escape the heat and congestion below. Be sure to visit the **Duomo (Cattedrale di San Romolo)** on the main square, Piazza Mino da Fiesole, which was built in 1028. Also definitely worth a visit is the archaeological area, which includes Roman and Etruscan remains (**Teatro Romano e Museo Civico,** Via Partigiani 1; ☎ **055-59-477;** Open: winter Wed–Mon 9:30 a.m.–5 p.m., summer daily 9:30 a.m.–7 p.m.). The theater, built in the first century B.C., is the site of outdoor concerts in the summer. Among the other sights in Fiesole are the **Museo Bandini** near the Duomo, with its 13th- to 15th-century Tuscan art. The combination ticket *Biglietto Fiesole Musei,* includes roundtrip bus fare from Florence and admission to the archaeological area with the Roman theater, the archeological museum, the Museo Bandini, and the Cappella San Jacopo — all for 7.20€ ($8.30). The *biglietto* is sold at the ATAF booth at the SMN train station and in bars and newsstands displaying a sticker advertising it.

✔ On a hill in the southeast part of Florence is the beautiful church of **San Miniato al Monte** (Via Monte alle Croci; ☎ **055-234-2731;** Admission: free; Open: summer Mon–Sat 8 a.m.–7:30 p.m., Sun and holidays 3–7:30 p.m.; winter Mon–Sat 8 a.m.–noon and 3–6 p.m., Sun and holidays 3–6 p.m.) set on a square that affords a superb view over the city. A masterpiece of Romanesque Florentine architecture, it was built between 1018 and 1207, in green and white marble. The elegant interior divided in three naves is graced by a beautiful marble inlay floor. The *cappella del Crocifisso,* at the end of the central nave is decorated by Michelozzo (1448) and has a majolica ceiling by Luca della Robbia. Also noteworthy are the marble gate and pulpit in the **presbytery** (sculpted in 1207), the **crypt** of the 11th century — with frescoes executed by Taddeo Gaddi in 1341, and the round ceiling decorations also by della Robbia in the **cappella del Cardinale del Portogallo.** The easiest way to reach the church is by bus: lines 12 and 13 from the SMN train station will bring you there.

Seeing Florence by guided tour

Walking tours with professional guides arranged through the tourist office (see "Finding more information after you arrive," earlier in this chapter) are extremely well organized and a great way to explore Florence's pedestrian-only historic center and its museums and churches.

If you contact the **Ufficio Guide Turistiche** (Viale Gramsci 9a; ☎ 055-247-8188), you can organize a guided tour tailored to your specific needs or even arrange for a private tour.

If you want to participate in a **bus tour**, the best is the **Florence Citysightseeing** "hop on and off" organized by ATAF, the city bus company (☎ 800-424-500). For 20€ ($23) adults and 10€ ($11) children 5 to 15 you can hop on and off two bus itineraries for 24 hours. **Linea A** departs the SMN railroad station every 30 minutes (winter 9 a.m.–7 p.m., summer till 11 p.m.) and tours the *centro storico* making 15 stops. **Linea B** runs every 60 minutes (winter 9 a.m.–6 p.m., summer till 10 p.m.) between Porta San Frediano in Oltrarno all the way to Fiesole, making 23 stops.

Following 1-, 2-, and 3 days itineraries

You could easily spend a week in Florence and not tire of it. For most, however, a visit to Florence is part of a larger tour of Italy. The following itineraries are designed to help you figure out how to get the most out of your time here.

Florence in 1 day

If you only have one day in Florence, you'll have to do some homework before getting there, and make your reservations to the Uffizi and the Bargello (if you decided to visit it) ahead of time. Start your day at the **Duomo,** enjoying the sight of the cathedral and of **Giotto's Bell Tower,** but visit only the **Baptistry,** since you are short of time. Proceed then down Via dei Calzaiuoli, stopping on your way at the **Coronas Cafe** for a gelato or a cappuccino (see the sidebar "Looking for a gelato break?" earlier in this chapter). Walk across **Piazza della Signoria** to the **Uffizi** and get your tickets for the gallery and for the Bargello. Then take a deep breath and plunge in — the Uffizi is one of the most important museums of the world! After your visit, you'll be ready for lunch. Try **Hosteria Da Ganino** nearby (see "Dining Out," earlier in this chapter). After lunch, walk to the **Bargello** for your dose of sculpture: The collection here is much richer than at the Accademia and you don't need to crane your neck over somebody's shoulder to have a glimpse at Michelangelo's work — *and* you can also take in some Donatello works in the bargain. Once you are done, head for **Ponte Vecchio** on Via Por Santa Maria, and cross over to **Oltrarno.** Check in some of the shops on your way, such as **C.O.I.** for gold, and **Cirri** for their embroidered linen, **Madova Gloves** for, well, gloves, and **Giulio Giannini & Figlio** for marbleized paper (see "Shopping the Local Stores," later in this chapter). After a nice stroll along the Arno, it is now time for *aperitivo,* and what best to sample than the Florentine invention *Negroni?* Try it at the **Negroni Florence Bar** (see "Bars and pubs," later in this chapter). For dinner, take the D bus to Santo Spirito or Piazza del Carmine (a few blocks away, but your feet must hurt by now) for dinner at **Il Cantinone** for regular Tuscan, at **Ricchi** for fish, or at **Cavolo Nero,** for more inventive Tuscan fare with an accent on veggies.

Florence in 2 days

Again, you'll need to do your homework and reserve tickets in advance for the Uffizi, the Bargello, and/or the Accademia. On **day 1**, check into your hotel, and then head for the **Uffizi**, where you'll pick up all the tickets you have reserved and visit the Gallery. After your visit, you'll be ready for lunch. Try **Le Mossacce**, or **Hosteria Da Ganino** nearby (see "Dining Out," earlier in this chapter). After lunch, walk across **Piazza della Signoria** and towards **Ponte Vecchio.** Follow our recommendations in "Florence in 1 day," above, for some leisurely shopping, only take in also the open air **Mercato della Paglia** before crossing over to Oltrarno. If you are not a shopping maven, visit the **Giardino di Boboli** instead, before your *aperitivo* and dinner (see "Florence in 1 day," for restaurant recommendations).

On **day 2**, start with the **Duomo, Giotto's Bell Tower,** the **Baptistry,** and the **Museo dell'Opera del Duomo.** Then have lunch in the other of the two restaurants we recommended for day 1. After lunch, walk to the **Bargello** or take bus 1, 6 or 11 to the **Accademia.** After your visit, stroll to Piazza Santissima Annunziata for a peek at one of Florence's nicest squares and stop for a gelato at **Carabé** (see the sidebar "Looking for a gelato break?" earlier in this chapter). Then, walk — or take bus 1,6,7,10, or 11 — to the **Basilica of San Lorenzo** or to the **Basilica di Santa Maria Novella,** and visit one of these beautiful churches and their cloisters. Alternatively, stroll through the **Mercato San Lorenzo** for some shopping. For *aperitivo* have your *Negroni* at the cafe that invented it, **Giacosa** (see "Bars and pubs," later in this chapter). For dinner, treat yourself at Buca Mario or Cantinetta Antinori, or take a taxi to the best restaurant in Florence, **Cibreo** (see "Dining Out," earlier in this chapter).

Florence in 3 days

Follow day 1 and 2 as in "Florence in 2 days." On **day 3** head for the **Basilica Santa Croce,** the **Cappella Pazzi,** and the **Museo dell'Opera di Santa Croce.** Once you are done with the visit, don't forget to have a look at the leather goods of the **Scuola del Cuoio di Santa Croce** (see "Shopping the Local Stores," below). Have lunch at **Cibreo** (see "Dining Out," earlier in this chapter). In the afternoon, visit one or two of the alternative attractions you didn't have time to see in the previous days: the **Giardino di Boboli,** the **Bargello,** the **Accademia,** the **Basilica of San Lorenzo** or the **Basilica di Santa Maria Novella.** For dinner, take your pick from the restaurants we recommend earlier in this chapter, or return to one you particularly liked.

Shopping the Local Stores

With a long tradition in crafts, Florence offers some very nice specialty products, such as leather, fine woven straw, jewelry, embroidered linens and lace, and fine paper products. It is also a center for casual fashion.

Many of these goodies are still available at the historic outdoor markets, which are fun to go to even if you don't intend to buy anything.

 Remember that all crowded areas, including the outdoor markets we recommend, are the preferred hunting ground for pickpockets and purse-snatchers. Don't display your money too liberally and keep an eye on your pockets and purse — otherwise your shopping spree will be very short indeed.

The outdoor markets of Florence

There are two famous markets in Florence: **San Lorenzo** (Piazza del Mercato Centrale, one block north of the Basilica of San Lorenzo) and the **Mercato della Paglia** (Straw Market, Via Por Santa Maria, off Ponte Vecchio); both markets are open daily in the summer, and Tuesday through Saturday in the winter. San Lorenzo is the leather market, and if you look hard and sharp you can find some good items — although Alessandra has always found the fashion style in Florence a little trashy, but then again she is from Rome. Good buys can be had but don't expect to find the greatest leather jacket on earth and pay peanuts for it. San Lorenzo is also a good place to shop for T-shirts and small gifts. San Lorenzo's food market is held every morning in the market building and is great, offering a large variety of produce, cheeses, cured meats, and breads in a lively atmosphere — it is an excellent place to pick up some picnic fixings. The Straw Market traditionally sold straw goods (hats, chairs, bags) of unique quality, but real craftmanship is today hard to find, but still present. If you are careful you will be able to find some great gifts among all the cheap trinkets and tourist souvenirs.

If you keep in mind a few simple shopping rules, these lively historic markets can be great fun and you can make some great buys:

✔ **Don't expect quality items to be cheap.** A good leather jacket will cost a few hundred dollars, whether at a market or at a proper store, but you should be able to get a level of quality that would be difficult to find back home, especially at that price.

✔ **Light bargaining is allowed in outdoor markets**, but don't expect to cut a quoted price in half. If the vendor does, the quality might not be what you think.

✔ **If you are out to buy an expensive item,** try to have a fair idea in your mind of what things are worth as well as what you can afford to pay for them. If you aren't an expert on the items you want to buy, shop around and find out as much as you can before making your decision.

The bottom line? Have fun and remember that there are no free rides. Buy an item if you really like it for what sounds to you a fair price, without worrying too much about getting the best bargain in the world — being happy with what you bought matters more than saving $20.

Retail shops are generally open Monday through Saturday from 10 a.m. to 1:30 p.m. and 4 to 8 p.m. and closed on Monday mornings; open-air markets are usually open during lunchtime but close earlier in the evening. As in all other Italian cities, many shops shut down for the month of August but department stores don't and are sometimes open during the lunch recess. Some stores are starting to open on Sundays.

Best shopping areas

For elegant shopping, the place to go is **Via de' Tornabuoni** in the *centro storico* near Santa Maria Novella (between Piazzetta degli Antinori and Piazza di Santa Trinità). This street is at the heart of the elegant shopping district which includes **Via Strozzi** and **Via della Vigna Nuova** (both off Via de' Tornabuoni; you'll find all the big names of Italian fashion here, such as **Ferragamo** (Via Tornabuoni 16), **Loro Piano** (Via della Vigna Nuova 37r), and **Giorgio Armani** (Via della Vigna Nuova 51r), and a choice of reliable but expensive boutiques. Other elegant stores line the **Lungarno Corsini** (take a left from Via della Vigna Nuova and continue along the river); here you'll find the luxury linen shop **Pratesi** (see later in this section), and other nice smaller shops. This shopping district extends east, all the way to **Via Roma, Piazza della Repubblica, Via del Corso, Via dei Calzaiuoli,** and **Via Calimala** off the Ponte Vecchio. Here you'll find lots of real-life stores, including the Italian style department stores (mostly clothes and house goods) **La Rinascente** (Piazza della Repubblica 1; ☎ 055-219-113) and **COIN** (Via dei Calzaiuoli 56r; ☎ 055-280-531).

What to look for and where to find it

Embroidery and Linens

Cirri (Via Por Santa Maria. ☎ 055-239-6593; Bus: B to Ponte Vecchio) is a good place for Florentine embroideries, but they don't come cheap.

Pratesi (Lungarno Corsini 32–34r. ☎ 055-211-327; Bus: D; www.pratesi. com) is the place to go for beautifully crafted luxury linens of all kinds.

Gold

C.O.I. (Via Por Santa Maria 8r, second floor; ☎ 055-283-970; Bus: B) is one of the reputable jewelry stores in town, with a very large selection organized by type — bunches of bracelets, drawers of earrings, and so on. Go with a precise idea in mind; this isn't the place for browsing. The staff is overworked, and the shop is always crowded.

Housewares and accessories

Controluce (Via della Vigna Nuova 89r; ☎ 055-239-8871; Bus: 6, 11, 36, or 37 to Tornabuoni) has a beautiful assortment of designer lamps and accessories.

Emporium (Via Guicciardini 122r; ☎ 055-212-646; Bus: D to Pitti) is good for a variety of stylish accessories.

Ponte Vecchio's gold

It is commonly assumed that Ponte Vecchio is the place to go for gold jewelry: Indeed, in that area, you will find one jewelry shop after the next, but all with pretty much the same merchandise. The prices are no longer great and it's difficult to find something original — maybe after 500 years and a trillion tourists, the street has gotten a tad stale.

Viceversa (Via Ricasoli 53r; ☎ **055-239-8281**; Bus: C, 6 to Santissima Annunziata) is a great place for browsing and also for some neat gift ideas.

Leather products

Beltrami (Via de' Tornabuoni 48r; ☎ **055-287-779**; Bus 6, 11, 36, or 37 to Tornabuoni) is the place to go for beautiful leather accessories, including shoes, bags, and luggage.

Beltrami outlet (Via de' Panzani 1, near the church of Santa Maria Novella; ☎ **055-212-661**; Bus: A, 1, 6, 11, 36, 37 to SMN) offers last season's inventory at a discount.

Madova Gloves (Via Guicciardini 1r; ☎ **055-239-6526**; www.madova.com; Bus: D to Pitti), is the place for gloves; this is actually a traditional glove maker's workshop.

Scuola del Cuoio di Santa Croce (Santa Croce's leather school) (Piazza Santa Croce, enter from the church's right transept; ☎ **055-244-533**; www.leatherschool.it; Bus: A to Piazza Santa Croce) is the place to go if you want to learn about the ancient art of leather embossing; the beautifully crafted goods don't come cheap though.

Stationery and paper goods

Giulio Giannini & Figlio (Piazza Pitti 37r; ☎ **055-212-621**; Bus: D to Pitti), is an historical paper provider that has specialized in marbleized goods since the 19th century. You'll find an excellent choice of stationery here.

Pineider (Piazza della Signoria 13r; ☎ **055-284-655**; Bus: B. Also in Via de' Tornabuoni 76; ☎ **055-211-605**; Bus: 6, 11, 36, or 37), opened in 1774, has been a purveyor of paper to many crowned heads.

Living It Up After Dark

As is true in the rest of Italy, the most common version of nightlife in Florence is hanging out in a pub with a group of friends, going for a drink in a trendy bar, or taking a stroll and enjoying some gelato in the historic center. The other preferred activity is listening to some music in a club or (mainly for the younger crowds) dancing in one of the popular discos out of town.

The performing arts

During the month of May, Florence blossoms with music. It's the month of the **Maggio Musicale Fiorentino,** which is Italy's oldest music festival (☎ **800-112-211** or 055-213-535; Fax: 055-277-9410; reservations accepted starting in Sept). Tickets are sold online, too (www.maggiofiorentino. com), and cost 20€ to 155€ ($23–$178). Continuing until the end of June, this concert and dance series includes famous performers and world premiers. The final concert is held in the Giardino di Boboli and is a magical experience. At the core of the event is the **Teatro Comunale** (Corso Italia 16; ☎ **055-213-535;** Tues–Fri 10 a.m.–4:30 p.m. and Sat 10 a.m.–1 p.m.), which also has a regular program of ballet and opera at other times of the year.

Many churches present **evening concerts,** especially in the fall. The easiest way to find out about these performances is to check the church's posters for announcements and pick up a free copy of the listing of events at the Via Cavour tourist office (see "Where to get information after you arrive," earlier in this chapter). The most sought-after are the concerts of the **Florentine Chamber Orchestra** (☎ **055-783-374;** www. orcafi.it) in the Orsanmichele church. The season runs March through October and tickets are available at the box office (Via Luigi Alamanni 39, by Fortezza de Basso; ☎ **055-210-804)** or online at www. boxol.it.

The **Teatro Verdi** (Via Ghibellina 99; ☎ **055-212-320)** is a smaller theater that offers mainly dance and classical music performances.

Bars and pubs

The oldest *caffè* in town is **Gilli** (Piazza della Repubblica 39r/Via Roma 1r; ☎ **055-213-896;** Bus: A to Orsanmichele), which dates back to the 18th century. Not only is it in a great location, but it has an elegant decor. **Giacosa** (Via de' Tornabuoni 83r; ☎ **055-239-6226;** Bus: 6, 11, 36, or 37 to Tornabuoni; closed on Sun) is known for its drinks, particularly the Negroni (the ancestor of Italian *aperitivo,* the bittersweet pre-lunch or pre-dinner drink), which apparently was invented here by Mr. Negroni and his barman. Named in honor of that drink, the **Negroni Florence Bar** (Via de'Renai 17r, off Ponte delle Grazie in Oltrarno; ☎ **055-243-647)** becomes a lively spot in the evening with music almost every night (open 8 a.m.–2 a.m.).

Also hot with the elegant crowds are the restaurants and bars of many hotels in the city, such as the **Savoy** (Piazza della Repubblica 7; ☎ **055-27-351),** the **Lungarno** (Borgo San Jacopo 14r; ☎ **055-27-261),** and the **Fusion Bar** (Gallery Hotel, Vicolo dell'Oro 5; ☎ **055-27-263).** Florence has been swept up in the Italian passion for Irish pubs. The beer is original but the atmosphere a little less so. Try the **Fiddler's Elbow** (Piazza Santa Maria Novella 7r; ☎ **055-215-056**; Bus: A, 1, 6, 11, 36, 37), a very successful branch of the Italian chain, or the **Dublin Pub** (Via Faenza 27r; ☎ **055-293-049**; Bus: A to Orsanmichele).

Discos

The latest fad seems still to be the disco **Universale** (Via Pisana 77r, Oltrarno, between Via di Monte Oliveto and Viale B. Gozzoli; ☎ **055-221-122**; www.universalefirenze.it; Bus: 6). It's open September through May only, Thursday through Sunday. Admission is 11€ to 18€ ($13–$21), depending on the evening. Another hotspot is **Jaragua** (Via Erta Canina 12r, Oltrarno, off Viale Michelangiolo; ☎ **055-234-3600**), a disco and tropical bar with plenty of Caribbean and Latin music — a genre that has been going strong in Italy over the past few years — with free dance classes and more. Jaragua is open daily 9:30 p.m. to 3 a.m.; admission is free.

Gay and lesbian bars

Tabasco (Piazza Santa Cecilia 3r, by Piazza della Signoria. ☎ **055-213-000**; Bus: B) is Florence's — and Italy's — oldest gay dance club, near Piazza della Signoria, housed in a 15th-century building. The crowd is mostly men in their 20s and 30s. The dance floor is downstairs, while a small video room and piano bar are up top. There are occasional cabaret shows and karaoke. It's open Tuesday through Saturday 10 p.m. to 3 a.m.; cover charge is 8€ to 16€ ($9.20–$18). Tabasco owns two other venues in town: **Silver Stud** (Via della Fornace 9; ☎ **055-688-466**) a cruising bar, and **Florence Baths** (Via Guelfa 93r; ☎ **055-216-050**) a gay club sauna.

In summer at **Discoteca Flamingo** (Via del Pandolfini 26r, near Piazza Santa Croce; ☎ **055-243-356**; Bus: A), the crowd is international. Thursday through Saturday it's a mixed gay/lesbian party; the rest of the week, it's men only. It's open Sunday through Thursday 10 p.m. to 4 a.m. and Friday and Saturday 10 p.m. to 6 a.m. The bar is open year-round; the disco open only September through June. Cover, including the first drink, is 6.20€ ($7.15) Sunday through Thursday and 7.75€ to 10.33€ ($8.90–$12) Friday and Saturday.

Fast Facts: Florence

American Express

The main office is at Via Dante Alighieri 22R (☎ 055-50-981; Bus: A to Condotta), open Monday through Friday 9 a.m. to 5:30 p.m. and Saturday 9 a.m. to 12:30 p.m.

Area Code

The country code for Italy is 39. The area code for Florence is 055; use this code when calling from anywhere outside or inside Italy, even within Florence itself (include the 0 every time, even when calling from abroad).

ATMs

Numerous banks and exchange offices are located along Via dei Calzaiuoli, between the Duomo and the Palazzo Vecchio.

Doctors

Call your consulate or the American Express office for a current list of English-speaking doctors and dentists. The Tourist Medical Service (Via Lorenzo il Magnifico 59; ☎ 055-475-411) is open 24 hours and can be reached by buses 8 and 80 (to Lavagnini) or bus 12 (to Poliziano).

Embassies and Consulates

United States: Lungarno Amerigo Vespucci, 38 (☎ 055-239-8279 or 055-7283-780; Bus: 12 to Palestro), near the intersection with Via Palestro. United Kingdom: Lungarno Corsini, 2 (☎ 055-284-123 or 055-289-556; Bus: 11, 36, or 37 to Lungarno Corsini). For citizens of Canada, Ireland, Australia, and New Zealand, see Chapter 12 for the addresses of embassies and consulates in the capital.

Emergencies

Ambulance, ☎ 118 or 055-212-222; Polizia ☎ 113; Carabinieri ☎ 112; Fire, ☎ 115.

Hospitals

The Ospedale di Santa Maria Nuova (Piazza Santa Maria Nuova; ☎ 055-27-581) is just a block northeast from the Duomo. Pronto Soccorso (first aid) Careggi is in Viale Morgagni 85 (☎ 055-427-7247).

Information

See "Finding information after you arrive," earlier in this chapter.

Internet Access

The Internet Train chain has several locations, the most convenient being Via Guelfa 24a, near the train station (☎ 055-214-794); Via dell'Oriuolo 40r, near the Duomo (☎ 055-263-8968); and Borgo San Jacopo 30r, near the Ponte Vecchio (☎ 055-265-7935). EasyEveryThing has a shop near the Duomo in Via Martelli 22 (open daily 9 a.m.–8 p.m.; no phone).

Maps

Any newsstand will have a good selection of local maps, especially those near the train station.

Pharmacies

There are many pharmacies in Florence, but the Farmacia Molteni (Via Calzaiuoli 7r; ☎ 055-215-472; Bus: A to Orsanmichele) is open 24 hours, as is the Farmacia Communale, inside the Santa Maria Novella train station (☎ 055-216-761).

Police

There are two police forces in Italy; call either one. For the Polizia, call ☎ 113; for the Carabinieri, call ☎ 112.

Post Office

The main post office is the Ufficio Postale in Via Pellicceria 3, just off Piazza della Repubblica (open Mon–Fri 9 a.m.–6 p.m. and Sat 9 a.m.–2 p.m.).

Restrooms

As elsewhere in Italy, public restrooms aren't plentiful and are often closed. Your best bet is to go to a cafe; better yet, because Florence is full of museums, use one while you're inside. Department stores are also a good bet, such as the Rinascente in Piazza della Repubblica.

Safety

Florence is quite safe; your only major worries are pickpockets and purse snatchers because of the huge concentration of tourists. Avoid deserted areas after dark (such as behind the train station and the Cascine Park) and exercise normal urban caution.

Smoking

Smoking is allowed in *caffès* and restaurants and is very common. Unfortunately for nonsmokers, it's difficult to find a restaurant with a separate no-smoking area, but it's slowly getting better.

Taxes

See Chapter 5 for detailed information on IVA (value-added tax).

Taxi

For radio taxi, call ☎ 055-4390, 055-4798, or 055-4242, or 055-4499.

Transit/Tourist Assistance

For air travel, call the airport at ☎ 055-373-498 or ☎ 050-500-707. For buses, call SITA (☎ 800-373-760); for trains call ☎ 848-888-088.

Weather Updates

For forecasts, the best bet is to look at the news on TV (there's no phone number to get weather forecasts). On the Web, you can check `http://meteo.tiscali.it`.

Web Sites

The city maintains a useful site at `www.comune.firenze.it`. Much of it, however, is in Italian. At `www.florence.ala.it`, most of the places listed are ranked — hotels by luxury, restaurants by price, and museums by importance. If you're going to Florence to see its magnificent works of art, first take a peek at `www.arca.net/florence.htm` for a combined tour-guide and Florence art-history lesson that includes a glossary of art terms.

Chapter 15

Northern Tuscany and the Cinque Terre

In This Chapter

▶ Exploring city ramparts in Lucca
▶ Checking out the Leaning Tower in Pisa
▶ Discovering fishing villages in the Cinque Terre

*N*orthern Tuscany is an area rich in history and natural beauty. In this book, we concentrate on its eastern part, near the beautiful Tyrrhenian Sea, where you'll find **Pisa**, with its justly famous Leaning Tower, and **Lucca,** one of Italy's most delightful medieval walled cities. However, no trip to the area could be complete without a glimpse of the Italian Riviera, especially as it is experienced in the national park of the **Cinque Terre,** a group of five picturesque villages clinging to abrupt cliffs and recently declared a World Heritage site by UNESCO.

Three days is the minimum you will need to visit these destinations, but of course, if you have the leisure and the disposition, this region could justify a longer stay. Pisa makes an excellent base for visiting any of the destinations in this chapter; it's not only central but it's also a pleasant city to visit, with a choice of moderately priced hotels. Alternatively, you can easily visit any of these destinations in this area as a day trip from Florence.

Lucca

The great English poet Percy Bysshe Shelley passed by here and wrote "The Baths of Lucca," celebrating the unspoiled medieval town surrounded by powerful red ramparts. Lucca's architecture speaks of its past glory: an important city under the Romans, it later became a republic, fighting for its independence against Pisa (see Chapter 2). It was — and still is — famous for the works produced in its music school, founded in A.D. 787. A famous student of the school was Giacomo Puccini, who gave the world some of its greatest operas, such as *Madame Butterfly* and *Tosca.*

Lucca is an easy day trip from Florence or Pisa, but if you have time, it's also a wonderful place to spend a couple of days leisurely strolling the walls or enjoying an opera or a concert, especially during the September festival (see "More cool things to see and do," later in this section).

Getting there

Lucca is about 64km (40 miles) west of Florence, and 22km (14 miles) north of Pisa, easily reached by train, bus, or car.

Trains for Lucca leave Florence every hour — and sometimes even more frequently. The trip takes about 1¼ hours and costs about 4.55€ ($5.20). Trains from Pisa to Lucca travel as frequently, but the trip is only 20 to 30 minutes and costs 2.05€ ($2.40). **Lucca's rail station** (☎ 0583-467-013) is just south of the walls, on Piazzale Ricasoli, off Porta San Pietro (St. Peter's Gate). You can easily walk to the center of town — if you don't have luggage or if you left it at the train station — or take a taxi or bus (see "Getting around," later in this section).

By **bus,** the company **Lazzi** (☎ 055-363-041; for schedule information: 050-46-288 in Pisa, 055-215-155 in Florence, 0583-584-896 in Lucca; www.lazzi.it) runs regular service to Lucca from both Pisa and Florence. The trip takes about an hour from Florence (for 4.70€/$5.40), and about 30 minutes from Pisa (for 2.20€/$2.50). Buses arrive at Piazzale Verdi, within Lucca's walls, on the west side.

If you have a **car,** from Florence take *autostrada* A11 toward Prato, Pistoia, and Lucca. From Pisa, you can take A12 north toward Viareggio and turn off toward Florence on A11; Lucca is the first exit after the junction with A11. You can also take the local road SS12 from Pisa to Lucca — it's narrower (two lanes) but shorter. You'll have to park your car outside the walls unless you are going to drop your luggage at your hotel — only locals are allowed to drive inside.

Parking lots are located near most of the six city gates; make a note of the city gate you parked near and of the bus route number that takes you there.

Getting around

To fully enjoy the medieval flavor of the town, the best way to visit is on foot. However, Lucca is larger than one might think and, if you get tired, public transportation comes in handy: the electric *navette* (shuttle bus) system runs regularly with routes to and from most of the city gates and all parking lots, and through the center of town. You'll find a map at the city bus office (CLAP; Piazzale Verdi ☎ 800-602-525 toll-free in Italy or 058-35-411) and you can buy tickets (0.60€/70¢ for 1 ride and 6€/$7 for 12) at any tobacconist, newsstand, or bar displaying the CLAP sign.

On Sundays the *navette* service is less frequent and most ticket vendors are closed.

Tuscany and Umbria

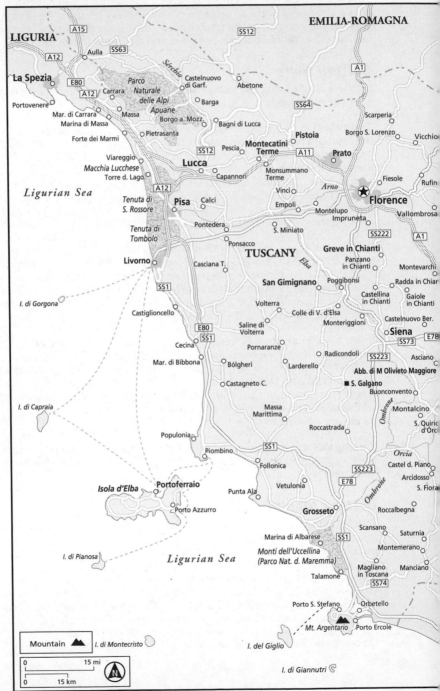

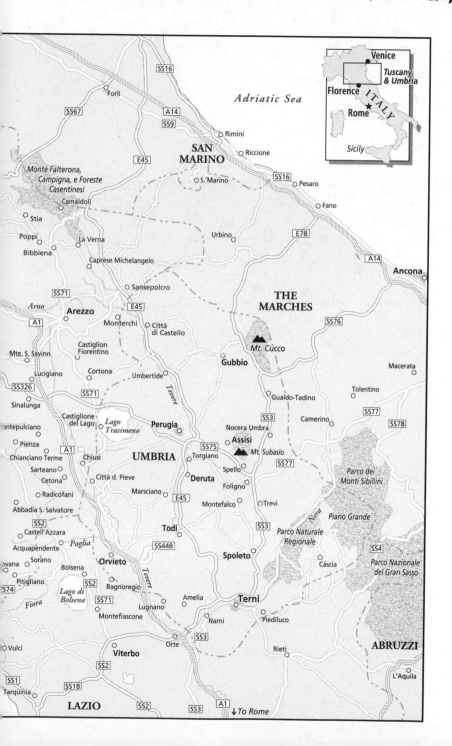

Lucca

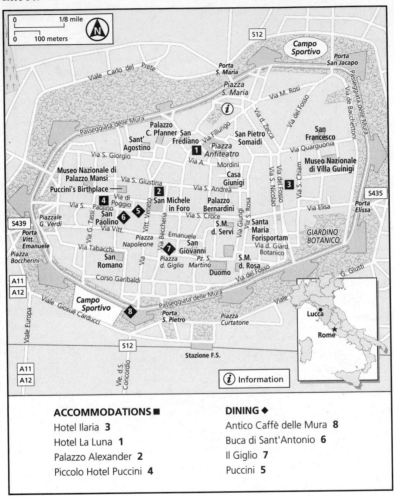

ACCOMMODATIONS ■	DINING ◆
Hotel Ilaria **3**	Antico Caffè delle Mura **8**
Hotel La Luna **1**	Buca di Sant'Antonio **6**
Palazzo Alexander **2**	Il Giglio **7**
Piccolo Hotel Puccini **4**	Puccini **5**

Taxis are also a great way to get around — and they operate on a regular schedule on Sundays. There are stands at the railroad station on Piazzale Ricasoli (☎ **0583-494-989**); Piazza Napoleone (☎ **0583-492-691**); Piazza Santa Maria (☎ **0583-494-190**); and Piazzale Verdi (☎ **0583-581-305**).

Another possibility is to do like the Luccans do: Although residents' cars are allowed within the city walls, Luccans seem to prefer **biking** (see "More cool things to see and do," later in this chapter.).

Spending the night

Hotel Ilaria
$$ Via Santa Croce

Tasteful guest rooms, breakfast on a quiet terrace overlooking a beautiful park, free use of bicycles, a parking garage on premise — all right in the center of Lucca. What else do you want? Discount prices at the best restaurants in town? You got it: The management of Hotel Ilaria has an agreement with three restaurants in town, including the well-recommended Giglio and Buca di Sant'Antonio (see "Dining locally," later in this chapter). Beautifully renovated, this elegant hotel is housed in the former stables of the Villa Bottini and overlooks the villa's park — a quiet location near the canal that crosses the city toward the east. Guest rooms are spacious and pleasant, with modern dark wood furniture and good-sized bathrooms. Some rooms are accessible to people with disabilities.

See map p. 242. Via del Fosso 26, off Via Santa Croce. ☎ *0583-47-615. Fax: 0583-991-961.* www.hotelilaria.com. *Free parking. Rack rates: 230€ ($265) double. Rates include buffet breakfast. AE, DC, MC, V.*

Hotel La Luna
$ Anfiteatro

This well-maintained hotel, renovated in 2003, offers a great value right in the historic center. It's divided between two buildings; some of the ceilings have 17th-century frescoes. All the guest rooms are spacious, decorated in warm tones, and furnished in classic style. Bathrooms are relatively small, but a few have Jacuzzi tubs. The hotel also has a number of suites — some quite grand, with large beds and high ceilings (for 175€/$201).

See map p. 242. Corte Compagni 12, off Via Fillungo. ☎ *0583-493-634. Fax: 0583-490-021.* www.hotellaluna.com. *Free parking. Rack rates: 110€ ($127) double. Rates include buffet breakfast. AE, DC, MC, V.*

Palazzo Alexander
$$ Piazza San Michele

This hotel, which opened in 2000, offers luxurious accommodations right in the center of town, with a staff committed to your service. The palace, originally from the 12th century, was restored according to the style of the original furnishings and decorations. Guest rooms are quite magnificent, in what the management defines as *stile nobile Lucchese* (Luccan aristocratic style), with much gilded furniture and stuccoes and damasqued fabrics; the bathrooms are decorated with marble and other local stones and some have Jacuzzis.

See map p. 242. Via Santa Giustina 48, near Piazza San Michele. ☎ *0583-583-571. Fax: 0583-583-610.* www.palazzo-alexander.it. *Free valet parking. Rack rates: 170€ ($196) double. AE, DC, MC, V.*

Piccolo Hotel Puccini
$ Piazza San Michele

In the heart of the historic center, this is a romantic hotel, offering moderate-sized rooms cozily furnished at low rates. Situated just across from the house where Puccini was born — hence its name — it is housed in a small 15th-century four-story *palazzo*. All the bathrooms were being completely renovated at press time and should be completed by the time you arrive. Note that there is no elevator or air conditioning. This popular hotel is always full, so book well in advance.

See map p. 242. Via di Poggio 9, off Piazza San Michele. ☎ *0583-55-421. Fax: 0583-53-487.* www.hotelpuccini.com. *Parking: 15€ ($17) in nearby garage. Rack rates: 83€ ($95) double. AE, DC, MC, V.*

Dining locally

There are fewer good restaurants in Lucca than you would expect, but most provide a decent meal — you are in Tuscany after all — although sometimes it's overpriced. Those listed below are the best in town. See Chapter 2 for more in-depth information about Tuscan and Luccan cuisine.

Antico Caffè delle Mura
$$ City Ramparts   LUCCAN/TUSCAN

With its fantastic location atop the city walls, this elegant restaurant tries to revive 19th-century atmosphere. In the paneled formal dining rooms and, during the good weather season, in the gardens at the back, you will be able to choose from traditional Luccan dishes or other Tuscan favorites, such as the homemade fresh pasta and some of the delectable *secondi* (main courses), including such specialties as rabbit, duck, and lamb.

See map p. 242. Piazza Vittorio Emanuele, at Baluardo Santa Maria. ☎ *0583-47-962. Reservations necessary. Secondi: 14€–18€ ($16–$21). AE, DC, MC, V. Open: Lunch and dinner Wed–Mon; closed 3 weeks in Jan.*

Buca di Sant'Antonio
$ Piazza San Michele   LUCCAN

Lucca's best restaurant, Buca di Sant'Antonio, boasts excellent food at very reasonable prices. The cuisine is strictly traditional, and you wouldn't expect anything else from a restaurant that's been around since 1782. The *capretto garfagnino allo spiedo* (spit-roasted baby goat from the Garfagnana area) is a classic well worth the trip, as are the *tortelli lucchesi al sugo* (special round ravioli with a meat sauce); the *petto di faraona all'uva moscato* (*faraona* hen breast with a *moscato* raisin sauce) gained our full approval as well. The remarkable atmosphere is characterized by a labyrinthine succession of small rooms decorated with musical instruments and copper pots. The service is professional and very kind.

See map p. 242. Via della Cervia 3, near Piazza San Michele. ☎ *0583-55-881.*
Reservations necessary. Secondi: 12.50€–13.50€ ($14–$16). AE, DC, MC, V. Open:
Lunch Tues–Sun; dinner Tues–Sat; closed 3 weeks in July.

Il Giglio
$ **Piazza Napoleone   LUCCAN**

Less formal than Antica Caffè delle Mura (reviewed above), Il Giglio offers
excellent traditional Luccan specialties and a friendly atmosphere. Dine
indoors or, during pleasant weather, you can dine *al fresco* under an
awning. Try the famed *zuppa di farro* (thick spelt soup) or the homemade
tortelli al ragù (round ravioli in meat and tomato sauce). The *secondi* are
also very tasty; you can never go wrong with the *coniglio alla cacciatora*
(rabbit in a wine and herbs sauce) or the roasted lamb.

See map p. 242. Piazza del Giglio 3, near Piazza Napoleone. ☎ *0583-494-058.*
Reservations recommended. Secondi: 14€–16€ ($16–$18). AE, DC, MC, V. Open:
Lunch Thurs–Tues, dinner Thurs–Mon; closed 2 weeks in Feb.

Puccini
$$ **Piazza San Michele   FISH/LUCCAN**

Specializing in seafood, you'll always get a fine meal but you may not receive
the service to match it. The cuisine mixes tradition with innovation, and the
offerings vary with the season and the daily catches. More creative dishes
such as *tortelloni neri di crostacei con asparagi e pomodorini* (black round
seafood ravioli with asparagus and cherry tomatoes) and *salmone marinato
al pepe rosa* (marinated salmon in a pink pepper sauce), are offered side by
side with great classics, such as the excellent *frittura di paranza* (fried small
fish) — one of our favorites. They also have a special children's menu offer-
ing simpler dishes, with fewer spices and special ingredients.

See map p. 242. Corte San Lorenzo 1/2, near Piazza San Michele. ☎ *0583-316-116*
Reservations necessary. Secondi: 16€–21€ ($18–$24). AE, DC, V. Open: Lunch
Thurs–Mon; dinner Wed–Mon; closed Jan–Feb.

Exploring Lucca

You might want to take advantage of the **Cityphone Guided Tour,** a
recorded tour — available in Italian, English, French, Spanish, and
German — that offers explanations and historic facts on all of Lucca's
sights. Rent one Cityphone for 9€ ($10), two for 14€ ($16), and each
additional one costs 7€ ($8.05). Together with the **free city map,** it's all
you need to explore the city in as much depth as you like. Both are avail-
able at the tourist office in Piazzale Verdi. (See "Fast Facts: Lucca," later
in this chapter.)

You can buy a **cumulative ticket** that includes the Duomo and Sacristy,
the museum of the Cathedral, and the church and baptistry of Santi
Giovanni e Reparata for 5€ ($5.75). Another cumulative ticket includes the
Museo Nazionale Palazzo Mansi and the Villa Guinigi for 6.50€ ($7.50).

The top attractions

Chiesa e Battistero Santi Giovanni e Reparata
Piazza San Martino

The 12th-century church of Santi Giovanni e Reparata was partly rebuilt in the 17th century. Together with the adjacent baptistry, adorned with a Gothic dome, they are a lovely sight. However, the real attraction here are the excavations under the church that take you back in time through layers of history. Beneath the later constructions, you can see the remains of a previous basilica, beneath which are the remains of a paleo-Christian church, itself built over a Roman temple, which was built atop a more ancient Roman house. The excavations are accessible to the public by guided tour, and it is best to make a reservation in advance. Expect to spend about an hour here.

Piazza San Giovanni. ☎ 0583-490-530 for reservations. Admission: 2.50€ ($2.90). Open: Winter Sat–Sun 10 a.m.–5 p.m.; summer daily 10 a.m.–6 p.m.

Duomo (Cattedrale di San Martino)
Piazza San Martino

Sitting on a medieval square, this cathedral is a perfect example of Luccan-Pisan Romanesque architecture. Striped with green and white marble, the facade is decorated with three tiers of polychromed small columns. Take some time to walk behind the church and admire the imposing apse, surrounded by a small park. The interior is Gothic, divided into three naves, and contains several fine pieces, the most important in the **Sacristy:** Ghirlandaio's **Madonna with Saints** and **Ilaria del Carretto Guinigi's funeral monument,** a Jacopo della Quercia masterpiece that's one of the finest examples of 15th-century Italian sculpture. Ilaria was the first wife of Paolo Guinigi, ruler of Lucca, and he had the monument built to commemorate her death (she died at 26 after only 2 years of marriage) and beauty. Other interesting works are the **Last Supper (Tintoretto Ultima Cena)**, on the third altar of the right nave, and several sculptures by 15th-century Luccan artist Matteo Civitali (among which are the two angels in the Chapel of the Sacrament [Cappella del Sacramento] and the altar dedicated to San Regolo in the adjacent chapel). Also by Matteo Civitali is the marble housing for the Duomo's relic: the **Volto Santo,** a wooden crucifix showing the real face of Christ, said to have been miraculously carved. Adjacent to the cathedral is a museum containing artworks once housed in the cathedral. Count about 30 minutes for your visit to the Duomo and another 40 minutes for the museum.

Piazza San Martino. ☎ 0583-494-726. Admission: Duomo free; Sacristy 2€ ($2.30); Museum 3.50€ ($4);. Open: Duomo daily winter 7 a.m.–5 p.m., summer till 7 p.m.; Museum, Nov–Mar Mon–Fri 10 a.m.–3 p.m., Sat–Sun 10 a.m.–6 p.m; Apr–Oct daily 10 a.m.–6 p.m.

Museo Nazionale Palazzo Mansi and Pinacoteca Nazionale
Porta San Donato

This lavish 17th-century palace is still decorated with some of its original furnishings and frescoes. Of special note are the **Music Room (Salone della Musica)** and **Nuptial Room (Camera degli Sposi).** The collection of paintings in the *pinacoteca* (picture gallery) includes Italian and foreign artists from the Renaissance to the 18th century; highlights are a portrait by Pontormo of a youth and works by a few big names, such as Andrea del Sarto, Veronese, and Domenichino. For a quick tour, allow about one hour.

See map p. 242. Via Galli Tassi 43. ☎ *0583-55-570. Admission: 4€ ($4.60). Open: Tues–Sun 9 a.m.–7 p.m.*

Museo Nazionale Villa Guinigi
Porta Elisa

Formerly the residence of the Guinigi family, this villa contains an interesting collection of Lucchese artworks, including paintings and sculptures from the 13th to the 18th century, and also a small collection of ancient Roman and Etruscan artifacts. The Guinigi ruled Lucca during the Renaissance, and some of the furnishings dating from that period remain. Allow one hour.

See map p. 242. Via del Quarquonia. ☎ *0583-496-003. Admission: 4€ ($4.60). Open: Tues–Sat 9 a.m.–7 p.m. and Sun 9 a.m.–2 p.m.*

San Frediano
Piazza Anfiteatro

Built in the early 12th century, this **church** has a simple facade decorated with a beautiful Byzantine-style mosaic depicting the ascension of Christ, as well as a soaring bell tower. Among the works inside the church are noteworthy Jacopo della Quercia **carvings** in the left nave's last chapel, the 12th- and 13th-century **mosaic floor** around the main altar, and the beautifully carved **Romanesque font** at the right nave's entrance. Allow about 20 minutes for your visit.

See map p. 242. Piazza San Frediano. ☎ *0583-493-627. Admission: Free. Open: Mon–Sat 9 a.m.–noon and 3–6 p.m., Sun 9 a.m.–1 p.m. and 3–5 p.m.*

San Michele in Foro
Piazza San Michele

Probably one of the greatest examples of Luccan-Pisan Romanesque architecture, the church of San Michele was built between the 12th and 14th centuries. The church derives its name from the fact that it was built over the ancient Roman city's **Forum.** The facade is graced by four tiers of small columns and is luxuriously decorated with different colors of marble, while the apse powerfully illustrates the Pisan influence. Inside is a beautiful

Filippino Lippi painting on wood representing Saints Sebastian, Jerome, Helen, and Roch. Piazza San Michele, which surrounds this wonderful church, is itself lovely. Allow about 20 minutes for your visit.

See map p. 242. Piazza San Michele. ☎ *0583-48-459. Admission: Free. Open: Daily 7:40 a.m.–noon and 3–6 p.m.*

More cool things to see and do

Lucca is more than just churches and palaces. Herewith, more to explore:

✔ Lucca is a city of music, and you may enjoy catching an opera at the historic **Teatro del Giglio** (☎ 0583-46531 or 0583-467-521 for tickets; www.teatrodelgiglio.it), if you're there in season (Oct–Feb). The theater also organizes **Lucca in Musica,** a series of concerts in the Basilica di San Frediano and in the Auditorium di San Romano from April through December. A great time to visit Lucca is during the **Settembre Lucchese,** when a variety of events liven the city, including many concerts. Another great musical event is the **Sagra Musicale Lucchese** (organized by Cappella Musicale Santa Cecilia; ☎ 0583-48-421; Apr–June), when concerts of religious and classic music are performed in the city's churches. Contact the tourist office for a schedule of concerts during your stay (see "Fast Facts: Lucca," later in this chapter).

✔ Overlooking the whole city, the **Passeggiata delle Mura** (promenade over the city walls) is one attraction enjoyed by visitors and Luccans alike. Erected between 1544 and 1650, this is the third and final set of city walls built by the independent Republic of Lucca (the first set was built in Roman times in the 2nd or 3rd c. A.D., the second between the 11th and 13th c.). In fact, they're Europe's only practically undamaged set of defense ramparts from the Renaissance — maybe thanks to their monumental scale measuring 35m (115-ft.) thick at the base and soaring 12m (40-ft.) high, and with *baluardi* (projecting defense works) at 11 different points. The tops of the walls were transformed into a tree-lined 4.2km (2½-mile) long public promenade in the early 19th century, with access ramps at 9 of the 11 *baluardi*. Today, after a short spell when cars where allowed on it, this scenic boulevard is restored to its peaceful beauty; do as the Luccans do and rent a bike at the **city-run stand** (Casermetta San Donato, near the city walls in Piazzale Verdi; ☎ 0583-583-150), or at one of these shops: Barbetti Cicli (Via Anfiteatro 23; ☎ 0583-954-444); Cicli Bizzarri (Piazza S.Maria 32; ☎ 0583-496-031) and Poli Antonio Biciclette (Piazza S.Maria 42; ☎ 0583-493-787). Prices range from about 6€ ($6.90) per hour to about 20€ ($23) per day.

✔ Lucca is dominated by two medieval towers, **Torre Guinigi** (Via Sant' Andrea, off Via Guinigi; ☎ 0583-316-846; open Nov–Feb 9 a.m.–5:30 p.m., Mar–Sept 9 a.m.–8 p.m., Oct 10 a.m.–6 p.m.) and **Torre delle Ore** (Via Fillungo, between Vicolo San Carlo and Via Sant'Andrea; ☎ 0583-316-846; open Oct–Feb 9 a.m.–5:30 p.m.,

Mar–Apr 10 a.m.–6 p.m., May–Sept 9 a.m.–8 p.m.). Torre Guinigi is topped by a garden with trees (entrance on Via Sant'Andrea), whereas the Torre delle Ore has marked the passing of time since the 14th century (the clocks have been replaced over the centuries and the current one dates from 1754). Recently restored, admission to the towers is 3.10€ ($3.60) each, or 5€ ($5.75) entrance to both.

✔ You can still visit the house (now museum) where the famous musician Giacomo Puccini was born: the **Casa Natale di Giacomo Puccini** (Corte San Lorenzo 9, off Via di Poggio; ☎ **0583-584-028).** The house is open October through December and March through May on Tuesday through Sunday from 10 a.m. to 1 p.m. and 3 to 6 p.m. and June through September daily from 10 a.m. to 6 p.m.; admission is 3€ ($3.45).

Fast Facts: Lucca

Area Code

The area code for Lucca is 0538; use this code when calling from anywhere outside or inside Italy and even within Lucca (including the 0, even when calling from abroad).

ATMs

There are many banks in town, especially in Piazza San Michele, Piazza San Martino, and Via Vittorio Veneto, where you can find ATMs and change your money. There's a *cambio* (exchange office) in the rail station and one near the tourist office on Piazzale Verdi, as well as others around town.

Emergencies

Ambulance, ☎ **118**; fire, ☎ **115**; road assistance, ☎ **116**.

Hospital

The Ospedale Generale Provinciale Campo di Marte is on Via dell'Ospedale (☎ 0583-9701 or toll-free 800-869-143).

Information

The APT office is in Piazza Santa Maria 35 (☎ 0583-919-931; www.luccaturismo.it; open daily Apr–Oct 9 a.m.–8 p.m., Nov–Mar 9 a.m.–1 p.m and 3 –6 p.m); and in Piazza Napoleone (open Apr–Oct Mon–Sat 10 a.m.–6 p.m., Nov–Mar 10 a.m.–1 p.m). Other tourist information offices are inside Porta Sant'Anna on Piazzale Verdi (☎ 0583-442-944; open daily from 9:30 a.m. –6:30 p.m. [to 3:30 p.m. in winter], and at Porta Elisa (☎ 0583-462-377), open daily from 9:30 a.m. –6:30 p.m. Apr–Oct.

Police

There are two police forces in Italy; call either one. For the Polizia, call ☎ **113**; for the Carabinieri, call ☎ **112**.

Post Office

The post office (ufficio postale) is at Via Vallisneri Antonio 2, behind Piazza San Martino and near Via Guinigi (☎ 0583-492-991).

Pisa

Famous for its Leaning Tower, **Pisa's** medieval buildings overlooking the curving Arno offer some of Italy's nicest riverside views.

The origins of Pisa stretch back to Roman times, when the Italic settlement that had existed since 1000 B.C. was transformed into a commercial harbor (in the 2nd c. B.C.). The city's maritime power was realized in the 11th century, when Pisa was one of the four powerful Italian Maritime Republics, along with Venice, Amalfi, and Genoa. These rival ports developed far-flung mercantile empires (see Chapter 2 for a brief history of Italy). Pisa controlled Corsica, Sardinia, and the Balearic Islands, competing with Genoa for commerce with the Arabs. Centuries later, the city lost its water access (the river silted up) and its power: In 1284, Genoa finally won its struggle against Pisa, whose fleet was destroyed. Genoa became the dominant power in the Tyrrhenian Sea, while Pisa shrank to a possession of Florence. During the three centuries of its splendor, however, the wealth coming from far-flung commerce funded the construction of the monumental town that you can still admire today.

You can see Pisa's most famous attraction on a day trip from Florence. However, Pisa makes a perfect base for exploring most other destinations in northern Tuscany and, like Lucca, has a good selection of moderately priced hotels and restaurants.

Getting there

Only 3km (2 miles) south of town, Pisa's **Aeroporto Galileo Galilei** (☎ 050-849-111; www.pisa-airport.com) is Tuscany's main airport, with daily flights from other major towns in Italy and Europe. From the airport, you can take a taxi to the center of town; it will cost you about 5€ to 7€ ($5.75–$8.05) and take about ten minutes. You can also take the **train** to **Pisa Centrale** (Pisa's rail station), a five-minute ride for 1€ ($1.15); trains depart the airport about every hour. If you're driving, rental-car counters are at arrivals, inside the airport. Once you have your car, from the airport, just follow the signs for **Pisa Centro** (center of town).

From other point in Italy, the **train** is an excellent way to get into Pisa. The **Pisa Centrale** station (☎ 050-41-385) is only about 3½ hours from Rome and a little over an hour from Florence. Trains run about every hour from Rome and every half-hour from Florence, and the trip costs about 4.95€ ($5.70) from Florence and 23€ ($26) from Rome. You can take the electric *navette* A across the Arno to the Duomo.

If you are arriving by **car,** you'll be able to drive the 96km (60 miles) from Florence in about an hour or less. From Florence, take *autostrada* (toll road) A11 to Lucca and follow the signs for A12 toward Livorno; watch for the exit for Pisa shortly after the junction with A12 South. From Florence, you can also follow the signs for Empoli-Livorno to reach Pisa by the more direct but slower *superstrada* (small highway). Three large free parking lots are located near the center of Pisa, just north of the town's walls; each is linked to the center by bus service (electric or otherwise), which costs 80€ (90¢) per ticket. The lots are on **Via Pietrasantina,** only a few hundred yards from the Duomo (*navette* A); **Via di Pratale**, a few hundred yards from the Via del Brennero (Bus 7); and **Via del Brennero**, near Via Paparelli and Porta Zeno, 1km (.6 miles) from the Duomo (*navette* E); this last lot is closed on Wednesday and Saturday from 7 a.m. to 4 p.m. because of an open-air market. Paid parking can be found at Piazza dei Miracoli and in a lot at Via Cammeo for 1.50€ ($1.70) per hour, the same rate as metered street parking.

Getting around

Most of Pisa's attractions are clustered together, so that you can easily visit everything on foot. Walking will also allow you to discover Pisa's network of charming little streets and fully enjoy the beautiful views of the Arno River and its bridges.

CPT, the town's system of city buses (toll-free ☎ 800-012-773 or ☎ 050-884-111), connects all major points in town, and special *navettes* connect the main parking lots with the town's attractions. You can get tickets and a map at the train station or at the **CPT office** in Piazza San Antonio 1, by Piazza Vittorio Emanuele II. Chances are, though, that the only bus you may need is the A, which runs between the Pisa Centrale station and the Duomo. All bus rides cost .80€ (90¢).

Of course you can always take a taxi; there are taxi stands in Piazza della Stazione (call station for info: ☎ 050-41-252) and Piazza del Duomo (☎ 050-561-878); from anywhere in town you can call ☎ 050-541-600.

Spending the night

Grand Hotel Duomo
$$ Duomo

Right off Piazza del Duomo, this hotel offers comfortable guest rooms with high ceilings and parquet floors; front rooms offer views of the piazza. Guest rooms are spacious and furnished with modern elegance, and a few leftover 1970s details; bathrooms are good sized. The hotel has a covered roof garden with great views of the city, a restaurant, and full bar.

See map p. 252. Via Santa Maria 94. ☎ *050-561-894. Fax: 050-560-418.* www.grand hotelduomo.it. *Parking: 16€ ($18). Rack rates: 180€ ($207) double. Rates include buffet breakfast. AE, DC, MC, V.*

Hotel Leonardo
$ Piazza dei Cavalieri

Walking distance from Campo dei Miracoli and the Arno River, this new hotel offers quiet accommodations at a moderate price. The hotel is housed in a building that used to be the study of Galileo Galilei; later, it

Pisa

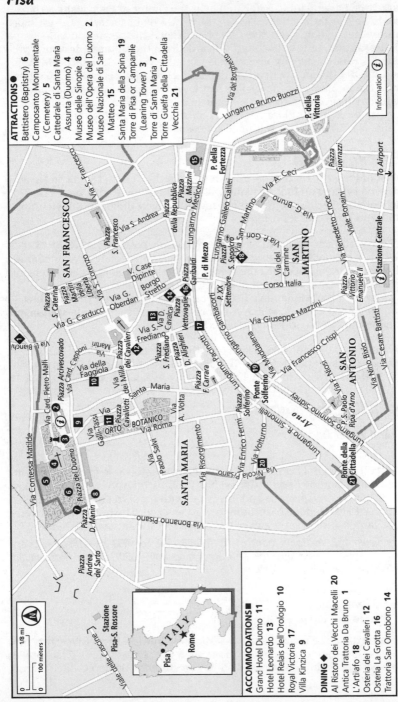

ATTRACTIONS ●
Battistero (Baptistry) **6**
Camposanto Monumentale
(Cemetery) **5**
Cattedrale di Santa Maria
Assunta (Duomo) **4**
Museo delle Sinopie **8**
Museo dell'Opera del Duomo **2**
Museo Nazionale di San
Matteo **15**
Santa Maria della Spina **19**
Torre di Pisa or Campanile
(Leaning Tower) **3**
Torre di Santa Maria **7**
Torre Guelfa della Cittadella
Vecchia **21**

Information ⓘ

ACCOMMODATIONS ■
Granci Hotel Duomo **11**
Hotel Leonardo **13**
Hotel Relais dell'Orologio **10**
Royal Victoria **17**
Villa Kinzica **9**

DINING ◆
Al Ristoro dei Vecchi Macelli **20**
Antica Trattoria Da Bruno **1**
L'Artiafo **18**
Osteria dei Cavalieri **12**
Osteria La Grotta **16**
Trattoria San Omobono **14**

was the residence of a duc, Duca Salviati. Today, the building has been completely renovated and transformed into a hotel. Guest rooms are pleasant, with bright, whitewashed walls relieved by vibrant fabrics and simple but stylish modern furnishings. Some of the rooms afford a beautiful view over Pisa and the Leaning Tower.

See map p. 252. Via Tavoleria 17. ☎ *050-579-946. Fax: 050-598-969. Free parking on street with hotel permit. Rack rates: 115€ ($132) double. Rates include continental breakfast. AE, DC, MC, V.*

Hotel Relais dell'Orologio
$$$ **Duomo**

Steps from Campo dei Miracoli, this historical palace was restored in 2004 and transformed into a hotel with stylish accommodations. Guest rooms are decorated with a subdued elegance that enhances the arched window frames and beamed ceilings typical of this style medieval building. The guest rooms and bathrooms alike are large and comfortable. The garden in back of the palace is the perfect place to have breakfast in the fair season. Ask about specials when you make your reservation (usually a discount and a free dinner on two-night stays).

See map p. 252. Via della Faggiola 12/14. ☎ *050-830-361. Fax: 050-551-869.* www. hotelrelaisorologio.com. *Free parking. Rack rates: 326€ ($375) double. Rates include breakfast. AE, DC, MC, V.*

Royal Victoria
$ **Lungarno-Ponte di Mezzo**

This hotel, located right on the Arno and walking distance of all major attractions, affords old-fashioned elegance, romantic views, moderate prices, and friendly service. Opened in 1839 as Pisa's first hotel, it is still run by the same family. The hotel occupies several medieval buildings, including the remains of a tenth-century tower; as a result, guest rooms differ greatly — some have frescoed ceilings and others are more simply decorated — but all are furnished with antiques and kept extremely clean. If you are planning to use the parking garage, you must reserve for that as well.

See map p. 252. Lungarno Pacinotti 12. ☎ *050-940-111. Fax: 050-940-180.* www.royal victoria.it. *Parking: 18€ ($21). Rack rates: 125€ ($144) double. Rates include breakfast. AE, DC, MC, V.*

Villa Kinzica
$ **Duomo**

Located just across from the Leaning Tower, the hotel is an excellent value, offering bright, clean rooms, most of which afford a glimpse of the famous monument. The hotel name comes from a Pisan heroine who saved the city from the Saracens. The guest rooms have whitewashed walls with simple yet tasteful furnishings and are extremely well kept. Bathrooms are small. A nice touch is the homemade rolls for breakfast.

See map p. 252. Piazza Arcivescovado 2. ☎ 050-560-419. Fax: 050-551-204. www. hotelvillakinzica.it. *Parking: Free on street with hotel permit. Rack rates: 108€ ($124) double. Rates include breakfast. AE, DC, MC, V.*

Dining locally

It is very difficult to have a bad meal in Pisa: restaurants and trattorie are plentiful and excellent. Feel free to try those that appeal to you — it was impossible to list all the restaurants that appealed to us! Food in Pisa includes typical Tuscan fare, such as *ribollita* (here called *zuppa pisana,* or Pisan soup — old rivalries die hard) and, because the sea is nearby, lots of seafood. See Chapter 2 for more in-depth information on Tuscan and Pisan cuisine.

Al Ristoro dei Vecchi Macelli
$$ Piazza Solferino   PISAN/SEAFOOD

A little outside the historic district, this is Pisa's best traditional restaurant and a local favorite. Housed in a 15th-century slaughterhouse *(macello)*, it nonetheless offers a cozy atmosphere, with beamed ceilings and dark wood floors. This family-run restaurant offers traditional Pisan recipes that are reinterpreted with genius and elegance. The homemade ravioli are stuffed with fish and served with a shrimp sauce or stuffed with pork and served with broccoli sauce. Other inventions are gnocchi with pesto and shrimp, stuffed rabbit with creamy truffle sauce, and sea bass with onion sauce and oysters au gratin. If you're looking for a refined dining experience, this is the place to go.

See map p. 252. Via Volturno 49, south of the Campo dei Miracoli. ☎ 050-20-424. Reservations necessary. Secondi: 13€–18€ ($15–$21). AE, DC. Open: Lunch and dinner Thurs–Tues; closed 2 weeks in Aug.

Antica Trattoria Da Bruno
$ Duomo   PISAN

Walking distance from the Duomo and just outside the city walls, this trattoria offers traditional homemade food in a warm atmosphere. You can dine in one of the various sized dining rooms, including a small "private" room which is the quietest; all of them have tables covered with pink tablecloths, beamed ceilings, and whitewashed walls decorated with photographs and copper utensils. The dishes are chosen from the traditional local cuisine and include homemade fresh pasta like the *pappardelle al sugo di lepre* (pappardelle pasta with hare sauce), *baccalà coi porri* (codfish with fresh tomatoes and leeks), *coniglio* (rabbit), and lamb.

See map p. 252. Via Luigi Bianchi 12, 3 block east of Piazza dei Miracoli. ☎ 050-560-818. Reservations recommended. Secondi: 10€–15€ ($12–$17). AE, DC, MC, V. Open: Lunch Wed–Mon; dinner Wed–Sun.

L'Artilafo
$ Ponte di Mezzo/Piazza San Martino   PISAN/TUSCAN

The best restaurant in town according to the younger crowd, this is a place where you will enjoy masterly prepared Tuscan dishes with a twist. The menu changes according to market offerings and the restaurant is open only for dinner. Now in a new location, the restaurant is divided into several small, intimate dining rooms — each painted in a different pastel color. Among the *primi*, the *pasta con seppie e bietole* (pasta with squid and chard) is delicious, and so are the more unusual *cannoli con anatra in salsa d'arancia e porri* (tubes of savory pastry filled with orange-glazed duck and leeks). Among the *secondi*, the *faraona con farcia di fegato e con ciliegie marascate* (guinea hen with liver-pâté stuffing and maraschino cherries) was outstanding.

See map p. 252. Via San Martino 33. ☎ 050-27-010. Reservations necessary. Secondi: 10€–16€ ($12–$18). AE, DC, MC, V. Open: Dinner Mon–Sat. Closed Aug.

Osteria dei Cavalieri
$ Piazza dei Cavalieri   PISAN

One of the most lively restaurants in Pisa, this osteria offers simple and tasty food at moderate prices. The two small and bright dining rooms are a perfect background for the food which delicately mixes tradition with innovation. We loved the *gnocchi ai fiori di zucca e pistacchi* (potato dumplings with zucchini flowers and pistachio nuts) and the *tagliata di manzo ai funghi pioppini con cannellini,* a perfect steak served with wild local mushrooms and white beans.

See map p. 252. Via San Frediano 16, off Piazza dei Cavalieri. ☎ 050-580-858. Reservations recommended. Secondi: 8€–10€ ($9.20–$12). AE, DC, MC, V. Open: Lunch Mon–Fri; dinner Mon–Sat. Closed 4 weeks in Aug.

Osteria La Grotta
$ Ponte di Mezzo   TUSCAN

A favorite among locals and visitors alike, this friendly restaurant has an interesting decor — a papier-mâché grotto — and a lively atmosphere. The traditional food is nicely prepared and includes such specialties as *tortelli* (a special kind of stuffed pasta), *pappardelle alla lepre* (pappardelle pasta in hare sauce), *gnocchi di ricotta e spinaci* (gnocchi with ricotta cheese and spinach), and a variety of *secondi* such as stuffed rabbit and roasted meats.

See map p. 252. Via San Francesco 103. ☎ 050-578-105. Reservations recommended. Secondi: 8€–14€ ($9.20–$16). AE, DC, MC, V. Open: Lunch and dinner Mon–Sat.

Trattoria San Omobono
$ Ponte di Mezzo   PISAN

Near the food market, this trattoria offers traditional Pisan fare at very moderate prices. Try the homemade pasta specialties, or such typical Tuscan fare as *ribollita* (thick bread, beans, and vegetable soup). Among

---

Fixings for a Pisa picnic

An excellent place to eat around town is the **food market** on **Piazza delle Vettovaglie,** just north of Piazza Garibaldi and the Ponte di Mezzo, and off Via Domenico Cavalca on the west side of the market. Every day from 7:00 a.m. to 1:30 p.m., food producers from the countryside offer their specialties for sale. You can save a few bucks and have a great picnic, perhaps along the riverbanks, with fresh produce and Tuscan specialties. The food market can supply bread, salami, fruit, and everything else you'll need for a picnic.

---

the tasty *secondi,* we enjoyed the *baccalà alla livornese* (codfish with onion and fresh tomatoes) and *maiale arrosto* (savory roasted pork).

See map p. 252. Piazza San Omobono 6. ☎ 050-540-847. Reservations recommended. Secondi: 9€ ($10). No credit cards. Open: Lunch and dinner Mon–Sat. Closed 2 weeks in Aug.

Exploring Pisa

The monumental **Piazza del Duomo,** also known as the **Field of Miracles (Campo dei Miracoli),** is where Pisa's top attractions are concentrated. The square was built in medieval times abutting the city walls — a quite unusual location for the city's cathedral, as far as cities in Italy go. Another unusual feature is that the piazza is covered with shining green grass — a perfect background for the carved marble masterpieces in the monumental compound.

If you're traveling between March and October and want to visit several or all of the sights of Pisa, you may want to buy the *biglietto unico,* which includes admission to the ten top attractions in Pisa, except the Leaning Tower, for 13€ ($15). The pass is valid for eight days, and includes admission to the Duomo, Camposanto Monumentale, Battistero, Museo delle Sinopie, Museo dell'Opera del Duomo, Museo Nazionale di San Matteo, Museo Nazionale di Palazzo Reale, Santa Maria della Spina, Torre di Santa Maria e camminamento sulle Mura Urbane, and Torre Guelfa della Cittadella Vecchia. It can be purchased only at the ticket booth of one of the four participating museums and at Santa Maria della Spina. Other passes, also available March through October, grant admission to your choice of two, four, or all five of the museums and monuments in Campo dei Miracoli, always excluding the Leaning Tower; they cost 6€ ($6.90), 8.50€ ($9.80), and 10.50€ ($12), respectively.

If you prefer to see Pisa via a guided tour from Florence, contact **American Express** (☎ 055-50-981) or **SitaSightseeing** (☎ 055-214-721) in Florence. Both offer a tour of Pisa from Florence for about 26€ ($30).

The top attractions

Battistero (Baptistry)
Campo dei Miracoli

Standing across from the Duomo, the Battistero was built between the 12th and 14th centuries, and its architecture reflects the passage from the Romanesque to the Gothic style during those years. It is the largest Baptistry in Italy and is actually taller — counting the statue on top — than the famous Leaning Tower. The exterior was once richly decorated with Giovanni Pisano statues, but many have been removed to the Museo dell'Opera del Duomo (see the listing, later in this chapter) for safekeeping, and only a few were replaced with plaster casts. Inside is a **hexagonal pulpit** carved by Nicola Pisano (father of Giovanni) between 1255 and 1260 and a **baptismal font** carved and inlaid by Guido Bigarelli da Como. Allow about 20 minutes for your visit.

See map p. 252. Piazza del Duomo ☎ *050-560-547.* www.opapisa.it. *Admission: 5€ ($5.75). Open: Daily Apr–Sept 8 a.m.–7:30 p.m.; Nov–Feb 9 a.m.–4:30 p.m.; Mar and Oct 9 a.m.–5:30 p.m.*

Camposanto Monumentale (Cemetery)
Campo dei Miracoli

On the edge of Piazza del Duomo stands the beautiful wall of the cemetery *(camposanto)*. Designed by Giovanni di Simone and built in 1278, this monumental cemetery has been the burial ground for Pisa's constables, and you can find sarcophagi, statues, and marble bas-reliefs here. The dirt used in the cemetery isn't common dirt but holy dirt from Golgotha in Palestine — where Christ was crucified — brought back by ship after a Crusade. During the 1944 U.S. bombing of Pisa to dislodge the Nazis, the cemetery's loggia roof caught fire, and most of the magnificent frescoes were destroyed. Parts of the frescoes that were salvaged — particularly interesting are the *Triumph of Death* and the *Last Judgment* — are exhibited inside, along with photographs showing the Camposanto before the destruction. Allow about 20 minutes for your visit.

See map p. 252. Piazza del Duomo. ☎ *050-560-547.* www.opapisa.it. *Admission: 5€ ($5.75). Open: Daily Apr–Sept 8 a.m.–7:30 p.m.; Nov–Feb 9 a.m.–4:30 p.m.; Mar and Oct 9 a.m.–5:30 p.m.*

Cattedrale di Santa Maria Assunta (Duomo)
Campo dei Miracoli

The center of Campo dei Miracoli is occupied by the magnificent cathedral, Pisa's Duomo, built by Buschetto in the 11th century. However, its current facade, with four layers of open-air arches diminishing in size as they ascend, is from the 13th century. In 1595, the cathedral was heavily damaged by a fire that destroyed the three bronze exterior doors and much of the art inside. The cathedral was restored during the 16th century, integrating some baroque elements. Still original is the **monumental bronze door** at the south entrance (the Porta San Ranieri) cast by Bonanno Pisano in 1180, the Andrea del Sarto painting of *Sant'Agnese* at the choir entrance, the 13th-century mosaic of *Christ Pantocrator,* and the Cimabue *San Giovanni Evangelista* in the apse. The **polygonal pulpit** carved by Giovanni Pisano was restored in 1926 when the original pieces were found; they had been put in storage after the fire in the 16th century. Plan to spend about 30 minutes here.

See map p. 252. Piazza del Duomo. ☎ *050-560-547.* www.opapisa.it. *Admission: Duomo 2€ ($2.30). Open: Apr–Sept Mon–Sat 10 a.m.–7:30 p.m., Sun and holidays 1–7:30 p.m.; Nov–Feb Mon–Sat 10 a.m.–12:45 p.m. and 3–4:30 p.m., Sun and holidays 3–4:30 p.m.; Mar and Oct Mon–Sat 10 a.m.–5:30 p.m., Sun and holidays 1–5:30 p.m.*

Museo delle Sinopie
Campo dei Miracoli

On the other side of Piazza del Duomo, across from the Camposanto, this museum houses the *sinopie* (preparatory sketches for frescoes) found under the charred remains of the frescoes in the Camposanto after the fire that destroyed most of them. Each *sinopia* faces an engraving that shows what the Camposanto frescoes looked like before their destruction. It is very well done and very expressive, allowing us to re-live what the magnificent camposanto must have looked like before 1944. Allow 30 minutes for your visit.

See map p. 252. Piazza del Duomo. ☎ *050-560-547. Admission: 5€ ($5.75). Open: Daily Apr–Sept 8 a.m.–7:30 p.m.; Nov–Feb 9 a.m.–4:30 p.m.; Mar and Oct 9 a.m.–5:30 p.m.*

Museo dell'Opera del Duomo
Campo dei Miracoli

On the south side of the Leaning Tower is the Museo dell'Opera del Duomo, which houses plans for the Duomo, ancient artifacts found on the site at the time the Duomo was constructed, illuminated books and religious paraphernalia, and original artworks that were removed from the Duomo and other monuments for preservation. Particularly notable are the **griffin** that decorated the Duomo's cupola before being replaced by a copy (an 11th-century Islamic bronze, booty from a Crusade) and Giovanni Pisano's **Madonna col Bambino,** carved from an ivory tusk in 1299. Also interesting are the Carlo Lasinio **etchings,** which were prepared for the 19th-century restoration of the Camposanto's frescoes. Colored by Lasinio's son, they're the best record of the frescoes that were made before their destruction in World War II. Allow about one hour for your visit.

See map p. 252. Piazza del Duomo. ☎ *050-560-547. Admission: 5€ ($5.75). Open: Daily Apr–Sept 8 a.m.–7:30 p.m.; Nov–Feb 9 a.m.–4:30 p.m.; Mar and Oct 9 a.m.–5:30 p.m.*

Museo Nazionale di San Matteo (National Museum of S. Matteo)
Piazza Mazzini

The monuments on Campo dei Miracoli steal the show in Pisa, but this very important museum should not be overlooked if you are interested in Italian Renaissance art. Its collection of paintings from the 12th to the 15th centuries is one of the best in the world, and its sculpture gallery — including works from the Middle Ages to the 16th century — is very rich. Some of the works come from nearby churches, particularly from Santa Maria della Spina (see below), others from ecclesiastical buildings farther away in the town's territory. Important masterpieces include the 1426 painting *San Paolo* by Masaccio, two paintings of the *Madonna con i Santi* by Ghirlandaio, the sculpture of the *Madonna del Latte* by Andrea and Nino Pisano, and sculptures by Donatello. Depending on your level of endurance, it could take you one to several hours to visit this museum.

See map p. 252. Lungarno Mediceo-Piazza San Matteo, near Piazza Mazzini. ☎ *050-541-865. Admission: 4€ ($4.60). Open: Tues–Sat 9 a.m.–7 p.m., Sun 9 a.m.–2 p.m.*

Santa Maria della Spina
Ponte Solferino

This small church, which has survived in spite of its dangerous location above unstable ground near the river bed, is a trove of marble carvings. Built on the river shore in 1230 as an oratory near a bridge that was destroyed in the 15th century, the church was enlarged during the 14th century and decorated by some of the town's best artists of the time. Its foundations were strengthened several times during the centuries, and in 1871, as a final drastic effort to consolidate the ground on which the church was built, the entire structure was taken apart and re-built on a 1.2m (4-ft.) high base. During this process, many of the original sculptures were moved to the Museo Nazionale di San Matteo and replaced with copies, and the entire sacristy was destroyed. Although this loss somewhat ruined the proportions of the building, it remains one of the most delightful examples of Tuscan Gothic architecture. The many delicate carvings on the external walls as well as the elegant arches and windows and the simple interior in contrasting stripes of marble make a wonderful encasing for the sculptural masterpiece by Andrea and Nino Pisano, the *Madonna della rosa* (1345-1348). Plan to spend about a half-hour here.

See map p. 252. Lungarno Gambacorti, near Ponte Solferino. ☎ *055-321-5446 Admission: 1.50€ ($1.70). Open: Nov–Feb Tues–Sun 10 a.m.–2 p.m., second Sun of the month 10 a.m.–1 p.m. and 2:30–5 p.m.; Mar–Oct Tues–Fri 10 a.m.–1:30 p.m. and 2:30–5 p.m., Sat–Sun 10 a.m.–7 p.m.*

Torre di Pisa or Campanile (Leaning Tower)
Campo dei Miracoli

Behind the Duomo is the famous Leaning Tower, the Duomo's Campanile (bell tower). Started in 1173 by the architect Bonnano, this beautiful eight-story carved masterpiece, with open-air arches matching those on the

Duomo, was finally finished in 1360. It took so long to build because it started leaning almost from the beginning, so the Pisans stopped construction in 1185. In 1275, they started again and built up to the belfry, cleverly curving the structure as they went to compensate for the lean. The construction stopped again, until 1360, when the belfry was added. Later architects and engineers studied the problem — the shifting alluvial subsoil, saturated with water — but couldn't devise a solution (one attempt to fix it made it lean more). In 1990, the lean became so bad — 4.5m (15 ft.) out of plumb — that the tower was closed to the public. Two years later, a belt of steel cables was placed around the base, and in 1993, it was decided to stop ringing the bells to prevent vibrations from shaking the tower, and visits to the tower had to be stopped. But after a $24-million restoration, engineers succeeded in reducing the tower's lean by 15 inches. It reopened in December 2001.

The visit is guided and tours start every 30 minutes; your ticket is valid only for the time stamped on it. You can now make advance reservations online at www.opapisa.it for an additional cost of 2€ ($2.30) per ticket; you must pick up your printed voucher from the ticket office at least one hour before your reserved slot. Tickets can be purchased up to 15 days in advance.

There are no elevators in the tower, and access is through the original — and very narrow — staircase. It's 300 steep steps to the top and it is impossible to stop or turn around, making the climb physically and psychologically taxing. Anybody suffering from vertigo or claustrophobia should not attempt it. Children under 8 are not allowed in the tower.

See map p. 252. Piazza del Duomo. ☎ *050-560-547.* www.opapisa.it. *Admission: 15€ ($17). Open: Daily 8:30 a.m.–8:30 p.m.*

More cool things to see and do

✔ Some of the town celebrations are great fun: a traditional event is the **Gioco del Ponte,** held on the last Sunday in June, when teams from the north and south sides of the Arno fight each other. Wearing Renaissance costumes, the teams use a decorated 6300kg (7-ton) cart to push each other off the Ponte di Mezzo, the Roman bridge at the center of town. Another town celebration is the **Festa di San Ranieri,** on June 16 and 17, held in honor of Pisa's patron saint. The Arno is lit with torches all along its length, which makes quite a beautiful sight. Contact the tourist office for more information (see "Fast Facts: Pisa," later in this chapter).

✔ To get a different perspective on the town, you can visit one, or both, of Pisa's **medieval towers.** The **Torre di Santa Maria** (Piazza del Duomo; ☎ 050-560-547; admission: 2€/$2.30, free for children under 10; open: daily Mar–Oct 11 a.m.–2 p.m. and 3–6 p.m.) overlooks the Campo dei Miracoli while the **Torre Guelfa della Cittadella Vecchia** (Piazza Tersanaia; ☎ 055-321-5446; admission 2€/$2.30, free for children under 10; open: Mar–Oct Fri–Sun 3–7 p.m., Nov–Feb Sat–Sun 2–5 p.m.; second Sun of month 10 a.m.–1 p.m. and 3–5 p.m.), affords great views over the Arno River and the surrounding countryside.

▸ **The Cooperativa il Navicello** (Lungarno Galilei 7; ☎ **050-540-162** or 338-980-8867) operates several **cruises,** including the "Tour Lungarno," a cruise along the urban portion of the river Arno (by reservation only; Apr–Oct weekends and holidays). This is the best way to fully savor the medieval flavor of Pisa. Boats leave from San Paolo a Ripa d'Arno on the hour from 10 a.m. to noon and from 3 to 6 p.m.; from May through September there is an additional cruise at 7 p.m. The trip lasts about an hour and tickets are 5€ ($5.75) per person.

Fast Facts: Pisa

Area Code

The area code for Pisa is 050; use this code when calling from anywhere outside or inside Italy, even within Pisa (include the 0 every time, even when calling from abroad).

ATMs

There are many banks in town with ATMs, especially on Corso Italia and Via G.Mazzini There's a *cambio* (exchange office) at the airport and several in town, including one on Piazza del Duomo.

Emergencies

Ambulance, ☎ **118;** fire, ☎ **115;** road assistance, ☎ **116.**

Hospital

The Ospedale Santa Chiara is at Via Roma 67, nearby the Duomo (☎ 050-554-433).

Information

The tourist office (☎ 050-929-777; Fax: 050-929-764) maintains three information booths, one outside Pisa Centrale, just to the left when you exit (☎ 050-42-291; open Mon–Sat 9 a.m.–7 p.m. and Sun 9:30 a.m.– 3:30 p.m.); one near the Duomo at Via Cammeo 2 (☎ 050-560-464; open Mon–Sat 9 a.m. –6 p.m. and Sun 10:30 a.m. –4:30 p.m.); and at the airport (☎ 050-503-700; open daily 10:30 a.m. –4:30 p.m. and 6 –10 p.m.).

Internet Access

Internet Surf is at Via Carducci 5, west of the Duomo, by Piazza Martiri della Libertà (☎ 050-830-800; www .internetsurf. it; open Mon–Fri 10 a.m.–11 p.m., Sat 10:30 a.m.–11 p.m., Sun 3–11 p.m.).

Police

There are two police forces in Italy; call either one. For the Polizia, call ☎ **113 ;** for the Carabinieri, call ☎ **112.**

Post Office

The Central Post Office is in Piazza Vittorio Emanuele II 7/8 (☎ 050-519-41), near the railroad station of Pisa Centrale.

The Cinque Terre

If you push on a bit farther along the coast, into neighboring Liguria and the Riviera di Levante (part of the Italian Riviera), you discover the **Cinque Terre,** a fishing and agricultural area of great natural beauty. Nested here at the water's edge and insulated from the inland by towering promontories are its five small towns: **Monterosso al Mare, Vernazza, Corniglia, Manarola,** and **Riomaggiore.**

The **Cinque Terre,** together with the sea surrounding them, were declared a national park a few years back — the first example of a national park created to protect a man-made environment, such as the almost vertical terraces where the locals have nurtured their vineyards and lemon orchards for centuries.

The Cinque Terre region is a great place to spend some time with your kids. The breathtaking views, the sea, the swimming, and the hiking provide a great respite from the usual cultural attractions.

While it is possible to "do" the Cinque Terre in a day, the area is definitely worth more than one day if you can spare the time — especially if you are into hiking and swimming.

Getting there

The best way to reach the Cinque Terre is by train or boat. You can catch a direct **train** from Pisa, but from most other places you'll need to change in La Spezia — the largish town at the southeastern end of the Gulf of the Poets and the gateway to the natural park of the Cinque Terre — to the local train line for Levanto. Riomaggiore, and Monterosso are the two village stations where the most trains stop, but trains run frequently to each of the five villages; and the entire ride from La Spezia to Levanto costs only about 2.60€ ($3). Note that you can purchase a special pass including admission to and transportation within the park; see "Getting around," later in this chapter.

The railroad tracks that run through the Cinque Terre are literally carved into the mountain, and in some stations, part of the platform is in the tunnel, making it difficult to know where you are. Pay attention and, if in doubt, ask the conductor or another passenger to alert you to your stop — just pronounce the name of the village with an interrogative inflection, they'll understand you.

In this magnificent land sloping steeply to the sea, boats are often better friends than cars. Even if you intend to use the train, consider taking a **boat** at least for one leg of your trip: viewing the Cinque Terre from the sea is a part of the magic that shouldn't be missed. The **Consorzio Marittimo Turistico 5 Terre** *Golfo dei Poeti* (☎ 0187-732-987; www. navigazionegolfodeipoeti.it) runs half- and full-day cruises during the season (Mar 27–Nov 1), leaving from Molo Italia (dock Italia) in the harbor of the town of La Spezia at 9:15 a.m. and 10 a.m. (for the full-day excursion) or at 2:15 p.m. (for the afternoon trip) and returning by 6:30 p.m. The cost is 20€ ($23) for the whole day and 15€ ($17) for the afternoon only; children aged four to ten pay 11€ ($13) for either cruise; children under 4 travel free. The ticket also includes unlimited rides on the boat service between the villages (see "Getting around," later in this chapter) and you can hop on and off between the villages as you please.

We do not recommend visiting the Cinque Terre by **car,** especially during the summer months, when cars are completely off limits in the villages — even for unloading luggage at your hotel. If you are traveling by car you

The Cinque Terre

can leave it at the ACIPARK lot in La Spezia (Via Crispi 73; ☎ **0187-510-545**) for 4€ ($4.30) and proceed by train or boat. If you insist on driving the whole way, the easiest route is to take the *autostrada* A12 toward Genova and take the exit for Carrodano-Levanto; follow signs for the Cinque Terre towards Monterosso al Mare. In Monterosso, you can stow your car in the **large parking lot** (☎ **0187-802-050**) provided for visitors (about 8.25€/$9.50 per day). From there you can get a taxi to town for about 7€ ($8.05) or take the shuttle bus (price included in the Cinque Terre Pass; see "Getting around," later in this section). Beware, though, this lot does get full in the height of the summer season.

Getting around

Trains and boats are the best way to move from one village to another, although the walking trails offer a unique experience. All of the five villages are connected by frequent **train service,** and a service of electric *navettes* (minibuses) connects each train station with the village harbors, trail heads, and other destinations in the park.

Be aware that most of the train run is through tunnels — the line was excavated along the cliff, after all. So don't expect scenic train rides — you'll see mostly solid rock!

The **Cinque Terre Card,** available at any rail station, is the best way to get around: the pass gives you unlimited rides on trains between Levanto, each of the Cinque Terre, and La Spezia, on the *navettes,* as well as free access to the trails within the park. For a small additional fee, you can also get unlimited rides by boat with the regular boat service. The daily card costs 5.40€ ($6.20) for adults and 2.70€ ($3.10) for children aged 4 to 12; the 3-day card costs 13€ ($15) for adults and 6.50€ ($7.50) for children aged 4 to 12. The daily card with boat service costs 13.60€ ($15.60) for adults and 6.80€ ($7.80) for children aged 4 to 12 (the 3-day card with boat service is not available).

Regular **boat service** runs between Monterosso and Riomaggiore, with stops in Vernazza and, every other trip, also in Manarola. Service starts at 9.20 a.m. in Riomaggiore and 10 a.m. in Monterosso and boats run about every hour; the last boat leaves Riomaggiore at 5:25 p.m. and Monterosso at 6 p.m. A day pass costs 11.50€ ($13) for adults and 6.50€ ($7.50) for children between four and ten years of age. It is provided by the Consorzio Marittimo Turistico 5 Terre *Golfo dei Poeti* (see "Getting to the Cinque Terre," earlier in this section).

If you are fit, **walking** is the only way to fully discover the beauty of the villages and the surrounding cliffs, with their paths carved into the earth. There are trails between each of the villages and to the *Santuari* (churches) up the hills. There is a fee to access each section of the main trail connecting the villages, unless you purchase the Cinque Terre Card.

If you intend to walk, you'll need to schedule enough time and, if you're traveling in the hot season, you'll need to hit the trails early, when the air is still cool and the sea breeze is with you, or you'll be broiling-hot. Plan to arrive at the head of the trail you have chosen early enough so that you can be done with your walk by around 10 o'clock (see our estimated walking times in "More cool things to see and do," later in this chapter). This will give you some leeway in case you decide to linger, and still keep you from the hottest hours of the day.

Although it is permissible to **drive** between the five villages, we don't recommend it; the local road SS370, is a twisty and narrow mountain road, and parking facilities — small and expensive — exist only in Riomaggiore, Corniglia, and Manarola.

Spending the night

Bed and Breakfast Il Vigneto
$ **Manarola/Riomaggiore**

The friendly atmosphere, the location up high in the promontory overlooking the sea, and the lush gardens, all contribute to make this one of our favorite places to stay in the area. The whitewashed walls with dark wood or iron-work furniture give the guest rooms a faint Mission feeling; the rooms are spacious and so are the bathrooms. The terrace, where breakfast is served in the good season, offers a breathtaking view sweeping over the sea and the dry wall terraces. There is no air-conditioning, but the mountain air will keep you cool. A *navette* service takes you to the center of town and to the railroad station.

Via Pasubio 64 in Volastra, a small village above Riomaggiore and Manarola. ☎ *0187-762-053. Fax: 0187-762-173.* www.ilvigneto5terre.com. *Rack rates: 75€–120€ ($86–$138) double. Rates include breakfast. AE, MC, V.*

Hotel Gianni Franzi
$ **Vernazza**

Each of the guest rooms in the new wing of this hotel has a private little garden cut into the cliff, overlooking the sea. The rooms are bright, with whitewashed walls, checkered terracotta floors, and beamed ceilings; the elegant furniture makes up for the fact that guest rooms and bathrooms are small, but you wouldn't expect anything different for a hotel housed in the truly old buildings in the heart of the village.

Piazza Marconi 5 (note: this is the address of the restaurant where reception is located; the hotel buildings are further up the hill). ☎ *and Fax: 0187-821-003.* www.giannifranzi.it. *Rack rates: 76€ ($87) double. Rates include continental breakfast. AE, DC, MC, V. Closed Jan–Mar.*

Hotel Marina Piccola
$ **Manarola**

Small, bright rooms with a beautiful view at moderate prices. This hotel is the way to go if you want to keep a lid on expenses and can do without air conditioning or an elevator (guest rooms go up to the 5th floor). The iron-work beds and whitewashed walls give a very Mediterranean feeling to the guest rooms; bathrooms are quite small though. The hotel restaurant is excellent (see "Dining locally," later in this section).

Via Birolli 120. ☎ *and Fax: 0187-920-103.* www.hotelmarinapiccola.com. *Rack rates: 105€ ($121) double. Rates include continental breakfast. AE, DC, MC, V. Closed Jan.*

Hotel Pasquale
$$ **Monterosso**

This family-run hotel is right on the beach in the center of town. Each of the rooms offer terrific views above the ocean and coastline. The rooms are medium-sized, with a clean modern look, and most bathrooms have only showers. The common areas include a bar (a real one, with a seating area — not one of those skimpy affairs) that doubles as a restaurant offering local cuisine. The family also owns the Hotel Villa Steno (see later in this section).

Via Fegina 4. ☎ *0187-817-477 or 0187-817-550. Fax: 0187-817-056.* www.pasini. com. *Rack rates: 135€–180€ ($155–$207) double. Rates include continental buffet breakfast. AE, MC, V.*

Hotel Porto Roca
$$$ Monterosso

This is a beautiful luxury hotel offering spectacular views from its high cliff location above town. The luminous guest rooms have whitewashed walls and wooden furniture; they are very spacious and comfortable, and most have large balconies and full baths. The hotel's amenities include a bar, a restaurant with an extensive cellar of Italian wines, a private beach, a beautiful sun terrace, and free parking — a real rarity in this area. The hotel accepts pets for a charge and provides a free car service to the train station. Book early during the high season.

Via Corone 1. ☎ *0187-817-502. Fax: 0187-817-692.* www.portoroca.it. *Free parking. Rack rates: 195€–280€ ($224–$322) double. Rates include buffet breakfast and use of beach chairs and umbrellas. AE, DC, MC, V. Closed Nov–Mar.*

Hotel Villa Steno
$$ Monterosso

Each room of this family-run modern hotel has a private terrace or small garden, with great views over the sea and the village. Located in the upper part of town, and surrounded by olive and lemon trees, it is unpretentious and offers comfortably appointed guest rooms with a minimalist look and bright white walls. The hotel is run by the same family that owns the Hotel Pasquale (see earlier in this section). Parking is limited, so call on the morning of your arrival and they'll do their best to reserve you a spot.

Via Roma 109. ☎ *0187-817-028 or 0187-818-336. Fax: 0187-817-354.* www.pasini. com. *Free parking. Rack rates: 135€–180€ ($155–$207). AE, MC, V.*

Dining locally

Being a highly touristy area, you'll want to avoid the few overpriced tourist traps, although the quality of the food is usually adequate. In this section, we give you the best of the good ones. The cuisine of the Cinque Terre is typical Ligurian, with a lot of fresh fish and fresh herbs — such as the basil for the pesto sauce, now famous around the world. See Chapter 2 for more in-depth information about Ligurian cuisine.

Al Carugio
$ Monterosso LIGURIAN

This is a classic Italian restaurant at its best: white linen, good food and wine, perfect service, and moderate prices. You can find all the typical dishes of Ligurian cuisine proudly prepared and served in a friendly atmosphere. Among the *primi,* go for the classic *troffie al pesto* (a rustic sort of linguine traditionally made with chestnut flour), or try their wonderful

Use these handy Post-It® Flags to mark your favorite pages.

risotto ai frutti di mare (seafood *risotto*), both delicious; among the *secondi* a must is the *acciughe*, the famous local anchovies, which are prepared *al tegame* (stewed) or *fritte* (fried).

Via S. Pietro 9 ☎ *0187-817-367. Reservations recommended. Secondi: 7€–15€ ($8.05–$17). AE, MC, V. Open: Lunch and dinner Fri–Wed; closed 4 weeks in Dec, 2 weeks in Jan.*

Gambero Rosso

$$ **Vernazza** LIGURIAN

Set in the picturesque square at the heart of town, this is one of the best fish restaurants in town, offering some of the less common local dishes and friendly yet professional service. The *spaghetti alle vongole* is truly excellent, but if you want to try something more typical, then go for the *tian,* the local specialty of oven-roasted anchovies, potatoes, tomatoes, and rosemary. You will also enjoy the complimentary glass of *Sciacchetrà* at the end of the meal (the famous local — and rare — *passito,* a sweet wine).

Piazza Marconi 7. ☎ *0187-811-265. Reservations recommended. Secondi: 8€–21€ ($9.20–$24). AE, DC, MC, V. Open: Summer, lunch and dinner daily; winter, lunch and dinner Tues–Sun. Closed Jan–Feb.*

Marina Piccola

$$ **Manarola** FISH

This unpretentious trattoria of Hotel Marina Piccola is liked by locals and known for its grilled fish. During the high season diners can enjoy wonderful sunsets on the terrace overlooking the sea. All the specialties are excellent, but we do recommend to do as the locals do and gorge on the splendid grilled fish, masterly cooked with garlic and fresh herbs; some of the best are the *spigola alla griglia* or the *San Pietro.*

Via Birolli 120. ☎ *0187-920-103.* www.hotelmarinapiccola.com. *Reservations recommended. Secondi: 9€–21€ ($10–$24). AE, DC, MC, V. Open: Lunch and dinner Wed–Mon. Closed mid-Nov–mid-Dec.*

Ripa del Sole

$$ **Riomaggiore** LIGURIAN

This new restaurant, run by a brother-and-sister team, offers cooking that's true to the best local tradition with a menu that's certified organic. The warm yellow walls, wood accents, and beautiful linen and real crystal on the table create a sunny atmosphere, a perfect setting to enjoy your meal. The terrace — open for dinner in the high season — is high above the sea and the view is breathtaking. We definitely recommend the antipasto platter, with all the Cinque Terre fish specialties: stuffed mussels and anchovies, marinated octopus and anchovies, *baccalà* (codfish) dumplings.

Via de Gasperi 282, on the mountain side of the village. ☎ *0187-920-143.* www.ripa delsole.it. *Reservations recommended. Secondi: 8€–21€ ($9.20–$24). AE, MC, V. Open: Summer, lunch and dinner daily; winter, lunch and dinner Tues–Sun. Closed Nov.*

Ristorante l'Alta Marea
$$ Monterosso   LIGURIAN

In the center of town, this lively restaurant offers a casual atmosphere that appeals to younger crowds. Although trendy, the food is as good as in more old-fashioned, traditional restaurants. The delicious *linguine al pesto* is tangy and fresh.

Via Roma 54. ☎ *0187-817-331. E-mail:* altamarea@monterossonet.com. *Reservations recommended. Secondi: 9.50€–18€ ($11–$21). AE, DC, MC, V. Open: Summer lunch and dinner daily; winter, lunch and dinner Thurs–Tues. Closed Dec.*

Trattoria Gianni Franzi
$$ Vernazza   LIGURIAN

Tradition is the key word at Gianni's, where the recipes of Ligurian cuisine are prepared with care and attention to detail and served in a refined surrounding. From late spring to mid-fall you can dine al fresco and enjoy gorgeous sunsets by the sea. You can find all the classics prepared with local fish, herbs, and vegetables; our favorites include a fantastic *zuppa di pesce* and excellent *troffie al pesto* (the linguine is made from chestnut flour); the *ravioli di pesce* (fish ravioli) are very good and so are the local anchovies, stuffed or marinated.

Piazza Marconi 5. ☎ *0187-821-003. Reservations recommended. Secondi: 9.50€–20€ ($11–$23). MC, V. Open: Summer, lunch and dinner daily; winter, lunch, and dinner Thurs–Tues. Closed Jan–Mar.*

Exploring the Cinque Terre

The National Park of the Cinque Terre was recently declared a World Heritage site by UNESCO. The **Cinque Terre Trail** (see "More fun things to see and do," later in this section) is the best way to see up close the real attraction of the Cinque Terre: the amazing cliffs, cultivated for centuries using dry stone walling — over 7,000m (21,000 ft.) of it — to build narrow terraces. Vineyards are planted all the way down to the edge of the sea, together with luscious lemon and olive trees. During the harvest, farmers secure themselves with ropes to keep from falling. Progress has come to the area, however, so here and there you may notice small lifts that look something like monorails.

The top attractions

Corniglia
The only inland village of the Cinque Terre — though you can reach the sea by way of an old flight of steps — it is also the most agricultural of the villages. The cobblestone streets of Corniglia wind from door to door and to its church, **San Pietro.** Built in 1334 above a chapel from the 11th century, the church was redone during the baroque period, but the Romanic facade, graced with a beautiful rosette, was preserved. The whole town is like a step back in time, and there are several medieval buildings of interest, such as the arched gothic building made of black

stone, believed to have been the postal station of the Fieschi family. Its agricultural tradition goes back millennia: Corniglia was already exporting wine to Pompeii during the Roman period.

Manarola

Manarola, a lovely sight from a distance with its gaily colored houses, is a real fisherman's village, still dependent on and closely related to the sea. The village is enclosed in a gorge opening to a small harbor between two rocky cliffs; Manarola contains the 14th-century Romanic **church of San Lorenzo,** highlighted by a splendid rose window. From Manarola starts — or ends — the famous **Via dell'Amore** (love trail), the easiest of the trails joining the villages (see "Riomaggiore," for more information).

Monterosso al Mare

This is the largest of the five villages that compose the Cinque Terre; it's also the only one of the villages to have a nice sandy beach, giving Monterosso the feeling of an old-fashioned seaside resort. It's wonderful for swimming here, even though most of the beach is divided into private swaths for the hotels lining the beachfront. It is also the busiest of the villages, and some say the least authentic. In reality, it is just different: because high cliffs don't surround it on all sides, the old town has seen the growth of a modern section towards the rail station and the beach, called Fegina. But the heart of Monterosso is still beautiful and unspoiled.

The **medieval tower Aurora** separates the modern town from the old; where you'll find the late-Romanic church San Giovanni Battista in black and white stripes with a beautiful rosette on the facade and an elegant portico at back facing the sea. Further up, you'll climb to the other church in town, **San Francesco,** within the complex of the **convent of the Capuchins.** Built in 1619, it is a nice example of Tuscan/Ligurian Gothic in green-and-white-striped marble. Inside you can admire a fine crucifixion attributed to Van Dyck.

Riomaggiore

Like Manarola, fishing is still an important industry in this village. Noteworthy attractions include the **church of San Giovanni Battista,** a fine example of late-Romanic architecture with two beautiful lateral portals from the 14th century. Uniting this village with Manarola is the most famous section of the coastal path: the **Via dell'Amore** (the love trail) — a romantic path which was excavated in the cliff and offers fabulous views. It was closed for more than five years after a landslide and has only recently reopened.

Vernazza

Vernazza is a very tiny fishing village with a strong medieval flavor. Dominated by its castle, it was founded around the year 1000. Overlooking the village is the Gothic church of **Santa Margherita di Antiochia,** built in blackstone right on the water with an unusual octagonal bell tower. The fishing harbor offers a fine view over the rest of the bay.

More cool things to see and do

✔ The **Cinque Terre Trail** (difficulty level: easy) requires five hours —
that is, if you are one of those tourists in excellent shape with iron
will; otherwise, plan on about six hours, plus any additional time
you would want to spend in the villages. We found that the best way
to follow this path is to do only part of the trail and travel the rest of
the way by train or boat; this way you get the full Cinque Terre experience without getting exhausted. It is also more adapted to a varied
party, including children or less fit people. As a national park, walking the trails between one village and the other is no longer free. If
you've purchased the recommended **Cinque Terre Card** (see
"Getting around," earlier in this section), admission to the trail is
free. If not, you can also just pay at the entrance of the section you
want to hike. The hike from Riomaggiore to Manarola along the
fairly flat stretch known as the **Via dell'Amore** (see section on
Riomaggiore), takes only 30 minutes. To this you can add the two
sections from Manarola to Corniglia and Corniglia to Vernazza, each
taking about 45 minutes. Between Corniglia and Vernazza the trail
gives you access to the romantic small sandy beach of **Guvano,**
where you can pause for a dive into the clean waters of the park; in
Vernazza you can catch the boat to Monterosso. The section of the
trail from Vernazza to Monterosso takes about 1½ hours and is quite
different, with windy ups and downs, and a precipitous descent into
Monterosso. We do not recommend it unless you feel you are fit or
you are here for the specific purpose of hiking: it doesn't add anything to your visit except a few more sore muscles!

Although the easy trail requires you to be only moderately fit, you
should go with at least one companion, bring at least a quart of
water per person (especially in summer, when it gets very hot), and
wear sturdy walking shoes. The trail is along a cliff, and landslides
are not uncommon. If you're lucky, during your walk you may see a
local farmer standing where you'd think only goats can stand, lovingly tending to one of his plants.

✔ Five **Santuari** (churches dedicated to the Madonna) line SS370, the
local road between the villages, but they can also be reached on
foot or by public transportation, including taxis, from each of the
village they overlook. Destination of religious processions, their
position — dominating the surrounding countryside and high
above the sea — make them fantastic stages for the breathtaking
views. Some are more interesting than others. **Nostra Signora di
Soviore,** overlooking Monterosso, sports the oldest campanile in
Liguria, dating back to the 8th century; the 14th-century facade has
an interesting rosette and portal. The area in front of the church
offers breathtaking views and is the seat for classical music concerts during the good season (inquire with the local information
office for the schedule). **Nostra Signora di Montenero** overlooks
Riomaggiore 340m (1120 ft.) above sea level; the church was built
in 1335, perhaps over an 8th-century chapel, and the monastery
now houses a good restaurant (**Ca' de Cian; ☎ 0187-920992;**

cadecian.tsx.org; reservations necessary. Prix-fixe lunch or dinner: 20€/$23. American Express accepted. Open: Lunch and dinner Thurs–Sun. Closed Nov–Mar). **Nostra Signora della Salute** in Volastra is a Romanic church with a noteworthy portal and gothic *bifora,* a delicate window with two arches.

✔ The sea along the national park is a protected **marine park** which can be best enjoyed with snorkeling and scuba-diving excursions. The **Coopsub Cinque Terre** in Riomaggiore (Via San Giacomo; ☎ **0187-920-011;** utenti.lycos.it/diving_5terre/) is a licensed diving center offering guided excursions and equipment rental. Excursions cost about 22€ ($25) per person; equipment rental is an extra 17.50€ ($20).

Fast Facts: The Cinque Terre

Area Code

The area code for the Cinque Terre is 0187; use this code when calling from anywhere outside or inside Italy, even within the Cinque Terre (include the 0 every time, even when calling from abroad).

ATMs

You can exchange money at the Pro loco office in Monterosso (see "Information," below); there are ATMs in the banks of Monterosso and Vernazza.

Emergencies

Ambulance ☎ **118,** or in Riomaggiore, ☎ **0187-920-777,** in Manarola ☎ **0187-920-766,** in Monterosso ☎ **0187-817-475,** and in Vernazza ☎ **0187-821-078.** Fire ☎ **115;** road assistance ☎ **116.**

Hospital

The nearest hospital is San Nicolo Levanto, in the town of Levanto, just west of Monterosso al Mare (☎ 0187-800-409); there is also a larger hospital in La Spezia (☎ 0187 -5331).

Information

In Monterosso al Mare, the Pro loco office (tourist office) is at Via Figena 38 (☎ 0187-817-506), open Monday through Saturday from 10 a.m. to noon and 5:00 to 7:30 p.m. and Sunday 10 a.m. to noon. From June through September, there's an additional office on Via del Molo (☎ 0187-817-204), which is open the same hours. A tourist office can be found inside the train stations of each of the villages: Monterosso (☎ 0187-817-059), Corniglia (☎ 0187-812-523), Vernazza (☎ 0187-812-533), Manarola (☎ 0187-760-511), and Riomaggiore (☎ 0187-760-091).

Internet Access

Located in Monterosso is The Net (Via Vittorio Emanuele 55; ☎ 0187-817-288; e-mail: info@monterossonet.com).

Police

There are two police forces in Italy; call either one. For the Polizia, call ☎ **113;** for the Carabinieri, call ☎ **112.**

Post Office

The main post office for the area is in Monterosso al Mare, on Piazza Garibaldi, in the center of town.

Chapter 16

Southern Tuscany

● ●

In This Chapter

▶ Discovering the glorious Tuscan landscapes in Chianti
▶ Exploring medieval Siena
▶ Checking out medieval towers in San Gimignano

● ●

*Y*ou could spend many weeks exploring the rich trove of cities and hills surrounding Florence. This region's incomparable beauty matches the richness of its artistic heritage. A castle or walled city seems to surmount each hill.

Lying between Florence and Siena is the **Chianti region,** famous for its flavorful ruby-red wine. This region is an agricultural area of uncommon beauty, the soft slopes of its hills blooming with magnificent colors in every season, with terraced rows of vineyards, shimmering olive groves, and stately cypress trees, and the tallest hills topped by medieval walled towns and *pieve* (fortified churches). The deceptively simple cuisine of the Chianti is much celebrated as well.

South of the Chianti is **San Gimignano,** famous for its medieval towers. During the 13th century, the city experienced an economic boom, and the city's rich merchants marked their increasing wealth and pride by building palaces, each with its own tower. This started a competition, and the towers became so high that the city's government had to intervene, dictating that no tower could be higher than the tower of the municipal palace. Of the original 72 or so towers, only 15 remain, but the view is still quite impressive. Continuing southeast, you arrive at **Siena,** Italy's most beautiful medieval town, in our opinion. Famous for the Palio delle Contrade (a furiously contested horse race that has been held in the city's main square, the Piazza del Campo, since medieval times), which occurs in July and August, Siena is a jewel of a town, giving unending pleasure to those who stroll its streets and visit its monuments.

If you have the time, you could base yourself in Siena, if you prefer to be in a town, or in the Chianti, should you prefer the charm of the country-side, and spend a few rewarding days enjoying the local food and wine and exploring southern Tuscany. If you choose to tour the region on your own, you get the most freedom by renting your own car, especially if you want to cover a lot of ground — but the driving can be stressful (see "Getting around," in the Chianti section of this chapter); as an alternative, you could try the public bus system. If your time is limited, you can easily visit each destination in this chapter as a day trip from Florence. Frequent buses visit each of the destinations described in this chapter (see "Getting there," in each of the regional sections below).

To see the scope of the entire Tuscan landscape, see the "Tuscany and Umbria" map in Chapter 15.

The Chianti

Break our rule about driving in Italy and put the pedal to the metal in the Chianti region (or at least take a bus tour). This gorgeous region between Florence and Siena has it all: velvety hills, tiny medieval walled towns, and acres of vineyards and olive groves. You can visit the area as a day trip from Florence, but the area has so many breathtaking sights that you're likely to long for more travel time. The region's tourist office is in **Greve in Chianti** (see "Fast Facts: The Chianti," later in this section).

Getting there

The **Chiantigiana,** or *strada statale* (state road) SS222, crosses the Chianti region, linking Siena to Florence. Going along the 66 kilometers (41.3 miles) of this winding road (winding because it was established as the route to collect wine from each vineyard in the region and bring it to Florence), is the best way to explore the Chianti. It passes through each of the major points of interest in the area.

Alternatively, you can take a **guided bus tour** from Florence, a solution that requires less organization on your part and may allow you to see more in less time (see "Exploring the Chianti," later in this section). It is a particularly good solution if you're pressed for time.

Taking a **public bus** is another option, affording you more independence than a guided tour (see "Getting around," below, for more information).

Getting around

While renting a car allows for the most independent travel, we've had a number of American friends make the trip, looking forward to a couple of relaxing weeks in the Tuscan countryside, only to return with white hair they didn't have when they left. Driving here is still way better than motoring the Amalfi coast, but reckless driving has reached even the back country areas; also, the smaller roads are truly narrow and often in bad repair or unpaved. It is difficult to enjoy a scenic drive if you have to grip your wheel and keep your eyes glued on the grey ribbon — or muddy potholes. If you feel up to the challenge, though, all you need is a good map of the region; the one from the tourist office in Florence is good, but for a larger map get one from a newsstand, souvenir shop, or bookstore in Florence or Siena.

If you choose to drive, note that you'll get the best deals by renting from abroad, either from one of the agencies that specialize in European rentals — such as AutoEurope, Europe by Car, Kemwel, Maiellano — or one of the three international car rental companies that operate in Italy — Hertz, Avis, or National/Maggiore (see "Car Rental Agencies," in the Appendix for Web sites and phone numbers).

If you pack light or go for a day trip from Florence, you can get a good glimpse of the region at your own pace by using the **public bus system.** You can get a good view of the countryside on the way, stop for an excellent meal in one of the villages we recommend, then catch a bus back. The bus company **SITA** (☎ **800-373-760** or 055-47-821; www.sita-on-line.it) runs lines that connect Florence with most small towns in the Chianti. We feel that the best destination is Greve in Chianti, at the center of the region and the main town in Chianti; the trip takes about an hour and costs about 3€ ($3.45). The same line also goes further, to Radda and then Castellina. A number of buses also depart Siena with the bus company **TRA-IN** (☎ **0577-204-245;** www.trainspa.it) for the same small towns.

Spending the night

The Chianti is rich in not only hotels and inns in the main towns but also rural accommodations (*agriturismo,* as Italians call it), and luxurious country villas.

Albergo del Chianti
$ Greve in Chianti

With large and bright guest rooms, immaculately kept and moderately priced, and excellent service, this hotel offers a great value. Located on Greve's beautiful main square, you can also enjoy the hotel's lovely garden — where breakfast and dinner are served in pleasant weather — and swimming pool, both a big hit if you have kids. The management is also very accommodating with special family needs.

Piazza G. Matteotti 86, in the center of Greve. ☎ *055-853-763. Fax: 055-853-764.* www.albergodelchianti.it. *Free parking. Rack rates: 104€ ($120) double. AE, DC, MC, V.*

Castello di Spaltenna
$$$$–$$$$$ Gaiole in Chianti

If your fancy is to stay in a real medieval castle, this is your chance: This historic landmark offers a variety of accommodations ranging from relatively simple guest rooms — wrought-iron beds and canopies, fine fabrics, and a few antiques — to a suite, with its private heliport. Prices range as widely and the simpler doubles are more affordable, especially during the off season. In the castle's beautiful park grounds you can enjoy a swimming pool (with a small waterfall), a tennis court, and free use of bikes; indoors, you'll find a heated swimming pool, an exercise room, a sauna, and a billiards room. The hotel's restaurant, Ristorante della Pieve, is rather elegant.

The Chianti

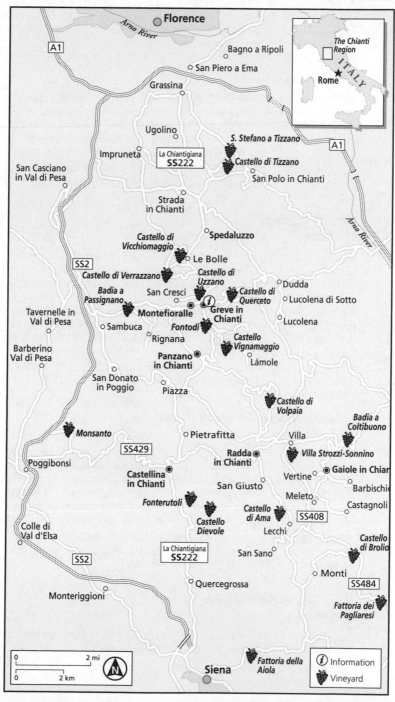

Via Spaltenna 13, just west of Gaiole in Chianti. ☎ **0577-749-483.** *Fax: 0577-749-269.* www.spaltenna.com. *Free parking. Rack rates: 320€–540€ ($368–$621) double. AE, DC, MC, V.*

Hotel il Colombaio
$ Castellina in Chianti

Surrounded by a large garden, this 16th-century stone squire house has guest rooms appointed with rustic elegance — whitewashed walls, beamed ceilings, and terracotta floors. The wrought-iron beds have thick mattresses and fresh, starched sheets. There is a nice swimming pool in the garden and the hotel is only a five-minute walk from the center of town.

Via Chiantigiana 29. ☎ **0577-740-444.** *Fax: 0577-740-402.* www.albergoil colombaio.it. *Free parking. Rack rates: 104€ ($120) double. AE, DC, MC, V.*

La Villa Miranda
$$ Radda

The old inn — housing an excellent restaurant (see "Dining locally," later in this section) — is the center of a large, recently renovated complex that includes two pools, tennis courts, and open, grassy spaces. You can stay in a room in the old inn; there's plenty of charm there but the rooms are, well, *old* (and smaller and darker than the new rooms). The new units are beautiful, large, and appointed with antique furnishings. The baths are a little small but have modern fixtures and a bright decor. It's a ten-minute walk from the center of town.

Hamlet of La Villa, 1km (0.6 miles) east of Radda in Chianti. ☎ **0577-738-021.** *Fax: 0577-738-668. Free parking. Rack rates: 145€ ($167) double. MC, V.*

Villaggio Albergo Tenuta di Ricavo
$$$$ Ricavo

If you have a car and want to splurge, you can stay at this beautiful estate — once a medieval hamlet — with large guest rooms that are elegant and comfortable and furnished with country-style antiques, plus an excellent restaurant, **La Pecora Nera** (reviewed later in this section). This 15th-century villa created from medieval houses boasts two tennis courts, a golf course, an 8km (5-mile) horse-riding path, bike paths, a pool, a terrace, and a garden.

Ricavo (3.2km/2 miles north of Castellina in Chianti). ☎ **0577-740-221.** *Fax: 0577-741-014.* www.ricavo.com. *Free parking. Rack rates: 360€ ($414) double. Rates include buffet breakfast. AE, DC, MC, V. Closed Nov–Mar.*

Villa Rosa di Boscorotondo
$ Panzano

Surrounded by vineyards, this pink villa offers large guest rooms with beamed ceilings; all have been individually decorated, with wrought-iron beds and canopies and quality Italian fabrics. The private baths are comfortably sized and some of the rooms open onto two large terraces overlooking the countryside. Managed by the same owners of the hotel Torre Guelfa in Florence, this resort also has a swimming pool that affords a panoramic view.

Via San Leolino 59, 5km (3 miles) south of Greve on SS222. ☎ *055-852-577. Fax: 055-856-0835.* www.resortvillarosa.com. *Free parking. Rack rates: 135€ ($155) double. Rates include breakfast. AE, DC, MC, V.*

Dining locally

It is very difficult to have a bad meal in the Chianti — and impossible to have a bad glass of wine, provided you stick to the local red — but it is possible to overpay. Some restaurants offer an upscale cuisine and atmosphere, but we recommend that you stick to simpler options: the more rustic tend to be the better. You can stop to sample wines in the region's many wineries, accompanied by tasty local specialties.

Albergaccio
$$ Castellina TUSCAN

The rustic atmosphere of a barn shouldn't mislead you — this restaurant offers a sophisticated cuisine that merges tradition with creativity. The menu is seasonal, but may include homemade *pici al sugo d'agnello* (homemade spaghetti with lamb sauce) and *zuppa di funghi e castagne* (local chestnuts and mushroom soup). You are in luck if they have the *semifreddo di pistacchi con salsa allo zafferano* (a pistachio cream with saffron sauce) for dessert. A special menu for children offers smaller portions and simpler dishes such as pasta with plain tomato sauce or fried chicken.

Via Fiorentina 63, just outside the city walls. ☎ *0577-741-042.* www.albergaccio cast.com. *Reservations necessary. Secondi: 16€–21€ ($18–$24). AE, DC, MC, V. Open: Lunch and dinner Mon–Sat. Closed 3 weeks in Nov/Dec.*

Bottega del Moro
$ Greve in Chianti TUSCAN

In Greve's center, this restaurant is a perfect place for a not-too-heavy lunch. The cooks prepare Tuscan specialties with an eye to tradition but also to modern health standards (read: less fat). This restaurant is a favorite with locals, who come for the grilled or stewed meats and the fresh pasta. We thoroughly enjoyed the *coniglio arrosto* (rabbit with black olives), the scrumptious ravioli, and the *pappardelle alla lepre* (homemade pasta with wild hare sauce).

Piazza Trieste 14r, behind the church at the narrow end of Greve's main square. ☎ *055-853-753. Reservations necessary. Secondi: 12€–18€ ($14–$21). AE, DC, MC, V. Open: Lunch and dinner Thurs–Tues. Closed Nov and 1 week in May/June.*

Giovanni da Verrazzano
$$ Greve in Chianti TUSCAN

On the first floor of the hotel of the same name, this excellent restaurant, which doubles as a cooking school, serves all the specialties of the region in a warm, inviting atmosphere. The simple wooden tables covered with white tablecloths, whitewashed walls, arched doorways, and beamed ceilings are the perfect setting for one of the best dinners you're likely to ever have. The kitchen turns out the classics — such as *pappardelle al cinghiale* (fresh homemade pasta with wild boar sauce) and a superb *fiorentina* steak, for example — but it also excels at other rarer traditional specialties, such as an excellent Tuscan pot roast made with Chianti wine, called *stracotto*.

Piazza G. Matteotti 28, on Greve's main square. ☎ **055-853-189.** *Reservations recommended. Secondi: 12€–21€ ($14–$24). AE, DC, MC, V. Open: Lunch and dinner Mon–Tues and Thurs–Sat. Closed 2 weeks in Aug.*

La Cantinetta
$ Spedaluzzo TUSCAN

In this two-centuries-old farmhouse surrounded by a garden, you can taste real Tuscan countryside food. Savor the regional specialties, including some that are more difficult to find, such as *involtini* (veal rolls) and *piccione farcito* (stuffed pigeon). The Tuscan equivalent of prime rib, known as *tagliata,* is excellent and so is the *tiramisù.*

Via Mugnano 93, in Spedaluzzo, 2.25km (1.4 miles) north of Greve on SS222. ☎ **055-857-2000.** *Reservations necessary. Secondi: 8€–16€ ($9.20–$18). AE, DC, MC, V. Open: Lunch and dinner Tues–Sun. Closed 3 weeks in Feb/Mar.*

La Pecora Nera
$$ Ricavo TUSCAN

The dining room of this luxurious farm-villa measures up to what you'd expect of a fine country inn in this region. It has a fireplace, white walls and red bricks, arched passageways, and wooden beams. The excellent food includes very well prepared traditional Tuscan dishes — *ragu di cinghiale* (wild boar sauce), *tagliata ai porcini* (steak with porcini mushrooms), *arista* (special cut of pork) — as well as some more imaginative options. Still unusual in Italy, this is a non-smoking restaurant.

At the Hotel Tenuta di Ricavo, in Ricavo (3.2km/2 miles north of Castellina in Chianti). ☎ **0577-740-221.** *Reservations recommended. Secondi: 12€–23€ ($14–$26). AE, DC. Open: Lunch and dinner Mon–Tues and Thurs–Sat. Closed 2 weeks in Aug.*

Villa Miranda
$$ Radda TUSCAN

Inside an old roadside inn (see "Spending the night," earlier in this section), this restaurant is intensely atmospheric and decorated with country-style furnishings. The food is well-prepared traditional Florentine. You can't go wrong with the grilled meat (such as the *fiorentina*) or the homemade pastas. If you're in the mood for typical vegetable soup, the *ribollita* is wonderful.

Hamlet of Villa, 1.12km (¾ miles) east of Radda in Chianti. ☎ *0577-738-021. Reservations recommended. Secondi: 10€–20€ ($12–$23). MC, V. Open: Lunch and dinner Tues–Sun.*

Exploring the Chianti

If you don't intend to drive in Italy, which is a sensible idea, you can take a guided tour of the Chianti. **SITA bus lines** (☎ 055-214-721; www.sita-on-line.it) organizes day tours from Florence every day for about 32€ ($37) per person. These trips allow you to get a good taste of the region without having to drive the snaking back roads.

The top attractions

Castellina in Chianti

Still surrounded by most of its 15th-century walls and dominated by a fortress with crenellated walls known as the **Rocca,** Castellina is where the medieval flavor of the region is strongest. The town, however, was already an Etruscan and then a Roman center. Built in the 15th century around a tower of the 14th century, the Rocca houses the town hall; in the entrance are some local Etruscan findings. The vaulted street around the walls — **Via delle Volte** — was once used by the soldiers for defense during the wars between Florence and Siena.

See map p. 275. 10km (6.2 miles) west of Radda.

Gaiole in Chianti

Ancient market place for the surrounding area, Gaiole was the third member of the Chianti League (an alliance of wine-producing towns working against the hegemony of Florence and Siena), together with Radda and Castellina. Today, it is a quiet small town, with a pleasant main street and a small museum (Via Ricasoli 48; near the tourist information office) housing Etruscan remains from the site of **Cetamura,** an archeological area including an Etruscan village and Roman baths on the road towards Radda. Also just outside Gaiole, are two fortified hamlets, well worth a visit. **Spaltenna** has a castle (see "Spending the night," earlier in this section) and the *pieve di Santa Maria* from the 12th century (but altered in the 18th). **Vertine,** 2 km (3.2 miles) away, is an imposing castle surrounded by a picturesque village from the 12th–13th century. About 2.7km (3.6 miles) away lays the castle of **Meleto,** a fortified medieval farmhouse which is the archetypical castle, with powerful round crenellated towers.

See map p. 275. 10km (6.2 miles) east of Radda on SS408.

Greve in Chianti

On the river Greve, this medieval small town began developing during the 13th and 14th centuries as marketplace for the castle of Montefioralle (see below), and today is the capital of the Chianti. Thanks to its central location, it hosts the annual **Rassegna del Chianti** (☎ 055-854-6287), a market fair of producers and sellers of Chianti Classico — the highest in the hierarchy of Chianti wines — during the second weekend of September, with food, wine tasting, and music. The picturesque center of town has a unique triangular main square, **Piazza Matteotti,** surrounded by arcades full of shops, restaurants, and hotels. The square hosts a lively open air market on Saturday mornings. At the narrow tip of the square is the church of **Santa Croce,** with a nice triptych of the *Madonna e Santi* by Bicci di Lorenzo.

See map p. 275. On SS222, 30km (19 miles) south of Florence, about halfway to Siena.

Montefioralle

This tiny hamlet is one of the few remaining perfectly preserved medieval fortified villages. Built on a steep hill and surrounded by walls, it can be easily reached on foot by a 20-minute uphill walk from Greve in Chianti. Montefioralle's houses and diminutive cobblestone squares are decorated with bright red geraniums; walking around the circular main road during the good weather is a real delight. Look for the house marked by a relief of a wasp and "V" on the stone, it is where Amerigo Vespucci, the sailor that gave his name to the American continent, was born. If you happen to be in the area on the Sunday after the 19th of March (the feast of San Giovanni), don't miss the *festa delle frittelle* when traditional sweet rice fritters are cooked in a huge pan.

See map p. 275. 1.28km (.8 miles) west of Greve on Via del Castello di Cintoia.

Panzano

This small and charming medieval town affords superb views over the surrounding countryside. The main square hosts a nice market on Sunday mornings and a lively **wine festival,** "Vino al Vino," on the third weekend of September (Call ☎ 055-854-6287 for possible date changes) with music and, of course, wine tastings. Also interesting is the 14th-century church of **Santa Maria Assunta,** integrated in the castle and the *Annunciazione* inside, attributed to the Ghirlandaio. Leaving Panzano towards the south on SS222 you'll see a sign on your left for the *pieve* of **San Leolino.** This fortified church was probably built over a church of the eighth century. The current three-naved church dates from the 12th century whereas the facade and portico are from the 16th century. Inside, there is a triptych attributed to the "Maestro di Panzano," two tabernacles by Giovanni della Robbia and, in the left nave, a *Madonna con S. Pietro e S Paolo* of the 13th century by Meliore di Jacopo. Also beautiful the small cloister of the 14th century. Ring the bell to be admitted in the church.

See map p. 275. 5.2km (3.2 miles) south of Greve on SS222.

Radda in Chianti

Built on a steep hill about 20km (12.5 miles) from Greve, **Radda in Chianti** is much smaller than Greve, with parts of its defense walls still standing. The town conserves a more definite medieval character. The **city hall (Palazzo Comunale)** boasts an interesting 15th-century fresco under its portico. In the Gardens off Viale Matteotti, you'll find the **Ghiacciaia Granducale,** a medieval ice house — at one time used to pack snow during the winter and as a "refrigerator" and source of ice for ice cream during the summer — which has been completely restored and transformed into an antique shop (☎ 0577-738-739; open daily). Head of the Chianti League in the middle ages, Radda still hosts the historical seat of the **Consorzio del Chianti Classico,** in the fattoria Vignale, just outside town. About 3km (4.8 miles) south of town going toward Lecchi is the *pieve di San Polo in Rosso,* a major Florentine defensive work. Built in A.D. 1000, this church was in a strategical position right on the border with Sienese territory. But is spite of all Florentine efforts, the Sienese won it over and the Florentine have never been able to get it back. Behind the mighty towers and walls, the three nave church has a frescoed walls and a beautiful vaulted roof with an almost Gothic style. The castle is privately owned and has been transformed into a hotel, but the whole *pieve* is open to visits on Thursdays at 4 p.m. (admission is 8€/$9.20 and includes a wine tasting).

See map p. 275. 20km (12.5 miles) south of Greve on SS222 and then Strada Provinciale SP2 bis.

More cool things to see and do

. . . and more wine to drink.

✔ No visit to the Chianti is complete without a stop at the **Castello di Brolio** (☎ 0577-749-066; www.ricasoli.it), about 11.2km (7 miles) southeast of Radda. Owned by the Baron Ricasoli, this is one of the region's oldest wine-producing estates (the vineyards trace back to at least the 11th century) and the birthplace of the Chianti Classico we know today, a masterly mix of grapes finalized in the mid-19th century. You can visit part of the spectacular grounds and gardens (Admission: 3€/$3.45; open: summer 9 a.m.–noon and 3–6 p.m.; winter 9 a.m.–noon and 2–5 p.m.) and take a wine-tasting tour of the cellars (by appointment) for 23€ ($26). The on-site store sells the estate's award-winning wines.

✔ Among all the other castles and wine-producing estates of the region, we like **Dievole,** one of the more modern vineyards located 12km (5½ miles) northeast of Siena. You can visit, have a wine tasting, or even stay overnight in the Villa (☎ 0577-322-613 [estate] or ☎ 0577-322-632 [Villa]; www.dievole.it). A pleasant shop sells wines and other products of the estate.

✔ The 11th-century **Castello di Uzzano** (☎ 055-854-032; Fax: 055-854-375; open: Apr–Oct daily from 8:30 a.m.–6 p.m.; winter, by reservation only), was transformed into an imposing villa in the 16th century. The surrounding estate produces both wine and olive oil. Located just northeast of Greve in Chianti, it can also be reached on foot by a pleasant hour-long hike (on a side road from the SS222; about 5km/3 miles from Greve). You can visit the cellars (admission: 5€/$5.75) and tour the famous Italianate Renaissance gardens (admission: 6€/$6.90).

> ✔ Obviously the temptation will be strong to **shop** at the estates and village shops you pass, and to bring back home some of those wonderful **cured meats** and a piece of that delightful **pecorino cheese**. Unfortunately, you can't. U.S. regulations are quite strict, especially against importing meats. You can bring cheese, but it has to be in air- sealed packaging. On the other hand, you could bring home some of the best **olive oils** and **herbed vinegars** in the world without restriction, and of course some **wine**. **La Cantinetta del Chianti** (Via B. Ricasoli 33, Gaiole in Chianti; ☎ **0577-749-125**; e-mail: cantinetta@chiantinet.it) is a good wine shop that will ship to most destinations. If you are interested in another specialty of the region, the ancient craft of wrought-iron work, visit **Vernifer** (Via Marconi 28; ☎ **0577-749-626**) in Gaiole in Chianti.

Fast Facts: The Chianti

Area Code

The country code for Italy is 39. The city code for towns within the province of Florence is 055, whereas the city code for towns within the province of Siena is 0577; use these codes when calling from anywhere outside or inside Italy, even within the same town (include the 0, even when you call from abroad).

Currency Exchange

There is at least one ATM in the center of the major towns in the area — Greve, Castellina, Gaiole, and Radda — but we recommend that you get your cash before coming to the Chianti (it's a farming area with few services).

Emergencies

Ambulance, ☎ **118**; fire, ☎ **115**; road assistance (Italian Automobile Club, ACI), ☎ **116.**

Hospital

There is a small unit in Gaiole in Chianti (Via Casa Bianca; ☎ 0577-749-500) and one in Castellina in Chianti (Via Ferruccio; ☎ 0577-740-897).

Information

The tourist office for the region is in Greve in Chianti (Via Luca Cino 1; ☎ 055-854-6287. open Mon–Sat 10 a.m.–1 p.m. and 3–6 p.m. in summer and 9 a.m.–2 p.m. in winter). There are other information offices in Radda in Chianti (Piazza Ferrucci 1; 0577-738-494, open daily from 9 a.m.–1 p.m. and 3–5 p.m.); and in Gaiole in Chianti (Via Ricasoli 50; ☎ 0577-749-605; e-mail: staff@chiantinet.it).

Internet Access

There is an Internet Train shop (Via Roma 36; ☎ 055-853-384), and an Internet Train corner inside the Bar Lepanto (Piazza Matteotti 4; ☎ 055-854-6077) in Greve in Chianti.

Police

There are two police forces in Italy; call either one. For the Polizia, call ☎ 113; for the Carabinieri, call ☎ 112.

Post Office

A post office (ufficio postale) is at Via Chiantigiana (☎ 0577-741-000) in Castellina in Chianti.

Siena

With its rich orange tones and myriads of tiled roofs baking in the strong sun, Siena is a sculpture in its own right. It is a magnificent medieval city surrounded by sun-drenched countryside, but Siena is far from being a museum piece. Passion pervades Sienese life, from the love the residents have for their town and their traditions to their time-honored Palio horse race (see "The top attraction," later in this section). Far from just a tourist attraction, the Palio is a deeply felt and hotly contested competition among the city's 17 districts *(contrade)* — trust us, the Super Bowl doesn't incite as much passion as this race.

To do justice to Siena, you should set aside a couple of days, and steep yourself in the local flavors. But if you don't have the time, you can also visit the town as a day trip from Florence.

Getting there

Siena is 62km (37 miles) south of Florence, and the easiest way to get to Siena from Florence is to take a **bus**. TRA-IN (☎ **0577-204-246**; www.train spa.it), with a ticket booth at Piazza Gramsci, in the La Lizza pedestrian underpass, has buses leaving the SITA station in Florence (near SMN train station) every half-hour. It also offers bus runs to many other Tuscan cities. The ride from Florence lasts about 1¼ hours (less than the train) and costs about 5€ ($5.75). **SITA** (☎ **800-373-760**; www.sita-on-line.it) also offers daily rides from Via Santa Caterina da Siena, near SMN in Florence. **SENA** (Via Montanini 92, ticket booth at Piazza Gramsci, in the La Lizza pedestrian underpass; ☎ **800-930-960** or 0577-283-203; www.sena.it) runs seven daily rides between Siena and Rome from Rome's Stazione Tiburtina for 17€ ($20). Reservations are required from Rome to Siena, but not from Siena to Rome. SENA also makes runs to/from Milan and other Italian cities. You can make a reservation and buy a ticket online, or by phone at **Eurolines** (☎ **06-4425-2461**), which will deliver your ticket by messenger service to your hotel. (In Siena, SENA provides the delivery service.)

From Florence, Siena is an easy **train** ride of about 1½ hours for about 6€ ($6.90). Because Siena is on local rail line, you usually have to change in Chiusi when you come from Rome, and in Florence or Empoli when you come from Venice. The trip from Rome takes about 3 hours and costs about 17€ ($20), and the trip from Venice takes about 5 hours and costs about 28€ ($32). Siena's rail station (☎ **0577-280-115**) is on Piazza Fratelli Rosselli, about 2.5km (1½ miles) from the town center. You can take a taxi or minibus C, which takes you from the train station to Piazza Gramsci, the northern tip of the historic district, a pedestrian-only area.

By **car,** Siena is an hour drive on the Florence/Siena highway or on one of the older and more scenic roads; just follow the signs (green for the highway, blue for the local road). From Rome, take *autostrada* A1 north toward Florence and exit at Val di Chiana for SS326, or alternatively take the Via Cassia from Rome (one of Italy's old consular roads, it's a bit narrow).

Siena

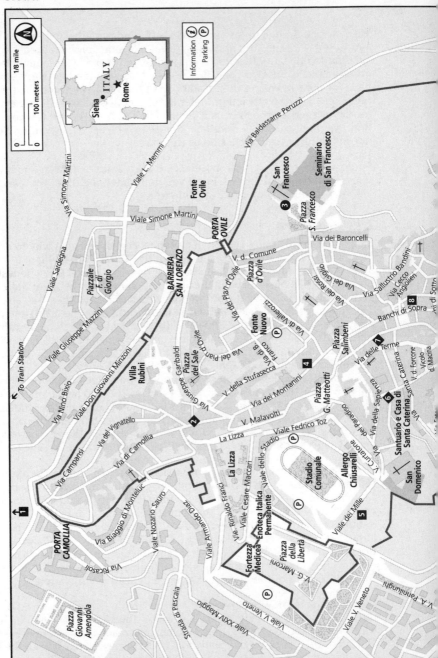

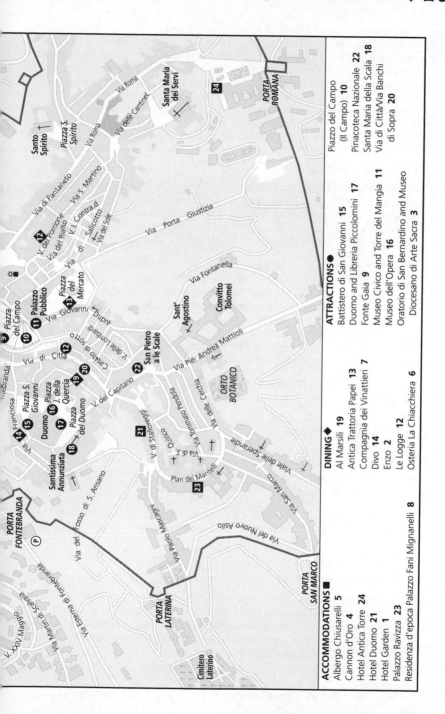

ACCOMMODATIONS ■
Albergo Chiusarelli **5**
Cannon d'Oro **4**
Hotel Antica Torre **24**
Hotel Duomo **21**
Hotel Garden **1**
Palazzo Ravizza **23**
Residenza d'epoca Palazzo Fani Mignanelli **8**

DINING ◆
Al Marsili **19**
Antica Trattoria Papei **13**
Compagnia dei Vinattieri **7**
Divo **14**
Enzo **2**
Le Logge **12**
Osteria La Chiacchiera **6**

ATTRACTIONS ●
Battistero di San Giovanni **15**
Duomo and Libreria Piccolomini **17**
Fonte Gaia **9**
Museo Civico and Torre del Mangia **11**
Museo dell'Opera **16**
Oratorio di San Bernardino and Museo
Diocesano di Arte Sacra **3**
Piazzo del Campo
(Il Campo) **10**
Pinacoteca Nazionale **22**
Santa Maria della Scala **18**
Via di Città/Via Banchi
di Sopra **20**

Traffic in the historic district is completely restricted, so when you arrive in Siena, you will need to park for the duration of your stay in one of the parking lots (Siena Parcheggi; ☎ 0577-228-711; www.sienaparcheggi.com) at the various gates of town charging 1.50€ ($1.70) per hour, which makes 36€ ($41) per day. Don't even dream of parking for free outside the town walls if you don't want your car broken into or stolen. Many hotels in town offer discounted rates for the use of the parking lots, but we think the cost of parking is just another good reason to use public transportation, unless you are on a driving itinerary.

Getting around

Built on three hills, historic Siena is divided in *terza* (districts that cover a third of town each). North, along Via Banchi di Sopra, is the **Terza di Camollia;** southwest, along Via di Città, is the **Terza di Città** (with the Duomo); and southeast, along Via del Porrione, is the **Terza di San Martino.** The three *terza* meet at **Piazza del Campo.**

You can best visit Siena **on foot,** especially because a large part of the historic district is pedestrian only, but also because most of Siena's attractions are very close to one another. The handy *pollicini,* the diminutive buses that link the Siena train station and the major parking lots with the center of town, will also shuttle you around. The *pollicini* are color-coded, depending on which *terza* they service. One ticket, valid one hour, costs 0.90€ ($1); ten tickets cost 8€ ($9.20); and a daily pass cost 3.50€ ($4); the buses run daily from 6 a.m. to 9 p.m.

For a taxi call ☎ 0577-49-222 (radio taxi) or ☎ 0577-289-350 (in Piazza Matteotti).

Spending the night

Siena has many hotels, but unlike other Italian towns, Siena's hotels in the historic district tend to be modest properties — most likely due to architectural constraints. The more luxurious ones are away from the center, near the city walls or beyond them. If you're planning to visit during the Palio delle Contrade (see "More cool things to see and do," later in this section), remember that hotels accept reservations for the Palio period as far as a year in advance. Plan ahead!

Albergo Chiusarelli
$ Piazza San Domenico

This 19th-century building, a five-minute walk from Piazza del Campo, has been renovated and features plain but modern guest rooms and bathrooms. The facade displays Ionic columns and a second-floor loggia and is shaded by palm trees, but you may want to get a room toward the back to avoid street noise. There is no elevator.

See map p. 284. Viale Curtatone 15. ☎ *0577-280-562. Fax: 0577-271-177.* www.chiusarelli.com. *Bus: C to Piazza San Domenico. Parking: Free in small parking garage. Rack rates: 117€ ($135) double. Rates include buffet breakfast. AE, MC, V.*

Cannon d'Oro
$ Piazza Salimbeni

This 15th-century *palazzo* is on a commercial street and offers simple but large guest rooms, furnished with wrought-iron beds and some old pieces that make you feel as if you've stepped back in time. It's a nice mix of the once grand and the now economical. The bathrooms are small but have modern fixtures. Management is very accommodating to the needs of families with children. No air conditioning or elevator.

See map p. 284. Via Montanini 28. ☎ **0577-44-321.** *Fax: 0577-280-868.* www.cannon doro.com. *Bus: C to Piazza Salimbeni. Rack rates: 90€ ($104) double. AE, MC, V.*

Hotel Antica Torre
$ Porta Romana

This small, family-run hotel has only eight rooms, but they are in a real 16th-century tower (*torre* — hence the name) and very romantic, elegantly appointed with marble floors and antique furniture. The two rooms on the top floors offer views of Siena and the countryside. Because it's a tower, however, don't expect huge rooms. There is no air conditioning or elevator.

See map p. 284. Via di Fieravecchia 7. ☎ *and Fax:* **0577-222-255.** *Bus: A, B, or N to the Porta Romana. Rack rates: 120€ ($138) double. AE, MC, V.*

Hotel Duomo
$ Duomo

You can't beat this hotel's location halfway between Piazza del Campo and the Duomo, and its guest rooms are simply but tastefully decorated, with whitewashed walls, wrought-iron beds, and new bathrooms. Ask for a room with a view on the Duomo and the hilly countryside. You can also enjoy the view from the hotel roof terrace.

See map p. 284. Via Stalloreggi 38. ☎ **0577-289-088.** *Fax: 0577-43-043.* www.hotel duomo.it. *Bus: A to Duomo. Parking: Free in nearby garage. Rack rates: 130€ ($150) double. AE, DC, MC, V.*

Hotel Garden
$$ North of Siena

This elegant 1700 villa is only 1.5km (1 mile) north of the city walls, up a hill among vineyards, olive groves, and a park full of oaks. (The walk downhill to town is very pleasant if you feel up to it, but take a taxi on your way back.) Guest rooms are divided among the villa itself and three annexes and are all large and tastefully furnished, some in period style, others with modern furniture. The rooms we prefer are in the Belvedere annex, large and bright and decorated in period style with some antiques, and the rooms in the Poggiarello annex, also bright and luminous but modern in decor. Guests have access to a tennis court and a large outdoor pool, and the terrace affords panoramic views over Siena and the countryside. The hotel's restaurant is elegant but with a very warm atmosphere.

See map p. 284. Via Custoza 2. ☎ 0577-47-056. Fax: 0577-46-050. E-mail: garden@ venere.it. *Free parking. Rack rates: 190€ ($219) double. Rates include breakfast. AE, DC, MC, V.*

Palazzo Ravizza
$$$ Duomo

The lenghty renovation of this 17th-century family palace has finally brought this hotel to its full potential: the beautiful architectural details — vaulted ceilings, checkered tiled floors, hardwood parquet — have been completely restored. Guest rooms are bright, with white plastered walls and some with frescoed ceilings; furnishings include elegant contemporary classics and a few antiques. There is a garden with beautiful views, where a typical American breakfast is served in the high season, as well as dinner, should you decide to take advantage of the hotel's restaurant, which is perfectly adequate.

See map p. 284. Pian dei Mantellini 34. ☎ 0577-280-462. Fax: 0577-211-597. www.palazzoravizza.it. *Bus: A to Duomo. Parking: Free in a garage nearby. Rack rates: 270€ ($311) double. Rates include buffet breakfast. AE, DC, MC, V.*

Residenza d'epoca Palazzo Fani Mignanelli
$$ Piazza San Domenico

This tiny five-room hotel — occupying the third floor of an historic building right in the heart of Siena, only steps from Piazza del Campo — is small but it's the best way to experience old-fashioned Sienese elegance. Its large, bright rooms have beamed ceilings and terracotta tile floors and are individually decorated with dark wood country antique furniture, and fine fabrics. Some beds have canopies and the hotel is air-conditioned and serviced by an elevator.

See map p. 284. Banchi di Sopra 15 and 15/B. ☎ 0577-283-566. Fax: 0577-217-732. www.residenzadepoca.it. *Bus: A. Rack rates: 200€ ($230) double. AE, MC, V.*

Dining locally

Sienese cuisine shares many of the specialties of Florentine cooking (see Chapter 14), with few fish dishes but plenty of game and prepared meats. Among the *primi* (first course) are *pici* (hand-rolled spaghetti), usually prepared with breadcrumbs and tomato sauce, and *pappa col pomodoro* (a soup of tomatoes and bread). Among the cold cuts are *finocchiona,* a fennel-flavored salami famous all over Italy.

Al Marsili
$$ Duomo SIENESE

If you've come to Siena for a romantic getaway or you just feel like splurging on a great dinner, Al Marsili is a superb choice. The service is formal, the atmosphere is elegant but warm, and the food lives up to its reputation. Here you can find staples of Sienese cuisine, such as the ubiquitous *pici,* but also specialties like *faraona alla Medici* (guinea hen with pine nuts, almonds, and prunes), and an excellent selection of wines.

See map p. 284. Via del Castoro 3, between Via di Città and the Duomo. ☎ **0577-47-154.** *Reservations recommended. Bus: A to Duomo; then walk past the Museo dell'Opera Metropolitana toward Via di Città. Secondi: 10€–18€ ($11–$21). AE, DC, MC, V. Open: Lunch and dinner Tues–Sun.*

Antica Trattoria Papei
$ **Piazza del Mercato   SIENESE**

This charming trattoria, close to Piazza del Campo, is a favorite with the Sienese. The food is good, sometimes remarkable. Try the *anatra alla Tolomei* (duck stewed with tomatoes), the Sienese favorite *pici alla Cardinale* (homemade spaghetti with hot tomato sauce) or the *pappardelle al sugo di cinghiale* (homemade noodles with wild boar sauce). They welcome families with kids and provide a choice of half-portion dishes for the younger ones.

See map p. 284. Piazza del Mercato 6, behind the Palazzo Pubblico. ☎ **0577-280-894.** *Reservations suggested. Bus: A to Piazza del Campo; then walk behind the Palazzo Pubblico. Secondi: 7€–12€ ($8.05–$14). AE, MC, V. Open: Lunch and dinner Tues–Sun.*

Compagnia dei Vinattieri
$$ **Santa Caterina   SIENESE**

The excellent cuisine is a fine match for this wonderful *enoteca* (winery) with over a thousand choices of wine, including the best of Tuscany but also of Italy and abroad. The menu offers lighter choices for lunch and heartier ones at dinner — all made with local ingredients. We recommend the *ravioli maremmani* (ravioli with a sauce of goat cheese and basil) and, if you don't mind the head, an unusual *collo di gallina ripieno in salsa verde* (stuffed neck of hen with green sauce). Wine is stored in cellars that are part of an ancient aqueduct running under the building. Should you be lucky enough to come during a lull in business you could even ask for a tour.

See map p. 284. Via delle Terme 79, at Via dei Pittori. ☎ **0577-236-568.** www. vinattieri.net. *Reservations recommended. Bus: A to Santa Caterina. Secondi: 9€–21€ ($10–$24). AE, DC, MC, V. Open: Summer, lunch and dinner daily; winter, lunch and dinner Wed–Mon.*

Divo
$$ **Duomo   SIENESE**

Even if you are a bit put off by the idea of dining in ancient Etruscan tombs, the quality of the food will more than make up for it. Under the vaulted tufa ceilings, you'll find a seasonal sophisticated menu including flavorful choices sech *involtini di zucchine con lardo di Colonnata* (rolled zucchini with gourmet local bacon), *piccione farcito ai profumi toscani su letto di polenta* (stuffed pigeon on polenta), and *scaloppa di agnello in croccante di olive con peperoncini* (lamb cutlet on a napoleon of olives and red peppers).

See map p. 284. Via Franciosa 29. ☎ *0577-284-381. Reservations recommended. Bus: A to Duomo. Secondi: 16€–24€ ($18–$28). MC, V. Open: Lunch and dinner daily.*

Enzo
$$ Duomo   SIENESE/FISH

This pleasant restaurant offers unusual traditional Tuscan dishes, including some tasty fish choices. The menu is seasonal but you might find the *terrina di ortiche* (stinging nettle terrine), the *margherite di grano saraceno agli scampi con calamari e pesto al dragoncello* (homemade buckwheat pasta with prawns, squid, and tarragon pesto), the *millefoglie di mare* (seafood napoleon), and the *costoletta di cinghiale in agrodolce* (wild boar cutlet in a sweet and sour sauce).

See map p. 284. Via Camollia 49. ☎ *0577-281-277. Reservations recommended. Bus: A to Duomo. Secondi: 12€–23€ ($14–$26). AE, MC, V. Open: Lunch and dinner Mon–Sat. Closed 2 weeks in July.*

Le Logge
$$ Duomo   SIENESE

Creative Tuscan cuisine paired with selections from their notable wine cellar are served in pleasant and rustic dining rooms, making this restaurant an excellent choice. The menu includes both traditional and more sophisticated dishes, from the simpler *pappa al pomodoro* (tomato and bread soup) and *pici* (homemade spaghetti) to the *ravioli di coniglio pecorino e menta* (hare, local pecorino cheese, and fresh mint ravioli), *costolette di coniglio con melanzane e polenta* (rabbit cutlets with eggplant and polenta), and *petto d'anatra con salsa di patate e raviolo al melograno* (duck breast with potato sauce and pomgranate raviolo).

See map p. 284. Via del Porrione 33. ☎ *0577-48-013. Reservations recommended. Bus: A to Duomo. Secondi: 14€–20€ ($16–$23). AE, DC, MC, V. Open: Lunch and dinner Mon–Sat. Closed 1 month Jan/Feb.*

Osteria La Chiacchiera
$ San Domenico   SIENESE

This *osteria* is cheap, with a minimum of decor and really good Tuscan peasant food — and it's welcoming to families. Try dishes like *pici alla boscaiola* (homemade spaghetti with tomato-and-mushroom sauce) and *salsicce e fagioli* (sausage and Tuscan beans). Anything on the daily menu is good and recommended.

See map p. 284. Costa di Sant'Antonio 4. ☎ *0577-280-631. Reservations recommended. Bus: A to San Domenico; then walk up Via di Sapienza and turn right. Secondi: 6€–9€ ($6.90–$10). No credit cards. Open: Lunch and dinner daily.*

Exploring Siena

Although strolling the narrow medieval streets is one of Siena's great pleasures, there's plenty to see indoors, from the Duomo to the collections of Siena's unique Renaissance school of art.

You can now make reservations for the sites you want to visit in Siena. Reservations are free and actually give you a discount off the admission price of 1€ ($1.15) or .50€ (60¢), depending on the site. You can make the reservation by contacting the **Comune di Siena** (☎ **0577-41-169;** Fax: 0577-226-265; e-mail moira@comune.siena.it), which will reply with a confirmation and an account number for a bank transfer; once that has cleared, they will send you a receipt. Pick up your tickets at the museum entrance at the time of your visit.

Siena offers several cumulative-ticket options. Most comprehensive are the **Siena Itinerari d'Arte (SIA) Inverno** (Siena Art Itineraries winter), which includes entrance to Museo Civico, Palazzo delle Papesse (a 15th-century palace housing contemporary art exhibits), Santa Maria della Scala, Museo dell'Opera, Battistero, and Libreria Piccolomini for 13€ ($15) per person; and the **SIA Estate,** including all the above plus San Bernardino and the Museo Diocesano, for 16€ ($18). Both passes are valid for seven days. Note that during the exposure of the floor in the Duomo (see later in this section), the Duomo and the Libreria Piccolomini are excluded.

If you are less ambitious, or you don't have the time, you can take advantage of the **Biglietto cumulativo Musei Comunali,** which includes entrance to Museo Civico, Palazzo delle Papesse, and Santa Maria della Scala for 10€ ($12) and is valid two days.

The best resource for guided tours is the **Centro Guide-Associazione guide turistiche** (☎ **0577-43-273;** www.guidesiena.it), which organizes daily highlights tours leaving from the tourist office in Piazza del Campo as well as custom-designed tours, such as a visit to Siena's museums. Prices vary according to the number of participants and the kind of tour. For a bus tour from Florence, call **American Express** (☎ **055-50-981**) or **SITA bus lines** (☎ **055-214-721;** www.sita-on-line.it) in Florence. Both offer similar tours of the major attractions in Tuscany, visiting the most important places and monuments, and give a tour of Siena for about 50€ ($58).

The top attractions

Battistero di San Giovanni (Baptistry of St. John)

Built in the 14th century, the Baptistry's unfinished Gothic facade is by Domenico di Agostino. But you won't care about the facade when you're inside admiring the lavish frescoes, most of which depict the lives of Christ and St. Anthony and were painted in the 15th century. At the center of it all is the baptismal font, a splendid masterpiece of monumental proportions made of six bronze panels depicting scenes of the life of St. John the Baptist, divided by figurines representing the virtues, each carved by one of the best artists of the time. The *Feast of Herod* and the figurines of *Faith* and *Hope* are by Donatello; Lorenzo Ghiberti carved the *Baptism of Christ* and the *Arrest of the Baptist;* Jacopo della Quercia the *Annunciation to Zacharias of the birth of the Baptist;* Giovanni di Turino did the *Preaching of the Baptist* and, with Turino di Sano, the *Birth of the Baptist.* Crowning the font is the marble ciborium with the statue of St. John the Baptist carved by Jacopo della Quercia. The angels are by Donatello and Giovanni di Turino.

See map p. 284. Piazza San Giovanni, behind the Duomo. ☎ *0577-283-048. Bus: A red or A green to Piazza del Duomo. Admission: 2€ ($2.30). Open: Daily Mar 15–Sept 30 9 a.m.–7:30 p.m.; Oct 9 a.m.–6 p.m.; Nov 1–Mar 14 10 a.m.–5 p.m.*

Duomo and Piccolomini Library (Libreria Piccolomini)

Some consider this Romanesque-Gothic cathedral the most beautiful in Italy. Decorated with contrasting colored marble both inside and out, it was built during the first half of the 13th century in Romanesque and Gothic styles. It contains many artworks, including a superb **13th-century pulpit** carved by Nicola Pisano — the artist who crafted the magnificent pulpit in Pisa's Baptistry and father of Giovanni Pisano (who carved the pulpit in Pisa's Duomo). The Cathedral pavement is another work of art upon which many famous artists of the time worked. Unfortunately, in order to protect it, it is visible only between August 23 and October 27, in honor of the Palio. Another masterpiece inside the Duomo is the **Piccolomini Library (Libreria Piccolomini),** built by Cardinal Francesco Piccolomini (later Pius III) to honor his uncle, Pope Pius II. The library was beautifully frescoed by Pinturicchio with scenes from the life of the Pope and contains the *Three Graces,* an exquisite Roman sculpture of the third century B.C. designed after a Greek model.

See map p. 284. Piazza del Duomo. ☎ *0577-283-048.* www.operaduomo.it. *Bus: A red or A green to Piazza del Duomo. Admission: Duomo free; Library 3€ ($3.45) except during the exposure of the floor when admission for Duomo plus Library is 6€ ($6.90). Open: Duomo March–Oct Mon–Sat 10:30 a.m.–7:30 p.m., Sun and holidays 10:30 a.m.–6:30 p.m. except during the exposure of the floor when it is opened daily 9:30 a.m.–7:30 p.m.; Nov–Feb Mon–Sat 10:30 a.m.–6:30 p.m. and Sun and holidays 1:30–5:30 p.m.*

Museo Civico and Torre del Mangia

The Museo Civico is housed in the beautiful 13th-century **Palazzo Pubblico**, the seat of the government in Siena's republican period and today Town Hall. Its richly frescoed rooms host some of Siena's important artworks. On the second floor, the loggia is the showcase for the eroded panels from the masterpiece fountain that decorated Piazza del Campo — the 14th-century **Fonte Gaia** was carved by Jacopo della Quercia and replaced by a replica in the 19th century. In the **Sala del Mappamondo (Globe Room),** just off the chapel, are two important pieces by 14th-century Sienese painter Simone Martini: the *Maestà* and the magnificent fresco of *Guidoriccio da Fogliano,* captain of the Sienese army (though there's been debate about the attribution of the latter work to Martini). In the **Sala della Pace (Peace Room)** — the meeting room of the Council of Nine that governed Siena, is a famous series of frescoes by another 14th-century Sienese painter, Ambrogio Lorenzetti: the secular medieval *Allegory of the Good and Bad Government and Its Effects on the City and the Countryside.* From the *palazzo*'s 14th-century **Torre del Mangia** — accessible from the courtyard — is a breathtaking view of the town and the surrounding hills (if you're up to climbing the 503 steps, that is). At 100m (335 ft.), the Torre del Mangia is the second-tallest medieval tower in Italy (the tower in Cremona is taller).

See map p. 284. Piazza del Campo. ☎ *0577-292-226. Bus: A pink, B, or N to Piazza del Campo. Admission: Museo 7€ ($8.05), 6€ ($6.90) with reservation; Tower 6€ ($6.90), 5€ ($5.75) with reservation. Both: 10€ ($11.50). Open: Museum daily Mar 16–Oct 31 10 a.m.–7 p.m.; Nov 1–Mar 15 10 a.m.–5:30 p.m. except Dec 25–Jan 6 when it closes at 6:30 p.m. Tower daily 16 Mar 16–Oct 31 10 a.m.–7 p.m.; Nov 1–Mar 15 10 a.m.–4 p.m.*

Museo dell'Opera

This museum occupies a part of the originally projected Duomo, which was never built. The ambitious plan was to create a cathedral of such huge proportions that the current Duomo would have been just the transept, but it never happened because of engineering problems and the plague of 1348. The gallery contains artworks that were removed from the Duomo for safekeeping and to prevent further decay. The main works are the statues that Giovanni Pisano carved for the façade; Duccio di Buoninsegna's famous painting of the Virgin, the *Maestà* (Duccio was a forerunner of Martini); and Pietro Lorenzetti beautiful triptych depicting the **Birth of the Virgin.**

See map p. 284. Piazza Jacopo della Quercia, adjacent to Duomo. ☎ *0577-283-048.* www.operaduomo.it. *Bus: A red or A green to Piazza del Duomo. Admission: 6€ ($6.90). Open: Daily, Mar 15–Sept 30 9 a.m.–7:30 p.m.; Oct 9 a.m.–6 p.m.; Nov 1–Mar 14 9 a.m.–1:30 p.m.*

Palio delle Contrade
Piazza del Campo

Siena's main sight isn't a site but an event. This famous festivity is a medieval-style derby in which riders representing the town's 17 *contrade* (neighborhoods) compete on horseback for top honors. This frantic horse race has been going on since the early Middle Ages at least — the origin of the Palio is uncertain and could even go back to the Etruscan, but the first written document mentioning the race is from 1238. It was only in the 17th century that the Palio started to be run on Piazza del Campo; before that, it was run in the streets, a bit in the style of the Monte Carlo car race. It was also during the 17th century that rules and regulations were written down and enforced, including the rule stating that participants had to ride bareback horses.

The Palio in its present form dates back to the 19th century, but whatever the origin, the passion continues unabated and the riders fight dearly to win. During race time, Piazza del Campo is temporarily filled with dirt for what is the world's most difficult horse race, and to some the most brutal — injuries aren't uncommon. A colorful parade in medieval costumes — each *contrada* has its own colors — accompanies the race; particularly famous is the flag juggling. The pageantry shows are competitive as well, and at the end of the Palio, the *contrada* with the best behavior, costumes, and skills wins the *Masgalano,* traditionally a silver bowl weighing at least 1kg (2.2 lbs.) and decorated with Palio scenes, though it could be a different work of art.

If you want to attend the Palio, you don't need to buy expensive tickets, unless you really want to see the horse racing up close. Standing in the center of the square is free — and could be a lot more fun. Note, though, that if you do seat yourself in the middle, you won't be able to get out until the race is over. Wherever you sit, bring lots of refreshments and a hat, as the sun gets very strong, and get there early, the square quickly fills to capacity. Although the horse race in itself is breathtaking, we like going just for the fun of watching all the pageantry and the parade at the end of the race, when the colors of the winning *contrada* are brought in triumph around town.

See map p. 284. Piazza del Campo. www.comune.siena.it. *Tickets for a seat in the grandstands or at a window of one of the buildings surrounding the piazza are controlled by the building owners and the shops in front of which the stands are set up.* **Palio Viaggi** *(Piazza La Lizza 12;* ☎ *0577-280-828; Fax: 0577-289-114) can help you score a seat. Seats can cost anywhere from 200€ to over 1,000€ ($230 to over $1,150) and need to be reserved as far as 6 months in advance. Final races: July 2 and August 16. Trials start on June 29 and August 13.*

The Palio day by day

The Palio is still organized by the town government and strictly regulated. Only 10 of the 17 *contrade* (town neighborhoods) participate in each of the two races: the 7 that didn't run the previous year in the same race plus 3 that are drawn from the remaining 10. The drawing, which takes place at least 20 days before each race, signals the beginning of the competition, but the official opening of the festivities occurs three days before the race and is marked by the ceremony of the drawing of the horse — when each of the ten chosen animals is assigned to a *contrada* — and the first of six trial runs on Piazza del Campo, three days before the Palio. At 3 p.m. on the day of the Palio, each horse is blessed in the church of its *contrada,* and then is lead to join the historical cortege. After the cortege has assembled, it tours the town before convening with the other horses in Piazza del Campo around 5 p.m. for the race. The alignment of the horses for the start is also decided by a drawing, and the last horse starts on the run from the back: when he moves the rope at the front, it is hastily lowered and the race begins. The horses then run around the square three times while riders can hit the horses — and each other — with a short whip. And remember, it's a *horse* race: the horse that arrives first wins, even if it has thrown his rider! The winning *contrada* will celebrate all night — and indeed till the next year. The victory dinner for the whole *contrada* — with thousands of participants — takes place around the end of September.

Pinacoteca Nazionale

This picture gallery is housed in the 15th-century Palazzo Buonsignori and contains an expansive collection of art showing the unique Sienese Renaissance style, which retained Greek and Byzantine influences long after realism came into play elsewhere (notably Florence), and emphasized rich coloration. It includes works from the 12th century to the first half of the 17th century. Guido da Siena, an early developer of the Sienese school, is well represented, along with the more famous Duccio, the real founder of the style; his painting of the Virgin is a marvel of delicacy and pathos. Also represented is Giovanni di Paolo — don't miss his beautiful little painting of the Virgin.

See map p. 284. Via San Pietro 29. ☎ *0577-281-161. Bus: A red or A green to Piazza del Duomo. Admission: 4€ ($4.60). Open: Tues–Sat 8 a.m.–7:15 p.m., Sun–Mon 8:15 a.m.–1:15 p.m.*

Santa Maria della Scala

Housed in the former Hospital of Siena, this huge complex of buildings has been recently opened to the public. Many of its rooms had been lavishly decorated with frescoes during the Renaissance and later periods and almost all the great Sienese artists worked for the hospital at one time or another. One of the most surprising rooms is the *Pellegrinaio,* which held hospital beds until only a few years ago. Built in the 14th century, it saw its original wooden ceiling replaced in the 15th century by a beautiful vaulted ceiling decorated with frescoes narrating the history of the hospital — note that the last vault by the window was added in the 16th century. The **Cappella del Sacro Chiodo** — or *Sagrestia Vecchia* (old sacristy), was also built in 1444 to hold the relics and reliquaries bought by the Spedale from the imperial palace of Byzantium. It was frescoed by Lorenzo Vecchietta with a cycle on the New and Old Testament. The chapel also holds the famous fresco by Domenico di Bartolo *Madonna della Misericordia,* painted in 1444 in the Cappella del Manto, but moved to its present location in 1610.

See map p. 284. Piazza Duomo 2. ☎ *0577-224-811. Fax: 0577-224-829.* www.santa maria.comune.siena.it. *Admission: 6€ ($6.90), 5.50€ ($6.30) with reservation. Open: daily Nov 1–Mar 15 10:30 a.m.–4:30 p.m., except Dec 25–Jan 6 when it is open 10 a.m.–6 p.m.; Mar 16–Oct 31 10:30 a.m.– 6:30 p.m.*

More cool things to see and do

✔ If you have some room in your mind left for more Renaissance paintings, the **Oratorio di San Bernardino and Museo Diocesano di Arte Sacra** (Piazza San Francesco 10; ☎ 0577-283-048; www.operaduomo.it) is worth a visit. Of San Bernardino's two chapels, the lower one was frescoed by the best Sienese painters of the 17th century, whereas the upper one is a beautiful example of Italian Renaissance with frescoes by Beccafumi, Sodoma, and Pacchia. Next door, the museum holds works collected from churches and convents in the area, including the famous *Madonna del Latte* by Pietro Lorenzetti. Admission is 3€ ($3.45). Open: March 15 to October 31 daily from 10:30 a.m. to 1:30 p.m. and 3 to 5:30 p.m.

✔ You might like to visit the **Santuario and Casa di Santa Caterina** (Vicolo del Tiratoio 8; ☎ **0577-247-393**; www.caterinati.org), the Sienese saint's house and the sanctuary (which includes several works of art) that was built around it in 1464, when Catherine was sanctified. Caterina Benincasa was born here in 1347, the daughter of a fabric dyer and launderer and one of 26 children (!); she fought for peace and for the Papacy to come back to Rome from its exile in Avignon at a time when women had little say in political questions. Admission is free and the site is open daily from 9 a.m. to 12:30 p.m. and from 3 to 6 p.m.

✔ Here is a new, wonderful experience, which we highly recommend — a ride on the **Treno natura** (Ferrovia della Val d'Orcia; ☎ **0577-207-413**; www.ferrovieturistiche.it). When the local train line, the Siena-Asciano-Monte Antico, closed a few years ago due to lack of interest, a group of volunteers, in cooperation with the Italian Railroads Company, decided that it was too bad to let this very scenic ride go to waste. They restored some antique engines and some carriages and reopened the line as a cultural- and nature-discovery activity. It's a hit, and kids love it, too. Diesel trains run on weekends and holidays and some weekdays, typically at 8:30 a.m., 11:15 a.m., and 3:45 p.m., but check with the organization as the schedule wasn't finalized at press time. Steam engine tours run only on special dates. Diesel engine runs cost 15€ ($17) and steam engine runs cost 25€ ($29); children under 10 ride for free. You can buy tickets on board, but reservations are required; make them through the APT tourist office in Siena (☎ **0577-280-551**).

✔ For a different experience of Siena, and one that suits this medieval town perfectly, try a **Giro di Siena a Cavallo** (Associazione Cavalieri Senesi; ☎ **339-185-7530** or 340-781-5935; note that these are cell-phone numbers, hence the unique area codes without the zero), a tour of Siena on horseback. Horses are still very important in Sienese life — think about the Palio (see "The top attractions," earlier in this section) — and this association is out to promote horseback riding. Tours can last as little as an hour or longer, taking in Sienese countryside. Prices are arranged, based on the tour.

Shopping the local stores

Siena offers a variety of elegant and interesting shops. Besides the usual Italian shops, where you find clothing, shoes, leather goods, and personal and home accessories, Siena has a few shops that sell specialized Sienese crafts. Among the city's specialties is the wine of the surrounding hills, which you can find at *enoteche* (wine stores). Note that, like all spirits, *grappa* (clear Italian brandy) travels better than wine, which "bruises" and has to be left to sit for months after being carried on a plane. Try the **Enoteca San Domenico** (Via del Paradiso 56; ☎ **0577-271-181**), which offers a good selection of local wines as well as an assortment of the region's food specialties. Another good address is the **Antica Drogheria Manganelli** (Via di Città 71/73; ☎ **0577-280-002**), a beautiful store that sells high-quality local products — including oils, vinegars, and cured meats, and makes its own **panforte** (the typical Sienese honey-and-almond fruitcake) since 1879.

Local products include embroidery and fine fabrics. You can find a variety of hand-embroidered goods at **Siena Ricama** (Via di Città 61; ☎ **0577-288-339**), where you can also place an order for custom-made items fashioned after Renaissance patterns; **Antiche Dimore** (Via di Città 115; ☎ **0577-45-337**) is another store where you can find beautiful linen, both sold by the yard and made into embroidered house linen. Another interesting shop is **Ceramiche Santa Caterina** (Via di Città 51, 74 and 76; ☎ **0577-283-098**), the showroom of local master ceramicist Marcello Neri, who makes beautiful Sienese ceramics.

Fast Facts: Siena

Area Code

The area code for Siena is 0577; use this code when calling from anywhere outside or inside Italy, as well as within Siena. Include the 0 every time, even when calling from abroad.

ATMs

You can change money at the many exchange offices in town, located near major attractions, or get cash from the many ATMs located at banks, especially in Via di Città and by the pedestrian underpass La Lizza.

Emergencies

Ambulance, ☎ **118**; fire, ☎ **115**; road assistance (Italian Automobile Club, ACI), ☎ **116**.

Hospital

The Policlinico Le Scotte is at Viale Bracci Mario 16 (☎ 0577-585-111).

Information

APT Siena (Piazza del Campo 56 ☎ 0577-280-551; Fax: 0577-281-041; www.terresiena.it) is open Monday through Saturday from 8:30 a.m. to 7:30 p.m. in summer and Monday through Friday from 8:30 a.m. to 1 p.m. and 3:30 to 6:30 p.m. and Saturday from 8:30 a.m. to 1 p.m. in winter.

Internet Access

The Internet Train chain of shops has a branch at Via Pantaneto 54, near Piazza del Campo (☎ 0577-247-460) and one at Via di Città 121 (☎ 0577-226-366).

Police

There are two police forces in Italy; call either one. For the Polizia, call ☎ **113**; for the Carabinieri, call ☎ **112**.

Post Office

The main post office is at Piazza Matteotti 37 (☎ 0577-42-178).

San Gimignano

A perfectly preserved medieval town, **San Gimignano delle Belle Torri**
(San Gimignano of the Beautiful Towers), is one of southern Tuscany's
most famous destinations. The city actually began as a small Etruscan
village in the third century B.C., but it was only centuries later that it
became an important town. The medieval "Francigena," the main route
from Italy to France, went right through San Gimignano and accounted
for much of its wealth. Once the symbol of the palace owners' wealth,
the towers flourished in San Gimignano during the city's period of great
economic success in the 13th century. So much competition existed in
tower-building — always taller and taller — that the government made
a law forbidding any tower taller than the tower on the Palazzo del
Popolo — the seat of the government. The town's economic boom was
suddenly wiped out by the plague (which hit San Gimignano several
times between the 14th and 17th centuries), a disaster that ultimately
preserved the town, allowing it to remain basically intact as a typical
walled medieval town, with no modern additions.

San Gimignano has been called "The Manhattan of Tuscany" because of
its soaring towers, but when you visit the town you'll see that the comparison is a bit silly. Unlike Florence or even Siena, San Gimignano was
too small to survive as a thriving center into the modern period, and its
magical medieval atmosphere still pervades its streets.

San Gimignano is an easy day trip from Siena or even Florence, but it can
be a romantic place to spend the night, with its view of the twinkling lights
of other Tuscan hill towns, and it could make a good base for some countryside exploring.

 If possible, try to visit San Gimignano in the off-season so you won't be
overwhelmed by summer's throngs of tourists. The village is small and
gets crowded fast.

Getting there

With a **car,** you can reach San Gimignano (which is on a secondary route
southwest of Florence and northwest of Siena) using the *autostrada*
Florence-Pisa. There are two ways to proceed: follow directions to
San Gimignano from the Colle di Val d'Elsa exit, which takes you along
picturesque small roads through the countryside. It's also the slow
way. Alternatively, you can exit at Poggibonsi, a busy industrial town.
The sign on the highway doesn't say San Gimignano, but after you exit,
the way to San Gimignano is well-marked; follow the directions for San
Gimignano on S324. The trip takes about 1½ hours from Florence and
slightly less time from Siena. Once there you'll need to park outside the
town's walls, because San Gimignano is closed to private traffic, except

to deposit your luggage at your hotel, but you need to have the authorization arranged by the hotel (ask when you make your reservation, and allow enough time for the paperwork to go through). The town is quite small, and you can explore it easily on foot.

The companies **TRA-IN** (☎ 0577-204-246; www.trainspa.it) in Siena and **SITA** (☎ 800-373-760; www.sita-on-line.it) in Florence offer regular **bus service** to San Gimignano, usually with a transfer at Poggibonsi. The bus ride from Siena takes about 50 minutes and costs 3.62€ ($3.25); the trip from Florence takes half an hour longer and costs approximately 4.13€ ($3.70).

You can also utilize the regular **train service** from Siena to Poggibonsi. The ride takes only about 30 minutes and costs about 5€ ($5.75). From Florence to Poggibonsi, the trip is a little longer because you must change trains in Empoli (the whole trip takes about an hour for about the same money). If you're traveling from Venice or Rome, you must go to Florence first. From Poggibonsi, a regular bus service starts from outside the train station and arrives in the center of San Gimignano in about 20 minutes, but be aware that there's little service on Sundays (especially in winter, when there are only two runs — one in the early morning and one around noon).

Getting around

San Gimignano is closed to private traffic. Only public buses and taxis are allowed in the center of town. The only exception is for tourists, who are allowed to use their cars to reach their hotels and deposit their luggage, but you need to have the authorization arranged by the hotel (ask when you make your reservation, and allow enough time for the paperwork to go through). The town is quite small, and you can explore it easily on foot.

Spending the night

In the low season of January and February, there may be only one hotel open in town; four of the major hotels take turns staying open so there is always a place to stay.

Hotel La Cisterna
$ Duomo

Opening onto San Gimignano's most picturesque square, this old hotel offers large rooms and baths as well as a sweeping panoramic view from some of the rooms (and from the breakfast room at the top of the building). The rooms are furnished with a mixture of reproduction antique furniture and more modern furnishings. Some rooms have balconies that are large enough for a table and chair and make a nice place to relax. The hotel's restaurant is the renowned **Le Terrazze** (see "Dining locally," later in this section).

See map p. 301. Piazza della Cisterna 23. ☎ *0577-940-328. Fax: 0577-942-080.* www.hotelcisterna.it. *Parking: 16€ ($18) in lot outside the walls of town. Rack rates: 120€ ($138) double. Rates include breakfast. AE, DC, MC, V.*

L'Antico Pozzo
$$ Duomo

This elegant hotel is housed in a 15th-century *palazzo* and the nicely appointed rooms are large, some with frescoed ceilings, other with beamed ceilings. Some of the rooms afford nice views over the city, and all are furnished with antiques — mostly from the 19th century. During the good weather, breakfast is served on the hotel's terrace.

See map p. 301. Via San Matteo 87. ☎ *0577-942-014. Fax: 0577-942-117.* www.antico pozzo.com. *Parking: 16€ ($18) in garage or lot outside the walls of town. Rack rates: 160€ ($184) double. Rates include breakfast. AE, DC, MC, V.*

Relais Santa Chiara
$$ Duomo

This beautiful hotel/resort is a ten-minute walk outside the town walls. Overlooking the luscious countryside and surrounded by private gardens, it's the grand way to see San Gimignano, and yet it isn't really that expensive, especially if you get some of their special rates or stay in one of the smaller rooms. The guest rooms and public areas are beautifully decorated, and some rooms have private terraces. There's also a pool and Jacuzzi.

See map p. 301. Via Matteotti 15. ☎ *0577-940-701. Fax: 0577-942-096.* www.rsc.it. *Free parking. Rack rates: 220€ ($253) double. Rates include buffet breakfast. AE, DC, MC, V.*

Dining locally
You can dine very well in San Gimignano. The famous local wine is the white Vernaccia di San Gimignano.

Dorandò
$$ Duomo   SAN GIMIGNANO

On a tiny street near the Duomo, this excellent restaurant is a popular destination for locals and Italian tourists. The food is classic Tuscan, with all the local specialies, and the menu changes seasonally or even daily, depending on the market. This is home-cooking of the best tradition.

See map p. 301. Vicolo dell'Oro 2; off Piazza del Duomo, turn right at the beginning of Via San Matteo. ☎ *0577-941-862.* www.ristorantedorando.it. *Reservations required. Secondi: 18€–22€ ($21–$25). AE, MC, V. Open: Lunch and dinner Tues–Sun. Closed 8 weeks in Jan/Mar.*

San Gimignano

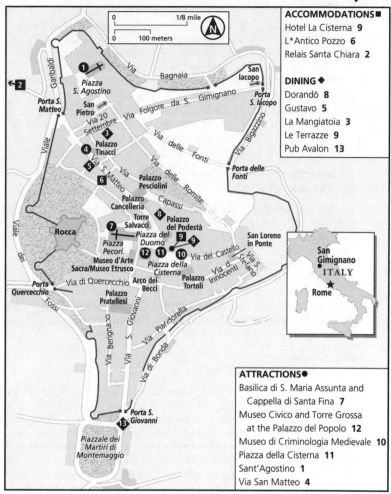

ACCOMMODATIONS■
Hotel La Cisterna **9**
L*Antico Pozzo **6**
Relais Santa Chiara **2**

DINING◆
Dorandò **8**
Gustavo **5**
La Mangiatoia **3**
Le Terrazze **9**
Pub Avalon **13**

ATTRACTIONS●
Basilica di S. Maria Assunta and
  Cappella di Santa Fina **7**
Museo Civico and Torre Grossa
  at the Palazzo del Popolo **12**
Museo di Criminologia Medievale **10**
Piazza della Cisterna **11**
Sant'Agostino **1**
Via San Matteo **4**

Gustavo
$ Duomo SIENESE

Gustavo is good for lunch or a light meal, with a very good wine list and an excellent selection of local cured meats and cheese as well as a variety of *bruschetta* or *fett'unta* (toasted bread with extra-virgin olive oil and veggie toppings) and of *crostini senesi* (the local variety of the Tuscan *crostini*, with warm meat or bean toppings). This is the place to try some Vino Nobile and Vernaccia, or even a Brunello.

See map p. 301. Via San Matteo 29. ☎ *0577-940-057. Reservations not accepted. Secondi: 8€–12€ ($9.20–$14). MC, V. Open: Lunch and dinner daily.*

La Mangiatoia
$ Duomo SIENESE

This may be the best restaurant in San Gimignano. Here, you can try all the traditional favorites in an elegant yet rustic atmosphere beneath white-washed brick arched passageways. The Medieval-inspired cuisine is strong on wild game: We recommend the *pappardelle al cinghiale* (large home-made noodles with wild boar sauce), the *cinghiale con le noci* (wild boar with walnut sauce), the *anatra al tartufo* (duck with a truffle sauce) — or anything else that appeals to you from the seasonal and daily offerings.

See map p. 301. Via Mainardi 5. ☎ *0577-941-528. Reservations recommended. Secondi: 12€–16€ ($14–$18). MC, V. Lunch and dinner Wed–Mon. Closed 4 weeks Nov/Dec.*

Le Terrazze
$$ Duomo TUSCAN

Located in **Hotel La Cisterna** (see "Spending the night," earlier in this section), this restaurant is one of the classiest places to dine in San Gimignano. It features two dining rooms — one of which is original from the 13th century — and has a classic Tuscan countryside feeling, with medieval beamed ceilings and wooden furniture. Both rooms have large windows that provide a breathtaking view of the surrounding valley. Try the *crostini,* grilled meat, or game *ragù.*

See map p. 301. Piazza della Cisterna 24. ☎ *0577-940-328. Reservations recommended. Secondi: 12€–21€ ($14–$24). AE, DC, MC, V. Open: Lunch and dinner daily.*

Pub Avalon
$ San Giovanni TUSCAN

Located just outside the main entrance to town, the cavernous Pub Avalon offers a little of everything. The first thing you'll notice is the outdoor beer garden, a popular hangout in summer. Inside, live music often starts around 10 p.m. The food runs the gamut from the Tuscan equivalent of "pub grub" (*crostini, bruschetta,* and other finger food) to substantial entrees like grilled chicken, risotto, and steak with porcini mushrooms.

See map p. 301. Viale Roma at Porta S. Giovanni. ☎ *0577-940-023.* www.avalon-pub. com. *Reservations recommended in summer. Secondi: 8€–15€ ($9.20–$17). AE, DC, MC, V. Open: Lunch and dinner daily.*

Exploring San Gimignano

The **medieval towers** attached to the local *palazzi* have become the symbol of the town, but time has clearly taken its toll, and some of the buildings have collapsed. Of the original 72 or so towers, only 15 remain today, including the tower on the Palazzo del Popolo (53m/177 ft.).

A **cumulative ticket** includes entrance to the Museo Civico (Palazzo del Popolo/Pinacoteca), the Torre Grossa, and the archaeological museum and other minor attractions. It costs 7.50€ ($8.65).

If you want to participate in a bus tour, call **American Express** (☎ 055-50-981) or **SITA** (☎ 055-214-721; www.sita-on-line.it) in Florence. Both companies offer tours of the major attractions in Tuscany, including San Gimignano, for about 50€ ($58).

The top attractions

Basilica di S. Maria Assunta and Cappella di Santa Fina

Still called the Duomo by locals — long ago, the town lost its bishop and the cathedral was downgraded to a Collegiata — the basilica opens onto the beautiful square connected to Piazza della Cisterna. Built in the 12th century, the Collegiata has a very plain unfinished facade but a gorgeously decorated Romanesque interior with tiger-striped arches and a galaxy of gold stars. Among the treasures inside are the wooden statues of *Gabriele* and *Annunziata* by Jacopo della Quercia and the 14th-century frescoes decorating the naves. The right nave's last chapel is the **Chapel of St. Fina (Cappella di Santa Fina),** one of the most beautiful from the Tuscan Renaissance. Designed by Giuliano and Benedetto da Maiano — Benedetto also carved the panel of the altar — its glorious cycle of frescoes by Domenico Ghirlandaio describes the life of a local girl named Fina, who became the town's patron saint.

See map p. 301. Piazza del Duomo. ☎ *0577-940-316. Admission: 3.50€ ($4). Open: Apr–Oct Mon–Fri 9:30 a.m.–7:30 p.m., Sat 9:30 a.m.–5 p.m., Sun and holidays 1–5 p.m.; Nov–Mar Mon–Sat 9:30 a.m.–5 p.m., Sun and holidays 1–5 p.m. Closed Jan 21–Feb 28.*

Museo Civico and Torre Grossa at the Palazzo del Popolo

The Palazzo del Popolo (the government's palace) waas built between 1288 and 1323 — the crenels were added in the 19th century. Its tower, the **Torre Grossa (Big Tower)** — the tallest in town — was added in 1311. Visiting the Torre Grossa awards you with a superb view over the town. The interior of the palace is decorated with great frescoes and furnishings from the 14th and 15th centuries. Particularly worth visiting in the **Museu Civico** inside the palace is the *Sala di Dante (Dante's Room),* which you reach via an external staircase from the courtyard. (This external staircase is decorated with splendid frescoes by Lippo Memmi — his *Maestà* is considered a masterpiece.)

See map p. 301. Piazza del Duomo 1. ☎ *0577-990-312 or 0577-990-340. Admission: 5€ ($5.75). Open: Daily Mar–Oct 9:30 a.m.–7:30 p.m.; Nov–Feb 10 a.m.–5:30 p.m.*

Piazza della Cisterna
Duomo

This triangular piazza, together with the attached **Piazza del Duomo,** constitutes the heart of the town. Piazza della Cisterna is an elegant example of medieval architecture, is one of the most attractive sights in San Gimignano. At the center of the square, beautifully paved with bricks, is the well that gives access to the underlying cistern. Surrounding the square are some of the town's important palaces, such as the Palazzo Tortoli-Treccani at no. 22, with its elegant double row of *bifora* ("bifold," divided by a stone arch) windows.

See map p. 301.

More cool things to see and do

San Gimignano is a small town but rich in sights. If you have more time, you may want to explore more of its medieval delights. Here are a few more choices:

- ✔ **Sant'Agostino** (Piazza Sant'Agostino; ☎ 0577-940-383) is a beautiful 13th-century Romanesque-Gothic church. Its plain facade hides a superb cycle of frescoes by Benozzo Gozzoli on the life of St. Augustine; also interesting is his fresco of St. Sebastian on the third altar to the left. The church is open daily from 7 a.m. to noon and 3 to 6 p.m. (until 7 p.m. in summer), and admission is free.

- ✔ **Via San Matteo** is a section of the Via Francigena, the medieval highway to France. Besides its historic interest — it was the most important communication path between northern and southern Europe — it's a beautiful section of medieval San Gimignano, lined with palaces and towers.

- ✔ The **Museo di Criminologia Medievale (Medieval Criminology Museum)** (Via del Castello 1, off Piazza della Cisterna; ☎ 0577-942-243) is housed in the Torre del Diavolo (Devil's Tower) and contains an ample choice of torture instruments as well as a collection of drawings and etchings concerning their use, complete with descriptions in English. These displays are horrifying but soberingly relevant, especially considering that modern versions of these instruments are still used today. *Note:* We designate this museum with the Kid Friendly icon because teenagers may be interested in these ghoulish instruments; this museum is definitely not appropriate for young children. Admission: 8€/$9.20. It's open daily from 10 a.m. to 6 p.m., but later in the high season, and until midnight mid-July to mid-September.

Fast Facts: San Gimignano

Area Code

The area code for San Gimignano is 0577; use this city code when calling from anywhere outside or inside Italy, even within San Gimignano, and always include the 0 whether you are calling from Italy or from abroad.

ATMs

You'll find ATMs inside the banks in town. You can exchange money at the tourist office (see Information, later in this section) and the Protur booth (Piazza San Domenico; ☎ 0577-288-084; open Mon–Sat 9 a.m.–7 p.m. in winter and until 8 p.m. in summer).

Emergencies

Ambulance and Pronto Soccorso (first aid) ☎ **118**; fire ☎ **115**; road assistance (Italian Automobile Club, ACI), ☎ **116**.

Hospital

The nearest hospital is the Ospedale Poggibonsi (Via Pisana 2; ☎ 0577-915-555).

Information

The Pro Loco tourist office is on Piazza Duomo 1 (☎ 0577-940-008; Fax: 0577-940-903; www.sangimignano.com).

Summer hours are daily 9 a.m. to 1 p.m. and 3 to 7 p.m. Winter hours are 9 a.m. to 1 p.m. and 2 to 6 p.m. daily.

Police

There are two police forces in Italy; call either one. For the Polizia, call ☎ **113**; for the Carabinieri, call ☎ **112**.

Post Office

The post office (ufficio postale) is at Piazza delle Erbe 8 (☎ 0577-941-983).

Chapter 17

Umbria

● ●

In This Chapter

▶ Discovering medieval Perugia and sweet Baci
▶ Visiting saints and monasteries in Assisi
▶ Thrilling to the music festivals in Spoleto

● ●

*U*mbria is a small region tucked away between Latium and Tuscany, with no access to the sea. Famous for its deep green hills and natural beauty, Umbria is traversed north-to-south by the river **Tiber (Tevere),** the river of Rome that ends at the sea near Ostia Antica (see Chapter 13). In its early segment, the river goes through ravines and steep valleys, which explains why **Perugia,** the region's capital, wasn't built along the river. At the heart of Umbria, this delightful city is rich in art and historic sights and is a lively university town. It was the hometown of painter Pietr Vannucci, who brought fame to himself and his town under the name "Il Perugino." The city's highlights are the **Palazzo dei Priori** and its magnificent art and the famous **Fontana Maggiore** — and nowhere else will you find a chocolate kiss as big as your (Italian) car!

Not far away to the east is **Assisi,** hometown of San Francesco (St. Francis), Italy's patron saint, and Santa Chiara (St. Clare). The 1997 earthquakes luckily didn't destroy the town's monuments entirely and spared most of the masterpieces by the major artists of the Renaissance. The highpoints of Assisi are the **Basilica di San Francesco** and its frescoes, the **Basilica di Santa Chiara,** and the **Eremo delle Carceri. Spoleto** is famous for its music and art festivals — the **Festival di Spoleto** and the **Stagione Lirica** — but it's also a delightful small medieval town offering beautiful vistas, a majestic **Duomo,** and the **Ponte delle Torri.** Of course, like other parts of Italy, Umbria has its own food specialties: *tartufi* (truffles) as well as porcini mushrooms. Perugia and Spoleto make excellent starting points from which to visit the rest of this region. Keep in mind, though, that you can reach all destinations in Umbria as day-trips from Florence or Rome.

To see the scope of the entire Umbrian landscape, see the "Tuscany and Umbria" map in Chapter 15.

Perugia

Etruscan in origin, Perugia developed as an important urban center during the Middle Ages and the Renaissance. It was infamous during the Renaissance for its fierce battles and was finally subjugated by the popes, who imposed a few hundred years of steady rule. Today the city is renowned for its universities and art — and for its chocolate. It's the home of the famous chocolate house of Perugina.

Getting there

Because Perugia lies on a secondary line, only a few **direct trains** connect it to Florence or Rome. From Rome, the ride takes about 2¼ hours and costs around 15€ ($17); from Florence, it's 2½ hours and 12€ ($14), and you have to change trains in Terontola. Perugia's **FS** train station (☎ 075-500-6865) is on Piazza Vittorio Veneto. From there you can catch one of many buses to Piazza Italia in the town center (about a 15-min. ride). Perugia is also on a privately run line connecting Sansepolcro to Terni with a frequent schedule. These trains arrive and depart from the **Stazione Sant'Anna** (☎ 075-572-3947) in the center of town.

The company **SULGA** (☎ 800-099-661 or 075-500-9641; www.sulga.it) has three daily **bus runs** from Rome and one from Florence; the ride from Rome takes 2½ hours and costs 23€ ($26) roundtrip; the one from Florence is 1¾ hours and costs about 16€ ($18) roundtrip. The company **SITA** (☎ 055-214-721; www.sita-on-line.it) also makes one daily run to and from Florence for about the same price. Perugia's Transit Authority **APM** (☎ 800-512-141 or 075-506-781; www.apm.perugia.it) connects Perugia with Assisi on a daily basis for 2.80€ ($3.25) and with other cities in Umbria. Buses arrive in Perugia in Piazza Partigiani, an escalator ride from Piazza Italia at the center of town.

Perugia is 180km (115 miles) from Rome and 150km (94 miles) from Florence. If you're **driving** from Florence, take A1 to the Val di Chiana Bettolle-Sinalunga exit and switch to SS75bis to Perugia. From Rome, take A1 to Orte and then SS204 to SS36 to Perugia. The center of the historic town is at the top of a steep hill; because the center has restricted traffic, you have to leave your car in one of the numerous parking lots — a convenient one is Piazza Partigiani's underground parking lot, just south of the historic center, but they're all linked to the center by elevators or escalators.

You're allowed to drive up into town to bring your luggage to your hotel before parking — but keep an eye on it (someone broke the window of our rental car in the few minutes we left it unattended). Maybe because of its bloody past, Perugia has a reputation for having a slightly violent edge (though, as elsewhere in Italy, physical violence isn't as much a concern as theft).

Getting around

The historic center has a relatively simple layout along **Corso Vannucci,** with bus and train arrivals at one end (at the bottom of a public escalator) in **Piazza Italia** and the major sites on **Piazza IV Novembre** at the other end. As often in small medieval towns, Perugia is easily visited on foot; however, the city has a system of buses with the central hub in Piazza Italia. For a **taxi,** call ☎ **075-500-4888.**

Spending the night

Castello dell'Oscano

$$ **Localita Cenerente**

Seven kilometers (4.3 miles) from the center of Perugia, this is a fantastic place to stay in full luxury; it is a real castle — crenellated towers and all — beautifully restored, including the frescoed ceilings and the wooden or terracotta floors. The guest rooms are large and nicely appointed. The castle has a lovely garden and a big swimming pool.

Strada della Forcella 37, Localita Cenerente. ☎ *075-584-371.* Fax: 075-690-666. E-mail: oscano@perugiaonline.com. *Free parking. Rack rates: 230€ ($265) double. Rates include breakfast. AE, DC, MC, V.*

Etruscan Chocohotel Perugia

$ **Piazza dei Partigiani**

This almost glitzy hotel offers style at a moderate price. All the guest rooms have contemporary Italian designer furniture and large baths. The real draw, though, is staying in a "chocohotel": Each floor is dedicated to a type of chocolate (milk, dark, gianduia) and each room has a "chocodesk" . . . we'll leave you to discover that surprise. The restaurant features a cocoa-based menu. Non-chocolate amenities include a large roof deck with a panoramic view and a good-sized swimming pool.

Via Campo di Marte 134. ☎ *075-583-7314.* Fax: 075-583-7314. www.chocohotel.it. *Free parking. Rack rates: 120€ ($138). AE, DC, MC, V.*

Hotel La Rosetta

$$ **Piazza Italia**

Considered one of the best hotels in town, La Rosetta is very convenient and boasts a national historic landmark in one of its guest rooms (Suite 55, which is richly decorated with frescoes). The rooms vary widely in furnishings but are uniformly comfortable, airy, and well kept.

Piazza Italia 19. ☎ *and Fax: 075-572-0841.* E-mail: larosetta@perugiaonline. com. *Parking: 20€ ($23). Rack rates: 135€ ($155) double. Rates include buffet breakfast. AE, DC.*

Perugia

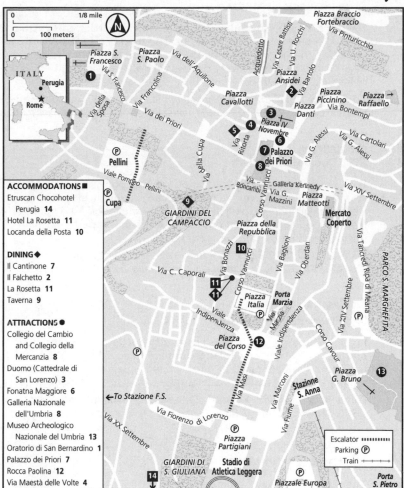

0 1/8 mile
0 100 meters

ITALY
Perugia
Rome

Piazza S. Francesco **1**
Piazza S. Paolo
Via dell'Aquilone
Via Cesare Battisti
Via U. Rocchi
Via Pinturicchio
Piazza Braccio Fortebraccio
Acquedotto
Piazza Ansidei
Via Bartolo
Via S. Francesco
Via Francolina
Piazza Cavallotti
Piazza IV Novembre **3**
Piazza Danti
Piazza Piccinino
Via Bontempi
Piazza Raffaello
Via della Sposa
Via dei Priori
5 **4**
6
7 Palazzo dei Priori
8
Via Ritorta
Via della Cupa
Via Cartolari
Via G. Alessi
Via G. Alessi
P Pellini
Viale Pompeo Pellini
Via Boncambi
Corso Vannucci
Via G. Mazzini
Galleria Kennedy
Via XIV Settembre
Piazza Matteotti
P Cupa
9
GIARDINI DEL CAMPACCIO
Piazza della Repubblica
Mercato Coperto
Via Tancredi Ripa di Meana
PARCO S. MARGHERITA

ACCOMMODATIONS ■
Etruscan Chocohotel
  Perugia **14**
Hotel La Rosetta **11**
Locanda della Posta **10**

Via C. Caporali
Via Bonazzi
Corso Vannucci
10
Via Baglioni
Via Oberdan

DINING ◆
Il Cantinone **7**
Il Falchetto **2**
La Rosetta **11**
Taverna **9**

11
11
Piazza Italia
Viale Indipendenza
Porta Marzia
Via Marzia
Viale Indipendenza
Via XIV Settembre
Corso Cavour
P

ATTRACTIONS ●
Collegio del Cambio
  and Collegio della
  Mercanzia **8**
Duomo (Cattedrale di
  San Lorenzo) **3**
Fonatna Maggiore **6**
Galleria Nazionale
  dell'Umbria **8**
Museo Archeologico
  Nazionale del Umbria **13**
Oratorio di San Bernardino **1**
Palazzo dei Priori **7**
Rocca Paolina **12**
Via Maestà delle Volte **4**

Piazza del Corso
12
Via Masi
←To Stazione F.S.
Via Fiorenzo di Lorenzo
Via XX Settembre
Piazza Partigiani
GIARDINI DI S. GIULIANA
Stadio di Atletica Leggera
14
Piazza G. Bruno
13
Stazione S. Anna
Via Marconi
Via Fiume
Piazzale Europa
Porta S. Pietro

Escalator ●●●●●●●●●
Parking **P**
Train ←——+——→

Dining locally

A university town, Perugia has a lot of *pizzerie* and cheap trattorie where you can have a bite in a lively, casual atmosphere, as well as some really nice places. The food is typically Umbrian (see Chapter 2 for more in depth coverage of this cuisine) and relies heavily on *tartufi* (truffles) and *porcini* mushrooms.

Il Cantinone
$ Piazza Italia   UMBRIAN

Just off Piazza IV Novembre, in the medieval district, this restaurant has vaulted ceilings and a simple decor. The food is traditional and excellent, including the homemade ravioli, the *grigliata mista* (a variety of grilled meats) and the *torello alla Perugina* (veal with a chicken livers sauce), one of Perugia's specialties.

Via Ritorta 6. ☎ *075-573-4130. Reservations recommended. Secondi: 7€–15€ ($8.05–$17). AE, DC, MC, V. Open: Lunch and dinner Wed–Mon. Closed 10 days for Christmas.*

Il Falchetto
$$$ Duomo   UMBRIAN

With a real medieval atmosphere (one dining room is from the 14th century) and a traditional menu, Falchetto is an excellent place for discovering Umbrian cuisine — especially if you're in the mood for a splurge. Try the *lepre alle olive* (hare with olives). The terrace is particularly in demand during the summer Umbria Jazz concerts.

Via Bartolo 20. ☎ *075-573-1775. Reservations recommended. Secondi: 15€–30€ ($17–$35). AE, DC, MC, V. Open: Lunch and dinner Tues–Sun. Closed Jan.*

La Rosetta
$$ Piazza Italia   UMBRIAN

In the hotel of the same name, La Rosetta is a famous restaurant in Perugia, offering a large choice of dishes prepared according to the best Umbrian tradition. Try the *spaghetti alla Norcina* (spaghetti with truffles) or the *scaloppine alla Perugina* (veal sautéed with wine and chicken livers).

Piazza Italia 19. ☎ *075-572-0841. Reservations recommended. Secondi: 8€–21€ ($9.20–$24). AE, DC, MC, V. Open: Lunch and dinner daily.*

Taverna
$$ UMBRIAN/CREATIVE

This lively restaurant, located in a historical palace, offers regional specialties and some tasty innovations. If you are in luck, the seasonal menu might include *crostini al tartufo* (an Umbrian version of the Tuscan variety), *lasagnette al tartufo* (small lasagna with truffles), or the *medaglioni di filetto al tartufo* (truffle beef medallions). Try the *agnello al forno* (roasted lamb) should you not like truffles.

Via delle Streghe 8. ☎ *0755-724-128. E-mail:* taverna9@interfree.it. *Secondi: 10€–18€ ($12–$21). AE, DC, MC, V. Open: Lunch and dinner Tues–Sun.*

Exploring Perugia

The **Perugia Città Museo** card is just the ticket if you are planning to visit more than one museum or monument in Perugia. It comes in several "types": **Tipo A** is a one-day card giving you access to any 4 out of 12 sights and museums for 7€ ($8.05); **Tipo B** is valid for three days and gives you access to all sites for 12€ ($14); **Tipo C2** is a family or group card giving access to a maximum of four people to all 12 sites for one year for 35€ ($40). The 12 sites include the Galleria Nazionale dell'Umbria, the Museo Archeologico Nazionale dell'Umbria, the Collegio del Cambio and Collegio della Mercanzia, and the Rocca Paolina (see later in this chapter), as well as Palazzo della Penna and Palazzo Baldeschi al Corso (two interesting Renaissance palaces), Pozzo Etrusco and Ipogeo dei Volumni (two Etruscan sites), Museo Capitolare (Renaissance art collection in the cloisters of the Cathedral of San Lorenzo), Cappella San Severo (with the first — yet damaged — fresco of Raffaello), and Museo delle Porte e delle mura Urbiche (the city walls). The card is for sale at any of the participating sites.

The top attractions

Collegio del Cambio and Collegio della Mercanzia

On the Palazzo dei Priori's ground floor, the Collegio del Cambio was the city's goods exchange in Renaissance times. This section of the palace is very interesting for its architecture and also for its magnificent frescoed ceilings, in particular those of the **Hall of the Audience (Sala dell'Udienza)** by Perugino and his assistants, one of whom was a young Raphael. These frescoes illustrate the life of Christ; there's also a **self-portrait of Perugino** himself. Also of interest is the **Chapel of Saint John the Baptist (Cappella di San Giovanni Battista),** with frescoes by Giannicola di Paolo. If you enter at Corso Vannucci 15, you'll find the **Merchant's Guild (Collegio della Mercanzia),** decorated with intricately carved wood paneling and beautiful vaulted ceilings.

Collegio del Cambio, Corso Vannucci 25. ☎ *075-572-8599. Collegio della Mercanzia, Corso Vannucci 15.* ☎ *075-573-0366. Admission: Cambio 2.60€ ($3); Mercanzia 1.05€ ($1.20); combined ticket to both 3.10€ ($3.60). Open: Cambio: daily 9 a.m.–1 p.m. and 2:30–5:30 p.m.; Mercanzia: Tues–Sat 9 a.m.–1 p.m. and 2:30–5:30 p.m., Sun 9 a.m.–1 p.m.*

Galleria Nazionale dell'Umbria

On the Palazzo dei Priori's third floor, this gallery's collection of Umbrian art from the 13th to the 19th centuries is indeed rich, including a number of marvelous Peruginos, a Gentile da Fabriano *Madonna and Child,* and a famous (and stunning) Piero della Francesco polyptych. This museum is strong in the late-medieval/early-Renaissance period, documenting the important phase during which Giotto and Cimabue revolutionized painting techniques. It's probably the most enjoyable Italian museum after the more famous ones in the larger cities.

Palazzo dei Priori, Corso Vannucci 19. ☎ *075-572-1009.* www.gallerianazionale dellumbria.it. *Admission: 3€ ($3.45). Open: Daily 8:30 a.m.–7:30 p.m. Closed the first Mon of every month.*

Museo Archeologico Nazionale del Umbria

Founded at the end of the 18th century, this museum occupies a former convent and is divided into a prehistoric section and an Etruscan-Roman section. The latter includes jewelry, funerary urns, statues, and other objects. Of particular interest are the sets of objects that, according to Etruscan custom, were entombed with the dead.

Piazza G. Bruno 10. ☎ *075-572-7141.* www.archeopg.arti.beniculturali. it/musei. *Admission: 2€ ($2.30). Open: Mon 2:30–7:30 p.m. and Tues–Sun 8:30 a.m.– 7:30 p.m.*

Oratorio di San Bernardino

Built in 1461 and designed by Agostino di Duccio, this oratory is a particularly attractive example of northern Italian Renaissance architecture. Constructed of multicolored marble, the church has a facade decorated with intricate reliefs illustrating the life of the saint. A paleo-Christian sarcophagus (fourth century) is now the main altar.

Piazza San Francesco al Prato, at the end of Via dei Priori. Admission: Free. Open: Daily 8 a.m.–12:30 p.m. and 3–6 p.m.

Palazzo dei Priori

Built between 1298 and 1353, this *palazzo* was created as the seat of the government and is one of the finest examples of Gothic architecture in Italy. The *palazzo* is a striking travertine building with white and red marble inlays. The main portal — accessible by a wide semicircular staircase — is off-center in the facade; it leads to the spacious **Hall of the Notables (Sala dei Notari).** There are two bronzes over the door of the griffin and the lion, symbols of the city. You can visit the *palazzo*'s many frescoed rooms It also houses the Collegio del Cambio and the Galleria Nazionale dell'Umbria (see later in this section). The *palazzo* opens on **Piazza IV Novembre** — once a Roman reservoir, which is graced by the **Fontana Maggiore,** a Gothic masterpiece carved by the famous Pisan sculptors Nicola and Giovanni Pisano (it had been under restoration for many years but is now visible again), which has been called the most beautiful fountain in the world. Carved from white and pink marble, it has allegorical panels representing each month of the year. On one side is the 15th-century facade of the **Duomo (Cattedrale di San Lorenzo)** — a beautiful face on an otherwise dull baroque church. Departing from the piazza is **Via Maestà delle Volte,** a typical medieval street with covered passages.

Piazza IV Novembre. ☎ *075-577-2339. Admission: free. Open: Summer daily 9 a.m.– 1 p.m. and 3–7 p.m.; winter Tues–Sun 9 a.m.–1 p.m. and 3–7 p.m.*

More cool things to see and do

✔ The **Rocca Paolina,** built in 1540 by Pope Paul III (hence the name) and designed by the famous architect Antonio da Sangallo the Younger, is a fortress that was constructed on top of medieval buildings and even earlier structures (you can still see an arch from the original Etruscan city walls). The upper part of the Rocca was demolished in 1860, but the lower sections were preserved, and the archaeological site has now been excavated. By a series of escalators, you can see the inside, viewing the fortification's huge walls, parts of dwellings and ancient streets, and even fragments of the ancient stadium where a forerunner of soccer was played. The Rocca is open daily from 9 a.m. to 7 p.m., and admission is free. Free guided tours — ocassionally offered in English — bring it all to life; they begin every 15 minutes and reservations are required (☎ **075-572-5778**).

✔ Perugia owes its fame to the world-famous chocolate manufacturer **Perugina,** and Perugina's claim to fame is its brilliant creation of Baci ("kisses") — bonbons of soft chocolate mixed with finely chopped hazelnuts and wrapped in silver paper speckled with purple-blue stars. Call ☎ **075-52-761** to schedule a free tour of the **Perugina chocolate factory,** in the neighborhood of San Sisto, 6km (3 miles) west of the city center (take a cab).

Fast Facts: Perugia

Area Code

The country code for Italy is **39.** The area code for Perugia is **075;** use this code when calling from anywhere outside or inside Italy, even within Perugia itself (include the 0 every time, even when calling from abroad).

ATMs

You will find many banks and ATMs, especially along Corso Vannucci and Piazza Italia. You can also exchange money at the F.S. rail station in Piazza Vittorio Veneto and Genefin at Via Pinturicchio 14–16.

Emergencies

Ambulance and first aid (Pronto Soccorso), ☎ **118;** fire, ☎ **115;** road assistance, ☎ **116.**

Hospital

The Ospedale Monteluce is on Piazza Monteluce (☎ 075-57-81).

Information

You can write for information to Perugia's main tourist office: APT (Via Mazzini 21; ☎ 075-572-3327; Fax: 075-573-6828). Once in town, visit its tourist booth just off the stairs of the Palazzo dei Priori at Piazza IV November 3 (☎ 075-573-6458; e-mail: info@iat.perugia.it), open daily from 8:30 a.m. to 1:30 p.m. and 2:30 to 6:30 p.m.

Internet Access

There is an Internet Train shop on Via Ulisse Rocchi 30, near the cathedral (☎ 075-572-0107).

Police

There are two police forces in Italy; call either one. For the Polizia, call ☎ **113**; for the Carabinieri, call ☎ **112**.

Post Office

The ufficio postale is on Piazza Matteotti.

Assisi

The hometown of Italy's patron saint, St. Francis (San Francesco), Assisi is famous around the world for its art and religious monuments. Many of its visitors are actually pilgrims who come to honor the humble man who was said to speak to animals and who created the Franciscan order. San Francesco was born in 1182 to a wealthy merchant family and died in 1226 in a simple hut. How he traversed the social scale and caused a revolution in Christianity is a remarkable story.

In 1209, after a reckless youth and even imprisonment, Francis experienced visions that led him to sell his father's cloth and give away the proceeds. He tried to follow the Bible literally and live the life of Christ, publicly renouncing his inheritance and rejecting wealth absolutely (this didn't endear him to the rich medieval church hierarchy). Two years before his death, he received the stigmata on a mountaintop — this and other scenes from his life were popular subjects for painters of the late medieval period and the Renaissance.

Assisi is only a small town of about 3,000 souls, though millions flock to it every year. You can easily visit it on a day-trip from Florence or Rome, but you can also stay overnight.

Getting there

Assisi lies on a spur track off the main **train line** so you'll have to switch trains to get here. If you're coming from Perugia or Rome, you'll have to change at Foligno; from Florence, you'll have to change in Terontola. Trains for Assisi are frequent from each of these stations. A ticket from Rome and Florence (a 3-hr. trip) costs about 13€ ($15) and from Perugia (a half-hour away) about 2€ ($2.30). Trains arrive at the rail station of Santa Maria degli Angeli, a small town 6km (3¾ miles) from Assisi. The station is well connected to the historic center of Assisi by a shuttle bus departing every half-hour and stopping in Piazza Matteotti, within Assisi's walls; the price is 1.29€ ($1.50). Taxis are also available at the station.

Perugia's Transit Authority **APM** (☎ **800-512-141** or 075-506-781; www.apm.perugia.it) has several **bus** runs between Perugia and Assisi. Buses leave Perugia from Piazza Partigiani and arrive at Piazza Matteotti behind the Duomo for 2.80€ ($3.25); tickets are more expensive if you buy them on board. The company **Sulga** (☎ **800-099-661** or 075-500-9641; www.sulga.it) has runs from Rome (a 3-hr. trip) and Florence (a 2½-hr. trip) for about 18€ ($21) round trip.

Assisi is 27km (17 miles) from Perugia. If you're **driving,** take SS3 in the direction of Foligno, then look for the exit for Assisi. The town is almost totally closed to traffic, so you have to park outside. You can park under Piazza Matteotti where there's a large lot — but "large" doesn't mean much when the place is packed with thousands of tourists and pilgrims. If you're going in summer, get there early or use public transportation. All parking lots outside the walls are connected with the town center by public minibuses; you can buy tickets at bars, tobacconists, and newsstands, or on the bus at a surcharge. If you prefer to take a **taxi,** look for the several stations in town where taxis wait for their fares or call ☎ 075-813-193.

Getting around

Assisi is small and you can see it on foot — the town's attractions are concentrated around the main square. However, outside Assisi are some interesting sights you can walk to — but getting there by public transportation or taxi is far easier. The public **minibus service** links all the major sites (see "Getting there," earlier in this chapter). You can also buy tickets on the bus at a surcharge. If you prefer to take a **taxi,** look for the several stations in town where taxis wait for their fares or call ☎ 075-813-19.

Spending the night

If you want to come to Assisi for religious holidays like Easter, the Feast of St. Francis (Oct 3–4), and the Calendimaggio in May, you'll have to reserve as much as half a year or more in advance. Otherwise, the only choices left may be big, ugly hotels in Santa Maria degli Angeli, the nearby little town.

Hotel Subasio
$$ Piazza San Francesco

Housed in a 16th-century *palazzo,* just steps from the Basilica, this large hotel offers spacious guest rooms that are individually decorated and furnished with antiques — including some nice 17th- and 18th-century pieces; all rooms have renovated bathrooms. Rooms overlooking the terrace have beautiful views of the surrounding valley.

Via Frate Elia 2. ☎ *075-812-206. Fax: 075-816-691. E-mail:* s.elisei.hotel subasio@interbusiness.it. *Parking: 11€ ($13). Rack rates: 233€ ($268) double. Rates include buffet breakfast. Closed Nov–Feb. AE, DC, MC, V.*

Hotel Umbra
$ Piazza del Comune

Housed in an old *palazzo* — some of the foundations are Roman, this quiet hotel offers relaxing guest rooms with Deruta tiles on the floors and decorated with some antique furniture, views of the surrounding hills and valleys, renovated bathrooms, and balconies. The Umbra's **restaurant** (see "Dining locally," below) is particularly good and is popular with locals as well as guests. The walled garden is an especially nice place to take a meal if you're in town in summer.

Via degli Archi 6, just off Piazza del Comune (west side). ☎ *075-812-240. Fax: 075-813-653.* www.hotelumbra.it. *Parking: 11€ ($13). Rack rates: 123€ ($141) double. Rates include breakfast. Closed mid-Jan–mid-Mar. AE, DC, MC, V.*

Dining locally

La Fortezza
$ Piazza del Comune   UMBRIAN/CREATIVE

This family-run restaurant is a good address for good food at moderate prices. The *cannelloni* are good (filled tubes of homemade pasta baked in Parmesan and tomato sauce) and so are the *gnocchi* (potato dumplings); for *secondo* you will not go wrong with any of the seasonal stews or with the local typical grilled meats.

Vicolo della Fortezza, off via San Rufino. ☎ *075-812-418. Reservations recommended. Secondi: 8€–12€ ($9.20–$14). MC, V. Open: Lunch and dinner Fri–Wed. Closed Feb and 1 week in July.*

Medio Evo
$$ Piazza del Comune   UMBRIAN/ITALIAN

A little south of Piazza del Comune, this family-run restaurant may be the town's most interesting place to eat. It combines traditional Umbrian cuisine with accents from other cultures. The building rests on 1,000-year-old foundations (note the name, which means "Middle Ages") and has vaulted medieval ceilings. For a *primo,* try the *tortelloni ai tartufi* (large ravioli with truffles); for a *secondo,* try one of the variety of grilled and roasted meats, or the *fritto misto* (fried meats and vegetables).

Via dell' Arco dei Priori 4/b. ☎ *075-813-068. Reservations recommended. Secondi: 11€–18€ ($13–$21). AE, DC, MC, V. Open: Lunch and dinner Thurs–Tues. Closed 1 month in Jan/Feb and 3 weeks in July.*

Ristorante Buca di San Francesco
$$ Piazza del Comune   UMBRIAN

In the center of town, this restaurant is housed in a medieval building and serves traditional, if pricey, food. The menu is excellent and changes with the seasons and what's available at the market. One dish we particularly like is the *cannelloni* (homemade pasta tubes filled with cheese or meat and baked with tomato sauce and Parmesan). The garden provides a view of Assisi's historic center.

Via Brizzi 1. ☎ *075-812-204. Reservations recommended. Secondi: 14€–22€ ($16–$25). AE, DC, MC, V. Open: Lunch and dinner Tues–Sun. Closed 2 weeks in July.*

Assisi

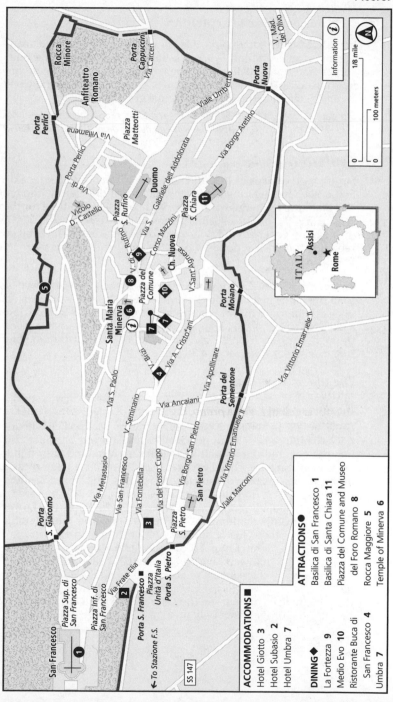

ATTRACTIONS●

Basilica di San Francesco **1**
Basilica di Santa Chiara **11**
Piazza del Comune and Museo
del Foro Romano **8**
Rocca Maggiore **5**
Temple of Minerva **6**

ACCOMMODATIONS■

Hotel Giotto **3**
Hotel Subasio **2**
Hotel Umbra **7**

DINING◆

La Fortezza **9**
Medio Evo **10**
Ristorante Buca di
San Francesco **4**
Umbra **7**

Umbra

$ Piazza del Comune   UMBRIAN

In the hotel of the same name, this popular restaurant opened nearly 80 years ago and is an institution. Don't miss the garden if the weather is fine. Umbra serves traditional dishes from the countryside, including *primi* with truffles (including the coveted white ones, when in season) and well-prepared *secondi,* including the local traditional grilled meats.

Via degli Archi 6. ☎ 075-812-240. Reservations recommended. Secondi: 9€–16€ ($10–$18). AE, DC, MC, V. Open: Lunch and dinner daily. Closed mid-Jan–mid-Mar.

Exploring Assisi

Severe earthquakes in 1997 did severe damage to the Basilica di San Francesco, endangering the very structure of the church and monastery. The ambitious schedule of repairs was completed in time for the Papal Jubilee in 2000 (pretty amazing, given that one fresco was in 50,000 pieces) through the generosity of donors all over the world. The total cost of repairing the destruction in the region was estimated at more than $1 billion.

Free tours of Assisi are given by the Franciscan order in town, starting from the office just outside the entrance to the lower basilica on the left in Piazza Inferiore di San Francesco (☎ 075-819-0084; Fax: 075-819-0035; e-mail: chiu@krenet.it). Tours last about an hour and take place Monday through Saturday from 9 a.m. to noon and Monday through Sunday from 2:00 to 5:30 p.m. (winter to 4:30 p.m.).

The top atttractions

Basilica di San Francesco

Begun in 1228 to house the bones of St. Francis, the basilica is not one church but two churches — an upper basilica and a lower basilica. The scaffolding that covered the church has been removed, and although the quake destroyed some frescoes beyond repair, some have been reassembled — from immense puzzles of thousands of pieces. The **Upper Basilica** contains Cimabue's *Crucifixion* and Giotto's celebrated cycle of frescoes on the life of the saint, including *St. Francis Preaching to the Birds.* The **Lower Basilica** is a somber Gothic monument to Francis's life, from which stairs descend to the crypt where his coffin was hidden (rediscovered in the 19th century). The **Magdalen Chapel (Cappella della Maddalena)** was frescoed by Giotto and his followers. Pietro Lorenzetti's beautiful *Deposition* is in the left transept; on the right is Cimabue's *Madonna Enthroned with Four Angels and St. Francis.* Friars assist visitors and even give church tours, some of them in English (though the tour is free, making a donation is customary because the order exists only on alms).

Piazza Superiorie di San Francesco/Piazza Inferiore di San Francesco. ☎ *075-819-001. Admission: Basilica free; Treasury and Perkins Collection 2.07€ ($1.85). Open: Basilica Mon–Sat 8:30 a.m.–6:50 p.m., Sun and holidays 2–7:15 p.m.; lower church opens at 6 a.m.; both close in winter at 6 p.m.; Treasury and Perkins Collecton summer Mon–Sat 9:30 a.m.–7 p.m.*

Basilica di Santa Chiara

Pilgrims come to this cavernous 1260 church to see the **tomb of Santa Chiara (St. Clare).** Canonized in 1255, she was the founder of the order of the Poor Clares. Chiara left her family to follow St. Francis, abandoning wealth and worldly pretensions as he did and cutting off her hair to symbolize her renunciation of the world. A number of miracles are attributed to her, one of which, a vision, led to her being proclaimed the patron saint of TV (saints don't get asked whether they want these honors). The other object attracting pilgrims is in the **Oratorio** — the crucifix that miraculously spoke to St. Francis and led him to start on his difficult path in the face of family, church, and society. Only some of the church's original frescoes remain. Note that Santa Chiara was closed at press time but should be open by the time you arrive.

Piazza di Santa Chiara. ☎ *075-812-282. Admission: Free. Open: Summer daily 6:30 a.m.– noon and 2–7 p.m.; winter daily 6:30 a.m.–noon and 2–6 p.m.*

Eremo delle Carceri

Eremo means "hermitage," and this is the site where St. Francis retired to meditate and pray, on the peaceful slopes of Mount Subasio. The name of the site comes from the fact that Francis and his followers withdrew here as though to a prison *(carcere).* Several of his miracles occurred here, and you can still see the sites — such as the ancient tree believed to be the one where he preached his sermon to the birds (see Giotto's fresco of this scene in the Basilica di San Francesco). Also here are the unforgiving stone bed where he slept and the dried-out stream he quieted because its noise was interrupting his prayers. If you want to partake of the silence of Mount Subasio yourself, stroll the marked trails in the park. You can reach the Eremo on foot, or by taking a taxi or a minibus.

4km (2½ miles) east of Assisi, out the Porta Cappuccini. ☎ *075-812-301. Bus: A minibus links the major sights in Assisi. Admission: Voluntary by donation. Open: Summer daily 6:30 a.m.–7:15 p.m., winter closes at sunset.*

Piazza del Comune and Museo del Foro Romano

At the end of Via San Francesco, this is the heart of Assisi. With so much religious art to see in Assisi, many people forget it was actually a Roman town. Graced with Renaissance fountains, this medieval piazza was built over the Roman Forum. The Temple of Minerva from the first century B.C.

still stands with its portico of six Corinthian columns — it was preserved as such only because early Christians converted it into a church which was still used after the Renaissance, when it was given a baroque overhaul. It is today one of the best-preserved Roman temples in Italy. Adjoining the temple is the 13th-century *torre* (tower), built by the Ghibellines. The site is open daily from 7 a.m. to noon and 2:30 p.m. to dusk. You can visit the Romans remains underneath the Piazza by entering the **Museo del Foro Romano di Assisi.**

Via Portica 2, off Piazza del Comune. ☎ *075-813-053.* www.sistemamuseo.it. *Admission: 2.50€ ($2.90). Open: Daily summer 10 a.m.–1 p.m. and 4–6 p.m.; winter 10 a.m.–1 p.m. and 2–5 p.m.*

Rocca Maggiore

Built by the Albornoz, this is a monument to a spirit opposite that of St. Francis. With foundations going back to Etruscan and Roman times, this 14th-century fort was built by the papacy when it subdued Assisi and brought the area under Vatican rule. It's somber and dark inside, but from the top you have a fabulous view of the walls, the town, and the surrounding valley. In the spring of 2000, lightning struck the Rocca and a tower partially collapsed, so the site was closed for restoration. As the restoration work advances, parts of the fortress are re-opening. At press time you could visit the *torretta* (one tower), and the long corridor leading to the polygonal watch tower, affording glorious views. Bring a flashlight — it may get quite dark in the corridor.

At the end of Via della Rocca. ☎ *075-815-292.* www.sistemamuseo.it. *Admission: 1.70€ ($2). Open: Daily 10 a.m.–sunset.*

More cool things to see and do

✔ In the nearby Santa Maria degli Angeli (4 km/2.5 miles from Assisi), the **Museo and Basilica di Santa Maria degli Angeli** (☎ 075-805-1430) is a grandiose basilica, built between 1569 and 1679 and graced by a superb cupola. The basilica was built around the **Porziuncola,** the first Franciscan convent where Santa Chiara was ordered by San Francesco in 1211 and where he died in 1226. The church and the museum have a collection of frescoes and paintings from the 14th to the 18th centuries. Admission is by voluntary donation. The site is open Thursday to Tuesday from 9 a.m. to noon and 3 to 6 p.m. in winter and Thursday to Tuesday from 9 a.m. to noon and 3:30–6:30 p.m. in summer.

✔ The **Santuario di San Damiano** (☎ 075-812-273), 2.5km (1.6 miles) from Assisi out the Porta Nuova, was built around the place of worship where St. Francis, praying before a wooden crucifix (today in the Basilica di Santa Chiara), had his first vision. This simple convent and its oratory, refectory, and cloister are beautifully decorated with frescoes from the 14th to the 16th centuries. You can also visit the dormitory where St. Clare died. It's open daily summer 10 a.m. to noon and 2 to 6 p.m., winter closes at 4:30 p.m.; admission is free.

Fast Facts: Assisi

Area Code

The country code for Italy is **39**. The area code for Assisi is **075**; use this code when calling from anywhere outside or inside Italy, even within Assisi itself (include the 0 every time, even when calling from abroad).

ATMs

You can change money in the ticket office at the rail station in Santa Maria degli Angeli, the small town nearby, which also has banks and ATMs.

Emergencies

Ambulance and Pronto Soccorso, ☎ **118**; fire, ☎ **115**; road assistance (Italian Automobile Club, ACI), ☎ **116**.

Hospital

The Ospedale di Assisi is just outside town in the direction of San Damiano (☎ 075-81-391).

Information

The main tourist office is on Piazza del Comune 27 (☎ 075-812-450; Fax: 075-813-727; www.umbria2000.it). It's open summer daily 8 a.m. to 6:30 p.m.; winter Monday to Saturday 8 a.m. to 2 p.m. and 3:30 to 6:30 p.m., and Sunday 9 a.m. to 1 p.m.

Internet Access

You can find Internet points at the Bar Caffe Duomo (Piazza S. Rufino 5; ☎ 075-813-794) and at the bar in Via Portica 29/B.

Police

There are two police forces in Italy; call either one. For the Polizia, call ☎ **113**; for the Carabinieri, call ☎ **112**.

Post Office

The Ufficio Postale is at Largo Properzio 4 (☎ 075-812-355).

Spoleto

A small medieval city in the shadow of an imposing fortress, Spoleto is one of the most picturesque towns in Umbria as well as one of the most famous. The city's development began in pre-Roman times, with the Umbri people who founded it. During the Roman period, Spoleto valiantly resisted the advances of Hannibal; under the emperors it was the resort of wealthy Romans. In the Middle Ages, Spoleto was devastated by the black plague and an earthquake; still, this jewel set among the Umbrian hills was a coveted prize fought over by Perugia and the Papacy. Today it is known the world over as a city of music and culture.

Spoleto is surrounded by the countryside that has made Umbria famous: olive groves, green hills, and beautiful mountains. Small enough to be visited as a day-trip from Rome or Florence, it's also a wonderful place to spend some days of leisure, especially during one of its art and music festivals. For the location of the tourist office, see "Fast Facts: Spoleto," later in this section.

Getting there

Spoleto is well connected by **rail** to all major destinations. There's direct service from Rome (the trip takes 1½ hours and costs about 15€/$17); you need to change in Foligno if you're traveling to and from Perugia (a trip of less than an hour, costing about 8€/$9.20). Trains arrive at Spoleto's **Stazione FS** on Piazza Polvani (☎ 0743-48-516), across the river Tessino to the north of the city's center. The station is well connected with the town by bus (circolare A, B, C, or D).

The **bus company SIT** (☎ 0743-212-211) has two daily runs to Perugia (a 90-minute trip for about 7€/$8.05) and many daily runs to Terni, where you can switch to one of the two daily trips to Rome (the whole thing takes about 2½ hours).

Spoleto lies about 130km (80 miles) from Rome on the Flaminia (SS3), the scenic but narrow consular road heading north from Rome. If you're **driving**, a faster possibility is A1; you exit at Orte and take the *superstrada* for Terni (follow the directions for Terni). The *superstrada* merges back into SS3 right after Terni; then just follow the directions for Spoleto.

Getting around

Spoleto is a small town on the slope of a mountain. Although the city developed on two levels (a lower one around the river Tessino and an upper one toward the fortress), the historic center *(centro storico)*, with most of Spoleto's attractions, is on the upper level, and you can easily visit it on foot — easily, that is, if you are in relatively good shape, for some of the streets are quite steep. However, you can also make use of the well-organized **bus service;** tickets cost .62€ (71¢) and are sold at the usual places (tobacconists and bars). As in other medieval towns, some of the narrower or stepped streets are closed to traffic.

Spending the night

Note that hotel reservations for the Spoleto Festival are made as much as a year in advance, so plan ahead if you'd like to attend the festival.

Hotel Charleston
$ Centro

An excellent choice in the historic center *(centro storico)*, the recently renovated Charleston occupies a 17th-century building and offers large, comfortable guest rooms. Each room is decorated differently, many with bright colors recalling the Renaissance. The bathrooms are not always large but they are nicely tiled and appointed; some have bathtubs, others showers. The public areas have terra-cotta floors, and an open fireplace is on the ground floor in the lounge area. The family-run hotel is constantly being upgraded; most rooms now have air-conditioning, and there are designated no-smoking rooms.

Spoleto

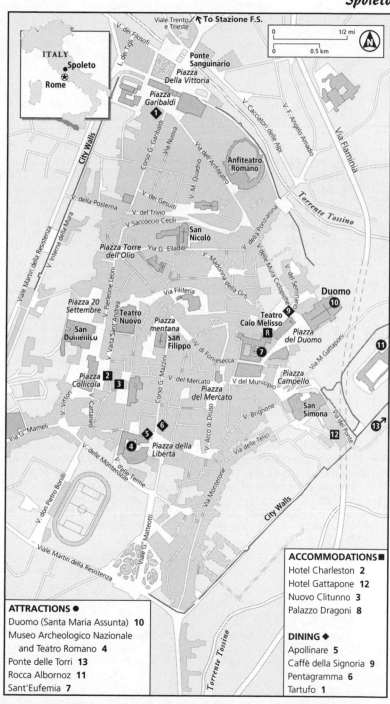

ITALY
Spoleto
Rome

To Stazione F.S.

Viale Trento e Trieste
V. dei Filosofi
L. dei Tigli
Ponte Sanguinario
Piazza Della Vittoria
Piazza Garibaldi ❶
City Walls
Corso G. Garibaldi
Via Nuova
Via dell'Anfiteatro
V. M. Quadrio
V. Cacciatori delle Alpi
V. F. Angelo Arnaldo
Via Flaminia
Anfiteatro Romano
V. della Posterna
V. dei Gesuiti
V. del Trivio
V. Saccoccio Cecili
San Nicolò
Via G. Elladio
Piazza Torre dell'Olio
V. Interna della Mura
Viale Martiri della Resistenza
Torrente Tossino
V. della Ponzianina
V. delle Mura Ciclopiche
V. Madonna della Orfi
Via Filiteria
V. del Seminario
Duomo ❿
Piazza 20 Settembre
V. Vaita Sant'Andrea
V. Pierleone Leoni
Teatro Nuovo
Piazza mentana
San Filippo
V. di Fontesecca
Teatro Caio Melisso ❽
❾
Piazza del Duomo
⓫
San Domenico
❼
Piazza Collicola ❷
❸
Corso G. Mazzini
V. del Mercato
Piazza del Mercato
V del Municipio
Piazza Campello
Via M. Gattaponi
V. Vittori
V. G. Cattaneo
❺ ❻
❹
Piazza della Libertà
V. Arco di Druso
V. Brignone
San Simona
Via del Ponte
⓬
⓭
Via G. Mameli
V. delle Monterozze
V. delle Terme
Via delle Felici
Via Monterone
City Walls
V. don Pietro Bonilli
Viale Martiri della Resistenza
Via G. Matteotti
Torrente Tossino

0 ——— 1/2 mi
0 ——— 0.5 km
N

ATTRACTIONS ●
Duomo (Santa Maria Assunta) 10
Museo Archeologico Nazionale
 and Teatro Romano 4
Ponte delle Torri 13
Rocca Albornoz 11
Sant'Eufemia 7

ACCOMMODATIONS ■
Hotel Charleston 2
Hotel Gattapone 12
Nuovo Clitunno 3
Palazzo Dragoni 8

DINING ◆
Apollinare 5
Caffè della Signoria 9
Pentagramma 6
Tartufo 1

Piazza Collicola 10. ☎ *0743-220-052. Fax: 0743-221-244.* www.hotelcharleston.it. *Free parking. Rack rates: 130€ ($150) double. Rates include buffet breakfast. AE, DC, MC, V.*

Hotel Gattapone
$$ Rocca

Named after the architect who built the Rocca Albornoz (see "More cool things to see and do," later in this section), this hotel is the nicest in Spoleto. The two 17th-century buildings forming the hotel dominate the town from a splendid location on the side of the Rocca. The antique-appointed guest rooms are spacious, with good beds and modern baths.

Via del Ponte 6. ☎ *0743-223-447. Fax: 0743-223-448.* www. hotelgattapone.it. *Free parking. Rack rates: 230€ ($265) double. Rates include breakfast. AE, DC, MC, V.*

Nuovo Clitunno
$ Centro

Located in the older part of town, the Clitunno is housed in a recently renovated building, and offers large guest rooms divided between old style (wood beams on the ceiling and decorated with antique reproduction furnishings in Renaissance style) and new style (modern but tasteful and comfortable, with king-size beds and fine fabrics). A restaurant and bar as well as a handicapped-accessible room have recently been added.

Piazza Sordini 6. ☎ *0743-223-340. Fax: 0743-222-663.* www.hotelclitunno.com. *Free parking. Rack rates: 130€ ($150) double. Rates include buffet breakfast. AE, DC, MC, V.*

Palazzo Dragoni
$$$ Centro

This hotel is housed in a 15th-century *palazzo* built over older structures (in the basement you can see the remains of tenth-century houses and a medieval street). From its magnificent lobby and common areas you ascend to rooms (no two alike) elegantly decorated with antiques, fine fabrics, wooden floors, pastel plastered walls, and painted, coffered, or vaulted ceilings. Some have balconies overlooking the Duomo and a panoramic view on the valley extending as far as Assisi. Book early — the hotel only has 15 rooms.

Via del Duomo 13. ☎ *0743-222-220. Fax: 0743-225-225.* www.palazzodragoni.it. *Free parking in nearby piazza. Rack rates: 250€ ($288) double. Rates include buffet breakfast. AE, DC, MC, V.*

Dining locally
Spoleto offers a number of good places to sample Umbrian cuisine and the famous *tartufo* (truffle) — which exist in white and black varieties; the former, which has a milder flavor, is the most coveted.

Apollinare
$ Teatro Romano NOUVELLE UMBRIAN

One of the best restaurants in town, the Apollinare is situated underneath the hotel Aurora, across the square from the Sant'Agata monastery. The food is excellent and includes traditional Umbrian dishes as well as imaginative — and delicious — interpretations of the classics. Be prepared for the crowds, especially if you're coming on a weekend.

Via Sant'Agata 14. ☎ *0743-223-256. Reservations necessary. Secondi: 11€–16€ ($13–$18). AE, DC, MC, V. Open: Lunch and dinner Wed–Mon. Closed 2 weeks in Jan or Feb and in Aug.*

Caffè della Signoria
$ Piazza della Signoria UMBRIAN

Particularly pleasant in the summer, when you can enjoy the scenic view over the garden and the surrounding countryside, this small restaurant offers simple cuisine true to Umbrian tradition. Excellent are the *torte di verdure* (savory greens pie), the *crespelle al forno* (crepes filled with ricotta and spinach and baked with tomato sauce and cheese), the *strangozzi al ragout bianco di vitello e tartufo di Norcia* (rustic homemade spaghetti with veal and white truffle sauce), and the local sausages.

Piazza della Signoria, 5b. ☎ *0743-46-333. Reservations recommended. Secondi: 8€–14€ ($9.20–16). DC, MC, V. Open: Lunch and dinner Thurs–Tues. Closed 2 weeks in Jan.*

Pentagramma
$ Teatro Romano UMBRIAN

Pentagramma specializes in pasta, homemade or not. You have a choice of sauces, including — of course — truffles and porcini mushrooms, fresh when in season. In addition, it serves a variety of soups, like the *zuppa di farro* (spelt soup), and a delicious *risotto al radicchio*.

Via Martani 4. ☎ *0743-223-141. Reservations recommended. Secondi: 10€–15€ ($12–$17). DC, MC, V. Open: Lunch and dinner Thurs–Tues. Closed Aug and 2 weeks in Jan/Feb.*

Tartufo
$$ Piazza Garibaldi UMBRIAN/CREATIVE

Il Tartufo — as its name suggests — specializes in dishes based on truffles, but its culinary offerings go well beyond that, including homemade bread, and delicious *grissini* (breadsticks), and simple, though uncommonly good, pastas and desserts. This is traditional Umbrian cuisine at its best, with a modern twist. Try the *ravioli neri di baccalà e tartufo* (truffle and cod ravioli), or the *maltagliati con broccoli, lenticchie e salsiccia* (homemade pasta with broccoli, lentils, and sausages). We definitely recommend the tasting menus.

Piazza Garibaldi 24. ☎ 0743-40-236. Reservations necessary. Secondi: 12€–19€ ($14–$22). AE, DC, MC, V. Open: Lunch Tues–Sun, dinner Tues–Sat. Closed 2 weeks in Feb and 10 days in Aug.

Exploring Spoleto

The two-week long Festival di Spoleto is immensely popular, but there's much more to explore in this picturesque town.

The top attractions

Duomo (Santa Maria Assunta)

This 12th-century Romanesque cathedral has a majestic facade, graced by rose windows and a beautiful 1207 mosaic by Solsterno depicting Christ in typical Byzantine style, flanked by saints against a magnificently gilded background. Because of the position of the church in a declivity on the slope of the hill, you can get a spectacular view looking down on the Duomo and its piazza. The Duomo's **campanile (bell tower)** was pieced together using stone looted from Roman temples. The church's interior, refurbished in the 17th century, still has the original mosaic floor in the central nave. In a niche at the entrance is the bronze bust of Urban VIII by Gian Lorenzo Bernini. Among all the treasures inside, the most important are in the **apse,** which was decorated in the 15th century with great Filippo Lippi frescoes, including the brooding and powerful *Morte della Vergine (Death of the Virgin Mary)*. The final concert of the Spoleto Festival is held every year in the piazza in front of the Duomo.

See map p. 323. Piazza del Duomo. Admission: Free. Open: Summer daily 8 a.m.–1 p.m. and 3–6:30 p.m.; winter daily 8 a.m.–1 p.m. and 3–5:30 p.m.

Festival di Spoleto

Also known as the **Festival dei Due Mondi** (Festival of Two Worlds), the Spoleto Festival was created by Gian Carlo Menotti in 1958 as a way to bring together the best of "two worlds," Europe and America. Now a two-week festival (end of June to the beginning of July), it attracts major performing-arts figures from around the world in a variety of disciplines, including theater, dance, music, and even cinema (Spoletocinema). Performances are held all over town, but the most important are held outdoors in the **Teatro Romano** (Piazza della Libertà; ☎ 0743-223-419), the Rocca, and the scenic Piazza del Duomo; and indoors in, the **Teatro Nuovo** (Via Filetteria 1; ☎ 0743-223-419), and the **Teatro Caio Melisso** (Piazza del Duomo; ☎ 0743-222-209).

Box office Piazza del Duomo 8 or buy online (☎ 800-565-600 in Italy or 0743-220-320; Fax: 0743-220-321; www.spoletofestival.it). Once in Spoleto, you can get tickets at the Teatro Nuovo. Tickets: 8€–50€ ($9.20–$58), depending on the event.

Museo Archeologico Nazionale and Teatro Romano

This theater dates back to the first years of the Roman Empire and is one of numerous vestiges of ancient Spoleto that are still visible. It was uncovered by a local archaeologist under Piazza della Libertà at the end of the 19th century and excavated in the 1950s, revealing some well-preserved structures. The Museum has interesting archeological findings from the area, including some sculpture and the famous *Lex Spoletina* (set of tablets bearing the carved law protecting the sacred wood of Monteluco nearby). A little farther east of the theater is the first-century **Arco di Druso (Via Arco di Druso)**, once the monumental arched entry to the Forum (now Piazza del Mercato). The impressive **baroque fountain** in the piazza was built on the site of the facade of a Romanesque church, of which a few pieces survive.

See map p. 323. Via Sant'Agata 18 Piazza della Libertà. ☎ *0743-223-277. Admission: 2€ ($2.30). Open: Daily 8:30 a.m.–7:30 p.m.*

Fast Facts: Spoleto

Area Code

The country code for Italy is **39**. The area code for Spoleto is **0743**; use this code when calling from anywhere outside or inside Italy — you must add the codes even within Spoleto itself (and you must include the 0 every time, even when calling from abroad).

ATMs

You can exchange money at the numerous banks and ATMs in town.

Emergencies

Ambulance and Pronto Soccorso (first aid), ☎ **118**; fire, ☎ **115**; road assistance ACI, ☎ **116**.

Hospital

There's an Ospedale on Via San Matteo (☎ 0743-21-01).

Information

The tourist office is on Piazza della Libertà (☎ 0743-220-311). Summer hours are Monday through Friday 9 a.m. to 1 p.m. and 4 to 7 p.m. and Saturday and Sunday 10 a.m. to 1 p.m. and 4 to 7 p.m.; winter hours are Monday through Saturday 9 a.m. to 1 p.m. and 3:30 to 6:30 p.m. and Sunday 10 a.m. to 1 p.m.

Police

There are two police forces in Italy; call either one. For the Polizia, call ☎ **113**; for the Carabinieri, call ☎ **112**.

Post Office

The Posta Centrale is on Piazza della Libertà (☎ 0743-40-231).

Part V
Venice and the Best of the Pianura Padana

"Funny—I just assumed it would be Carreras too."

In this part . . .

American poet Mark Rudman once wrote, "Venice is anti-simile; it isn't like any other place." It may be one of the few cities where you'll never hear an automobile (though the growling diesel motors of boats are never very far away). Venice, arguably the world's most romantic city, has grown up over thousands of years on marshy ground where people once hid in the reeds from barbarian hordes. From those humble beginnings, Venice became one of the greatest maritime empires history has ever seen and gave birth to great art, great institutions, and a unique architecture. And still, when you think of Venice, you first think of water — beguiling, mesmerizing, relaxing. The artistic and cultural influence of Venice spread to the surrounding region of the Pianura Padana, whose towns offer many splendid sights.

In Chapter 18, we take you through the watery roads and alleys of Venice and the most interesting of the nearby lagoon islands. In Chapter 19, we introduce you to the Pianura Padana's other three important cities: Padua and Verona, with their own beauties and treasures, and Milan, the business and industrial capital of Italy.

Chapter 18

Venice

● ●

In This Chapter

▶ Making your way to Venice and getting around without getting your feet wet
▶ Finding the best in Venice lodging and food
▶ Experiencing the sights, smells, and tastes of Venice
▶ Getting the scoop on the best shopping areas and nightlife attractions

● ●

A s soon as you arrive in **Venice (Venezia),** you'll see that this city
goes beyond all you have imagined or seen. The important public
structures and elegant private *palazzi* lining the canals bear witness to a
past of tremendous wealth, power, and culture. It's truly a magnificent
human achievement. And yet people have been calling Venice a dead
city for a century and a half. Henry James wrote, "She exists only as a
battered peep-show and bazaar." Just 70,000 people actually live in
Venice, but if you're ever alone anywhere for more than five minutes,
consider yourself lucky. The crowds are unbelievable: Everywhere you
go, someone is already there.

And yet . . . the Grand Canal at sunset, St. Mark's Square, the Academy
Gallery, the lagoon, the Lido, the Canaletto skies, and the stillness beneath
the hubbub are sights you just have to experience. And Venice's famous
serenity (the republic was called *La Serenissima,* the "serene one") is as
seductive as ever. Cranky Henry James and many other famous travelers
have succumbed to Venice before you. James conceded that "the only
way to care for Venice as she deserves it is to give her a chance to touch
you often — to linger and remain and return."

Venice became independent from Bisance (Constantinople, the capital
of the Eastern Roman Empire) in the eighth century A.D. with its first *doge*
(the head of the government). The word *doge* is the Venetian mutation of
the Latin word *dux* ("leader"). Venice became a harbor of international
importance in the tenth century, when the Republic started regulating
commerce between Europe and the Orient. The city we know today
started developing around St. Mark's Basilica (Basilica di San Marco),
constructed to house the relics of the saint. The group of islands in the
lagoon was built up, the canals drained, and their edges reinforced. The
city had begun its metamorphosis.

The Venetian Republic was a great experiment in government. Over the centuries, a complicated network of institutions and checks and balances was built to limit the power of the *doge* and all the other political institutions that governed the city-state. At the heart was the *Maggior Consiglio* (Great Council) who elected the *doge*. Originally elective, membership to the Maggior Consiglio became hereditary in 1297. The smaller Council of Ten was established in 1310 to judge conspirators in a failed plot, but it became permanent (the *doge* and his counselors were also members). It became so powerful that the Maggior Consiglio passed legislation to limit its powers in 1582, 1628, and 1762. Most powerful of all, perhaps, was the Grand Chancellor, who, as the head of the secret police, knew all the dark secrets of the nobility, so other institutions were established to limit his power. The experiment was successful: Venice remained a republic until May 12, 1797, when Napoleon invaded northern Italy and established a new European order.

Venice has weathered wars, dictators, and conspiracies and enjoyed more than a thousand years of democracy. But its most treacherous foe may be the very ground beneath it. The increase in the sea levels registered all over the planet in recent years has had especially dramatic consequences for Venice, and the city is literally sinking into the muddy lagoon on which it was built. In spite of advice from experts all over the world, cement injections, and the ongoing work of restoration and solidification of the canals, the city continues to sink. The search for ways to save one of the most beautiful and extraordinary cities ever built continues.

Getting There

Regardless of Venice's unique location, it is easily accessible by plane, train, ship, or car. But no matter which way you arrive, remember to pack light: unless your hotel has a water access, you'll have to carry your luggage from the closest waterway to the door of your hotel.

By air

Small but not too small, Venice's **Aeroporto Marco Polo** (☎ 041-260-9260; www.veniceairport.it) is situated in a mainland locality called Tessera, about 10km (6¼ miles) from the city. **Alitalia** (☎ 041-258-1333; www.alitalia.com) has several flights a day to Venice from other Italian cities. Some other European companies fly direct to Venice from some European capitals.

Getting oriented at the airport

The airport is well organized and very easy to get around. You will find an ATM, a currency-exchange counter, and a tourist information desk at the arrivals area of the airport terminal (there's only one terminal). Passing customs is usually not a big issue as you arrive in Venice via a connecting flight from in Rome, Milan, or another European airport — which means that you have already cleared customs in the city that your flight originated.

Getting from the airport to your hotel

From the airport, you can reach the city by bus or water. The *motoscafo* (**shuttle boat**) run by **Cooperativa San Marco/Alilaguna** (☎ 041-523-5775; www.alilaguna.it) takes about 50 minutes to Piazza San Marco, with stops at Murano and Lido, and costs 10€ ($12) per person. Though romantic and convenient, a **water taxi** (☎ 041-541-5084) costs a whopping 70€ ($80) on average for two to four persons. A less expensive option is to take the **shuttle bus** to Piazzale Roma (Venice's car terminal on the mainland) operated by **ATVO** (☎ 041-520-5530; www.atvo.it). It runs every hour and costs 3€ ($3.45) per person. The trip takes about 20 minutes. When you arrive at Piazzale Roma, you can take a water taxi or a *vaporetto* (see "Getting Around Venice," later in this chapter).

By train

Venice's rail station is the **Stazione Ferroviaria Santa Lucia.** Many trains head directly to **Santa Lucia,** but sometimes you have to change in **Mestre,** Venice's inland rail hub, and switch to a shuttle train. The trip from Mestre to Santa Lucia takes about ten minutes, with connections every few minutes, but it still is inconvenient; definitely try to get one of the direct trains. Here you can find a (usually mobbed) branch of the tourist office, the hotel association (in case you don't have a reservation), and, just in front of the exit, the ticket booth for the *vaporetto* (water bus; see "Getting Around Venice," later in this chapter), as well as water taxis.

When you buy your train ticket, remember that there is no "Venezia" rail station. Many tourists get confused and frustrated when trying to buy a ticket to Venice from an Italian railroad employee. When they ask you if you want to go to Santa Lucia, your answer should be "Yes!" Because that's the station in historic Venice, right on the Canal Grande.

The fastest train to Venice is the **Eurostar,** which gets you to Venice in about 5 hours from Rome and 3½ hours from Milan; the **Intercity** takes just a little longer. Both trains travel directly to Santa Lucia. Try to avoid the slower regular train that makes many stops. A one-way ticket from Rome costs about 40€ ($46), depending on the category of train you choose.

By ship

Traditionally, Venice was accessible only by water — the bridge to the mainland was built only in 1846. You can still get to Venice by ship, but pleasant as it is, it's also rare. Several international cruising companies offer cruises to Venice; your travel agent can help you sort through the options. Remember that it's a long way to Venice from most international ports of call, usually a minimum of a month (most travelers don't have that kind of time). Your ship arrives at the **Marine Terminal (Stazione Marittima)** in Santa Croce, in the heart of Venice. From there, the regular city transportation is at your disposal.

By car

If you drive to Venice from Rome or Florence, take A1 to Bologna, then A13 to Padua, and then A4 to Venice. The distance is 530km (327 miles from Rome and 243km (151 miles) from Florence.

No cars are allowed to enter Venice. The closest you can get is the car terminal in Piazzale Roma, where you have to say goodbye to your mechanical pet. Expect to pay 20€ ($23) or more per day for a garage, depending on the size of your car. (Don't even think about leaving your car on the street for a day or two, or you'll say goodbye for good.) The **ASM Garage** (☎ **041-272-7301**; www.asmvenezia.it) and the **Garage San Marco** (☎ **041-523-2213**; www.garagesanmarco.it) are convenient to boat stops. A cheaper alternative is on the island of **Tronchetto**, where the **COMPARK** (☎ **041-520-7555**) costs about 15€ ($17) per day.

Note that all these parking places are hard to get to in summer and on weekends because of monstrous traffic jams. Leaving your car on the mainland, in Mestre, where there are parking lots at the train station or on Via Stazione, is a better (and cheaper) idea. There are two garages in the city of Mestre: **Garage Serenissima** (☎ **041-938-021**) and **Crivellari** (☎ **041-929-225**).

Orienting Yourself in Venice

Today's Venice comprises three major areas: the ***centro storico* (historic district)**, a cluster of islands linked by small bridges and crossed by **Canal Grande;** the **Terraferma,** a modern development on the mainland which includes **Mestre** — where a large part of the city's population actually lives; and the larger islands of the ***laguna* (lagoon),** including **Lido** and **Murano.** The lagoon stretches from the Adriatic Sea to the mainland, enclosing Venice proper and many other islands.

The *centro storico* is the heart of Venice. It is divided into *sestieri* (a *sestiere* is a sixth of the city), three on each side of the **Canal Grande** — the central canal, shaped as a reversed S. Canal Grande is crossed by three bridges: the **Ponte dell'Accademia,** the famous **Ponte di Rialto,** and the **Ponte degli Scalzi** (at the rail station). The canal divides the historic district in two — *de citra* ("this side" of the canal), the side of **San Marco** and the **Ca' d'Oro,** and *de ultra* ("the far side"), where the **Gallerie dell'Accademia** are located.

Introducing the neighborhoods

Venice is very safe — and the only real danger is being served a bad meal at a touristy restaurant. Seriously, no matter how narrow a *calle* (street) may be or how poor a place may look, there's no "bad neighborhood" in the historic district, even at night. That shouldn't induce you, though, to do foolish things such as display large quantities of money or leave your expensive camera unattended. Plenty of pickpockets (and some bag snatchers, too) are still around.

Cannaregio

This is an authentic neighborhood, where locals still live and work. The painter Tintoretto was born here, near the Madonna dell'Orto church, not far from the Ghetto. On the Grand Canal end are the **Ca' d'Oro,** and, farther up, the **Rail Station Santa Lucia.** In Cannaregio, you will find no-frills restaurants, a bit of nightlife (toward the Canal Grande), and a number of moderately priced hotels. It's from this borough, on the lagoon side, that you find the **Fondamenta Nuove station,** from which you can take the *vaporetto* (water bus) to the islands of **Murano, Burano,** and **Torcello.**

Castello

Behind **St. Mark's Basilica,** and inland from the **Riva degli Schiavoni** — the grandiose promenade overlooking the bay of San Marco with some expensive hotels and restaurants — this is an authentic working district. Running through the heart of **Castello** is **Via Garibaldi,** a street lined with neighborhood shops and *osterie* and an outdoor market. Highlights are the **Arsenale (Naval Armory)** the **Giardini Pubblici** — where **La Biennale di Venezia,** the famous international art show, is held — and the **Basilica dei Santi Giovanni e Paolo.**

Dorsoduro

This is where the university is located; the neighborhood offers plenty of interesting restaurants and many small hotels. It's a more artsy and trendy area where you can find the **Gallerie dell'Accademia, Ca' Rezzonico,** and the **Peggy Guggenheim Collection.** You can stroll along the beautiful promenade of the **Zattere** — famous for its outdoor cafes — to the majestic church of **Santa Maria della Salute.** This area also includes the **Isola della Giudecca,** a small island across from the promenade of the Zattere, separated by the Canale della Giudecca, the second canal in importance after the Grand Canal, and the main water route to the maritime terminal.

Lido

The **Lido** is the long barrier island that protects the lagoon from the open sea. Inhabited since ancient times, it bloomed at the end of the 19th century with the development of an elegant Art Nouveau resort that includes the **Excelsior Palace,** the **Hotel des Bains,** and the **casino.** It's here that Venetians come to swim and tan on the long beaches. Many tourists choose to stay here because it's only a short *vaporetto* ride from San Marco and you get much better hotels for your money.

Murano

Smaller than Venice, Murano keeps exactly the same spirit but in a quieter way. It is the island of the glassmakers, famous for centuries. It has the **Glass Museum (Museo Vetrario di Murano),** and you can find a few glassworks that still produce artistic glass. There are a few restaurants but no hotels.

San Marco

Named after the famous Basilica, this *sestiere* is the central tourist destination, containing some of the major attractions in Venice: **Basilica di San Marco, Palazzo Ducale, Ponte dei Sospiri, Correr Museum,** and **Palazzo Gritti.** San Marco is a neighborhood with lots of hotels — including some of the most expensive in the city — and a number of city offices. The many restaurants tend to be "touristy" and the streets overcrowded. To appreciate its picturesque side, explore the area at night, when the crowds have receded. San Marco is connected to other *sestieri* by two of the three bridges crossing the Grand Canal: the **Rialto,** connecting San Marco to San Polo, and the **Accademia,** connecting San Marco to Dorsoduro.

San Polo

Just across from the rail station Santa Lucia, and over the Rialto Bridge from San Marco, this is a less touristy neighborhood. San Polo was the main market in Venice at the time when Rialto was the marine terminal of the medieval city. It is still a commercial neighborhood with many shops, some simple restaurants, and just a few hotels. You can also find the **Scuola Grande di San Rocco** and the **Basilica dei Frari** here.

Santa Croce

This is the borough in which you arrive when you come by car. It has the marine and automobile terminal but also some very interesting churches and a beautiful promenade. It's the least visited part of Venice.

Finding information after you arrive

The tourist offices are worth a visit if only to get the current opening hours of churches and museums — they change all the time, as in the rest of Italy. If you need wheelchair access, special maps are available. Following is a list of Venice's tourist offices:

- ✔ **Aeroporto Marco Polo** (☎ 041-529-8711); located in the Arrivals area, open daily 9:30 a.m. to 7:30 p.m.

- ✔ **APT,** the central tourist office of Venice), is in Palazzo Ziani at 5050 Fondamenta San Lorenzo (☎ **041-529-8700;** www.turismovenezia.it). It's open Monday through Friday 8:30 a.m. to 5 p.m.

- ✔ **Lido** (☎ 041-526-5711), at the *vaporetto* arrival station; open daily June to September 9 a.m. to 12:30 p.m. and 3:30 to 6 p.m.

- ✔ **Piazzale Roma** (☎ 041-529-8711) in the **Garage Azienda Sevizi Mobilità;** open daily 9:30 a.m. to 6:30 p.m.

- ✔ **San Marco all'Ascensione** (☎ 041-529-8711) at San Marco 71/F; open daily 9 a.m. to 3:30 p.m.

- ✔ **Train Station Santa Lucia** (☎ 041-529-8711); open daily 8 a.m. to 6:30 p.m.

- ✔ **Venice Pavillion** (San Marco Ex Giardini Reali; ☎ 041-529-8711); open daily 10 a.m. to 6 p.m.

Venice Orientation

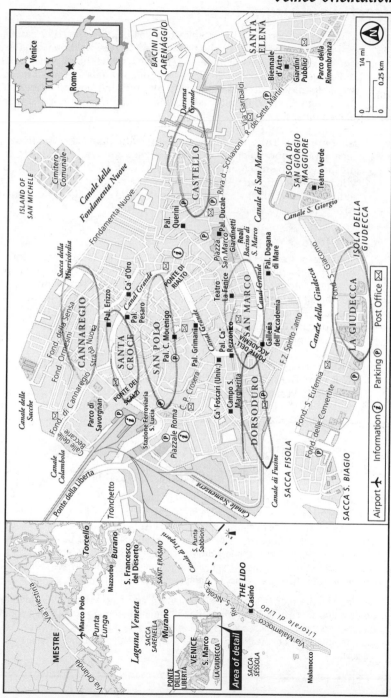

Getting Around Venice

Made up of over 100 islands linked by 354 bridges over 177 canals, Venice can be quite confusing to the uninitiated. These waterways have always been the main means of access to houses, which is why the facades of buildings are on the canals. Crossing these canals are small bridges with steps up and down — a major difficulty for anything on wheels. You can just imagine how difficult loading and unloading for shops and catering places must be.

Here are a few rules to have a good time and gain lots of kudos with the locals: Get a good map, remember to keep your right — yes, even walking, and not to stop on narrow bridges blocking the circulation; also, put your backpack down when you travel in a *vaporetto*. If you have a problem you would like to report, please do so at the Ufficio Reclami of the APT central office (see earlier in this chapter).

On foot

Walking is the best way to visit Venice, and you'll be doing a lot of it. The only things you need are a **good map** (try the smartly folded Falk map, available at many bookstores and newsstands), comfortable shoes, and perhaps good foot balm (an end-of-the-day treat for your faithful "wheels"). We've seen many a tourist, unprepared for the rigors of walking Venice, slumped in dismay in front of the steps of yet another bridge. Although it might appear daunting and maze-like, you can't get lost in Venice as you would in a regular city: there are really few streets and a canal will always stop you — at worst, you'll have to backtrack and then try the next turn. Big deal — you'll have discovered yet another fantastic view of the city you came to visit.

How to get around if you're wheelchair-bound

Although the city has made big efforts, Venice still isn't easy for wheelchair-bound visitors. The only real problem, but a major one, are the bridges over the canals, all with steps up and down. Any longish route passes over a canal, hence the steps; otherwise, you're condemned to go around in circles on the same tiny island. Still, the main attractions are all accessible by water (boats are boarded by gangways, which have no steps), you can take strolls without crossing a bridge, and a few bridges have been equipped with motorized lifts (alas, we saw a number that were inoperable).

Fortunately, the tourist board has prepared a **city map with yellow-highlighted wheelchair-accessible itineraries.** The lifts on the few bridges equipped with them require a key to work, and the key is available free at the APT tourist information offices (see earlier in this chapter). You can also learn the latest information online at www.comune.venezia.it/handicap/.

As you wander, look for those ubiquitous signs with arrows (sometimes a little old, but still readable) which, just like trailblazers, direct you toward major landmarks: **Ferrovia** (the train station), **Piazzale Roma** (the car terminal), **vaporetto** (the *vaporetto* stop), **Rialto** (the bridge), **Piazza San Marco,** and **Accademia** (the bridge). If you decide to ask someone for directions, be aware that people are more likely to know the name of the actual place you're looking for than the name of a small street, often unmarked.

The famous *acqua alta* (high water) shouldn't be a concern. From November through March, in periods of high tides, many streets of the historic district are inundated with water. To facilitate walking, wooden platforms are placed around, so you don't have to pack your waders, unless you want to wander in the smallest or out-of-the-way streets. Many hotels ($$$ and above) actually provide plastic boots in an ample choice of sizes for you to borrow (ask when you reserve if you're planning your visit for the *acqua alta* season). Particularly high tides (*acqua alta*) are announced by a siren.

By vaporetto

The bus system of the historic district is the *vaporetto* (water bus) run by Venice Transportation Authority **ACTV** (☎ **041-272-2111;** www.actv.it). Riding these strange motorboats — something between a small barge and a ferry — is great fun: *Vaporetti* are relatively slow, but what a view you get! One must-do experience is the ride down the Grand Canal, both by day and by night (see "Exploring Venice," later in this chapter).

See the Cheat Sheet at the front of this guide for a map of Venice's *vaporetto* system.

A regular *vaporetto* ride for any line except the Canal Grande lines costs 3.50€ ($4), and a ride along Canal Grande (a 90-minute ticket) is 1.80€ ($2.07). If you plan to use the *vaporetto* a lot, go for a ***giornaliero* (daily pass)** at 10.50€ ($12), or a ***biglietto tre giorni* (three-day pass)** at 22€ ($25), or 15€ ($17) if you have the Rolling Venice Card (see "Exploring Venice," later in this chapter). The pass gives you access to the whole public transportation system, including the beautiful islands of Torcello, Murano, and Burano (see "More cool things to see and do," later in this chapter) as well as the Lido.

Take advantage of **Venice Card** (see "Exploring Venice," later in this chapter), which includes a public transportation pass.

By gondola and traghetto

Yes, we know, gondolas are for, ahem, *tourists* . . . but really, what can be more romantic than being rowed in a gondola along the Grand Canal? These traditional crafts are still built and conducted according to the strictest rules, and not taking a ride in one is something you might regret forever after. Alas, a gondola ride is very expensive: The official rates (set by Ente Gondola; ☎ **041-528-5075;** www.gondolavenezia.it) are

62€ ($71) for 50 minutes for a maximum of six people and 31€ ($36) for each additional 25 minutes during the day; and in the evening the rates are 77€ ($89), for up to six for 50 minutes, and 39€ ($45) for each additional 25 minutes during the night. Many *gondolieri* (the guys who row) contend that they'd be underpaid if they respected those rates. It is true that official rates have not gone up in quite a few years — as a result, they try to charge whatever the market will bear. So be sure to establish the price in advance before you get in the boat! Your chances of getting a good deal at any of the gondola stations along the Grand Canal are about equal. What really makes the difference is how busy the *gondolieri* are. Use only authorized gondolas and make sure you know the proper tariffs before boarding. Two of the gondola companies are the **Consorzio dei Gondolieri** in San Marco (☎ 041-522-8637) and the **Cooperativa Gondolieri** in Santa Maria del Giglio (☎ 041-522-2073).

Although the tide excursion is not very high in the Mediterranean, you might still want to have your tour at high tide — to be more level with the pavement, instead of the "architectonically interesting," but kind of scummy canal sidewalls. You also always want to avoid Canal Grande, which gets very choppy and can therefore be quite unpleasant for a small boat.

Many people don't know that a traditional type of boat is still used as public transportation: the *traghetto,* very similar to the gondola, only it's moved by two rowers instead of one and is much less fancy in decoration. Because only three bridges span the Grand Canal, *traghetti* take you across at eight points for a mere .40€ (46¢) per person; the *traghetto* stations are San Tomà, Santa Maria del Giglio, Dogana, Ferrovia, Rialto, San Marcuola, San Samuele, and Santa Sofia. You just walk down to the small wooden dock, indicated by a sign saying "TRAGHETTO" (often the street leading to the dock is called Calle del Traghetto), and wait for the boat to come. Note that Venetians ride *traghetti* standing, proudly displaying their sea legs. The only drawbacks are that the *traghetti* operate for limited hours (most only mornings, a few also in the afternoon) and that the ride won't last more than five minutes.

By water taxi

Though a little expensive, *taxi acquei* (water taxis) are a great way to get to and from your hotel with your luggage or to have a taste of luxury. They cost 14€ ($16) for the first seven minutes and then .25€ (30¢) for each additional 15 seconds; a ride from Piazzale Roma to Piazza San Marco is about 42€ ($47) for up to four passengers. Remember that certain locations — and hotels — even water taxis can't reach, in which cases you have to walk the rest of the way. Among the several companies in town are the **Cooperativa San Marco** (☎ 041-523-5775), **Cooperativa Veneziana** (☎ 041-716-000) in Cannaregio, and **Cooperativa Serenissima** (☎ 041-522-1265) in Castello.

Finding your way around Venice

To deal with its very unique geography, Venice had to develop its own unique jargon. A *calle* (pronounced with a hard l) is a narrow street; a paved road is a *salizzada* or a *calle larg;* a *rio terà* is a canal that was filled in to make a street; a *fondamenta* is a long street running alongside a canal; and a *sottoportico* is a passage under a building. Note that there's only one piazza in Venice and that's **Piazza San Marco** — all the others are either a *campo* (square) or a *campiello* (a smaller square). As if that weren't enough to confuse visitors, buildings are numbered in a unique way too: "2534 San Marco" and "2536 San Marco" may well be on two different streets — oops, *calli!* Those numbers are only postal addresses and that's why all hotels and restaurants have small maps printed on the back of their business cards and why even Venetians call for directions before going to an address they haven't been to before. And always make sure you have the name of the *sestiere* (borough): Venice has many streets of the same name!

 Be aware of "gypsy" water taxis that will offer you a ride. Official taxis do not cruise around looking for passengers. You must call one by phone (numbers listed above), or go to one of the official taxi stands in Aeroporto Marco Polo, Piazzale Roma, Ferrovia, Rialto, Piazza San Marco, and Lido.

Staying in Style

Because Venice is such a major tourist attraction, it has a wide variety of hotels to choose from. Most of our choices are accessible by water or by a short walk without crossing bridges.

Luggage is your enemy in Venice. Pack as light as you can. No vehicles are allowed in the city, so whatever you bring with you you'll have to carry. Beware also that the bridges over the canals have steps — not many of them, but enough to transform that luggage with wheels into an unbearable load. Therefore, find out how accessible your hotel is by water before booking.

 If you want to see Venice during Carnevale (Carnival, better known in the U.S. as Mardi Gras), reserve your hotel room way in advance — up to a year for the most sought-after accommodations.

 You can get special discounts with the **Venice Card** (see "Exploring Venice," later in this chapter) by reserving your hotel through the **Hotel Association of Venice** (AVA; ☎ 800-843-006 toll-free in Italy or 041-522-2264; www.veneziasi.it). The following hotels (reviewed below) are AVA members and offer discounts of 10 to 15 percent to Venice Card carriers: Al Sole Palace, Boscolo Hotel Bellini, Hotel Bernardi-Semenzato, Hotel Campiello, Hotel Cipriani e Palazzo Vendramin, Hotel Flora, Hotel Marconi, Hotel Pantalon, Hotel San Cassiano Ca' Favretto, Hotel Santo Stefano, Hotel Violino d'Oro, La Calcina, and Pensione Accademia Villa Maravegie.

The top hotels

Albergo La Meridiana
$$ Lido di Venezia

This small hotel offers quality accommodations and excellent service on the island of Lido, only a short *traghetto* ride from San Marco. All the guest rooms are spacious, and decorated in pastel colors with simple but quality modern furniture. The nicest rooms are those that have rows of casement windows and look out over the garden. The hotel also has a private beach and offers such perks as free bicycles and free entrance to the casino.

Via Lepanto 45, Lido di Venezia. ☎ *041-526-0343. Fax: 041-526-9240.* www.lameridiana.com. *Free parking. Vaporetto: 62 to Casino; walk left on Via Dardanelli, turn left on Via Lorenzo Marcello, and right on Via Lepanto. Rack rates: 230€ ($265) double. Rates include breakfast. AE, DC, MC, V. Closed Nov 15–Jan 31.*

Al Sole Palace
$$$ Santa Croce

Away from the tourist crowds near the university and Ca' Foscari (see "More cool things to see and do," later in this chapter), this hotel occupies a delightful 15th-century *palazzo* that was originally the home of the prominent Marcello family. The rooms have old Venetian furniture and beamed ceilings, and some have nice views over the canal. A restaurant is on the premises. Note that the hotel sometimes runs specials and affordable package deals including sightseeing tours.

Fondamenta Minotta, 136 Santa Croce. ☎ *041-710-844. Fax: 041-714-398.* www.alsolepalace.com. *Vaporetto: 1, 82, 41, 42, 51, or 52 to Piazzale Roma; follow the Fondamenta Croce to your left, turn right on Fondamenta dei Tolentin along the Canali, and continue to Fondamenta Minotta on your left. Rack rates: 260€ ($299) double. Discount available with purchase of Venice Card. Rates include buffet breakfast. AE, DC, MC, V.*

Boscolo Hotel Bellini
$$$$ Cannaregio

Although only steps from Santa Lucia train station, this elegant hotel is surprisingly well insulated from the lively street below. Housed in a *palazzo* overlooking Canal Grande, it offers grand guest rooms furnished in luxurious Venetian style, with damask fabrics and gilded furniture. Some of the rooms have a beautiful view over the canal. It is a way to stay in style at a fraction of what you would pay in one of the hotels on Canal Grande closer to San Marco.

See map p. 344. Lista di Spagna, 116/a Cannaregio. ☎ **041-524-2488.** *Fax: 041-715-193.* www.bellini.boscolohotels.com. *Vaporetto: 1, 82, 71, 72, 51, 52, 41 or 42 to Ferrovia stop and turn right . Rack rates: 450€ ($518) double. Discount available with purchase of Venice Card. Rates include breakfast. AE, DC, MC, V.*

Gritti Palace
$$$$$ **San Marco**

If you can afford it, staying at the magnificent residence of Doge Andrea Gritti, an ornate 16th-century palace, will bring you back in time and offer you a truly unique experience. Guest rooms are spacious and decorated with antique paintings and furniture in the Venetian style. A must, of course, is to arrive by water transportation and the staff will meet you at water's edge. Service is perfect.

See map p. 344. Campo Santa Maria del Giglio, San Marco 2467. ☎ **800-325-3535** *in the U.S. and Canada, or 041-794-611. Fax: 041-520-0942.* www.starwood.com/italy. *Vaporetto: 1 to Giglio. Rack Rates: 1,107€ ($1,273) double. AE, DC, MC, V.*

Hotel Bernardi-Semenzato
$ **Cannaregio**

Renovated in 1995, this hotel a few minutes from the Ponte di Rialto combines an antique look with modern amenities; the annex three blocks away offers the same amenities. The guest rooms are good sized and the baths mostly new; but you can get a really cheap room if you're willing to do without a private bath. Nearby Strada Nuova is a busy shopping street where Venetians actually outnumber tourists and linger for a chat, a coffee, or an ice cream. The hotel has a 40 percent-off deal with a parking lot in Tronchetto. The management welcomes families and tries its best to meet their special needs.

See map p. 344. Calle dell'Oca, 4366 Cannaregio. ☎ **041-522-7257.** *Fax: 041-522-2424.* www.hotelbernardi.com. *Vaporetto: 1 to Ca' d'Oro; walk up to Strada Nuova, turn right, then turn left on Calle del Duca and right on Calle dell'Oca. Rack rates: 115€ ($132) double. Discount available with purchase of Venice Card. AE, DC, MC, V.*

Hotel Campiello
$$$ **Castello**

This pink 15th-century building is easy to find — just off posh Riva degli Schiavoni — and it's a bargain for the area. The location is just about perfect, nearby Riva degli Schiavoni but somewhat quieter. The recently renovated guest rooms are decorated either in Venetian Liberty (Art Nouveau) style or in a modern Italian look, and all have new bathrooms. The expert staff of this family-run hotel is friendly. The buffet breakfast is more substantial than many and is served in a rather glitzy hall. The hotel also has suites, triples, and quads, which are great for families.

Venice Accommodations and Dining

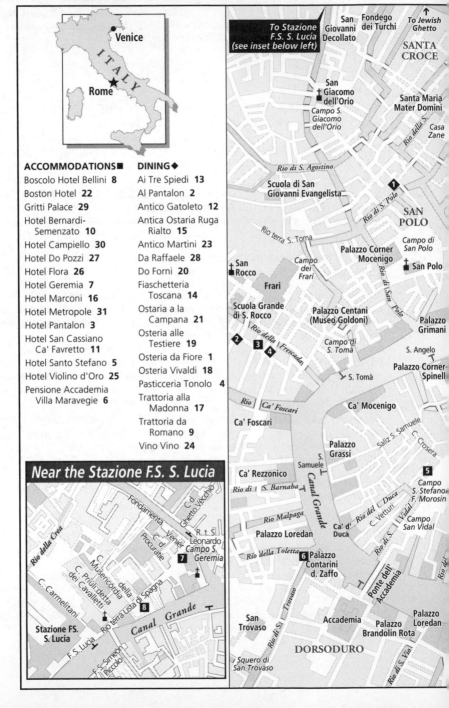

ACCOMMODATIONS■

Boscolo Hotel Bellini **8**
Boston Hotel **22**
Gritti Palace **29**
Hotel Bernardi-
Semenzato **10**
Hotel Campiello **30**
Hotel Do Pozzi **27**
Hotel Flora **26**
Hotel Geremia **7**
Hotel Marconi **16**
Hotel Metropole **31**
Hotel Pantalon **3**
Hotel San Cassiano
Ca' Favretto **11**
Hotel Santo Stefano **5**
Hotel Violino d'Oro **25**
Pensione Accademia
Villa Maravegie **6**

DINING◆

Ai Tre Spiedi **13**
Al Pantalon **2**
Antico Gatoleto **12**
Antica Ostaria Ruga
Rialto **15**
Antico Martini **23**
Da Raffaele **28**
Do Forni **20**
Fiaschetteria
Toscana **14**
Ostaria a la
Campana **21**
Osteria alle
Testiere **19**
Osteria da Fiore **1**
Osteria Vivaldi **18**
Pasticceria Tonolo **4**
Trattoria alla
Madonna **17**
Trattoria da
Romano **9**
Vino Vino **24**

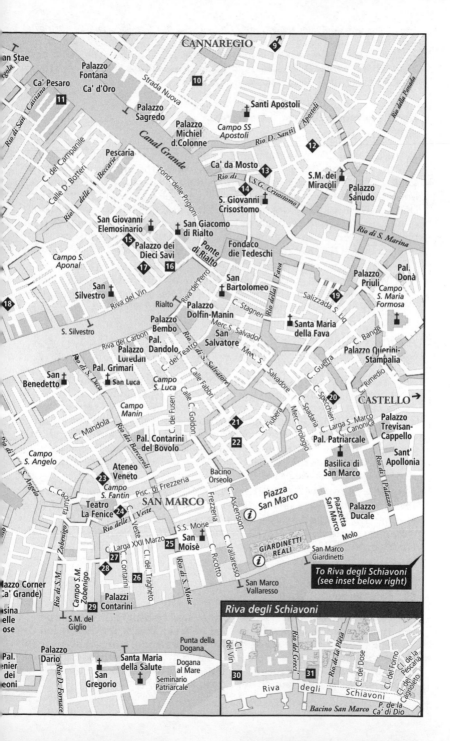

See map p. 344. Campiello del Vin, 4647 Castello. ☎ *041-523-9682. Fax: 041-520-5798.* www.hotelcampiello.it. *Vaporetto: 1, 14, 41, 42, 51, 52, 71, 72, or 82 to San Zaccaria; walk up Calle del Vin. Rack rates: 300€ ($345) double, 230€ ($265) triple, 270€ ($310) quad, and 300€ ($345) suite. Discount available with purchase of Venice Card. Rates include buffet breakfast. AE, MC, V.*

Hotel Cipriani e Palazzo Vendramin
$$$$$ Dorsoduro

At the tip of Giudecca — the island a few minutes from San Marco by free shuttle boat, this hotel offers one of the most romantic experiences in Venice. The individually decorated rooms are spacious and elegant, but not with the ornate — and somewhat tiring — elegance of the Gritti Palace. Detailed with pastel colors, quality linens, and fine fabrics and with windows opening above the canal or the gardens and private swimming pool, make for a very relaxing experience. The **Cipriani** restaurant inside the hotel is one of the best restaurants in Venice and in Italy.

Isola della Giudecca 10. ☎ *041-520-7744. Fax: 041-520-7745* www.hotelcipriani. com. *Vaporetto: 41, 42, 82, N to Zitelle. Rack rates: 852€ ($980)standard double. Discount available with purchase of Venice Card. Rates include full American breakfast. Children 12 and under stay free in parent's room. AE, DC, MC, V.*

Hotel des Bains
$$$$$ Lido

Now owned by Starwood, this grand Art Nouveau hotel is one of Venice's most famous, and beautiful. Everybody who was anybody in the early 1900s stayed here (Thomas Mann's *Death in Venice* was set here). The guest rooms are large and bright, and furnished with handsome antiques as well as modern conveniences. The hotel offers a motorboat shuttle between Lido and Venice, plus tennis courts and a pool in the surrounding park and horseback riding. Ask about their low-season prices — they usually have very good deals.

Lungomare Marconi 17, Lido di Venezia. ☎ *800-325-3535 in the U.S. or 041-526-5921. Fax: 041-526-0113.* www.starwooditaly.com. *Vaporetto: 1, 6, 14, 51, 52, 61, 62, or 82 to the Lido; walk up Gran Viale Santa Maria Elizabetta and turn right (the hotel is in the park) or take bus A, B, or C. Rack rates: 704€ ($810)double. Rates include buffet breakfast. AE, DC, MC, V. Closed Nov–Mar.*

Hotel Flora
$$ San Marco

Friendly, handicapped accessible, and with a charming private garden (a rare treasure in Venice), this hotel lies between Piazza San Marco and the Teatro La Fenice. All the guest rooms are furnished Venetian style; many have views of the garden and rooms 3 and 47, the most beautiful rooms, also have views of the dome of La Salute — try to score one of these. Hotel guests enjoy a private launch service to Murano.

See map p. 344. Calle dei Bergamaschi, 2283/A San Marco. ☎ *041-520-5844. Fax: 041-522-8217.* www.hotelflora.it. *Vaporetto: 1 to Giglio; walk up Calle Gritti, turn right on Calle delle Ostriche, cross the bridge and continue onto Calle Larga XXII Marzo, then turn right on Calle dei Bergamaschi. Rack rates: 230€ ($265) double. Discount available with purchase of Venice Card. Rates include breakfast. MC, V.*

Hotel Marconi
$$$ San Polo

At the foot of the Ponte di Rialto and overlooking the Grand Canal, the Marconi has an understated elegance. Refurbished in 1999, the building dates from the 1500s and is in a beautiful — particularly at night — part of Venice that has many cafes and restaurants. All the guest rooms are furnished in perfect Venetian style; only four open onto the canal, so reserve early for one of these. In fair weather, breakfast is served in the terrace by the Grand Canal.

See map p. 344. Riva del Vin, 729 San Polo. ☎ *041-522-2068. Fax: 041-522-9700.* www.hotelmarconi.it. *Vaporetto: 1 and 82 to Rialto; walk to the Rialto Bridge and cross over and turn left along the canal on Riva del Vin. Rack rates: 342€ ($393) double. Discount available with purchase of Venice Card. Rates include breakfast. AE, MC, DC, V.*

Hotel Pantalon
$$ Dorsoduro

In the nice neighborhood between San Polo, the Accademia, and Santa Maria de' Frari, this hotel has been renovated with care and is a good alternative to the more pricey ones around San Marco. Some of the moderate-sized guest rooms have beamed ceilings, and a few have terraces; one has a handicapped-accessible bathroom. All the rooms are decorated with tasteful reproductions. The decor in the common areas has a French feel (the place is popular with French tourists).

See map p. 344. Crosera San Pantalon, 3941 Dorsoduro. ☎ *041-710-896. Fax: 041-718-683. Vaporetto: 1 or 82 to San Tomà; walk up to Campo San Tomà, turn left on Calle Campanièl, cross a bridge onto Calle Balbi, turn right on Fondamenta del Fornèr, then left onto the bridge and Calle Larga Foscari and right on Crosera. Rack rates: 240€ ($276) double. Discount available with purchase of Venice Card. Rates include breakfast. AE, MC, V.*

Hotel San Cassiano Ca' Favretto
$$$$ Santa Croce

This moderately priced (for what it is) hotel occupies a 14th-century *palazzo* on the Grand Canal. It's just across from the Ca' d'Oro and left of the Ca' Corner della Regina. The hotel has been completely renovated, and all the guest rooms have quality dark wood furniture, relieved by brightly colored wallpaper, fine fabrics, and large windows. Many have views of the Ca' d'Oro or the smaller canal on the side. The hotel also has a beautiful terrace overlooking the canals.

See map p. 344. Calle della Rosa, 2232 Santa Croce. ☎ **041-524-1768.** *Fax: 041-721-033.* www.sancassiano.it. *Vaporetto: 1 to San Stae; walk to the left of Campo San Stae, cross the canal and turn right on Fondamenta Rimpetto Mocenigo, then left on Calle del Forner, cross the bridge, continue on Calle del Ravano, cross the bridge, and turn left on Calle della Rosa. Rack rates: 342€ ($393) double. Discount available with purchase of Venice Card. Rates include breakfast. AE, V.*

Hotel Santo Stefano
$$$ San Marco

Recently renovated, this already pleasant tiny hotel has become even better, with Frau beds (the best Italian maker of modern quality sofas and beds), quality reproduction furniture in Venetian style, fine fabrics, and marble and mosaic bathrooms. Housed in the 15th-century watch tower of a convent opening on the beautiful Campo Santo Stefano, it has coffered ceilings, Murano chandeliers, and a nice terrace.

See map p. 344. Campo S. Stefano, 2957 San Marco. ☎ **041-520-0166.** *Fax: 041-522-4460.* www.hotelsantostefanovenezia.com. *Vaporetto: 82 to S. Samuele stop, walk salizzada S. Samuele and turn right on Calle Crosera. Rack rates: 280€ ($322) double. Discount available with purchase of Venice Card. Rates include breakfast. AE, MC, DC, V.*

Hotel Violino d'Oro
$$$ San Marco

This new family-run hotel overlooking Rio San Moisè (a minor canal), is small but offers a good location and guest rooms elegantly and brightly decorated with fine fabrics and Venetian-style furniture. Some of the rooms are larger than others, but all have Murano chandeliers and marble bathrooms (only a few with bath tub). A very pleasant roof terrace and friendly service round out the good experience.

See map p. 344. Campiello Barozzi, 2091 San Marco. ☎ **041-277-0841.** *Fax: 041-277-1001.* www.violinodoro.com. *Vaporetto: 1 or 82 to San Marco-Vallaresso stop; walk up calle Vallaresso, turn left on Salita San Moisè, and cross the bridge over the canal. Rack rates: 300€ ($345) double. Discount available with purchase of Venice Card. Rates include breakfast. AE, DC, MC, V.*

La Calcina
$$ Dorsoduro

This historical hotel, recently taken over by a young couple, has been completely renovated but refitted with its original antique furniture. This is where Victorian writer John Ruskin stayed in 1876. The location overlooking the Canale della Giudecca is both beautiful and less hectic than the area around San Marco. All the guest rooms are large — especially the corner rooms — and have parquet floors. In warm weather, the buffet breakfast is served on the large terrace by the water. The hotel also has a *solarium* (roof terrace). Note that you need to reserve six months in advance for summer. La Calcina now also rents suites and small apartments.

Zattere ai Gesuati, 780 Dorsoduro. ☎ **041-520-6466**. *Fax: 041-522-7045. Vaporetto: 51, 52, 61, 62, or 82 to Zattere; turn right along the Canale della Giudecca to the Rio di San Vio.* www.lacalcina.com *or* www.warmhospitality.com *for apartments. Rack rates: 182€ ($209) double, 170€–245 ($196–$282) suites and apartments. Discount available with purchase of Venice Card. Rates include buffet breakfast. AE, DC, MC, V.*

Pensione Accademia Villa Maravegie
$$$ Dorsoduro

In a beautiful location two steps from the Accademia, this hotel occupies a 17th-century villa with a garden, and the whole place has a wonderfully old-fashioned feeling. The guest rooms contain 19th-century furnishings, and all have decent-sized private bathrooms. It's very popular, so you have to reserve well in advance to secure a room with a view of the garden.

See map p. 344. Fondamenta Bollani, 1058 Dorsoduro. ☎ **041-521-0188**. *Fax: 041-523-9152.* www.pensioneaccademia.it. *Vaporetto: 1 or 82 to Accademia; turn right on Calle Corfù, left on Fondamenta Priuli, right on the first bridge, and then again right on Fondamenta Bollani. Rack rates: 275€ ($316) double. Discount available with purchase of Venice Card. Rates include breakfast. AE, DC, MC, V.*

Runner-up accommodations

Boston Hotel

$$$ San Marco   The Boston Hotel isn't too expensive, especially for its location just off St. Mark's Square. Some of its elegantly appointed guest rooms have views of the canal from their tiny balconies. *See map p. 344. Ponte dei Dai, 848 San Marco.* ☎ **041-528-7665** *or 041-523-8857. Fax: 041-522-6628.* www.bostonhotel.it.

Hotel Do Pozzi

$$ San Marco   The Hotel Do Pozzi has a quiet yet central position between St. Mark's Square and the Teatro La Fenice. The guest rooms have been renovated but are still furnished in antique style; guests receive a ten-percent discount at the Ristorante Da Raffaele (see "Dining Out," later in this chapter). A discount is available with the purchase of Venice Card. *See map p. 344. Corte dei Do Pozzi, 2373 San Marco.* ☎ **041-520-7855**. *Fax: 041-522-9413.* www.hoteldopozzi.it.

Hotel Falier

$$ Santa Croce   Although moderate in price, the guest rooms of this hotel have been furnished with taste and care, and decorated with lace curtains and bright bedspreads. A discount is available with the purchase of Venice Card. *Salizada S. Pantalon, 130 S. Croce.* ☎ **041-710-882**. *Fax: 041-520-6554.* www.hotelfalier.com.

Hotel Geremia

$ **Cannaregio** The Hotel Geremia is within walking distance of the rail station — a nice hotel in an area where many are not. A lot of care has been put into the renovation, especially the bathrooms, and the service is good. *See map p. 344. Campo San Geremia, 290/A Cannaregio.* ☎ *041-716-245. Fax: 041-524-2342.*

Hotel Metropole

$$$$ **Castello** This romantic property has an entrance on a canal and baroque furnishings inside. A discount is available with the purchase of Venice Card. *See map p. 344. Riva degli Schiavoni, 4149 Castello.* ☎ *041-520-5044. Fax: 041-522-3679.* www.hotelmetropole.com.

Hotel Olimpia

$$$ **Santa Croce** Elegant guest rooms are done up in Venetian style, and some rooms overlook the hotel's pleasant private garden. A discount is available with the purchase of Venice Card. *Fondamenta delle Burchielle 395 Santa Croce.* ☎ *041-711-041. Fax: 041-524-6777.* www.hotel-olimpia.com.

Dining Out

Fish and shellfish from the lagoon and the Adriatic served on rice, pasta, or *polenta* (cornmeal) are the staples of Venetian cuisine (see Chapter 2 for more details). Wine is as important as — more important than, some locals would say — the food in Venice. The best local wines are Amarone and Valpolicella (red) or, if you prefer it white and fizzy, try Cartizze or Prosecco.

If you want to seek out your own finds, the best places to hunt are along **Via Garibaldi** in Castello, **Strada Nuova** in Cannaregio, and **Rialto** in San Polo, but be aware that Venice has the reputation (well founded, unfortunately) of having an inordinate number of bad and expensive restaurants. (It's our personal theory that the more a restaurant advertises, the worse the place is likely to be.) Small *osterie* and *bacari,* often with wooden tables and paper atop the tablecloths (or directly on the tables), are often your best bet. At the other end of the spectrum, Venice has a number of well-established restaurants that serve excellent fare, but at much higher prices. Both of these kinds of restaurants have steady customers.

Ai Tre Spiedi
$$ **Cannaregio** VENETIAN

This formal but friendly *trattoria* is a favorite with locals who like to come with their families. The cuisine is traditional and you'll find many choices of fresh fish as well as a variety of meat and vegetable dishes. The many spaghetti *primi* are excellent and for *secondo* try the *fegato alla veneziana* (veal liver sauteed with onions), or the *bisato in umido* (eel stew), both served with polenta.

See map p. 344. Salizada San Canciano, 5906 Cannaregio. ☎ *041-520-8035. Reservations not accepted. Vaporetto: 1, 4, 82, N to Rialto, walk up and turn left on Salizada S. Giovanni Grisostomo, cross the bridge, continue and turn right on Salizada San Canciano. Secondi: 10€–18€ ($11–$21). AE, MC, V. Open: Lunch Tues–Sat, dinner Tues–Sun.*

Al Pantalon
$$ Dorsoduro VENETIAN

This is a great place for lunch in the busy area near the university, and lots of Venetians know it — go early if you want to avoid the line. The food is traditional, extremely fresh, and served by a friendly young staff. Try the *antipasto di pesce* (mixed seafood appetizer) or the *baccalà mantegato* (creamed cod) as a starter, and continue with excellent *spaghetti alle vongole* (spaghetti with clams) and one of the many *secondi* (main courses).

See map p. 344. Campo San Fantin, 3958 Dorsoduro. ☎ *041-710-849. Reservations not accepted. Vaporetto: 1 or 82 to San Tomà; follow the red signs to the Scuola di San Rocco but just before the Scuola turn left on Sottoportego San Rocco and cross the bridge. Secondi: 12€–22€ ($14–$25). No credit cards. Open: Lunch and dinner daily.*

Antica Besseta
$$ Santa Croce VENETIAN/FISH

This small trattoria from 1700 is very popular with locals — and no wonder, the food is very good and moderately priced, so making a reservation is a good idea. The seasonal menu includes many excellent *risotti* — such as a very well prepared *risotto al nero di seppia* (squid ink risotto). The fish *secondi* also vary with the season and the market, but all are delicious renditions of traditional Venetian dishes.

Salizada de Ca' Zusto, 1395 Santa Croce. ☎ *041-721-687. Reservation recommended. Vaporetto: 1 to Riva de Biasio; walk up Calle Zen, turn left, and make an immediate right on Salizada de Ca' Zusto. Secondi: 16€–22€ ($18–$25). AE, MC, V. Open: Lunch Thurs–Mon; dinner Wed–Mon.*

Antica Ostaria Ruga Rialto
$ San Polo VENETIAN

Italians who don't have a lot of money still manage to eat well at places like this, where the decor is minimal, the tablecloth is likely to be a piece of paper, and all the food is local and fresh. Popular with students, this *ostaria* serves an excellent antipasto, specialties like *baccalà mantegato* (creamed cod), and abundant and tasty pastas. There's lots of space, lots of people, and (sometimes) lots of noise, but you never have a bad meal.

See map p. 344. Ruga Vecchia San Giovanni, 692 San Polo. ☎ *041-521-1243. Reservations recommended for large parties. Vaporetto: 1 or 82 to Rialto; walk to the Rialto Bridge and cross over, continue straight through the arcades and make your first left on Ruga Vecchia San Giovanni. Secondi: 9€–14€ ($10–$16). No credit cards. Open: Lunch and dinner Tues–Sun.*

Antico Gatoleto
$ Castello   VENETIAN

Although this restaurant is in Castello, it's in the northwest corner and so isn't far from the Ponte di Rialto. It's on a quiet little square and has some tables outside. In addition to Venetian specialties and seafood — including *bigoli in salsa* (similar to spaghetti, with a special tomato sauce), *risotto alla pescatora* (seafood risotto), and *fegato alla veneziana* (veal liver with onions) — you can get inexpensive pasta dishes and even pizza.

See map p. 344. Campo Santa Maria Nova, 6055 Castello. ☎ *041-522-1883. Reservations recommended on Sat. Vaporetto: 1 or 82 to Rialto; turn left and pass the bridge, make a right when you can't go any farther, take your first left on Salizada San Giovanni Crisóstomo, follow it, and immediately after the second bridge take a right on Salizada San Canciano; when you reach Campo San Canciano, take the dogleg to the right that leads to Campo Santa Maria Nova. Secondi: 8€–14€ ($9.20–$16). DC, MC, V. Open: Lunch and dinner daily.*

Antico Martini
$$$$ San Marco   VENETIAN/CREATIVE

This elegant restaurant on the site of an 18th-century cafe is one of the city's best, and as such comes with a high price. You can sample Venetian specialties — the excellent *fegato alla veneziana* (veal liver with onions), as well as other innovative dishes, such as a wonderful *sformato di scampi e carciofi* (young artichokes and prawn torte). This gourmet spot is famous for its *involtini di salmone al caviale* (rolled salmon and caviar).

See map p. 344. Campo San Fantin, 1983 San Marco. ☎ *041-523-7027.* www.antico martini.com. *Reservations recommended. Vaporetto: 1 to Giglio; walk up Calle Gritti, turn right on Calle delle Ostreghe, continue into Calle Larga XXII Marzo, turn left on Calle delle Veste and follow it to Campo San Fantin. Secondi: 25€–36€ ($29–$41). AE, DC, MC, V. Open: Lunch Thurs–Mon; dinner Wed–Mon.*

Taking a sweet break

Venetians definitely have a sweet tooth! They not only make scrumptious pastries but, together with Rome, Florence, and Sicily, are contenders for the best *gelato* (ice cream) in Italy and maybe in the world. One of the best places for gelato is **Algiubagiò** (☎ 041-523-6084; www.algiubagio.com), on Fondamenta Nuove right in front of the *vaporetto* stop of that name. It also has a coffee shop and restaurant. (Twenty yards down Fondamenta Nuove, there's a little storefront selling just ice cream.) Sample some of the delicious flavors — and definitely try the fantastic *crema Veneziana,* a cream-flavored ice cream with chunks of chocolate (the recipe is a secret). For typical and delicious pastries, head to **Pasticceria Tonolo** (San Pantalon, 3764 Dorsoduro; Vaporetto: San Tomà). Of course, Venice has many, many other ice cream and pastry shops. Don't be afraid to stop and sample; you'll rarely find a bad one.

Bar Pizzeria di Paolo Melinato
$ Castello   PIZZA

Pizza? In Venice? After two or three days of nonstop meat and shellfish consumption, your body may be asking for a break. This pizzeria, in front of the Arsenale, is simple to find and has really good pizza, especially for the north of Italy. You can get all the classics — *margherita, capricciosa,* and so on. The small campo with the Arsenale and its canal in the background are especially quiet and picturesque at night.

Campo Arsenale, 2389 Castello. ☎ *041-521-0660. Reservations not necessary. Vaporetto: 1, 41, or 42 to Arsenale; follow Calle dei Forni to its end, turn left on Calle di Pegola, and turn right into Campo Arsenale. Secondi: 8€–15€ ($9.20–$17). No credit cards. Open: Lunch Tues–Sat; dinner Mon–Sat.*

Corte Sconta
$$ Castello   VENETIAN/FISH

This simple yet elegant restaurant offers quality cuisine in a quiet neighborhood and a pleasant private courtyard for dining *al fresco*. Among the many delicious seasonal and daily offerings, you might find *alici marinate in salsa di capperi* (marinated anchovies with a caper sauce), and *moscardini* (baby squid). Fresh pasta is homemade and served in a variety of ways. Polenta often accompanies the daily catches.

Calle del Pedestrin, 3886 Castello. ☎ *041-522-7024. Vaporetto: 1, 41, or 42 to Arsenale, walk west along Riva degli Schiavoni, cross the bridge, turn right on Calle del Forno, left on Calle Va in Crosera and immediately right. Secondi: 14€–21€ ($16–$24). MC, V. Open: Lunch and dinner Tues–Sat. Closed 4 weeks in Jan/Feb and 4 weeks in July/Aug.*

Da Raffaele
$$ San Marco   VENETIAN

Go to this canal-side restaurant for excellent fresh fish and other specialties. If you're tired of seafood, try the very tasty pastas and grilled meats. Everything on the menu is reliable — which is why this place has been a major tourist magnet for years (make a reservation). A nice plus is the terrace, so you can dine outdoors in the summer.

See map p. 344. Ponte delle Ostreghe, 2347 San Marco. ☎ *041-523-2317. Reservations recommended on weekends. Vaporetto: 1 or 82 to San Marco–Vallaresso; walk up Calle Vallaresso, turn left on Salizzada San Moisè, and continue into Calle Larga XXII Marzo and Calle delle Ostreghe. Secondi: 13€–21€ ($15–$24). AE, DC, MC, V. Open: Lunch and dinner Wed–Mon.*

Do Forni
$$$ San Marco   VENETIAN

A very popular restaurant especially with younger people, Do Forni is constantly busy, but the food justifies the wait. The room in back has a country-style coziness, whereas the front room is practically opulent. The specialties of the house are *risi e bisi* (a thick soup of rice and beans) and *bigoli in salsa* (similar to spaghetti, but with a special tomato sauce), but the menu is extensive and includes some Italian specialties as well.

See map p. 344. Calle degli Specchieri, 457–468 San Marco. ☎ *041-523-2148.* www. doforni.it. *Reservations recommended. Vaporetto: 1 or 82 to San Marco–Vallaresso; cross Piazza San Marco, turn right in Piazzetta dei Leoni on the left side of the Basilica di San Marco, and turn left on Calle degli Specchieri. Secondi: 20€–26€ ($23–$30). AE, DC, MC, V. Open: Lunch and dinner daily.*

Fiaschetteria Toscana
$$$ Cannaregio   VENETIAN

The Venetian-Tuscan merging gave birth here to a refined cuisine, making this one of Venice's best restaurants. You can still get steaks in true Tuscan style, but the traditional Venetian cuisine has taken over much of the menu. Excellent are the *bigoli in salsa* and the *spaghetti al cartoccio ai frutti di mare* (spaghetti with seafood cooked in a pouch), as well as the *frittura della Serenissima* (deep-fried seafood and vegetables). Leave room for dessert, they are homemade and delicious.

See map p. 344. Salizzada San Giovanni Crisostomo, 2347 Cannaregio. ☎ *041-528-5281.* www.fiaschetteriatoscana.it. *Reservations required. Vaporetto: 1 or 82 to Rialto; walk past the Rialto Bridge along the Canal Grande, then turn right and left onto Salizzada San Giovanni Crisostomo. Secondi: 13€–33€ ($15–$38). AE, DC, MC, V. Open: Lunch Wed–Sun; dinner Wed–Mon. Closed July.*

Ostaria ai Vetrai
$$ Murano   VENETIAN

If you're on Murano and looking for lunch, this *ostaria* serves excellent seafood at a more affordable price than many comparable restaurants in Venice. It prepares every type of local fish and also serves pastas with seafood. The huge antipasto for two at 12.91€ ($15) contains all the Venetian seafood specialties — it's virtually a meal in itself — and you can eat it at a canal-side table.

Fondamenta Manin 29, Murano. ☎ *041-739-293. Reservations not necessary. Vaporetto: 41, 42, 71, or 72 to Colonna; walk along the canal to the right until you come to the first bridge, then cross over to Fondamenta Manin and turn left. Secondi: 10€–21€ ($12–$24). DC, MC, V. Open: Lunch Wed–Sun.*

Ostaria a la Campana
$ San Marco   VENETIAN

This *ostaria* is really small but neat and simple, and you can get a plate of steaming pasta with a delicious sauce for the equivalent of about $5. A half-liter of wine runs another $1.75. This is good hearty food with a complete absence of tourist ambience. The place is convenient because it's on Calle dei Fabbri, the main drag (very straight, for Venice) between Piazza San Marco and the Ponte di Rialto.

See map p. 344. Calle dei Fabbri, 4720 San Marco. ☎ *041-528-5170. Reservations not accepted. Vaporetto: 1 or 82 to Rialto; turn right and walk along the canal, then turn left on Calle Bembo, which turns into Calle dei Fabbri. Secondi: 6€–10€ ($6.90–$12). No credit cards. Open: Lunch and dinner Mon–Sat.*

Osteria alle Testiere
$$ Castello   VENETIAN/FISH/CREATIVE

This tiny *osteria* is unassuming, but you will find delicious food served in a simple and friendly atmosphere. The chef performs subtle and masterly variations on traditional recipes: the classic *spaghetti alle vongole veraci e allo zafferano* (with clams and saffron), *ravioli agli asparagi e ricotta in salsa di capesante* (asparagus and ricotta cheese ravioli served with scallops), the *filetto di sanpietro alle erbe aromatiche* (fish filet with herbs and citrus sauce) are all excellent.

See map p. 344. Corte del Mondo Novo, off Salizada San Lio, 5801 Castello. ☎ *041-522-7220. Vaporetto: 1, 4, 82, N to Rialto stop, walk to Campiello San Bartolomeo and across to your left up Calle Bissa, cross the bridge, continue on Calle San Antonio and across Campo San Lio to Salizzada San Lio. Secondi: 15€–22€ ($17–$25). MC, V. Open: Lunch and dinner Tues–Sat. Closed 3 weeks Dec/Jan and July–Aug.*

Osteria da Fiore
$$$$ San Polo   VENETIAN/FISH

One of the most exclusive restaurants in Venice, it is also one of the best. The extremely well-prepared dishes are made with only the freshest ingredients and local fish, and are carefully served in the subdued elegance of the two dining rooms. Excellent are the *spaghetti al cartoccio* (cooked in a pouch), the *scampi al limone con sedano e pomodoro* (prawns with a lemon, tomato, and celery sauce), and the many seasonal *antipasti*.

See map p. 344. Calle del Scaleter, 2202/A San Polo. ☎ *041-721-308. Reservations required. Vaporetto: 1 or 82 to San Tomà; walk straight ahead to Campo San Tomà, continue straight on Calle larga Prima toward Santa Maria dei Frari and the Scuola di San Rocco and a block before the Scuola and behind the Frari, turn right on Calle del Scaleter. Secondi: 25€–32€ ($29–$37). AE, DC, MC, V. Open: Lunch and dinner Tues–Sat.*

Osteria Vivaldi
$$ San Polo   VENETIAN

This charming and small *osteria,* with its wood interior and bar, low ceilings, and musical decor, is a cozy place for dinner. The new management has only improved on an already good offering. The typical Venetian cuisine, including *risotto di pesce* (fish risotto) and *fegato alla veneziana* (veal liver with onions) are well accompanied by the small but excellent selection of wines. Other good dishes are the *tagliolini Vivaldi* (home made pasta with vegetables and prawns), and the *tagliata di tonno all'aceto balsamico* (tuna steak in balsamic vinegar sauce).

See map p. 344. Calle Madonnetta, 1457 San Polo. ☎ 041-523-8185. Reservations necessary. Vaporetto: 1 to San Silvestro; follow the narrow street behind the Palazzo Barzizza to Campo Aponàl, turn left toward Campo San Polo, and cross the bridge onto Calle Madonnetta. Secondi: 12€–19€ ($14–$22). AE, DC, MC, V. Open: Lunch and dinner daily.

Sole sulla Vecia Cavana
$$$ Cannaregio   VENETIAN

This justly renowned restaurant is housed in a 17th-century boat house (*gondole* were repaired and stationed here), completely restored and decorated in bright colors. The cuisine is typically Venetian, with many "turf" options beside the "surf" ones. The *granchio al forno* (oven-roasted crab) is an excellent antipasto, as are the *baccalà mantecato* (creamed cod) and the *sarde in saôr* (savory sardines). Also very good the *risotto al basilico con le capesante* (risotto with basil and scallops) and the *frittura mista* (fried calamari and small fish).

Rio Terrà dei Franceschi, 4624 Cannaregio. ☎ 041-528-7106. www.ilsolevenezia.it. *Reservations recommended. Vaporetto: 1 to Ca' d'Oro; walk straight ahead to Strada Nuova and turn right, bear left around Campo dei Apóstoli and the church, take Rio Terrà SS Apóstoli, and turn left at Rio Terrà dei Franceschi. Secondi: 20€–28€ ($23–$32). AE, DC, MC, V. Open: Lunch and dinner Tues–Sun. Closed 2 weeks in July.*

Trattoria alla Madonna
$ San Polo   VENETIAN/FISH

Seafood and more seafood! In this local trattoria, celebrated by both locals and tourists, you find all the bounty the Adriatic has to offer, some existing only in the Venetian lagoon, prepared in various traditional ways — grilled, roasted, fried, or served with pasta, risotto, or polenta. The moderate prices attract crowds, so be prepared for a long wait.

See map p. 344. Calle della Madonna, 594 San Polo. ☎ 041-522-3824. Reservations accepted only for large parties. Vaporetto: 1 or 82 to Rialto; cross the Rialto Bridge, turn left on Riva del Vin along the Canal Grande, and turn right onto Calle della Madonna. Secondi: 11€–15€ ($13–$17). AE, MC, V. Open: Lunch and dinner Thurs–Tues.

Trattoria da Romano
$ Burano   VENETIAN/FISH

A very busy address in Burano, this restaurant is renowned for its *risotti*. You may choose among squid risotto, mixed seafood risotto, and other delicious combinations. If you're still hungry after one of these dishes, try the excellent fish *secondi*.

See map p. 344. Via Baldassarre Galuppi 221, Burano. ☎ 041-730-030. Reservations recommended. Vaporetto: 12 from Fondamenta Nuove to Burano; walk up and then left onto Via Baldassarre Galuppi. Secondi: 10€–14€ ($12–$16). AE, MC, V. Open: Lunch and dinner Wed–Mon.

Vino Vino
$ San Marco VENETIAN

Vino Vino is a Venetian *bacaro* (wine bar) just behind the remains of the Teatro La Fenice; the service is simple but the food is very good. You can find traditional Venetian fare, including *sarde in saôr* (savory sardines) and *risotto al nero di seppia* (squid ink risotto), as well as some *Terraferma* dishes such as *stufato di manzo al Barolo* (Barolo braised beef) and *gallina faraona arrosto* (roasted Guinea hen) and a large choice of wines.

See map p. 344. Calle del Caffettier, 2007/A San Marco. ☎ *041-523-7027. Vaporetto: 1 or 82 to San Marco–Vallaresso, walk up calle Vallaresso, turn left on Calle XXII Marzo, cross the bridge, continue, turn right on Calle del Sartor da Veste and cross the bridge. Secondi: 8.50€–12€ ($12–$16). AE, DC, MC, V. Open: Wed–Mon 10:30 a.m.–midnight.*

Exploring Venice

Public museums in Venice are divided into three groups: **Museums of Piazza San Marco,** including Palazzo Ducale, Biblioteca Marciana, Museo Correr, and Museo Archeologico Nazionale; **Museums of the Venetian 18th century,** including Museo del Settecento Veneziano Ca' Rezzonico, Palazzo Moncenigo, and Casa Goldoni; and the **Museums of the Islands**, the Museo del Vetro in Murano and the Museo del Merletto in Burano. We recommend that you make some reservations in advance, especially for the **Palazzo Ducale** and for the **Gallerie dell'Accademia;** by doing so you go directly to the booth and buy your ticket (or show one of the special cards listed later in this section) without standing in line. Reserve entrance by calling the numbers in the individual listings below

The city of Venice owns and runs the following museums: **Museums of Piazza San Marco,** including Palazzo Ducale, Biblioteca Marciana, Museo Correr, and Museo Archeologico Nazionale; **Museums of the Venetian 18th century,** including Museo del Settecento Veneziano Ca' Rezzonico, Palazzo Moncenigo, and Casa Goldoni; and the **Museums of the Islands**, the Museo del Vetro in Murano and the Museo del Merletto in Burano. Tickets for these museums are actually **Museum Cards,** which grant admission to all the museums within the group: 11€ ($13) for the Museums of Piazza San Marco, 8€ ($9.20) for the Museums of the Venetian 18th century, and 6€ ($6.90) for the Museums of the Islands. You can purchase a **Museum Pass** for all of the city-run museums for 15.50€ ($18), which allows entry to any of the museum in any group. Children under 5 enter free.

Among the many discount cards available in Venice, the best is the most comprehensive **Venice Card** (☎ **041-2424**; www.venicecard.it for reservation and purchase). It is a personal pass that gives you access to all public transportation, public bathrooms, bathrooms, all the city-run museums (see earlier in this section), and the Casinò di Venezia. It also grants you discounts at a number of hotels (members of AVA, the Hotel

Association of Venice), shops, restaurants, and attractions. The one-day pass costs 28€ ($32) senior (above 29 years of age) and 18€ ($21) junior (under 29); the three-day pass costs 47€ ($54) senior and 35€ ($40) junior. The card is free for children under 4. You can also get seven-day passes or a pass that includes only public transportation and bathrooms — useful for children between 4 and 5 who get to enter free at museums but not on public transportation. For an additional fee you can include the airport shuttle boat or parking at the ASM Garage at Piazzale Roma (you need to pay this online at the moment of reservation), and even some travel insurance. Cards must be reserved at least 48 hours in advance. After you arrive in Venice, you can pick up your card at ticket booths at Piazzale Roma, Tronchetto, the rail station Santa Lucia, Marco Polo airport, or directly at your hotel, provided you made your hotel reservation through **AVA** (☎ **800-843-006** in Italy or 041-522-2264; www.veneziasi. it), which you should do anyway in order to get your discount.

Another good option if you're aged 14 to 29, is the **Rolling Venice card** (☎ **041-241-3908**; www.comune.venezia.it), which gives you substantial discounts — from 10 to 40 percent — on hotels, restaurants, museums, public transportation, and shops. If you decide to get the Venice card, the Rolling Venice discounts are additional to the ones you already get through the Venice card Junior. To have access to the discounts you need only register — remember to bring a photo ID — and pay 3€ ($3.45) at one of the Rolling Venice information kiosks, the easiest being the **Stazione Ferroviaria Santa Lucia booth** (☎ **041-524-2852**; open daily 8 a.m–8 p.m. July–Oct). Purchase of the card includes a map of Venice charting the location of all the participating hotels, restaurants, clubs, and shops, as well as a small guidebook including facts about Venetian history and culture and smart itineraries. You can also get the **ACTV Rolling Venice Rover ticket,** a three-day pass for all public boats and buses for 15€ ($17).

Chorus, the Association of Churches in Venice (☎ **041-274-0462**; www. chorusvenezia.org) also offers a pass, the **Chorus Card**, which gives you access to 15 churches rich in paintings and works by famous artists of the 15th and 16th centuries, and a free audioguide in each church. The pass is valid for one year and costs 8€ ($9.20), 5€ ($5.75) if you have the Venice Card); you can purchase it at any of the participating churches except the Frari. The churches honoring the Chorus Card are Sant'Alvise, Madonna dell'Orto, San Stae, San Giovanni Elemosinario, Santa Maria Formosa, San Pietro di Castello, Santa Maria del Giglio, Santo Stefano, Chiesa del Redentore, San Sebastiano, Santa Maria Gloriosa dei Frari, Gesuati (Santa Maria del Rosario), San Polo, and San Giacomo dell'Orio.

Finally, a combo ticket for the Ca' d'Oro, Ca' Pesaro, and Gallerie dell'Accademia is available for 13.50€ ($16); you can purchase it at the ticket booth of any of the three museums.

The top attractions

Basilica dei Frari (Santa Maria Gloriosa dei Frari minori Francescani)
San Polo

This church is a magnificent example of the Venetian Gothic, built in the first half of the 14th century and enlarged in the 15th. Beside it is the 14th-century **campanile (bell tower)**. The Frari contains many significant artworks, none more so than Titian's *Pala Pesaro (Pesaro altarpiece)* and *L'Assunta (Assumption)* over the main altar, a glorious composition that combines billowing forms with exquisite colors and a feeling of serenity. Also important are Giovanni Bellini's triptych *Vergine con il Bambino e Quattro Santi (Virgin and Child with Four Saints)* and Donatello's *San Giovanni Battista (St. John the Baptist)*, a rare sculpture in wood. Be sure to visit the original wooden choir, where monks participated in Mass — this is the only extant choir of its kind in Venice. The triangular marble monument dedicated to sculptor Antonio Canova was actually designed by Canova to be a monument to Titian (Canova's followers appropriated the design for their master after he died in 1822). A bit of trivia: If you look carefully at the walls near the monument, you see an **Austrian bomb** that was dropped on the church during World War I but miraculously failed to explode.

See map p. 360. Campo dei Frari. ☎ *041-522-2637. Vaporetto: 1 or 82 to San Tomà; walk up to Calle Campaniel, turn right, turn left on Campo San Tomà, continue onto Calle larga Prima, and turn right. Admission: 2.50€ ($2.90); audioguide .50€ (60¢). Open: Mon–Sat 9 a.m.–6 p.m., Sun 1–6 p.m.*

Ca' d'Oro
Cannaregio

The Ca' d'Oro (Gold House), as its name suggests, was once richly decorated with gold, now worn away to reveal the pink and white marble beneath. Begun in 1422, it's one of the most beautiful of the *palazzi* fronting the Grand Canal. Its elegant tracery of carvings, even without the gold, are evocative of the Venetian spirit — ornate without being gaudy, Gothic but without the broodingly morbid feel of north European Gothic. The building was bought in 1895 by musician/art collector Giorgio Franchetti, who donated the Ca' d'Oro and his collections to the public in 1916. The collection's primary works are Mantegna's *San Sebastian,* Titian's *Venus at the Mirror,* works by Carpaccio and Tintoretto, and **Venetian ceramics** from as far back as the 12th century.

See map p. 360. Calle Ca' d'Oro. ☎ *041-523-8790. Vaporetto: 1 to Ca' d'Oro. Admission: 5€ ($5.75); children under 12 free. Open: Mon 8:15 a.m.–2 p.m., Tues–Sun 8:15 a.m.–7:15 p.m.; ticket booth closes 30 min. before closing time.*

Venice Attractions

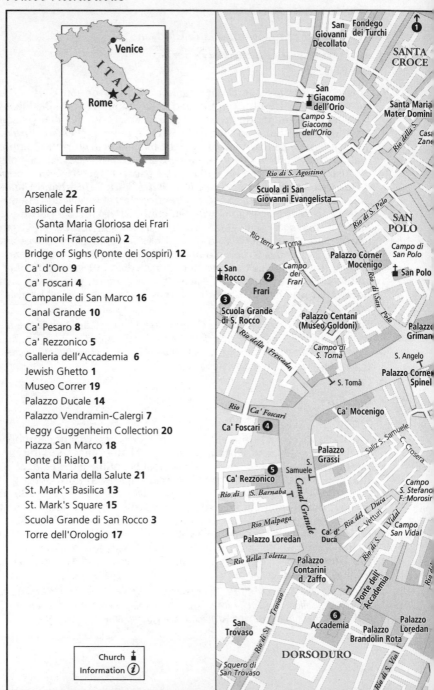

Arsenale **22**

Basilica dei Frari
(Santa Maria Gloriosa dei Frari
minori Francescani) **2**

Bridge of Sighs (Ponte dei Sospiri) **12**

Ca' d'Oro **9**

Ca' Foscari **4**

Campanile di San Marco **16**

Canal Grande **10**

Ca' Pesaro **8**

Ca' Rezzonico **5**

Galleria dell'Accademia **6**

Jewish Ghetto **1**

Museo Correr **19**

Palazzo Ducale **14**

Palazzo Vendramin-Calergi **7**

Peggy Guggenheim Collection **20**

Piazza San Marco **18**

Ponte di Rialto **11**

Santa Maria della Salute **21**

St. Mark's Basilica **13**

St. Mark's Square **15**

Scuola Grande di San Rocco **3**

Torre dell'Orologio **17**

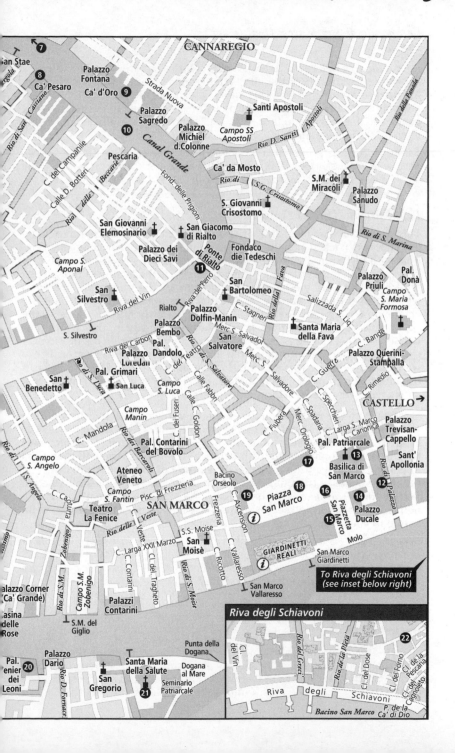

CANNAREGIO

San Stae

Palazzo Fontana
Ca' Pesaro
Ca' d'Oro

Palazzo Sagredo

Strada Nuova

Santi Apostoli

Palazzo Michiel d.Colonne

Campo SS Apostoli

Canal Grande

Rio D. Santi

Rio di Sant' Cassiano

Ca' da Mosto

S.M. dei Miracoli

Palazzo Sanudo

Rio di S.G. Crisostomo

Pescaria

C. del Campanile

Calle D. Botteri

Beccarie

Fond. delle Prigioni

Rio di

S. Giovanni Crisostomo

Rio di S. Marina

San Giovanni Elemosinario

San Giacomo di Rialto

Palazzo dei Dieci Savi

Ponte di Rialto

Fondaco die Tedeschi

Palazzo Priuli

Pal. Donà

Campo S. Aponal

Campo S. Maria Formosa

San Silvestro

Riva del Vin

San Bartolomeo

C. Stagneri

Rio della Fava

Salizzada S. Lio

C. Bande

S. Silvestro

Rialto

Palazzo Dolfin-Manin

Merc. S. Salvador

Santa Maria della Fava

Palazzo Querini-Stampalla

Palazzo Bembo

San Salvatore

Riva del Carbon

Pal. Dandolo

Rio del Teatro di S. Salvatore

Salvadore

Palazzo Loredan

C. del Teatro di S. Salvatore

Calle Fabbri

C. Rimedio

San Benedetto

Pal. Grimani

San Luca

Campo S. Luca

Rio di S. Luca

Merc. Orologio

C. Guerra

CASTELLO →

Campo Manin

C. Mandola

Rio di S. Baccaroli

C. dei Fuseri

Pal. Contarini del Bovolo

C. dei Goldin

Mercerie

C. Frubera

C. Spadaria

Pal. Patriarcale

Palazzo Trevisan-Cappello

Campo S. Angelo

Ateneo Veneto

Campo S. Fantin

Bacino Orseolo

C. Larga S. Marco

C. Canonica

Sant' Apollonia

Rio di S. Angelo

C. Caodura

Pisc. di Frezzeria

17

Piazza San Marco

18

16

Basilica di San Marco

13

14

12

Rio di Palazzo

Teatro La Fenice

C. Veste

SAN MARCO

Frezzeria

19

i

15

Piazzetta San Marco

Palazzo Ducale

Rio delle Veste

S.S. Moise

San Moisè

C. Larga XXII Marzo

C. Ricotto

C. Vallaresso

GIARDINETTI REALI

i

Molo

San Marco Giardinetti

Palazzo Corner (Ca' Grande)

Campo S.M. Zobenigo

Palazzi Contarini

Rio di S. Moise

San Marco Vallaresso

To Riva degli Schiavoni (see inset below right)

Casina delle Rose

S.M. del Giglio

Pal. enier dei Leoni

20

Palazzo Dario

Rio D. Fornace

San Gregorio

Santa Maria della Salute

21

Punta della Dogana

Dogana al Mare

Seminario Patriarcale

Riva degli Schiavoni

Ci. del Vin

Rio di La Pietà

Ci. del Dose

Ci. del Forno

22

Ci. de la Pescaria

Ci. de la Cagnoleto

Riva degli Schiavoni

P. de la Ca' di Dio

Bacino San Marco

Campanile di San Marco (bell tower)
San Marco

From atop this bell tower, located on St. Mark's Square, you can admire a 360-degree panorama of the city — and you can do so without climbing hundreds of steps (there's an elevator). The campanile is 97m (324-ft.) high and was originally built in the ninth century and added to in the following centuries. It suddenly collapsed in 1902, but was faithfully rebuilt using much of the same materials.

See map p. 360. Piazza San Marco. ☎ *041-522-4064. Vaporetto: 1 or 82 to San Marco–Vallaresso. Admission: 6€ ($6.90). Open: Oct–Feb daily 9:30 a.m.–4 p.m.; Mar–June daily 9 a.m.–7 p.m.; July–Sept daily 9 a.m.–9 p.m. Closed Jan 7–31.*

Canal Grande (Grand Canal)

This Grand Canal was and still is the heart of Venice. Whether you're riding in a *vaporetto* packed as tight as a can of tuna or whispering along in a gondola with just your significant other by your side, you will find the procession of buildings stunning — nowhere else is the feeling of the past so bittersweet and mesmerizing. The *vaporetto,* by the way, is the preferred way to travel this canal; the large canal gets quite choppy with all the engine-powered boats that steam along and across it at all times so the *vaporetto* is your sturdiest bet. It is the best way to admire the city's showcase of Venetian Gothic architecture — the delicate marble decorations of the *palazzi* opening onto the canal are best seen from the water. These were once the residences of Venice's wealthiest families. Many have been transformed into museums or hotels, others are still lived in (lucky tenants!), and a few seem forlorn and abandoned.

Starting from the rail station Santa Lucia, you will first see the **Palazzo Vendramin-Calergi** (hosting the casino in winter) on the left; the **Ca' Pesaro** on the right; the famous and delightful **Ca' d'Oro** (a Gothic jewel built at the beginning of the 15th century) on the left. You will then pass underneath the beautiful red-and-white **Ponte di Rialto.** Farther down on the right you'll see the **Ca' Foscari** (one of the best examples of Venetian Gothic, today the seat of the university). After passing beneath the **Ponte dell'Accademia** you will see the imposing white dome of the **Basilica della Salute** to your right and enter the harbor of San Marco and the lagoon.

See map p. 360. For a leisurely ride take vaporetto 1 which makes every stop; for a faster ride take the 82, the express line; at night take the N. Admission: 1.80€ ($2.07) for a 90-minute ticket (you can hop on and off during the period of validity; remember to stamp it as soon as you board the first time).

Ca' Rezzonico
Dorsoduro

Despite its name, the Ca' Rezzonico was begun in 1649 for the Bon, an important Venetian family. The Rezzonico acquired it a hundred years later and completed the structure — now one of the most magnificent *palazzi* on the Grand Canal. The most famous resident, however, was the English poet Robert Browning, who died here in 1889. The Ca' Rezzonico contains the **Museum of the 18th century in Venice (Museo del Settecento Veneziano),** and among its elegant rooms is the Throne Room, whose ceilings were painted by Giovanni Battista Tiepolo. You can step out onto the balcony and gaze down at the Grand Canal like a tortured lover or brooding poet and get a feel for the life of a Venetian aristocrat.

See map p. 360. Fondamenta Rezzonico 3136. ☎ *041-241-0100. Vaporetto: 1 to Ca' Rezzonico. Admission: 6.50€ ($7.50). Open: Wed–Mon, Apr–Oct 10 a.m.–6 p.m.; Nov–Mar 10 a.m.–5 p.m.*

Correr Museum
San Marco

Housed in the Procuratie Nuove building, the Correr, which gets less press than the more famous Venetian museums, offers an interesting and eclectic collection, including not only art but also items that make up a history of daily Venetian life, like games, cards, coins, and weapons. Among the clothing are robes worn by the *doges.* The artwork highlights are Canova **bas-reliefs;** a Cosmé Tura *Pietà* from 1460, a fanciful and in some ways surreal painting with a red Golgotha in the background; the famous Carpaccio *Two Venetian Ladies* (familiarly called *The Courtesans* but now known to be a pair of respectable Venetian ladies, a fragment from a larger painting); and a strange Lucas Cranach, with Christ rising from the tomb and two bearded soldiers looking trollish. Hugo van der Goes's emotional small *Crucifixion* is striking.

Attached to the Procuratie Nuove is the **Biblioteca Nazionale Marciana** or **Sansovino Library,** named for its architect, Jacopo Sansovino. Built between 1537 and 1560 to house the collection of Greek and Ancient Roman manuscripts, this historical library has over one million volumes, and about 13,000 manuscripts, including many works in miniature (made available only to scholars). It also hides beautifully decorated rooms and works of art. Sansovino also built the nearby **Zecca** (where the Republic's coins where made), then transformed into the Library's reading rooms; among the paintings and frescoes are **Tiziano's** *La Sapienza* in the Vestibolo, and **Veronese's** and **Tintoretto's Philosophers** in the main room. We recommend the Library's free guided tour, available at press time on Saturdays and Sundays at 10 a.m., noon, 2 p.m., and 4 p.m.

See map p. 360. Piazza San Marco. ☎ *041-522-5625 or 041-240-7233 for reservations for free guided tours. Vaporetto: 1 or 82 to San Marco–Vallaresso. Admission: 11€ ($13) Museum Card, which admits you to all the Museums of Piazza San Marco (see earlier in this section). Open: Summer daily Apr–Oct 9 a.m.–7 p.m., Nov–Mar 9 a.m.– 5 p.m.; ticket booth closes 1 hour before museum closing.*

Gallerie dell'Accademia
Dorsoduro

Rivaling Florence's Uffizi Gallery and Rome's Galleria Borghese, Venice's Academy Gallery contains great paintings from the 13th through the 18th centuries. Its 24 rooms are housed in a former church (deconsecrated in

1807), its monastery, and its **Scuola Grande di Santa Maria della Carità,** one of Venice's religious associations. The complex also houses Venice's **Academy of Fine Arts.** You can follow the development of art from the medieval period to the Renaissance through the galleries, while also walking through the history of Venetian art.

In room 1 you find the luminous, influential works of Veneziano, still very medieval in feeling. Then you pass into the totally different world of the 15th century, marked by greater naturalism, fuller figures, and the introduction of perspective. For example, Jacopo Bellini's *Madonna and Child* shows the figures in three-quarter view rather than head-on, giving an intimate feeling. In succeeding rooms are Mantegna's *St. George,* works by Mantegna's brother-in-law Giovanni Bellini, and examples of Tintoretto's revolutionary work (radical postures, greater looseness, and theatricality, as well as an instantly recognizable palette).

There's too much in the Accademia to even give an adequate summary, but don't miss Lorenzo Lotto's striking **portrait of a young man** watched by a small lizard on a table; Giorgione's haunting **portrait of an old woman;** and the Tiepolo **ceiling paintings** rescued from a now destroyed building. One of the most famous works is Veronese's incredible, enormous *Last Supper.* Its frenzied energy and party atmosphere (with wine flowing and dwarf figures in the foreground) brought a charge of heresy (and a hasty change of title to *The Banquet in the House of Levi*). At the end of room 15 is Palladio's gravity-defying **staircase.** Room 20 contains a fascinating series of paintings by Carpaccio, Bellini, and others, all commissioned to illustrate miracles of the True Cross, a fragment of which was brought to Venice in 1369, but also illustrating Venice as it once was.

See map p. 360. Campo della Carità, at the foot of the Accademia Bridge. ☎ *041-522-2247 or 041-520-0345 for reservations. Vaporetto: 1 or 82 to Accademia. Admission: 9€ ($10), children under 12 free. Open: Mon 8:15 a.m.–2 p.m., Tues–Sun 8:15 a.m.–7:15 p.m.; ticket booth closes 1 hour before museum closing.*

Palazzo Ducale and Ponte dei Sospiri
San Marco

Don't be misled by the exterior; the Palazzo Ducale is huge, especially when you count the labyrinthine prison next door, through which you can wander (and shudder at the medieval conditions — the place was used into the 1920s). You can easily spend four hours inside, especially if you take one of the special tours. At press time, a three-year restoration program for the facade was underway; it will not hinder the visit of the palace but certainly hide most of the outside to view.

Once the private home of the *doges* (the *doge* was leader of the republic, elected for life), the seat of the government, and a court of law, the pink-and-white marble Palazzo Ducale was the Republic's heart. The present Gothic-Renaissance building was begun in 1173 and integrated walls and towers of an A.D. 810 castle. The *palazzo* was enlarged in 1340 with the addition of the new wing housing the **Sala del Maggior Consiglio (Great**

Piazza San Marco

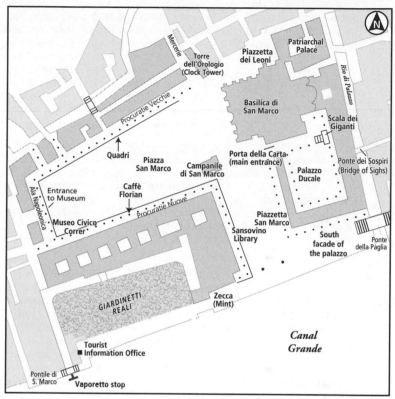

Council Room), a marvel of architecture for the size of the unsupported ceilings. On the left side of the courtyard is the **Scala dei Giganti (Staircase of the Giants),** guarded by two giant stone figures. At the top of these steps, you enter the loggia, from which departs the famous **Scala d'Oro (Golden Staircase);** it leads to the **Appartamento Ducale (doges' apartments)** and **Sale Istituzionali (government chambers),** where are conserved beautiful paintings by the major artists of the 16th century (all the work by 15th-century artists decorating the older wing was destroyed by fires at the end of the 16th century), such as **Titian, Tintoretto, Veronese,** and **Tiepolo.** Tintoretto's *Paradiso,* in the Sala del Maggior Consiglio, is said to be the largest oil painting in the world (not Tintoretto's best, however). A little-known part of the palace's collection is a group of paintings bequeathed by a bishop, including interesting works by **Hieronymous Bosch.**

On the ground floor, in the Doge's kitchens, there is a modern cafeteria and a space for special exhibits, currently occupied by an exhibit on the restoration of the **Orologio della Torre** — the clock tower built in 1496, just to the right of St. Marks Basilica. The clock indicates the phases of the moon and signs of the zodiac, while above it a complicated mechanism propels wooden statues of the Magi (the three kings bringing offerings to Jesus) guided by an angel to come out at the striking of the hour and pass in front of the Virgin and Child. Above this, yet another mechanism propels two bronze Moors to strike a bell on the hour. A gruesome legend has it that when the clock was completed, it was such a wonder that the workman who designed and built it was blinded so he could never duplicate it anywhere else. You can admire the restored figures before the whole thing is put together after the restoration of the tower is completed (the clock tower was scheduled to reopen for visitors in 2004, but at press time it still hadn't; you might find the clock back in place and the tower open when you get to Venice).

From the palace you continue your visit on the famous **Ponte dei Sospiri (Bridge of Sighs),** which didn't get its name from the lovers who met under it. The bridge connects the palace to the 16th-century **Prigioni Nuove (New Prisons),** and those condemned to death had to pass over this bridge (supposedly sighing heavily) both on their way into the prison and eventually on their way out to be executed in Piazzetta San Marco. The two red columns in the facade of the Ducal Palace mark the place where the death sentences were read out.

If you're interested in the dark history of these ages, you'll love the special guided tour, the **Secret Itineraries** offered in several languages at fixed hours. The tour takes you into the doges' hidden apartments and the **Palazzo di Giustizia (Palace of Justice),** where the most important decisions were made. You also visit the famous **Piombi** ("leads"), the prisons under the lead roof of the palace; horribly hot in summer and cold in winter — this is where Casanova was held and from where he made his illustrious escape. You then visit the Prigioni Nuove, built when the palace's limited facilities became insufficient. The guided tour is available in English, and you need to book in advance.

See map p. 360. Piazza San Marco; the entrance to the palace is from the Porta del Frumento on the water side. ☎ *041-522-4951 or 041-520-9070 for reservations. Vaporetto: 1, 14, 41, 42, 51, 52, 71, 72, or 82 to San Zaccaria. Admission: 11€ ($13) Museum Card for the Museums of Piazza San Marco (see earlier in this section); 12.50€ ($14) with the "Secret Itineraries" tour. Audio-guide: 5.50€ ($6). Open: Daily Apr–Oct 9 a.m.–7 p.m., Nov–Mar 9 a.m.–5 p.m.; ticket booth closes 90 minutes before. At press time the "Secret Itineraries" tour was scheduled at 9:55 a.m., 10:45 a.m., and 11:35 a.m. in English, and at 9:30 a.m. and 11:10 a.m. in Italian; reserve at least 48 hours in advance.*

Peggy Guggenheim Collection
Dorsoduro

In the Palazzo Venier dei Leoni on the Grand Canal, this museum holds one of Italy's most important collections of avant-garde art. The reason the building looks so short is that it's the ground floor of a 1749 *palazzo* that was never completed. American expatriate collector Peggy Guggenheim lived here for 30 years; after her death in 1979, the building and collection became the property of New York's Guggenheim Foundation. Guggenheim protégés included Jackson Pollock, represented by ten paintings, and Max

Ernst, whom she married. From dada and surrealism to expressionism and abstract expressionism, the collection is rich and diverse, with works by Klee, Magritte, Mondrian, De Chirico, Dalí, Kandinsky, Picasso, and others. The sculpture garden includes works by Giacometti. Temporary exhibits are also mounted.

See map p. 360. Calle San Cristoforo 701. ☎ *041-240-5411.* www.guggenheim-venice.it. *Vaporetto: 1 or 82 to Accademia; walk left past the Accademia, turn right on Rio Terrà A. Foscarini, turn left on Calle Nuova Sant'Agnese, continue on Piscina Former, cross the bridge, continue on Calle della Chiesa and then Fondamenta Venier along the small canal, and turn left on Calle San. Cristoforo. Admission: 8€ ($9). Open: Wed–Mon 10 a.m.–6 p.m.; Apr–Oct, Sat until 10 p.m.*

Ponte di Rialto
San Marco/San Polo

The original wooden bridge here started rotting away, and the citizens of Venice couldn't decide what to do. Finally, in 1588, they decided to replace it with the current stone marvel. The bridge opens onto the Rialto district in San Polo, the merchant area of the past. Ships arrived here after stopping at the **Dogana (Customs house)** at the tip of Dorsoduro and discharged their merchandise in the large warehouses. Goods were then sold at the market surrounding the warehouses. The fish and vegetable market had survived until 1998, when it was moved to the current merchant and maritime area of Venice, near the Stazione Ferroviaria Santa Lucia.

See map p. 360. Across the Canal Grande, between Riva del Vin and Riva del Carbon. Vaporetto: 1 or 82 to Rialto.

Don't eat or drink while visiting Piazza San Marco and its surroundings: it is considered an open-air museum and you will be fined if caught eating, drinking, or littering outside the authorized areas.

San Marco (St. Mark's Basilica)
San Marco

The basilica, the symbol of Venice, dominates beautiful **Piazza San Marco.** Built in A.D. 829 to house the remains of San Marco (martyred by the Turks in Alexandria, Egypt), the city's patron saint, the church burned down in 932, was rebuilt, and was rebuilt again in 1063, taking its present shape. The five portals of the basilica are topped by domes that were originally gilded; above the portals is the **loggia** from which the *doges* presided over the public functions held in the square, under the shade of the famous gilded bronze horses. Just inside the entrance on the right, and up a long and steep flight of stone steps, is the access to the **Galleria (gallery),** the **Marciano Museum,** and the **loggia** — affording beautiful views over St. Mark's Square. From the Gallery you can have a close-up view of the mosaic decorations. In the loggia you will find multilingual audio boxes giving a brief description of the sites around the piazza. The museum holds the original horses of the **Triumphal Quadriga** (the ones outdoors are copies), as well as other mosaics, altarpieces, and other sculptures. Experts

St. Mark's Basilica

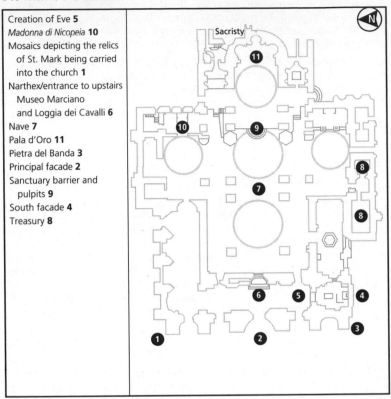

Creation of Eve **5**
Madonna di Nicopeia **10**
Mosaics depicting the relics
   of St. Mark being carried
   into the church **1**
Narthex/entrance to upstairs
   Museo Marciano
   and Loggia dei Cavalli **6**
Nave **7**
Pala d'Oro **11**
Pietra del Banda **3**
Principal facade **2**
Sanctuary barrier and
   pulpits **9**
South facade **4**
Treasury **8**

Sacristy

have estimated that the horses — brought from Constantinople in 1204 after the Fourth Crusade are Greek sculptures from the fourth century B.C. Also from the Fourth Crusade are the bronze doors of the Basilica main portal and of the **Cappella Zen** inside, named for a family, not the religion. Only one of the mosaics above the doorways is original — the one in the first doorway to the left. The others are 17th- and 18th-century reproductions.

We recommend taking advantage of the free tour of the basilica (available in English); reserve it 48 hours in advance by phone or online at www.alata.it.

Entering the portal, you may be overwhelmed by the luxury of the decorations: gold mosaics and colored inlaid marble. The lower part of the basilica is decorated in Byzantine and Venetian style and the second story in Flamboyant Gothic. The atrium's ceiling mosaics date from 1225 to 1275 and depict Old Testament scenes. The floors are in geometric marble mosaics of typical Byzantine style from the 11th and 12th centuries. The inner basilica mosaics, depicting scenes from the New Testament, were begun in the 12th century and finished in the 13th. The **Tesoro (Treasury)** holds the basilica's rich collection of relics and art, including booty from Constantinople and the Crusades. Behind the main altar is the famous **Pala d'Oro**, a magnificent altarpiece in gold and enamel started in the 10th century and further decorated in the 14th and 15th centuries. Finely chiseled in Byzantine-Venetian style, it is encrusted with over 2,000 precious stones.

As in Rome's Basilica di San Pietro, bare shoulders, halter tops, tank tops, shorts or skirts above the knee all lead to your being turned away from the Basilica di San Marco — no kidding, and no matter your age and sex.

See map p. 360. Piazza San Marco. ☎ *041-522-5205. Vaporetto: 1 or 82 to San Marco–Vallaresso. Admission: Basilica free; Pala d'Oro 1.50€ ($1.70); Treasury 2€ ($2.30); Galleria and Museo Marciano 3€ ($3.45). Audioguides: 5.50€ ($6). Open: Basilica (including Treasury and Pala d'Oro) May–Sept Mon–Sat 9:45 a.m.–5 p.m.; Oct–Apr Mon–Sat 9:45 a.m.–4:30 p.m.; Sun and holidays 2–4 p.m.; Gallery and Museo Marciano daily Apr–Oct 9:45 a.m.–5 p.m.; Nov–Mar 9:45 a.m.–4 p.m.*

Santa Maria della Salute
Dorsoduro

Built after the 1630 black plague epidemic as an *ex-voto* (thanks offering to God), the octagonal St. Mary of Good Health is an enduring baroque landmark at the end of Dorsoduro, almost across from Piazza San Marco. On the main altar is a 13th-century **Byzantine icon** and Titian's *Discesa dello Spirito Santo (Descent of the Holy Spirit);* in the Sacristy are three Titian **ceiling paintings** as well as Tintoretto's wonderful *Le Nozze di Cana (Wedding at Cana).* If you happen to be in town on November 21, you can see the feast of the Madonna della Salute, a centuries-old commemorative pageant in which a pontoon bridge is constructed across the Canal Grande, linking La Salute with the San Marco side.

See map p. 360. Campo della Salute. ☎ *041-522-5558. Vaporetto: 1 to Salute. Admission: Church voluntary offering; Sacristy 1.50€ ($1.75). Open: Daily 9 a.m.–noon and 3–5:30 p.m.*

Scuola Grande di San Rocco
San Polo

San Rocco is Jacopo Tintoretto's Sistine Chapel. From 1564 to 1587, Tintoretto, a brother of the school, decorated the **Sala dell'Albergo**, the *sala inferiore* **(lower hall)**, and the *sala superiore* **(upper hall)** with an incredible series of paintings on biblical and Christian subjects. There are 21 paintings on the upper hall ceiling alone (mirrors are available so you don't have to strain your neck). The most impressive is his *Crucifixion,* a painting of almost overpowering emotion and incredible detail (the tools used to make the cross are strewn in the foreground); the painter shows the moment when one of the two thieves' crosses is raised. The upper hall is also decorated with a fascinating collection of Francesco Pianta **wood sculptures** from the 17th century; some depict artisans and the tools of their trade with an amazing realism. Works by Bellini, Titian, and Tiepolo are also on display.

See map p. 360. Campo San Rocco 3058. ☎ 041-523-4864. www.sanrocco.it.
Vaporetto: 1 or 82 to San Tomà; walk up to Calle Campaniel, turn right, turn left on Campo
San Tomà, continue onto Calle Larga Prima and Salizzada San Rocco, and turn left.
Admission: 5.50€ ($6). Open: Summer daily 9 a.m.–5:30 p.m.; winter daily 10 a.m.–4 p.m.

More cool things to see and do

✔ Built in the 12th century, the **Arsenale** (Vaporetto: 1, 41, or 42 to Arsenale; follow Calle dei Forni to its end, turn left on Calle di Pegola, and turn right into Campo Arsenale) was the Venetian Republic's shipyard — the name comes from the Arab word *darsina'a* (shipyard or docks) — the largest in the Mediterranean. At its heyday, when there were as many as 100 galleons ready to sail, crews could assemble a vessel from prefab timbers in a single day! And a crew at that time could number as many as 16,000! The Arsenale has finally commenced restoration, if only partial restoration, and is now open to the public for special exibits only, such as **Navalis** — the wooden boat show — and **La Biennale di Venezia** in 2005. If you don't happen to visit during an exhibit, you can still admire the beautiful portal and the canal flowing into the Arsenale's large pond.

Nearby is the **Museo Storico Navale** (Campo San Biagio, 2148 Castello; ☎ 041-520-0276; Open: Mon–Sat 8 a.m.–1 p.m.) housed in the 15th-century Granary of the Venetian Republic and in part of the Arsenale. It is the largest in Italy and includes a beautiful collection of historical boats and models. You can also admire the famous **Bucintoro,** the Doge's ceremonial boat still used for traditional celebrations.

✔ The word *ghetto* has been used to name the neighborhood once set apart for Jews in European cities, but the **Venetian Ghetto (Ghetto Novo)** was Europe's first. It was established in 1516 on a small island accessible by only one bridge that was closed at night (you can still see the grooves in the marble *sottoportico* (portico interior) where the iron bars fitted). In 1541, when groups of Jews from Germany, Poland, Spain, and Portugal fled to Venice, the government allowed the community to expand into the **Old Ghetto (Ghetto Vecchio),** the area between the Ghetto Novo and the Rio di Cannaregio, which has the two largest places of worship — the Levantine and Spanish synagogues **(Scola Levantina** and **Scola Spagnola).** To accommodate the growing population, buildings were made taller and taller, so that this area has some of the tallest buildings in Venice. Every hour daily beginning at 10:30 a.m., guided tours of the Ghetto (6.20€/$5.58) start at the **Museo Ebraico** (Campo del Ghetto Novo; ☎ 041-715-359; Vaporetto: 1 or 82 to San Marcuola); the museum is open daily from 10 a.m. to 7 p.m. in summer and Sunday through Friday from 10:00 a.m. to 4:30 p.m. in winter; admission is 3€ ($3.45) and 8€ ($9.20) for the tour including the Synagogues (or 2€/$2.30 and 6.50€/$7.50, respectively, with the Venice Card).

✔ A visit to Venice isn't complete without a trip to the lagoon. Of the three famous islands near Venice, **Murano** is the closest and largest (connected via a *navette* direct from the rail station and *vaporetti* 41, 42, 71, 72, 12, and 13). This community of more than 6,000 contains about 70 glass factories, some of which allow you to sit and watch glass being blown. You'll find many shops selling glass of all kinds and several good seafood restaurants (see "Dining Out," earlier in this chapter). At the **Museo Vetrario di Murano** (Fondamenta Giustinian; ☎ 041-739-586; Admission 4€/$4.60 Open Thurs–Tues Apr–Oct 10 a.m.–5 p.m.; Nov–Mar 10 a.m.–4 p.m.; ticket booth closes 1 hour before museum closing), you can see a wonderful selection of glass, including a number of antique masterpieces. Also on Murano, the Venetian-Byzantine **Chiesa di Santa Maria e Donato** is really one of the wonders of the whole Venetian region. Founded in the 7th century, it was rebuilt in the 12th. The floor is decorated with a mosaic of birds and animals dating from 1140. In the apse is a dramatic and simple mosaic of the Virgin Mary.

✔ The second island of the trio (*vaporetto* 12 from Fondamenta Nove), **Torcello** is where the civilization of the lagoon began. In 639, the diocese of Altino was moved here because of the barbarian invasions. It grew into a town of 20,000 inhabitants and was the focus of the lagoon — until this area became more and more marshy and the population center shifted to Venice. Torcello today is abandoned, and because Venice used it as a quarry, few buildings are left. The **Cattedrale di Santa Maria Assunta**, however, is magnificent, founded in 639 and added to over the centuries (in 824 and in 1004). Its main attractions are the 13th-century **Byzantine mosaics** inside — a striking *Madonna and Child* and an almost Boschian *Last Judgment*. Open daily from 10:00 a.m. to 12.30 p.m. and 2:00 to 6:30 p.m., the church sits in the middle of a grassy plain reached by a canal from the dock; you can do the walk in 15 minutes or so, but there may be gondoliers hanging around to convince you to make the trip by boat.

✔ The farthest island from Venice — about half an hour by vaporetto 12 from Fondamenta Nove — **Burano** is a fishing village renowned for its lacemaking. The houses on Burano are famous for their bright colors, ranging from purple to mustard to bright yellow. The town itself is almost wholly given up to lace shops, and the **Scuola di Merletti di Burano** (San Martino Destra 183; ☎ 041-730-034), the lace school, is right in the middle of town on Piazza Baldassare Galuppi. Attached to the school, is the **Museo del Merletto** (lace museum) where you can study some of the amazing creations of this world-renowned center at leisure, without people pressing you to buy (Piazza Galuppi 187; ☎ 041-730-034. Admission 4€/$4.60. Open Wed–Mon Apr–Oct 10 a.m.–5 p.m.; Nov–Mar 10 a.m.–4 p.m.). The **Duomo,** with its tilting campanile, is just across the street and features a Tiepolo *Crucifixion;* it's open daily from 9:00 a.m. to 12:30 p.m. and 3 to 6 p.m.

✔ The island of **Lido** (take *vaporetto* 1, 6, 14, 41, 42, 61, 62, or 82 to Lido) is the stretch of sand protecting the lagoon from the open sea. It's called *Lido* (beach) because it's here that Venetians come to enjoy the beaches on the open-water side. On the lagoon side, you have a fantastic view of Venice. The Lido is also the seat of some of the most elegant hotels from the early 1900s, such as the Art Nouveau **Hotel des Bains** (see "Staying in Style," earlier in this chapter). The two best things to do here are spend a decadent evening at the elegant historical casino (still functioning in summer), and bike around this barrier island, which extends for 11km (6.9 miles). If you choose the second option, you can rent a bike at the shop on Piazzale Santa Maria Elisabetta where the ferry arrives or in the three shops on Gran Viale leading away from the *vaporetto* station (**Gardin Anna Vallè,** Piazzale Santa Maria Elisabetta 2/a, ☎ 041-276-0005; **Lazzari Bruno,** Gran Viale Santa Maria Elisabetta 21/b, ☎ 041-526-8019; or **Barbieri Giorgio,** Via Zara 5, ☎ 041-526-1490). You can take either of the two parallel roads, the one running on the lagoon side or the one running on the sea side. If you go left from the *vaporetto* station, you soon arrive at the end of the island and can take a ride along the narrow sandbar leading to the lighthouse. It overlooks one of the three entry channels to the lagoon. If you prefer a more urban landscape, go toward the right and the sea; you come to the casino and the Art Nouveau buildings. If you're in good shape, you can reach **Malamocco** (one of the lagoon's oldest settlements) and, even farther, **Alberoni** (a fishing village protected by dikes).

✔ The period before Lent — celebrated as Mardi Gras in New Orleans — is celebrated as **Carnevale** all over Italy, but Venice's celebrations are spectacular, beginning the week before Ash Wednesday (usually in February) and culminating on the last day, *martedi grasso* (Fat Tuesday). In 1797, Napoleon suppressed Carnevale, which had grown into a month-long bacchanal. But this festive holiday was revived in 1980 and is a big deal in Venice, famous for the elaborate costumes and masks, which are historic and elegant rather than Halloween-ish. Music events take place at all times, and crowds — big crowds — surge all over. Some of the events are reserved only for those who are in disguise, such as the Gran Ballo in Piazza San Marco, with prizes given for the best costume. Other events include a Children's Carnevale daily on Piazza San Polo, a cortege of decorated boats on the Grand Canal, and a market of Venetian costumes at Santo Stefano (see "Shopping the Local Stores," for other sources of masks and authentic Venetian getups). Costumes are for rent at **Tragicomica di Gualtiero dell'Osto** (Campiello dei Meloni, 2800 San Polo; ☎ 041-721-101; Vaporetto: 1 to San Staè).

Guided tours

If you'd like your own personal guided tour, you might want to take advantage of the **PlanetAudio guide,** the first outdoor audio tour in Italy, automatically activated by your walking, thanks to the complex technology of the GPS (Global Positioning System). (☎ **041-528-5051;** www.planetaudioguide.com). It is available at the APT tourist info points (you'll get 10 percent discount with the Venice card).For a more traditional tour, many travel agencies organize tours of Venice, but the best are offered by **American Express** (Salizzada San Moisè, 1471 San Marco; ☎ **041-520-0844;** Vaporetto: 1 or 82 to San Marco–Vallaresso). At about 21€ ($24) for a 2-hour tour and 34€ ($49) for a full day, a guide walks you around the sights and keeps you from getting lost. American Express also has the best prices — half that of other guide services.

Suggested 1-, 2-, and 3-day itineraries

For a stay of any duration, consider purchasing the **Venice Card,** which includes museum admissions, public transportation, access to public bathrooms, and a variety of other discounts (see "Exploring Venice," earlier in this chapter).

Venice in 1 day

If you have only one day in Venice, you definitely want to make your reservations ahead of time — 48 hours in advance for a guided tour of St. Mark's Basilica and as early as you can for the Gallerie dell'Accademia. Hit St. Mark's in the morning and the Academy in the afternoon; if your one day here is on a Sunday or a Monday, however, reverse your appointments. Also make your lunch and dinner reservations at least a day ahead (we make recommendations later in this tour). Start your day on **Piazza San Marco** with a visit to the **Basilica,** including the climb to the **loggia** upstairs, where the light is at its most beautiful in the morning. You will not have time for the Palazzo Ducale, but you will get your fill of paintings later on at the Accademia. Have a *caffè* or *cappuccino* in one of the terraces of the two historic cafes on the square — expensive, but oh so romantic: **Caffè Florian** and **Caffè Quadri** (see "Living It Up After Dark," later in this chapter). After, have a look at the beautiful Murano glass — and maybe even buy something — in **Venini** and **Pauly & C.** or at the more affordable **Marco Polo** (see "Shopping the Local Stores," later in this chapter). Walk to the Accademia, taking the foot bridge over the Canal Grande and have lunch in the lively area nearby at **Al Pantalon** or have a snack — for a sweet one, the **Pasticceria Tonolo** is wonderful (see "Dining Out", earlier in this chapter). After lunch, visit the **Gallerie dell'Accademia.** Have an *aperitivo* — a *cicchetto* here in Venice: a glass of dry wine accompanied by some savory tidbits — in one of the small bars near the Accademia, or across the Canal Grande at the **Antico Martini,** where you can also have an excellent dinner. Actually, you could have an excellent dinner in most places; see what appeals to you in our "Dining Out" section, earlier in this chapter. After dinner, take a magical **gondola** ride if you can afford it or settle for the *vaporetto* ride up **Canal Grande** (see "Getting Around," earlier in this chapter).

Venice in 2 days

Again, make your reservations in advance. Follow our itinerary above for the morning of day 1, but have lunch in the area and, after lunch, take a tour of **Palazzo Ducale.** After your visit, walk to the **Antico Martini** for drinks and dinner or to **Corte Sconta** (see "Dining Out," earlier in this chapter). On day 2 visit the **Gallerie dell'Accademia.** Follow our lunch recommendations in our "Venice in 1 day" itinerary. After lunch visit the **Basilica de' Frari** and the **Scuola Grande di San Rocco.** Have dinner at **Osteria Vivaldi,** or another restaurant of your choice (see "Dining Out," earlier in this chapter). Take a gondola ride after dinner or ride the *vaporetto* on **Canal Grande.**

Venice in 3 days

Follow our 2-day itinerary, but skip the glass shopping on day 1 — you can always substitute some other shopping or a visit to the **Biblioteca Marciana** in the **Museo Correr.** On day 3, visit the islands. On Murano, check out the **Glass Museum** or the show rooms of one of the most famous glassmakers (see "Shopping the Local Stores," later in this chapter). In **Burano,** you'll need only about an hour, unless you want to spend a little extra time and visit the **Lace Museum.** If you have the time, make a short detour to explore **Torcello.** Have lunch in Murano or Burano. For dinner, treat yourself to a nice restaurant in San Polo, or any other restaurant that strikes your fancy (see "Dining Out," earlier in this chapter), including the **Cipriani** in the hotel by the same name (see "Staying in Style," earlier in this chapter).

Shopping the Local Stores

Venice's most renowned wares reflect the city's aura of delicate, shimmering beauty. Where else would you find exquisite goblets tinged with gold and lace as fine as snowflakes? Where else would fine paper be fashioned from molds from the 18th century? The good stuff is definitely here, but so is the not-so-good: be careful to buy only from reputable merchants. Our recommendations should give you a head start.

Generally, shopping hours are daily, from 9 a.m. to 1 p.m. and 3:30 to 7:30 p.m. Only local neighborhood shops close on Sunday in Venice.

Best shopping areas

In Venice, you feel like a bull in a china shop — there's glass here, there, and everywhere. Some of it is low quality, however, and some isn't even from Venice! If you already know a lot about glass, you'll be fine. If not, be very careful. Some of the big names of glassmaking in Murano have showrooms in Venice, and galleries usually carry a selection of works by many glass artists. Another option, of course, is to go to Murano itself and shop around; a huge array of glass shops and showrooms lines both sides of the **Rio dei Vetrai,** which means "the small canal of the glass-makers" (see "More cool things to see and do," earlier in this chapter). Prices will be the same as in town, but the selection will be much larger.

The deal with lace is the same as with glass: You may find something handmade in Venice, not handmade in Venice, or not handmade at all and actually produced thousands of miles away. You can go to **Burano** — go there anyway just for the experience (see "More cool things to see and do," earlier in this chapter) — but some of the shops there feel very fake and others apply heavy sales pressure. We also hear rumors about lace coming from other parts of Italy or even the Far East. Again, if you know your linens and laces, you can tell what you're buying. If not, going to a reputable shop in Venice may be better.

For browsing, the best streets are the **Mercerie** (the zigzag route from the Piazza San Marco clock tower to the Ponte di Rialto) and the path leading from Piazza San Marco to Campo Santo Stefano and includes **Calle Larga XXII Marzo.** Here you can find big-name Italian stores specializing in everything from shoes to housewares to clothing. Of course, you'll also find these kinds of shops in Florence or Rome.

The **Ponte di Rialto** is famous for its shops, which spill over into the surrounding neighborhood, particularly on the Dorsoduro side. Many of these merchants, however, aren't selling Murano chandeliers and Burano tablecloths, but T-shirts with pictures of Piazza San Marco and plastic Campaniles. Don't count on finding much more here than a few souvenirs and trinkets for the folks back home.

What to look for and where to find it

Venice is known for its exquisite blown glass, lace, and fine paper, among other things. Here are the best places to find them.

Glass

Founded in the early 1920s, **Venini** (Piazzetta dei Leoncini, just to the left of St. Marks Basilica, 314 San Marco; ☎ 041-522-4045; Vaporetto: 1 or 82 to San Marco-Vallaresso; and at Fondamenta Vetrai, Murano 47/50; ☎ 041-273-7211; www.venini.com) is world renowned. Prices are what you'd expect for works of art; one drinking glass could cost up to $1,000.

Pauly & C. (Palazzo Trevisan Cappello, Ponte dei Consorzi 4391/A San Marco, off Calle Larga San Marco; ☎ 041-520-9899; www.paulyglass factory.com) has three nice boutiques in Piazza San Marco (Piazza San Marco 73, ☎ 041-523-5484; Piazza San Marco 77, ☎ 041-277-0279; and Piazza San Marco 316, ☎ 041-523-5575). If you have the time, though, visit the company headquarters on Rio di Palazzo, where you'll see a large collection of antiques and high-quality copies of ancient models.

Barovier & Toso (Fondamenta Vetrai, Murano 28; ☎ 041-739-049; www.barovier.com) has been a family business since the 13th century. You can visit their showroom as well as a museum with their historical pieces, both housed in a 17th-century *palazzo* in Murano.

Marco Polo (Frezzeria, west of Piazza San Marco, 1644 San Marco; ☎ 041-522-9295; Vaporetto: 1 or 82 to San Marco–Vallaresso), has an exceptional selection of Murano glass.

The **Murano Collezioni** gallery (Fondamenta Manin, Murano 1CD; ☎ 041-736-272) has a selection of works by the three biggest names in Venetian glass — Barovier & Toso, Venini, and Carlo Moretti — and is a good one-stop location if you are short of time.

Lace

Jesurum (Mercerie del Capitello, 4857 San Marco; ☎ 041-520-6177; www.jesurum.it; Vaporetto: 1 or 82 to San Marco–Vallaresso) is a reliable lace shop that's been in business since the 1870s. High quality is expensive, but the range of items, from cocktail napkins to bed linens, means that you stand a good chance of finding something within your budget.

Another good address is **Martinuzzi** (Piazza San Marco, 67/A San Marco; ☎ 041-522-5068), with an extensive selection of beautiful lace and embroidered linen.

Masks and costumes

If you're in town to enjoy Carnevale and didn't pack your 18th-century finery, you're going to need a mask at the very least. The **Laboratorio Artigianale Maschere,** just a short way from SS. Giovanni e Paolo (Barbaria delle Tole, 6657 Castello; ☎ 041-522-310; Vaporetto: 41, 42, 51, or 52 to Ospedale) has some of the most beautiful costumes.

Another good shop is the more affordable **Mondonovo** (Rio Terra Canal, 3063 Dorsoduro; ☎ 041-528-7344; Vaporetto: 1 or 82 to Accademia). Still, expect to pay 16€ ($18) for a basic mask; for the beautiful and artful masks, prices run much higher.

Paper

Handmade marbleized paper is a specialty of Venice, and **Piazzesi** (Campiello della Feltrina, just off Santa Maria del Giglio, 2511 San Marco; ☎ 041-522-1202; Vaporetto: 1 to Giglio) is said to be one of the oldest in the business — founded in 1900.

Living It Up After Dark

As often is the case in Italy, nightlife for the locals means visiting pubs, sitting at outdoor terraces in well-placed cafes, going to concerts, and (for the younger crowd) dancing at discos. Nightlife ends early in Venice and you'll be hard-pressed to find a place that stays open much past midnight. For the big discos you have to go to Lido or the Terraferma (mainly in Mestre).

The performing arts

Venice is famous for music; it seems there are always a dozen perform-ances and concerts going on, whether in the major theaters or in a former church. Advertisements are plastered everywhere there's a free wall. The **Teatro Goldoni** (Calle Goldoni, 4650/B San Marco; ☎ 041-520-7583; Vaporetto: 1 or 82 to Rialto) is one of Venice's premier theaters. Venice's largest opera theater, the **Teatro La Fenice** (Campo San Fantin, 1965 San Marco; ☎ 041-786-562; www.teatrolafenice.it) has finally been given back to the public after the fire that gutted it in 1996 and the ensuing lengthy reconstruction. Tickets are about 12€ to 50€ ($14–$58), depending on the performance.

Bars and pubs

Since Hemingway's days in Venice, one of the classic things for visitors to do is head to **Harry's Bar** (Calle Vallaresso, 1323 San Marco; ☎ 041-528-5777; Vaporetto: 1 to San Marco–Vallaresso) for a martini or a Bellini (made with Prosecco, a champagne-like white wine, and the juice of white peaches). Harry's also has great food, but the prices are as huge as the reputation. Attached to the Antico Martini restaurant is the **Martini Scala** (Campo San Fantin, 1980 San Marco, left of the La Fenice theatre; ☎ 041-522-4121) open till 3:30 a.m. with good live jazzy piano bar. Another, somewhat younger, place is **Vino Vino** (see "Dining Out," earlier in this chapter). The **Devil's Forest Pub** (Calle Stagneri, 5185 San Marco; ☎ 041-520-0623; Vaporetto: 1 or 82 to Rialto) is very popular and often crowded.

You won't find any gay or lesbian bars in Venice, but you can find some in nearby Padua, a lovely old city about 35 minutes from Venice by train (see Chapter 19).

Cafes

Right on St. Mark's Square are two packed cafes that square off (sorry!) against each other with classical music groups. They've been there for centuries: **Caffè Florian** (☎ 041-528-5338) since 1720 and **Caffè Quadri** (☎ 041-522-2105) since 1638. You won't find a more central place in Venice. If you want something a little more authentic, **Le Cafe** (Campo Santo Stefano, 2797 San Marco; ☎ 041-523-7201; Vaporetto: 1 or 82 to Accademia, then cross the bridge) serves at its outdoor tables a large assortment of drinks, good coffee, and salads.

Fast Facts: Venice

Area Code

The country code for Italy is **39**. The area code for Venice is **041;** use this code when calling from anywhere outside or inside Italy and even within Venice itself (including the 0, even when calling from abroad).

American Express

The office is at Salizzada San Moisè, 1471 San Marco (☎ 041-520-0844; Vaporetto: 1 or 82 to San Marco–Vallaresso). Summer hours are Monday through Saturday 8 a.m. to 8 p.m. (currency exchange) and 8:00 a.m. to 5:30 p.m. (everything else); winter hours are Monday through Friday 9:00 a.m. to 5:30 p.m. and Saturday 9:00 a.m. to 12:30 p.m.

ATMs

You can find banks with ATMs all around town, especially in the commercial areas of Mercerie, Campo Santo Stefano, Calle Larga XXII Marzo, and Strada Nuova.

Doctors

The U.K. consulate and the American Express office keep a list of English-speaking doctors and dentists.

Embassies and Consulates

The U.K. Consulate is at Campo della Carità, 1051 Dorsoduro (☎ 041-522-7207), by the Accademia Bridge. All other consulates are in Milan.

Emergencies

Ambulance, ☎ **118**; fire, ☎ **115**; First Aid (Pronto Soccorso), ☎ **041-520-3222.**

Hospital

The Ospedali Civili Riuniti di Venezia (Campo SS. Giovanni e Paolo; ☎ 041-260-711; Vaporetto: 41, 42, 51, or 52 to Ospedale) has English-speaking doctors.

Information

APT in Palazzo Ziani on Fondamenta San Lorenzo (Castello 5050, 30122 Venezia; ☎ 041-529-8700; www.turismo venezia.it) is the central tourist office. Aeroporto Marco Polo (☎ 041-529-8711. Open daily 9:30 a.m.–7:30 p.m.). Piazzale Roma (☎ 041-529-8711. Open daily 9:30 a.m.–6:30 p.m.) Train Station Santa Lucia (☎ 041-529-8711. Open daily 8 a.m.–6:30 p.m.) Lido (☎ 041-526-5711. Open daily Jun–Sept 9 a.m.–12:30 p.m. and 3:30 p.m.–6 p.m.) San Marco all'Ascensione (☎ 041-529-8711. Open daily 9 a.m.–3:30 p.m.) Venice Pavillion (San Marco Ex Giardini Reali ☎ 041-529-8711. Open daily 10 a.m.–6 p.m.)

Internet Access

Venetian Navigator(Calle della Casselleria, 5300 Castello; ☎ 041-277-1056; www.venetiannavigator.com; open 10 a.m.–10 p.m in summer and 10 a.m.–7.30 p.m. in winter) is only steps behind San Marco Basilica.

Maps

One of the best maps is Falk, but many other maps are available at most bookstores and newsstands around town.

Newspapers and Magazines

Most newsstands in town sell English papers. One of the largest is in the Stazione Santa Lucia. A helpful small publication, available in all major hotels, is *Un Ospite a Venezia,* a guide on everything useful, from public transportation to special events.

Pharmacies

A centrally located one is the International Pharmacy (Calle Larga XXII Marzo, 2067 San Marco; ☎ 041-522-2311; Vaporetto:

1 or 82 to San Marco–Vallaresso). If you need a pharmacy after hours, ask your hotel or call ☎ 192 to get a list of those open near you.

Police

Call ☎ **113**; for the Carabinieri (other police force), call ☎ **112.**

Post Office

You can find many post offices around town, but the central one is the Ufficio Postale (Fontego dei Tedeschi, 5550 San Marco; ☎ 041-271-7111) near Ponte di Rialto.

Restrooms

The new and clean public toilets — disabled accessible — are open 8 a.m.– 8 p.m. and located at the Giardini Reali off Piazza San Marco; at the Ascensione in sestiere San Marco; at San Bartolomeo near Ponte di Rialto; at the Ponte dell'Accademia in Dorsoduro; at Bragora in sestiere Castello; at San Leonardo in Cannaregio; on Murano; in Piazza Galuppi on Burano; on Torcello. You need to pay, unless you have the Venice Card (see "Exploring Venice," earlier in this chapter).

Safety

Venice is very safe, even in the off-the-beaten-path solitary areas. The only real danger are pickpockets, always plentiful in areas with lots of tourists: Watch your bags and cameras and don't display wads of money or jewelry.

Smoking

Smoking is allowed in cafes and restaurants and is very common, but restaurants are starting to set aside separate no-smoking areas when their size allows it.

Taxes

See Chapter 5 for information on IVA (VAT).

Taxis

Cooperativa San Marco (☎ 041-523-5775) in San Marco; Cooperativa Veneziana (☎ 041-716-000) in Cannaregio, and Cooperativa Serenissima (☎ 041-522-1265) in Castello;.Coop. Bucintoro Motoscafi (☎ 041-520-3144) in Dorsorduro; Radio Taxi (☎ 041-522-2303).

Weather Updates

For forecasts, your best bet is to look at the news on TV. On the Internet, you can check http://meteo.tiscalinet.it.

Chapter 19

Padua, Verona, and Milan

· ·

In This Chapter

▶ Discovering Padua and the famous Giotto frescoes

▶ Thrilling to Verona, the setting for the legend of Romeo and Juliet

▶ Shopping 'til you drop in bustling Milan

· ·

Though Venice towers over all other cities of northern Italy for its art and unique setting, many other towns in the region are well worth your time. **Padua (Padova),** just inland of Venice, has a wealth of churches and museums, including Giotto's famous frescoes in the **Cappella degli Scrovegni,** so breathtaking that they dwarf the other worthy attractions in town. Farther inland, to the west, is pleasant **Verona,** an ancient city whose development dates back to the Romans, as the famous **Roman theater** in the middle of town attests. Known for its Romanesque churches, beautiful squares, and attractive Renaissance architecture, Verona also draws visitors from all over the world who want to see the **House of Juliet** with its balcony, where people like to believe that Shakespeare's tragic Juliet once lived. Finally, there's **Milan (Milano),** the economic heart of northern Italy and Italy's main industrial and manufacturing region. Milan is such an important business center — renowned for both its sizzling fashion and incredible shopping opportunities — that one forgets its art: **Leonardo da Vinci's** *Last Supper* and Milan's grandiose gothic **Duomo,** for example, seem all but trifles. We recommend that you take the time to see both sides.

Padua: Home of Giotto's Fabulous Frescoes

Padua (Padova) began as a fishing village and became a Roman *municipium* (municipality) in 45 B.C. Ever prosperous, Patavium (the ancient Roman name of Padova) was the site of great public buildings and an amphitheater, but much was destroyed by the barbarian Longobards in A.D. 602. Padua rose from the ashes in the late Middle Ages and early Renaissance, and the university was founded in 1222, making it the second university in Italy. Today it is a small but bustling modern town and the Veneto's economic heart; the presence of the university makes for an active cultural life. Padua is also the adoptive hometown of St. Anthony, who's buried in the basilica bearing his name.

The Pianura Padana and Milan

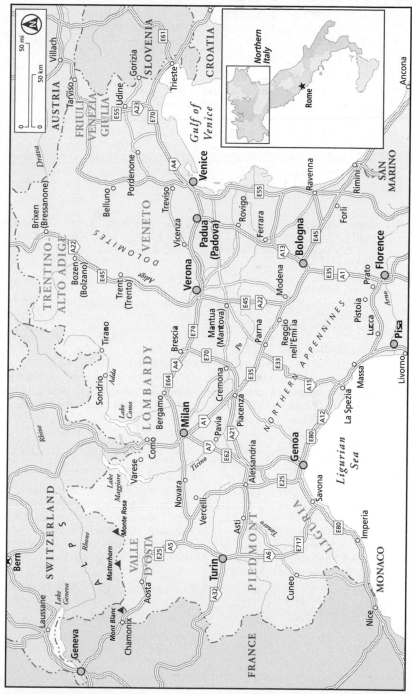

To fully enjoy the town, you might want to spend the night, however, you can also see the highlights in one day. Many like to stay in Padua as a base for their visit to Venice — it is less expensive and much less crowded.

Getting there

On the main line from Rome to the northeast, Padua enjoys excellent **rail connections.** The city is only 30 minutes from Venice, with trains running as frequently as every few minutes during rush hours; the fare is about 4€ ($4.60). The train trip from Rome lasts about five hours and costs about 35€ ($40). The **Stazione FS** (rail station) is on Piazza Stazione (☎ 049-875-1800) and only 10 to 15 minutes north of the major attractions. If you don't feel like walking, though, you can use the excellent bus service for .85€ ($1). Get a bus map from the tourist office in the train station.

Buses leave for Padua about every half-hour from Venice. The ride lasts less than an hour and costs about 4€ ($4.60). Padua's **bus station** is on Via Trieste (☎ 049-820-6844), off Piazza Boschetti, not far from the train station.

If you're **driving,** Padua lies at the convergence of the *autostrada* **A4** (east-west) and **A13** (north-south); you can easily reach it by car from any direction.

Spending the night

You'd expect to find delightful hotels tucked away in the heart of Padova's romantic historic district — but you'd be wrong. Instead, most of these hotels are old fashioned and lack style. The service is professional and kind, but the decor is always a bit drab. The best hotels tend to be in the more modern part of town.

Hotel Grand'Italia
$$ Rail Station

Housed in a beautiful 19th-century Liberty (Italian Art Nouveau) building which was recently completely restored, this hotel offers large and bright guest rooms decorated with pleasant colors, fine fabrics, and contemporary furnishings. The service is excellent and the location very central, which, together with the historical setting, makes it our preferred stay in town. The public spaces have been carefully restored and decorated with fine antiques and carpets.

See map p. 384. Via P. Bronzetti 62, just across from the train station. ☎ *049-871-2555. Fax: 049-871-3923.* www.hotelmilano-padova.it. *Parking: 15€ ($17). Rack rates: 175€ ($202) double. Rates include breakfast. AE, MC, V.*

Hotel Plaza
$$$ Center

The most popular hotel in town with businesspeople, the Plaza offers accommodations in line with international standards — large, carpeted rooms decorated with modern European furniture and stylish public areas — but it is housed in a large modern building. A nearby annex offers rooms with slightly more character and the same level of amenities.

See map p. 384. Corso Milano 40. ☎ *049-656-822. Fax: 049-661-117. Parking: 15€ ($17). Rack rates: 195€ ($224) double. Rates include buffet breakfast. AE, DC, MC, V.*

Majestic Hotel Toscanelli
$$$ Center

Just off of an old market square, this is one of the best hotels in town and a charming place to stay. The lobby has marble floors and fine furnishings. The guest rooms have been renovated with fine fabrics and stylish furniture — some in Venetian baroque and others Victorian. You won't lack for atmosphere, comfort (the beds are large), or something to eat (there's an excellent pizzeria in the hotel).

See map p. 384. Via dell'Arco 2. ☎ *049-663-244. Fax: 049-876-0025. E-mail:* majestic @@toscanelli.it. *Parking: 19€ ($22) valet. Rack rates: 169€ ($194) double. Rates include buffet breakfast. AE, DC, MC, V.*

Dining locally

Padua's cuisine is typically Italian, with a Venetian influence. As a university town, it offers a variety of cheap lunch spots, particularly on Piazza Cavour and Via Matteotti, where you can enjoy anything from pasta and pizza to sandwiches.

Angelo Rasi
$ Centro PADUAN

This moderately priced *osteria* is famous for its excellent cuisine and friendly service. During the summer, you can dine in the pretty garden, which children seem to enjoy. Good choices include *ravioli alle erbe* (ravioli with fresh herbs) and *baccalà mantecato* (creamed cod), as well as a variety of surf or turf *secondi;* half-portions are available for the little ones. The wine list is excellent.

See map p. 384. Riviera Paleocapa 7. ☎ *049-871-9797. Reservation recommended. Secondi: 11€–15€ ($13–$17). MC, V. Open: Dinner Tues–Sun.*

Casa Veneta
$$ Centro PADUAN/CREATIVE

This more elegant restaurant near the Chiesa del Carmone, popular at lunch with businessmen, offers well prepared traditional dishes with a twist. Very good are the *pesce spada affumicato con finocchi freschi e*

Padua

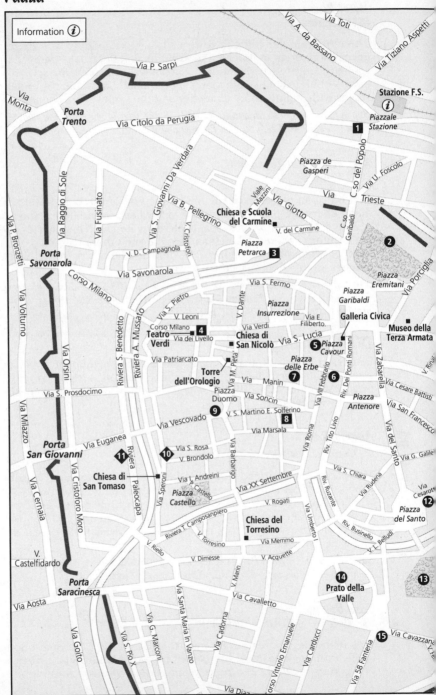

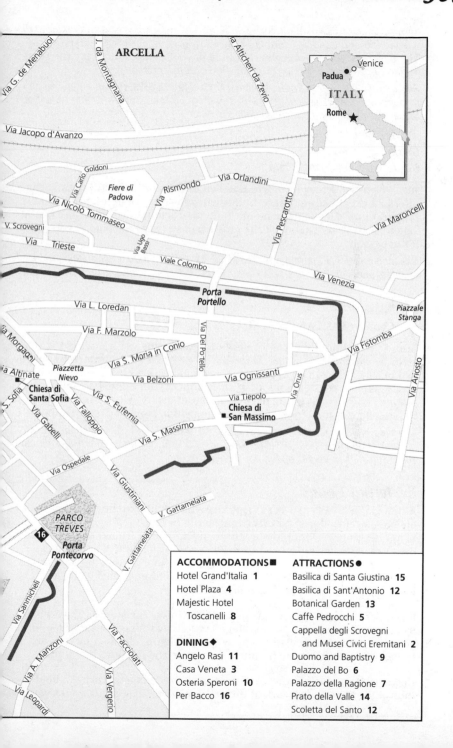

ARCELLA

Via G. de Menabuoi
J. da Montagnana
Via Alticheri da Zevio
Via Jacopo d'Avanzo

Venice
Padua
ITALY
Rome

Goldoni
Via Carlo
Via Rismondo
Via Orlandini
Fiere di
Padova
Via Nicolò Tommaseo
V. Scrovegni
Via Pescarotto
Via Maroncelli
Via   Trieste
Via Ugo Bassi
Viale Colombo
Via Venezia

Porta
Portello
Via L. Loredan
Piazzale
Stanga
Via F. Marzolo
Via Del Po'tello
Via Fistomba
Via Ariosto
Via Morgagni
Via S. Maria in Conio
Piazzetta
Nievo
Via Belzoni
Via Ognissanti
Via Orus
Via Altinate
Chiesa di
Santa Sofia
Via S. Eufemia
Via Falloppio
Via Tiepolo
Chiesa di
San Massimo
S. Sofia
Via Gabelli
Via S. Massimo

Via Ospedale
Via Giustiniani
V. Gattamelata

PARCO
TREVES
16
Porta
Pontecorvo
V. Gattamelata

Via Sanmicheli
Via A. Manzoni
Via Facciolati
Via Vergerio
Via Leopardi

ACCOMMODATIONS■	ATTRACTIONS●
Hotel Grand'Italia **1**	Basilica di Santa Giustina **15**
Hotel Plaza **4**	Basilica di Sant'Antonio **12**
Majestic Hotel	Botanical Garden **13**
Toscanelli **8**	Caffè Pedrocchi **5**
	Cappella degli Scrovegni
DINING◆	and Musei Civici Eremitani **2**
Angelo Rasi **11**	Duomo and Baptistry **9**
Casa Veneta **3**	Palazzo del Bo **6**
Osteria Speroni **10**	Palazzo della Ragione **7**
Per Bacco **16**	Prato della Valle **14**
	Scoletta del Santo **12**

agrumi (smoked swordfish with fresh fennel and citrus) and the *insalata di misticanza con asparagi bianchi* (mesclun greens with white asparagus). The desserts, too, are excellent; if they have it on the menu, try the *semifreddo al pistacchio* (pistachio cake/ice cream creation).

See map p. 384. Vicolo Ponte Molino 11. ☎ *049-875-8699. Reservations recommended. Secondi: 12€–16€ ($14–$18). Open: Lunch Tues–Sat and dinner Mon–Sat. Closed Aug and during Christmas holidays.*

Osteria Speroni
$$ Center PADUAN/FISH

Just down the street from the Basilica di Sant'Antonio, this restaurant offers an excellent antipasto buffet with a variety of fish and vegetable preparations. The regular menu includes regional dishes from coastal Veneto, with an accent on fish. Try the *capitone* (a special kind of eel) when it's in season.

See map p. 384. Via Speroni Sperone 32/36. ☎ *049-875-3370. Reservations recommended. Secondi: 10€–16€ ($12–$18). AE, MC, V. Open: Lunch and dinner Mon–Sat.*

Per Bacco
$$ Centro PADUAN/ENOTECA

True to its name, this is a a temple to good wine, with a wine list that includes hundreds of labels by the glass — all of it accompanied by excellent cuisine. The *ravioli di ricotta alla crema* (ricotta cheese ravioli with a cream sauce) are delicious and for secondo you might try the *composizione Per Bacco,* a tasting of three different dishes, which may including the excellent stuffed quail on a bed of zucchini, mint, and green apple.

See map p. 384. Piazzale Pontecorvo 10. ☎ *049-875-4664. Reservations recommended. Secondi: 11€–21€ ($13–$24). AE, CD, MC, V. Open: Lunch and dinner Tues–Sun. Closed 1 week in Jan and 2 weeks in Aug.*

Exploring Padua

Although Padova isn't a very large city, you might like the new hop-on-and-off tour offered by **City Sightseeing** (www.padova.city-sightseeing.it), offered May through September from 9 a.m. to 6 p.m. Buses depart Sant'Antonio church every 20 to 30 minutes and you can buy tickets on the bus. The itinerary last one hour if you stay onboard; tickets cost 13€ ($15) adults, 6.50€ ($7.50) children ages 5 to 15, and free for kids under 5, and are valid 24 hours.

If you prefer a walking tour, **Associazione Guide Turistiche** (☎ 049-820-9741; www.guidepadova.it) offers a variety of tours — classical, religious, scientific, and more — and will even custom-design one for you. Prices vary, based on the number of persons and the length of tour.

However, if you visit in the good season, we recommend taking a **boat tour** of the historic network of the urban canals; these inner waterways have been used for centuries and afford a very special view of Padua (see "More cool things to see and do," later in this section).

For 13€ ($15), the **PadovaCard** (☎ **049-876-7927;** www.apt.padova.it) is an excellent deal, granting one adult (and one child under 13) admission to the major museums in town, plus free access to public transportation and the APS parking lots (in **Prato della Valle**, **rail station**, and **Via Fra' Paolo Sarpi).** It also includes free bicycle rental and discounts in shops, and on cruises with the **Padovanavigazione** and guided tours. The card is valid 48 hours and is available at the tourist booths and all participating sights, including the parking lots. Participating museums include Cappella degli Scrovegni (plus 1€/$1.15 reservation fee), Musei Civici Eremitani, Palazzo della Ragione, Piano Nobile Caffè Pedrocchi, Battistero del Duomo, Orto Botanico, Palazzo Suckermann, Museo del Risorgimento, Loggia and Odeo Cornaro, Oratorio di San Michele, Oratorio di San Rocco, and Casa del Petrarca in Arquà Petrarca.

The top attractions

Basilica di Sant'Antonio

Built in the 13th century, this basilica houses the remains of St. Anthony of Padua (including his tongue, still amazingly undecayed). Its distinctive Romanesque-Gothic style reveals Eastern influences, most visible in the eight round domes and the several *campanili* (bell towers) vaguely reminiscent of minarets. Several prominent Renaissance artists worked on the interior: The basilica's treasures include Donatello's **bronze crucifix, reliefs,** and **statues** on the high altar (1444–1448), as well as **frescoes** by 14th-century artists Altichiero and Giusto de' Menabuoi. In the square in front of the church is Donatello's **equestrian statue of Gattamelata** (considered one of his masterpieces). Attached to the basilica is the 14th-century **Oratorio di San Giorgio (Oratory of St. George),** which opened in 2000 for the Papal Jubilee after a period of restoration; here you'll find a fine cycle of frescoes by Altichiero da Zevio. To visit, you need to ask the gatekeeper at the attached building between San Giorgio and the **Scoletta del Santo,** a small church built in the 15th century, on its right. The second floor was added at the beginning of the 16th century and decorated with sculptures and paintings by various artists, among which three beautiful frescoes and a sinopia by **Titian** of 1511. The **Museo Antoniano**, accessible from the cloisters, contains works of art of the Basilica, including a fresco by **Mantegna** and a painting by **Tiepolo.**

See map p. 384. Piazza del Santo 11. Basilica: ☎ *049-878-9722. Museum: 049-822-5650.* www.santantonio.org. *Admission: Basilica free; Oratorio di San Giorgio 1.50€ ($1.70); Scoletta 1.55€ ($1.39); Musei Antoniani 2.50€ ($2.90). Open: Basilica summer daily 6:20 a.m.–7:45 p.m., winter daily 6:20 a.m.–7 p.m.; Oratorio and Scoletta summer daily 9 a.m.–12:30 p.m. and 2:30–7 p.m., winter daily 9 a.m.–12:30 p.m. and 2:30–5 p.m.; Musei Antoniani summer daily 9 a.m.–1 p.m. and 2:30–6:30 p.m., winter Tues–Sun 9 a.m.–1 p.m. and 2–6 p.m.*

Cappella degli Scrovegni and Musei Civici Eremitani

The **Cappella degli Scrovegni** (Scrovegni Chapel) is surrounded by the archaeological remains of the **Roman Arena** — hence its other name, Cappella dell'Arena — and is accessible from the courtyard of the **Civic Museums (Musei Civici Eremitani).** Housed in the monastery attached to the chapel, these museums include the gallery upstairs — a large collection of paintings by Venetian masters from the 15th to the 19th centuries such as Giorgione, Titian, Veronese, and Tintoretto, as well as the archeological museum downstairs, a collection of artifacts documenting the history of Padua.

But it is the Scrovegni Chapel that makes Padua an artistic pilgrimage site. In 1267, Giotto di Bondone was born in a village not far from Florence and went on to become an apprentice of the great painter Cimabue. The frescoes Giotto executed in the chapel are absolute masterpieces. Construction of the chapel itself began in 1303 by banker Enrico Scrovegni, partly as an act of contrition because of his family's ill-gotten (in Christian terms) wealth. (In his *Inferno,* Dante put Enrico's father, Reginaldo, in the circle of hell reserved for usurers, because usury was considered sinful.) Ironically, the jewel that the chapel became under Giotto's hands led local monks to complain about the excessive luxury of the Scrovegni family — sometimes you just can't win. The chapel is an early example of a complex project that reflects the vision of a single artist. The unusual design — windows on one side but not the other, no internal architectural decorations — made it a perfect canvas for Giotto's work. The stories that he depicts move from left to right. The top row or band contains scenes from the life of Joachim and Anna, parents of the Virgin Mary. The middle and lower levels of the chapel contain scenes from the life of Jesus. Giotto also painted allegorical figures representing six virtues and six vices.

Giotto's frescoes broke with tradition in a number of ways, making them striking and important in art history. His composition is dramatic rather than static, as in Byzantine art; he chose scenes that weren't usually depicted; and, above all, he represented human beings with much greater psychological realism, which a glance at these beautiful faces shows. On the altar are a Madonna with child and two angels by the sculptor Giovanni Pisano.

To protect the invaluable frescoes, when the Scrovegni Chapel reopened in March 2002 after a major restoration, a special access gate was installed — to filter the air and control the humidity and other factors — and the number of visitors, as well as the length of their stay, were severely restricted. You now need to make a reservation for a precise time slot (usually 15 min. but at special times up to 30 min.). Note that reservations are required also for children under 6 even though they enter for free — they breath too.

See map p. 384. Piazza Eremitani 8, off Corso Garibaldi. ☎ 049-820-45450 or 049-201-0020 for reservations. Reservations online at www.cappelladegli scrovegni.it. *Admission: 12€ ($14) adults, children under 6 free; obligatory reservation fee 1€ ($1.15) per person. Admission also includes entry to Palazzo Zuckermann. Open: Summer daily 9 a.m.–7 p.m., winter daily 9 a.m.–6 p.m.*

Duomo

Built between the 16th and 18th centuries, the Duomo was partly designed by Michelangelo. Behind the unfinished facade, the two points of interest are the paintings in the **Sacristy (Sagrestia dei Canonici)** and the statues by Florentine artist Giuliano Vangi in the new **Presbetery.** Attached to the Duomo, the beautiful Romanesque **Baptistry** from 1075 is especially remarkable. The interior is decorated with Giusto de' Menabuoi frescoes; among the masterpieces of the 14th century; they have been recently restored and illustrate scenes from the lives of John the Baptist and Christ. A vision of paradise is gloriously depicted on the domed ceiling.

See map p. 384. Piazza Duomo. ☎ *049-656-914. Admission: Duomo free; Battistero 2.50€ ($2.90). Open: Duomo Mon–Sat 7:30 a.m.–noon and 3:45–7:30 p.m., Sun 7:45 a.m.–1p.m. and 3:45–8:30 p.m.; Battistero daily 10 a.m.–6 p.m.*

Palazzo della Ragione

Known as **Il Salone (the Great Hall),** this elegantly colonnaded structure was built in 1218 and an upper level was added in 1306. It served as the seat of the city's courts of law and its assembly hall. Today, after a complete restoration that ended in 2002, it houses special exhibitions. On the ground floor, it divides the **Piazza delle Erbe (green market)** from the **Piazza della Frutta (fruit market).** (These markets still occupy the squares today and are lively affairs.) The top floor is the *salone,* one huge open hall covered by a beautifully crafted wooden vaulted roof — a fine example of medieval architecture and one of the largest of its kind in the world (81m x 27m x27m high / 265 ft. x 89 ft. x 89-ft. high). The rich wall frescoes, illustrating religious and astrological themes, date from the 15th century and replace the original 13th-century frescoes by Giotto and its school which were destroyed by fire. The *palazzo*'s largest conversation piece is a giant wooden horse built for a jousting event in 1466.

See map p. 384. Via VIII Febbraio, between Piazza delle Erbe and Piazza della Frutta. ☎ *049-820-5006. Admission: 8€ ($9.20). Open: Tues–Sun 9 a.m.–7 p.m.*

More cool things to see and do

✔ **Caffè Pedrocchi** (Piazza Pedrocchi, just off Piazza Cavour; ☎ **049-820-5007** or 049-878-1231; www.caffepedrocchi.it) has been the main intellectual gathering place of the city's intelligentsia since its opening in 1831. At that time, Padua was under Austrian rule, and the cafe became a meeting place for patriotic and political groups; it maintained this role through the years and as late as 1948 it was the scene of a student uprising against the fascist regime. Completely restored to its elegant 19th-century glory, the cafe is open daily 9 a.m. to 9 p.m. (until midnight Thurs–Sat) for regular business and live music — mostly jazz — in the evening. The upper floor, with its elegant 19th-century furniture, can be visited for a fee of 3€ ($3.45); it's also open daily, but only 9:30 a.m. to 12:30 p.m. and 3:30 to 8:00 p.m. Closed two weeks in August.

✔ The seat of the University of Padua, the **Palazzo del Bo** (Via VIII Febbraio, just off Piazza delle Erbe; ☎ **049-827-3044** or 049-827-3047 for reservations; admission: 3€/$3.45) was built in the 16th century and later enlarged. Founded in 1222, the University of Padua is Italy's second oldest and counted among its scholars Galileo Galilei. It was the first university in the world to have an **Anatomy Theater (Teatro Anatomico),** an architectural masterpiece by G. Fabrici d'Acquapendente, built in 1594. Here medical students observed dissections of cadavers (sometimes in secret, for it was long forbidden by the church) in order to learn about the human body. You can visit only by guided tour; call for reservations or go at one of the set visiting times: Monday, Wednesday, and Friday at 3:15 p.m., 4:15 p.m., and 5:15 p.m. or Tuesday, Thursday, and Saturday at 9:15 a.m., 10:15 a.m., and 11:15 a.m.

✔ Padua boasts the world's first **Botanical Garden (Orto Botanico;** off Via San Michele, behind the Basilica di Sant'Antonio; ☎ **049-827-2119** or 049-827-2127; admission: 4€/$4.60). It was founded in 1545 as the garden for the university's faculty of medicine, where medicinal plants and herbs were grown. Today it houses a very important collection of rare plants. You can also visit the old library and the university's collection of botanical specimens. There's nothing dusty and academic about this garden, however; it's organized as a Renaissance garden and makes for a very pleasurable stroll. Summer hours are Monday through Saturday 9 a.m. to 1 p.m. and 3 to 6 p.m., and winter hours are Monday through Saturday 9 a.m. to 1 p.m.

✔ In a lesser way than Venice, Padua is also a town of water, crossed by many canals, which link Padua to the Brenta River, and, further, to the sea and Venice. During the Renaissance, rich Venetians had their country "houses" built along the Brenta, many of them designed by Palladio, one of the greatest architects of all times, noted for the grace and balance of his designs. Among the various companies offering boat tours in Padua, the **Consorzio Battellieri di Padova e Riviera del Brenta** (P.ggio de Gasperi 3; ☎ **049-820-9825;** www.padovanavigazione.it) offers several itineraries, all very interesting, particularly the tour of the villas along the **Riviera del Brenta.** The tour starts in Padua and brings you to Venice (we took this one and definitely recommend it). The same company also offers a shorter urban tour. Boats run from March to October.

Fast Facts: Padua

Area Code

The country code for Italy is **39.** The area code for Padua is **049;** use this code when calling from anywhere outside or inside Italy, even within Padua, and include the 0 every time.

ATMs

There are many banks in Padova with ATMs, particularly on Via Trieste and Via S. Lucia, and Piazza Duomo. You can also change money at the train station (open Mon–Sat 8 a.m.–8 p.m.), as well as in the exchange office at Via L. Belludi 15 (☎ 049-660-504).

Emergencies

Ambulance, ☎ **118**; fire, ☎ **115**; road assistance, ☎ **116**; First Aid (Pronto Soccorso), ☎ **049-821-2856** or 049-821-2857.

Hospital

The Ospedale Civile is at Via Giustiniani 1 (☎ 049-821-1111).

Information

The tourist office (www.turismo padova.it or turismopadova. tecnoteca.com) maintains throo

offices: Stazione FS (☎ 049-875-2077; open: Mon–Sat 9:15 a.m.–7 p.m. and Sun 9 a.m.–noon); Galleria Pedrocchi (☎ 049-876-7927; Mon–Sat 9 a.m.–1:30 p.m. and 3–7 p.m.); Piazza del Santo (☎ 049-875-3087; open: Mar–Oct daily 9 a.m.–5 p.m.).

Police

There are two police forces in Italy; call either one. For the Polizia, call ☎ **113**; for the Carabinieri, call ☎ **112**.

Post Office

The post office (ufficio postale) is at Corso Garibaldi 33 (☎ 049-820-8511).

Taxi

Call ☎ 049-651-333.

Verona: City of Juliet and Romeo

Like Padua, **Verona** was a Roman city whose historic center is now surrounded by a bustling modern urban area (Verona, too, is a major economic hub). After its glory during the reign of Augustus, Verona suffered under barbarian invasions and went into decline. The Scaligeri (or della Scala) family ruled it during the 13th and 14th centuries, much as the Medici family ruled Florence. Venice absorbed Verona in 1405, and Venetian rule lasted until Napoleon made everybody equal (sort of). Austrian domination followed, which continued until 1866 and the unification of Italy.

Today Verona is a popular destination — even though Romeo and Juliet may never have existed, there's plenty to see here — but because of its contemporary vitality, it's not as overwhelmed with tourists as Venice. While you can easily visit the sights as a day trip from Venice, Padua, or Milan, we recommend that you spend the night, which will enable you to savor the unique spirit of this beautiful medieval town — and maybe catch an opera (see later in this section).

Getting there

The **train** to Verona takes two hours from Venice and six from Rome. The fare is approximately 6€ ($6.90) from Venice and 23€ ($26) from Rome.

Trains arrive at the **Stazione Porta Nuova** on Piazza XXV Aprile (☎ 045-590-688).

Verona's **Aeroporto Valerio Catullo** (☎ 045-809-5666), in Villa Franca, is 16km (10 miles) from the center. **Meridiana** offers hour-long flights daily from Rome (☎ 06-4780-4222 or 02-864-771; www.meridiana.it) for about 150€ ($170) round-trip. You can take a taxi from the airport (about 15 min.), or you can take a regular city bus running from the airport to the town center (.80€/90¢) in about 20 minutes.

If you're **driving** from Rome, take **A1** to Campogalliano and then **Autostrada del Brennero (A22)** to the Verona Sud exit (about 6 hrs. to cover the 505km/315 miles). From Venice, take **A4** heading west; the 110km (68- mile) drive takes about two hours. The center of Verona is closed to private cars; you will have to leave your car in a parking garage — the main parking lot is **Arsenale** (Piazza Arsenale 8, ☎ 045-830-3281).

Spending the night

Domus Nova
$$ Center

This family-run hotel, housed in a medieval building, opens onto the elegant Piazza dei Signori in the heart of Verona. The welcoming guest rooms are tastefully furnished with antiques and have new bathrooms.

See map p. 393. Piazza dei Signori 18. ☎ *045-801-5245. Fax: 045-804-3459. Parking: 26€ ($30) valet. Rack rates: 220€ ($253) double. Rates include breakfast. AE, DC, MC, V. Closed 5 weeks in Jan/Feb.*

Hotel Aurora
$ Piazza delle Erbe

Recently renovated, this hotel is housed in a 15th-century building and offers nicely appointed guest rooms and a great location. Some of the guest rooms offer views over the famous piazza — the one on the top floor even has a balcony — and the bathrooms are of a decent size.

See map p. 393. Piazzetta XIV Novembre 2, off Piazza delle Erbe. ☎ *045-594-717. Fax: 045-801-0860.* www.hotelaurora.biz. *Parking: 10€ ($12). Rack rates: 130€ ($150) double. Rates include buffet breakfast. AE, DC, MC, V.*

Hotel Colomba d'Oro
$$ Arena

A couple of steps from the Roman Arena, this elegant but moderately priced historic hotel — it has been an inn since the 19th century — occupies what was once a monastery. The hall is decorated with original

Verona

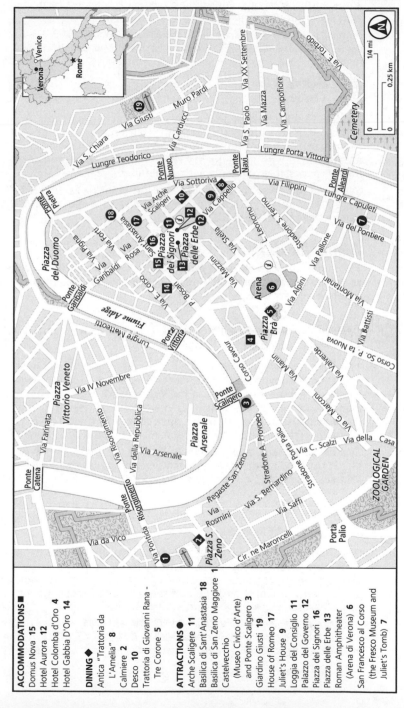

ACCOMMODATIONS ■
Domus Nova **15**
Hotel Aurora **12**
Hotel Colomba d'Oro **4**
Hotel Gabbia D'Oro **14**

DINING ◆
Antica "Trattoria da
  L'Amelia" **8**
Calmiere **2**
Desco **10**
Trattoria di Giovanni Rana -
  Tre Corone **5**

ATTRACTIONS ●
Arche Scaligere **11**
Basilica di Sant'Anastasia **18**
Basilica di San Zeno Maggiore **1**
Castelvecchio
  (Museo Civico d'Arte)
  and Ponte Scaligero **3**
Giardino Giusti **19**
House of Romeo **17**
Juliet's House **9**
Loggia del Consiglio **11**
Palazzo del Governo **12**
Piazza dei Signori **16**
Piazza delle Erbe **13**
Roman Amphitheater
  (Arena di Verona) **6**
San Francesco al Corso
  (the Fresco Museum and
  Juliet's Tomb) **7**

15th-century frescoes, and the large guest rooms are furnished in style with some antiques and a careful attention to details.

See map p. 393. Via C. Cattaneo 10. ☎ *045-595-300. Fax: 045-594-974.* www.colomba hotel.com. *Parking: 16€ ($18). Rack rates: 214€ ($246) double. AE, MC, V.*

Hotel Gabbia D'Oro
$$$$ **Center**

Small but very well kept, with a keen attention to detail, this elegant hotel is housed in an 18th-century building that opens onto a delightful year-round garden. Guest rooms are not large but some have balconies and all are furnished with good-quality reproductions and some antiques. The hotel is accessible to people with disabilities.

See map p. 393. Corso Porta Borsari 4/a. ☎ *045-800-3060. Fax: 045-803-0347.* www.hotelgabbiadoro.it. *Parking: 26€ ($30) valet. Rack rates: 351€ ($404) double. Rates include breakfast. AE, DC, MC, V.*

Dining locally

The important wine-growing region of the Veneto supplies Verona with an interesting assortment of fine wines, and the city maintains restaurants for every purse.

Antica "Trattoria da L'Amelia"
$$ **Center   ITALIAN**

This historic trattoria (open since 1876) offers nice views over the river and a cozy atmosphere. The service is friendly and they are welcoming to families. It serves food typical of the Veneto, with an accent on fresh home-made pastas and *risotti,* plus a good selection of desserts. Try the *bigoli all'anatra* (rustic spaghetti with a duck sauce), or the *risotto con capesante e zucchine* (risotto with scallops and zucchini), and don't forget the wine.

See map p. 393. Lungadige B. Rubele 32, near the Anfiteatro. ☎ *045-800-5526.* www.trattoriaamelia.com. *Reservations recommended. Secondi: 10€–18€ ($12–$21). AE, DC, MC, V. Open: Lunch Tues–Sat, dinner Mon–Sat.*

Calmiere
$ **San Zeno   VERONESE**

Opening onto what is arguably the most beautiful square in Verona, this restaurant offers excellent food true to the best Veronese tradition in a friendly and welcoming atmosphere. Try the *luccio con polenta* (pike served with polenta) and the *carrello dei bolliti* (assortment of boiled meats and sausages served with several sauces).

See map p. 393. Piazza San Zeno, 10. ☎ *045-803-0765.* www.calmiere.com. *Reservations recommended. Secondi: 10€–13€ ($12–$15). AE, DC, MC, V. Open: Lunch Fri–Wed and dinner Fri–Tues. Closed 2 weeks during Christmas holidays.*

Desco
$$$$ Center VERONESE/CREATIVE

It doesn't come cheap, but it is heavenly: This is one of the best restaurants in Italy. The menu changes with the seasons and the whims of the chef/owner, with such creations as *scaloppa di foie gras al Recioto con pere* (foie gras with pears and a local wine sauce), *petto di faraona con purea di topinambour e salsa all'aceto balsamico e cioccolato* (breast of guinea hen with Jerusalem artichokes and a chocolate and balsamic vinegar sauce), *tortelli di baccalà mantecato con pomodori e capperi* (large ravioli filled with cod in a tomato and capers sauce). Whatever you eat, absolutely leave room for dessert, each fantastic concoction is a perfect balance of flavor, texture, and temperature and is accompanied by a complementary glass of wine on the house!

See map p. 393. Via Dietro San Sebastiano 7. ☎ 045-595-358. Reservations recommended. Secondi: 28€–36€ ($32–$41). AE. DC, MC, V. Open: Lunch and dinner Tues–Sat. Closed 2 weeks in June and 2 weeks for Christmas holidays.

Trattoria di Giovanni Rana - Tre Corone
$$$ Center NORTHERN ITALIAN

In its large and elegant dining room, decorated with Murano chandeliers and marble floors, you will taste the best the local culinary tradition has to offer. The menu is seasonal but you will always find the well-prepared classics: *lasagne al forno* (lasagna), *tortellini burro e salvia* (filled pasta in a butter and sage sauce), *cotoletta alla milanese* (deep-fried veal cutlet), and *baccalà alla vicentina* (cod in a tomato sauce).

See map p. 393. Piazza Bra 16. ☎ 045-800-2462. Secondi: 14€–22€ ($16–$25). AE, DC, MC, V. Open: Lunch Tues–Sun and dinner Tues–Sat.

Exploring Verona
If you visit during the good season, you can take advantage of the **Bus Romeo** (☎ 045-840-1160 or e-mail romeo@amt.it for reservations), a 90-minute guided tour that's accompanied by an audioguide (available in several languages). Tours depart from Piazza Bra and are offered June to September only, Tuesday through Sunday, four times a day (10 a.m.; 11:30 a.m.; 1 p.m., and 3:30 p.m.). Tickets are 15€ ($17) for adults, 7€ ($8.05) for youth aged 5 to 18, and free for children under 5. The last run on Saturdays has a live guide — in Italian and English, depending on the audience — and costs 5€ ($5.75) more.

If you spend the night in any hotel — or even camping — in the province of Verona, you will receive the **Welcome Card,** granting discounts on many attractions, guided tours, public transportation, and even some shops and restaurants in the area. Ask for it upon check-in should your host forget to give it to you.

You can get a **cumulative ticket** for the five most interesting churches in town — San Zeno, Duomo, Sant'Anastasia, San Lorenzo, and San Fermo — for 5€ ($5.75) per person. The ticket can be purchased at any of the participating churches (☎ 045-592-813; www.chieseverona.it).

The top attractions

Arche Scaligere

Just off Piazza dei Signori and adjoining the Romanesque church **Santa Maria Antica,** are the **Arche Scaligere,** the outdoor tombs of the Scaligeri princes, enclosed behind wrought-iron gates bearing the representation of ladders, the family's heraldic symbol. The grandest of the monuments is that of Cangrande I (he was certainly top dog — his name means "Big Dog"), which stands over the portal of the church and is crowned by the equestrian statue of Cangrande (a copy — the original is at the Castelvecchio, see later in this section). The two other major monuments are for Cansignorio (more or less "Sir Dog") and Mastino II ("Mastiff"). All richly decorated, the monuments are sculptural masterpieces. The church — originally built in the 8th century, but rebuilt in the 12th century after it was severely damaged by the earthquake of 1117 — still contains part of a mosaic floor believed to belong to the original 8th-century church. Note that in winter you can see the Arche only from outside the gates. Tickets are sold at the booth by the Torre dei Lamberti (see Piazza dei Signori, later in this section).

See map p. 393. Via Arche Scaligere, off Via Sant'Anastasia and Via P. Bosari; Torre dei Lamberti: Cortile Mercato Vecchio. ☎ *045-803-2726. Admission: 2.10€ ($2.40) including Torre dei Lamberti (add .50€/60¢ for the elevator). Open: June–Sept Mon 1:45–7:30 p.m. and Tues–Sun 9:30 a.m.–7:30 p.m. Ticket booth closes at 7 p.m.*

Basilica di San Zeno Maggiore

 A wonderful example of the Romanesque style and the most beautiful in northern Italy, this church and campanile were built between the 9th and 12th centuries above the tomb of Verona's patron saint (the original church dates from the 4th and 5th centuries). Some of its most fascinating artworks are the 11th- and 12th-century **bronze door panels** illustrating San Zeno's miracles; like other works in this part of Italy (notably Venice), they reflect a mix of Byzantine, Gothic, and Turkish influences. Over the entrance is the famous **Ruota della Fortuna (Wheel of Fortune),** a beautiful rose window from the early 12th century. Inside, the church is decorated with graceful Romanesque capitals on the columns and frescoes (dating from the 12th to 14th centuries). The **timbered roof** is still the original 14th-century one. At the north end of the church you can access the peaceful Romanesque **cloister**.

See map p. 393. Piazza San Zeno, just west of the Arena. ☎ *045-800-4325 or -6120. Admission: 3€ ($3.45). Open: Mar–Oct Mon–Sat 8:30 a.m.–6 p.m., Sun and holidays 1–6 p.m.; Nov–Feb Tues–Sat 10 a.m.–1 p.m. and 1:30–4 p.m., Sun and holidays 1–5 p.m.*

Castelvecchio (Museo Civico d'Arte) and Ponte Scaligero

The 14th-century **Castelvecchio,** perched over the Adige River, was the fortress and residence of the Scaligeri family, set to defend the famous bridge **Ponte Scaligero.** Built between 1355 and 1375, the bridge was destroyed by the Nazis during their retreat at the end of World War II, but was painstakingly rebuilt using the pieces that remained in the river. Today this castle, complete with crenellated towers and walls, houses a picture gallery containing paintings by **Paolo Veronese** and its school, as well as Venetian artists like **Tiepolo** and **Tintoretto.** The castle is worth a visit, with its labyrinthine passageways and the tower from which you can see sweeping vistas of the city and its environs. In the courtyard is the **equestrian statue** of Cangrande I.

See map p. 393. Corso Castelvecchio 2, at the western end of Corso Cavour. ☎ *045-594-734. Admission: 3.10€ ($3.60). Free the first Sun of each month. Audioguide 3.60€ ($4.10). Open: Mon 1:45 p.m.–7:30 p.m. and Tues–Sun 8:30 a.m.–7:30 p.m. Ticket booth closes at 6:45 p.m.*

 ### Piazza dei Signori

One of northern Italy's most beautiful piazze, surrounded by beautiful palaces, this square was the center of Verona's government during its heyday. The **Palazzo del Governo** is where Cangrande della Scala (one of the first Scaligeri) extended the shelter of his hearth and home to the fleeing Florentine poet Dante Alighieri. A marble statue of Dante stands in the center of the square. The **Palazzo della Ragione,** on the south side of the piazza, was built in 1123 but underwent changes many times in later centuries, including receiving a Renaissance facade in 1524. From its courtyard rises a tower, the majestic **Torre dei Lamberti** (84m/277 feet), also called the Torre del Comune. An elevator takes you to the top, and the views are magnificent. On the north side of the piazza is the 15th-century **Loggia del Consiglio,** which was the town council's meeting place; it's surmounted by five statues of famous Veronese citizens. Five arches lead into Piazza dei Signori.

See map p. 393. Torre dei Lamberti: Cortile Mercato Vecchio. ☎ *045-803-2726. Admission: 1.50€ ($1.70) on foot and 2.10€ ($2.40) by elevator; in summer admission includes Arche Scaligere 2.10€ ($2.40) on foot, 2.60€ ($3) by elevator. Open: Tues–Sun 9:30 a.m.–7:30 p.m., Monday 1:45–7:30 p.m. (ticket booth open to 7 p.m.).*

Piazza delle Erbe

The piazza (its name means Square of the Herbs) was built where the Forum stood in Roman times. Today, it's the fruit-and-vegetable market where Veronese shoppers and vendors mill about, surrounded by Renaissance palaces. In the center is the **Berlina,** a canopy supported by four columns where the election of the town's *signore* (elected prince) and the *podestà* (the governor) took place. On the north side is a 14th-century **fountain** and the *Madonna Verona,* which is actually a restored Roman statue. Important buildings on the piazza include the early-14th-century **House of the Merchants (Casa dei Mercanti),** restructured in 1870 to restore its original 1301 form; the baroque **Palazzo Maffei;** the adjacent **Torre del Gardello,** a tower built in 1370; and the **Casa Mazzanti,** another Scaligeri palace, decorated with frescoes.

See map p. 393. Intersection of Via Mazzini and Via Cappello.

Roman Amphitheater (Arena di Verona)

This famous elliptical Roman arena dates from the reign of Diocletian (it was built around A.D. 290) and remains in surprisingly good condition. The inner ring is basically intact, though a 12th-century earthquake destroyed most of the outer ring (only four of the arches remain). This was Italy's third-largest Roman amphitheater and the second most important to have survived after Rome's Colosseum.

The arena's overall length was 152m (470 feet) and its height 32m (97½ feet). Its 44 rows of seats could originally hold as many as 20,000 spectators, who watched gladiators and animals sparring. These days, however, the arena hosts more civilized entertainments: One of the greatest experiences in Verona is attending an opera or a ballet here during July or August. The setting speaks for itself. Tickets cost from about 20€ to 160€ ($23–$180); for schedule and reservations call ☎ **045-800-5151** or visit www.arena.it.

*See map p. 393. Piazza Brà. ☎ **045-800-3204.** Admission: 3.10€ ($3.60), 1€ ($1.15) first Sun of every month. Open: Tues–Sun 8:30 a.m.–7:30 p.m., Monday 1:45–7:30 p.m.; ticket booth closes 45 min. before amphitheater closing. During the performance season (June–Aug), arena closes at 3:30 p.m.*

More cool things to see and do

✔ The small **Juliet's House (Casa di Giulietta),** at Via Cappello 23 (☎ **045-803-4303**), is a 12th-century house that the city bought in 1905 and turned into a tourist site (the famous balcony was added in 1935). Shakespeare's Capulets and Montagues (from his famous play *Romeo and Juliet*) were indeed versions of two historic Veronese families, the Capuleti (or Cappello) and the Montecchi. No proof exists that a family of Capulets ever lived in this house, but that doesn't stop people from flocking here to see the balcony where Juliet would've stood, if she'd been here at all. Tradition calls for you to rub the right breast of the bronze statue of Juliet for good luck. The house is open Tuesday through Sunday from 8:30 a.m. to 7:30 p.m., and Monday from 1:30 to 7:30 p.m.; admission is 3.10€ ($3.60). Of course, you can't have a Juliet without a Romeo, and there's a so-called **House of Romeo (Casa di Romeo),** at Via Arche Scaligeri 2 (east of Piazza dei Signori), a 13th-century house which is said to have been the home of the Montecchi family. It now houses a small, cute restaurant serving excellent Veronese fare called the **Osteria dal Duca** (☎ **045-594-474**); it's open for lunch and dinner Monday through Saturday. Reservations are not accepted and a prix-fixe menu is available for 13€ ($15).

✔ The **Fresco Museum (Museo degli Affreschi G. B. Cavalcaselle)** and **Juliet's Tomb (Tomba di Giulietta)** are housed in the 13th-century complex of **San Francesco al Corso** (Via Shakespeare; ☎ 045-800-0361). It was inaugurated in 1935 with the display of a sarcophagus that, according to legend, holds the bodies of Romeo and Juliet. The museum displays an interesting collection of frescoes from a number of buildings in Verona, as well as 19th-century sculptures. The church of San Francesco houses several paintings from the 15th, 16th, and 17th centuries and a large collection of Roman amphoras in the vaults. The complex is open Monday from 1:45 to 7:30 p.m. and Tuesday through Sunday from 8:30 a.m. to 7:30 p.m. Admission is 2.60€ ($3) per person, free the first Sunday of each month.

✔ The **Basilica di Sant'Anastasia** (Piazza Sant'Anastasia; ☎ 045-800-4325) is Verona's largest church. Built between 1290 and 1481, it is graced by an unfinished Gothic facade adorned by a beautiful arched portal and an ornate campanile. Although the architecture (rather than the contents of the church) is its noblest feature, it does contain a Pisanello fresco of San Giorgio pictured with a princess in the **Cappella Giusti,** and terra cotta works by Michele da Firenze in the **Cappella Pellegrini.** It's open March through October, Monday to Saturday, from 9 a.m. to 6 p.m., and Sunday and holidays from 1 to 6 p.m.; November to February it's open Tuesday through Saturday from 10 a.m. to 1 p.m. and 1:30 to 4 p.m. and Sundays and holidays from 1 to 5 p.m. Admission is 2€ ($2.30).

✔ If you have ever wondered what an "Italian Garden" really should look like, visit the **Giardino Giusti** (Via Giardino Giusti 2; ☎ 045-803-4029). Built in the 14th century and given its current layout in the 16th, this renaissance garden has survived for centuries more or less intact. Crossed by a main alley lined with secular cypress trees, the garden is embellished with grottoes, statues, and fountains. From a balcony at one end of the garden, known as the "monster balcony," you can enjoy a panoramic view of the city. It's open daily in the summer, from 9 a.m. to 8 p.m. and until sunset during winter; admission is 4.50€ ($5.20).

Fast Facts: Verona

Area Code

The country code for Italy is **39**. The area code for Verona is **045;** use this city code when calling from anywhere outside or inside Italy, even within Verona and always include the 0.

ATMs

You can change currency inside the rail station or at numerous banks around town (for example, on Corso Cavour, where you can also find ATMs).

Emergencies

Ambulance, ☎ **118**; fire, ☎ **115**; road assistance, ☎ **116**; first aid (Pronto Soccorso), ☎ **045-807-2120**.

Hospital

The Ospedale Civile Maggiore Borgo Trento is at Piazzale Stefani 1 (☎ 045-807-1111). At night and during weekends and holidays, you can reach a doctor by calling ☎ 045-807-5627.

Information

Verona tourist board (www.tourism. verona.it) maintains three tourist

offices: Piazza Bra (Via degli Alpini 9; ☎ 045-806-8680); Porta Nuova railroad station (Piazza XXV Aprile; ☎ 045-800-0861); and airport "V. Catullo," Villafranca (☎ 045-861-9163).

Police

There are two police forces in Italy; call either one. For the Polizia, call ☎ **113**; for the Carabinieri, call ☎ **112**.

Post Office

The post office (ufficio postale) is at Piazza Viviani 7 (☎ 045-805-1111).

Milan: Italy's Business and Fashion Center

Milan (Milano) is a large industrial city that has deep roots in Italy's history. Its charm as a tourist destination, however, is much tarnished by its fast-paced modern Milanese lifestyle and its inclement climate, which includes much fog in winter and steamy heat in summer. Still, Milan is home to several gems, making it well worth a detour. You can certainly see the highlights in one day, but we recommend you spend the night if you can spare the time.

Getting there

The main international airport of Milan is **Malpensa** (☎ **02-7485-2200**), located 50km (31 miles) to the north of the city. Malpensa has the dubious distinction of being called the "worst airport in Europe," but that's mainly thanks to the frequent fogs that prevent take-offs and landings. Italians try to avoid flying to this airport if they possibly can. If you actually do land there, you can take a **shuttle train** which brings you to the rail station **Cadorna** (one of Milan's secondary rail stations) in 40 minutes, and runs every 20 minutes, or a **shuttle bus** which brings you to the railway station **Milano Centrale** (the primary rail station in Milan) in 50 minutes and runs every 30 minutes.

The **Linate Airport** (☎ **02-7485-2200**) is 10km (6.2 miles) to the east of town. It is a smaller airport, which handles some European and most domestic flights. We prefer this airport, but it offers fewer flight choices. From Linate it is an easy taxi ride to the center of town, or you can take the **city bus** (bus 73), which runs every ten minutes and connects to the subway (M1).

Milan is an important transportation hub in Italy, second only to Rome. The **train** trip from Rome lasts about five hours and costs about 40€

($46). **Milano Centrale** (Piazza Duca d'Aosta; ☎ **1478-88-088** toll-free in Italy), is the city's main rail station for arrivals.

If you're **driving,** Milan is at the intersection of the following highways: **A1** (Milano-Napoli); **A4** (Torino-Trieste); **A7** (Milano-Genova); **A8** (Milano-Varese); and **A9** (Lainate-Chiasso). Take the exit "Milano centro" for the center of the city. Avoid driving into Milan, however — the traffic is bad and parking is expensive. If you choose to do so anyway, use the public parking marked by blue lines on the ground: You have to buy a card from a news kiosk or a tobacconist (or from an attendant when available) and display it inside your car.

Getting around

Although walking is the best way to see the town, you may want to use public transportation to get yourself to more distant corners of Milan. The city transportation authority (☎ **800-80-8181;** www.atm-mi.it) runs a system of three **subway lines** and several **buses and trams.** The **Metro (subway)** is the fastest and simplest means to get around, but you'll see more from traveling on buses and trams. If you want to use the buses and trams, pick up a public transportation **map** from the information booth inside the Duomo subway station (open Mon–Sat 8:30 a.m.–8 p.m.)

Buses, trams, and subways use the same tickets, which are sold at newsstands, tobacconists, and bars. A **75-minute ticket** costs 1€ ($1.15), but you can also buy a **carnet of ten tickets** for 9.20€ ($10), a **one-day travel card** for 3€ ($3.45), or a **two-day travel card** for 5.50€ ($6.35).

Spending the night

As Italy's business center, Milan has many hotels; mostly keyed to business travelers, they tend to offer good weekend deals.

Four Seasons
$$$$$ Center

This luxury hotel is housed in a 15th-century convent, whose columned cloister now forms an inner courtyard. The rooms are large and tastefully decorated, with modern and antique details and marble bathrooms; the service is top notch, and you're right in the center of everything. It comes at a price, of course, but the hotel does run weekend and other specials.

See map p. 402. Via Gesù 8, off Via Montenapoleone. ☎ *02-77088. Fax: 02-7708-5000.* www.fourseasons.com. *Parking: 51€ ($59) valet. Rack rates: 737€ ($848) double. AE, DC, MC, V.*

Grand Hotel et de Milan
$$$$ Center

This family-run luxury hotel provides a more intimate feeling than the Four Seasons yet a similarly high level of services. The spacious and elegant

Milan

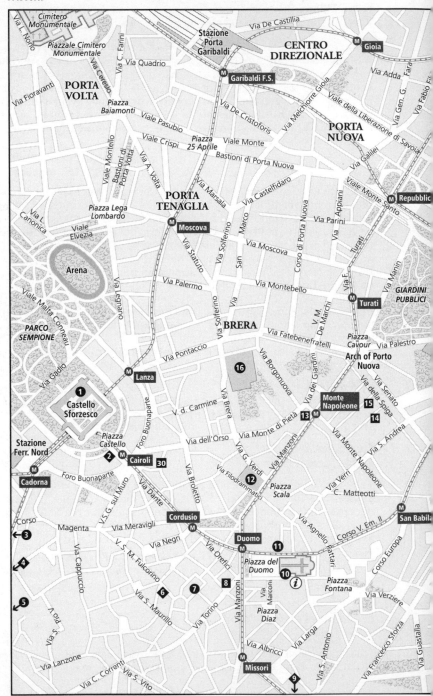

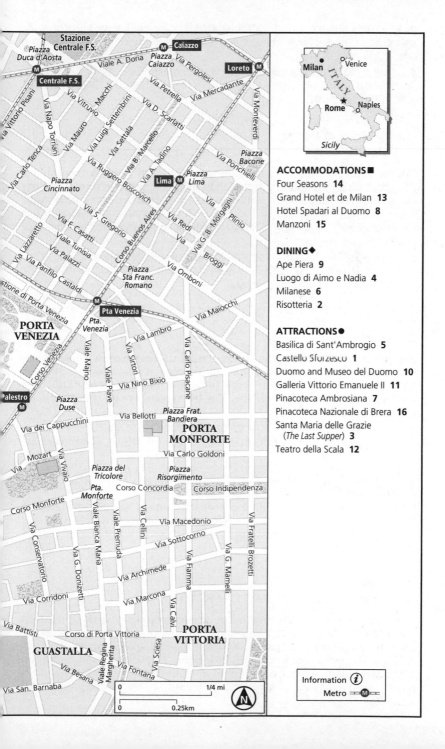

ACCOMMODATIONS ■
Four Seasons **14**
Grand Hotel et de Milan **13**
Hotel Spadari al Duomo **8**
Manzoni **15**

DINING ◆
Ape Piera **9**
Luogo di Aimo e Nadia **4**
Milanese **6**
Risotteria **2**

ATTRACTIONS ●
Basilica di Sant'Ambrogio **5**
Castello Sforzesco **1**
Duomo and Museo del Duomo **10**
Galleria Vittorio Emanuele II **11**
Pinacoteca Ambrosiana **7**
Pinacoteca Nazionale di Brera **16**
Santa Maria delle Grazie
  (*The Last Supper*) **3**
Teatro della Scala **12**

Information (*i*)
Metro ━M━

guest rooms are decorated with fine fabrics, canopied beds, and antiques, and graced by marble bathrooms. The hotel's restaurant, Dos Carlos, is one of the best in Italy.

See map p. 402. Via A. Manzoni 29, near Via Montenapoleone. ☎ *02-723-141. Fax: 02-8646-0861.* www.grandhoteletdemilan.it. *Parking: 43€ ($49). Rack rates: 520€ ($598) double. AE, DC, MC, V.*

Hotel Spadari al Duomo
$$$ **Duomo**

Not far from La Scala, this small, elegant, family-run hotel is decorated in the chic and contemporary style Milan is known for. The rooms are spacious and have large beds, sofas, desks, and modern baths with multidirectional shower heads or bath tubs. A few rooms have balconies or views over the Duomo and a Jacuzzi tub. Specials rates are available on weekends and in August.

See map p. 402. Via Spadari 11. ☎ *02-7200-2371. Fax: 02-861-184.* www.spadari-hotel.com. *Parking: 25€ ($29). Rack rates: 208€–268€ ($239–$308) double. AE, DC, MC, V. Closed 3 days around Christmas.*

Manzoni
$$ **Center**

In a good central location, the Manzoni is an affordable choice in an expensive city. Housed in a modern postwar building, it offers comfortable and attractive guest rooms with large beds and tastefully decorated with modern or reproduction furniture. The bathrooms are unusually large for Italian standards.

See map p. 402. Via Santo Spirito 20. ☎ *02-7600-5700. Fax: 02-784-212.* www.hotel-manzoni.com. *Rack rates: 195€ ($224) double. AE, DC, MC, V. Closed August and Christmas.*

Dining locally

One of the best areas for finding new restaurants is Navigli, once a small Venice with canals that have now been mostly covered over; the area is teaming with various venues, from trendy bars to romantic small restaurants.

Ape Piera
$$$ **Centro**   **MILANESE/ITALIAN/CREATIVE**

This modern and elegant restaurant offers tasty, light cuisine in a warm and friendly atmosphere. The seasonal menu may include some of our favorites: *ravioloni farciti con pesto patate fagiolini e olive taggiasche* (large ravioli with pesto, potatoes, green beans, and local olives), *spaghetti Latini "Taganrog"* (with prawns, onions, and fresh tomatoes), *millefoglie di pesce spada con melanzane al profumo di menta* (swordfish napoleon with minted eggplants), and *anatra alle spezie* (spicy duck). Dishes in the two tasting menus — including a vegetarian menu — may be paired with wines.

See map p. 402. Via Lodovico il Moro 11. ☎ *02-8912-6060.* www.ape-piera.com. *Reservations recommended. Secondi: 16€–22€ ($18–$25). AE, DC, MC, V. Open: Lunch and dinner Mon–Sat. Closed Aug and 10 days in Jan.*

Luogo di Aimo e Nadia
$$$$ **Centro** **CREATIVE/ITALIAN**

This wonderful place is one of the best restaurant in Milan — but it'll cost you. Using simple, yet excellent ingredients, the menu changes with the seasons and the whims of the chef. Among the best offerings are the *ricottine mantecate agli asparagi* (baby ricotta sauteed with asparagus), *zuppa etrusca profumata al finocchio selvatico* (vegetable soup with wild fennel), and *trio di pesce con tortino di melanzane* (triglia, gallinella, and prawns with eggplant torte).

See map p. 402. Via Montecuccoli 6. ☎ *02-416-886.* www.aimoenadia.com. *Reservations recommended. Secondi: 20€–32€ ($23–$37). AE, DC, MC, V. Open: Lunch Mon–Fri and dinner Mon–Sat. Closed Aug and 10 days in Jan.*

Milanese
$$$ **Duomo** **MILANESE**

This traditional trattoria offers a choice of typical Milanese dishes in a pleasantly old-fashioned ambience. The *risotto alla Milanese* (with saffron and bone marrow) is excellent, but you can also enjoy some of the very good meats for a *secondo,* such as a perfect *cotoletta alla Milanese* (deep-fried beef cutlet), and a juicy *ossobuco* (braised veal shank cutlet).

See map p. 402. Via Santa Marta 11. ☎ *02-8645-1991. Metro: M1 to Cordusio. Reservations recommended. Secondi: 9€–18€ ($10–$21). AE, DC, MC, V. Open: Lunch and dinner Wed–Mon.*

Risotteria
$ **Center** **MILANESE**

This is a simple restaurant specializing in, you guessed it, Milan's traditional staple dish. Risotto is prepared here in many varieties, prices are moderate, and the service is professional.

See map p. 402. Via Dandolo 2. ☎ *02-5518-1694. Secondi: 7€–14€ ($8.05–$16). MC, V. Open: Lunch and dinner Mon–Sat.*

Exploring Milan

The company **Autostradale** (☎ 02-3391-0794; www.autostradale.it) runs the new **Tram Turistico Ciao Milano,** line number 20 — a great way to visit Milan. You travel on historical street cars from the 1920s and listen to a commentary in the language of your choice; you can hop on and off as you please, but plan your stops well because there are only two or three runs a day. Tickets are valid one day and cost 20€ ($23) per person; rides start in Piazza Castello April through October daily at 11 a.m., 1 p.m., and 3 pm; and November through March Saturday, Sunday, and holidays only at 11 a.m. and 1 p.m. Trams don't operate January 1, May 1, December 25, December 31, and the second and third weeks in August. You can buy tickets at the tourist office in Piazza Duomo. Autostradale also runs **City Sightseeing,** a traditional bus tour for 40€ ($46), which includes admission to see Leonardo's *Last Supper.* Tours — one in the morning and one in the afternoon — start in front of the tourist office in Piazza Duomo and last three hours.

For a walking tour, the **Centro Guide Turistiche Milano** (Via Marconi 1; Fax: 02-863-210; www.centroguidemilano.net) offers basic three-hour tours as well as other specialized formulas.

 You can get a **cumulative ticket** including Leonardo's *Last Supper,* Brera Picture Gallery, and the Museo Teatrale alla Scala for 10€ ($12); you still have to pay for the 1.50€ ($1.70) reservation fee.

The top attractions

 ### Castello Sforzesco

The castle embraces centuries of the history of Milan, from its construction as a small defensive *rocca* by the Visconti family in the 14th century to its enlargement as a palace by the Sforza family, who dominated Milan during the Renaissance, and finally to its military development under the Austrian domination. Badly damaged during the Italian wars for independence in the 19th century, the castle seemed doomed, but the powers that be finally decided to restore it to its original Renaissance design. Kids will love the storybook crenellated walls, the underground passages, and the towers. The *castello* houses several museums. The **Museo di Scultura** — located in the former ducal public apartments, contains a large sculpture collection ranging from Roman times to the Renaissance. The star is **Michelangelo**'s famous **Pietà Rondanini**, his last — and unfinished — work, finally visible again after a lengthy restoration and cleaning. In the former ducal private apartments is the **Pinacoteca,** a collection of Italian art from the 13th to the 18th centuries, including the *Madonna in Gloria con Santi* by Andrea Mantegna and the *San Benedetto* by Antonello da Messina. Also on premises is a great collection of arms and armors, and a museum of musical instruments dating from the 15th to the 19th century. Underground is the **archaeological collection.** Inside the inner castle, around which later circles of defenses were added, is the beautiful **Argo,** with frescoes probably by Bramante.

See map p. 402. Porta Umberto. ☎ 02-8846-3651. www.creval.it/sforzesco. *Metro: M1 Cairoli or M2 Lanza/Cadorna. Admission: Free. Open: Castle Tues–Sun summer 7 a.m.–7 p.m., winter 7 a.m.–6 p.m.; museums daily 9 a.m.–5:30 p.m.*

Duomo and Museo del Duomo

This grandiose cathedral — second in Italy only to San Pietro, covers about 10,034 sq. m (108,000 sq. ft.), and is 107m (356-ft.) high; its construction lasted for centuries. Founded in 1386, the facade was completed at the beginning of the 19th century, and the last bronze portal was posed in 1965. Outside it is decorated with about 3,400 statues and 135 marble spires; its 1,394 sq. m (15,000 sq. ft.) of windows feature about 3,600 different characters. Some of the best artists of all periods have participated in the project, a history illustrated by the very interesting collection in the **Museo del Duomo.** The museum is on the first floor of the **Royal Palace,** by the cathedral, and houses a huge collection of artwork assembled over the centuries of construction and ongoing restoration, including **Tintoretto's** *Gesù al Tempio.* An important sculpture collection is organized chronologically and offers a unique panorama of Italian sculpture from the late 14th to the 19th centuries. There is also a fascinating array of stained-glass windows. The Baptistry is from the 4th century. At press time, the facade of the Duomo was covered in scaffolding for restoration; no date has been set for completion of the project.

See map p. 402. Cathedral Piazza Duomo; Museum Piazza Duomo 14 (inside Palazzo Reale). ☎ *02-860-358. Metro: M1 and M3 to Duomo. Admission: Cathedral free; crypt 1.55€ ($1.75); Baptistry 1.55€ ($1.75); roof 3.50€ ($4) and 5€ ($5.75) with elevator; museum 6€ ($6.90). Open: Cathedral daily 7 a.m.–7 p.m.; crypt daily 9 a.m.–noon and 2:30–6p.m.; Baptistry Tues–Sun 10 a.m.–noon and 3–5 p.m.; roof daily 7 a.m.–7 p.m.; Museum Tues–Sun 9:30 a.m.–12:30 p.m. and 3–6 p.m.*

Santa Maria delle Grazie and Leonardo's Last Supper

Built in the 15th century, this church was supposed to be the burial place of Ludovico il Moro and his descendants; the beautiful sculpted cover for the tomb is still here. But it's not tombs that draw tourists from all over the world. In the refectory of the church is the famous Leonardo da Vinci painting the *Ultima Cena,* or *Last Supper.* Painted by the master with an experimental technique (tempera over a plaster preparation) over four years of work between 1494 and 1498. The fresco was already looking quite bad by the end of the 16th century, so it required continuous repainting and restoration during the following centuries. The most recent restoration lasted 20 years and was completed in 1999; it removed the many previous restorations, revealing Leonardo's original work. Unfortunately, there are many gaps, but what remains is still a wonderful example of Leonardo's artistic achievement. Audioguides are available. *Note:* You need to reserve entry at least 24 hours in advance.

See map p. 402. Piazza S. Maria delle Grazie 2, off Corso Magenta. ☎ *02-8942-1146 for reservations.* www.cenacolovinciano.it. *Metro: M1 Conciliazione. Admission: 6.50€ ($7.50) plus an additional 1.50€ ($1.70) for mandatory reservation. Open: Tues–Sun 8:15 a.m.–7 p.m.; last admission 6:45 p.m.*

Pinacoteca Nazionale di Brera

Open since 1809 and housed in a beautiful 18th-century palace, this art museum was started by the Austrian Hapsburgs in the late 18th century as a small collection for the use of the students at the attached Art Academy. During the Napoleonic period, though, it was vastly enlarged with artworks confiscated by the French from museums as well as from the churches and monasteries that were shut down all over northern Italy. This already rich art collection was further enlarged with two private collections of modern art. It includes paintings by famous masters from the 14th to the 18th centuries — **Piero della Francesca's** famous *Pala di Urbino,* **Raffaello's** *Sposalizio della Vergine,* **Andrea Mantegna's** *Cristo Morto,* and **Caravaggio's** *Cena di Emmaus* among others, as well as important 19th- and 20-century paintings by artists such as Carrà and Morandi.

See map p. 402. Via Brera 28 (at the Accademia di Brera). ☎ *02-8942-1146. Metro: M2 to Lanza. Admission: 5€ ($5.75) Open: Tues–Sun 8:30 a.m.–7:30 p.m.; last admission 6:45 p.m.*

More cool things to see and do

✔ Originally built in 386 by the Roman Magistrate Ambrogio on the burial site of two martyrs, Gervaso and Protaso, the **Basilica di Sant'Ambrogio** is the church of Milan's patron saint and an interesting example of Romanesque church (Piazza S. Ambrogio 15; ☎ **02-8645-0895;** Metro: M2 S. Ambrogio; open: Church daily 9:00 a.m.–12:30 p.m. and 3:30–5 p.m.; museum Wed–Sun 10 a.m.– noon and 3–5 p.m.; closed August; admission: church free, museum 2€/$2.30). Under the main altar is a ninth-century masterpiece housing the church's relics and decorated with scenes from the life of Jesus in gold, toward the front, and the life of St.Ambrose in silver, toward the back. You can still view the remains of the two martyrs, together with those of Ambrogio. The **chapel of San Vittore in Ciel d'Oro (St.Victor in the Golden Sky),** in the apse area, is the only visible part of the church that dates from the fifth century. The **Museum of the Basilica** was recently reopened after a complete overhaul and is also worth a visit. Of particular interest is the **Urna degli Innocenti,** a jewelry masterpiece from the 15th century and a **stucco portrait of Saint Ambrose** from the 11th century.

✔ Among the many other museums of Milan, you might like to visit the **Pinacoteca Ambrosiana** (Piazza Pio XI; ☎ **02-806-921;** www. ambrosiana.it; Metro: M1 and M3 to Duomo), the oldest museum in town (opened in 1618). Among the artwork are **Caravaggio's** *Canestra,* **Botticelli's** *Madonna del Padiglione,* and **Leonardo's** *Musico* — although this last attribution is debated. It's open Tuesday through Sunday 10 a.m. to 5:30 p.m.; admission is 7.50€ ($8.60).

✔ The famous **Teatro della Scala** (see "Living it up after dark," later in this section) is a landmark in the history of Milan and Italian opera; if you love theater and opera you shouldn't miss the interesting

Museo Teatrale della Scala in Palazzo Busca, nearby Leonardo's *Last Supper* (Corso Magenta 71; ☎ 02-469-1528; Metro: M1 Conciliazione or M2 Cadorna). It's open daily from 9 a.m. to 6 p.m. and admission is 5€ ($5.75)

✔ Take a stroll under the **Galleria Vittorio Emanuele II** (off Piazza Duomo), a beautiful construction of wrought iron and glass covering four streets, built in the 1870s. Under the elegant canopy you'll find a number of shops, cafes, and small boutiques.

Shopping the local stores

The heart of Italy's fashion industry, Milan is prêt-à-porter galore. Do not leave without doing at least a bit of window-shopping.

The most famous shopping street for clothing and accessories is the world-renowned **Via Montenapoleone,** the fashion heart of Milan. Also worthy are the nearby streets of **Via della Spiga** and **Via Sant'Andrea.** Here, you'll find all kinds of shops and boutiques along with some of the top names of Italian fashion (**Valentino** and **Versace** are in Via Montenapoleone, **Dolce & Gabbana** is in nearby Corso Venezia, and **Armani** is in Via Manzoni). The shopping district, now with more down-to-earth shops, has spilled over all the way to **Piazza Duomo.**

If you aren't interested in haute couture, another excellent shopping area is the **Brera district.** In its backstreets, you'll find elegant boutiques, with many young designer names and open-air market stalls.

Living it up after dark

If you have the time, viewing an opera performance at the grand **Teatro della Scala** (Piazza della Scala; ☎ 02-7200-3744; www.teatroalla scala.org) is an unforgettable experience. You need to reserve well in advance, though. Tickets cost from about 6€ to 90€ ($6.90–$104). *Note:* At press time, La Scala was closed for renovations and scheduled to reopen in December 2004. During restoration performances have been moved to Teatro degli Arcimboldi.

For a simpler evening out, you may want to head for one of the two major nightlife destinations in Milan, the more elegant Brera district (Metro M2 to Lanza or M3 to Montenapoleone) or the more casual Ticinese/Navigli district. Both offer a large choice of restaurants, bars, and clubs.

Brera is a trendy district of Old Milan, with narrow streets and alleys (the name Brera comes from ancient German, meaning "meadows"). It used to be the artsy neighborhood of Milan, but of late it has become much more classy and established. Having undergone a transformation similar to New York's SoHo, it's still where you'll find some of the major art galleries of the city, but it is also home to some top fashion boutiques.

The **Ticinese/Navigli** is a charming neighborhood of canals (although most of them have been paved over) and narrow streets to the southwest of the city center. Places are open late here and attract a more mixed crowd, with lots of hangouts for young people, trendy bars, small restaurants, and clubs with live music. If dance clubs are your thing, the hottest address in town is **Plastic,** at Viale Umbria 120 (☎ 02-733-996; Metro: Vittoria). It's open Friday to Sunday only.

Popular with the locals, *enoteche* abound in Milan. You can drink a glass — or a bottle — of excellent wine and accompany it with a tasty something to eat. Our favorites include **Cotti** (Via Solferino 42; ☎ 02-2900-1096; open till the wee hours); **Ronchi** (Via S. Vincenzo 12; ☎ 02-8940-2627), where they also have a wine museum; and **Enoteca Wine & Chocolate** (Foro Buonaparte 63; ☎ 02-862-626), which also features chocolate tasting.

Milan is also the center of Italy's gay scene. A popular disco and restaurant is the mostly lesbian **After Line** (Via Sammartini 25; ☎ 02-669-2130; open: Tues–Sun). The **G-lounge** (Via Larga 8; ☎ 02-805-3042) is a trendy disco-bar, with quality music.

Fast Facts: Milan

Area Code

The country code for Italy is **39.** The area code for Milan is **02;** use this code when calling from anywhere outside or inside Italy, even within Milan, and always include the 0.

Consulates

Australia: Via Borgogna 2 (☎ 02-777-041); Canada: Via V. Pisani 19 (☎ 02-67581 or for emergency ☎ 02-6758-3994); United Kingdom: Via San Paolo 7 (☎ 02-723-001, or for emergency ☎ 02-862-490); Ireland: Piazza S. Pietro In Gessate 2 (☎ 02-5518-7569); U.S.A.: Via Principe Amedeo 2/10 (☎ 02-290-351); New Zealand: Via Guido D'Arezzo 6 (☎ 02-4801-2544).

ATMs

An exchange bureau is located at the airport and another is inside Stazione Centrale (the main train station). Otherwise, change offices are scattered all around town and concentrated in the *centro.*

Also, outside many banks and at the airport are automatic exchange machines that operate 24 hours a day.

Emergencies

Ambulance, ☎ **118;** fire, ☎ **115;** road assistance, ☎ **116;** Croce Rossa (Red Cross), ☎ **3883;** Polizia Municipale, ☎ **77271;** first aid (Pronto Soccorso), ☎ **02-5503-3209.**

Hospital

Ospedale Policlinico (☎ 02-5503-3209) is at Via Francesco Sforza 35, near the Duomo.

Information

Milan tourist board is in **Piazza Duomo** (APT, Via Marconi 1; ☎ **02-7252-4301;** www.milanoinfotourist.com; open Mon–Fri 8:45 a.m.–8 p.m., Sat 9 a.m.–1 p.m. and 2–7 p.m., and Sun till 5 p.m.). An information booth is inside the **Stazione Centrale**, near the "Gran Bar" (☎ 02-7252-4360; open Mon–Fri 8 a.m.–7 p.m., Sat

9 a.m.–6 p.m., and Sun 9 a.m.–12:30 p.m. and 1:30–6 p.m.).

Internet Access

There is an easyInternetCafe in Piazza Duomo 8 (www.easyinternetcafe. it) open daily 10 a.m.–midnight.

Police

There are two police forces in Italy; call either one. For the Polizia, call ☎ **113**; for the Carabinieri, call ☎ **112**.

Post Office

One of many post offices is at Via Orefici 15 (☎ 02-855-0081), off Piazza Mercanti steps from the Duomo.

Taxi

Radio Taxi ☎ 02-8585, 02-4040, 02-5353, 02-8383, or 02-6767.

Part VI

Naples, Pompeii, and the Amalfi Coast

"He had it made after our trip to Italy. I give you Fontana di Clifford."

In this part . . .

Naples is the capital of Campania, a beautiful region south of Rome. Campania is in many ways the heart of Italy — warm, welcoming, and mysterious. Naples borrows some of its character from Mount Vesuvius, the unpredictable volcano in whose shadow the city lies.

Chapter 20 covers the best of Naples, a city rich in art and a real jewel — especially after the recent restorations and reorganizations in various museums — opening on the most beautiful bay in Italy. Chapter 21 guides you to nearby excursions, including the Roman ruins of Herculaneum and Pompeii, which are really more than just ruins. In fact, their violent instant destruction by Vesuvius's eruption gives them a poignancy that peaceful ruins, eroded over centuries, don't have. Another day trip is to the beautiful isle of Capri, which has entranced the artistic and well-to-do since the Roman Emperor Tiberius rioted here with his playthings. And Chapter 22 leads you along the most celebrated stretch of Italian coast, the justly renowned Amalfi Coast.

Chapter 20

Naples

● ●

In This Chapter

▶ Finding your way to and around the city

▶ Choosing where to stay and where to eat

▶ Soaking up the Neapolitan atmosphere and activities

● ●

Naples (Napoli) can be daunting or seductive, depending on how you look at it. But either way, the former capital of the Kingdom of the Two Sicilies is rich in art, churches, historic sights, and character — and one of the most vital cities anywhere. In a sense, if you haven't seen Naples, you haven't seen Italy. The city used to get a bad rap from the rest of Italy because of its poverty and grunginess — it's legendary for its terrible drivers, thieves, and dirt (a cholera outbreak occurred as late as the 1970s) — but it underwent a real renaissance during the 1990s. During that time, monuments were refurbished and the main squares cleaned up and reclaimed for pedestrians; as a result, the marvelous treasures of Naples are again available to be seen and enjoyed.

Born from the two original Greek colonies of Partenope and Neapolis, the city grew under successive dominations, from the Romans to the Normans to the Angevins (house of Anjou) and finally to the Spanish and the Borbone (the Bourbons). Each group left its mark, making Naples one of the richest art cities in Italy.

You should not try to visit Naples as a day trip. Take the time to explore this vivid, intense destination by spending at least one night. Naples could also be an excellent starting point for exploring sites in the region (see Chapters 21 and 22) or a jumping-off point for Sicily, if you go by boat (see Chapter 23).

Getting There

Although Naples may feel a world apart from Rome or Florence, it is quite convenient to reach by rail, air, sea, or road.

By train

One or more trains per hour leave Rome for Naples; the trip takes about 2½ hours and costs around 15€ ($17). The trip from Florence is about 4½ hours and costs about 35€ ($40), and the trip from Venice 7½ hours and 50€ ($58). Naples's surprisingly pleasant **Stazione Centrale** (☎ 081-554-3188) is on Piazza Garibaldi, in the city center. (Naples's other train station, **Stazione Mergellina,** on Piazza Piedigrotta, is convenient to the western part of town.) Piazza Garibaldi is a major hub for city buses and the subway line and also has a taxi station. The city center lies only a few blocks west, but the area around the station is grungy, so you may want to catch a cab or public transportation to get to the city center; walking through the area surrounding the station could spoil your first impression of this otherwise beautiful town.

By plane

About 7km (4 miles) from the city center, the small **Aeroporto Capodichino** (☎ 081-789-6111; www.gesac.it) receives daily flights from other cities in Italy. The easiest way to get into town is by taking a taxi directly to your hotel; expect to pay about 30€ ($35) for the 15-minute trip.

By ferry

Naples's harbor is the major port of central Italy, with ferries and cruise ships pulling in and out from various destinations daily. Sailing into the **Stazione Marittima** seaport, just off Via Cristoforo Colombo, is the best way to arrive in Naples: you will get the full effect of the magical beauty of the bay, and you will arrive in the heart of town, where most of the attractions lie. One of the most interesting possibilities is taking a ferry to or from Sicily, saving many hours of driving (see Chapter 23 for complete details on rates and schedules), but you could also come in from other destinations.

By car

Driving in Naples is challenging, even for Italians, and we do not recommend it. Also, Naples is infamous for car theft, even from inside guarded parking lots. If you think you need a car to explore further destinations such as the Amalfi Coast, think again, and see Chapter 22 for better options.

Orienting Yourself in Naples

Forced by the shape of the surrounding land — high cliffs overlooking the sea — Naples developed like a crescent along the bay. Some neighborhoods are up on the cliff, but the part of town where you'll spend most of your time is down by the water and on the slopes under the cliff.

The Gulf of Naples and Salerno

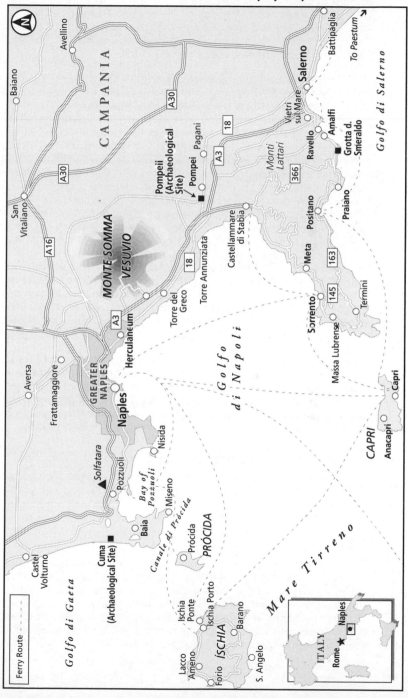

Riviera di Chiaia lies at northern part of the crescent, with the promenade of **Via Partenope** overlooking the sea and **Castel dell'Ovo,** on a small island at the end of a causeway. At the other tip of the crescent are the more industrial and popular neighborhoods of Naples. The **Stazione Centrale** is just southeast of the *centro storico.*

The ***centro storico*** (historic center) occupies the center of the crescent. Between Chiaia and the *centro storico* is the small neighborhood of **Santa Lucia.** Towards the sea is the **Stazione Marittima (seaport),** and just inland are the major monuments of the Neapolitan political establishment: the **Palazzo San Giacomo** — today the city hall; **Castel Nuovo** — built by the Angevins as the center for their two-century-long kingdom; and **Palazzo Reale** on **Piazza del Plebiscito** — the Royal Palace built under the Spanish. Going uphill from Piazza del Plebiscito, **Via Toledo** is Naples's main street, lined with elegant palaces and fashionable shops. On the left are the **Quartieri Spagnoli,** the tight grid of narrow streets built by the Spanish in the 16th century, mainly to house their troops; today it's the embodiment of "Neapolitanness" — laundry drying at windows, mammas screaming at their kids down in the street, motor scooters rushing past, and so on. Branching east from Via Toledo are **Via Benedetto Croce** and **Via Biagio dei Librai** — colloquially referred to by the name **Spacca Napoli** because they seem to divide the center of town in two parts. Parallel to the north is **Via dei Tribunali**, and parallel to the south runs **Corso Umberto I.** Along those streets are concentrated some of the most important attractions, including important churches and *palazzi,* as well as the university.

Above the *centro storico* lies the **Vomero** — with **Castel Sant'Elmo** and the **Certosa di San Martino** and, on a separate hill **Capodimonte,** with its royal palace, park, and museum. Technically not Naples proper, **Mergellina,** the pleasure harbor of Naples, lies at the northern tip of the crescent and to the west is the towering promontory lined by **Via Posillipo** leading to the very pretty small square of **Marechiaro.**

Introducing the neighborhoods

With the exception of the area around Stazione Centrale, which is seedy, all the central neighborhoods of Naples are safe, but you will want to watch your purse and your belongings carefully no matter where you are: pickpockets and purse grabbers are a sad — and abundant — reality.

Centro storico

This is the city's heart, historically and geographically turned toward the sea. This is where you will find Naples's most important churches and monuments, but this is also where the political buildings and the university are located. The area is alive with local life in every age range and very authentic. If you can spare having views over the bay, this is a very convenient part of town to find your hotel, and it's also rich with shops, restaurants, and nightlife.

Naples

Legend:
- ✝ Church
- ⓘ Information
- 🗼 Lighthouse
- – – Ⓜ Metro

0 — 1/4 mi
0 — 0.25 km

PARCO DI CAPODIMONTE **1**

CAPODIMONTE

Albergo dei Poveri

ORTO BOTANICO

ITALY
Rome ★
Naples ●

PIAZZA CAVOUR Ⓜ

Stazione Centrale ⓘ

CENTRALE

Piazza Garibaldi

Castel Capuana

Duomo **4**

Piazza Bellini

San Lorenzo Maggiore

San Domenico Maggiore ✝

MONTESANTO Ⓜ

Stazione Cumana

Piazza Dante

Piazza del Mercato

CENTRO STORICO Università

Stazione Circumvesuviana

Via Marinella

Bacino del Piliero

Stazione Marittima

Piazza Municipio

Molo Beverello ⓘ

Bacino Angiono

Piazza Plebiscito

SANTA LUCIA

Golfo di Napoli

←To Chiaia & Mergellina

Castel dell'Ovo **26**

ACCOMMODATIONS ■
Chiaja Hotel **17**
Grand Hotel Santa Lucia **25**
Hotel Miramare **24**
Hotel Rex **22**
Il Convento **10**
Mercure Angioino **13**

ATTRACTIONS ●
Castel dell'Ovo **26**
Castel Nuovo or Maschio Angioino and Museo Civico **20**
Castel Sant'Elmo/ Certosa di San Martino **9**
Catacombe di San Gennaro **2**
Duomo (Cattedrale di Santa Maria Assunta) **4**
Galleria Umberto I **14**
Museo Archeologico Nazionale (Archaeological Museum) **3**
Museo e Gallerie Nazionali di Capodimonte **1**
Palazzo Reale **19**
Santa Chiara **7**
Sant'Anna dei Lombardi **8**
Teatro San Carlo **18**

DINING ◆
Amici Miei **23**
Brandi **16**
Ciro a Santa Brigida **11**
Europeo di Mattozzi **12**
I Re di Napoli **5, 15**
La Cantinella **21**
Pasticceria Scaturchio **6**

Mergellina

This is where Neapolitans come for a romantic dinner by the sea. It is a very pleasant area but you are a bit distant from the center of town.

Riviera di Chiaia

Along the sea, this area is famous for its elegant hotels and view over the bay — which, by the way, was much better before the 19th century, when they filled the waterfront and advanced the *lungomare* (promenade) of **Via Partenope** to its present position. Along the pleasant green of the **Villa Comunale** and the gardens of the **Villa Pignatelli,** you will be a short distance from the *centro storico* and its attractions and in one of the best shopping areas in town.

Santa Lucia

Right behind the **Castel dell'Ovo,** this secluded area by the sea also affords beautiful views over the bay from some elegant hotels, but it doesn't have the glamorous life — shopping or nightlife — of the Riviera di Chiaia.

The Vomero

The higher part of town, the **Vomero,** is where the *Napoli bene* (the city's middle and upper classes) live. The air here is fresher — an important plus in summer — and the views over the city and the bay spectacular, but don't expect much in terms of shopping or nightlife.

Finding information after you arrive

You will find the main tourist office off the Riviera di Chiaia (Piazza dei Martiri 58; ☎ 081-405-311) and small tourist booths in the railroad stations **Stazione Centrale** (Piazza Garibaldi; ☎ 081-268-799; Metro: Piazza Garibaldi) and **Stazione Mergellina** (Piazza Piedigrotta; ☎ 081-761-2102; Metro: Mergellina). However, you get the best assistance at the tourist offices of **Via San Carlo** (Via San Carlo 9; ☎ 081-402-394. www.inaples.it), **Piazza del Gesù** (☎ 081-551-2701), **Palazzo Reale** (Piazza del Plebiscito 1; ☎ 081-252-5711), and **Via Marino Turchi** (Via Marino Turchi 16; ☎ 081-240-0911).

Getting Around Naples

On foot

Naples is a large, bustling city. But the parts that attract tourists are relatively concentrated, and you can cover a lot of this ground on foot. Naples offers beautiful walks, particularly near the major sights. All the areas we describe in the preceding sections are safe to explore on foot.

By subway, bus, funicular, and tram

The city transportation authority (☎ 800-482-644; www.ctpn.it), maintains an information booth at Stazione Centrale on Piazza Garibaldi where you can get an excellent public transportation map. Individual tickets cost .77€ (90¢) and are valid for unlimited travel for 90 minutes. You can buy them at bars, tobacconists, and newsstands around town. You can also buy a **giornaliero,** valid for unlimited travel for one day for 2.32€ ($2.70). Both tickets are labeled **GiraNapoli** and may be used on the funicular, tram, bus, and metro. **Unico** tickets are used for the larger metropolitan area of Naples. An individual ticket is valid 100 minutes and costs 1.29€ ($1.50) and the **giornaliero** is valid from 10 a.m. to midnight and costs between 2.07€ ($2.40) and 3.10€ ($3.60), depending on which day of the week and how large an area your ticket covers.

The **Metropolitana (subway)** line makes a few widely spaced stops but is quite useful for avoiding the city traffic. Surprisingly, little of it is actually underground; it's an urban railroad more than a subway and is, in fact, linked to the rail system. It runs daily from 5:00 a.m. to 11:30 p.m.

Because of traffic, regular **buses** are slow and crowded — **tram lines** are only slightly better because most of their tracks are not on separated lanes. Most tourist destinations, though, are served by special fast lines *(linee rosse,* red lines, marked by a letter *R)* running much more frequently. The *linee rosse* run daily from roughly 5:30 a.m. to midnight; other bus and tramway lines stop earlier, some as early as 8:30 p.m. A number of *linee notturne* (night lines) usually start around midnight and run with an hourly frequency.

Given the city's development over the cliffs surrounding the bay, Naples enjoys a special kind of transportation: the **funicular** (railway pulled up and over hills by cables) — here called the *Funivia.* Three funiculars connect the lower town to the higher one: **Montesanto** (at the metro station Montesanto, running daily 7 a.m.–10 p.m.), **Chiaia** (from Piazza Amedeo, running Mon–Thurs 7 a.m.–9 p.m. and Fri–Sun 7 a.m.–1 a.m.), and **Centrale** (from Via Toledo, off Piazza Trieste e Trento, running daily 6 a.m.–1 a.m.). **Mergellina** also has a funicular, from Via Mergellina by the harbor (running daily from 7 a.m.–10 p.m.). The Funivia accepts regular transportation tickets (see the preceding section).

By taxi

Naples has a number of taxi stations, where taxis wait in line for customers near major hubs and attractions. You can also call a **radio taxi** at ☎ 081-556-4444. Beware, though, that the driving in Naples is reckless — even if you're in a taxi — and Neapolitans are known for rounding up their fares to make a little extra money (try not to look so gullible — you'll be an easy target for such things). Although practices have changed a lot, a few taxi drivers still pretend their meter is broken in order to charge a little more. If this happens to you, take another cab.

A number of destinations have fixed fares, and *not* using the meter is therefore legal. For example, if you're traveling from the airport to your hotel, or to the Museo Capodimonte, you're charged a set fare. If you are planning a different trip from those above, ask your concierge for an estimate of what a reasonable fare might be. Get a quote from the taxi driver before boarding: if it is not extravagant, it is probably correct.

Beware of illegal taxis, the main reason why Naples cabbies get a bad rap. Always take a taxi from an official taxi stand or make sure you only get in authorized vehicles, painted white (or yellow for the older models) and sometimes emblazoned with a *Comune di Napoli* (Naples municipality) mark.

Staying in Style

Naples offers a big selection of hotels ranging from glitzy to modest. Naples is a cheaper destination than Rome, Florence, or Venice, so you will be able to treat yourself to a higher caliber of hotel. Which is good because, frankly, you don't want to stay in a marginal area of Naples just to save a few euro.

Chiaja Hotel
$$ **Centro storico**

On the second floor of the restored residence of the Marquis Lecaldano Sasso La Terza, this new hotel offers guest rooms with a decor that manages to be both elegant (in an ornate Neapolitan style) and cozy. Located just steps from all the major attractions in Naples, it also provides excellent service — you can even get someone to sing a real Neapolitan serenade to your loved one!

See map p. 419. Via Chiaja 216, just off Piazza Plebiscito. ☎ *081-415-555. Fax: 081-422-344.* www.hotelchiaia.it. *Bus: R2 to Piazza Municipio. Parking: 16€ ($18). Rack rates: 160€ ($184) double. Rates include buffet breakfast. AE, DC, MC, V.*

Grand Hotel Parker's
$$$$ **Vomero**

Dating from 1870, this historic hotel sits on the hill overlooking the center of Naples and the harbor and affords grand views of the beautiful bay; its neoclassical interior and ornate Liberty (Italian Art Nouveau) plasterwork have been completely preserved and restored. The large, elegant guest rooms are decorated in period furniture and many offer views. The roof garden houses **George's,** maybe the best restaurant in Naples, where you can enjoy creative regional cuisine and a magnificent view in an elegant setting (the restaurant was just renovated in 2004).

Corso Vittorio Emanuele 135. ☎ *081-761-2474. Fax: 081-663-527.* www.grandhotelparkers.com. *Metro: Piazza Amedeo. Parking: 16€ ($18). Rack rates: 350€ ($403) double. Rates include buffet breakfast. AE, DC, MC, V.*

Grand Hotel Santa Lucia
$$$ Riviera di Chiaia

One of the best, and reknowned in Napoli, this elegant historic hotel offers beautiful rooms with great views over the Castel dell'Ovo and the bay. The bright guest rooms are decorated with pastel colors and period furniture (antiques and good-quality reproductions) and the service is excellent.

*See map p. 419. Via Partenope 46. ☎ **081-764-0666**. Fax: 081-764-8580.* www.santa lucia.it. *Bus: R2 to Piazza Municipio. Parking: 18€ ($21). Rack rates: 255€ ($293) double. Rates include buffet breakfast. AE, DC, MC, V.*

Hotel Miramare
$$ Santa Lucia

Built in 1914 as a private villa, this charming hotel right on the water offers bright guest rooms with beautiful baths, decorated with quality modern furniture, many with views over the sea. Recently renovated, this villa was the American consulate before being converted into a hotel. The public areas are still decorated in the original Liberty style and breakfast is served on a terrace overlooking the bay. A second panoramic terrace is used as solarium. Guests at the hotel received a 10-percent discount at the nearby **La Cantinella** restaurant (see "Dining Out," later in this chapter).

*See map p. 419. Via Nazario Sauro 24. ☎ **081-764-7589**. Fax: 081-764-0775.* www. hotelmiramare.com. *Bus/Tram: Bus R3 or tram 4 to Via Acton. Parking: 22€ ($25). Rack rates: 190€ ($219) double. Rates include buffet breakfast. AE, DC, MC, V.*

Hotel Rex
$ Santa Lucia

The Rex is well known (read: reserve well in advance) as a moderately priced hotel in the waterside neighborhood of Santa Lucia. It offers simply but carefully decorated guest rooms, some with a view over the harbor or Vesuvio, and all with private balconies. Housed in a 19th-century palace, most rooms and baths are good-sized; contrasting with its lavish exterior, the room furniture is simple (many rooms are decorated in a 1960s style) but in good repair. A very nice breakfast is served in your room.

*See map p. 419. Via Palepoli 12. ☎ **081-764-9389**. Fax: 081-764-9227. Bus/Tram: Bus R3 or tram 4 to Via Acton. Parking: 22€ ($25). Rack rates: 100€ ($115) double. Rates include breakfast. AE, V.*

Il Convento
$ Centro Storico

Housed in a 17th-century palace in the heart of Naples, this hotel offers carefully restored guest rooms and public spaces at a moderate price. Guest rooms have pastel-colored plaster walls and quality modern furniture in dark wood. Some guest rooms have wooden beams, others have arches or private roof gardens.

See map p. 419. Via Speranzella 137/a. ☎ *081-403-977. Fax: 081-400-332.* www.hotel ilconvento.it. *Bus: R2 to Piazza Municipio. Parking: 16€ ($18). Rack rates: 130€ ($150) double. Rates include breakfast. AE, DC, MC, V.*

Mercure Angioino
$$ Piazza Municipio

Located between the university and the harbor, this recently opened hotel is within sight of the Angioino castle and is both modern and convenient. Housed in a beautiful, restored 19th-century building, the Mercure offers rooms that are simple, with large beds, modern furniture, and carpeting; one floor is nonsmoking.

Via Depretis 123. ☎ *081-552-9500. Fax: 081-552-9509. E-mail:* mercure.napoli angioino@accor-hotels.it. *Bus: R2 to Piazza Municipio. Parking: 15€ ($17). Rack rates: 180€ ($207) double. Rates include buffet breakfast. AE, DC, MC, V.*

Dining Out

Although Naples has not yet been fully touched by the wave that has hit the northern part of the Italian peninsula, you can eat well enough in Naples — in a good, simple and traditional way. There are not as many restaurants, though, as you would think.

If you have a sweet tooth, try Naples's specialties (see Chapter 2 for details) at the **Pasticceria Scaturchio** (Piazza San Domenico Maggiore 19–24; ☎ 081-551-6944; Bus: R2), one of the oldest pastry shops in town, established in 1903. Besides wonderful pastries, you may also want to sample their *Ministeriale,* a medallion of dark chocolate with a liqueur cream filling.

Amici Miei
$ Centro Storico   NEAPOLITAN/ITALIAN

Popular with locals, this restaurant offers a refreshing change from the somewhat trite menu in most Neapolitan restaurants, with a large variety of meat choices, including unusual ones such as *struzzo* (ostrich), and *oca* (goose), usually grilled or roasted. Among the *primi,* the *panzerottini alla ricotta* (homemade pasta filled with ricotta), the *risotto ai fiori di zucchine* (risotto with zucchini flowers), and the *pappardelle al sugo di agnello* (homemade pasta with a lamb sauce) are very good. The homemade breads are excellent.

See map p. 419. Via Monte di Dio 77/78. ☎ *081-764-6063. Fax: 081-245-5995. Reservations required. Secondi: 11€–13€ ($13–$15). AE, DC, MC, V. Open: Lunch Tues–Sun, dinner Tues–Sat; closed 2 weeks in July and Sept.*

Brandi
$ **Centro Storico** PIZZA

Literally fit for a queen, this pizzeria opened in the 19th century and is the place where *pizza margherita* was invented. It takes its name from Margherita di Savoia, first queen of Italy, who graciously accepted having a pizza named after her (how many sovereigns can say that?). The pizza comes with tomato, basil, and mozzarella — red, green, and white, not coincidentally the colors of the united Italy. Brandi's menu includes many dishes other than pizza, all well prepared.

See map p. 419. Salita Sant'Anna di Palazzo. ☎ *081-416-928. Reservations required. Bus: R2 or R3 to Piazza Trieste e Trento. Secondi: 7€–18€ ($8.05–$21). No credit cards accepted. Open: Lunch and dinner Tues–Sun.*

Ciro a Santa Brigida
$$$ **Centro Storico** NEAPOLITAN

This famous historical restaurant offers excellent food and professional service. The extensive menu — accompanied by an equally extensive wine list — includes the best dishes of the Neapolitan tradition, all prepared with attention to detail and the freshest ingredients. In addition to its homemade pastas and daily fish dishes, this restaurant is famous for its *fritti* (deep-fried specialties), and for the quality and variety of traditional vegetable *contorni*. They also serve excellent pizza and a large selection of desserts.

See map p. 419. Via Santa Brigida 71, off Via Toledo and the Galleria Umberto I. ☎ *081-552-4072. Reservations required. Bus: R2 or R3 to Piazza Trieste e Trento. Secondi: 18€–25€ ($21–$29). AE, DC, MC, V. Open: Lunch and dinner Mon–Sat.*

Don Salvatore
$$$ **Mergellina** NEAPOLITAN/FISH

On the Mergellina waterfront, near the dock where the ferries leave for Capri, Don Salvatore is the perfect example of a Neapolitan seaside trattoria, down to the large families of locals who like to come for lunch on weekends. Children are welcome and the kitchen is ready to accommodate their special needs. In this atmospheric restaurant (it's housed in a former boat shed) you can enjoy nicely grilled fresh fish, accompanied by local vegetables, or else opt for some of the seafood pasta or *risotti*. Very good is the *linguine incaciate* (pasta with cheese). The restaurant features an excellent wine list.

Strada Mergellina 4/a. ☎ *081-681-817. Reservations recommended. Metro: Mergellina. Secondi: 10€–21€ ($12–$24). AE, DC, MC, V. Open: Lunch and dinner Thurs–Tues winter; daily in summer.*

Europeo di Mattozzi
$$ Centro Storico NEAPOLITAN/FISH

In the welcoming atmosphere of this historical dining room, the modern chef offers you tasty choices inspired to the local tradition. Excellent choices in include the *zuppa di cannellini e cozze* (bean and mussel soup) and the *pasta e patate con provola* (pasta and potatoes with melted local cheese), the *scorfano all' acquapazza* (scorpion-fish in a light herbed broth), and the *stoccafisso alla pizzaiola* (codfish in a tomato, garlic and oregano sauce). The *pizze* are also very good. Leave room for the great traditional desserts such as the *babà* (sort of liquor-soaked brioche with a dollop of pastry cream), and the *pastiera* (tart filled with a creamy wheatberry and candied fruit mixture).

See map p. 419. Via Marchese Campodisola 4. ☎ *081-552-1323. Reservations required. Bus: R2 or R3 to Piazza Trieste e Trento. Secondi: 11€–16€ ($13–$18). AE, DC, MC, V. Open: Lunch Mon–Sat and dinner Thurs–Sat; in summer dinner Thurs–Fri only. Closed 2 weeks in Aug.*

1 Re di Napoli
$ Piazza Plebescito NEAPOLITAN/PIZZA

With a view of the open space and grand buildings of the Piazza Plebescito, and with outdoor dining in good weather, this is a nice place to sample Naples's greatest culinary contribution. In addition to its fine pizza, it has a full range of *antipasti* and vegetable dishes. A second location is near the archaeological museum (Piazza Dante 16, off via Toledo), which is also open from lunch until 1 a.m.

See map p. 419. Piazza Trieste e Trento 7. ☎ *081-423-013.* www.netlab.it/redi napoli. *Reservations recommended. Bus/Tram: Bus R3 or R2 to Piazza Trieste e Trento. Pizza: 5€–9€ ($5.75–$10). AE, DC, MC, V. Open: Lunch and dinner daily.*

La Cantinella
$$$$ Santa Lucia NEAPOLITAN/CREATIVE/FISH

One of the best and most-loved restaurants in Naples, this waterfront spot has plenty of style. It feels like a 1930s nightclub or something out of a movie, but the food is pure Neapolitan, with excellent *antipasto* and grilled seafood. Try the *pappardelle "sotto il cielo di Napoli"* (homemade pasta with zucchini, prawns, and green tomatoes) and the excellent *fritto misto* (deep-fried calamari, small fish, and shrimp). Do not forget the wine — the selection is excellent — or the dessert (if you have the patience for the lengthy preparation, choose the fantastic soufflé).

See map p. 419. Via Cuma 42. ☎ *081-764-8684. Reservations required. Bus/Tram: Bus R3 or tram 4 to Via Acton. Secondi: 19€–31€ ($22–$36). AE, DC, MC, V. Open: Lunch and dinner Mon–Sat. Closed 1 week in January and 3 weeks in Aug.*

Exploring Naples

If you visit Naples during the spring you will be able to enjoy special openings — both extended hours and opening of usually closed sights — during the **Napoli Museo Aperto** initiative.

Naples's **artecard** (☎ **800-600-601** or 06-3996-7650; www.campani artecard.it) is a really good deal, which comes in several money-saving versions. The most comprehensive is the "**3 day all the sites,**" which costs 25€ ($29) and gives you free admission to two attractions of your choice and a 50-percent discount on all the others, plus access to all public transportation, including the regional trains and special buses you need to get to certain sights. A simpler version is the 13€ ($15) "**3 day Napoli e Campi Flegrei**" card which gives you free admission to two attractions of your choice and a 50-percent discount on all the others *within* Naples and the Campi Flegrei, plus access to urban public trans-portation and the Archeobus to Campi Flegrei. Even if you are not going to the Campi Flegrei, this is a good deal. The card also grants discounts at a number of other attractions, shops, and entertainment venues. Sites included within Naples are Museo Archeologico, Museo di Capodimonte, Certosa and Museo Di San Martino, Castel Sant' Elmo, Museo Civico di Castelnuovo, Palazzo Reale, and Città Della Scienza; sites outside Naples are Pompei and Ercolano (Herculaneum) as well as Caserta, Capua, Paestum, Velia, and Padula, and of course the Campi Flegrei. The card is for sale at all participating sites as well as at the Capodichino airport, the molo Beverello (harbor), the train stations of Napoli Cantrale and Mergellina, major hotels, and news kiosks.

The top attractions

Castel dell'Ovo (Castle of the Egg)

The promontory projecting into the harbor where the castle stands is where the first Greek colonists landed in the ninth century B.C., and where, in Roman times, the celebrated gourmand Lucullus had his villa — or so it is believed. A symbol of the city and an important landmark, the current fortress was built by Frederick II and enlarged by the Angevins. The name originated in the Middle Ages and was probably based on the belief that Virgil (author of the *Aeneid* and reputed magician) placed a magic egg under the castle's foundations to protect it; this ploy apparently wasn't too successful, because the castle collapsed and the present one was built over the site. You have a beautiful view of the castle from **Via Partenope,** the promenade overlooking the sea, which merges into the **Riviera di Chiaia** farther west. Inside, the castle is a fortified citadel wth some very interesting architectural gems, such as the **Sala delle Colonne (Hall of the Columns)** and the **Loggiato**. From its wall you can enjoy a superb view over the city. Currently, the castle is open only for special exhibits.

See map p. 419. Borgo Marinari. ☎ 081-764-0590. Bus/Tram: Bus R3 or tram 4 to Via Acton, Porto Santa Lucia. Admission: Depending on the exhibit.

Castel Nuovo or Maschio Angioino and Museo Civico

Built in the 13th century by Carlo d'Angió (Angevin dynasty) as the new royal residence — the Castel dell'Ovo and Castel Capuano didn't fit the needs of the new kingdom — this castle was renovated in the 15th century. The inland facade is graced by the grandiose **Triumphal Arch of Alfonso I of Aragona,** a splendid example of early Renaissance architecture, the work of Francesco Laurana to commemorate the 1443 expulsion of the Angevins by the forces of Alphonso I. Inside beyond the courtyard and up the stair is the **Sala dei Baroni (Barons Hall),** a monumental room with a star-shaped ceiling which was once decorated by Giotto, but his frescoes have been lost. Also lost are most of the sculptures that had decorated the room, all destroyed by a fire in 1919. Today the Hall is the seat of the Municipal Council. Also inside is the **Civic Museum (Museo Civico),** through which you can visit the **Cappella Palatina** or of Santa Barbara, the chapel opening onto the castle's courtyard. The carved portal and rose window are from the 15th century — the originals were destroyed by an earthquake. The Cappella Palatina was also completely decorated by Giotto, but only a few fragments remain. The chapel houses a collection of 14th-century frescoes from nearby churches and a fine collection of 15th-century sculpture including Domenico Gagini's (pupil of Donatello and Brinelleschi) altarpiece of Madonna and child, and two Madonnas by Francesco Laurana. The second and third floor contain a collection of paintings from the 15th to the 20th century and church ornaments.

See map p. 419. Piazza Municipio. ☎ *081-795-5877. Bus: R1 or R4. Admission: 5.16€ ($6). Open: Mon–Sat 9 a.m.–7 p.m.*

Duomo or Cattedrale di Santa Maria Assunta

The 14th-century Duomo may not be the most interesting church in town, but it houses the **Cappella di San Gennaro,** named after the patron saint of Naples. The chapel is richly decorated with goldwork, and protects the gold bust of the saint that contains his skull and a vial of his blood — the blood is said to become liquid each May and September; it's a sign of great misfortune for the whole town if the miracle doesn't take place. In the left nave is the original paleo-Christian basilica of **Santa Restituta;** it and its adjoining baptistry are decorated with beautiful mosaics and were absorbed into the Duomo and refurbished in the 17th century. In the transept is the **Cappella Minutolo** with **Perugino's** *Assunta*. Ask in the sacristy if you'd like to see Santa Restituta and Cappella Minutolo.

See map p. 419. Via Duomo 147. ☎ *081-449-097. Metro: Piazza Cavour. Admission: 2.60€ ($3). Open: Mon–Sat 8 a.m.–12:30 p.m. and 4:30 p.m.–7 p.m; Sun and holidays 8 a.m.–1:30 p.m. and 5–7:30 p.m.*

Museo Archeologico Nazionale (Archaeological Museum)

The National Archaeological Museum contains one of the greatest collections of treasures from antiquity in the world. If you want to visit just one archaeological museum in Italy, make it this one. Among the holdings is a superb collection of **Roman sculptures,** many copied from Greek originals of the fourth and fifth centuries B.C. and reflecting the Roman incorporation of Hellenism into its art. The most stunning is the massive *Toro Romano,* which depicts several warriors trying to harness the surging figure of a bull — a dramatic scene come to life in marble. In addition, the museum is the repository for objects from archaeological excavations in southern Italy, particularly Pompeii and Herculaneum. One of the stars in the vast collection of mosaics and frescoes on display is the huge mosaic of the victory of Alexander the Great over the Persians. Other mosaics naturalistically depict fish, animals, birds, and themes from mythology. The diversity of other objects in the museum is amazing; whether it's a **gladiator's helmet, exquisite cameo vases,** or the tiny **head of a centurion carved in bone** with great psychological realism, you will marvel at the artistic heights Rome achieved. The **Gabinetto segreto (secret room)** is a historic collection of Roman erotica (famous already in Goethe's day). It is now housed in a special room and documents the ancient attitude toward sexuality (guilt-free and frank, to say the least). We recommended that you rent an audioguide for your visit.

See map p. 419. Piazza Museo Nazionale 18–19. ☎ *081-440-166. Metro: Piazza Cavour. Admission: 6.50€ ($7.50). Audioguide: 4€ ($4.60). Open: Wed–Mon 9 a.m.– 8 p.m. Ticket booth closes 1 hour before museum closing.*

Museo e Gallerie Nazionali di Capodimonte

Recently restored and reorganized, this museum holds a first-class painting collection that contains several masterpieces On the second floor, the Farnese collection includes Masaccio's *Crucifixion,* Perugino's *Madonna and Child,* Bruegel's *Misanthrope,* and Filippino Lippi's *Annunciation and Saints,* plus works by Mantegna, Raphael, Titian, and Botticelli; on the third floor the *pinacoteca* **Borbonica D'Avolos** (a 16th-century family) includes the famous 16th-century **tapestry series** of the Battle of Pavia as well as important paintings such as Simone Martini's *San Ludovico di Tolosa,* Tiziano's *Annonciation,* and Caravaggio's *Flagellation.* The building is itself a masterpiece: The **Palazzo Capodimonte** and the surrounding park were built in the 18th century as a royal hunting residence and museum, situated to afford beautiful views over the city and bay. You can also see what the palace was like originally in the **royal apartments** on the second floor, full of priceless objects, tapestries, and statuary.

See map p. 419. Palazzo Capodimonte, Via Miano 1 and Via Capodimonte. ☎ *081- 749-9111. Bus: 24 to Parco Capodimonte. Admission: 7.50€ ($8.60); 6.50€ ($7.50) from 2–5 p.m. Audioguide: 4€ ($4.60). Open: Tues–Sun 8:30 a.m.–7:30 p.m. Ticket booth closes 1 hour before museum closing.*

Palazzo Reale

The imposing neoclassical Royal Palace was designed by Domenico Fontana and built by the Bourbons in the 17th century; the eight statues on the facade are of Neapolitan kings. Inside you can visit the **royal apartments,** richly appointed with marble floors, tapestries, frescoes, and baroque furniture. The **library,** established by Charles de Bourbon, is one of the greatest in the south, with more than 1,250,000 volumes. The *palazzo* retains its glamour to this day and was used as the venue for a G7 summit meeting in 1994. If it is still there, do not miss the splendid 18th-century Presepio del Banco di Napoli (crèche), at press time exposed in the **Cappella.** Many of its characters have been carved by famous Neapolitan sculptors of the time. To bring the *palazzo* to life, you might want to reserve a guided tour, available in English.

See map p. 419. Piazza del Plebiscito 1. ☎ *081-580-8111. Bus: R2 or R3 to Piazza Trieste e Trento. Admission: 4€ ($4.60), courtyard and gardens free. Guided tour by reservation 3€ ($3.45). Open: Thurs–Tues 9 a.m.–8 p.m. Ticket booth closes 1 hour before museum closing.*

Santa Chiara

Built at the beginning of the 14th century as the burial church for the d'Angió dynasty, Santa Chiara was once the center of a large monastic complex for the order of the Clarisse. The church was severely damaged by World War II bombing and an ensuing fire, but it has been restored somewhat to its original look. Although damaged, the monumental **tomb of Roberto d'Angió** at the end of the nave is still a magnificent example of Tuscan-style Renaissance sculpture. Also interesting is the **Coro delle Clarisse (Choir of the Clarisses),** where the nuns can sit protected from the public during mass. The key attraction is the **Chiostro delle Clarisse,** the uniquely beautiful cloister behind the church (turn around the church to the left). On the piazza outside the church is one of Naples's several baroque spires, the **Guglia dell'Immacolata,** a tall pile of statues and reliefs from 1750.

See map p. 419. Via Santa Chiaa 49. ☎ *081-552-6280. Metro: Montesanto. Admission: Church free, cloister 3.10€ ($3.60). Open: Thurs–Sat and Mon–Tues 9 a.m.–1 p.m. and 4–6 p.m.; Sun 9 a.m.–1 p.m.*

Sant'Anna dei Lombardi aka Santa Maria di Monteoliveto

Recently restored, this church — built in the 15th century and transformed in the 17th — is famous for its rich collection of Renaissance sculpture. The Cappella Piccolomini houses the tomb of Maria d'Aragona by Antonio Rossellino and Benedetto da Maiano, whereas in the Cappella Mastro Giudice, you will find the *Annunciazione* by Benedetto da Maiano; also noteworthy are the Cappella Terranova and the Tuscan-influenced Cappella Tolosa, decorated in the styles of Brunelleschi and della Robbia. In the sacristy are frescoes by Giorgio Vasari and helpers, as well as the spectacular wood inlay work by Giovanni da Verona (created 1506–1510) depicting classical panoramas, musical instruments, and other scenes with thousands of tiny slivers of wood of various kinds and colors.

See map p. 419. Piazza Monteoliveto 44. ☎ *081-551-3333. Metro: Montesanto. Admission: Free. Open: Mon–Sat 8:30 a.m.–noon; Sat also 5:30–6:30 p.m.*

More cool things to see and do

Here are some more sights to explore:

- Built at the end of the 19th century (20 years after its larger Milanese counterpart), the **Galleria Umberto I** (Bus: R2 or R3 to Piazza Trieste e Trento) is a splendid example of the Liberty style (Italian Art Nouveau). Opening to the right of Via Toledo as you come from Piazza del Plebiscito, the glass-and-iron galleria is an enormous airy space with a soaring glass ceiling, and is lined with graciously decorated buildings and elegant shops. Come to marvel at the architecture and even to shop (see "Shopping the Local Stores," later in this chapter).

- Built by the Borbone at the beginning of the 18th century, the **Teatro San Carlo** (Via San Carlo 98/f; ☎ 081-400-300 for reservations; Bus: R2 or R3 to Via San Carlo) is among Europe's most beautiful opera houses, a neoclassical jewel with an ornate gilded interior. It is also the first opera theater in the world and it is said to have even better acoustics than Milan's famous La Scala. You can appreciate its architecture and decoration by taking the free guided tour (by reservation), but of course you can also come for a performance (see "Living it Up After Dark," later in this chapter) and hear the building in its full glory.

- If you want an excuse to take the funicular, head to the **Certosa di San Martino (Carthusian Monastery of St. Martin),** set in a beautiful park that has great views over the city from terraced gardens. The monastery was built in the 14th century but rebuilt in the 17th; the church is considered the most important baroque church in the city. The monastery houses the **Museo Nazionale di San Martino** (☎ 081-578-1769; admission: 6€/$6.90 and includes admission to Castel Sant'Elmo. Open: Tues–Sun 8:30 a.m.–7:30 p.m.), which displays several collections — paintings, sculpture, and porcelain — but the most important is the recently restored collection of *presepi* (crèches). Crèches in Naples evolved into an art form which reached its peak in the 18th and 19th century, and the tradition is still alive today (see "Shopping the Local Stores," later in this chapter). This collection includes the most famous historical *presepio,* the **Cuciniello** from 1879, to the creation of which collaborated sculptors and architects. Near the Certosa is **Castel Sant'Elmo** (Via Tito Angelini 20; ☎ 081-578-4030. *Funivia:* Centrale from Piazza Trento e Trieste to the last stop), a 14th-century castle restored in the 16th century. It's open Tuesday through Sunday from 8:30 a.m. to 7:30 p.m.; admission is 1€ ($1.15) or free with paid admission to Museo Nazionale di San Martino.

- In use between the second and ninth centuries, the **Catacombe di San Gennaro (Catacombs of St. Gennaro),** located at Via Capodimonte 13, down a small alley running alongside the church Madre del Buon Consiglio (☎ 081-741-1071; Bus: 24 to Via Capodimonte; admission: 2.58€/$3), are particularly famous for the well-maintained frescoes decorating the large corridors — different from the Roman catacombs. Also buried in these catacombs is San Gennaro, the patron saint of Naples — hence the name — whose remains were moved here in the fifth century. You can visit only by guided tour Tuesday through Sunday at 9 a.m., 10 a.m., 11 a.m., and noon.

Guided tours

If you like hop-on-and-off tours, Napoli finally has its own variation, offered by **CitySightseeing** (☎ 081-551-7279; www.napoli.city-sight seeing.it). Two one-hour itineraries start from Piazza Municipio/Parco Castello: Line A travels inland up to the Museo di Capodimonte, and Line B moves along the seaside to Posillipo. Buses depart every 30 minutes daily, October to May from 9 a.m.–6:30 p.m. From June to September, Line A should run extended hours to 7:30 p.m. and line B until 11 p.m, but check this schedule, however, as it was still being finalized at press time. You can get tickets on board for 16€ ($18) adults and 8€ ($9.20) children ages 5 to 15 (under 5 ride for free). Tickets are valid for both itineraries for 24 hours. You get a 10-percent discount if you have the **artecard** (see earlier in this chapter).

The agency **Every Tours** (Piazza del Municipio 5; ☎ 081-551-8564; Metro: Garibaldi) is the American Express antenna in Naples and organizes tours of the city as well as day excursions to Vesuvio and other sights. It's open Monday through Friday from 9:00 a.m. to 1:30 p.m. and 3:30 to 7:00 p.m., and Saturday from 9 a.m. to 1 p.m. Another agency, **NapoliVision** (☎ 081-559-5130; www.napolivision.it), offers guided tours of Naples, Pompei, and Capri.

Suggested 1-, 2-, and 3-day itineraries
Naples in 1 day

If you have only one day, start it early and plan to use the **CitySightseeing** bus (Line A; see "Guided tours," earlier in this chapter) to move between attractions. Go directly up to **Capodimonte** and visit this splendid museum; after your visit, take in the view from the gardens of the **Certosa di San Martino** (see "More cool things to see and do," earlier in this chapter). If you like crèches, take the time to visit the *presepio* exhibit inside that museum. Hop back on the bus and head in the heart of town for a well-deserved lunch at **Ciro** or **Europeo** (see "Dining Out," earlier in this chapter). Skip dessert and after lunch, stroll in the beautiful old streets of *Spacca Napoli* (see "Orienting Yourself in Naples," earlier in this chapter); you can get your coffee and pastry at the **Pasticceria Scaturchio** (see "Dining Out," earlier in this chapter). For the afternoon, head to the **Museo Archeologico.** After your visit, take the bus back towards the harbor and enter the courtyard of **Castel Nuovo.** Switch to the seaside bus and ride it to Posillipo, stopping along the way for some shopping along the **Riviera di Chiaia** area (see "Shopping the Local Stores," later in this chapter). Have dinner at **Don Salvatore** in Mergellina, or at **La Cantinella** in Santa Lucia, taking in the romantic beauty of the bay.

Naples in 2 days

If you have two days, follow our one-day itinerary up to (and including, of course) the pastry stop, and then take time to visit some of the attractions in the old streets of *Spacca Napoli,* including the **Duomo, Santa Chiara** and **Sant'Anna dei Lombardi**. Return towards **via Toledo** and visit the **Galleria Umberto I** — where you can also do some shopping. Have dinner at **La Cantinella** in Santa Lucia.

On day 2, head for **Teatro San Carlo** and take a guided tour. After, have a *caffè* and *sfogliatella* at the **Gran Caffè Gambrinus** or the nearby **Caffè del Professore** (See "Living It Up After Dark," later in this chapter) and proceed to the **Museo Archeologico.** Have lunch at **Amici Miei** or a pizza at **Brandi** (see "Dining Out," earlier in this chapter). In the afternoon visit **Palazzo Reale** and then take the **CitySightseeing** bus tour of the seaside (see "Guided tours," earlier in this chapter), stopping for shopping and browsing along the **Riviera di Chiaia;** have dinner at **Don Salvatore** in Mergellina. Alternatively, have an unforgettable dinner at **George's** of the **Grand Hotel Parker's** up in Vomero (see "Staying in Style," earlier in this chapter).

Naples in 3 days

Follow our itinerary for "Naples in 2 days." On day three, head for Pompei and Ercolano, spending the day visiting these archeological sites (see Chapter 21).

Shopping the Local Stores

Although not a shopping mecca, Naples does offer some serious possibilities. In the elegant area behind the **Riviera di Chiaia** and **Via Partenope** are all the big names of **Italian fashion**, such as Valentino, Versace, Ferragamo, and Prada. The best places for such high-end shopping are **Via dei Mille, Piazza dei Martiri,** and **Via Calabritto.** Among the local designers, **Marinella** (Via Riviera di Chiaia 287; ☎ 081-764-4214; open Mon–Sat 6:45 a.m.–8 p.m.) is the most famous: a designer specializing in cravats and ties, offering a new collection almost every week. Also in this area are many **antiques** dealers. Naples is an excellent place to buy antiques if you know what you are doing (Naples is reputed for its experts in the tricky art of *antiquing,* or making something new look old). The **Fiera Antiquaria** (☎ 081-621-951) in the Villa Comunale di Napoli on Viale Dohrn, is an important event held every third Saturday and Sunday of each month 8 a.m. to 2 p.m. (except in Aug). Nearby is **Via Domenico Morelli,** home of the city's most established antiques dealers, specializing in 18th-century furniture and paintings. Two reputable stores are **Regency House** (Via D. Morelli 36; ☎ 081-764-3640) and **Navarra** (Piazza dei Martiri; ☎ 081-764-3595). For these shops, take bus R3 to Riviera di Chiaia.

Another good area for shopping is **Via Roma,** the animated street leading into **Via Toledo.** The most interesting shop here is **Gay-Odin Fabbrica di Cioccolato** (Via Toledo 214 and up the street at no. 427–428), an historical chocolate factory making delicious, 100-percent pure chocolate (what you usually get is 30-percent chocolate at best), and such daring concoctions as chocolate *con peperoncino* (with hot pepper): try it, it is great!

Naples used to be famous for its crafts, and you can still find some specialized crafts typical of the region. Among them, the most dear to Neapolitans probably is the carving of figurines for the ***presepio* (crèche).** Far from being a little display of established characters, Neapolitan crèches are alive with the passions and happenings of the historical and political present, and among the figures offered for sale you will recognize such characters as Lady Diana and Madre Teresa di Calcutta, and even Gianni Versace! **Via San Gregorio Armeno** near Riviera di Chiaia, is where most of the historic workshops are located; you will find not only characters, but also rocks, grottoes, miniature pumps to make "rivers," miniature street lamps, and so on. A vividly painted figure or figurine — some of them are life-sized — can be a beautiful souvenir of Naples and Italy, but remember that these carvings don't come cheap: a shepherd dressed in 18th-century clothes could be as much as 300€ ($345).

Other traditional crafts include **porcelain** figurines and **hand-painted majolica** in the style of the historical royal plant of Capodimonte; and **cameos** (delicately carved jewels using colored stone like agathe or coral), traditionally from Torre del Greco. You can find some shops specializing in these crafts in the **Galleria Umberto I,** off Via Toledo (see "More cool things to see and do," earlier in this chapter); in particular, you can visit an exhibit on the cameo and coral carving, organized by **Ascione 1855 (☎ 081-421-111** for reservations).

Living It Up After Dark

Seeing an opera at the **Teatro San Carlo** (Via San Carlo 98/f; ☎ **081-797-2412** or 081-797-2331; Fax: 081-400-902; www.teatrosancarlo.it; Bus: R2 or R3 to Via San Carlo) is an unforgettable experience. This is a world-class venue (see "More cool things to see and do," earlier in this chapter) where the best international stars come to perform. The acoustics are excellent, and the program always includes some grandiose production. The season opens in December and closes in June, with shows Tuesday through Sunday and tickets costing 45€ to 90€ ($52–$104).

The beautiful former dancing hall of the Palazzo Marigliano — of the duc Marigliano-Caracciolo — has been completely restored into the Sala Teatro Tintadi Rosso and is now a venue for a variety of trendy shows including avant-garde theater (Via San Biagio 39; ☎ **081-790-1270;** Bus: E1 to Via Duomo).

As a real harbor town, Naples offers a lively nighttime scene with discos and clubs. One of the most popular is **Chez Moi** (Via del Parco Margherita 13; ☎ 081-407-526), a small, chic hangout in the Riviera di Chiaia. Nearby is **La Mela** (Via dei Mille; ☎ 081-401-0270), where the best night is Thursday. For either of these clubs, take bus R3 or tram 2 or 4 to Riviera di Chiaia or the Metro to Amadeo.

For a gay atmosphere, go to **Tongue** (Via Manzoni 202; ☎ 081-769-0888; Metro: Mergellina, then take a cab), where you'll find a mixed crowd but with a large proportion of gays and lesbians.

If you feel like relaxing over a nice glass of wine, **Berevino** (Via Sebastiano 62; ☎ 081-290-313) is an *enoteca* with lots of room and many wines to sample. With its beamed ceiling and warm interior, it will make you feel as if you've stepped into the countryside. Berevino also serves food and has a full bar. Best of all, maybe, is that it has a non-smoking room — not an easy thing to find in Italy.

Like other Italians, Neapolitans like to stroll in the evening, maybe having an ice cream or sitting on the terrace of a popular cafe, such as the oldest cafe in Naples, the **Gran Caffè Gambrinus** (Via Chiaia 1; ☎ 081-417-582; Bus: R2 or R3 to Piazza Trieste e Trento). The cafe has been beautifully restored to its full glory; the ornate gilded interior dates from the 1860s. If Gambrinus is too full, the nearby **Caffè del Professore** (Piazza Trieste e Trento 46; ☎ 081-403-041) serves an excellent coffee, and you'll rub shoulders with locals taking an espresso break.

Fast Facts: Naples

Area Code

The country code for Italy is **39**. The area code for Naples is **081**; use this code when calling from anywhere outside or inside Italy and even within Naples itself (including the 0, even when calling from abroad).

American Express

American Express business is handled by Every Tours (Piazza del Municipio 5; ☎ 081-551-8564; Bus: R2 or R3 to Piazza del Municipio). It's open Monday through Friday 9:00 a.m. to 1:30 p.m. and 3:30 to 7:00 p.m., and Saturday 9 a.m. to 1 p.m.

ATMs

ATMs are available everywhere in the city center and near hotels. Most banks are linked to the Cirrus network; if you have access only to the Plus system with your card, look for a BNL (Banca Nazionale del Lavoro), with several locations in Naples.

Currency Exchange

There are three exchange offices on Piazza Garibaldi (Metro: Piazza Garibaldi) and four on Corso Umberto at nos. 44, 92, 212, and 292 (Bus: R2 to Corso Umberto); Thomas Cook is on Piazza del Municipio (Bus: R2 or R3 to Piazza del Municipio).

Doctors

Call the 24-hour Guardia Medica Specialistica at ☎ 081-43-1111, or contact any consulate to get a list of English-speaking doctors.

Embassies and Consulates

The U.S. Consulate is at Piazza della Repubblica (☎ 081-583-8111); the U.K. Consulate is at Via Francesco Crispi 122 (☎ 081-663-511). For other embassies and consulates, See "Fast Facts: Rome" in Chapter 12.

Emergencies

Ambulance, ☎ **118**, 081-780-4296, or 081-584-1481; fire, ☎ **115**; first aid (pronto soccorso), ☎ **081-752-0696**.

Hospital

The Ospedale Fatebenefratelli is at Via Manzoni 220 (☎ 081-769-7220).

Information

APT (Piazza dei Martiri 58, by the Riviera di Chiaia; ☎ 081-405-311) maintains tourist booths in the Stazione Centrale on Piazza Garibaldi (☎ 081-268-799; Metro: Piazza Garibaldi) and in the Stazione Mergellina on Piazza Piedigrotta (☎ 081-761-2102; Metro: Mergellina). The town tourist office (www.inaples.it) also maintains tourist information points, in Via S. Carlo 9 (☎ 081-402-394); in Piazza del Gesù (☎ 081-551-2701) and in Via Marino Turchi 16 (tel 081-240-0911). There is also a tourist point inside Palazzo Reale (☎ 081-252-5711).

Internet Access

Try the ClickNet Internet Café (Via Toledo 393; ☎ 081-552-9370; www.mbx.clic net.it; Bus: R1 or R4).

Maps

You can buy a good map of Naples in any newspaper kiosk in the station or in town.

Newspapers/Magazines

You can find foreign newspapers and magazines in the kiosks, particularly at the train station and nearby the American Consulate.

Do not miss *QuiNapoli,* the free monthly prepared by the city tourist office and listing all the latest events (also online at www.inaples.it/quinapoli.htm).

Pharmacies

A good one is the large one near the Stazione Centrale, Farmacia Helvethiam (Piazza Garibaldi 11; ☎ 081-554-8894; Metro: Piazza Garibaldi).

Police

There are two police forces in Italy; call either one. For the Polizia, call ☎ **113**; for the Carabinieri, call ☎ **112**.

Post Office

The post office (Ufficio Postale) is at Piazza Matteotti (☎ 081-551-1456; Bus: R3 to Piazza Matteotti).

Restrooms

There are very few public toilets in town, so your best bet is to go to a nice-looking cafe (though you'll have to buy something, like a cup of coffee).

Safety

Naples is considered less safe than other cities in Italy, although notable efforts have been made in recent years, with tremendous improvement. Still, pickpocketing and car theft are popular. In dark alleys off the beaten track, getting mugged is also possible, but that's quite rare in the city center or in the areas we describe in this book. Definitely seedy at night is the area around the train station.

Smoking

Smoking is allowed in cafes and restaurants and very common. Unfortunately for nonsmokers, finding a restaurant with a separate no-smoking area is still a bit difficult.

Taxes

See information on VAT in Chapter 5.

Taxi

There are five radio taxi companies: ☎ 081-570-7070, 081-551-5151, 081-556-4444, 081-556-0202, or 081-552-5252.

Transit info

Call Trenitalia for railroad information (☎ 892-021; www.trenitalia.it) and Naples transportation authority (☎ 800-482-644; www.ctpn.it) for local trains, buses, trams, metro, and funiculars.

Weather Updates

For forecasts, the best bet is to watch the news on TV. On the Internet, you can check http://meteo.tiscalinet.it.

Chapter 21

Going Beyond Naples: Three Day Trips

* *

In This Chapter

▶ Checking out the crater of Mount Vesuvius

▶ Seeing the eerie sights of Herculaneum and Pompeii

▶ Enjoying the beauty of Capri

* *

Campania, the region surrounding Naples, is rich in history and natural beauty. Its beauty and proximity to Rome made Campania a favorite resort of the ancient Romans. Ancient historians reported that Caligula had a bridge of ships built the entire four or so miles across the nearby Bay of Pozzuoli — maybe there's always been something a little nutty about this place! Tiberius retreated to the nearby island of Capri to concentrate on his own decadent pleasures. Idyllic (now only in the off season) and full of charm (in any season), **Capri** (pronounce it *Cap*-ree), with its famous Blue Grotto and emerald water, makes a perfect getaway from busy Naples. It's just a ferry ride south of the city off the peninsula of Sorrento, in the heart of the beautiful bay that made Naples famous. From Naples, you can also visit **Mount Vesuvius (Vesuvio),** the volcano loved and feared by Neapolitans, which could never deter visitors from this beautiful land, not even after it swallowed Herculaneum and Pompeii in its A.D. 79 eruption. Few archaeological sites are as moving as the towns that shared a similar catastrophic destiny. Each is still unique: **Pompeii (Pompei)** was buried beneath volcanic ash and pumice stone, transforming Pompeiians taking flight into human statues that remain to this day. **Herculaneum (Ercolano)** was buried beneath volcanic mud that preserved its houses to a remarkable extent.

While Mount Vesuvius, Hercolaneum, and Pompeii all make good day trips, Capri is well worth a longer stay if you have the time.

Mount Vesuvius

Some think Neapolitans live below a sleeping monster: Of the two major kinds of volcanoes — some slowly ooze magma, like the ones on Hawaii; others build and build and build the pressure inside and then blow their tops — Vesuvius is a top-blower. Although Vesuvius has belched only a few puffs of smoke since the last real eruption in 1944, no one really knows whether the volcano is losing its punch or just biding its time. It got everybody on their toes when it puffed again in 1999, in case anyone thought it was sleeping. Luckily, one of the best (and the first) observatories for the study of vulcanology is right there on the mountain, taking its pulse daily.

You will need only a few hours to visit Mount Vesuvius; allow about an hour for the panoramic walk and add another two hours for visits to the crater, the museum, and the gift shop. There is not much else at the site, but you might decide to have a picnic or to eat a bite at the historic *osteria* on premises.

Getting there

You can easily reach Vesuvius from Naples via the **Circumvesuviana Railway** (☎ 800-053-939; www.vesuviana.it), which leaves from the Stazione Circumvesuviana (Corso Garibaldi, off Piazza Garibaldi; Metro: Garibaldi). Get off at the **Ercolano** station — about 15 minutes away, and take the *navette* (electric minibus) to the entrance of the park, just out of the station. The trip costs about 1.50€ ($1.70). Alternatively, you can take a guided tour from Naples (see "Taking a tour," later in this section), or hire a limousine service such as **ANA Limousine Service** (Piazza Garibaldi 73; ☎ and Fax **081-282-000**; e-mail: anatrasp@hotmail.com), which has several branches in Naples, including the railroad station Centrale (☎ **081-266-908**); the airport Capodichino (☎ **081-789-6716**); and the Harbor (☎ **0339-664-5490**).

Note that all transportation only gets you as far as the entrance to the park at 1,017m (3,106 feet) altitude; you will have to walk the rest of the way — uphill another 264m (838 feet) and about the same downhill should you decide to descend into the crater with a guided tour.

Taking a tour

You can join a tour group organized from Naples — for example, by the agency that handles American Express business, **Every Tours** (Piazza del Municipio 5; ☎ **081-551-8564**).

It is also worth taking one of the tours starting on Mount Vesuvius itself, such as those offered by **La Porta del Vesuvio** (☎ **081-274-200**; www.laportadelvesuvio.it; for reservations, call from 9 a.m.–1:30 p.m.), which organizes scenic night tours of the crater as well as a nature trail visit in the heart of the park on Sundays at 11 a.m.; or the **Centro Visite** (☎ **081-777-5720**, 081-739-1123, or 033-794-2249) of the Parco Nazionale del Vesuvio itself, taking place daily from 10 a.m. to sunset. You can take a tour of the crater itself — indeed, you can closely approach the crater only with a guide — for 3€ ($3.45); sign up at the site's entrance.

Seeing the sights

Mount Vesuvius is the only continental volcano still active in Europe, and it is now a national park. Rising 1,281m (3,944 feet), the slopes of Vesuvius are green with vineyards, and they become more rugged only as you approach the top. At the entrance of the park, there is a visitor center where you can sign up for a guided tour, as well as an historical *osteria* that was recently restored and is now open for business. There you can taste the local cuisine and the famous local wine, the Lacrima Christi, made from the vineyards on Mount Vesuvius. In the small shop you can buy local products, including the wine. Nearby, at 608m (1,994 feet), you can visit the **Vesuvian Observatory,** the top-notch center that has observed the volcano's activity day by day since around 1850. Attached to the observatory are the geological museum and a rich scientific library.

Entering the park, you follow a dirt trail to the crater. Closer to the top, the dirt trail becomes lava, the typical black-and-purple rough pieces of stone. The trail circles the crater and you can have a good look at it, but to descend closer you will need to follow a guide (see earlier in this chapter). From the top on a good day, you can enjoy a fantastic view over the Bay of Naples. Since the June 2002 alert about a possible explosion, there has been no new warning of upcoming activity and everything has been normal; the visitor center will keep you informed should there be any development by the time you visit. Admission to the park is 4.50€ ($5) and it's open daily from 9 a.m. until sunset; last admission is 1 hour before sunset.

Pompeii and Herculaneum

The two archeological sites are very different and both well worth a visit; excavations still go on. In the 1990s, a boat was found near the water at Herculaneum, still filled with the corpses of victims caught in frantic postures. These are unforgettable sights, and the towns have yielded great numbers of artifacts and sculptures as well. You can see many of the finds on display in Naples's National Archaeological Museum. A recent overhaul of the museum facilities on-site has much improved the already interesting experience.

You can visit either — or both — of these towns as a day-trip from Naples. Consider spending at least two hours in Herculaneum and four hours in Pompeii.

Getting there

The **Circumvesuviana** railway (☎ 800-053-939; www.vesuviana.it), which leaves from the Stazione Circumvesuviana (Corso Garibaldi, off Piazza Garibaldi; Metro: Garibaldi) makes stops at both archeological sites. For Herculaneum, get off at the **Ercolano Scavi** stop on the **Sorrento** or the Poggiomarino line; outside the station there are *navettes* to the site. For Pompeii, also take the **Sorrento** line and get off at the **Pompei Scavi** stop; you can walk from there. Be aware that there is a Pompei stop on the Poggiomarino line, but it is modern Pompei. The 20-minute ride to Ercolano Scavi costs 1.70€ ($2) and the 45-minute ride to Pompei Scavi is 2.20€ ($2.50); trains leave every half-hour.

Taking a tour

You can take a guided tour to either or both sites from Naples (see Chapter 20). You can also book a guided tour with an official guide at the **Ufficio Scavi** of each sight. We recommend this option; among other reasons, these guides can show you those houses that are protected by gates. If you're on your own, you can't enter the locked structures and you'll have to squint between the iron frames for a peek. If you're with a tour that originated in Naples you'll probably be allowed to enter the gated houses, but it's not guaranteed. While you can get a tour of the whole archeological area in Ercolano, you will have to choose a more selective tour for Pompeii — the whole site is too large. Note that you can sign up for a guided tour directly at the ticket booth when you arrive, but we recommend making reservations ahead of time, especially if you're going to be there on the weekend.

Somewhat unusual, **Virtual Pompei** (Via Plinio 105, Pompei; ☎ and Fax: **081-861-0500** from 11 a.m. to 4 p.m. or 081-578-3593 or 329-173-5876; www.virtualpompei.it) is not a tour of the excavations but a way of reliving what Pompeii must have looked like in antiquity. The center is open daily from 11:30 a.m. to 5 p.m. and admission is 6€ ($6.90); 10 percent discount with the artecard (see Chapter 20).

Seeing the sights

Unless you're visiting in the dead of winter, remember to bring a hat, plenty of sunscreen, and water. There are no trees among the ruins, and it can get really hot. Remember to wear comfortable shoes as well, especially if you're visiting larger Pompeii.

If you have time to visit both Herculaneum and Pompeii, you can get a cumulative ticket for 18€ ($21); it is valid for three days and gives you access to three other archeological sites in the region — Oplonti, Stabia, and Boscoreale.

Herculaneum is easier to see because it's smaller, but it's less impressive than Pompeii — though the sites share the feeling of having been abandoned not very long ago. Pompeii is some four times larger than Herculaneum, and visiting the whole thing is somewhat laborious. Count on a minimum of four hours just to get a general idea of the place and have a quick look at most of the attractions.

Ercolano (Herculaneum)

Herculaneum is the smaller of the two ancient towns and has the smaller archeological area; much of it still lies under the present-day town and has never been excavated (digging into the solidified volcanic mud is quite a chore). It is especially interesting, however, because many of Herculaneum's buildings were more elaborate than Pompeii's — this was the glitzier seaside resort for rich Romans. Among the most interesting public buildings are the two sets of *terme* **(thermal baths)** — particularly the smaller but more elegantly decorated **Terme Suburbane (Suburban Baths),** and the **Palestra** — a sports arena, where games were staged to satisfy the spectacle-hungry denizens.

You will also admire the private architecture, with the typical townhouses built around one or more uncovered atriums and lavishly decorated. Herculaneum also had the forerunner to the modern apartment house — a building with several stories where poorer people lived. Important private homes to seek out are the **Casa del Bicentenario (House of the Bicentenary),** the **Casa a Graticcio (House of the Latticework),** the **Casa del Tramezzo di Legno (House of the Wooden Partition),** and the **Casa di Nettune (House of Neptune),** which contains the most striking mosaic found in the ruins. The finest example of how the aristocracy lived is the **Casa dei Cervi (House of the Stags),** so-named for the sculpture found inside. Note that several houses are locked and opened only by official guides during a tour. Recently opened in March 2004 is the **Villa dei Papiri,** a grandiose building taking its name for the thousand of papyrus rolls found there, and extending for over 250m (820 feet) along the coast. You can visit the lower and upper floors, with rich mosaics and frescoes, but only by guided tour reserved in advance.

See map. p. 443. Corso Resina, Ercolano. Call Ufficio Scavi (☎ 081-857-5347) daily from 10 a.m.–1:30 p.m. for information and tour reservations. Admission: 10€ ($12). Open: Daily Nov–Mar 8:30 a.m.–5 p.m. and Apr–Oct 8:30 a.m.–7:30 p.m. Last entrance 90 minutes before site closing.

Pompei (Pompeii)

Pompeii was an important commercial town as well as a residential resort, and its urban fabric was a mix of elegant villas, shops, and more modest housing. The town was buried under volcanic ash and pumice stone that then solidified, which allowed the residents who had escaped to come back and salvage some of their treasures. Of course, this same situation also made it easier for the treasure hunters of later centuries to loot the place. In spite of all the scavengers, the city was very well preserved, and the archaeological excavations have uncovered much about the life of the times.

Among the patrician villas, decorated with inner courtyards, sculptures, and frescoes, the most elegant is the **Casa dei Vettii (House of the Vettii).** Here you can admire a frescoed dining room in the coloring that has become famous as Pompeiian red. The house was occupied by two brothers named Vettii, both of whom were wealthy merchants, hence the rich

Herculaneum

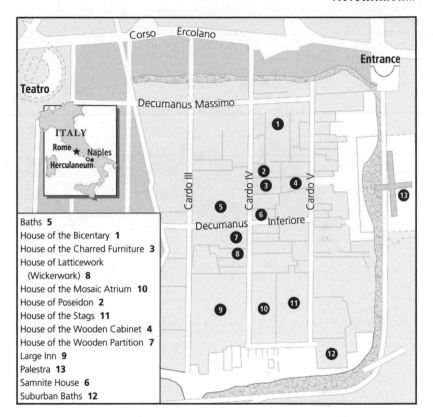

Corso Ercolano

Entrance

Teatro

Decumanus Massimo

ITALY
Rome ★ Naples
Herculaneum

Cardo III Cardo IV Cardo V

Decumanus Inferiore

Baths **5**
House of the Bicentary **1**
House of the Charred Furniture **3**
House of Latticework
   (Wickerwork) **8**
House of the Mosaic Atrium **10**
House of Poseidon **2**
House of the Stags **11**
House of the Wooden Cabinet **4**
House of the Wooden Partition **7**
Large Inn **9**
Palestra **13**
Samnite House **6**
Suburban Baths **12**

decorations and statuary. Another treasure is the **Casa dei Misteri (House of the Mysteries),** near the Porto Ercolano outside the walls, decorated with frescoes of mythological scenes related to the cult of Dionysus (Bacchus) — one of the cults that flourished in Roman times. The most famous and the largest of the houses is the **Casa del Fauno (House of the Faun),** so called because of the bronze statue of a dancing faun that was found there; the house takes up a city block and has four dining rooms and two spacious inner gardens.

Also interesting are the public areas of the ancient city. In the center of town is the **Forum,** surrounded by three important buildings: the **Basilica** (the meeting hall, the city's largest single structure), the **Tempio di Apollo (Temple of Apollo),** and the **Tempio di Giove (Temple of Jupiter).** Interestingly, the forum had been severely damaged in an earthquake 16 years before the eruption of Vesuvius and you can see how parts of it had not yet been repaired when the final destruction came. The **Terme Stabiane (baths)** are among the finest baths to survive from antiquity and are still in good condition. Other buildings of interest are the **Teatro**

Pompeii

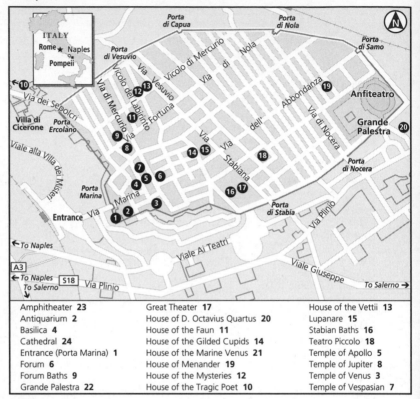

Amphitheater **23**	Great Theater **17**	House of the Vettii **13**
Antiquarium **2**	House of D. Octavius Quartus **20**	Lupanare **15**
Basilica **4**	House of the Faun **11**	Stabian Baths **16**
Cathedral **24**	House of the Gilded Cupids **14**	Teatro Piccolo **18**
Entrance (Porta Marina) **1**	House of the Marine Venus **21**	Temple of Apollo **5**
Forum **6**	House of Menander **19**	Temple of Jupiter **8**
Forum Baths **9**	House of the Mysteries **12**	Temple of Venus **3**
Grande Palestra **22**	House of the Tragic Poet **10**	Temple of Vespasian **7**

Grande, built in the fifth century B.C.; the **Casa degli Amorini Dorati (House of the Gilded Cupids),** a flamboyant private home; and the **Casa del Poeta Tragico (House of the Tragic Poet),** which gets its name from a mosaic discovered here (but later sent to Naples). In this house you can observe a picture and warning that it is still common to see on gates in many private houses in central Italy: the depiction of a chained watchdog with the words CAVE CANEM ("Beware of the dog").

Particularly evocative — and disturbing — are the "statues" of the victims: as the ash hardened on the dead bodies, it became a shell that preserved all the details, including agonizing facial expressions. Archaeologists made casts of these bodies, by pouring plaster into the cavities. They are conserved in the museum.

Note that on Saturdays and Sundays, the tour of the thermal baths also includes a visit to two Roman houses, the Casa di Polibio and Casa Menandro. For a virtual reconstruction of Pompeii, see Virtual Pompei under "Taking a tour," earlier in this section.

See map p. 444. Porta Marina, Pompei. Call Ufficio Scavi (☎ 081-857-5347) daily from 10 a.m.–1:30 p.m. for information and tour reservations. Admission: 10€ ($12). Open: Daily Nov–Mar 8:30 a.m.–5 p.m. and Apr–Oct 8:30 a.m.–7:30 p.m. Last entrance 90 minutes before closing time.

Dining locally

There's little to eat at the excavations, so packing a picnic lunch to bring with you is a good idea (don't forget plenty of water during the summer). If you want to eat in a restaurant, you have to head for the modern town. Herculaneum is relatively poor, but it has a few snack bars near the center; Pompeii offers better options.

Capri and the Blue Grotto

Ever since Emperor Tiberius sought amusement at Villa Jovis here, this famous island has been a haunt for eccentric characters (such as movie stars hiding out, artists in exile, and the like). Whether you stay for a day or a year, remember to bring very little luggage or expect to hire a porter when you land: The island is quite steep and you may have to walk up many steps to get to your hotel.

Getting there

Ferries leave from **Molo Beverello** at Naples's Stazione Marittima frequently for Capri. In addition to the several competing private companies, the newly created **Metrò del Mare** (☎ 199-446-644; www.metro delmare.com) makes one daily run (a 50-min. trip) to Capri at 4:25 p.m. with return from Capri at 10:50 a.m. Take the line MM4 from **Molo Beverello;** you can use the special ticket **Terra and Mare,** which includes ground transportation for 45 minutes before and 45 minutes after the ferry link for about 4.50€ ($5.20). **Caremar** (☎ 081-551-3882 in Naples and 081-837-0700 in Capri; www.caremar.it) has four runs a day for 4.90€ ($5.65) with a regular ferry — a 90-minute trip; **SNAV** (☎ 081-761-2348 in Naples and 081-837-7577 in Capri), and **NLG** (☎ 081-552-7209 in Naples and 081-837-0819 in Capri; www.navlib.it) have several runs a day by *aliscafo* (hydrofoil) for 12€ ($14) — a 35-minute trip.

You can also get to Capri from other towns along the coast; in particular, the company **Alicost** (☎ 081-761-1004 or 081-837-6995 in Capri; www.alilauro.it) offers several daily runs to and from **Amalfi** (hydrofoil 13.50€/$16; regular ferry 11€/$13) and **Positano** (hydrofoil 13€/$15; regular ferry 10.50€/$12).

Ferries and hydrofoils arrive at **Marina Grande** in Capri. From the ferry terminal you can take the *funicolare* (funicular) up the steep coast to the town of Capri. Also, regular **bus** service links Marina Grande, Capri,

Marina Piccola, Anacapri, Faro (lighthouse), and Grotta Azzurra. A regular ticket costs 1.30€ ($1.50) for either bus or funicular; you can also get a 60-minute ticket for 2.10€ ($2.40), valid for one funicular run and unlimited bus runs during the time limit, and a day pass for 6.70€ ($7.70) valid for two funicular rides and unlimited bus service.

Taking a tour

Boat tours of the island leave from **Marina Grande** (where the ferry and hydrofoil from Naples arrive). The **Gruppo Motoscafisti** (www.motoscafisticapri.com) runs boat tours of the island for 10.50€ ($12) and excursions to the Faraglioni — Capri's famous cliffs — for 9€ ($10) per person. **Laser Capri** (www.lasercaprisrl.com) also runs boat tours of the island for 9€ ($10) per person.

Seeing the sights

Capri boasts beautiful cliffs and views of the sea and over the Bay of Naples and Vesuvius. The windy roads climbing up the promontory are picturesque, though less entertaining when clogged with tourists. If you're moderately fit, you may enjoy exploring the island on foot. Most of the footpaths offer fantastic views. If you like to swim, you won't be disappointed: The water is beautiful and marvelously refreshing under the hot sun. Because Capri is very rocky, though, beaches are small, and the easy-to-reach beaches are often crowded. The best approach is to avail yourself of one of the small boats that take you to a difficult-to-reach beach for about 8€ ($9.20).

The **Bagni di Tiberio** is a nice sandy beach on the north side of the island, near the ruins of an ancient villa. You can take a boat there from Marina Grande or walk (it takes about half an hour). The beach is freely accessible and not too crowded.

Anacapri

This is the other, smaller town in the island. The steep climb from Capri through the old **Scala Fenicia** (Fenician staircase) is a must if you are fit (of course you can also **descend** the stairs from Anacapri). This steep path linking Anacapri to Capri was built by Greek colonists almost three thousands years ago and affords spectacular views. It's so steep that it is actually a staircase (*scala* means "stairs") with over 500 steps. You can also reach Anacapri by bus — a hair-raising ride along the cliff road. Although there are some nice restaurants and hotels in Anacapri, you come up here mostly for the natural beauty of the place.

Capri

A picturesque little town which is the largest of the two on the island, this is where you can find the most glamorous hotels, cafes, and shops. We know of people who come to Capri to shop — there are indeed some nice clothing and jewelry shops that you wouldn't find on the mainland: happy hunting.

Grotta Azzurra (Blue Grotto)

Kids will love visiting this underwater cave that can be reached only by small boat. This natural wonder conjures up visions of pirates and buried treasure. Alas, this is also Capri's top attraction, and as such it has been overexploited by entrepreneurs. When you board that big boat going there, don't think that's how you'll see the grotto. You have to get off onto a rowboat that takes you into the grotto, which is reached by a narrow passage — so narrow and low that if you're not limber or have claustrophia you won't like it. The slow sinking of the grotto over time has reduced the opening to slightly more than 3 feet above sea level. You can reach the Grotto from Anacapri and skip the motorboat ride. From there you can directly take the row boat. Technically, you could also swim inside the grotto, though you still need to pay the 4€ ($4.60) admission; however, we strongly advise against this option because of the incessant boat traffic.

When you get inside, you'll understand the reason for all the commotion and even forget about the outrageous money you've paid to see it. The grotto was known to the ancients — you'll see a little landing just inside the entrance dating back to Roman times, but was later lost to the world until an artist stumbled upon it in 1826. Inside the cavern, light refraction (the sun's rays entering from an opening under the water) creates incredible colors and a magical atmosphere — stunning, indeed. Alas, chances are you won't be able to stay as long as you'd like, because at the height of tourist season no lingering is allowed. For all these reasons, we think that the grotto, like Capri in general, should be seen in the off season if possible.

Near the northwestern tip of the island. Admission: Boat tour 15.10€ ($17) including motorboat trip from Marina Grande, row boat trip inside the Grotto and admission. Land excursion from Anacapri 8.10€ ($9) including row boat trip inside the Grotto and admission. Boat operators welcome a tip. Open: Daily 9 a.m.–1 hour before sunset.

Marina Piccola and the Faraglioni

A tiny and picturesque harbor on the south shore of the island, this is where you can admire the famous **Faraglioni,** the tall cliffs off the island's southeastern tip. The local beach offers perfect views, but you can also hire a boat to take you closer to this natural attraction.

Monte Solaro

From Anacapri you can take the chairlift up to the highest point on the island. The views from uphere are absolutely breathtaking, especially on a clear day, when you can see Mount Vesuvius and the whole bay.

Pick up the chairlift at Via Caposcuro 10, Anacapri. ☎ 081-837-1428. Ticket: 4€ ($4.60) one-way and 5.50€ ($6.30) for the 12-min. round-trip ride. Ride operates Mar–Oct 9:30 a.m.–sunset; Nov–Feb 10:30 a.m.–3 p.m.

Villa Jovis

Emperor Tiberius built several villas on the island during his self-imposed exile here, where he could enjoy all sorts of illicit pleasures far away from

Capri

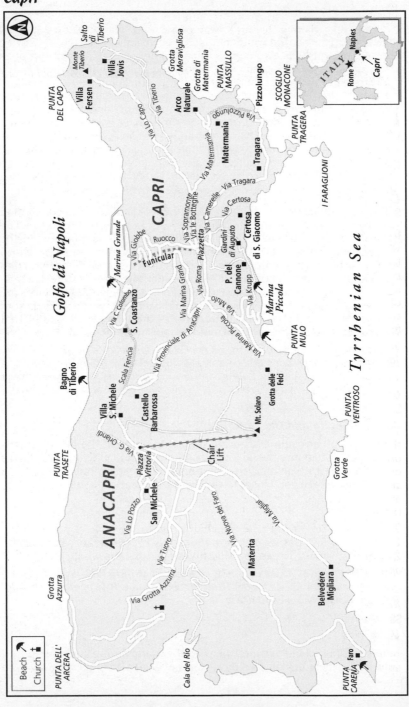

the prying eyes of the Roman Senate. The Villa Jovis, the palace where Tiberius lived, extended over several levels for an estimated 5,850 sq. m (63,000 sq. ft. — just a modest summer home) but is now only a romantic ruin from which you get beautiful views.

Viale Amedeo Maiuri, at the eastern tip of the island. www.villajovis.it. *Admission: 2€ ($2.30). Open: Daily 9 a.m.–sunset; ticket booth closes 1 hour before sunset.*

Dining locally

Restaurants on Capri can be excellent although expensive. Don't be afraid to explore — many very nice small trattorie are tucked away on this magnificent island.

Cantinella
$$$ Capri   CAPRESE

If you don't get too distracted by the great view over the Faraglioni, you will be able to enjoy the very good cuisine of this restaurant. Among the local dishes, the *paccheri con frutti di mare e rucola* (homemade largish pasta with seafood and arugula) was excellent as were the other home-made pastas. The fish *secondi* change daily and meat and vegetarian dishes are available as well; we enjoyed the *carpaccio di melanzane, zucchine e provola* (eggplant, zucchini, and cheese carpaccio). Leave room for the delicious homemade desserts.

Viale Matteotti 8. ☎ *081-837-0616. Reservations necessary for dinner. Secondi: 18€–29€ ($21–$33). AE, DC, MC, V. Open: Lunch and dinner Wed–Mon.*

Olivo del Capri Palace
$$$$ Capri   CAPRESE/CREATIVE

The best restaurant in Capri is also one of the most elegant, housed in the the Capri Palace. The menu changes often, but you might find such tasty offerings as *ravioli capresi con caciotta e maggiorana* (local ravioli with cheese and marjoram) or *astice con zucchine e pesche gialle all'olio di zucca* (local lobster with yellow peaches and zucchini with pumpkin oil) and *zuppa di albicocche al tamarindo e menta con gelato e latte di mandorle* (apricots with tamarind and mint served with ice cream and sweet almond milk) for dessert.

Via Capodimonte 2b, Capri. ☎ *081-978-0111. Reservations necessary. Secondi: 25€–36€ ($29–$41). AE, DC, MC, V. Open: Lunch and dinner daily. Closed Nov–Feb but open 10 days for new year.*

Rondinella
$$ Anacapri   CAPRESE

This excellent restaurant is right in the center of the tranquil Anacapri and serves some of the best food in the island; a plus is the possibility of dining outdoors in the good season. Do try the *tagliatelle alle cozze* (homemade pasta with mussels) — it's the best we've had — and enjoy the local and fragrant bread with the daily catch or one of the meats. We recommend the *torta di mandorle* (almond cake) for dessert.

Via G. Orlandi 245, Anacapri. ☎ *081-837-1223. Reservations necessary for dinner. Secondi: 12€–16€ ($14–$18). AE, DC, MC, V. Open: Lunch and dinner daily; closed first 2 weeks in Feb.*

Spending the night

If you want to stay overnight, hotels in Anacapri are cheaper, and quieter, located among the vineyards of the hills; Capri hotels, on the other hand, are glitzier and offer much more in the way of nightlife.

Grand Hotel Quisisana Capri
$$$$$ Capri

What was a sanatorium in the 19th century is today the chic place to stay on Capri — Georgio Armani has been a regular for years — and the place to come for elegant bars open till late. If you can't afford one of the ritzy guest rooms, lounge in the terrace of the hotel cafe, maybe sipping the blue-colored house cocktail, or take a sauna or a swim in the pool. Guest rooms are quite stylish; indeed, some of the best rooms are decorated with fine antiques, marble columns, and extravagant baths. Prices are cut in the off season by more than half.

Via Camerelle 2. ☎ *081-837-0788. Fax: 081-837-6080.* www.quisi.com. *Rack rates: 700€ ($805) double. Rates include buffet breakfast. Closed Nov–mid-Mar.*

Hotel Luna
$$$$ Capri

A less pricey choice than the Grand Hotel Quisisana but still upscale, Hotel Luna offers beautiful vistas over the Faraglioni and the bay from its location atop a cliff. Most guest rooms have private terraces overlooking the cliffs or gardens, and all are quite luxurious.

Viale Matteotti 3. ☎ *081-837-0433. Fax: 081-837-7459.* www.lunahotel.com. *Rack rates: 365€ ($420) double. Rates include breakfast. Closed end of Oct–Easter.*

Hotel San Michele
$$ Anacapri

A beautiful pool (the largest on Capri), gardens overlooking the sea, pleasant guest rooms, and a relaxed atmosphere make Hotel San Michele an excellent moderately priced (for Capri) choice. Every room has some kind of view, whether of the sea, the mountain, or the gardens.

Via G. Orlandi 1–3. ☎ *081-837-1427. Fax: 081-837-1420.* www.sanmichele-capri.com. *Rack rates: 200€ ($230) double. Rates include breakfast. AE, MC, V. Closed Nov–Mar.*

Chapter 22

The Amalfi Coast

In This Chapter

▶ Sunning and swimming on the beaches of the Amalfi Coast
▶ Living the good life in Positano
▶ Taking in the sights in lovely Ravello and Amalfi

The **Amalfi Coast (Costiera Amalfitana)** is a stretch of shore famous for its natural beauty. Its terraced cliffs overlooking the sea are blanketed with lemon trees, olive groves, and vineyards interspersed with small villages and historic towns, among which the queen is **Amalfi.** It was one of the four Italian historic maritime republics, along with Siena, Genoa, and Venice.

The Amalfi Coast is only a couple of hours from Naples, so you can choose to have only a quick glimpse and take a day trip, but the best way to enjoy it is to spend at least one or two nights if you can spare the time. Base yourself in Amalfi or Positano, where it is easy to catch public transportation and you have a large choice of restaurants, hotels, and shops.

Getting There

Many think that the best way to enjoy the Amalfi Coast is by taking a scenic drive: that is true, but only if you are not the one driving. We have friends who insisted on driving themselves but, once on the road, they because so uncomfortable that they didn't even stop till they reached the highway to Naples! The result? They didn't see a thing. What makes the beauty of the place makes it also difficult to drive: The road is narrow and winding, sometimes without a guard rail, and it's cut on the side of tall cliffs. Traffic, and crazy, speeding locals seemingly attached to your rear bumper don't make it any easier. There are several ways to see the Amalfi Coast, as we discuss below — driving yourself is just not one of them.

By hired car

By far the best way to visit the Amalfi Coast if you are coming for a day trip, hiring a car allows you to enjoy the scenic drive in complete comfort and at your own pace. Here are a few reliable companies which use new cars and minivans with air conditioning and trained English-speaking

The Amalfi Coast

drivers: **ANA Limousine Service** (Piazza Garibaldi 73; ☎ and Fax **081-282-000**); **2golfi car service** (Via Deserto 30/e, 80064 Sant'Agata sui due Golfi; ☎ **339-830-7748** or 338-562-8649; Fax 081-533-0882; www.duegolfi carservice.it); and **Italy Limousine** (☎ **081-801-6184** or 335-673-2245; www.italylimousine.it). Prices vary depending on your needs, the car you choose, and the number of people in your group, but the average hourly rate is about 35€ ($40) for two people. For a leisurely tour of the coast, count on about eight hours.

By bus

The easiest and cheaper route to the coast is to take a train from Naples to Sorrento on the **Circumvesuviana Railway** (☎ **800-053-939**; www.vesuviana.it), which leaves from the Stazione Circumvesuviana (Corso Garibaldi, off Piazza Garibaldi; Metro: Garibaldi), and then switch to the **SITA bus** (☎ **089-871-016** or 089-871-009 in Amalfi) which makes daily runs from Sorrento to Positano, Amalfi, and Ravello — and a number of stops on the way. The whole trip should cost you about 4€ ($4.60) and take about two hours. The ride can be hair-raising at times — you will certainly be grateful that you're not driving the bus — but it's certainly panoramic.

By ferry

The newly created **Metrò del Mare** (☎ **199-446-644**; www.metrodel mare.com) makes several daily runs to Amalfi and Positano. The trip from **Molo Beverello** in Naples to Positano takes 75 minutes with the express line (MM2) and about two hours with the local line (MM3); count on 25 additional minutes to Amalfi on either line. You can use the special ticket **Terra and Mare,** which includes ground transportation for

45 minutes before and 45 minutes after the ferry link for about 8.50€ ($9.80). The company **Alicost** (☎ **081-761-1004** in Naples, 089-873-301 in Amalfi, and 089-875-032 or 089-811-164 in Positano) has several daily runs to and from Amalfi (hydrofoil 13.50€/$16; regular ferry 11€/$13) and Positano (hydrofoil 13€/$15; regular ferry 10.50€/$12) but you need to make reservations at least 24 hours in advance.

Spending the Night

Following are some of our favorite places to stay on the coast.

Albergo L'Ancora
$$ Positano

Not one of the most elegant choices in Positano, but this moderately priced hotel still offers good value. Most guest rooms have air-conditioning, and each boasts comfortable beds, some antiques, and a private terrace. Open only to guests, the hotel's restaurant serves meals on the terrace.

*Via Colombo 36. ☎ **089-875-318**. Fax: 089-811-784. www.htlancora.it. Free parking. Rack rates: 232€ ($267) double. Rates include breakfast. AE, DC, MC, V. Closed Nov–Mar.*

Hotel Le Sirenuse
$$$$$ Positano

This gorgeous 18th-century villa overlooking the bay is owned by the Marchesi Sersale family and was their residence until 1951. You may have seen the hotel featured in the film *Only You* with Marisa Tomei and Robert Downey, Jr. Guest rooms are elegantly furnished, with antiques and period reproductions, many have gorgeous views over the sea. The hotel also has a splendid swimming pool and serves a very nice buffet breakfast. Prices are significantly lower in the off season.

*Via Cristoforo Colombo 30. ☎ **089-875-066**. Fax: 089-811-798. www.sirenuse.it. Free parking. Rack rates: 680€ ($782) double. Rates include buffet breakfast. AE, DC, MC, V.*

Hotel Lidomare
$ Amalfi

This moderately priced hotel near the beach is housed in a 13th-century building. The guest rooms are brightly decorated in typical Amalfitan style (tiles, strong colors, lots of sparkling white). Most rooms have air-conditioning, the baths are small but very clean, and the staff is extremely friendly and welcoming to families with children.

*Largo Duchi Piccolomini 9. ☎ **089-871-332**. Fax: 089-871-394. Parking: 15€ ($17). Rack rates: 120€ ($138) double. Rates include breakfast. AE, MC, V.*

Hotel Luna Convento
$$$$ Amalfi

With a splendid position on the promontory of Amalfi, overlooking the sea, this family-run hotel offers elegant and romantic accommodations. An ancient monastery founded by Saint Francis in 1222, it was transformed into a hotel in 1822; you can still visit and enjoy the original cloister and chapel, as well as the watch tower from 1564. The large and bright guest rooms are individually decorated, with furnishing vaguely reminiscent of Moresque style, with whitewashed walls and fine fabrics. All guest rooms have views of the sea and large tiled bathrooms; some have private terraces. The hotel also has a large seawater swimming pool and a solarium.

Via P. Comite 33, Amalfi. ☎ **089-871-002.** *Fax: 089-871-333.* www.lunahotel.it. *Free parking. Rack rates: 350€ ($403) double. Rates include breakfast. AE, DC, MC, V.*

Villa Cimbrone
$$$–$$$$ Ravello

Residence of the Vuillemier family, this villa offers hospitality to a small number of guests (20 maximum) in great luxury and privacy. Each of the rooms is unique and decorated with antiques, some of them have views over the park, others — more expensive — have private terraces overlooking the sea. From Ravello, call the hotel; they'll send a porter to carry your luggage to the villa. The villa is an attraction in itself (see "The top attractions," later in this chapter).

Via Santa Chiara 26. ☎ **089-857-459.** *Fax: 089-857-777.* www.villacimbrone.it. *Rack rates: 280€–450€ ($322–$518) double. Rates include breakfast. AE, DC, MC, V. Closed Dec–Mar.*

Dining Locally

On the Amalfi Coast, the sea reigns, making it a paradise for seafood lovers.

Caravella
$$$$ Amalfi   AMALFITAN/CREATIVE

If ever a restaurant deserved being expensive, this is the one: the delicious concoctions are not only made from excellent ingredients, they are also extremely complicated and time-consuming preparations. You will find such dishes as *panzerottini al nero di seppia ripieni di provola e scampi con salsa di calamaretti mignon ripieni di zucchine* (homemade squid-ink pasta filled with prawns and local cheese, with a sauce of zucchini-stuffed calamari) or *zuppetta di polpo con il pane fritto alle alghe* (octopus stew with homemade bread with seaweed).

Via M. Camera 12, Amalfi. ☎ **089-871-029.** *Reservations necessary. Secondi: 20€–30€ ($23–$35). AE, DC, MC, V. Open: Lunch and dinner Wed–Mon. Closed 5 weeks Nov/Dec.*

Cumpà Cosimo
$$ Ravello AMALFITAN

At this great family-run restaurant, you can order all the local specialties prepared home-style but at a lower price than in the more "resorty" restaurants. You will see locals with their families, especially at lunchtime on weekends. The pasta is very good, and so are the *secondi* (main dishes of meat or fish), among which you'll find a good *zuppa di pesce* (fish stew) and a fine *fritto misto* (deep-fried mixed seafood). Half-portions and kid-friendly menu items will please your little ones.

Via Roma 44. ☎ *089-857-156. Reservations recommended. Secondi: 11€–28€ ($13–$32). AE, DC, MC, V. Open: Lunch and dinner daily.*

Da Gemma
$$$ Amalfi AMALFITAN

One of the best restaurants on this stretch of coast, Da Gemma serves all the typical regional dishes. The *zuppa di pesce per due* (fish stew for two) is definitely a winner; the *fritto misto* is one of the lighter fried mixed seafoods we've tasted, and the *polipo* (tender octopus) is great. The home-made *crostata* (a thick crust topped with jam, a typical Italian home-style dessert), prepared with local citrus fruit jam, also deserves a mention. Half-portions and child-friendly foods available.

Via Fra Gerardo Sassi 9. ☎ *089-871-345. Reservations necessary. Secondi: 16€–28€ ($18–$32). AE, DC, MC, V. Open: Lunch and dinner Thurs–Tues. Closed Jan.*

Donna Rosa
$$ Positano AMALFITAN

This very pleasant restaurant just outside the center of town serves traditional cuisine very carefully prepared. We warmly recommend all the homemade pastas, served with local vegetables, and the daily catches, but you will not be limited to fish: rather unusually for the region, the *secondi* include many very good meat choices such as *salsicce alla griglia* (grilled local sausages) and *agnello arrosto* (roasted lamb). You can dine on the terrace in the good season.

Via Montepertuso 97/99, Positano. ☎ *089-811-806. Reservations recommended. Secondi: 12€–21€ ($14–$24). AE, DC, MC, V. Open: Lunch and dinner June–Oct daily; Nov–May Wed–Mon. Closed 11 weeks Jan/Mar.*

Ristorante Luna Convento
$$ Amalfi AMALFITAN/ITALIAN

The restaurant of the Hotel Luna Convento (see "Spending the Night," earlier in this chapter), this is a popular and fashionable rendezvous where you can enjoy excellent food. Housed in a 16th-century watch tower, its restaurant and bar both afford fantastic views over the sea. The extensive menu includes delicious homemade pastas — many made with seafood — and daily fish offerings, but also several meat dishes.

Via Pantaleone Comite 33. ☎ 089-871-002. Reservations recommended. Secondi: 16€–25€ ($18–$29). AE, DC, MC, V. Open: Lunch and dinner daily.

San Pietro
$$$$ Positano   AMALFITAN/CREATIVE

The restaurant of the beautiful hotel by the same name, it offers an elegant but warm and friendly atmosphere, refined by beautiful sea views — you can dine on the terrace — and good food. The menu, which changes often, may include *paccheri di Gragnano con patelle e sconcigli* (homemade pasta with local shellfish), *zuppa di patate con mandorle e tonno* (stew of potatoes with almonds and tuna), and *pescatrice spadellata con salsa di vongole e lumachine di mare* (sauteed local fish with clams and sea snails).

Via Laurito 2, Positano. ☎ 089-875-455. Reservations recommended. Secondi: 25€–32€ ($29–$37). AE, DC, MC, V. Open: Lunch and dinner daily. Closed Nov–Mar.

Exploring the Amalfi Coast

Beaches, seaside resorts, small farming villages up the cliffs, fishing villages by the sea — the Amalfi Coast is varied and beautiful. The attractions of the Amalfi Coast are mainly natural; people come to drive along the spectacular cliffs, play in the sea, and eat delicious seafood.

The top attractions

Amalfi

The first of Italy's maritime republics, before Genoa and Venice, Amalfi knew its moment of glory between the 10th and the 12th centuries when it was the power dominating the southern Mediterranean. The town is rich in monuments that are mementos of its past importance. The grandiose **Duomo** (Piazza del Duomo; ☎ 089-871-059) — named in honor of Sant'Andrea — has a black-and-white facade that was redone in the 18th century; it was built around the original 10th-century cathedral, which you can still see inside, integrated into the Duomo as the **Cappella del Crocifisso (Chapel of the Crucifixion).** The Duomo is open daily from 7:30 a.m. to 8:00 p.m., and admission is free. To the left of the Duomo is the breathtakingly beautiful **Chiostro del Paradiso (Paradise Cloister);** dating from the 13th century, this cloister was once the cemetery for the city's religious and political elite. From it, you can gain access to the crypt containing the remains of St. Andrew. An interesting detail is that his face is missing — it was donated to the Cathedral of St. Andrew in Patras, Greece. Admission to the cloister is 3€ ($3.45), and it's open daily from 9 a.m. to 7 p.m. From July through September, concerts are held in the cloister on Friday nights.

The once-powerful republic was famous for its **paper industry** and paper from Amalfi — a particularly thick one called *bambagina* — was shipped all over Europe. This art has been preserved in town, where one of the descendants of the ancient master papermakers is still at work: **Antonio Cavaliere** (Via Fiume; ☎ **089-7871-954**). You can visit his workshop, complete with the traditional equipment of the trade, where he produces paper of an almost forgotten quality — though it's sold to the most exclusive paper shops in Italy, Europe, and the U.S. His shop is open during regular business hours. The water for this craft still comes from the covered river that crosses town and was the key resource in the development of the paper industry in Amalfi.

If you follow the river out of town toward the hills (start at Piazza del Duomo and head up Via Genova), you can explore the **Valle dei Mulini (Valley of the Mills),** the path stretching down the narrow valley of the river, along which the old paper mills that were the town's main economic resource are still visible. You can find out more about the industry at the very interesting **Museo della Carta (Museum of Paper)** (Via delle Cartiere; ☎ **089-830-4561**), filled with antique presses and yellowing manuscripts. It's open Tuesday, Thursday, Saturday, and Sunday from 9 a.m. to 1 p.m., and admission is 2€ ($2.30).

Besides paper, Amalfi is famous today for its **lemons.** Unique in size, sweetness, flavor, and color, the lemons of Amalfi are exported as rare gems to markets around Italy. Here you can see them turned into the famous *limoncello,* a yellow-colored sweet lemon liqueur, but also into delicious confections such as candied lemons, jams, and lemon ice cream.

Limoncello has a very nice taste, but few people can drink it straight. If you buy a bottle, you will probably want to use it to flavor cakes, cookies, and other sweet preparations.

Positano

Positano is a seaside resort made exclusive by its topography. The westernmost of the three most famous towns on the Amalfi Coast, **Positano** is also the most dramatic. Built in the narrow gap between two mountains, the village slopes steeply to the Tyrrhenian Sea.

The village develops vertically and, as you'll soon discover, is impossibly steep. You may prefer to wear comfortable shoes without heels to climb the steep alleys and many ramps of steps. Don't expect white Caribbean beaches here: The beach is gray and rather pebbly; however, the sea is splendid. Just off its coast are the legendary Sirenuse Islands, Homer's siren islands in the *Odyssey,* which form the privately owned mini-archipelago of Li Galli (The Cocks).

As an elegant resort, the village's small alleys and ramps are filled with boutiques, restaurants, and hotels. Aside from the picturesque alleys, the big attraction here — you'll notice it the moment you step into town — are the swimsuits. Whether maillot, bikini, or thong, all have colorful and unique patterns. Because people here spend two-thirds of their time in swimsuits, this local industry has exploded. We know someone who buys her bikinis only in Positano, no matter how far she has to travel to get them!

Ravello

The only one of the major towns not on the coast, **Ravello** opens into a splendid valley with intensive cultivation — vineyards and lemons and other fruit grow on its steep terraced flanks. The town has a feeling of subdued elegance, the evidence of its magnificent past. Indeed, Ravello continued, after the fall of Amalfi, to be an important center for commerce with the East during the 13th century. Celebrities and writers favor this town, and the reigning celeb of the moment is Gore Vidal, who purchased a villa as a writing retreat.

The 11th-century **Duomo** (Piazza Vescovado; ☎ 089-858-311; open: daily 9 a.m.–1 p.m. and 4–7 p.m.) has a beautiful portal, the center arch of which is closed by its famous bronze door — one of the nicest in Italy — sculpted in 1179 by Barisano da Trani; also interesting are the 13th-century campanile, and the crypt. Inside, to the left of the main altar, is the **Cappella di San Pantaleone,** the chapel of the patron saint of Ravello. It contains a relic of the saint (a cracked vessel with his blood, which miraculously fails to leak away when it liquefies once a year); the blood is a symbol of the saint's violent demise: He was beheaded in Nicomedia on July 27, 290. Ravello holds a festival on that day every year.

Going farther inland, you can reach the **Villa Cimbrone** (Via Santa Chiara 26; ☎ 089-858-072), built in the 19th century by an eccentric Englishman over a preexisting 15th-century villa. The views and the gardens are very beautiful, and spending the night here is well worth it (some of the rooms have been opened as a hotel accommodation — see "Spending the Night," earlier in this chapter). The villa is accessible only on foot after a somewhat steep walk of about ten minutes. If you ring the bell at the entrance, a member of the staff lets you in and even takes you inside the building to admire the strange architecture. It's open daily from 9 a.m. to 7 p.m., in winter until sunset; admission is 5€ ($5.75).

More cool things to see and do

Many people drive the Amalfi Coast and stop at only one or two of the towns, usually Amalfi or Positano. But the smaller towns and destinations are worth exploring, too. Here are a few recommendations:

✔ At 5km (3.1 miles) west of Amalfi — on foot or by boat — is the **Grotta dello Smeraldo (Emerald Grotto),** an underwater grotto less famous than Capri's Blue Grotto, but to the eyes of some, even more beautiful. What's unique about this grotto is its ancient formation of stalactites and stalagmites, which have been partially invaded by sea water. As a result, some of the formations are submerged, creating fantastic effects of light and shade. The boat takes you inside and around this bizarre world. It's open daily from 9 a.m. to 4 p.m., weather permitting. The cave is accessible from the sea — regular launch service is available from **Molo Pennello** in Amalfi from 9:30 a.m. to 4 p.m. for 10€ ($12) round-trip — or from land — you can walk or take the SITA bus toward Sorrento (get off at the km 26.4 milestone on SS163) and go down a steep staircase or elevator. Admission to the grotto is 5€ ($5.75) per person, which includes the elevator ride from the road down to sea level and the boat ride to and inside the cave.

✔ The Amalfi Coast is a seaside resort, and you can enjoy its many small sandy beaches. The one in Amalfi is nice, but even better are the beaches at the small towns of **Maiori** and **Minori,** two small villages farther south. There you can sunbathe and swim in the blue Mediterranean. Take to SITA bus to Maiori or to Minori.

✔ If you visit during the summer, you might like to catch a show at the **Ravello Festival** (Via Roma 10/12; ☎ and Fax: **089-858-422** or 199-109-910 for reservations; www.ravellofestival.com). Held in Ravello from June to September, this venue offers musical performances — mostly, but not all classical — by famous artists.

Fast Facts: The Amalfi Coast

Area Code

The country code for Italy is **39**. The area code for the towns along the Amalfi Coast is **089**; use this code when calling from anywhere outside or inside Italy, even within the towns themselves (include the 0 every time, even when calling from abroad).

ATMs

Banks in the three main town have ATMs on-site and also offer currency exchange.

Emergencies

Ambulance, ☎ **118**; fire, ☎ **115**; police, ☎ **113**; road assistance (ACI), ☎ **116**.

Hospital

There is a medical center in Amalfi (via Casamare ☎ 089-871-449), and one in Ravello (Guardia Medica Castiglione di Ravello. ☎ 118).

Police

There are two police forces in Italy; call either one. For the Polizia, call ☎ **113**; for the Carabinieri, call ☎ **112**.

Post Office

Ravello, Positano, and Amalfi each has an Ufficio Postale in the center of town; the one in Amalfi is at Via delle Repubbliche Marinare (☎ 089-872-996).

Part VII
Sicily

The 5th Wave   By Rich Tennant

"I appreciate that our room looks out onto several baroque fountains, but I had to get up 6 times last night to go to the bathroom."

In this part . . .

"**Y**ou cannot get a true idea of Italy without seeing Sicily. Sicily is where you can find the key to everything." These words, which Goethe wrote in 1787, still hold true. Sicily is a more intense version of Italy, where things from the past are preserved with a magic vitality and hit you with strength and clarity. As you'll see from reading this part of the guide, visiting Sicily is a unique experience if you abandon yourself to the task.

In Chapter 23, we tell you everything you need to know to explore Palermo, Sicily's capital and southern Italy's largest art center. In Chapter 24, we recommend three very interesting destinations worth exploring in Sicily: beautiful Taormina; Syracuse, rich in art and attractions; and Agrigento, with its breathtaking Valley of the Temples.

Chapter 23

Palermo

· ·

In This Chapter

▶ Discovering the treasures of Palermo

▶ Getting the best deal on lodging and the best meal

▶ Enjoying the sights and activities

· ·

The island of Sicily is almost like a country unto itself. Geographically separate from the Italian peninsula, it is hundreds of miles from Rome, Florence, and the other top tourist centers, and has developed its own unique culture over the centuries.

Why go all the way to Sicily, you ask? Well, if you don't, you'll be missing out on a big chunk of Italy — bigger than Tuscany, bigger than Lombardy. In fact, Sicily is the largest of the Italian regions. The island's central position in the Mediterranean — Africa is only a day's sail away — has made it a strategic base since ancient times, and its rich volcanic soil has attracted colonizers and pillagers alike. No wonder Rome and Carthage used the island as a battleground, and later, the Arabs and Normans. Though Sicily's northeast corner is separated from the mainland only by the sliver of the Straits of Messina, at its southernmost points it stretches farther south than Tunis.

Palermo is a busy modern port and is the political center of "new" Sicily — meaning from about 1060 onward. The mixture of Arab and Norman influences in Palermo brought about a cultural mix that's apparent both in stunning works of art and in Sicilian traditions and institutions. (The Sicilian Parliament meets in the building that was the Norman palace.) Palermo was severely damaged by earthquakes in the early 20th century and was bombarded in World War II; much of it seems to have never recovered. However, Palermo still boasts some of the region's finest art; its churches alone are worth the visit, and its museums, in a region where museums are rather inadequate, are very good. Although most visitors to Sicily arrive here, you'll find it easier to understand and appreciate Palermo after having seen other parts of the island.

Behind a decaying but elegant facade, Palermo holds unsuspected treasures. Similarly, behind more formal manners and customs, the Sicilians are a warm and welcoming people ready to help you enjoy your visit. Remember, though, that *respect* is the key word here.

Palermo is a good starting point for exploring Sicily, especially if you're planning to take a guided tour. Indeed, tours start from here for each of the major attractions on the island. The other good starting point is Taormina (see Chapter 24). For a map of Sicily, please see this book's inside back cover.

Getting There

There are many ways to get to Sicily, but the best way, in our opinion, is to take the ferry.

By ferry

Several ferry companies serve the island. **SNAV** (Via Giordano Bruno 84; ☎ **081-428-5555;** Fax: 081-428-5259; www.snav.it) has ferry service running between Naples and Palermo. It runs once a day, leaving from Naples around 9 a.m. and arriving in Palermo in the evening. The one-way fare, depending on the season, varies from about 115€ to 150€ ($132–$173). Transportation of a car with two adults is 175€ to 280€ ($201–$322), depending on the car size and the season, plus 2.25€ ($2.60) per person and 5€ ($5.75) per car in harbor taxes. The ferry run by **Tirrenia** between Naples and Palermo (☎ **091-333-300** in Naples and 06-474-2041 in Rome; www.tirrenia.com) is an overnight (10 hours) — a good deal because you save on a hotel for the night and don't use up daylight hours traveling. A one-way adult fare is 71€ to 85€ ($82–$98) for a double cabin (with bunk beds — very comfortable); a car costs from 69€ to 106€ ($79–$122).

By air

Flying is less romantic than taking the ferry but it's the fastest way to get to Sicily. Remember, though, that you can't fly directly in and out of Italy from Sicily — you have to fly into Rome or Milan first. **Alitalia** (☎ **8488-65641;** www.alitalia.com) has several flights a day from Italian cities to Sicily. To book from the U.S., call ☎ **800-223-5730. Meridiana** (☎ **0789-52-682;** www.meridiana.it) may offer better deals, and has some flights in conjunction with Alitalia.

Like Rome's Fiumicino, Palermo's airport, **Aeroporto Falcone Borsellino** (☎ **800-541-880** or 091-702-0111), is referred to by its location (Punta Raisi) and not by its actual name. The airport is open daily from 8 a.m. to 11 p.m. You can take the metro from Punta Raisi to Palermo for 4.50€ ($5.20). It runs approximately every half-hour.

The company **Prestia & Comande** (☎ **091-586-351**) runs the **bus** service between the airport and the Hotel Politeama and Stazione Centrale in Palermo. The bus runs every 30 minutes, takes about half an hour, and the fare is 4.80€ ($5.95). A **taxi** from the airport will cost about 40€ ($46).

By train

The train (☎ **147-888-088** toll-free in Italy or 091-616-1806; www. ferroviedellostato.it) from Rome takes 11 to 13 hours and costs 44€ to 89€ ($51–$102) per person, depending on whether it's a local or an express. A *cuccetta* (sleeping berth) runs about 24€ ($28). You don't save much over the ferry, and the train takes longer. The train is put on a train ferry at Messina and continues on to Palermo. The train arrives at Palermo's **Stazione Centrale FS (☎ 091-616-5914)** on Piazza Giulio Cesare, very near the center of town.

Orienting Yourself in Palermo

Palermo is a port city, organized around its busy waterfront. **Via Francesco Crispi** is the major thoroughfare running along the waterfront of **Porto,** the new harbor. To the east of the modern harbor is the original harbor, the **Cala,** today just a small yacht basin compared with nearby Porto and its piers for large ships. Inland of the Cala is the historical center of Palermo, with **La Kalsa,** the ancient Arab quarters, to the east, and the four *mandamenti* (neighborhoods) of the *centro storico* (old town) to the south. The *centro storico* is neatly divided along **Corso Vittorio Emanuele** and **Via Maqueda,** intersecting at **Piazza Vigliena,** a small square usually referred to as **Quattro Canti (four corners),** but also called *Teatro del Sole* (theater of the sun) because you can see the sun from sunrise to sunset. At the junction of La Kalsa and the *centro storico* is **Piazza Marina,** just off the Cala. Parallel to Via Maqueda to the north is **Via Roma.**

During the 19th century, the city expanded to the west and Via Maqueda was prolonged by **Via Ruggero VII,** across **Piazza Verdi,** and **Via della Libertà,** across **Piazza Castelnuovo.** To the south is **Monreale.**

Introducing the neighborhoods

The historic part of Palermo is, naturally, where most of the attractions are concentrated; it can be divided into an older section (going back to the Arabian rulers) and a more recent one (built at the turn of the 20th century) — but the rest of the city is worth exploring, too.

Centro Storico or Città Antica (Old Town)

The old town starts at the ancient **Cala** and stretches to the **Palazzo dei Normanni,** the castle and royal residence of the various powers that reigned over Palermo (from the Arab Emirs to the current Regional Assembly of Sicily). Besides some of Palermo's most important monuments, such as **La Martorana** and the **Cattedrale,** this area has many hotels and restaurants, an active nightlife, and lively shopping — including the famous **Vucciria open-air market.**

Palermo

ACCOMMODATIONS ■
Grand Albergo Sole **21**
Grand Hotel et des Palmes **9**
Grand Hotel Villa Igiea **1**
Joli Hotel **8**
Jolly Hotel **29**
Massimo Plaza **12**
President Hotel **7**
Principe de Villafranca **4**

DINING ◆
Capricci di Sicilia **5**
Casa del Brodo **25**
La Cambusa **27**
Osteria dei Vespri **26**

ATTRACTIONS ●
Casa Professa (Chiesa del Gesù) **22**
Catacombe dei Cappuccini **17**
Cattedrale **16**
Chiesa di Santa Maria dell'Ammiraglio (La Martorana) **23**
Fontana Pretoria **24**
Galleria Regionale Siciliana (Palazzo Abatellis) **28**
La Cuba **18**
La Kalsa **30**
La Zisa **10**
Monte Pellegrino and Santuario di Santa Rosalia **2**
Museo Archeologico Regionale **13**
Oratorio del Santissimo Rosariodi San Domenico **15**
Oratorio di Santa Cita **14**
Palazzo dei Normanni and Cappella Palatina **19**
San Giovanni dei Eremiti **20**
Teatro Massimo **11**
Teatro Politeama Garibaldi **6**
Villa Malfitano **3**

Città Nuova (New Town)

Less picturesque than the old town, but also interesting, this part of town was first developed in the late 19th century. Important sights here include the **Teatro Massimo,** the **Teatro Politeama** (its full name is the Teatro Politeama Garibaldi), and **Via Libertà** with its Liberty (Italian Art Nouveau) palaces. This is central Palermo's most pleasant area, and hence very popular with locals — the Politeama is the rendezvous place for people of every age. It is the place to head for boutiques, restaurants, and hotels.

La Kalsa

This neighborhood, centered around the ancient harbor of **La Cala,** has been the most famous and the most notorious in Palermo. La Kalsa is where the Arab part of Palermo grew up, beginning with the invasion of the Saracens in 831. Its winding streets are picturesque — and, at times, have been dangerous: There was a time when tourists wouldn't come here at all. That has changed. La Cala has been revitalized (although not entirely refurbished) and is a popular spot for cultural events and nightlife. Among the sights in this neighborhood are the **Galleria Regionale della Sicilia (Regional Gallery)** and the **Piazza Marina,** which is the focus of an exuberant nightlife and dining scene.

Monreale

A separate town overlooking the city, Monreale is to Palermo what Ficsole is to Florence, dominating the city from a beautiful hill. The great attraction here, sufficient alone to justify your whole trip to Sicily, is the **Duomo** with its cloister. Otherwise, it's a quiet little town with little activity and not much in terms of restaurants or hotels.

Porto (Harbor)

The harbor has been the focus of Palermo for ages, and as the city expanded, it outgrew the original Arab harbor and these new facilities were built. This is the first part of Palermo that you see when you arrive, but don't take it as representative of the city. It was heavily bombarded during the invasion in World War II and most of the buildings are new. It is a safe area and surprisingly quiet — the industrial part of the harbor is farther away. It has hotels — convenient to the ferries and liners — and a few restaurants and shops.

Finding information after you arrive

The walk-in public office of the **Azienda Autonoma Provinciale per l'Incremento Turistico** is at Piazza Castelnuovo 34, across from the Teatro Politeama (☎ **091-583-847** or 091-605-8351; www.palermo tourism.com). It's open Monday through Friday from 8:30 a.m. to 2:00 p.m. and 3:00 to 7:00 p.m. The agency also maintains **tourist information desks** at the airport (☎ **091-591-698**) and at the train station (☎ **091-616-5914**). The train station office is open Monday through

Friday from 8:30 a.m. to 2:00 p.m. and 3:00 to 7:00 p.m. The airport desk is open 8 a.m. to midnight on weekdays and 8 a.m. to 8 p.m. on Saturday and Sunday; if you arrive at the airport on a weekend, make sure to stop here before proceeding to town.

Getting Around Palermo

Although the modern town sprawls between the mountains and the sea, the historic center and its sights are fairly concentrated and can be visited on foot, provided you make a logical plan — as usual, avoiding the up and down, east and west itineraries is best.

On foot

Palermo is an interesting city to discover on foot; however, you should be aware that purse snatchers (particularly effective and dangerous ones operate from *motorini,* or motor scooters) and pickpockets are a common reality. They are especially active in the crowded open-air markets — such as the Vucciria, but also wherever tourists are; hence, don't be distracted and keep your valuables safe. Backpacks are especially susceptible, as their bottoms can be easily sliced without you noticing it. Also, there are still forlorn blocks with partially destroyed buildings — some by World War II bombings, others by earthquakes — in many parts of the old town. We have walked down some of these streets (by day) to look at the shuttered villas of the Sicilian aristocracy and never had any problem, but everyone has their own comfort level.

The only major sight that will require you to take public transportation is Monreale.

By bus

Palermo's transportation authority, **AMAT** (☎ **091-690-2690;** www.amat.pa.it), runs electric minibuses — called *Aquilotto* — that are convenient for visiting all the important attractions in Palermo. These special circular lines go through the *centro storico* Monday through Saturday from 7:45 a.m. to 7:30 p.m. and Sunday and holidays from 7:45 a.m. to 1:30 p.m.; use them as you would a hop-on-hop-off tour bus. The **Linea Gialla** goes from Stazione centrale (railroad station) through La Kalsa and the *centro storico;* the **Linea Rossa** goes from Piazza Marina to the Cattedrale, and via Maqueda. The ticket is valid 24 hours on both lines.

For information on both the electric special lines and regular buses, AMAT maintains an information office at Via Giusti 7 (open Mon–Wed 8 a.m.–1 p.m. and 3–5:30 p.m., and Thurs–Fri 8 a.m.–1 p.m.), where you can get bus maps and tickets, including a **rechargeable ticket card,** for the regular bus system. An individual ticket costs 1 € ($1.15) and is valid for 2 hours; you can also get a **giornaliero** ticket for 3.35€ ($3.85), which is valid for one day, or a carnet of 20 individual tickets for 18.10€ ($21).

When you need to reach sights out of town, note that the *provincia* of Palermo is served by the bus company **AST** (☎ **800-234-163** toll-free in Italy or 091-688-2906).

By taxi

Taxis are an excellent way to get around when your feet are tired and when it is very hot. You'll find taxi stands at all the major squares — Piazza Indipendenza, Piazza Verdi, Piazza Castelnuovo — at the Porto, and at the railroad station. Alternatively, you can phone a radio-dispatched taxi and be picked up anywhere; call ☎ **091-225-455** or 091-513-311. The basic charge for a taxi is 3.50€ ($4), and then .65€ (75¢) for every additional kilometer (.6 mile), but these official rates are old.

It is true — we checked — "official rates haven't been adjusted since 1991," one taxi driver told us after awarding himself an inflation increase over the meter. Expect to pay a few euro more than what the meter shows, depending on the length of the trip, but it should be reasonable. It's just a lot easier and will avoid friction on both sides if you confirm with the driver what the charge is likely to be for your destination up front, instead of being surprised by an extravagant charge upon arrival.

Staying in Style

Most of Palermo's sights are within walking distance of the center, and that's the best place to stay (plus, you don't have to transit any deserted neighborhoods on your way home after dark). Because tourism isn't as highly developed as in other major centers in Italy of comparable importance, hotels in Palermo are more old-fashioned than what you may be used to, and the pace of renovation seems to be slower. In Sicily, even more than elsewhere in Italy, family-run hotels tend to feel as if you stepped into someone's home. But never fear: For better or worse, things are changing.

For the same reasons we just explained, if you're planning to pick a hotel that's not from our recommendations, remember that going for cheapy accommodations in Sicily doesn't pay in the long run.

The top hotels

Grand Hotel et des Palmes
$$ Città Nuova

Once a private home, the Grand Hotel opened in 1874 and has since been the hotel to go to in central Palermo. Wagner finished writing his *Parsifal* here, and one of the guests in more recent times was Bill Clinton. The classically inspired lobby has marble floors, Greek columns, chandeliers, marble staircases, and Art Nouveau furnishings. It's no insult to say this is the poor man's grand hotel; some areas are updated, while others recall past glories. This makes it a great value; the overall feeling is grand, even if guest rooms (though large) are rather staid. Meals are served in La Palmetta Restaurant, and the Hall of Mirrors (Sala degli Specchi) is used not only for receptions but also as the breakfast room — the breakfast is great, with eggs, meat, *cornetti* (Italian croissants), juices, and good coffee.

See map 466. Via Roma 398, four blocks northeast of the Teatro Politeama. ☎ *800-179-217 or 091-602-8111. Fax: 091-331-545. E-mail:* des-palmes@cormorano. net. *Bus: 806. Parking: $14€ ($16). Rack rates: 95€–270€ ($109–$311) double. Rates include buffet breakfast. AE, DC, MC, V.*

Grand Hotel Villa Igiea
$$$$ Porto

This is not only a hotel, but a historic site; you are paying not just for a room, but a chance to stay in a beautiful residence full of beautiful things (and at much less cost than in the more touristed parts of Italy). Housed in a former private villa on the outskirts of town, the Grand Hotel Villa Igiea is a masterpiece of the Sicilian Liberty (Italian Art Nouveau) architect Ernesto Basile, who also designed the furnishings. The spacious guest rooms are as glamorous as the public areas, and the hotel is surrounded by splendid terraced gardens overlooking the bay. The two restaurants feature local and regional cuisine; in summer, meals are served on the terrace overlooking Palermo. Other features include a piano bar, a seawater pool, and a meeting center for those traveling with an entourage.

See map 466. Salita Belmonte 43. ☎ *091-631-2111. Fax: 091-547-654. E-mail:* villa_ igiea@amthotels.it. *Bus: 139 to Villa Igiea. Free parking. Rack rates: 157€–484€ ($181–$557) double. Rates include breakfast. AE, DC, MC, V.*

Joli Hotel
$ Città Nuova

This modest hotel, on a quiet square just north of the port, has undergone a several-year renovation that was completed in 2002. A bar was added and the number of rooms was increased to 30. All the air-conditioned guest rooms have small but functional bathrooms and private terraces; some have views of Monte Pellegrino, the mountain overlooking Palermo. Although the hotel is small, it offers a pleasant lounge for guests.

See map 466. Via Michele Amari 11, two blocks southeast of the Teatro Politeama. ☎ *and Fax: 091-611-1765 or 091-611-1766. Bus: 101. Free parking. Rack rates: 88€– 138€ ($101–$159) double. Rates include breakfast. AE, DC, MC, V.*

Massimo Plaza
$$ Centro Storico

Recently restored, this elegant hotel is one of the best in town, offering beautiful accommodations and an excellent location just across from the Teatro Massimo. The large guest rooms are decorated with tasteful modern furniture, pastel walls, and wooden floors.

See map 466. Via Maqueda 437. ☎ ***091-325-657.*** *Fax: 091-325-711.* www.massimo plazahotel.com. *Rack rates: 120€–190€ ($138–$219). AE, DC, MC, V.*

Principe di Villafranca
$$ Città Nuova

This family-run hotel offers palatial accommodations close to the heart of Palermo. With Turkish carpets and wooden floors, huge rooms and some antique furnishings, it is an excellent value. It even has a fitness club.

See map 466. Via G. Turrisi Colonna 4. ☎ ***091-611-8523.*** *Fax: 091-588-705.* www.principedivillafranca.it. *Bus: 101 to Piazza Sturzo. Rack rates: 130€–185€ ($150–$213). AE, DC, MC, V.*

Runner-up accommodations

Grande Albergo Sole

$$ Centro Storico   Located near the Duomo and the Palazzo Reale, this is considered one of the best hotels in Palermo. It has an indoor garden and a terrace with a panoramic view. The hotel is currently undergoing a renovation and some floors are closed. *See map 466. Corso Vittorio Emanuele 291.* ☎ ***091-604-1111.*** *Fax: 091-611-0182.*

Jolly Hotel

$$ Porto   A modern hotel with a garden, a pool, and a welcoming attitude toward children. Although the guest rooms are average in size, some have balconies. *See map 466. East of the harbor, near the train station.* ☎ ***091-616-5090.*** *Fax: 091-616-1441.*

President Hotel

$$ Porto   Across from the port where the ferries arrive, this hotel was renovated in 1999. Even if the modern port is ugly, the hotel has advantages (you won't have far to walk to reach it if you arrive by boat). As such, it appeals to Italian commercial travelers. There is air-conditioning and rates include a buffet breakfast served in the restaurant with sunny views of the port and mountains. *See map 466. Via Francesco Crispi 230, west of the harbor.* ☎ ***091-580-733.*** *Fax: 091-611-1588.*

Dining Out

Even within Italy, where every town seems to lay claim to a unique cuisine, Sicily is exceptional. Nobody else in Italy would attempt some of these daring creations. The Sicilians perfected multiculturalism centuries ago; you can find dishes like Italian-looking pasta with pistachio nuts and North African spices, and other dishes reflecting its checkered past. And because Sicily is an island, its cuisine is chock full of treasures from the sea (see Chapter 2 for more info).

Two excellent dining areas worth checking out are the ones most popular with locals. Attracting younger crowds is the area surrounding **Piazza Marina,** behind the recreational harbor of La Cala. Here you can find pizzerias with pounding music and fish restaurants that draw a professional clientele. The area around the **Teatro Politeama,** on Piazza Sturzo/Piazza Castelnuovo, is where locals go for more traditional and/or more elegant dining.

Capricci di Sicilia
$$ Città Nuova SICILIAN

In the more elegant part of the center, Capricci di Sicilia is an excellent restaurant offering typical recipes of the Sicilian tradition in a pleasant decor. Try the delicious *bucatini alle sarde e finocchietto selvatico* (pasta with sardines and wild fennel), *maccheroni alla Norma* (with eggplant), *involtini di pesce spada* (rolled and stuffed swordfish), and *trionfo di pesce azzurro* (several kinds of bluefish — grilled, sauteed, roasted, or poached).

See map 466. Via Istituto Pignatelli 6, off Piazza Sturzo to the northwest of the Teatro Politeama. ☎ *091-327-777. Reservations recommended. Bus: 101 to Piazza Sturzo. Secondi: 9€–14€ ($10–$16). AE, DC, MC, V. Open: Lunch and dinner Tues–Sun.*

Casa del Brodo
$ Centro Storico SICILIAN

This trattoria, opened in 1890, claims to be the oldest in Palermo. The buffet of *antipasti* includes a large variety of traditional specialties, all freshly prepared. The fish dishes are dependable, as are the traditional *primi* (*pasta alla Norma* [with eggplant], *pasta con le sarde* [with sardines], and so on). The old-fashioned ambience isn't a bit ruined by the air-conditioning. The restaurant is in a busy section of town and gets crowded at lunchtime.

See map 466. Corso Vittorio Emanuele 175, near the Vucciria. ☎ *091-321-655. Reservations recommended on weekends. Bus: 104 to Quattro Canti or 105 to Corso Vittorio Emanuele, east of Via Roma. Secondi: 6.50€–11€ ($7.50–$13). MC, V. Open: Lunch and dinner Wed–Mon.*

La Cambusa
$ Centro Storico SICILIAN

Here you find excellent homemade typical Sicilian fare. La Cambusa is very popular with the people of La Cala (the marina across the street) and other Palermitans, so come early — Sicilians eat at 9:00 or even 9:30 p.m. in summer — or be prepared to wait. Try the superb *pasta con le sarde* (pasta with sardines, fennel, and tomato sauce) or the *pasta alla carrettiera* (the Sicilian version of pesto sauce, with capers, almonds, and tomato).

See map 466. Piazza Marina 16. ☎ *091-584-574. Reservations recommended on weekends. Bus: 105 to Piazza Marina. Secondi: 6.50€–13€ ($7.50–$15). MC, V. Open: Lunch and dinner Tues–Sun.*

Mandarini
$$ Porto SEAFOOD/SICILIAN

This is an excellent place to sample Sicily's seafood bounty. It is especially pleasant to eat under the shade of the mandarin trees on the spacious terrace in summer. Another attraction is the comprehensive list of Sicilian wines, many of which are not commonly available, even elsewhere in Italy.

Via Rosario Da Partanna, 18, just north of the harbor. ☎ *091-671-2199. Reservations recommended. Secondi: 14€–20€ ($16–$23). AE, DC, MC, V. Open: Lunch and dinner Tues–Sun.*

Osteria dei Vespri
$$ Centro Storico ITALIAN/CREATIVE

Not everything in Palermo is traditional; this *osteria* specializes in innovative cuisine, for which chef and proprietor Alberto Rizzo has become renowned. Try the soup made with local mushrooms, or the *ravioli ripieni di funghi porcini e patate al profumo di timo su fondutina tartufata e prezzemolo riccio* (mushroom, potato, and thyme ravioli over cheese fondue with truffles and fresh parsley) and the *filetto di maiale in crosta di nocciole* (pork filet mignon in hazelnut crust). In a land known for idiosyncracy, Rizzo earns the reputation.

See map 466. Piazza Croce dei Vespri 6. ☎ *091-617-1631. Reservations recommended. Bus: 105 to Piazza Marina. Secondi: 9€–16€ ($10–$18). AE, DC, MC, V. Open: Lunch and dinner Mon–Sat.*

Exploring Palermo

Palermo's intertwined traditions have left behind a city like no other in the world, where "multiculturalism" flourished in the 12th century. Just wandering around can be fascinating; note the various styles and cultural overlays. It may help to remember that, by one of those quirks of history, Holy Roman emperor Frederick II (1194–1250) was born in Italy, and made Palermo his capital; it became one of most renowned and magnificent courts in the Western world. Although today the city may seem to be off the beaten track tourism-wise, its treasures attest that it was once the center of an empire.

There are two cumulative tickets you can buy if you are planning to see several of sights of Palermo. Each costs 8€ ($9.20). One gains you entrance to **La Zisa, La Cuba,** the cloister of **Monreale,** and **San Giovanni degli Eremiti.** The other is valid for the **Galleria Regionale Siciliana,** the **Museo Archeologico Regionale** and one of the Palermitan palaces. You can buy them at any of the participating attractions.

The top attractions

Casa Professa aka Chiesa del Gesù

Most commonly called the Casa Professa, so named for the library attached to the church, this is the first church in Sicily founded by the Jesuits. Its interior is rich in **stuccowork** by the Serpotta (famous 17th- and 18th-century Palermitan sculptors), and beautiful **marble inlays** in a large range of colors decorate the altar and walls. The original Renaissance church, in the form of a Latin cross (a nave and two short aisles), was designed by Giovanni Tristano in 1564. It was much changed in the following century by the Jesuit Natale Masuccio, who made it into one of the most ostentatious churches of the Sicilian baroque. A large part of the church was destroyed in 1943, but it was later restored.

See map 466. Piazza Casa Professa, off Via Ponticello from Via Maqueda. ☎ *091-607-6223. Bus: 101, 102, 103. Admission: Free. Open: Daily 7 a.m.–noon and 5–6:30 p.m.; no visits during mass. Open mornings only in Aug.*

Cattedrale

Palermo's cathedral was built in 1185 atop a mosque that was itself built atop a Byzantine church. In this mixed-up sandwich, some material was reused; for example, in the portico is a column (first on the left) with an engraved inscription from the Koran, an unusual feature for a Catholic church. In the 15th century, the south side became the main entrance, with a portico in Gothic-Catalan style. In the 18th century, the whole interior was redone in neoclassical style, and the lateral naves were added along with the dome. The apse is the original part of the church. The outside is Romanesque; after its warm, pale ochres, the inside is a shock of white and gray baroque. Look for the bas-reliefs by Vincenzo and Fazio Gagini on the altar and the **Madonna with Child** by Francesco Laurana in the seventh chapel of the left nave (Laurana's famous sculpture of Eleanora d'Aragona is in the Galleria Regionale Siciliana — see the description later in this chapter). The **imperial and royal tombs** include those of Frederick II (see earlier in this section) and Roger II. The **Cappella di Santa Rosalia (Chapel of St. Rosalia)** contains the saint's remains, which are carried through the streets in a procession every July (see "More cool things to see and do," later in this chapter). The **tesoro (treasury)** of the church contains a variety of precious objects, including chalices, vestments, and other utensils of the Catholic rite, as well as the **crown** of **Constance of Aragon,** the wife of Frederick II. The treasury and crypt are reached from inside the cathedral, but the entrance to the tombs is outside on the Via Matteo Bonello.

See map 466. Piazza della Cattedrale, on Via Vittorio Emanuele. ☎ *091-334-3736.* www.cattedrale.palermo.it. *Bus: 104, 110. Admission: 2€ ($2.30). Open: Mon–Sat 7 a.m.–5:30 p.m., Sun and holidays 7:30 a.m.–1:30 p.m. and 4–7 p.m. Treasury and Crypt: same hours, but closed on Sun except for groups. Closed to visitors during mass.*

Chiesa di Santa Maria dell'Ammiraglio aka La Martorana

This church was built by the admiral of Ruggero II, Giorgio di Antiochia, in 1143, but it was transformed during later centuries. However, the original structure's beautiful **Byzantine mosaics** remain. The central scene depicts the heavenly hierarchy; in a bit of artistic politicking, a mosaic on the balustrade shows Roger II getting his crown directly from Christ and not from the pope. Other scenes are from the life of Mary. The name *Martorana* comes from the nearby convent, founded by the Martorana family. Tradition says that the nuns there invented the little marzipan fruits that today are a typical — and delicious — souvenir from Sicily. They still sell the original creations: sculptures of bunches of grapes made of almond paste, each grape delicately painted with sugar and the stems made of candied orange peel covered in dark chocolate — a bit expensive, yes, but a treat fit for a king.

See map 466. Piazza Bellini 3, off Via Maqueda, near the Quattro Canti. ☎ *091-616-1692. Bus: 101. Admission: Free. Open: Mon–Sat 8 a.m.–1 p.m. and 3:30–6:30 p.m., Sun and holidays 8:30 a.m.–1 p.m.*

Duomo di Monreale

This 12th-century Romanesque church in Monreale is one of the most breathtaking in existence. It may not be exceptional for its Norman exterior — the Duomo in Palermo is more interesting — but the interior is extraordinary. The church is decorated with 6,000 sq. m (55,000 sq. ft.) of fabulous **Byzantine school mosaics,** whose subjects come from the Old and New Testaments, with the stories of Noah, Isaac, and Jacob most prominent (only in Constantinople itself, in the Hagia Sofia, did the Byzantines create a more extensive series of mosaics). In the dome is a **Christ Pantocrator** icon (an image of Christ as the ruler of the universe, with his fingers making the Greek symbol of his divine and human nature). The apse's decorations show an Islamic influence. The floors are comprised of remarkable marble mosaics, and the bronze doors by Bonanno Pisano (designer of Pisa's famous tower) are masterpieces. Annexed to the church is the **cloister** from 1180, one of the most beautiful in Italy. It has 228 double columns, some with mosaic inlay and each with an individual pattern; the carved stone capitals are amazingly intricate renderings of scenes such as battles, the punishment of the damned, and stories of obscure meaning with fanciful and incredibly detailed carvings.

Piazza del Duomo in Monreale. ☎ *091-640-4413 or 091-640-4403 (cloister). Bus: 389 from Piazza Indipendenza, off the Palazzo dei Normanni, to Piazza del Duomo, running every 20 minutes. Admission: Duomo free, cloister 4.50€ ($5.20). Open: Duomo daily 9 a.m.–6 p.m.; cloister Mon–Sat 9 a.m.–noon and 3:30–5:30 p.m., Sun and holidays 9 a.m.–12:30 p.m.*

Fontana Pretoria

This magnificent 16th-century fountain was created for a Florentine villa, but when the villa's owner died, his son sold the fountain to the Palermo

Senate. The nudes created a big scandal in town, and for a while it was called the "fountain of shame." The succession of concentric circular platforms are connected by stairways and balustrades. There are 4 basins on which 24 heads of monsters and animals face outward, 56 channels of water, 37 statues portraying mythological characters, and 4 large statues representing the rivers that fertilize the countryside around Palermo.

See map 466. Piazza Pretoria, off the Quattro Canti, where Via Vittorio Emanuele crosses Via Maqueda.

Galleria Regionale Siciliana (Palazzo Abatellis)

In late Catalan Gothic style, the 1490 Palazzo Abbatellis houses the principal museum of Sicilian art from the 13th to the 18th centuries. The 15th-century *Triumph of Death* is a powerful and intriguing fresco that came from the hall of the 1330 Palazzo Sclafani. A skeleton on horseback fires arrows at pleasure seekers, rich prelates, and other sinners as the poor and ill look on (the two artists who did the fresco painted themselves in this group). The faces are incredibly expressive; Picasso could have done the horse's head. One of the words that most comes to mind when seeing this work is "modern." It's unfortunate that its creator's identity is not known. Among other masterpieces, Antonello da Messina's **Madonna Annunziata,** looking out from under a blue mantle, displays the painter's uncanny ability to portray more than one emotion at the same time. Francesco Laurana's marble **bust of Eleonora d'Aragona** is one of the most famous artworks in Sicily. These works are definitely worth the visit, even if many other pieces are of minor importance or in poor condition.

See map 466. Via Alloro, near Piazza Marina. ☎ *091-623-0011. Bus: 101 or 102, or, from Piazza Marina, cross the garden and take Via Quattro Aprile to Via Alloro. Admission: 5€ ($5.75). Open: Daily 9 a.m.–1 p.m.; Tues and Thurs also 3–7:30 p.m.*

La Kalsa

One of the city's oldest neighborhoods (it was built by the Arabs as the emir's citadel), La Kalsa developed around **Piazza Magione,** southeast of **Piazza Marina.** The grandiose battle scene between Garibaldi and the Bourbons in the famous Visconti movie *Il Gattopardo (The Leopard)* was filmed on Piazza Magione. Piazza Marina is one of La Kalsa's main features, with its beautiful garden enclosed by elegant Liberty-style iron railings and graced by an impressive giant ficus. **Via Alloro** was the central street of La Kalsa, as you can see from the once-elegant palaces lining the street. The nearby **Cala** is Palermo's original harbor.

Unfortunately, the rest of the neighborhood is quite grungy, though it is slowly being revamped. Much of the Arabs' fine work was destroyed when the Spanish viceroys took over, adding their own architectural interpretations, and much of the later *palazzi* were damaged or destroyed by earthquakes and World War II, and are mostly semi-abandoned. For an idea of what they looked like in their former splendor, visit the restored 15th-century **Palazzo Abatellis,** seat of the Galleria Regionale Siciliana (see the description earlier in this chapter) and the **Palazzo Mirto** (Via Merlo 2;

☎ 091-616-4751); the latter is open Monday through Friday 9 a.m. to 1:30 p.m. and Tuesday and Thursday also 3 to 5:30 p.m., and Saturday and Sunday 9:00 a.m. to 12:30 p.m. Admission is free. The aristocratic family that occupied the *palazzo* for centuries donated it to the city in 1982. Its lavishly decorated rooms preserve the memory of the glory days of the Sicilian aristocracy. Among the neighborhood's churches, visit **Santa Teresa** (Piazza Kalsa; ☎ 091-616-1658), a good example of the irrepressible Sicilian baroque, and the 13th-century **San Francesco d'Assisi** (Piazza San Francesco d'Assisi, off Via Merlo; ☎ 091-616-2819), with a superb 14th-century portal and handsome carvings inside. Both churches are closed in the early afternoon.

Unless you're a diehard urbanite, check out La Kalsa during the daytime. Its dark alleys and decaying buildings can be intimidating at night.

See map 466. Defined by Via Maqueda, Corso Vittorio Emanuele, Via Lincoln, and the sea.

La Zisa

Also called Castello della Zisa, this building dates from 1165 to 1167 and is more a home than a castle. The castle is known for its elegant columns and mosaics and may have belonged to an Arab noblewoman, Azisa, or may have been built for King Guglielmo I (William) using Arab techniques and hence named Al-Aziz, "the Magnificent." The palace was surrounded by a park with an artificial lake in which the building was reflected (a few hundred years before the Taj Mahal) and with small rivers and ponds for fish. The surrounding garden has disappeared, and the building suffered partial collapse in 1971 but was then restored. The second floor opens onto a beautiful courtyard. La Zisa also houses a collection of **Islamic art,** including the characteristic carved wooden screens known as *musciarabia.*

See map 466. Piazza Guglielmo il Buono. ☎ 091-652-0269. Bus: 124. Admission: 2.50€ ($2.90). Open: Mon–Sat 9 a.m.–noon and 3–7 p.m., Sun and holidays 9 a.m.–noon.

Monte Pellegrino and Santuario di Santa Rosalia

Rosalia is Palermo's patron saint. The young girl, niece of Guglielmo II, abandoned the riches of her royal family and took refuge in a cave on the mountain, where she prayed until her death (not unlike St. Francis, who also spurned his family's wealth in order to live a purer religious life). After her body was found, the cave became the site of a shrine/convent. An unforgettable view is offered from this 600m (2,000-ft.) promontory — labeled by Goethe the most beautiful in the world — separating the bay of Palermo from the gulf of Mondello and its beaches. From its top, in good weather, you can see all the way to Etna and the Aeolian Islands. Toward the interior is a plain with beautiful villas. The flanks of Monte Pellegrino are filled with caves, some of which have Paleolithic carvings. The mountain is reached by Via Pietro Bonnano; the road to the top was finished only in the 1920s.

See map 466. Monte Pellegrino, northeast of Palermo. Sanctuary: ☎ *091-540-326. Bus: 812 from Piazza Sturzo, off the Teatro Politeama. Open: 7 a.m.–7:30 p.m daily.*

Museo Archeologico Regionale

This museum, built on the site of a monastery, is a good introduction to Sicily's ancient history. The best collections are on the ground floor, which has major art finds from Greek sites in southern Italy and some Roman art (as you pass through the cloister, you see a collection of Roman objects, including pieces from Pompeii). Also important are remains from Selinunte, the site of an ancient Greek colony on Sicily's southwestern tip and today much damaged by looters. The collection was begun during the 19th century when the first *metope* (part of the frieze) from the site were found. The main salon has important finds from several of the temples, including the famous **head of Medusa.** The basement houses a reconstruction of the **clay decorations of Temple "C"** (a Greek temple built in 500 B.C. in Selinus, Italy), and in the Sala Marconi there's a partial reconstruction of the **cornice moldings** with lion heads from the Temple of Victory in Himera. The museum also holds beautiful **Roman bronze statues** — note particularly the bronze statue of a ram — and a fair amount of **Etruscan** pottery and other objects. Also remarkable are the **Phoenician** artworks dating from the fifth century B.C., including sarcophagi depicting human images.

See map 466. Piazza P. Olivella 24, between Via Roma and Via Maqueda. Bus: 101, 102, 103. ☎ *091-611-6807. Admission: 5€ ($5.75). Open: Daily 9 a.m.–1:30 p.m. and Tues, Wed, Fri also 3–6:30 p.m.*

Oratorio del Santissimo Rosario di San Domenico

Sicilian sculptor Giacomo Serpotta belonged to this small chapel (oratory); though he excelled in the use of marble and polychrome, he chose stucco to lavishly decorate the oratory from 1714 to 1717, making it his masterpiece. Another member of the oratory was Pietro Novelli, who painted many of the walls and ceilings. The other great work of art within is Anthony van Dyck's *Madonna del Rosario (Madonna of the Rosary)* commissioned during his stay in Palermo in 1624 but painted four years later in Genoa. Note that as of press time, the oratorio is closed for restoration; no date is set yet for its reopening.

See map 466. Via dei Bambinai 2, off Via Roma, between La Cala and Via Maqueda. Closed for restoration.

Palazzo dei Normanni and Cappella Palatina

Now the seat of the Sicilian Parliament, this *palazzo* goes back even further than the period of the Normans for which it is named — perhaps even as far as the time when Sicily was ruled by the Romans, and before them the Carthaginians. In the 12th century, the Normans remodeled the palace, which had been the residence of the Arab Emir. It had four towers, of which only one remains today, the **Torre Pisana.** It was remodeled again in the 16th century as the residence of the Spanish viceroy. The royal apartments are open to the public, but because of the parliamentary meetings, access is restricted (see details in the following paragraph). On the third floor is the **Sala di Ruggero,** originally the bedroom of Ruggero II (1095–1154), with mosaics representing hunting scenes and striking animals and plant forms. On the second floor is the famous **Cappella Palatina (Palatine Chapel),** with its impressive decorations. The chapel, started by Ruggero II in 1132, took over ten years to complete and is a harmony of masterwork from different cultures — Arab artisans made the inlaid wooden ceilings (a type of work known as *muqarnas*), Sicilians did the stonecutting, and the mosaics are Byzantine. The walls and dome are completely covered with rich mosaics representing scenes from the Old Testament (the nave), Christ's life (the southern transept), and scenes from the lives of Peter and Paul (the aisles). Note by the entryway the **candlestick,** intricately carved from of a single piece of stone and over 3.9m (13-ft.) tall.

See map 466. Piazza Indipendenza, off Corso Calatafimi, through the Porta Nuova. ☎ *091-705-1111. Bus: 104, 105. Admission: 5€ ($5.75) when the Royal Appartments are open and 4€ ($4.60) otherwise. Open: Royal Appartments Mon, Fri, and Sat 9 a.m.–noon. Cappella Palatina Mon–Fri 9 a.m.–noon and 3–5 p.m., Sat 9 a.m.–noon; Sun 9–10 a.m. and noon–1 p.m.*

Teatro Massimo

Begun in 1875 but not completed until 1897, this building cost a fortune and was Italy's largest and most splendid theater at a time when Palermo didn't even have a good hospital. The theater is a masterpiece of Liberty style (Italian Art Nouveau) and was designed by Gian Battista and Ernesto Basile, the famous Sicilian father-and-son Art Nouveau stylists. The stage and back stage measure 1,280 sq. m (12,000 sq. ft.), the second largest in Europe after the Opéra Garnier in Paris. Its greatest marvel is a **painted ceiling** with 11 panels that open like flower petals to let heat escape from the interior during intermissions. The only change that has been made since the building's conception has been to lay a wood floor for better acoustics. The building was not only a theater but also a meeting place, and these rooms were used for important business and political meetings. The most famous is the **Sala Pompeiana,** at the level of the second loggia, where the men would meet; it's designed so that the sound of voices would keep bouncing from wall to wall and not get out of the room and disturb the performance. After 23 years of closure for restoration, the theater reopened in 1997.

See map 466. Piazza Verdi, west on Via Maqueda. ☎ *800-655-858. Admission: 3€ ($3.45). Open: Tues–Sun 10 a.m.–3:30 p.m.*

Villa Malfitano

This great Liberty-style villa lies within one of the city's most spectacular gardens. It was built in 1886 by Joseph Whitaker, who arranged to have trees shipped here from all over the world and planted around his villa. High society in Palermo flocked here for lavish parties, as did royalty from as far away as Great Britain. The villa is stocked with beautiful antiques and furnishings of various styles and periods. The most beautiful of the rooms, the **Sala d`Estata (Summer Room)**, is decorated with trompe-l'oeil frescoes on the walls and ceiling.

See map 466. Via Dante 167. ☎ 091-681-6133. Bus: 103, 108. Admission: 2.50€ ($2.90). Open: Mon–Sat 9 a.m.–1 p.m.

More cool things to see and do

The major sites of Palermo are stunning, but there's still much more to see and do — as well as things to eat. Here are a few recommendations:

✔ If you happen to be in Palermo in July, the **Festa di Santa Rosalia** (July 11–July 15) is an interesting event celebrating the anniversary of the discovery of the saint's remains many centuries after her death. Niece of Norman King Guglielmo II, Rosalia abandoned the palace for a cave on Monte Pellegrino (see the description earlier in this chapter) to live a life of prayer. During the terrible plague epidemic of 1624, her bones were found and brought down the mountain. As the procession bringing her remains traversed the city, the epidemic miraculously stopped (a good reason to keep celebrating her!). During the festival, a religious procession with a beautifully decorated, huge triumphal carriage carrying an orchestra wends through the town. There's also a spectacular candlelit procession up Monte Pellegrino to Santa Rosalia's cave. The end of the festival is marked by great fireworks.

✔ If you're into catacombs and you aren't squeamish, you will enjoy the **Catacombe dei Cappuccini** (Piazza Cappuccini; ☎ 091-212-117), which contain 8,000 mummified bodies of aristocratic Sicilians and priests, still dressed in the costumes of their time. The catacombs were used as a burial spot, or rather a repository, for mummified remains until 1920. Why, you ask? Because for some reason these catacombs seem to miraculously preserve the dead — or at least some of them. Some of these Sicilians look amazingly "well preserved," as they say, while others are missing some parts. It's open Monday through Saturday from 9 a.m. to noon and 3 to 5 p.m., with a 1.50€ ($1.70) admission charge. Needless to say, this is not a "kid-friendly" sight, unless you have teenagers.

✔ The city has three much-visited traditional **food markets,** where fruits, vegetables, meat, and fish provide an explosion of colors and flavors. **La Vucciria,** whose name comes from the French word *boucherie* ("meat store"), is in La Kalsa and goes along Via Argenteria to Piazza Garraffello. The **Ballarò** is our preferred market — Palermo's oldest, running from Piazza Casa Professa to Corso Tukory toward Porta Sant'Agata. It's connected to the market of Casa Professa (selling shoes and secondhand clothing); this market was called the *mercato americano* because, for a long time, secondhand clothes came to Italy from the United States in huge bundles, with everything from swimsuits to nightgowns to ski clothes and fur coats! Smaller and less lively, **Il Capo** covers Via Carini and Via Beati Paoli, crossing Via Sant'Agostino and Via Cappuccinelle. The three markets are shown in blue on the free city map you find in hotels and at the tourist office. In all the markets, beware of potential purse snatchers and pickpockets riding *motorini*.

✔ **La Cuba** (Corso Calatafimi 100, inside the Caserma Tukory; ☎ 091-590-299), a dome surrounded by gardens, is a striking example of Arab and early Norman architecture. It was built by Guglielmo II in 1180 in the Park of Genoardo; its beauty was so famous that Boccaccio used it in the Decameron. The building is only one floor, organized around a central space with a star-shaped fountain. Today only the external walls and giant arches remain. It's open Monday through Saturday from 9 a.m. to 7 p.m. and Sunday from 9 a.m. to 1 p.m., with a 2€ ($2.30) admission.

✔ If you fell in love with the work of Giacomo Serpotta, you should add to your schedule a visit to the **Oratorio di Santa Cita** (Via Valverde 3, off Via Squarcialupo, between Via Cavour and Via Roma, on the left of the church; ☎ 091-332-779). Famous for his stucco *putti* (cherubs), the Sicilian sculptor worked here between 1687 and 1718, creating a whole world of stucco figures and reliefs. Note that as of press time, the oratorio is closed for restoration; however, it should reopen in 2005, so you may find it open and more magnificent than ever.

✔ One of the most famous sights of Palermo is **San Giovanni degli Eremiti** (Via dei Benedettini 3; ☎ 091-651-5019). Although it is a Christian church it was built at the height of the Arab-Norman style, and thus it was given five round red domes. The church is a ruin and the inside is open to the elements; once you've seen it from the outside, you have seen most of its charm, although its 13th-century cloister is very nice. It is open April through October, Monday through Saturday from 9 a.m. to 7 p.m. and Sunday 9 a.m to 1 p.m. Admission is 4.50€ ($5.20).

Guided tours

Palermo's city bus company, **AMAT** (☎ 091-690-2690; www.amat.pa.it), offers a sightseeing tour of Palermo for 12€ ($14) per person. The bus leaves daily at 9 a.m. from the Teatro Politeama at Via E. Amari and makes stops at the Teatro Massimo, Santa Maria della Catena, San Giovanni degli Eremiti, Palazzo dei Normanni, Cattedrale, and Duomo di Monreale, before coming back to the Politeama. You can buy tickets from travel agencies and hotels, at the AMAT office at Via Giusti 7, or directly on the bus; entrance fees to attractions visited along the way are extra.

For a more do-it-yourself approach, take the *Aquilotto* bus lines (see "Getting Around," earlier in this chapter).

If you would like to arrange your own personal tour of the city by a local, **AGT** (Associazione Guide Turistiche di Palermo e Provincia; www.palermo guide.it; no phone) is an association of local expert guides who speak various languages, including English. Check the Web site for the names and phone numbers of the guides. The cost for a half-day tour for 1 to 50 people is 116€ ($133), and you can join a tour already organized, with an obvious price advantage. Another option is a two-hour "mini-tour" of the historic center of Palermo for up to eight people for 70€ ($81).

Suggested 1-, 2-, and 3-day Itineraries

Palermo deserves as much time as you can give it. You could easily spend several days here and not see everything. Here are our suggestions on how to manage the time you have.

Palermo in 1 day

If you arrive in the morning, head straight for the harbor — if you've arrived by boat, you're already there. Walk along the waterfront toward the old neighborhood of **La Kalsa,** noting the ancient horseshoe-shaped harbor of **La Cala** and stopping for a moment in **Piazza Marina**. (Be sure to pass by the open-air market of **La Vucciria,** which is busy from early morning to early afternoon.) Visit the nearby **Galleria Regionale Siciliana** housed in the Palazzo Abatellis, taking in at least the masterpieces we mention in our description (see review earlier in this chapter). Don't linger too long, however, because you need to get to the **Palazzo dei Normanni** and **Cappella Palatina,** the crowning achievement of the hybrid Arab-Norman culture of the Middle Ages. Then take a cab to the **Casa del Brodo** for lunch; it's a Palermitan institution. After lunch take the bus to **Monreale** to see the fabulous **Duomo** and its **cloister.** Return to the center and stroll past **San Giovanni degli Eremiti,** one of the symbols of Palermo, before having dinner in one our recommended restaurants (see "Dining Out," earlier in this chapter).

Palermo in 2 days

If you have 2 days in Palermo, follow the itinerary for "Palermo in 1 day," except: don't visit the **Galleria Regionale Siciliana** for now, which will relieve some pressure on your schedule and give you more time at the **Palazzo dei Normanni** and **Cappella Palatina.** Instead, visit the Galleria first thing on the morning of Day 2. Afterward, admire the stuccowork of Serpotta at the **Casa Professa,** and take a quick look at the nearby **Chiesa di Santa Maria dell'Ammiraglio,** know as **La Martorana,** and its lovely mosaics. Then have lunch at **La Cambusa,** a popular spot with locals. In the afternoon, explore Palermo's more ancient past at the **Museo Archeologico Regionale.** Afterward you can see Palermo's **duomo** from the outside, skipping the remodeled interior (though you might take a quick look in the **tombs.** If you are so inclined, you can then visit the **Catacombe dei Cappuccini,** a macabre but certainly unique sight. (Alternatively, see the marvelous **Oratorio di Santa Cita** if it has

reopened after renovation.) If possible, take in a performance at the
Teatro Massimo in the evening (see "Living it Up After Dark," later in
this chapter).

Palermo in 3 days

Follow the suggested itinerary for "Palermo in 2 days." On your third
day, begin by savoring the sights and sounds of another market, the
Ballarò. Afterward, explore the beautiful rooms of the **Villa Malfitana,**
before proceeding on in the same direction toward **La Zisa**. After lunch,
have a little adventure: take the bus to **Monte Pellegrino** and the
Santuario di Santa Rosalia, enjoying the spectacular view over Palermo
and beyond, perhaps even as far as **Etna**. Treat yourself to a wonderful
dinner of seafood and fine wine at **Mandarini** (see "Dining Out," earlier
in this chapter).

Shopping the Local Stores

Shopping isn't Palermo's strong suit, unless you're buying **swordfish,
tuna,** or **almond paste.** The city has some of Italy's best open-air food
markets (see "More cool things to see and do," earlier in this chapter),
notable for the freshness and quality of their produce, and they offer
some great deals. Alas, visitors can't turn this much to advantage. Of
course, you can buy provisions for a picnic (great for an out-of-town
excursions or for a snack in the gardens of Piazza Marina).

Palermitans are very keen on dressing up, and the center of town offers
some nice clothing shops. For the best shopping, try the streets south
of the Politeama, especially **Via Ruggero Settimo** (which becomes **Via
Maqueda**) and **Via Roma** and the smaller streets in between, such as
Via Principe di Belmonte.

As the central city and port for the island of Sicily, Palermo is a way sta-
tion for and place to buy all sorts of craft items. Besides the **models of
Sicilian carts** and **puppets** that you find in stands at most tourist sites,
Sicily is famous for its **pottery.** In Palermo are works from the three
Sicilian schools of Santo Stefano di Camastra, Caltagirone, and Sciacca.
Try **Via E. Amari,** running from the Politeama to the port; it has a
number of very reliable ceramic shops. **De Simone** has two shops, one
at Via Gaetano Daita 13/B (☎ 091-584-876) and one at Via Principe de
Scalea 698 (☎ 091-671-1005), where they also have their factory; **Verde
Italiano** at Via Principe di Villafranca 42 (☎ 091-320-282) also has a
shop and a factory that you can tour.

Another handmade item is **linen. Frette,** one of the finest makers of
linens in Italy, is on Via Ruggero Settimo (☎ 091-585-166). There is a
huge selection of **fabrics** at **Giuseppe Gramuglia** (Via Roma 412-414;
☎ 091-583-262), where you can outfit your home with hangings, curtains, or upholsteries fit for a Sicilian count.

Living It Up After Dark

Nightlife in Palermo has been picking up steadily after the dark years of the 1980s, when people were almost too afraid to walk the streets. Like all Italians, Sicilians like to eat out, especially at an outdoor terrace in the good season, as evening entertainment. Sicilians, especially young ones, love to dance, and Palermo is home to lots of discos.

The performing arts

Opera and ballet performances take place in the **Teatro Politeama Garibaldi** (Piazza Ruggero VII; ☎ **091-605-3315**). Like everything else in Sicily, tickets are reasonably priced at about 20€ to 40€ ($23–$46). The revived **Teatro Massimo** (Piazza Verdi; ☎ **800-655-858**) also hosts concert and opera performances. The season runs from October through June.

Another interesting entertainment is the traditional **Puppet Theater (Teatro dei Pupi).** The *pupi* became popular in the 18th century and, dressed in armor and bright-colored fabrics, tell tales of Orlando and the Paladins of France (who, however, think and act in a perfectly Sicilian way). They usually stage fights against the Saracens, in which the audience participates actively. A few decades ago, Palermo boasted more than ten companies, but today the companies that are left perform only on request or on weekends in summer. The best is at the **Teatro Arte Cuticchio — Opera dei Pupi e Laboratorio** (Via Bara all'Olivella 95; ☎ **091-323-400**; www.figlidartecuticchio.com). November through June and cost 6€ ($6.90) adults and 3€ ($3.45) children; the theater also contains a museum with a collection of *pupi,* machines, and special effects.

Discos, bars, and pubs

A popular disco is **I Candelai** (Via Candelai 65; ☎ **091-327-151**; www.candelai.it), a club for the young and energetic that plays the latest rock (loud). You can also try the well-established **Kandinsky** (Discesa Tonnara 4; ☎ **091-637-6511**) and the appropriately named **Dancing Club** (Viale Piemonte 16; ☎ **091-348-917**).

Pubs have also swept through Palermo (like other Italian cities). **Villa Niscemi** (Piazza Niscemi 55; ☎ **091-688-0820**) has music of various kinds, including, literally, pick-up groups (instruments provided), and stays open into the wee hours of the morning. **Pub 88** (Via Candelai 88; ☎ **091-611-9967**), just down the road from I Candelai, is a quieter place to have a drink and relax. At **Agricantus** (Via XX Settembre 82; ☎ **091-487-117**) you might find jazz playing in the background, or a group performing a skit. You can also just stop and relax with a glass of wine.

Speaking of wine, a more Italian institution is the *enoteca,* the Italian answer to an English pub. Very popular all over Italy, these are places where you can sample some nice wine and have a light snack — sometimes a real dinner. One noteworthy *enoteca* is **Ai Vini d'Oro** (Piazza Nascé 11; ☎ **091-585-647**).

Fast Facts: Palermo

Area Code

The country code for Italy is **39**. The area code for Palermo is **091**, whether you are outside or inside Italy, even within Palermo itself (always include the 0, even when calling from abroad).

ATMs

You can find ATMs at the many banks in town as well as exchange booths in the airport and scattered around town, especially in the center.

Doctors

The emergency doctor for tourists (Guardia Medica Turistica) is at ☎ 091-532-798.

Embassies and Consulates

The U.S. Consulate is at Via Vaccarini 1 (☎ 091-305-857) and the U.K. Consulate is at Via Cavour 117 (☎ 091-326-412).

Emergencies

Police, ☎ **112**; ambulance, ☎ **118**; Red Cross ambulance, ☎ **091-306-644**; fire, ☎ **115**.

Hospital

The Ospedale Civico is at Via Carmelo Lazzaro (☎ 091-606-2207).

Information

The Azienda Autonoma Provinciale per l'Incremento Turistico is at Piazza Castelnuovo 34, across from the Teatro Politeama (☎ 091-583-847 or 091-605-8351; www.palermotourism.com). Hours are Monday through Friday 8:30 a.m.–2:00 p.m.

and 3:00 p.m.–7:00 p.m., and Saturday 8:30 a.m.–2:00 p.m. There are also information booths at the train station (☎ 091-616-5914) and the airport (☎ 091-591-698). The one at the train station is open Monday through Friday from 8:30 a.m. to 2:00 p.m. and 3:00 to 7:00 p.m. The airport desk is open 8 a.m. to midnight on weekdays and 8 a.m. to 8 p.m. on Saturday and Sunday.

Internet Access & Cybercafes

A centrally located Internet point is Aboriginal Internet Café (Via Spinuzza 51; ☎ 091-662-2229; www.aboriginal cafe.com), only a couple of blocks from the Teatro Massimo (it's also a center for extreme sport enthusiasts and a bar, if that interests you). Two local bars, I Candelai and Villa Niscemi (see "Discos, bars, and pubs, " earlier in this chapter), also offer Internet access.

Pharmacies

Several pharmacies are open at night in Palermo. Among the most central are Farma Taxi (Via Libertà 54; ☎ 091-309-8098) and Farmacia Pensabene (Via Mariano Stabile 177, off Teatro Massimo; ☎ 091-334-482).

Police

There are two police forces in Italy; call either one. For the Polizia, call ☎ 113; for the Carabinieri, call ☎ 112.

Restrooms

Museums have public toilets. The best bet for a restroom is to go to a nice-looking cafe (though you'll have to buy something, like a cup of coffee).

Safety

Palermo's historic districts are quite safe except for the pickpockets and purse snatchers on *motorini*. They concentrate in tourist areas, on public transportation, and at crowded open-air markets, such as the the Vucciria.

Smoking

Smoking is allowed in cafes and restaurants and is very common. Unfortunately for nonsmokers, finding a restaurant with a no-smoking area is still quite hard, though some are beginning to appear.

Taxes

See Chapter 5 for information on VAT.

Transit info

The 24-hour tourist assistance hotline is toll-free ☎ 167-234-169. You can call toll free ☎ 147-888-088 daily 7 a.m. to 9 p.m. for the FS, the state railroad (www.ferro viedellostato.it). Call Palermo's transportation authority AMAT (☎ 091-690-2690; www.amat.pa.it) for urban bus and subway info; and AST (☎ 800 234 163 toll free from Italy, or 091-688-2906) for out-of-town bus connections.

Weather Updates

For forecasts, the best bet is to watch the news on TV. On the Web, you can check http://meteo.tiscalinet.it.

Chapter 24

Taormina and the Rest of Sicily

. . . .

In This Chapter

▶ Touring Taormina
▶ Viewing the past and present in Syracuse
▶ Visiting the Valley of the Temples in Agrigento

. . . .

*I*nhabited since prehistoric times, Sicily has been shaped, culturally and physically, by its many rulers: Phoenician, Greek, and Roman ruins mingle with stern Norman palaces and cathedrals, softened and embellished by Byzantine and Arab art (no complete Arab building remains — the 500 mosques that existed under their rule were destroyed — but they left a permanent mark with their introduction of citrus fruits, today one of the symbols of Sicily). Also, Sicily offers some of Italy's most splendid examples of baroque architecture. After the ravages of time, earthquakes, and World War II, most of these jewels were in bad need of repair. Luckily, a slow process of recuperation has started, bringing glory back to Sicilian architecture.

Among the many Sicilian destinations, **Taormina** — a city that flourished during the Roman period and again from the 19th century on — stands out for its fabulous position between the sea and Etna, the snow-capped volcano, and for its great **Teatro Greco-Romano (Greco-Roman Theater)** — one of the greatest of antiquity. Rivaling for importance with Athens during antiquity, **Syracuse (Siracusa)** was also important during the 17th and 18th centuries; the remains in its **Parco Archeologico (archeological area)** are grandiose and the baroque buildings on the island of **Ortigia** very nice. Dominating the southern shore, **Agrigento** was another important Greek city, one of the most beautiful of the ancient world.

If you have the time you can spend a night in each of these destinations, traveling between them by bus or rental car.

Taormina

On Sicily's eastern shore, near Etna and south of Messina, is **Taormina,** founded by Andromachus in 358 B.C. Taormina is actually the second town built at this location. In the fifth century B.C., Dionysius I of Syracuse destroyed the first, Naxos (today the seaside resort of Giardini Naxos), which lies below, near the water. The residents prudently moved to the top of the cliffs, though that didn't save them from further invasions. The Greek city-state backed the Romans in the Punic Wars, which resulted in a glorious period between the third century B.C. and the end of the Roman Empire. During this time Taormina thrived and received the coveted status of Roman colony under Augustus. After the empire ended, the city of Taormina declined and was twice laid waste by the Arabs. Roger II took over the city in 1078 for the Normans, but later Taormina sank into obscurity for several hundred years.

Taking its name from Monte Taurus, the cliff dominating the sea over **Taormina,** this small town was a forgotten medieval village until the end of the 18th century, when European artists, such as the German writer Goethe, began to celebrate it as the "ideal vista." Indeed, Taormina is a unique panorama, with the sea on one side and snow-capped Etna smoking on the other. Today, Taormina has about 10,000 residents and receives some 900,000 visitors per year — that's about 2,500 visitors a day. Consider that 80 percent of these visitors are non-Italians and that this figure includes only those visitors who stay overnight; many others just pass through for the day (you may find it odd that crowded Taormina was a haunt of Greta Garbo, who "wanted to be alone"). Taormina isn't a stranger to wealth and glamour, with many magnificent villas and famous visitors past and present.

Taormina makes an excellent starting point for visiting the rest of the region; many travel agencies based here offer guided tours to other destinations in Sicily (see "Exploring Taormina," later in this section).

Getting there

Catania is the most logical point of arrival for the eastern shore of Sicily; from Catania, you can easily catch a train or bus or rent a car to your next destination.

By **ferry, TTT Lines** (☎ **800-915-365** toll-free in Italy or 081 575 2192; www.tttlines.com) offers regular service from Naples for 50€ to 150€ ($58–$173) per person, depending on the cabin you choose (from single to quad); it costs about 80 € ($92) to transport a car. Ferries leave Naples' Molo Angioino daily at 9 p.m. and arrive in Catania the next morning at 7:30 a.m.; for the return, they leave Catania Monday through Saturday at midnight and arrive in Naples at 11 a.m. the next day; on Sunday ferries depart Catania at 7:30 p.m. and arrive in Naples Monday at 7 a.m.

Taormina

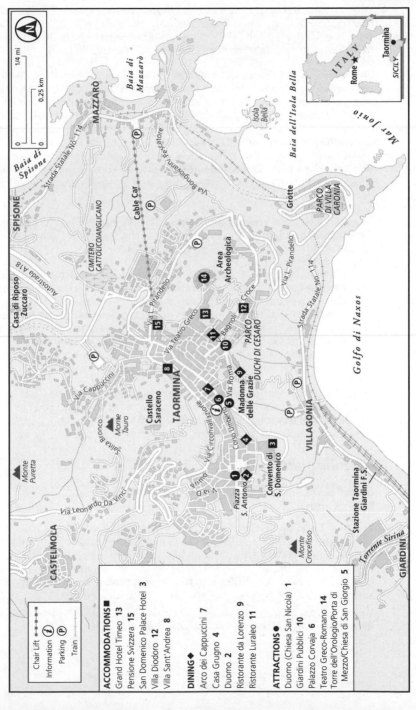

ACCOMMODATIONS ■
Grand Hotel Timeo **13**
Pensione Svizzera **15**
San Domenico Palace Hotel **3**
Villa Diodoro **12**
Villa Sant'Andrea **8**

DINING ◆
Arco dei Cappuccini **7**
Casa Grugno **4**
Duomo **2**
Ristorante da Lorenzo **9**
Ristorante Luraleo **11**

ATTRACTIONS ●
Duomo (Chiesa San Nicola) **1**
Giardini Pubblici **10**
Palazzo Corvaja **6**
Teatro Greco-Romano **14**
Torre dell'Orologio/Porta di
Mezzo/Chiesa di San Giorgio **5**

You can also arrive by **plane** at the **Fontanarossa** airport (☎ **800-605-656** toll-free in Italy; www.aeroporto.catania.it). From Catania's airport, the **Alibus** *navette* (electric minibus) operates every 20 minutes from 5 a.m. to midnight and brings you to the center of town.

Taormina is 50km (30 miles) north of Catania and 250km (150 miles) east of Palermo, and an easy 50-minute **train** ride from Catania railroad station; the ride from Palermo instead takes approximately 4½ hours (with one change in Messina). It will cost you about 4€ ($4.60) from Catania and 12€ ($14) from Palermo. Trains arrive at the **Stazione F.S. di Taormina** (Via Nazionale; ☎ **0942-51-026** or 0942-51-511), located a little down the hill, below Taormina's center, in Villagonia. From the station, you can take a **taxi** (☎ **0942-51-150** or 0942-23-800) or the *navette,* which runs every 15 to 45 minutes, depending on the season and hour of the day, for 1.20€ ($1.40).

The company **Etna Trasporti** (☎ **095-532-716;** www.etnatrasporti.it) runs regular and frequent **bus** service from the airport in Catania to Taormina; the ride is one hour and 15 minutes.

If you're **driving** from Catania, take the **A18** and exit at Taormina. From Palermo, the fastest route is **A19,** which runs briefly along the coast and then cuts cross-country to Catania, where you pick up A18. Taormina's center is pedestrian only, so you have to leave your car at the entrance of town. The best place to leave your car is just after the highway exit for Taormina, in the large city parking lot **Parcheggio Lumbi** at the base of the hill. A shuttle bus runs from the parking lot to town every few minutes. If your hotel has parking, park your car there.

From the center of town starts the *funivia* (funicular; ☎ **0942-23-906**), which connects Taormina with the beach down below and runs every 15 minutes all day long; a ticket is 3€ ($3.45) round-trip and 1.70€ ($2) one-way. It goes until 3 a.m. in the summer.

Spending the night

Grand Hotel Timeo
$$$$ Centro

The first hotel opened in Taormina, this beautiful villa dates back to the 18th century and sits just below the Greek theater, surrounded by its own garden. Guest rooms are spacious and elegantly decorated with fine fabrics and furniture; all have terraces or balconies and come with large marble bathrooms. The hotel also has its own private beach — with its own shuttle service for guests — as well as a sophisticated restaurant and bar.

Via del Teatro Greco 59, just off the Greek theater. ☎ *0942-23-801. Fax: 0942-628-501. Rack rates: 424€ ($488) double. Rates include breakfast. AE, DC, MC, V.*

Pensione Svizzera
$ Centro

This centrally located hotel offers nicely appointed guest rooms at a moderate price. Rooms are furnished with a German flavor, with whitewashed walls, tiled floors, and dark wood classic furniture; some have nice sea views. It offers a few frills, such as breakfast in the lovely garden when the weather is good. Other pluses are its convenient location near the beach, and its friendly, English-speaking owners.

Via Piradello 26, just off Porta Messina. ☎ **0942-23-790.** *Fax: 0942-625-906. E-mail:* info@pensionesvizzera.com. *Parking: 8€ ($9.20). Rack rates: 90€–120€ ($104–$138) double. Rates include breakfast. AE, DC, MC, V. Closed Jan.*

San Domenico Palace Hotel
$$$$ Centro

In a converted monastery amid magnificent terraced gardens, the San Domenico was the second hotel built in Taormina and has long been a haunt of the rich and famous. The eclectically furnished guest rooms feature fine furniture from various Mediterranean lands, and the superb **Bougainvillées** restaurant serves regional specialties on the terrace with a breathtaking view over Mount Etna. The hotel has a piano bar and a conference center housed in the church of the original convent and also boasts a heated pool with a view.

Piazza San Domenico 5, south of the Duomo. ☎ **0942-613-111.** *Fax: 0942-625-506.* www.sandomenico.thi.it. *Parking: 16€ ($18). Rack rates: 520€ ($598) double. Rates include buffet breakfast. AE, DC, MC, V.*

Villa Diodoro
$$ Centro

This elegant hotel is housed in an attractive villa near the center of town surrounded by its own garden. Guest rooms are spacious and tastefully decorated with fine fabrics and period furniture, including wrought-iron beds and oriental carpets. Most of the guest rooms feature private terraces and gorgeous ocean views. Amenities include a swimming pool, a solarium, a bar, and a restaurant.

Via Bagnoli Croci 75. ☎ **0942-23-312.** *Fax: 0942-23-391.* www.gaishotels.com/hp.htm. *Rack rates: 120€–194€ ($138–$223) double. Rates include breakfast. AE, DC, MC, V.*

Villa Sant'Andrea
$$$ Centro

Housed in an elegant villa built in 1830, this hotel overlooks the beautiful bay of Mazzarò, where it has its own private beach. The welcoming guest rooms are spacious and bright and are individually decorated with art and antiques. The hotel is surrounded by its private park and has two good restaurants, the Oliviero, for a special romantic dinner, and the Sant'Andrea, for a less formal experience.

Via Nazionale 137. ☎ *0942-23-125. Fax: 0942-24-838. Rack rates: 200€–297€ ($230–$342) double. Rates include breakfast. AE, DC, MC, V. Closed 4 weeks Nov/Dec.*

Dining locally

You will find plenty of restaurants in this lively resort, catering to a variety of styles; they are particularly easy to spot during the warm season when tables overflow on small outdoor terraces and sidewalks.

Arco dei Cappuccini
$ Centro SICILIAN/FISH

In a perfect location just off the main street in the center of town, this restaurant offers a menu that changes daily according to the market offerings; there could be *gamberi marinati* (marinated shrimp), *fettuccine fresche con i crostacei appena pescati* (fresh homemade pasta with shellfish, just harvested), *campanelle con pesce e zucchine* (pasta with fish and zucchini), and *pesce del giorno gratinato* (daily catch au gratin).

Via Cappuccini 1a. ☎ *0942-24-893. Reservations recommended. Secondi: 8€–14€ ($9.20–$16). AE, DC, MC, V. Open: Lunch and dinner Thurs–Tues. Closed 1 week in Nov/Dec and 4 weeks in Jan/Feb.*

Casa Grugno
$$ Centro SICILIAN/CREATIVE

The best restaurant in Taormina, Casa Grugno offers delicious concoctions of high-quality ingredients. The menu changes often, but we warmly recommend the *crema di crostacei al Marsala stravecchio* (Marsala-flavored seafood bisque), the *fusilli al limone con alici fresche capperi pan grattato e prezzemolo fritto* (pasta with lemon, fresh anchovies, capers, breadcrumbs, and parsley), the *tortelli ripieni di pollo ruspante su carciofo di Cerda* (large ravioli of free-range chicken, with fresh artichokes), the *filetto di pesce affumicato in casa su relish di cedro mango e zenzero* (house-smoked fish with a mango, citron, and ginger relish), and the *gamberoni in nido di vermicelli croccanti con salsa di arance* (jumbo shrimp over crispy pasta with citrus sauce).

Via Santa Maria dei Greci. ☎ *0942-21-208. Reservations recommended. Secondi: 16€–22€ ($18–$25). AE, DC, MC, V. Open: Lunch and dinner Thurs–Tues; daily in summer. Closed Feb and first 3 weeks in Dec.*

Duomo
$$ Centro SICILIAN

Opening on Piazza Duomo, this restaurant offers fine local cuisine that you can enjoy on the terrace with a view or inside in the very pleasantly appointed dining room — or, you can reserve the romantic table for two on a private balcony in summer. Excellent choices include the *tonno sott'olio fatto in casa* (home-preserved tuna in olive oil), *zuppa di ceci* (chickpea soup), *pasta ca' nocca* (pasta with anchovies, fried breadcrumbs, and wild fennel), *braciole di pesce spada alla messinese* (swordfish steaks, Messina style), *agnello "ngrassatu"* (roasted lamb chops). There is also a good choice of vegetarian dishes and great traditional desserts such as *cassata* (a ricotta, almond paste, and candied-fruit preparation) and *cannoli di ricotta.*

Vico Ebrei 11, off Piazza Duomo. ☎ *0942-625-656. Reservations recommended. Secondi: 12€–16€ ($14–$18). AE, DC, MC, V. Open: Lunch and dinner Tues–Sun. Closed 1 month in Jan/Feb and 10 days in Dec.*

Ristorante da Lorenzo
$$ Centro   SICILIAN

This excellent restaurant is a bit away from the crowds. It has a pleasant terrace, notable for the ancient tree that has given shade for some 800 years, or so they say. The food lives up to the setting and includes fresh fish, an excellent *antipasto,* and such unusual dishes as *spaghetti ai ricci di mare* (spaghetti with sea urchins), considered a real delicacy by Italians. The staff and the kitchen welcome families and the terrace makes a good outlet for your children's extra energy.

Via Roma, near via Michele Amari. ☎ *0942-23-480. Reservations recommended. Secondi: 12€–23€ ($14–$26). AE, DC, MC, V. Open: Lunch and dinner Thurs–Tues. Closed 1 month in Nov/Dec.*

Ristorante Luraleo
$$ Centro   SICILIAN

The romantic atmosphere and terrace help ensure a pleasant experience at this restaurant, which serves a variety of Sicilian specialties. You're always safe choosing the grilled fish if you don't want to try something more adventurous, such as the *risotto al salmone e pistacchi* (risotto with salmon and pistachios).

Via Bagnoli Croce 27. ☎ *0942-24-279. Reservations recommended. Secondi: 11€–20€ ($13–$23). DC, MC, V. Open: Summer lunch and dinner daily; winter lunch and dinner Thurs–Tues.*

Exploring Taormina

Because Taormina is so small, there are no tours of the village itself. **Sais Tours** (☎ 091-343-811; www.saistours.com) organizes guided tours and excursions to the nearby attractions of Etna and Gole dell'Alcantara (see "More cool things to see and do," later in this section), as well as to further destinations, such as Palermo (Chapter 23), Syracuse (see later in this chapter), and Agrigento also later in this chapter). **SAT Sicilian Airbus Travel** (Corso Umberto 73; ☎ 0942-24-653; Fax: 0942-21-128; www.sat-group.it) offers a similar array of tours, including a nice bus-and-jeep sunset Etna tour. For either company, tours cost between 35€ and 60€ ($40–$69) per person, depending on the length of the tour.

The top attractions

Corso Umberto 1

Taormina's central street, it stretches between the town's two main gates, the **Porta Catania** and the **Porta Messina.** In the Middle Ages, the city shrank to the area between the Porta Catania and the **Torre dell'Orologio (clock tower);** also called the Porta di Mezzo (Middle Gate), the Torre dell'Orologio was built during the early Middle Ages as the gate to the medieval village. After its partial destruction, the clock tower was rebuilt in 1679 and is attached to the **Chiesa di San Giorgio** with its 17th-century baroque facade. During the Renaissance, the city started expanding again; it reoccupied the whole hourglass-shaped area of the Greek city only in modern times. Along Corso Umberto I are some of Taormina's most interesting monuments, such as the **Palazzo dei Duchi di Santo Stefano,** the best preserved of the town's Norman buildings, and the **Chiesa di Sant'Agostino,** a 16th-century church opening on its nice square, **Largo IX Aprile,** above the sea. The church is closed to worship and used as the town library.

Duomo aka Chiesa San Nicola

Built in the 12th century in a Latin cross plan, this church was later remodeled and the central portal dates from 1633, while the lateral portals date from the 15th and 16th centuries, respectively. Inside, the nave is defined by gracious monolithic pink marble columns topped by capitals decorated with a fish-scale pattern, to recall Sicily's maritime tradition. In front of the Duomo is the beautiful baroque **Fontana Monumentale,** built in 1635 with two-legged female centaurs.

Piazza del Duomo, just off Corso Umberto. Admission: Free. Open: Daily for mass, usually early morning and early evening.

Giardini Pubblici (Public Gardens)

These garden were built by Miss Florence Trevelyan, who arrived in 1882, fell in love with the town, and bought a piece of land sloping toward the sea. She worked at transforming the land into a garden, training and employing local workers as gardeners. Taorminians were fond of her, and when she died in 1902, they threw flowers at her passage in the funeral procession. Her will forbade her heirs from building or industrially cultivating the land. Within the gardens, she designed and built the **Victorian Follies** — bizarre toy houses built with red bricks and light-colored stone containing inlaid archaeological materials.

Via Bagnoli Croce, just below Corso Umberto. Admission: Free. Open: Daily sunrise–sunset.

Palazzo Corvaja

This palace was built between the 12th and 15th centuries around a pre-existing Arab cubic tower — probably part of a fortress — in several additions. During the 14th century, the crenellated structure and beautiful entrance staircase were added to the tower. And in the 15th century, the right wing was built to serve as the meeting place for the Sicilian Parliament. This *palazzo* also houses the tourist office.

Piazza Santa Caterina off Corso Umberto. ☎ *0942-23-243. Admission: Free. Open: Mon–Sat 8 a.m.–2 p.m. and 4–7 p.m.*

Teatro Greco-Romano (Greek-Roman Theater)

With a capacity of 5,000 people, this theater carved out of rock is second in Sicily only to Syracuse's (see later in this chapter) in size and importance. It's the best preserved of all Greek and Roman theaters in Italy. Unusual for a Greek theater, the backdrop scene was a fixed structure: It represented a two-story house, part of which is still visible. As was the case for many buildings of antiquity, part of the theater's materials were taken to build other buildings, in this case by the Arabs and Normans. During its glory days, the walls of the theater (only a portion in the back remains) were covered with marble and decorated with frescoes. Although the theater was Greek in origin, the Romans modified it for gladiator battles. For example, a tunnel connected the cellar of the Roman arena with the outside; the orchestra of the theater was enlarged and closed off by a high podium in order to protect spectators. The theater is famous for the summer performances held there (see "More cool things to see and do," below).

Via del Teatro Greco. ☎ *0942-23-220. Admission: 4€ ($4.60). Open: Tues–Sun 9 a.m.–5:30 p.m.*

More cool things to see and do

✔ If you're in Taormina during summer, enjoy the **Taormina Arte** (Via Pirandello 31, 98039 Taormina; ☎ **0942-21-142;** Fax: 0942-23-348), a festival of cinema, theater, music, ballet, and video started in 1983. Included are shows at the Greek-Roman Theater (see earlier in this chapter).

✔ By the sea below Taormina lies the town of **Mazzarò,** with its beautiful beach and restaurants specializing in fish. It's easy to reach by funicular from Taormina. In front of Mazzarò is the **Isola Bella,** with its marine grottoes: some swim to it but you can hire a boat for the ride.

✔ If you have the time, take a day-trip to visit the great **Etna,** which dominates the background of Taormina. Europe's biggest and most active volcano, it is 3,300m (10,824-ft.) tall and still growing. Vulcanologists have charted its eruptions back to the Middle Ages and even to ancient eruptions, which were usually far more dramatic and catastrophic. Though these mega-eruptions ceased centuries ago, Etna's littlest grumbles and oozings can wipe out vast areas and human settlements. The 1669 eruption not only took out chunks of the not-so-close-by town of Catania (amazingly, the deposits by the side of the highway south of town look as if they were made yesterday) but also extended the coastline about a kilometer (more than half a mile) into the sea. Etna isn't all lava and debris; parts of its north slopes are covered with a soaring conifer forest that took root in the rich soil. The easiest way to visit Etna is to take an organized tour from Taormina (see earlier in this section) or, if you have a car, follow the signs for Linguaglossa and then Zafferana, where you take the small winding road to the Rifugio Sapienza. From the Rifugio starts the cable car to the summit. If you want to see the craters up close and personal, you need an authorized guide. Book one at **Guide Alpine Etna Sud** (☎ 095-791-4755).

Fast Facts: Taormina

Area Code

The country code for Italy is **39.** The area code for Taormina is **0942;** use this code when calling from anywhere outside or inside Italy, including within Taormina. (Include the 0 every time, even when calling from abroad.)

ATMs

There are banks with ATMs on Corso Umberto, just before the Porta Messina to the north. You can also find banks in Giardini Naxos, the town next to Taormina.

Emergencies

Ambulance, ☎ **118;** fire, ☎ **115;** road assistance ☎ **116;** first aid *(Pronto Soccorso),* ☎ **0942-625-419.**

Hospital

The Ospedale Sirina is on Piazza San Francesco di Paola (☎ 0942-53-745).

Information

The tourist office is inside the beautiful Palazzo Corvaja on Piazza Santa Caterina off Corso Umberto to the west (Azienda Autonoma di Soggiorno e Turismo, Palazzo Corvaja, 98039 Taormina; ☎ 0942-23-243; Fax: 0942-24-941). Hours of operation are Monday through Saturday 8 a.m. to 2 p.m. and 4 to 7 p.m.

Pharmacy

Visit Dr. Verso at Piazza IX Aprile 1 (☎ 0942-625-866).

Police

There are two police forces in Italy; call either one. For the Polizia, call ☎ **113;** for the Carabinieri, call ☎ **112.**

Post Office

The Ufficio Postale is on Piazza Medaglie d'Oro (☎ 0942-23-010).

Syracuse

South of Taormina and close to the island's southeast corner is **Syracuse (Siracusa);** the island on which Syracuse began, **Ortigia,** was the home of mythical Calypso, who kept Odysseus captive for seven years. The Corinthians founded Syracuse in the eighth century B.C. and the city flourished around its beautiful harbor, perfectly positioned to trade with and control the eastern and western Mediterranean, to the point of rivaling the great cities of the mother country (like Athens). Syracuse rose to become the Mediterranean's greatest power under its forceful tyrants (particularly Dionysius I). However, during the Punic Wars, Syracuse was caught between a rock and a hard place — the Romans and the Carthaginians. The Roman siege lasted two years, and in 215 B.C. they finally overwhelmed the city, despite the clever devices that Archimedes, the city's most famous son, constructed to thwart them and their siege engines. Archimedes died in the Roman siege, and Syracuse wound up on the losing side, which hampered its future development. Today Syracuse is a beautiful stone city shimmering somewhat sleepily by the sea (the summer heat is unbelievable). Nearby is the unique baroque city of **Noto.**

You can easily visit Syracuse's highlights in one day, but if you can spend one or even two nights, you will find that the city has much more to offer, especially if you plan to visit nearby Noto.

Getting there

The obvious port of entry for the east coast of Sicily is Catania (see the "Getting there," section in Taormina, earlier in this chapter), and Syracuse is only 63 km (39 miles) south of Catania. Palermo is 259km (162 miles) southwest of Syracuse.

From Catania, the fastest route to Syracuse is by **bus** (about a 70-minute ride). Frequent bus service is offered by **Interbus** (☎ **0935-565-111;** www.interbus.it), among other companies. Interbus also has frequent service to/from Palermo (a 3½-hour ride).

Frequent direct **train** service from Catania takes about 1½ hours; from Taormina, however, you usually must transfer in Catania, and the ride will take you slightly over two hours. The ride from Palermo takes five to seven hours and from Agrigento, six hours. Syracuse's train station **(Stazione FS)** is on the west side of town; it is approximately a 20-minute walk from there to either Ortigia or the Archaeological Zone. From the train station, city buses connect to the main sights or you can take a taxi.

We do not recommend **driving** yourself from Catania to Syracuse, because of a dangerous 21km (13-mile) long stretch where the road reduces to two lanes, much too small for the amount of traffic on it. Locals speeding and passing each other turn it into a hair-raising, potentially dangerous experience — you really have to pay attention to who is passing whom in both directions. If you insist, take **SS114,** also labeled **E14** on European maps, following the signs for Siracusa, and absolutely avoid it after dark. From Agrigento, a highway is under construction but not yet completed; until it is, you'll have to take the state road **SS115,** which is picturesque but a long haul — about five hours.

Spending the night

Gran Bretagna
$ Ortigia

This small hotel, recently upgraded, has the great advantage of being on Ortigia, the main historic center of town. It's very popular with Italian and foreign tourists alike. The guest rooms are still basic, but comfortable; a few rooms still have the orginal ceiling frescoes from the 19th century.

Via Savoia 21. ☎ *0931-68-765.* www.hotelgranbretagna.it. *Rack rates: 100€ ($115) double. Rates include breakfast. AE, MC, V.*

Grand Hotel
$$ Ortigia

This beautiful Liberty (Italian Art Nouveau) hotel offers guest rooms that are large and bright, decorated with pastel colors and elegant furnishings; floors are beautiful chequered tiles or wood intarsia (inlay). Most rooms have a beautiful view over the harbor and the sea. The public areas are pleasant and welcoming and service is professional.

Viale Mazzini 12. ☎ *0931-464-600. Fax: 0931-464-611.* www.grandhotelsr.it. *Rack rates: 225€ ($259) double. Rates include breakfast. AE, DC, MC, V.*

Gutkowski
$ Ortigia

This hotel offers excellent accommodations and service at moderate prices. Guest rooms vary in size, but all are bright, with comfortable beds and decorated in pastel colors in a modern yet welcoming style. Only five of the guest rooms have a sea view, so reserve in advance if you want to grab one of those, but be aware that they tend to be smaller.

Lungomare Vittorini 26. ☎ *0931-465-861. Fax: 0931-480-505.* www.guthotel.it. *Rack rates: 90€ ($104) double. Rates include breakfast. AE, MC, V.*

Dining locally

You will find many small restaurants tucked away in the historic streets of Ortigia, but don't expect a lively scene as in Taormina; Syracuse has yet to become a crowded tourist destination.

Don Camillo
$ Ortigia SICILIAN

This welcoming restaurant has a wine bar up front and a more formal dining room in the back where you can taste some excellent local cuisine. Smoked local tuna and swordfish make a typical appetizer and you can follow that with the unique *spaghetti delle sirene* (pasta with shrimp and sea urchins) or the delicious *crespelle mediterraneee* (crepes layered with eggplant, tomato, basil, and hot pepper), and one of the daily catches.

Via Maestranza 96. ☎ *0931-67-133. Reservations recommended. Secondi: 12€–16€ ($14–$18). AE, DC, MC, V. Open: Lunch and dinner Mon–Sat.*

Gambero Rosso
$$ Centro   SICILIAN

In an old tavern near the harbor, this restaurant is known for its seafood and has a terrace overlooking the port. It is popular with the locals, who come with their families, especially during weekends; you will find that children are welcome and half portions are available. Try the *cannelloni* (tubes of pasta filled with fish or meat) or one of the fish soups.

Via Eritrea 2, off to the right of Corso Umberto, just inland of the bridge leaving Ortigia. ☎ *0931-68-546. Reservations recommended. Secondi: 14€–18€ ($16–$21). AE, DC, MC, V. Open: Lunch and dinner Fri–Wed.*

Ristorante Jonico
$$ Castello di Eurialo   SICILIAN

On the main street running along the coast north of Ortigia, this elegant place overlooks the sea. The casual roof garden serves pizza and is a perfect choice if you have children: they'll be able to move around a bit and pizza is always a kid-pleaser. Down below is a very pleasant upscale dining room with a lovely view. The seafood is particularly good, such as the *antipasto misto* and the *pesce spada alla pizzaiola* (swordfish in tomato-and-garlic sauce).

A Rutta e Ciauli, Riviera Dionisio II Grande 194, just off Piazza dei Cappuccini and near the Castello di Eurialo. ☎ *0931-65-540. Reservations recommended. Secondi: 12€–18€ ($14–$21). AE, DC, MC, V. Open: Lunch and dinner Wed–Mon.*

Ristorante Rossini
$$ Ortigia   SICILIAN

This intimate restaurant, run by a renowned chef, offers a menu based mainly on seafood prepared in both traditional and imaginative ways. One specialty is *pesce alla stimpirata,* which creatively combines mint, garlic, and olive oil with fish. More familiar Sicilian-style preparations include roasted swordfish. The buffet *antipasto* is excellent.

Via Savoia 6. ☎ *0931-24-317. Reservations recommended. Secondi: 14€–22€ ($16–$25). AE, DC, MC, V. Open: Lunch and dinner Wed–Mon.*

Exploring Syracuse

You can easily visit Syracuse on foot, and enjoy some beautiful strolls, whether by the harbor or amid the ancient ruins. But if you get tired, remember that there are a number of taxi stands around (in front of the rail station, at the Darsena [entering Ortigia to the right], at Piazza

Pancali [at the entrance of Ortigia], and at the end of Corso Umberto I); or, you can also always call a radio taxi (see "Fast Facts: Syracuse," later in this section).

The top attractions

Galleria Regionale di Palazzo Bellomo

This museum is housed in a beautiful *palazzo,* originally built in the 13th century and remodeled in the 15th, which was incorporated into the nearby monastery of San Benedetto in the 18th century and ultimately was transformed into a museum in 1948; it was completely restored in the 1970s. Its large collection of Sicilian figurative art goes from the Byzantine period to the 18th century. The single most important piece is **Antonello da Messina**'s famous *Annunciation.*

Via Capodieci 16. ☎ *0931-69-617 or 0931-69-511. Admission: 5€ ($5.75). Open: Mon–Sat 9 a.m.–1:30 p.m. and Sun 9 a.m.–12:30 p.m.*

Museo Archeologico Regionale Paolo Orsi

This is the best archaeological museum in Sicily. Every time period is represented in the large, well-organized collection, from prehistoric objects to an extensive Hellenistic collection from Syracuse's heyday. The single-most famous piece is the second-century B.C. *Venus Anadyomene* that — though headless — powerfully evokes the birth of the goddess from the sea. The pre-Greek vases are lovely, too.

In the gardens of the Villa Landolina, Viale Teocrito 66, near the Zona Archeologica. ☎ *0931-464-022. Bus: 4, 5, 12, or 15 to Viale Teocrito. Admission: 5€ ($5.75). Open: Tues–Sun 9 a.m.–2 p.m.; Wed and Fri also 3:30–7:30 p.m.*

Ortigia

The island of **Ortigia,** connected to the modern town of Syracuse by a bridge (Ponte Nuovo), is where the city began back in the eighth century B.C. Surrounded by Syracuse's harbor, it is the heart of the historic city. Indeed, by the end of the 19th century, Ortigia was still all there was of Syracuse; the land side contained only the rail station and the Greek ruins. The mainland part of Syracuse has changed much since, but not Ortigia. As you cross the Ponte Nuovo, you will first see the remains of the **Tempio di Apollo (Temple of Apollo);** built in the sixth century B.C., reduced now to just a few columns. If you walk up Via Savoia, you come to the **Porta Marina,** from which you can enter the old town. Farther along the stone border of the harbor is the **Fonte Aretusa,** the magical spring which, according to classic mythology, was created when nymph Arethusa was turned into a spring to escape Alfeo, the marine god trying to seduce her. Famous since antiquity, this spring is rich in freshwater fish and separated from the sea only by a stone wall. Heading back to the center of Ortigia, you will see the seventh-century **Duomo** (Piazza del Duomo; admission: free; open: daily 8 a.m.–noon and 4–7 p.m.), built on the remains of a Greek temple to Athena (Minerva to the Romans). You can still see 12 of the temple's columns incoporated into the church structure. Toward the tip of Ortigia is the 13th-century **Palazzo Bellomo**, which houses the **Galleria Regionale** (see earlier in this section) and the church of **San Benedetto.** At the tip of the island is the **Castello Maniace,** an imposing defensive structure dating back to the 12th century. The castle is currently under restoration.

In the harbor, off Largo XXV Luglio and Ponte Nuovo.

Parco Archeologico della Neopolis (Archaeological Area)

On the edge of modern Syracuse, lies the **Neopolis,** the Greek new town — as opposed to the original settlement — of Ortigia. Because Syracuse did not expand beyond Ortigia until the 20th century, this archeological area is very large and well preserved.

Beware of the sun in the hot months — walking around the ruins at high noon can quickly exhaust and dehydrate you. Highlights of the park are the two theaters and the quarries from which stone was excavated to build all the monuments in the old town. The **Teatro Greco (Greek Theater)** is extraordinary: dating back to the fifth century B.C., it is actually a giant sculpture because it was carved out of the hillside, using the rock for other buildings and for decorations. It is a beautiful example of an ancient theater and is still used today (see "More cool things to see and do," later in this section). The tunnels you see in the stage area aren't original; they were dug later by the Romans so that they could use the theater for their blood sports. At the back of the theater are Byzantine tombs and a fountain served by the original Greek system of aqueducts fetching water from 40km (25 miles) away.

On the other side of the hill is the **Latomia del Paradiso (stone quarry).** What you see is a huge hole covering many acres, with a few pillars sticking up and giant stones scattered here and there. The central pillar held up the roof of the quarry, and the big blocks of stone were once the roof, which collapsed in the 1693 earthquake. One of the excavated caves, the **Grotta dei Cordari (Grotto of the Ropemakers),** was used in later centuries for ropemaking; it has been closed for years for safety reasons. After descending into the quarry, you can visit the **Orecchio di Dionisio (Dionysius's Ear),** a deep, very tall, pitch-black cave. The story that Dionysius used the cave to eavesdrop on conversations is a myth; the painter Caravaggio was said to have given the cave its name (perhaps he made up the story, too). Nearby is another important structure, the **Anfiteatro Romano (Roman Amphitheater),** built during the reign of Augustus and partially carved from the rock. Like other Roman theaters, it was used for life-and-death battles between humans as well as animals and was sometimes flooded and filled with crocodiles and other friendly creatures for water fights.

What you see today is only the bottom story — try to imagine how it looked when the top of the theater reached the present height of the surrounding trees. Holy Roman Emperor Charles V is the bad guy of many stories about Italy, and Syracuse is no exception. He did more damage than the earthquake and is responsible for turning this theater into a quarry. During his North African campaigns, he destroyed much of the Roman ruins for material to build fortifications.

Via Augusto, near the intersection of Corso Gelone and Viale Teocrito. ☎ *0931-66-206. Bus: 4, 5, or 6 to Parco Archeologico. Admission: 3€ ($3.45). Open: Daily 9 a.m.–sunset; last admission 2 hours before sunset.*

More cool things to see and do

✔ The antique **Teatro Greco** (Greek Theater) in the Parco Archeologico comes to life again when ancient dramas by Greek authors are presented as they were 2,500 years ago. The season usually run from mid-May through June. Contact the **Istituto Nazionale del Dramma Antico** (Corso G. Matteotti 29, 96100 Siracusa; ☎ **800-907-080** toll-free in Italy or 0931-67-415; www.drammantico.it) for information on programs and dates. Tickets run from 15€ to 35€ ($17–$40), depending on the quality of the seats.

✔ Only 32km (20 miles) south of Syracuse is the famous town of **Noto,** a wonderful example of Sicilian baroque. The town was reduced to rubble by the 1693 earthquake — the same that destroyed the whole southeast of Sicily — and the town's notables decided to rebuild a completely new town 10 miles south of its original location. The reconstruction happened very rapidly — in about 45 years — and the result was a town remarkably uniform in style, a real rarity in Italy where you can usually see the layers of history. Faithful to pure baroque standards, Noto was built on a regular street grid. Many important Sicilian artists contributed to the reconstruction and the whole town is considered a work of art. Carvings of grotesque animals and figures support the balconies, and the town is built in golden-yellow stone. Noto underwent a restoration that started in 1997. The **tourist office,** where you can also get a map of the town, is in the center at Piazza XIV Maggio (☎ **0931-573-779**); summer hours are daily from 9 a.m. to 1 p.m. and 3:30 to 6:30 p.m.; winter hours are Monday through Saturday from 8 a.m. to 2 p.m. and 3:30 to 6:30 p.m. Noto is a 50-minute bus ride from Syracuse; guided tours are also available (see earlier in this chapter).

Fast Facts: Syracuse

Area Code

The country code for Italy is **39**. The area code for Syracuse is **0931**; use this code when calling from anywhere outside or inside Italy. Add the codes even when calling within Syracuse itself, and include the 0 every time, even when calling from abroad.

Emergencies

Ambulance, ☎ **118**; fire, ☎ **115**; road assistance, ☎ **116**.

Information

The tourist office maintains one booth at Via San Sebastiano 43 (☎ 0931-481-200 or

0931-481-232) and one at the Zona Archeologica (Via Augusto); both are open Monday through Saturday 8:30 a.m. to 2:00 p.m. and 4:30 to 7:30 p.m. in summer; 3:30 to 6:30 p.m. in winter.

Police

There are two police forces in Italy; call either one. For the Polizia, call ☎ **113;** for the Carabinieri, call ☎ **112.**

Post Office

The Ufficio Postale is on Piazza Riva della Posta 15, to the left of the main bridge in Ortigia (☎ 0931-68-973). It's open Monday through Friday 8:10 a.m. to 6:30 p.m. (Sat to 1 p.m.).

Taxis

You can call a radio taxi at ☎ 0931-757-557, 0931-717-081, or 0931-781-864.

Agrigento and the Valley of the Temples

Dominating the southern shore, **Agrigento** was another important Greek city, one of the most beautiful of the ancient world; the Greek poet Pindar admired it deeply. Agrigento reached great heights in art and culture in the third century B.C. but saw its fortunes wax and wane with those of the Roman Empire. The **Valley of the Temples (Valle dei Templi),** where the ancient city once stood, is one of the most dramatic classical ruins in the Mediterranean. Farther up the hill from the ruins stands modern Agrigento, a small town that most visitors bypass.

Agrigento was founded in 581 B.C. on a gentle slope toward the sea shaped as a natural amphitheater and protected by two hills and two rivers. A prosperous city in antiquity, it was progressively abandoned during the decline of the Roman Empire. The Arabs and then the Normans later occupied the site, and the population moved up the hill to the current site of town. During the 13th and 14th centuries, the feudal Chiaramonte family promoted the construction of walls around the town, as well as numerous churches and monasteries.

Getting there

Several companies in Palermo offer tours of the Valle dei Templi (see "Taking a tour," later in this section), but you can easily get to Agrigento on your own.

Eleven **trains** a day run from Palermo to Agrigento's rail station, **Stazione Centrale** (Piazza Guglielmo Marconi; ☎ **0922-725-669**); the trip takes 1½ hours and costs about 7€ ($8.05).

Several **bus** companies have daily runs between Palermo and Agrigento, including **AST** (☎ **800-234-163** toll-free in Italy or 091-688-2906) in Palermo and **Omnia** (☎ **0922-596-490**) in Agrigento; the trip takes approximately two hours and costs about 7€ ($8.05). **Licata** (☎ **0922-401-360**) in Agrigento makes two daily runs directly from Palermo's airport to Agrigento for the same price.

The Greek temple

The Greek temple was conceived as the habitation of a god and always opened to the east because the god's statue had to face the rising sun (symbol of the beginning of light and life) and never the sunset (symbol of the night and death). Over a high rectangular platform with steps, the classic temple has a perimeter of columns and an inside wall enclosing three rooms: the *pronaos* (entrance), the *naos* (the cell with the statue of the god), and the *opistodomos* (where the treasure, the votive gifts, and the archives of the temple were kept). In fact, temples were so sacred that citizens used to leave their valuables there, thus using them as safes.

Agrigento is 126km (79 miles) from Palermo by regular road or 180km (112 miles) by *autostrada;* take **A19** to Caltanissetta, and then follow the directions to Agrigento and take **SS640** for the remaining 60km (37 miles). If you don't mind narrower roads, you can take **SS121/189** all the way from Palermo to Agrigento, which is shorter.

The Valley of the Temples (see "Seeing the sights," later in this section) is 3km (2 miles) south of the town center; a *navette* service connects the valley with the train station in Agrigento. You can also take a **taxi** from the taxi stand at the train station (☎ **0922-26-670)**; another taxi stand is on Piazzale Aldo Moro (☎ **0922-21-899**).

Taking a tour

CST (Via A. Amari 124; ☎ **091-582-294;** Fax: 091-582-218; 24-hour service at 0348-343-6104) offers guided tours of the Valley of the Temples from Palermo for about 45€ ($52).

Spending the night

Dioscuri Bay Palace
$$ San Leone

If you're going to stay in Agrigento, why not stay near the beach and swim in beautiful waters? Only 2.5km (1.4 miles) from the Valley of the Temples, this hotel is modern, and the small bay is delightful, with view of the temples. The spacious guest rooms are furnished in modern Mediterranean style, with bright white walls.

Lungomare Falcone e Borsellino 1, San Leone (off SS115 toward the sea from the Valle dei Templi). ☎ ***0922-406-111.*** *Fax: 0922-411-297.* www.framon-hotels.com. *Rack rates: 130€–185€ ($150–$213) double. Rates include breakfast. AE, DC, MC, V.*

Foresteria Baglio della Luna
$$$ **Valle dei Templi**

Near the Valley of the Temples, this hotel offers stylish accommodations with individually decorated guest rooms and an excellent restaurant, Dehor (see "Dining locally," later in this section).

Valle dei Templi, Contrada Maddalusa on SS 640 at km 4,150. ☎ *0922-511-061. Fax: 0922-598-802. Rack rates: 330€ ($386) double. Rates include breakfast. AE, DC, MC, V.*

Dining locally
Like the rest of Sicily, the cuisine of Agrigento relies heavily on seafood. In addition, Agrigento is at the center of the almond-growing industry, so almonds are used in a variety of preparations.

Dehor
$$ **Valle dei Templi**   **SICILIAN/CREATIVE**

This excellent restaurant inside the Hotel Foresteria Baglio della Luna will provide you with the perfect break after your visit to the temples. It is one of the best restaurants in Sicily. The menu changes with the seasons and the whims of the chef. Try such delicacies as *crema leggera di sedano verde all'aglio e fiori di timo con raviolini di lumache* (light creamy green celery soup with garlic, thyme flower, and snail-filled tiny ravioli), *tonno grigliato al couscous aromatico fonduta di peperoni e vellutata di pomodorini alla menta* (grilled tuna with herbed couscous, bell-pepper fondue, and minted cherry tomato puree), and *crema ghiacciata di mandorle e fichi secchi e miele al profumo di vecchio Marsala Florio* (iced almond cream with figs, honey, and aged Marsala wine sauce).

Valle dei Templi, Contrada Maddalusa on SS 640 at km. 4,150; in the Hotel Foresteria Baglio della Luna. ☎ *0922-511-061. Reservations recommended. Secondi: 15€–22€ ($17–$25). AE, DC, MC, V. Open: Lunch and dinner daily.*

Trattoria dei Templi
$$ **Valle dei Templi**   **SICILIAN**

This simple but pleasant restaurant is old-fashioned, down to the absence of a complete written menu — only the staple dishes figure on the menu whereas the many delicious specialties don't — and up to professional and kind service. You will be delighted with the great appetizer buffet, which includes all the local traditional specialties of fish and vegetables and is a great success with children, who get to see and choose what they want (half portions are available for every dish and the kitchen and staff will strive to meet all your special needs). The rest of the meal will include such fine choices as *spaghetti alle vongole veraci* (spaghetti with clams), *ravioli di pesce ai frutti di mare* (seafood ravioli), and *gamberoni alla griglia* (grilled jumbo shrimp).

Strada Panoramica dei Templi 15. ☎ *0922-403-110. Reservations recommended. Secondi: 12€–16€ ($14–$18). AE, DC, MC, V. Open: Lunch and dinner Sat–Thurs. Closed Sun July–Aug; closed 2 weeks in July.*

Exploring Agrigento

Casa Natale di Pirandello

This is the house where the writer Luigi Pirandello was born in 1867. Pirandello received the Nobel Prize for Literature in 1934. In his famous novel *Six Characters in Search of an Author,* Pirandello explored the theme of the mask that everyone must wear to have a role in society. The museum contains the author's memorabilia, and the grounds are beautiful; take the walk to the site's famous secular pine growing alone on a beautiful spot with a great view; it's where the author's ashes are buried.

Contrada Caos. ☎ *0922-511-102. Admission: 2.60€ ($3). Open: Daily 8 a.m.–8 p.m. Last admission for the promenade to the pine 1 hour before sunset.*

Chiesa di San Nicola

Built in the 12th century, this church is the first sight you encounter descending to the Valley of the Temples from Agrigento; it offers a perfect view above the temples. Inside, at the center of the second chapel, is the famous third-century *Sarcofago di Fedra,* one of the most gracious examples of Greek sculpture, evoking the myth of Phaedra and Ippolyte (a sad story of unrequited love in which the rejected Phaedra is delirious while Ippolyte goes hunting; he is killed in an accident).

Contrada San Nicola, Via dei Templi, Zona Archeologica. Admission: Free. Open: Daily 8 a.m.–1 p.m.

Museo Archeologico Regionale

This museum contains a large collection of Greek artifacts, many of which were found during the excavations in Agrigento. Besides the ample collection of Greek vases, an interesting piece is one of the Telamons (human figures supporting a structure) from the Tempio di Giove (see the description under the Valley of the Temples listing), which is in much better shape than the one on the ground at the temple.

Contrada San Nicola, Via dei Templi, Zona Archeologica. ☎ *0922-497-111. Admission: 4€ ($4.60). Open: Mon, Wed, Thu, Sat, and Sun 9 a.m.–1 p.m. and Tues and Fri 9 a.m.–5 p.m.*

Sagra del Mandorlo in Fiore (Festival of the Almond Flowers)

Held between the first and second Sunday in February, the festival was first created in 1938 as a celebration of spring — symbolized by the almond tree in blossom — accompanied by traditional dances and songs. Today the weeklong festival features folklore groups from around Sicily as well as from the rest of Italy and neighboring countries.

Town of Agrigento. Check with the local tourist office (Viale della Vittoria 255; ☎ *0922-401-352, 0922-20-391, or 0922-20-454; Fax: 0922-35-185) for a calendar of festival events.*

Valle dei Templi (Valley of the Temples)

The Valley of the Temples is the reason that most people come to Agrigento, and it's the most impressive Greek ruin outside Greece.

The archaeological area where the temples are located is quite wide and has very few trees. Bring comfortable shoes, a hat, sunscreen, and at least a quart of water per person. If you plan to visit as a day trip, we suggest you pack a picnic lunch to eat near the ruins — it's a nice spot, and you'll have more time to visit. The valley at sunrise or sunset is dramatic, and in summer the temperature at these times is cooler. You will need two to three hours for your visit, so if you want to be there at sunset plan to come early enough to see everything before dark.

From the **Porta Aurea,** a gate in the Greek walls of ancient Agrigento, you will find the three best-conserved temples on one side (Tempio di Ercole, Tempio della Concordia, and Tempio di Giunone) and the Tempio di Giove and Tempio dei Dioscuri by the river on the other.

The massive **Tempio di Giove (Temple of Jove or Zeus)** was built to celebrate the gratitude of the people of Agrigento for their 480–479 B.C. victory over the Carthaginians at Himera. One of the largest temples of antiquity, it covered approximately 6,317 sq. m (68,000 sq. ft.) and was 32.4m (108-ft.) tall. Each of the columns rose 26.3m (55.4 ft.) and measured 4.1m (13.8 ft.) at the base; probably alternated with the columns were the Telamons (or Atlases) — human figures supporting a structure. Each of these giants measured 7.5m (25-ft.) high, and you can see one that is now lying flat on the ground.

The **Tempio dei Dioscuri or di Castore e Polluce (Temple of Castor and Pollux)** is believed to have been built between 480 and 460 B.C. to honor the twin sons of Jupiter and Leda, queen of Sparta, protectors of athletes, hospitality, and sailors in difficulty. Of the 34 columns, only 4 remain standing (at the corner of the temple), which were restored in the 19th century. Nearby are the few remains of the **Tempio di Vulcano.**

On the other side of the entrance, the **Tempio di Ercole (Temple of Hercules)** is one of the most beautiful and the largest of the temples on this side: it occupied an area of about 2,043 sq. m (22,000 sq. ft.). Hercules was highly revered in Sicily and particularly in Agrigento; the god of strength, he was thought to free people from nightmares and unwanted erotic stimuli. Only nine columns are still standing, thanks to the generosity of the English Captain Hardcastle who paid for their restoration in the 1920s. The columns were originally painted white to simulate marble, whereas the cornice was decorated in red, blue, and turquoise. The temple was richly decorated with reliefs and sculptures.

The **Tempio della Concordia (Temple of Concordia),** built around 430 B.C., is remarkably well preserved, because it was transformed into a church

Agrigento and the Valley of the Temples

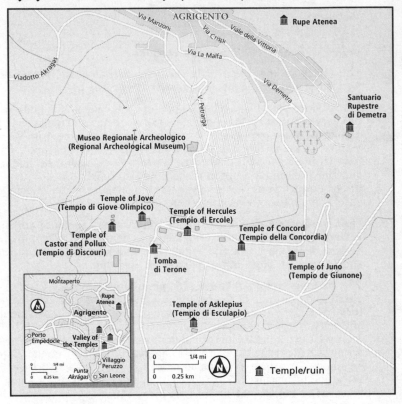

as far back as A.D. 597. Twelve arches were opened in the walls of the temple, and the space between the columns was walled in to make it a church with three naves. These alterations were reversed in 1743 when the temple was declared a national monument and restored. It's one of the best-conserved temples of this period, together with the one of Hera in Paestum and the Theseion in Athens.

The **Tempio di Giunone (Temple of Juno or Hera)** is also well preseved. Built in 450–440 B.C. in honor of Juno (Hera) — the mother goddess and protectress of marriage and fertility — it has 34 columns and a maximum height of 15.31m (50.2 ft.). It rises on a pretty hill, near one of the only trees in the whole archeological area!

Piazzale dei Templi/Posto di Ristoro, at the crossroad with SS115 Siracusa–Trapani. ☎ *0922-26-191. Bus: 8, 9, 10, or 11 to the Posto di Ristoro. Admission (ticket booth is at the Tempio di Giove entrance): 6.50€ ($7.50). Open: Tempio di Giove archaeological area, daily 8:30 a.m.–5 p.m.; Tempio della Concordia archaeological area, daily 8 a.m.–9 p.m.*

Part VIII
The Part of Tens

The 5th Wave   By Rich Tennant

"So far you've called a rickshaw, a unicyclist, and a Zamboni. I really wish you'd learn the Italian word for taxicab."

In this part . . .

Think you can't possibly make do in Italy knowing only ten Italian words? Believe it or not, you can, and in Chapter 25 we give you the few key words that will help you converse with the natives. In Chapter 26, we tell you more about ten Italian artists, maybe the greatest of all, but certainly some whose work you will encounter over and over during your visit.

Chapter 25

Non Capisco: The Top Ten Expressions You Need to Know

In This Chapter
- Using salutations
- Asking questions
- Knowing lifesavers

*T*raveling in a country where you don't know the language can be intimidating, but trying to speak the language can be amusing, at the very least. Local people often appreciate it if you at least make the effort. And you'll find that Italian is a fun language to try to speak.

Per Favore

Meaning "please," *per favore* (*per* fa-*voe*-ray) is the most important expression you can know. With it you can make useful phrases such as *Un caffè, per favore* ("A coffee, please") and *Il conto, per favore* ("The bill, please"). There's no need for verbs, and it's perfectly polite!

Grazie

Grazie (*gra*-tziay) means "thank you"; if you want to go all out, use *grazie mille* (*mee*-lay), meaning "a thousand thanks." Say it clearly and loudly enough to be heard. Saying *grazie* is always right and puts people in a good mood. *Grazie* has other uses as well: Italians often use it as a way to say goodbye or mark the end of an interaction. It's particularly useful when you don't want to buy something from an insistent street vendor: Say, *"Grazie,"* and walk away.

Permesso

Meaning "excuse me" (to request passage or admittance), *permesso* (per-*mess*-ow) is of fundamental importance on public transportation. When you're in a crowded bus and need to get off, say loudly and clearly, *"Permesso!"* and people will clear from your path (or feel less irritated as you squeeze your way through). The same thing applies in supermarkets, trains, museums, and so on. Of course, you may be surrounded by non-Italians and the effect may be a little lost on them.

Scusi

Scusi (*scoo*-sy) means "excuse me" (to say you're sorry after bumping into someone) and is more exactly *mi scusi,* but the shortened form is the one more people use. Again, it's a most useful word in any crowded situation. You'll note that Italians push their way through a narrow passage with a long chain of *"Scusi, permesso, mi scusi, grazie, permesso. . . ."* It's very funny to hear. *Scusi* has another important use: It's the proper beginning to attract somebody's attention before asking a question. Say *"Scusi?"* and the person will turn toward you in benevolent expectation. Then it's up to you.

Buon Giorno and Buona Sera

Buon giorno (bwon *djor*-know), meaning "good day," and its sibling *buona sera* (*bwon*-a *sey*-rah), meaning "good evening," are of the utmost importance in Italian interactions. Italians always salute one another when entering or leaving a public place. Do the same, saying it clearly when entering a store or restaurant. Occasionally, these words can also be used as forms of goodbye.

Arrivederci

Arrivederci (ah-rree-vey-*der*-tchy) is the appropriate way to say goodbye in a formal occasion — in a shop, in a bar or restaurant, or to friends. If you can say it properly, people will like it very much: Italians are aware of the difficulties of their language for foreigners.

You'll hear the word *ciao* (chow), the familiar word for goodbye, used among friends (usually of the same age). Note that using the word *ciao* with someone you don't know is considered quite impolite!

Dov'è

Meaning "where is," *dov'è* (doe-*vay*) is useful for asking for directions. Because the verb is included, you just need to add the thing you're looking for: *Dov'è il Colosseo?* ("Where is the Colosseum?") or *Dov'è la stazione?* ("Where is the train station?"). Of course you need to know the names of monuments in Italian, but don't worry! We always give you the Italian names in this book. It makes things much easier when you're there!

Quanto Costa?

Meaning "How much does it cost?", *Quanto costa?* (*quahnn*-tow *koss*-tah) is of obvious use all around Italy for buying anything from a train ticket to a Murano glass chandelier.

Che Cos'è?

Meaning "What is it?", *Che cos'è?* (kay *koss*-ay) will help you buy things, particularly food, and know what you're buying. But it could also be useful in museums and other circumstances. But then the tricky part begins: understanding the answer. If you don't understand the answer, you can get the person to repeat it by saying the next phrase on our list. . . .

Non Capisco

Non capisco (nonn kah-*peace*-koh) means "I don't understand." There's no need to explain this one: Keep repeating it and Italians will try more and more imaginative ways to explain things to you.

Chapter 26

Ten Great Italian Artists

In This Chapter

▶ Knowing who's who
▶ Charting the careers of the masters
▶ Getting background for what you'll be seeing

*A*dmittedly, hundreds of books have been written about the great figures of Italian art, so any choice of ten figures is apt to be personal. However, some artists would be on everybody's list: Leonardo, Michelangelo, Raffaelo . . . This chapter is intended to give you some background to attach to the names that you will encounter again and again in your travels in Italy.

Giotto

Immortalized by Dante in the *Divine Comedy*, Giotto di Bondone (1266 or 1276–1337) was famous in his own time and in later centuries came to be known as the father of modern painting. A practitioner of the **Gothic** style, he departed from the serene but flat and static mode of Byzantine painting and the somber, otherworldly beauty of medieval art. In works such as his masterpiece, the **Scrovegni Chapel** in Padua (see Chapter 19), he depicted human beings with a passion and emotion not seen since classical times, and paved the way for the Renaissance in the following century.

Donatello

In a sense, Donatello (1386–1466) did for sculpture what **Giotto** did for painting: pulled it out of the Middle Ages and gave it a new realism and psychological accuracy. He developed a new technique, *schiacciato*, which used flattened, shallow carving to make relief sculpture more pictorial and more like painting. Donatello executed works in marble, bronze, and wood, and many of his works survive in his native Florence, where he spent most of his long life. His crowning achievement is probably the carvings for the sacristy in the **Basilica di San Lorenzo**; the **Bargello** museum has two of his statues of *David,* one in bronze and the other in marble (see Chapter 14).

Giovanni Bellini

Born to an artistic family (his father and brother were painters, and his sister married Andrea Mantegna), Giovanni Bellini (1430–1516) began as a painter of austere religious pictures in the late **Gothic** tradition. He later developed one of the most recognizable styles and had a lasting effect on Venetian painting. His masterpiece is reputed to have been the large historical paintings he did for the hall of the Maggior Consiglio in **Venice**, but these were destroyed by fire in 1577. However, his luminosity and exquisite colors are fully on display in religious artworks (such as his famous Madonnas) and other pieces preserved in the museums and churches of Venice (see Chapter 18).

Leonardo da Vinci

Leonardo (1452–1519) grew up on his father's estate in Vinci, a Tuscan town under the rule of Florence. He was apprentice to the Florentine painter Andrea del Verrocchio. Leonardo later left Florence for Milan, where he spent 17 years. Leonardo's genius for observation manifested itself in portrayals of the human figure, such as the *Mona Lisa,* that were psychologically real to the point of being uncanny, while also showing a revolutionary sense of physicality, based on a profound grasp of anatomy. His use of *chiaroscuro* (contrast between light and dark) influenced later painters. Leonardo's attention to nature led him to become a scientist, engineer, and inventor as well. Leonardo's life and work are perhaps the most perfect expression of the spirit of the Renaissance. His *Last Supper* in **Milan** (see Chapter 19), though much damaged, is a pilgrimage site for art lovers.

Michelangelo

Michelangelo Buonarotti (1475–1564), like Leonardo, was a great painter but many other things as well, including an architect; **St. Peter's** in Rome (see Chapter 12) received its final form and its dome from him. This architectural masterpiece also contains his painterly masterpiece, the frescoes of the **Cappella Sistina,** and his sculptural masterpiece, the **Pietà**. A tempestuous genius, he was often embroiled in conflict. His patrons included **Lorenzo de' Medici** and **Pope Julius II.** Julius's successor, Leo X, was actually a son of Lorenzo and longtime friend of Michelangelo, and he employed the artist in the **Medici Chapels** in Florence (see Chapter 14). His use of color and monumental modeling of the human form pointed ahead to the style known as Mannerism.

Rafael

In a short life Raffaelo Sanzio (1483–1520) left a profound mark on European painting. He had already shown great talent as a draftsman before he was out of his teens. After studying painting with Perugino and other artists, he moved to Florence and fell under the spell of **Leonardo da Vinci.** But Raffaelo's figures have a radiant, peaceful composure that is all his own; his images have often been described as "sublime." Some of his finest work is in the rooms he frescoed at the **Vatican** for Pope Julius II (see Chapter 12). It is less known that Rafael was very interested in archaeology and was appointed commissioner of antiquities for the city of Rome. Rafael died on his birthday at the age of 37; his tomb is in the Pantheon.

Titian

Tiziano Vecellio (circa 1488–1576) moved to Venice with his brother at the age of nine and was apprenticed to a mosaicist. He found his true calling, however, when he began to study under the greatest Venetian painter of the time, Giovanni Bellini (see earlier in this chapter). Titian became famous for his depictions of mythological and idyllic scenes, powerful and revealing portraits (like the one of Pope Paul III and family in the Capodimonte museum in **Naples**–see Chapter 20), and stunning religious works such as the revolutionary *Assumption* in the Frari church in **Venice** (see Chapter 18), a truly glorious painting.

Tintoretto

Jacopo Robusti (1518–1594) was nicknamed "tintoretto" ("little dyer") because his father was a silk dyer. His unmistakable mature style involved dynamic, loose brushwork and a palette that could almost be described as moody. He was a colossal talent, the leading Mannerist painter of the time, and his presence is felt everywhere in **Venice,** particularly in **Scuola Grande di San Rocco,** which he literally filled with large canvasses (see Chapter 18). Inspired by **Michelangelo** and **Titian** (see earlier in this chapter), Tintoretto is nonetheless a unique and startlingly original painter, whose work is above all passionate.

Gian Lorenzo Bernini

If anyone personifies the Baroque period, it is Bernini (1598–1680). Although born in Naples, he did his major work in Rome, where one can hardly turn around without stumbling on one of his masterworks. He developed a style, which combined the psychological realism of earlier Renaissance sculptors with heightened decoration. His **baldaquin** inside

St. Peter's in Rome (see Chapter 12), a giant gilt-and-bronze canopy over four stories tall, has been called the first Baroque monument. His fountain in the **Piazza Navona** is one of the most beautiful in Rome, while the **Galleria Borghese** contains several sculptures of incredible mastery where he made marble behave like flesh. Bernini was so famous that when he visited the court of French king **Louis XIV** in 1665, crowds lined the streets to see him.

Caravaggio

One of the most beloved of Italian artists, Michelangelo Merisi da Caravaggio (1572–1610) appeals to the modern imagination for his romantic, tragic life as well as for his intense and unique art. He was considered a "wild spirit" by his contemporaries, and was a friend of prostitutes (some of whom were his models) and criminals. However, he was also protected and encouraged by cardinal Francesco del Monte. His religious paintings were often rejected for their emotional intensity and overpowering sensual impact (many can be found in the churches of **Rome** and in the **Galleria Borghese** — see Chapter 12). He fled Rome after a killing, or duel, which remains shadowy; he died soon thereafter. The lurid details of his life, however, are less important than his extraordinary use of light and shade, brilliant depiction of bodies in motion, and tremendous fusion of naturalistic art and spiritual faith.

Appendix

Quick Concierge

○ ○

Fast Facts

Automobile Club

Contact the Automobile Club d'Italia (ACI) at ☎ 06-4477 for 24-hour information and assistance. For **road emergencies** in Italy, dial ☎ **116.**

American Express

The Rome office is at Piazza di Spagna 38 (☎ 06-676-41; Metro: Line A to Spagna); the Florence office is at Via Dante Alighieri 22R (☎ 055-50-981); and the Venice office is at Salizzada San Moisè, 1471 San Marco (☎ 041-520-0844). The Milan office is Via Brera 3 (☎ 02-876-674); in Naples, Piazza Municipio 5 (☎ 081-551-2007); in Palermo, Via E. Amari 40 (☎ 091-587-144).

ATMs

ATMs are available everywhere in the centers of towns. Most banks are linked to the Cirrus network. If you require the Plus network, your best bet is the BNL (Banca Nazionale del Lavoro), but ask your bank for a list of locations before leaving on your trip.

Credit Cards

If your card is lost or stolen, contact these offices: American Express (☎ 06-722-0348, or 06-72-282 or 06-72-461; www.american express.it); Diners Club (☎ 800-864-064866 toll-free within Italy; www.diners club.com); MasterCard (☎ 800-870-866 toll-free within Italy; www.mastercard.com); or Visa (☎ 800-819-014 toll-free within Italy; www.visaeu.com)

Currency Exchange

You can find very good exchange bureaus (marked *cambio/change/wechsel*) at airports and at major train stations.

Customs

U.S. citizens can bring back $800 worth of merchandise duty-free. You can mail yourself $200 worth of merchandise per day and $100 worth of gifts to others — alcohol and tobacco excluded. You can bring on the plane 1 liter of alcohol and 200 cigarettes or 100 cigars. The $800 ceiling doesn't apply to artwork or antiques (antiques must be 100 years old or more). You're charged a flat rate of 10% duty on the next $1,000 worth of purchases — for special items, the duty is higher. Make sure that you have your receipts handy. Agricultural restrictions are severely enforced: no fresh products, no meat products, no dried flowers; other foodstuffs are allowed only if they're canned or in airtight sealed packages. For more information, contact the U.S. Customs Service, 1301 Pennsylvania Ave, NW, Washington, DC 20229 (☎ 877-287-8867) and request the free pamphlet *Know Before You Go*, which is also available for download on the Web at www.customs.gov.

Canadian citizens are allowed a Can$750 exemption and can bring back duty-free 200 cigarettes, 2.2 pounds of tobacco, 40 imperial ounces of liquor, and 50 cigars. In addition, you're allowed to mail gifts to Canada from abroad at the rate of Can$60 a day, provided they're unsolicited and don't contain alcohol or tobacco (write on the package "Unsolicited Gift, Under $60 Value"). Declare all valuables on the Y-38 form before your departure from Canada, including serial numbers of valuables that you already own, such as expensive foreign cameras. You can use the $750 exemption only once a year and only after an absence of seven days. For more information, contact the Canada Border Services Agency (☎ 800-461-9999 from within Canada, or 204-983-3500 or 506-636-5064 from outside Canada; www.cbsa-asfc.gc.ca).

There's no limit on what U.K. citizens can bring back from an EU country, as long as the items are for personal use (this includes gifts), and the necessary duty and tax has already been paid. However, Customs law sets out guidance levels. If you bring in more than these levels, you may be asked to prove that the goods are for your own use. Guidance levels on goods bought in the EU for your own use are 800 cigarettes, 200 cigars, 1kg smoking tobacco, 10 liters of spirits, 90 liters of wine (of this not more than 60 liters can be sparkling wine), and 110 liters of beer. For more information, contact HM Customs and Excise, Passenger Enquiry Point, 2nd Floor Wayfarer House, Great South West Road, Feltham, Middlesex, TW14 8NP (☎ 0845-010-9000; from outside the U.K. ☎ 44-208-929-0152), or consult their Web site at www.hmce.gov.uk.

Australian citizens are allowed an exemption of A$400 or, for those under 18, A$200. Personal property mailed back home should be marked "Australian Goods Returned" to avoid payment of duty. On returning to Australia, you can bring in 250 cigarettes or 250 grams of loose tobacco, and 1,125ml of alcohol. If you're returning with valuable goods you already own, such as foreign-made cameras, you should file

form B263. A helpful brochure, available from Australian consulates or Customs offices, is *Know Before You Go*. For more information, contact Australian Customs Services, GPO Box 8, Sydney NSW 2001 (☎ 02-9213-2000 or 1300-363-263 within Australia or 612-6275-6666 from outside Australia; www.customs.gov.au).

New Zealand citizens have a duty-free allowance of NZ$700. If you're over 17, you can bring in 200 cigarettes, 50 cigars, or 250 grams of tobacco (or a mix of all three if their combined weight doesn't exceed 250 grams); plus 4.5 liters of wine and beer, or 1.125 liters of liquor. New Zealand currency doesn't carry import or export restrictions. Fill out a certificate of export, listing the valuables you're taking out of the country. (That way, you can bring them back without paying duty.) You can find the answers to most of your questions in a free pamphlet available at New Zealand consulates and Customs offices: *New Zealand Customs Guide for Travelers, Notice no. 4*. For more information, contact New Zealand Customs, The Custom House, 17-21 Whitmore St. Box 2218, Wellington (☎ 04-473-6099; www.customs.govt.nz).

Driving

If you have a breakdown or any other **road emergencies,** call ☎ **116** (road emergencies and first aid of the Italian Automobile Club) or call the **police emergency** (☎ **113** and **112**).

Electricity

Electricity in Italy is 220 volts. To use your appliances, you need a transformer. Remember that plugs are different, too: The prongs are round, so you also need an adapter. You can buy an adapter kit in many electronics stores before you leave.

Embassies and Consulates

Rome is the capital of Italy and, therefore, the seat of all the embassies and consulates, which maintain a 24-hour referral service for emergencies: United States (☎ 06-46741), Canada (☎ 06-445-981), Australia (☎ 06-852-721), New Zealand (☎ 06-440-2928), United Kingdom (☎ 06-7-482-5441), Ireland (☎ 06-697-9121). For more information on embassies and consulates around Italy, see the "Fast Facts" sections in the chapters on the larger cities.

Emergencies

For an **ambulance or first aid**, call ☎ 118; for the **fire department**, call ☎ 115.

Information

See "Where to Get More Information," below, and in individual destination chapters throughout this book.

Internet Access and Cybercafes

Refer to the "Fast Facts" section in individual destination chapters.

Language

Italians speak Italian and although many know a bit of English, it is not widely understood. Luckily, you can survive with very little knowledge of the Italian language (see Chapter 26 for a few choice terms), especially because Italians are very friendly and ready to help foreigners in difficulty. However, you'll greatly enhance your experience if you master more than a dozen basic expressions. A good place to start your studies is *Italian For Dummies* (Wiley)!

Liquor Laws

There are no liquor laws in Italy. However, there are laws against disturbing the *quiete pubblica* (public quiet) — getting drunk and loud in bars, streets, and so on.

Italians consider public drunkenness disgraceful, and though they love wine, they very much frown upon drinking to excess. You can buy alcohol in all supermarkets and grocery stores, open usually from 9 a.m. to 1 p.m. and 4 to 7 p.m.

Maps

The tourist maps given at tourist information booths are usually adequate. If you want something more detailed, you can buy one at local newsstands, kiosks, and tobacconists — they all carry a good selection.

Police

There are two police forces in Italy; call either one. For the Polizia, call ☎ 113; for the Carabinieri, call ☎ 112.

Post Office

Each town has at least one post office, usually in the center. Mail in Italy used to be notoriously unreliable and many tourists still prefer to use the Vatican post office while they're visiting St. Peter in Rome (it's the same price as Italian post offices, but faster). Italian mail, though, has gotten a lot better with the introduction of *Posta Prioritaria* (express/priority). A letter to the U.S. costs .80€ (92¢) and can take as little as four to five days to get there. Beware, though, that postcards are always sent via the equivalent of U.S. third-class mail and will take a long time to arrive; if you want your postcards to arrive fast, slip them in an envelope and send them letter rate. Also, make sure you put your mail in the right mail box: The ones for international mail are blue, whereas the red ones are for national mail and sorting will take longer. The new priority mail also applies to packages; however, it is expensive and you might be better off using a private carrier like UPS or DHL, which will garantee your delivery, especially for valuables.

Safety

Italy is very safe, not considering petty theft. Pickpockets abound in tourist areas, public transportation, and crowded open-air markets. Bag snatchers on motor scooters are less frequent than they used to be, and Palermo is the only city where they're still common. Keeping your bag on the wall side of a sidewalk or between you and your companion is a good rule to follow, however. There are areas of poverty where a wealthy-looking tourist with an expensive camera may be mugged after dark, but those are usually on the out-skirt of cities. (Seedy areas are often behind rail stations, and we indicate when they exist in each destination.)

If you're a woman traveling alone in Italy — especially if you're young and fair-haired — you'll attract young Italian men. In fact, they'll approach you and try to charm you; however, it's unlikely that someone will touch you, let alone harm you. Still, it's a good idea to ignore and not make eye contact with anyone who approaches you. The way you dress sometimes has an effect. Italians have a stricter dress code than Americans do, and the farther south you go, the more traditional the society is. You can either dress however you feel like dressing (and steel yourself for the occasional look of disapproval or suggestive remark), or adapt your mode of dress to fit in with local traditions — the choice is yours.

Smoking

Smoking is allowed in caffés and restau-rants and is very common. Unfortunately for nonsmokers, finding a restaurant with a separate no-smoking area is not easy, but their number is growing. If dining in a no-smoking area is very important to you, call beforehand to make sure the restaurant or cafe you'll be visiting offers one.

Taxes

Please refer to Chapter 5 for VAT information.

Telephone

To call Italy from the U.S., dial the **interna-tional access code, 011;** then Italy's **coun-try code, 39;** and then the city code for the city you're calling (06 for Rome, 055 for Florence, 041 for Venice, and so on); and then the regular phone number. Note that cellphone numbers do not begin with a 0, nor do special phone numbers such as toll-free numbers (mostly starting with 800-) and paying services.

To make a call within Italy, remember to always dial city codes (including the 0) for every call, even local calls. All public pay phones in Italy take a *carta telefonica* (telephone card), which you can buy at a *tabacchi* (tobacconist, marked by a sign with a white *T* on a black background), bar, or newsstand. The cards can be pur-chased in different denominations, from 2€ to 7.50€ ($2.30–$8.05). Tear off the per-forated corner, stick the card in the phone, and you're ready to go. A local call in Italy costs .10€ (12¢).

To call abroad from Italy, dial the interna-tional access code, 00; then the country code of the country that you're calling (1 for the United States and Canada, 44 for the United Kingdom, 353 for Ireland, 61 for Australia, 64 for New Zealand); and then the phone number. Make sure that you have a high-value *carta telefonica* before you start; your 5€ won't last long when you call San Diego at noon. Lower rates apply after 11 p.m. and before 8 a.m. and on Sundays. The best option for calling home, though, is using your own calling card linked to your home phone. Some calling cards offer a toll-free access number in Italy, others do not and you must put in a *carta telefonica* to dial the access number (you're usually charged only for a local call or not at all). Check with your calling card provider before leaving on your trip. You can also make collect calls. For AT&T, dial ☎ 800-172-4444 and then your US phone number area code first; for MCI, dial ☎ 800-90-5825; and for Sprint, dial ☎ 800-172-405 or 800-172-406. To make a collect call to a country other than the United States, dial ☎ 170. Directory assistance for calls within Italy is a free call: Dial ☎ 12. International directory assistance is a toll call: Dial ☎ 176. Remember that calling from a hotel is convenient but usually very expensive.

Time Zone

In terms of standard time zones, Italy is six hours ahead of eastern standard time in the United States: When it is 6 a.m. in New York, it is noon in Italy. Daylight saving time goes into effect in Italy each year from the end of March to the end of September.

Tipping

Tipping is customary as a token of appreciation as well as a polite gesture in most occasions. A 10 to 15 percent service charge is usually included in your restaurant bill (check the menu when you order — if the service is included it will be marked at the beginning or at the end *servizio incluso*), but it is customary to leave an additional 5 to 10 percent if you appreciated the meal; if the service is not included, leave 15 to 25 percent. In bars, leave a 5 percent tip at the counter and a 10 to 15 percent tip if you sit at a table. Bellhops who carry your bags will expect about 1€/$1.15 per bag, and you might want to leave a small tip for the maid in your hotel; cab drivers will expect 10 to 15 percent of the fare.

Weather Updates

Before you go, you can check a local Web site such as `http://meteo.tiscalinet.it` or one of the U.S.–based ones, such as `www.cnn.com`. Once in Italy, your best bet is to watch the news on TV (there's no telephone weather number as there is in the U.S.).

Toll-Free Numbers and Web Sites

Airlines that fly to and around Italy

Air France
☎ 800-237-2747
`www.airfrance.com`

Air New Zealand
☎ 800-737-000
`www.airnewzealand.com`

Air One
☎ 199-207-080 within Italy or 06-488-800 from abroad.
`www.air-one.it`

Air Sicilia
☎ 06-6501-71046

Alitalia
☎ 1478-65-643 toll-free within Italy or 06-65643; ☎ 800-223-5730 in the U.S.; ☎ 800-361-8336 in Canada; ☎ 0990-448-259 in the U.K. and 020-7602-7111 in London; ☎ 1300-653-747 or 1300-653-757 in Australia.
`www.alitalia.it` or in the USA `www.alitaliausa.com`

American Airlines
☎ 800-433-7300
`www.aa.com`

British Airways
☎ 800-AIRWAYS (800-247-9297) in the U.S.
www.british-airways.com

Cathay Pacific
☎ 131-747 toll-free in Australia or 0508-800454 in New Zealand
www.cathaypacific.com

Continental Airlines
☎ 800-525-0280
www.continental.com

Delta Airlines
☎ 800-241-4141
www.delta.com

Lufthansa
☎ 800-645-3880 in the U.S.
www.lufthansa-usa.com

Meridiana
☎ 199-111-333 within Italy or 0789-52-682 from abroad
www.meridiana.it

Northwest/KLM
☎ 800-447-4747 or 800-374-7747
www.nwa.com or www.klm.nl

Qantas
☎ 13-13-13
www.qantas.com

United
☎ 800-538-2929
www.united.com

US Airways
☎ 800-428-4322
www.usairways.com

Car-rental agencies

AutoEurope
☎ 800-334-440 toll-free in Italy or 800-223-5555 in the U.S.
www.autoeurope.com

Avis
☎ 06-41-999 in Italy or 800-331-1212 in the U.S.
www.avis.com

Europe by Car
☎ 800-223-1516 in the U.S.
www.europebycar.com

Europcar
☎ 800-014-410 toll-free in Italy or 06-6501-0879
www.europcar.it

Hertz
☎ 199-112-211 in Italy or 800-654-3001 in the U.S.
www.hertz.com

Kemwel
☎ 800-678-0678 in the U.S.
www.kemwel.com

National/Maggiore
☎ 1478-67-067 toll-free in Italy or 800-227-7368 in the U.S.
www.maggiore.it

Hotel chains in Italy

Best Western
☎ 800-780-7234 in the U.S. and Canada, ☎ 0800-39-31-30 in the U.K., ☎ 131-779 in Australia, ☎ 0800-237-893 in New Zealand
www.bestwestern.com or www.bestwestern.it

Hilton Hotels
☎ 800-HILTONS
www.hilton.com

Holiday Inn
☎ 800-HOLIDAY
www.holiday-inn.com

Jolly Hotels
☎ 800-017-703 toll-free in Italy,
☎ 800-221-2626 toll-free in the U.S.,
☎ 800-247-1277 toll-free in New York
state, ☎ 800-237-0319 toll-free in
Canada, ☎ 0800-731-0470 toll-free in
the U.K.
www.jollyhotels.it.

ITT Sheraton
☎ 800-325-3535
www.sheraton.com

Sofitel
☎ 800-SOFITEL in the U.S. and
Canada, ☎ 020-8 283-4570 in the U.K.,
☎ 02- 2951-2280 in Italy, ☎ 800-
642-244 in Australia, ☎ 0800-44-44-22
in New Zealand
www.sofitel.com or www.accor-
hotels.it/sofitel.htm.

(Sofitel is part of the giant Accor
group, representing 3,400 hotels in
several chains. You can connect to all
of them through ☎ 800-221-4542 in
the U.S. and Canada and ☎ 0208-
283-4500 in the U.K.; www.accor.
com).

Where to Get More Information

For more information on Italy, you can visit the tourist offices and Web sites listed in this section.

Visitor information

The Italian National Tourist Board ENIT (www.enit.it) maintains a Web site where you can find all kinds of cultural and practical information — including hotel listings and mail and Web addresses of local tourist offices. It also maintains liaison offices abroad where you can get brochures and other info (all offices are open Mon–Fri, 9 a.m.–5 p.m. local time):

- **New York** (630 Fifth Ave., Suite 1565, New York, NY 10111; ☎ 212-245-5618 or 212-245-4822; Fax: 212-586-9249; E-mail: enitny@italian tourism.com)

- **Chicago** (500 N. Michigan Ave., Suite 2240, Chicago, IL 60611; ☎ 312-644-0996 or 312-644-0990; Fax: 312-644-3019; E-mail: enitch@ italiantourism.com)

- **Los Angeles** (12400 Wilshire Blvd., Suite 550, Los Angeles, CA 90025; ☎ 310-820-9807 or 310-820-1898; Fax: 310-820-6357; E-mail: enitla@earthlink.net)

- **Toronto** (175 Bloor St., Suite 907, South Tower Toronto M4W3R8 Ontario; ☎ 416-925-4822; Fax: 416-925-4799; E-mail: enit.canada@ on.aibn.com)

- **London** (1 Princes St., London, WIB 2AY; ☎ 0207-399-3562; Fax: 0207-493-6695; E-mail: italy@italiantouristboard.co.uk)

- **Sydney** (Level 26, 44 Market St. NSW 2000 Sydney; ☎ 02-9262-1666; Fax: 02-9262-1677; E-mail: enitour@ihug.com.au)

In the local tourist offices you can get detailed and up-to-date cultural and practical information, including a calendar of events, info on special exhibits, and hotel information:

- **AAPIT Palermo** (Piazza Castelnuovo 34, 90141 Palermo; ☎ 091-586-122; Fax: 091-582-788; www.palermotourism.com or www. aapit.pa.it)

- **APT Assisi** (Piazza del Comune 27; ☎ 075-812-450; Fax: 075-813-727; www.umbria2000.it).

- **APT Cinque Terre e Golfo dei Poeti** (Viale Mazzini 47, 19100 La Spezia; ☎ 0187-770-900; www.aptcinqueterre.sp.it)

- **APT Firenze** (Via A. Manzoni 16, 50121, Firenze; ☎ 055-23-320; Fax: 055-234-6286; www.firenzeturismo.it)

- ✔ **APT Roma** (Via Parigi 5, 00100 Roma; ☎ 06-3600-4399; www.roma turismo.it).

- ✔ **APT Lucca** (Piazza Santa Maria 35; ☎ 0583-919-931; E-mail: info@ luccaturismo.it).

- ✔ **APT Milano** (Via Marconi 1; ☎ 02-7252-4301; www.milanoinfo tourist.com).

- ✔ **APT Padova** (Galleria Pedrocchi; ☎ 049-876-7927 or 049-875-2077; www.turismopadova.it or turismopadova.tecnoteca.com).

- ✔ **APT Perugia** (Via Mazzini 21; ☎ 075-572-3327; Fax: 075-573-6828; www.umbria2000.it).

- ✔ **APT Pisa** (Via Cammeo 2; ☎ 050-929-777; Fax: 050-929-764; www.pisa.turismo.toscana.it).

- ✔ **APT Siena** (Piazza del Campo 56; ☎ 0577-280-551; Fax: 0577-281-041; www.terresiena.it).

- ✔ **APT Siracusa** (Via San Sebastiano 43; ☎ 0931-481-200 or 0931-481-232; www.apt-siracusa.it).

- ✔ **APT Spoleto** (Piazza della Libertà; ☎ 0743-220-311; www.umbria2000.it).

- ✔ **APT Venezia** (Palazzo Ziani, Fondamenta San Lorenzo, Castello 5050, 30122 Venezia; ☎ 041-529-8700. Fax: 041-523-0399. www.turismovenezia.it).

- ✔ **APT Verona** (Via degli Alpini 9; ☎ 045-806-8680; www.tourism.verona.it).

- ✔ **Gaiole in Chianti** (Via Ricasoli 50; ☎ 0577-749-605; E-mail: staff@ chiantinet.it).

- ✔ **Pro Loco Greve in Chianti** (Via Luca Cino 1; ☎ 055-854-6287).

- ✔ **Pro Loco Napoli** (Via S. Carlo 9; ☎ 081-402-394; www.inaples.it) or also **APT Napoli** (Piazza dei Martiri 58, 80100 Napoli; ☎ 081-405-311).

- ✔ **Pro Loco San Gimignano** (Piazza Duomo 1; ☎ 0577-940-008; Fax: 0577-940-903; www.sangimignano.com).

Other sources of information

If you love Italy or want to prepare for your trip you can browse one of the following magazines: They are the best Italian magazines about Italy in English and are all available from Amazon.com or by subscription, and also from some bookstores in the U.S.

- ✔ **Bell'Italia** (www.bellitalia.it) is a monthly magazine dedicated to discovering the most beautiful natural, cultural, and artistic destinations in Italy, with a gorgeous print quality.

✔ **Events in Italy** (Lungarno Corsini 6, 50123 Firenze; www.events-italy.it) is a beautiful bimonthly magazine in English, focusing on cultural and social events in Italy.

✔ **ItalyItaly Magazine** (Piazza Principe di Piemonte 9, Magliano Romano (RM), 00060 Italy; www.italyitalymagazine.com) is an elegant travel and lifestyle magazine about Italy, available by subscription (contact them directly or contact American Multimedia Corporation; P.O. Box 1255, New York, NY 10116; ☎ 800-984-8259 in the U.S.).

You can also find excellent information on a number of Web sites:

✔ **Ciao Italy** (www.ciao-italy.com) provides links to a variety of other Web sites, from museums to local news.

✔ **Dolce Vita** (www.dolcevita.com) is all about style — as it pertains to fashion, cuisine, design, and travel. Dolce Vita is a good place to stay up-to-date on trends in modern Italian culture.

✔ **In Italy Online** (www.initaly.com) provides information on all sorts of accommodations in Italy (country villas, historic residences, convents, and farmhouses) and includes tips on shopping, dining, driving, and viewing art.

✔ The **Italian Tourist Web Guide** (www.itwg.com) provides new itineraries each month, for art lovers, nature buffs, wine enthusiasts, and other Italophiles. It features a searchable directory of accommodations, transportation tips, and city-specific lists of restaurants and attractions.

✔ **Welcome to Italy** (www.wel.it) is a good source for all kinds of visitor information about Italy, from the cultural (monuments and history) to the practical (hotels and restaurants), with some curiosities thrown into the mix.

Index

• A •

Abbey Theatre Irish Pub (Rome), 177
Academy Gallery
  Florence, 220
  Venice, 9, 363–364
Academy of Fine Arts (Venice), 364
Accademia Nazionale di Santa
    Cecilia, 175
accessibility issues, 89, 338
accommodations
  accessibility issues, 89
  Agrigento, 504–505
  Amalfi Coast, 453–454
  amenities, 80
  Assisi, 315–316
  baby-sitting service, 87–88
  bars in, 234
  bathrooms, 50, 80
  beds, 79
  best, 11
  best rate, finding, 82–83
  best room, getting, 85
  breakfast, buying at hotel, 50
  budget for, 50–51
  Capri, 450
  Chianti region, 274, 276–277
  for children, 55
  Cinque Terre, 264–266
  Florence, 197–205
  hotel chains, 523–524
  Internet access at, 100
  Lucca, 243–244
  Milan, 401, 404
  Naples, 422–424
  package tours and, 69
  Padua, 382–383
  Palermo, 469–471
  Perugia, 308
  Pisa, 251, 253–254
  price of, 81
  rack rate, 51, 82, 119
  reservations, 82–83, 85, 120, 197
  Rome, 119–121, 124–130
  San Gimignano, 299–300
  Siena, 286–288
  Spoleto, 322–324
  Syracuse, 498
  Taormina, 490–492
  types of, 79–80, 85–86
  Venice, 341–343, 346–350
  Verona, 392, 394
  Web sites for, 82, 83–85
ACTV Venice Transportation
    Authority, 339
After Line (Milan), 410
Agostino di Duccio (artist), 312
Agricantus (Palermo), 484
Agrigento, 11, 19, 503–508
agriturismo, 80, 86
Ai Tre Spiedi (Venice), 350–351
Ai Vini d'Oro (Palermo), 485
air tour of Rome, 170
airfare, 54, 64–65, 66
airlines. See also airports
  contact information, 522–523
  European, 66
  flight, finding, 63–64
  in Italy, 71, 332
  package tours and, 70
  to Rome, 105–106
  security requirements, 100–101
airports
  Amerigo Vespucci (Peretola), 190
  Capodichino (Naples), 416
  Ciampino (Rome), 105, 107–108
  Falcone Borsellino (Palermo), 464
  Fiumicino (Rome), 105–106
  Fontanarossa (Taormina), 490
  Galileo Galilei (Pisa), 191, 250
  Internet kiosks at, 98
  Linate (Milan), 400
  Malpensa (Milan), 400
  Marco Polo (Venice), 332
  Valerio Catullo (Verona), 392
Al Carugio (Monterosso), 266–267

Al Marsili (Siena), 288–289
Al Pantalon (Venice), 351
Al Regno di Re Ferdinando II (Rome), 131, 171
Al Ristoro dei Vecchi Macelli (Pisa), 254
Al Sole Palace (Venice), 342
Albergaccio (Castellina), 277
albergo, 80
Albergo Cesàri Hotel (Rome), 120
Albergo Chiusarelli (Siena), 286
Albergo del Chianti (Greve), 274
Albergo del Senato (Rome), 129
Albergo del Sole al Pantheon (Rome), 120
Albergo La Meridiana (Venice), 342
Albergo L'Ancora (Positano), 453
Albergo Ristorante Adriano (Tivoli), 182–183
Albergo Santa Chiara (Rome), 11, 120–121
Alberoni, 372
Albert (Rome), 177
Aldrovandi Palace Hotel (Rome), 121
Alessandra (Florence), 197
Alexander VI (Pope), 218
Alexanderplatz (Rome), 176
Algiubagiò (Venice), 352
Alibi (Rome), 178
Alien (Rome), 177
Alpheus (Rome), 177
Altemps, Marco Sittico (architect), 153–154
Altichiero da Zevio (artist), 387
Amalfi, 456–457
Amalfi Coast, 27, 29, 451
amaro, 23
The Amazons (statues), 147
Amici Miei (Naples), 424
Anacapri, 446
Anatomy Theater (Padua), 390
Angelico, Fra Beato (artist), 159, 218
Angelo Azzurro (Rome), 178
Angelo Rasi (Padua), 383
Anthony of Padua (saint), 387
Antica Besseta (Venice), 351
Antica Drogheria Manganelli, 296–297
Antica Hostaria de' Carrettieri (Tivoli), 183
Antica Ostaria Ruga Rialto (Venice), 351

Antica Trattoria Da Bruno (Pisa), 254
Antica "Trattoria da L'Amelia" (Verona), 394
Antica Trattoria Papei (Siena), 289
Antico Caffè della Pace (Rome), 176
Antico Caffè delle Mura (Lucca), 244
Antico Gatoleto (Venice), 352
Antico Martini (Venice), 351
Antiquarium Forense (Rome), 152
antiques, shopping for, 172, 433
Antonello da Messina (artist), 152, 406, 476, 500
apartment, renting, 85, 86
Ape Piera (Milan), 404–405
APM buses, 307, 314
Apollinare (Spoleto), 325
Apollo and Daphne (Bernini), 152
Appian Way (Rome), 167
Arcangelo (Rome), 131
Arch of Constantine (Rome), 149
Arch of Septimius Severus (Rome), 150
Arch of Titus (Rome), 150, 152
Archaeological Area (Syracuse), 29, 501–502
Arche Scaligere (Verona), 396
architecture, 18–20, 215, 247–248. *See also specific architects*
Arciliuto (Rome), 177
Arco dei Cappuccini (Taormina), 492
Arena di Verona, 35
Ares Ludovisi (statue), 154
Arnolfo di Cambio (artist), 163
Arsenale (Venice), 370
art. *See also specific artists*
   in churches, viewing, 48
   itinerary for viewing, 42–43
   shopping for in Rome, 173
Assisi, 28, 306, 314–321
Assunta (Perugino), 428
ATAC bus system, 117, 118, 168
ATM, 58–59
attractions
   Agrigento, 506–508
   Amalfi Coast, 456–459
   Assisi, 318–320
   best, 12–13
   Capri, 446–449
   Chianti region, 279–282
   Cinque Terre, 268–271
   Lucca, 245–249
   Milan, 405–409

Naples, 427–432
Palermo, 473–481
Perugia, 311–314
Pisa, 256–261
San Gimignano, 302–304
Siena, 291–296
Spoleto, 326–327
Syracuse, 499–502
Taormina, 493–496
Venice, 357–359, 362–372
Verona, 395–399
ATVO bus service, 333

• B •

baby-sitting service, 87–88
Bacchus (Caravaggio), 152
Bagni di Tiberio (Capri), 446
Bandinelli (sculptor), 226
Baptism of Christ (Titian), 147
Baptistry of St. John
    Florence, 215
    Siena, 291–292
Baptistry (Pisa), 257
Bar Caffe Dell'Appia Antica, 167
Bar Pizzeria di Paolo Melinato
    (Venice), 352
bars and pubs
    Florence, 234–235
    Palermo, 484
    Rome, 177
    standing in, 52
    Venice, 377
Basile, Ernesto (architect), 470, 479
Basilica dei Frari (Venice), 359
Basilica della Salute (Venice), 362
Basilica di S. Maria Assunta and
    Cappella di Santa Fina
    (San Gimignano), 303
Basilica di San Francesco (Assisi),
    318–319
Basilica di San Giovanni in Laterano
    (Rome), 143, 146
Basilica di San Lorenzo (Florence),
    213. *See also* Medici Chapels
Basilica di San Marco (Venice), 20
Basilica di San Pietro. *See* St. Peter's
    Basilica
Basilica di San Zeno Maggiore
    (Verona), 396

Basilica di Santa Chiara (Assisi), 319
Basilica di Santa Croce (Florence), 214
Basilica di Santa Maria degli Angeli
    (Assisi), 320
Basilica di Santa Maria Maggiore
    (Rome), 146
Basilica di Santa Maria Novella
    (Florence), 214
Basilica di Sant'Ambrogio (Milan), 408
Basilica di Sant'Anastasia
    (Verona), 399
Basilica di Sant'Antonio (Padua), 387
Basilica of Constantine and Maxentius
    (Rome), 152
Baths of Caracalla, 175, 176
Battista, Gian (architect), 479
beaches
    Capri, 446
    Lido, 372
    Maiori and Minori, 459
    Monterosso al Mare, 269
    Positano, 457
    Vernazza, 270
Bed and Breakfast Il Vigneto
    (Cinque Terre), 264–265
Bell Tower (Florence), 215
Bellettini (Florence), 197
Bellini, Giovanni (artist), 359, 364,
    515, 516
Bellini, Jacopo (artist), 364
Benedizione Pasquale, 34
Benincasa, Caterina (Catherine of
    Siena, saint), 159, 296
Berevino (Naples), 435
Bernini, Gian Lorenzo (sculptor/
    architect)
    altar of, 162
    background, 516–517
    canopy of, 19, 162–163
    fountains of, 158, 160, 161, 182
    restoration of sculpture by, 154
    rococo apartments decorated
        by, 155
    sculpture of, 152, 159, 163, 326
    St. Peter's Square (Rome),
        19, 160–161
    tomb of, 146
Bernini, Pietro (artist), 157
Biblioteca Laurenziana (Florence), 213
Biblioteca Nazionale Marciana
    (Venice), 363

Biennale di Venezia, 36
Big Mama (Rome), 176
Bigallo (Florence), 197–198
bike rental, 167, 248
bistecca alla fiorentina, 21
Blue Grotto (Capri), 447
boat tours
  Capri, 446
  Emerald Grotto, 458–459
  gondola ride (Venice), 13, 339–340
  Ostia Antica, 184
  Padua, 386–387, 390
  Pisa, 261
  Rome, 167, 169
boat travel. *See also* ferry travel
  Cinque Terre, 262, 264
  Venice, 333, 339–340, 362
Boboli (Florence), 198
Boboli Gardens (Florence), 224–225
Bocca della Verità (Rome), 158–159
Boingo wi-fi network, 99
Bolognese (Rome), 132
Bonnano (architect), 259
books, 24–25, 173
Borghese, Scipione (cardinal), 152
Borromini, Francesco (architect), 146
Bosch, Hieronymous (artist), 365
Boscolo Hotel Bellini (Venice), 342–343
Boston Hotel (Venice), 349
Botanical Garden (Padua), 390
Bottega del Moro (Greve), 277
Botticelli, Sandro (artist), 219–220, 408
Brandi (Naples), 425
Brera district (Milan), 409
Brera Gallery, 10, 408
Bric (Rome), 132
Bridge of Sighs (Venice), 366
Bronzino, Il (artist), 225
Bruegel (artist), 429
Brunelleschi, Filippo (architect),
    213, 218–219, 221, 227
Brunello di Montalcino, 21–22
Bruno, Giordano (philosopher), 147
Buca di Sant'Antonio (Lucca), 244–245
Buca Mario dal 1886 (Florence), 206
bucket shops, 64–65
budget for trip, 47–56, 64–65, 76, 522
Buonaito, Andrea di (artist), 214
Burano, 371

bus travel
  to Agrigento, 503
  to Amalfi Coast, 452
  to Assisi, 314
  to Capri, 445–446
  to Chianti region, 274
  to and in Florence, 190, 196
  to and in Italy, 67, 73
  to Lucca, 239
  in Milan, 401
  in Naples, 421
  to Padua, 382
  to and in Palermo, 464, 468–469
  to Perugia, 307
  in Pisa, 251
  to and in Rome, 107, 117, 168
  to Siena, 283
  to Spoleto, 322
  to Syracuse, 497
  to Taormina, 490
  to Tivoli, 179–180
  in Venice, 333

• *C* •

Ca' de Cian (Cinque Terre), 270–271
Ca' d'Oro (Venice), 359, 362
Ca' Foscari (Venice), 362
Ca' Pesaro (Venice), 362
Ca' Rezzonico (Venice), 362–363
Caesar Augustus (emperor), 15–16
cafes
  Naples, 435
  Rome, 176
  Venice, 377
Caffè del Professore (Naples), 435
Caffè della Signoria (Spoleto), 325
Caffè Florian (Venice), 377
Caffè Greco (Rome), 176
Caffè Pedrocchi (Padua), 389
Caffè Quadri (Venice), 377
Caffè Rosati (Rome), 176
Caffè Sant'Eustachio (Rome), 176
calendar of events, 33–37
Calendimaggio, 35, 315
Caligula (ruler), 16
Callixtus III (pope), 149
Calmiere (Verona), 394
cammeo jewel, 13, 434

Campania region, 438
Campanile di San Marco (Venice), 362
Campo de' Fiori (Rome), 112, 147
campsites, 86
Canestra (Caravaggio), 408
Cannaregio neighborhood
   (Venice), 335
Cannon d'Oro (Siena), 287
Canova, Antonio (sculptor),
   152, 359, 363
Cantinella (Capri), 449
Cantinetta Antinori Tornabuoni
   (Florence), 206
Capannina (Ostia), 185
Capitoline Museums (Rome), 147–148
Cappella degli Scrovegni and Musei
   Civici Eremitani (Padua), 28, 388
Cappella del Crocifisso (Amalfi), 456
Cappella di San Pantaleone
   (Ravello), 458
Cappella Palatina (Sicily), 20
Cappella Pazzi (Florence), 214
Capri, 29, 91, 445–450
Capricci di Sicilia (Palermo), 472
car, renting, 49–50, 76, 77–78, 274, 523.
   See also driving
Caravaggio, Michelangelo Merisi da
   (artist)
  Bacchus, 152, 220
  background, 517
  Flagellation, 429
  Fortune Teller, 147
  John the Baptist, 147
  Milan, works in, 408
  Narcissus, 155
  Rome, works in, 156, 163, 165, 169
Caravella (Amalfi), 454
Carnevale (Venice), 34, 341, 372
Carpaccio, Vittore (artist), 363
carry-on luggage, 101
Cartiera Latina, 167
Casa del Brodo (Palermo), 472
Casa del Lago (Florence), 198
Casa Fontana (Milan), 12
Casa Grugno (Taormina), 492
Casa Kolbe (Rome), 121
Casa Natale di Giacomo Puccini
   (Lucca), 249

Casa Natale di Pirandello
   (Agrigento), 506
Casa Professa (Palermo), 474
Casa Valdese (Rome), 121
Casa Veneta (Padua), 383, 386
cash, carrying, 58–59
Casina delle Civitte (Rome), 166
casino (Venice), 372
Casino dei Principi (Rome), 166
Casino del Cavaliere (Florence), 225
Castel dell'Ovo (Naples), 427
Castel Nuovo (Naples), 428
Castel Sant'Angelo (Rome), 11, 148
Castel Sant'Elmo (Naples), 431
Castellina in Chianti, 279
Castello dell'Oscano (Perugia), 308
Castello di Brolio (Radda), 281
Castello di Spaltenna (Gaiole), 274, 276
Castello di Uzzano (Greve), 281
Castello neighborhood (Venice), 335
Castello Sforzesco (Milan), 406
Castelvecchio (Verona), 397
catacombs, 149, 431–432, 480
Caterina de' Medici (queen), 206
Catherine of Siena (saint), 159, 296
Cattedrale (Palermo), 474
Cattedrale di Santa Maria Assunta
  Naples, 428
  Pisa, 257–258
  Torcello, 371
Cavaliere, Antonio (papermaker), 457
Cavolo Nero (Florence), 207
Cellini, Benvenuto (author/artist),
   221, 226
cellphone, using outside U.S., 97–98
Cemetery (Pisa), 257
Cena di Emmaus (Caravaggio), 408
centro (Rome), 172
Centro Congressi (Florence), 194
centro storico
  Florence, 192
  Naples, 418
  Palermo, 465
ceramics, 297, 359
Certosa di San Martino (Naples), 431
Cesarina (Rome), 132
Cetamura (Gaiole in Chianti), 279
Chapel of the Scrovegni (Padua),
   28, 388

Charlemagne (king), 17
Checchino dal 1887 (Rome),
    12, 132–133, 171
Checco er Carettiere (Rome), 133
Chez Moi (Naples), 435
Chiaja Hotel (Naples), 422
Chianti League, 279, 281
Chianti region, 27, 49, 272–283
Chianti wine, 21–22
Chiara d'Assisi (saint), 306, 319, 320
Chiesa and Museo di San Marco
    (Florence), 218
Chiesa di San Nicola (Agrigento), 506
Chiesa di Santa Maria dell'Ammiraglio
    (Palermo), 475
Chiesa di Santa Maria e Donato
    (Murano), 371
Chiesa e Battistero Santi Giovanni e
    Reparata (Lucca), 246
children, 41, 55, 87–88
Chiostro del Paradiso (Amalfi), 456
chocolate, 313, 434
Christmas Blessing, 37
churches, 10, 48, 160, 369. *See also*
    specific churches
Cibreo (Florence), 12, 207
Cimabue (artist), 214, 219, 258,
    318, 388
Cimitero dei Cappuccini/Chiesa
    dell'Immacolata Concezione
    (Rome), 167–168
Cinque Terre, 27, 261–271
Cipriani (Venice), 12
Circo Massimo neighborhood
    (Rome), 112
Circus Maximus (Rome), 154, 156
Ciro a Santa Brigida (Naples), 425
Città Nuovo (Palermo), 467
Civitali, Matteo (artist), 246
Claudius (ruler), 16
climate, 30–33
clothing
    shopping for, 13, 173, 174, 409
    swimsuits, shopping for, 457–458
    for visiting churches, 160, 369
    for visiting Pompeii, 441
Club Picasso (Rome), 178
Cola di Rienzo (Rome), 112

Collegio del Cambia and Collegio
    della Mercanzia (Perugia), 311
Colosseo neighborhood (Rome), 112
Colosseum (Rome), 19, 149–150, 175
Compagnia de Navagazione Ponte San
    Angelo, 167, 169, 184
Compagnia dei Vinattieri (Siena), 289
Compagnia Siciliana Turismo, 69
concerts. *See also* music; opera
    Florence, 234
    Lucca, 248
    Rome, 166, 175
Concorso Ippico Internazionale di
    Roma, 35, 167
consolidators, 64–65
Consorzio Agrario Pane and Co.
    (Florence), 209
Consorzio del Chianti Classico, 281
Constantine (emperor), 17
conversion rate, 2, 3, 56, 58
Cooperativa il Navicello, 261
Cooperativa San Marco/Alilaguna, 333
Coopsub Cinque Terre, 271
Corniglia, 268–269
Coronas Cafè (Florence), 210
Correr Museum (Venice), 363
Corso Umberto I (Taormina), 494
Corte Sconta (Venice), 353
costumes, renting or buying in
    Venice, 372, 376
crafts, shopping for, 173, 434
Cranach, Lucas (artist), 363
Crèche Exhibit, 37
credit cards, 2, 59, 60
credit-reporting agencies, 61
crime
    car theft, 78
    at Fiumicino airport, 106
    in Florence, 231
    in Italy, 521
    in Naples, 436
    in Perugia, 307
    pickpocketing, 60
    in Rome, 116
    in Venice, 334
Croce di Malta (Florence), 198
cruises to Venice, 333. *See also*
    boat tours

cuisine
  Agrigento, 505
  Italy, 20
  Naples, 22
  Rome, 22, 130–131
  Sicily, 22–23, 471–472
  Siena, 288
  Tuscany region, 21, 206
  Umbria region, 21–22
  Venice, 23–24, 350
Cumpà Cosimo (Ravello), 455
Curia (Rome), 150
customs regulations, 518–519
cybercafes, 98

• D •

Da Benito e Gilberto (Rome), 133
Da Gemma (Amalfi), 455
Da Giggetto (Rome), 133
Da Maciste al Salario, Pizza, Vino e
    Cucina (Rome), 134
Da Raffaele (Venice), 353
Daddi, Bernardo (artist), 224
dance clubs
  Florence, 235
  Milan, 410
  Naples, 435
  Rome, 177–178
Dancing Club (Palermo), 484
Dante Alighieri (author), 214, 388,
    397, 514
Dante Taberna de'Gracchi (Rome),
    134–135
day trips
  Capri and Blue Grotto, 445–450
  Mount Vesuvius, 438–440
  Pompeii and Herculaneum, 440–445
  from Rome, 179–185
Dehor (Agrigento), 505
Della Robbia, Luca (artist), 221, 228
Desco (Verona), 395
Desirée (Florence), 199
Devil's Forest Pub (Venice), 377
Dievole, 281
dining. *See* cuisine; restaurants
Dioscuri Bay Palace (Agrigento), 504
disability, traveler with, 89–90, 338

Discoteca Flamingo (Florence), 235
discounts
  on accommodations, 83
  asking for, 55
  on car rental, 77
  Fiesole, 228
  Florence, 196
  Lucca, 245
  Naples, 427
  Padua, 387
  Palermo, 473
  Perugia, 311
  Pisa, 256
  Rome, 142–143
  San Gimignano, 302
  for seniors, 89
  Siena, 291
  Venice, 341–342, 357–358
  Verona, 395–396
Divo (Siena), 289–290
Do Forni (Venice), 353–354
documents for travel, 92–94, 100–101
Domenico di Bartolo (artist), 295
Domus Aurea (Rome), 150
Domus Nova (Verona), 392
Don Camillo (Syracuse), 498–499
Don Chisciotte (Florence), 207–208
Don Salvatore (Naples), 425
Donatello (sculptor)
  background, 514
  David, 221
  Florence, works in, 213, 214, 221, 225
  Padua, works in, 387
  Pisa, works in, 259
  San Giovanni Battista, 359
  Siena, works in, 292
Donna Rosa (Positano), 455
Dorandò (San Gimignano), 300
Dorsoduro neighborhood (Venice), 335
dress. *See* clothing
drinking liquor, 23, 520
driving
  emergency while, 519
  International Driver's License and, 74
  in Italy, 75–76
  motorini and, 76
  parking and, 30
  rules of road for, 74–75

Drunken Ship (Rome), 177
Dublin Pub (Florence), 235
Duccio di Buoninsegna (artist),
      293, 295
Duomo
   Amalfi, 456
   Burano, 371–372
   Fiesole, 228
   Florence, 10, 19, 218–219
   Lucca, 246
   Milan, 10, 407
   Naples, 428
   Ortigia, 500–501
   Padua, 389
   Pisa, 257–258
   Ravello, 458
   Siena, 19, 292
   Spoleto, 19, 326
   Taormina, 494
Duomo (restaurant, Taormina),
      492–493
Duomo di Monreale (Palermo),
      10, 475

• E •

embroidery, shopping for, 232, 297
Emerald Grotto (Amalfi), 458–459
emergency, 96, 520
Enoteca Ristorante Mario
      (Florence), 208
enoteche
   Milan, 410
   Naples, 435
   Palermo, 484–485
   Rome, 135
   Siena, 296–297
Enzo (Siena), 290
Epifania, 33
Eremo delle Carceri (Assisi), 319
Ernst, Max (artist), 366–367
escorted tour, 67–69
Estate Romana, 35
E-tickets, 100–101
Etruscan Chocohotel Perugia
      (Perugia), 308
Etruscans, 15, 153, 279, 312
euro, 2, 3, 56–58

Europeo di Mattozzi (Naples), 426
events, special, 33–37
exchange rate, 2, 3, 56, 58
expressions, Italian, 511–513

• F •

family. See children
Faraglioni (Capri), 447
fashion accessories. See clothing;
      leather goods, shopping for
fast facts
   Amalfi Coast, 459
   Assisi, 321
   Chianti region, 282
   Cinque Terre, 271
   Florence, 235–236
   Lucca, 249
   Milan, 410–411
   Naples, 435–437
   Palermo, 485–486
   Perugia, 313–314
   Pisa, 261
   Rome, 139–141
   San Gimignano, 304–305
   Siena, 297
   Spoleto, 327
   Syracuse, 502–503
   Taormina, 496
   Venice, 378–379
   Verona, 399–400
Fattoria la Parrina (Rome), 131
Feast of St. Francis (Assisi), 315
Federazione Italiana Campeggiatori, 86
Ferragosto, 36
Ferrara (Rome), 135
ferry travel. See also boat travel
   along Amalfi Coast, 452–453
   to Capri, 445
   to and in Italy, 67, 73–74
   to Naples, 416
   to Sicily, 464
   to Taormina, 488
Festa del Redentore, 36
Festa di San Francesco d'Assisi, 37
Festa di San Marco, 34
Festa di Santa Rosalia, 36, 480
Festival di Spoleto, 35, 326

Festival of the Almond Flowers
    (Agrigento), 506–507
festivals, 33–37
Fiaschetteria Toscana (Venice), 354
Fiddler's Elbow (Florence), 235
Fiesole (Florence), 194, 228
figurines, carved, for creche, 13
Florence, 27, 189
Florence Baths (Florence), 235
flying. *See also* airlines; airports
    deep vein thrombosis and, 96
    to Italy, 62–64
Fonclea (Rome), 176–177
Foresteria Baglio della Luna
    (Agrigento), 505
fountains
    of Boboli Gardens, 225
    in Florence, 226
    in Palermo, 475–476
    in Perugia, 312
    in Rome, 157, 158, 161
    in Spoleto, 327
    in Taormina, 494
    of Tivoli, 182
Four Seasons (Milan), 401
Francesca, Piero della (artist), 220
Francesco d'Assisi (saint),
    306, 314, 319
Franchetti, Giorgio (musician/
    art collector), 359
Frederick II (emperor), 473, 474
Fresco Museum (Verona), 399
Fuga, Ferdinando (architect), 146
funicular, 421, 445, 490

• G •

Gaddi, Taddeo (artist), 228
Gagini, Vincenzo and Fazio
    (artists), 474
Gaiole in Chianti, 279
Galilei, Alessandro (architect), 143
Galleria Borghese (Rome), 152–153
Galleria d'Arte Moderna
    (Florence), 224
Galleria del Costume (Florence), 224
Galleria Doria Pamphili (Rome),
    165–166

Galleria Nazionale d'Arte Antica
    (Rome), 155
Galleria Nazionale dell'Umbria
    (Perugia), 311–312
Galleria Regionale di Palazzo Bellomo
    (Syracuse), 500
Galleria Regionale Siciliana
    (Palermo), 476
Galleria Umberto I (Naples), 431
Galleria Vittorio Emanuele II
    (Milan), 409
Gallerie dell'Accademia (Academy
    Gallery, Venice), 9, 363–364
Gallerie Nazionali di Capodimonte
    (Naples), 10, 429
Gambero Rosso
    Cinque Terre, 267
    Syracuse, 499
gardens. *See also* parks
    Florence, 224–225
    Padua, 390
    Taormina, 494
    Tivoli, 181
    Vatican, 169
    Verona, 399
Garga (Florence), 208
Garibaldi, Giuseppe (soldier), 18, 166
gas stations, 76
gay or lesbian traveler
    in Capri, 91
    Florence, bars in, 235
    Milan, bars in, 410
    Naples, bars in, 435
    planning trip, 90–91
    Rome, bars in, 178
Gelateria alla Scala (Rome), 134
Gelateria Carabè (Florence), 210
Gelateria Trevi (Rome), 134
Gelateria Vivoli (Florence), 210
gelato, 20, 134, 210, 352
Gennaro of Naples (saint), 432
Ghiberti, Lorenzo (artist), 215, 221, 292
Ghirlandaio, Domenico (artist)
    Annunciazione, 280
    Florence, works in, 214
    Last Supper, 218
    Madonna with Saints, 246
    Pisa, works in, 259
    St. Zenobius Enthroned, 225

Giacosa (Florence), 234
Giambologna (artist), 226
Gianicolo (Rome), 166
Giannino in San Lorenzo (Florence), 208–209
Giardini Pubblici (Taormina), 494
Giardino Giusti (Verona), 399
Gilda (Rome), 178
Gilli (Florence), 234
Gioco del Ponte (Pisa), 260
Gioco di Calcio Storico Fiorentino, 35
Giolitti (Rome), 134
Giotto di Bondone (artist)
   background, 514
   Bell Tower, 215
   Crucifix, 214
   frescoes of, 28, 318, 388
Giovanni da Verrazzano (Greve), 278
Giovanni di Paolo (artist), 295
Giro di Siena a Cavallo (Siena), 296
glass, Murano, 13, 375–376
G-lounge (Milan), 410
Goes, Hugo van der (artist), 220, 363
gold, shopping for, 232, 233
Goldoni (Florence), 205
gondola ride (Venice), 13, 339–340
Gozzoli, Benozzo (artist), 227
Gran Bretagna (Syracuse), 498
Gran Caffè Gambrinus (Naples), 435
Grand Canal (Venice), 362
Grand Hotel (Syracuse), 498
Grand Hotel Cavour (Florence), 199
Grand Hotel Duomo (Pisa), 251
Grand Hotel et de Milan (Milan), 401, 404
Grand Hotel et des Palmes (Palermo), 469–470
Grand Hotel Parker's (Naples), 422
Grand Hotel Quisisana Capri (Capri), 450
Grand Hotel Santa Lucia (Naples), 423
Grand Hotel Timeo (Taormina), 490
Grand Hotel Villa Igiea (Palermo), 11, 470
Grand Hotel Villa Medici (Florence), 199
Grande Albergo Sole (Palermo), 471
grappa, 23, 296

Greek temple, 504
Greve in Chianti, 279–280
Gritti Palace (Venice), 11, 343
Grotta Azzurra (Capri), 447
Grotta dello Smeraldo (Amalfi), 458–459
Guggenheim, Peggy (art patron), 366
guided tours. *See* tours
Guido da Siena (artist), 295
Guinigi, Ilaria del Caretto (wife of ruler of Lucca), 246
Gustavo (San Gimignano), 301
Gusto (Rome), 135–136, 177
Gutkowski (Syracuse), 498

• *H* •

Hadrian (emperor), 180–181
Hadrian's Villa (Tivoli), 27, 180–181
Harry's Bar (Venice), 377
Hawkwood, John (mercenary), 219
Herculaneum, 29, 442, 443
Hermitage (Florence), 205
history
   of Etruscans, 15, 153, 279, 312
   of Italy, 14–18, 143, 147–148, 153–154
   itinerary for viewing, 42
holidays, 33–37
Holy Roman Empire, 17
Holy See (Rome), 14, 115–116, 160. *See also* Vatican
horse races. *See* Palio delle Contrade
horseback riding in Siena, 296
Hostaria L'Archeologia (Rome), 136
Hostaria Nerone (Rome), 136
Hosteria Da Ganino (Florence), 209
Hotel Antica Torre (Siena), 287
Hotel Art (Rome), 124
Hotel Aurora (Verona), 392
Hotel Barberini (Rome), 129
Hotel Barocco (Rome), 124
Hotel Bernardi-Semenzato (Venice), 343
Hotel Campiello (Venice), 343, 346
Hotel Casci (Florence), 199
Hotel Celio (Rome), 124
Hotel Charleston (Spoleto), 322, 324
Hotel Cipriani (Venice), 346

Hotel Colomba d'Oro (Verona), 392, 394
Hotel Columbia (Rome), 125
Hotel Columbus (Rome), 125
Hotel De La Pace (Florence), 202
Hotel de Russie (Rome), 125
Hotel des Bains (Venice), 346, 372
Hotel Do Pozzi (Venice), 349
Hotel Duomo (Siena), 287
Hotel Emmaus (Rome), 129
Hotel Falier (Venice), 349
Hotel Farnese (Rome), 126
Hotel Flora (Venice), 346–347
Hotel Gabbia D'Oro (Verona), 394
Hotel Garden (Siena), 287–288
Hotel Gattapone (Spoleto), 324
Hotel Geremia (Venice), 350
Hotel Gianni Franzi (Cinque Terre), 265
Hotel Grand'Italia (Padua), 382
Hotel Grifo (Rome), 126
Hotel Homs (Rome), 129
Hotel il Colombaio (Castellina), 276
Hotel Ilaria (Lucca), 243
Hotel La Cisterna (San Gimignano), 299–300
Hotel La Luna (Lucca), 243
Hotel La Rosetta (Perugia), 308
Hotel La Rovere (Rome), 130
Hotel Laurential (Rome), 126
Hotel Le Sirenuse (Positano), 453
Hotel Leonardo (Pisa), 251, 253
Hotel Lidomare (Amalfi), 453
Hotel Luna (Capri), 450
Hotel Luna Convento (Amalfi), 11, 454
Hotel Marconi (Venice), 347
Hotel Marina Piccola (Cinque Terre), 265
Hotel Metropole (Venice), 350
Hotel Miramare (Naples), 423
Hotel Navona (Rome), 126–127
Hotel Olimpia (Venice), 350
Hotel Pantalon (Venice), 347
Hotel Parlamento (Rome), 127
Hotel Pasquale (Cinque Terre), 265–266
Hotel Piazza di Spagna (Rome), 127
Hotel Plaza (Padua), 383
Hotel Porto Roca (Cinque Terre), 266

Hotel Ranieri (Rome), 130
Hotel Relais dell'Orologio (Pisa), 253
Hotel Rex (Naples), 423
Hotel San Cassiano Ca' Favretto (Venice), 347–348
Hotel San Michele (Capri), 450
Hotel Santa Prassede (Rome), 127
Hotel Santo Stefano (Venice), 348
Hotel Scalinata di Spagna (Rome), 128
Hotel Spadari al Duomo (Milan), 404
Hotel Subasio (Assisi), 315
Hotel Turner (Rome), 130
Hotel Umbra (Assisi), 315–316
Hotel Venezia (Rome), 130
Hotel Villa del Parco (Rome), 128
Hotel Villa Steno (Cinque Terre), 266
Hotel Violino d'Oro (Venice), 348
hotels. *See* accommodations; *specific hotels*
House of Romeo (Verona), 398
House of the Merchants (Verona), 397–398
housewares, shopping for, 232–233
humanism, 14, 17

• *1* •

I Candelai (Palermo), 484
I Re di Napoli (Naples), 426
identity theft or fraud, 61
Il Cantastorie (Florence), 209–210
Il Cantinone
  Florence, 210
  Perugia, 310
Il Convento (Naples), 423–424
Il Drappo (Rome), 136
Il Falchetto (Perugia), 310
Il Giglio (Lucca), 245
Il Guelfo Bianco (Florence), 202
illness during trip, 96
Imperial Forums (Rome), 151, 152
insurance, 77–78, 94–95
International Driver's License, 74
Internet
  access to outside U.S., 98–100
  booking flight on, 65–66
  booking hotel on, 82, 83–85
  comparing rental car rates on, 77

Isola Bella, 495
Italian expressions, 511–513
Italian National Tourist Board, 525
itineraries. *See also* tours
  ancient history tour, 42
  for art buffs, 42–43
  for children, 41
  Florence, 229–230
  Naples, 432–433
  one-week, 38–39
  Palermo, 482–483
  Rome, 170–171
  two-week, 39–40
  Venice, 373–374

• J •

Jacopo della Quercia (artist),
  246, 247, 292, 303
Jaragua (Florence), 235
jazz, 36, 176–177
Joli Hotel (Palermo), 470
Jolly Hotel (Palermo), 471
Juliet's House (Verona), 398
Juliet's Tomb (Verona), 399
Julius Caesar (general), 15

• K •

Kandinsky (Palermo), 484
Keats-Shelley House (Rome), 157

• L •

La Calcina (Venice), 348–349
La Cambusa (Palermo), 472
La Cantinella (Naples), 12, 426
La Cantinetta (Spedaluzzo), 278
La Cantinetta del Chianti (Gaiole), 282
La Carabaccia (Florence), 211
La Cuba (Palermo), 481
La Fortezza (Assisi), 316
La Kalsa (Palermo), 467, 476–477
La Mangiatoia (San Gimignano), 302
La Mela (Naples), 435
La Mossacce (Florence), 211

La Pecora Nera (Ricavo), 278
La Pergola (Rome), 12, 137
La Porta del Vesuvio, 439
La Rosetta (Perugia), 310
La Taverna Trevi da Tarquinio
  (Rome), 137
La Veranda (Rome), 137
La Villa Miranda (Radda), 276
La Zisa (Palermo), 477
Labor Day, 32
lace, shopping for in Venice, 376
Lachrymae Christi (wine), 22
language, 511–513, 520
L'Antico Pozzo (San Gimignano), 300
L'Artilafo (Pisa), 255
Lasinio, Carlo (artist), 258
Laurana, Francesco da (architect/
  sculptor), 428, 474, 476
Lazzi, 239
Le Cafe (Venice), 377
Le Cascine (Florence), 205
Le Cinque Statue (Tivoli), 183
Le Logge (Siena), 290
Le Nozze di Cana (Tintoretto), 369
Le Terrazze (San Gimignano), 302
Leaning Tower (Pisa), 259–260
leather goods, shopping for,
  172, 174, 233
Lido (Venice), 335, 372
Ligorio, Pirro (architect), 182
Liguria region (Cinque Terre),
  27, 261–271
limoncello, 457
limousine service, 451–452
linens, shopping for, 232, 297, 483
Lippi, Filippino (artist)
  Annunciation and Saints, 429
  frescoes by, 159, 214
  Lucca, works in, 248
  Madonna col Bambino e santi, 227
Lippi, Filippo (artist), 326
liquor, drinking, 23, 520
Livia's House (Rome), 153–154
lodging. *See* accommodations
Loggia del Consiglio (Verona), 397
Loggiato dei Serviti (Florence),
  11, 202

Lorenzetti, Ambrogio (artist), 293
Lorenzetti, Pietro (artist),
    293, 295, 318
Lucca, 238–239, 242–249
luggage, 76, 95, 101, 341
Luogo di Aimo e Nadia (Milan), 405

• *M* •

Machiavelli Palace (Florence), 203
Mad Jack (Rome), 177
Maderno, Carlo (architect), 161
magazines, 88–90, 526–527
Maggio Musicale Fiorentino,
    35, 227, 234
Maiano, Benedetto da, 303, 430
Maiano, Giuliano, 303
Maiori, 459
Majestic Hotel Toscanelli
    (Padua), 383
Malamocco, 372
Manarola, 269
Mandarini (Palermo), 473
Mantegna, Andrea (artist), 359, 364,
    387, 406, 408
Manzoni (Milan), 404
maps
  Agrigento and Valley of the
    Temples, 508
  Assisi, 317
  Capri, 448
  Chianti region, 275
  Cinque Terre, 263
  Florence, 193, 200–201, 216–217
  Gulf of Naples and Salerno, 417
  Herculaneum, 443
  Lucca, 242
  Milan, 381, 401–402
  Naples, 419
  Padua, 384–385
  Palermo, 466
  Perugia, 309
  Pianura Padana and Milan, 381
  Pisa, 252
  Pompeii, 444
  Rome, 110–111, 122–123, 143–144,
    151, 181

San Gimignano, 301
Siena, 284–285
Spoleto, 323
Taormina, 489
Tuscany and Umbria, 240–241
Vatican, 161, 164
Venice, 337, 344–345, 360–361, 365
Verona, 393
Marina Piccola
  Capri, 447
  Cinque Terre, 267
marine park, 271
Mario's (Florence), 205
markets
  Florence, 231
  Padua, 389
  Palermo, 480–481
  Pisa, 256
  Rome, 147
  Verona, 397
Martini Scala (Venice), 377
Martini, Simone (artist), 292–293, 429
Masaccio (artist), 214, 220, 259, 429
masks and costumes, shopping
    for, 376
Massimo Plaza (Palermo), 470–471
Masuccio, Natale (Jesuit), 474
Mazzarò, 495
Mazzini, Guiseppe (radical), 18
medical issues, 95–96
Medici Chapels (Florence), 215, 218
Medici family
  Basilica di San Lorenzo, 213
  Caterina, 206
  Cosimo, 225, 226–227
  Eleonora, 214
  Lorenzo, 219
  Palazzo Medici Riccardi, 227
  Palazzo Pitti, 224
Medio Evo (Assisi), 316
Meleto (castle), 279
Memmi, Lippo (artist), 303
Menabuoi, Giusto de' (artist), 387, 389
Merchant's Guild (Perugia), 311
Mercure Angioino (Naples), 424
Mergellina neighborhood (Naples), 420
Metro (subway), 116–117, 401, 421

Michelangelo Buonarotti (artist)
background, 515
Cristo Portacroce, 159
David, 220, 221, 226
Florence, works in, 213, 215,
218, 225
Genius of Victory, 225
Holy Family, 220
Madonna of the Steps, 227
Padua, works in, 389
Palazzo Farnese, 19
Pietà, 162, 221
Pieta Rondanini, 406
Rome, works in, 147, 162, 163, 164
Michelozzo (architect), 227, 228
Milan, 21, 381, 400–409
Milanese (Milan), 405
Minori, 459
money, 2, 3, 56–60
Monna Lisa (Florence), 203
Monreale (Palermo), 467
Monte Pellegrino and Santuario de
Santa Rosalia (Palermo), 477–478
Monte Solaro (Capri), 447
Montefioralle, 280
Monterosso al Mare, 269
Mostra delle Azalee, 34
motorini, 61, 76, 116, 119
Mount Etna (Sicily), 29, 495–496
Mount Subasio (Assisi), 319
Mount Vesuvius (Naples), 29, 438–440
movies about Italy, 25
Murano, 335, 371
Murano glass, 13, 375–376
Museo and Basilica di Santa Maria
degli Angeli (Assisi), 320
Museo Antoniano (Padua), 387
Museo Archeologico Nazionale
Naples, 10, 28, 428–429
Spoleto, 327
Museo Archeologico Nazionale del
Umbria (Perugia), 312
Museo Archeologico Regionale
Agrigento, 506
Palermo, 478
Museo Archeologico Regionale Paolo
Orsi (Syracuse), 500
Museo Bandini (Fiesole), 228

Museo Civico
Naples, 428
Torre del Mangia and (Siena),
292–293
Torre Grossa and (San
Gimignano), 303
Museo degli Argenti (Florence), 224
Museo del Duomo (Milan), 407
Museo del Merletto (Burano), 371
Museo della Carta (Amalfi), 457
Museo della Casa Buonarroti
(Florence), 227
Museo delle Porcellane
(Florence), 225
Museo delle Sinopie (Pisa), 258
Museo dell'Opera del Duomo
Florence, 221
Pisa, 258
Siena, 293
Museo dell'Opera di Santa Croce, 214
Museo di Criminologia Medievale
(San Gimignano), 304
Museo di Roma (Rome), 158
Museo di Santa Maria Novella
(Florence), 214
Museo Diocesano di Arte Sacra
(Siena), 295
Museo e Gallerie Nazionali di
Capodimonte (Naples), 10, 429
Museo Ebraico (Venice), 370
Museo Nazionale del Bargello
(Florence), 221
Museo Nazionale delle Paste
Alimentari (Rome), 166
Museo Nazionale di San Martino
(Naples), 431
Museo Nazionale di San Matteo
(Pisa), 259
Museo Nazionale Etrusco di Villa
Giulia (Rome), 153
Museo Nazionale Palazzo Mansi
and Pinacoteca Nazionale
(Lucca), 247
Museo Nazionale Villa Guinigi
(Lucca), 247
Museo Storico Navale (Venice), 370
Museo Teatrale della Scala (Milan),
408–409

Museo Vetrario di Murano, 371
Museum Card (Rome), 143
Museum of the 18th century in
    Venice, 363
museums. *See also specific museums*
    advance ticketing, 52, 143, 213, 357
    best of, 9–10
    Florence, 212
    line, standing in, 17
    Naples, 28
    Rome, 142–143
    ticket, cost of, 52
    Venice, 357
music. *See also* opera
    Festival di Spoleto, 35, 326
    Florence, 35, 234
    jazz, 36, 176–177
    Lucca, 248
    Ravello Festival, 459
    Rome, 166, 175, 176–177

• N •

Naples, 22, 28, 30, 76
Napoleon (ruler), 18, 372
National Archaeological Museum
    Naples, 10, 28, 428–429
    Spoleto, 327
Navigli neighborhood (Milan),
    404, 410
Negroni Florence Bar
    (Florence), 234
neighborhoods
    Florence, 192–194
    Milan, 409–410
    Naples, 418, 420
    Palermo, 465, 467
    Rome, 109, 112–115
    Venice, 334–336
Nero (ruler), 16
New Joli Coeur (Rome), 178
New Year's Eve, 37
nightlife
    budget for, 53
    Florence, 233–235
    Milan, 409–410
    Naples, 434–435

Palermo, 484–485
Rome, 175–178
Venice, 376–377
Nostra Signora della Salute
    (Cinque Terre), 271
Nostra Signora di Montenero
    (Cinque Terre), 270
Nostra Signora di Soviore
    (Cinque Terre), 270
Noto, 497, 502
Novelli, Pietro (artist), 478
Nuovo Clitunno (Spoleto), 324

• O •

OANDA (currency exchange), 58
obelisks in Rome, 156, 158, 161
Olivo del Capri Palace (Capri), 449
Oltrarno neighborhood (Florence), 194
one-week itinerary, 38–39
online check-in, 100
opera
    Lucca, 248
    Milan, 409
    Naples, 434
    Palermo, 484
    Rome, 175, 176
Oratorio (Assisi), 319
Oratorio del Santissimo Rosario di
    San Domenico (Palermo), 478
Oratorio di San Bernardino
    Perugia, 312
    Siena, 295
Oratorio di San Giorgio (Padua), 387
Oratorio di Santa Cita (Palermo), 481
Orsanmichele (Florence), 221, 224
Ortigia, 29, 496, 500–501
Ostaria a la Campana (Venice),
    354–355
Ostaria ai Vetrai (Venice), 354
Osteria alle Testiere (Venice), 355
Osteria da Fiore (Venice), 355
Osteria dal Duca (Verona), 398
Osteria dei Cavalieri (Pisa), 255
Osteria dei Vespri (Palermo), 473
Osteria del Caffè Italiano
    (Florence), 211

Osteria La Chiacchiera (Siena), 290
Osteria La Grotta (Pisa), 255
Osteria Ponte Sisto (Rome), 138
Osteria Speroni (Padua), 386
Osteria Vivaldi (Venice), 355–356
osterie, 22
Ostia Antica, 27, 183–185

• *P* •

package tours, 55, 69–70
packing for trip, 55. *See also* clothing;
    luggage
Padua
    accommodations, 382–383
    attractions, 386–390
    fast facts, 390–391
    map of, 384–385
    overview of, 380, 382
    restaurants, 383, 386
    transportation to, 382
Palatine Hill (Rome), 153–154
Palazzo Abatellis (Palermo), 476
Palazzo Alexander (Lucca), 243
Palazzo Altemps (Rome), 154
Palazzo Barberini (Rome), 155
Palazzo Benci (Florence), 203
Palazzo Braschi (Rome), 158
Palazzo Corvaja (Taormina), 495
Palazzo dei Conservatori Museum
    (Rome), 147
Palazzo dei Normanni and Cappella
    Palatina (Palermo), 478–479
Palazzo dei Priori (Perugia), 312
Palazzo del Bo (Padua), 390
Palazzo del Capitano del Popolo
    (Florence), 221
Palazzo del Freddo di G. Fassi
    (Rome), 134
Palazzo del Governo (Verona), 397
Palazzo del Popolo (San
    Gimignano), 303
Palazzo del Quirnale (Rome), 157
Palazzo della Ragione
    Padua, 389
    Verona, 397
Palazzo Dragoni (Spoleto), 11, 324

Palazzo Ducal (Venice), 364–366
Palazzo Farnese (Rome), 19, 147
Palazzo Massimo alle Terme
    (Rome), 155
Palazzo Medici Riccardi (Florence), 227
Palazzo Mirto (Palermo), 476–477
Palazzo Pitti (Florence), 224–225
Palazzo Ravizza (Siena), 288
Palazzo Reale (Naples), 429–430
palazzo, renting, 86
Palazzo Vecchio (Florence), 225
Palermo, 29, 463–464
Palio delle Contrade (Siena), 12, 36,
    293–294
Pantheon (Rome), 12, 113, 156
Panzano, 280
papal audience, 162
paper, 13, 233, 376, 457
Parco Archeologico della Neopolis
    (Syracuse), 501
Parco della Musica (Rome), 175
Parioli neighborhood (Rome), 113
parks. *See also* gardens
    Mount Vesuvius (Naples), 440
    Naples, 429
    Villa Borghese (Rome), 166–167
Passeggiata delle Mura (Lucca), 248
passport, 92–94
Pasticceria Scaturchio (Naples), 424
Pasticceria Tonolo (Venice), 352
Peggy Guggenheim Collection
    (Venice), 366–367
Pendini (Florence), 203–204
pensione, 80
Pensione Accademia Villa Maravegie
    (Venice), 349
Pensione Svizzera (Taormina), 491
Pentagramma (Spoleto), 325
Per Bacco (Padua), 386
Perchè No (Florence), 210
performing arts. *See also* music; opera
    Florence, 234
    Palermo, 484
    Rome, 175–176
    Venice, 377
Perugia, 28, 306, 307–314
Perugina chocolate factory, 313

Perugino, Il (artist), 220, 311, 428, 429
Phidias (sculptor), 155
phone numbers, 3
Pianta, Francesco (sculptor), 369
Pianura Padana region, 28, 381.
  See also Milan; Padua; Verona
Piazza dei Signori (Verona), 397
Piazza del Campidoglio (Rome), 147
Piazza del Commune and Museo del
  Foro Romano (Assisi), 319–320
Piazza del Duomo (Pisa), 256
Piazza del Popolo (Rome), 113, 156
Piazza del Quirinale (Rome), 157
Piazza della Cisterna (San Gimignano),
  303–304
Piazza della Rotonda (Rome), 156
Piazza della Signoria (Florence), 226
Piazza delle Erbe (Verona), 397–398
Piazza di Siena (Rome), 166–167
Piazza di Spagna (Rome), 113, 157
Piazza Farnese (Rome), 147
Piazza Magione (Palermo), 476
Piazza Marina (Palermo), 476
Piazza Matteotti (Greve in
  Chianti), 280
Piazza Navona (Rome), 113, 157–158
Piazza San Marco (Venice),
  341, 365, 367
Piazza San Pietro (Rome), 160–161
Piazzale Flaminio (Rome), 156
Pica (Rome), 134
Piccolo Hotel Puccini (Lucca), 244
Piccolomini Library (Siena), 292
pickpockets, 60, 116, 231
picnic
  food for, 131, 209, 256
  at Pompeii, 445
  saving money with, 52, 55
Pierreci (ticket broker), 143
Piero della Francesca (artist), 408
Pietro da Cortona (artist), 160
Pinacoteca Ambrosiana (Milan), 408
Pinacoteca Nazionale (Siena), 295
Pinacoteca Nazionale di Brera
  (Milan), 10, 408
Pincio (Rome), 156, 166
Pinturicchio (artist), 158

Pirandello, Luigi (author), 506
Pisa, 27, 250–261
Pisano, Andrea and Nino
  (sculptors), 259
Pisano, Bonanno (artist), 257, 258, 475
Pisano, Giovanni (artist), 257, 258,
  293, 312
Pisano, Nicola (artist), 292, 312
Pizzeria Ivo (Rome), 138
pizzerie, 22
planning trip. *See also* budget for trip;
  itineraries
  escorted tour, 67–69
  package tour, 55, 69–70
  transportation, 49–50
Plastic (Milan), 410
Plaza Hotel Lucchesi (Florence), 204
Pollock, Jackson (artist), 366
Pompeii, 13, 29, 442–445
Pompey (general), 15
Ponte dei Sospiri (Bridge of Sighs,
  Venice), 366
Ponte dell'Accademia (Venice), 362
Ponte di Rialto (Venice), 362, 367
Ponte Scaligero (Verona), 397
Ponte Vecchio (Florence), 226–227, 233
porcelain, shopping for, 13, 434
Porta Pia/Nomentana neighborhood
  (Rome), 113
Porto neighborhood (Palermo), 467
Portrait of a Man (Antonello da
  Messina), 152
Positano, 457–458
pranzo, 51
Prati neighborhood (Rome), 109, 112
Presentation of Mary in the Temple, 37
President Hotel (Palermo), 471
Presidente (Rome), 138
Principe di Villafranca (Palermo), 471
Pub Avalon (San Gimignano), 302
Pub 88 (Palermo), 484
pubs. *See* bars and pubs
Puccini (Lucca), 245
Puccini, Giacomo (composer),
  238, 249
Puppet Theater (Palermo), 484
purse, carrying, 60–61

• Q •

Quirino (Rome), 138

• R •

rack rate, 51, 82, 119
Radda in Chianti, 280–281
Rail Europe Group, 72
Raphael Sanzio (artist), 152, 155, 156, 163, 224
Rassegna del Chianti, 280
Ravello, 458
Ravello Festival, 459
Regata delle Grandi Repubbliche Marinare, 35
Regata Storica, 37
Regata sull'Arno, 33
Relais Santa Chiara (San Gimignano), 300
Relais Santa Croce (Florence), 204
Renaissance, 17–18
renting. *See also* car, renting
  apartment or palazzo, 85, 86
  bike, 167, 248
  cellphone, 97–98
  costumes for Carnevale, 372
  motorini, 119
reservations
  ferry service for car, 74
  Last Supper viewing, 407
  for rooms, 82–83, 85
  Scrovegni Chapel, 388
  Siena, 291
  tickets in advance, 52, 143, 213, 357
  traveling without, 85, 120, 197
Residenza d'epoca Palazzo Fani Mignanelli, 288
resources. *See also* Internet; tourist information; Web sites
  books about Italy, 24–25
  disability, traveler with, 90
  gay or lesbian traveler, 91
  movies about Italy, 25
  senior traveler, 89
  student traveler, 91
  for traveling with children, 88

restaurants. *See also* cuisine
  Agrigento, 505–506
  Amalfi Coast, 454–456
  Assisi, 316, 318
  best, 12
  budget for, 51–52
  Capri, 449–450
  Chianti region, 277–279
  Cinque Terre, 266–268
  cutting costs on, 55
  Florence, 205–212
  Lucca, 244–245
  Milan, 404–405
  Naples, 424–426
  Ostia, 185
  Padua, 383, 386
  Palermo, 471–473
  Perugia, 309–310
  Pisa, 254–256
  Rome, 122–123, 130–139
  San Gimignano, 300–302
  Siena, 288–290
  Spoleto, 324–326
  Syracuse, 498–499
  table-and-bread charge (pane e coperto), 51
  Taormina, 492–493
  Tivoli, 182–183
  Venice, 350–357
  Verona, 394–395
Riomaggiore, 269
Ripa del Sole (Cinque Terre), 267
Risotteria (Milan), 405
Ristorante Buca di San Francesco (Assisi), 316
Ristorante da Lorenzo (Taormina), 493
Ristorante Jonico (Syracuse), 499
Ristorante l'Alta Marea (Cinque Terre), 268
Ristorante Luna Convento (Amalfi), 455–456
Ristorante Luraleo (Taormina), 493
Ristorante Ricchi (Florence), 212
Ristorante Rossini (Syracuse), 499
Riviera di Chiaia neighborhood (Naples), 420
Robusti, Jacopo. *See* Tintoretto, Jacopo (artist)

Rocca (Castellina in Chianti), 279
Rocca Maggiore (Assisi), 320
Rocca Paolina (Perugia), 313
Rocca Pia (Tivoli), 180
Roman Amphitheater (Verona), 398
Roman Empire, 15–16
Roman Forum (Rome), 150–152
Roman National Museum, 142
Roman Summer, 175
Romanesque style, 19, 215, 247–248
Rome
  best ruins in, 10–11
  costs in, 48
  cuisine, 22
  overview of, 27, 30, 109
Rondinella (Capri), 449–450
Rosalia of Palermo (saint), 477, 480
Rose Garden Palace (Rome), 128
rosticcerie, 51
Royal Victoria (Pisa), 253
ruins, best, 10–11

• S •

safety issues. *See also* crime
  airline security, 100–101
  overview of, 521
  pickpockets, 60, 116, 231
Sagra del Mandorlo in Fiore
  (Agrigento), 506–507
Salvi, Nicola (artist), 160
San Damiano, convent of (Assisi), 320
San Domenico Palace Hotel
  (Taormina), 491
San Francesco (Monterosso
  al Mare), 269
San Francesco al Corso (Verona), 399
San Francesco d'Assisi (Palermo), 477
San Frediano (Lucca), 247
San Gimignano, 27, 298–305
San Giovanni (Rome), 114
San Giovanni Battista
  (Riomaggiore), 269
San Giovanni degli Eremiti
  (Palermo), 481
San Leolino (Panzano), 280

San Lorenzo
  Manarola, 269
  Rome, 114
San Ludovico di Tolosa (Martini), 429
San Marco neighborhood (Venice),
  336, 367–369
San Michele in Foro (Lucca), 247–248
San Miniato al Monte (Florence), 228
San Pietro (Corniglia), 268
San Pietro (restaurant, Positano),
  12, 456
San Pietro neighborhood (Rome), 114
San Polo in Rosso, 281
San Polo neighborhood (Venice), 336
San Silvestro (Tivoli), 180
Sangallo, Antonio da, the Younger
  (architect), 313
Sansovino, Jacopo (architect), 363
Santa Agnes (Rome), 158
Santa Chiara (Naples), 430
Santa Croce (Greve), 280
Santa Croce neighborhood
  (Venice), 336
Santa Lucia neighborhood
  (Naples), 420
Santa Margherita di Antiochia
  (Vernazza), 269
Santa Maria Antica (Verona), 396
Santa Maria Assunta (Panzano), 280
Santa Maria d'Aracoeli (Rome), 158
Santa Maria degli Angeli (Rome), 159
Santa Maria del Popolo (Rome), 156
Santa Maria della Salute (Venice), 369
Santa Maria della Scala (Siena), 295
Santa Maria della Spina (Pisa), 259
Santa Maria delle Grazie (Milan), 407
Santa Maria in Cosmedin (Rome),
  158–159
Santa Maria Maggiore (Tivoli), 180
Santa Maria sopra Minerva (Rome),
  19, 159
Santa Reparata (Florence), 219
Santa Teresa (Palermo), 477
Sant'Agostino (San Gimignano), 304
Sant'Anna (Rome), 128–129
Sant'Anna dei Lombardi (Naples), 430
Santo Spirito (Florence), 227

santuari in Cinque Terre, 270
Santuario and Casa di Santa Caterina (Siena), 296
Santuario di San Damiano (Umbria)
Sarto, Andrea del (artist), 224, 247, 258
Savonarola, Girolamo (reformer), 218
Scala Reale, 169
schiacciato, 514
Scoppio del Carro, 34
Scrovegni, Enrico (banker), 388
scuba diving, 271
Scuola di Merletti di Burano (Burano), 371
Scuola Grande di San Rocco (Venice), 369–370
seasons, 31–33
secondi, 2
Segesta, 19, 29
Senatorial Palace (Rome), 148
senior traveler, 88–89
Serpotta, Giacomo (sculptor), 478, 481
servizio incluso, 53
Settembre Lucchese, 37, 248
shoes, shopping for in Rome, 174
shopping. *See also* markets
  budget for, 53
  Chianti region, 282
  Florence, 230–233
  Milan, 409
  Naples, 433–434
  Palermo, 483
  Rome, 171–174
  Siena, 296–297
  for souvenirs, 13
  Venice, 374–376
Sicily
  Agrigento, 11, 19, 503–508
  architecture, 18–19, 20
  cuisine, 22–23
  Ortigia, 29, 496, 500–501
  overview of, 29, 463
  Palermo, 29, 463–464
  Syracuse, 29, 496–503
  Taormina, 29, 488–496
sickness during trip, 96

Siena. *See also* Palio delle Contrade
  accommodations, 286–288
  attractions, 12, 291–296
  cuisine, 21
  fast facts, 297
  map of, 284–285
  overview of, 27
  restaurants, 288–290
  shopping, 296–297
  transportation, 283, 286
sightseeing. *See* attractions
signs, traffic, 74–75
Silver Stud (Florence), 235
Sistine Chapel (Rome), 9, 163–164
smoking, 521
snorkeling, 271
Sole sulla Vecia Cavana (Venice), 356
Sora Lella (Rome), 139
souvenirs, best, 13
Spaltenna, 279
Spanish Steps (Rome), 157
Spoleto
  Duomo, 19
  festival in, 35, 326
  overview of, 28, 306, 321–327
St. Mark's Basilica (Venice), 367–369
St. Mark's Square (Piazza San Marco, Venice), 341, 365, 367
St. Peter's Basilica (Rome)
  architectural style of, 19
  neighborhood around, 114
  visiting, 10, 161, 162–163
St. Peter's Square (Rome), 160–161
Stadium of Diocletian (Rome), 157–158
standing
  in bar or cafè, 52
  in line at museum, 17
stationery and pens, shopping for, 174, 233
Stazione Santa Maria Novella (Florence), 191
Stazione Termini (Rome), 107, 108, 114
stolen item, 60–61, 93
student traveler, 91
Syracuse, 29, 496–503

• T •

Tabasco (Florence), 235
Taormina, 29, 488–496
Taormina Arte festival, 495
Tartufo (Spoleto), 12, 325–326
Taverna del Campo (Rome), 177
Taverna (Perugia), 310
tax, value-added (IVA), 60
taxi
  Florence, 190
  gypsy or pirate, 107, 108, 341, 422
  Lucca, 242
  Naples, 421–422
  Palermo, 464, 469
  Pisa, 250, 251
  Rome, 106–107, 108, 118
  Syracuse, 499–500
  water, Venice, 333, 340–341
Tazza d'Oro (Rome), 176
Teatro Arte Cuticchio (Palermo), 484
Teatro Comunale (Florence), 194, 234
Teatro della Scala (Milan), 408–409
Teatro dell'Opera di Roma, 175, 176
Teatro di Pompeo (Rome), 129
Teatro Goldoni (Venice), 377
Teatro Greco (Syracuse), 501, 502
Teatro Greco-Romano (Taormina),
    13, 495
Teatro La Fenice (Venice), 377
Teatro Marcello (Rome), 114
Teatro Massimo (Palermo), 479, 484
Teatro Politeama Garibaldi
    (Palermo), 484
Teatro Romano
  Fiesole, 228
  Ostia Antica, 183
  Spoleto, 327
Teatro San Carlo (Naples), 431
telephone calls, 521
temperature, average, 31
Tempio della Sibilla (Tivoli), 180
Temple of Antoninus and Faustina
    (Rome), 150
Temple of Jove or Zeus (Agrigento),
    11, 507

Temple of Minerva (Assisi), 319–320
Temple of Saturn (Rome), 152
Temple of the Dioscuri (Rome), 152
Terme di Diocleziano e Aula
    Ottagonale (Rome), 159
Testaccio neighborhood (Rome),
    114, 171, 178
theater in Rome, 175, 176
thrombosis, deep vein, and
    flying, 96
Tiber river, 167, 306
Tiberius (ruler), 16
tickets. *See also* discounts
  for papal audience, 162
  reserving in advance, 52, 143,
    213, 357
Tiepolo, Giovanni Battista
    (artist), 397
Tintoretto, Jacopo (artist)
  background, 516
  Gesù al Tempio, 407
  Venice, works in, 363, 364, 365, 369
  Verona, works in, 397
tipping, 53–54, 522
Titian (Tiziano Vecellio, artist)
  Annonciation, 429
  background, 516
  Padua, works in, 387
  Rome, works in, 147, 152, 155
  Venice, works in, 359, 363, 369
Tivoli, 179–183
Tomba di Cecilia Metella
    (Rome), 167
Tongue (Naples), 435
Torcello, 371
Toro Romano (sculpture), 429
Torre dei Lamberti (Verona), 397
Torre del Mangia (Siena), 293
Torre di Pisa, 259–260
Torre di Santa Maria (Pisa), 260
Torre Guelfa (Florence), 205
Torre Guelfa della Cittadella Vecchia
    (Pisa), 260
Torre Guinigi and Torre delle Ore
    (Lucca), 248–249

tourist information. *See also*
  Web sites
  Chianti region, 273
  Fiumicino airport, 106
  Florence, 194
  international, 525
  Italian National Tourist Board, 525
  local, 525–526
  Naples, 420
  Palermo, 467–468
  Rome, 115–116
  Tivoli, 180
  Vatican, 160
  Venice, 336
tours. *See also* boat tours; itineraries;
  walking
  Agrigento, 504
  Assisi, 318
  Chianti region, 273
  escorted, 67–69
  Florence, 228–229
  Lucca, 245
  Milan, 405–406
  Mount Vesuvius, 439
  Naples, 432
  Ostia Antica, 184
  package, 55, 69–70
  Padua, 386–387
  Palermo, 481–482
  Pisa, 256
  Pompeii and Herculaneum, 441
  Rome, 168–170
  Sicily, 464
  Siena, 291, 296
  specialty, 67
  Taormina, 493–494
  Tivoli, 180
  Venice, 366, 368, 373
  Verona, 395
traghetto in Venice, 340
train travel
  to Agrigento, 503
  to Amalfi Coast, 452
  to Assisi, 314
  in Cinque Terre, 262, 264
  to Florence, 191
  to and in Italy, 67, 72–73
  to Lucca, 239
  to Milan, 400–401

  to Mount Vesuvius, 439
  to Naples, 416
  to Ostia Antica, 184
  to Padua, 382
  to Perugia, 307
  to Pisa, 250
  to Pompeii and Herculaneum,
    440–441
  to Rome, 107, 108
  to San Gimignano, 299
  to Sicily, 465
  to Siena, 283
  to Spoleto, 322
  to Syracuse, 497
  to Taormina, 490
  to Venice, 333
  to Verona, 391–392
tram lines, 117, 401, 421
transportation. *See also* airlines;
    bus travel; taxi; train travel
  accessibility issues, 89
  budget for, 49–50
  ferry, 67, 73–74
  funicular, 421, 445, 490
  to and in Italy, 62–67, 71–74
  Metro (subway), 116–117, 401, 421
  public, 55, 107, 118
  vaporetto (Venice), 339, 362
Transportation Security
    Administration, 101
Trastevere (Rome), 114
Trattoria alla Madonna (Venice), 356
Trattoria Boboli (Florence), 212
Trattoria da Romano (Venice), 356
Trattoria dei Templi (Agrigento),
    505–506
Trattoria di Giovanni Rana-Tre Corone
    (Verona), 395
Trattoria Gianni Franzi (Cinque
    Terre), 268
Trattoria San Omobono (Pisa),
    255–256
trattorie, 51
travel insurance, 94–95
Travel Sentry locks, 101
travel times between cities, 72
traveler's checks, 59–60
Tre Scalini (Rome), 176
Trenitalia, 72, 108

Treno natura (Siena), 296
Trevi Fountain (Rome), 160
Trevi neighborhood (Rome), 115
Trinità del Monte church (Rome), 157
trip-cancellation insurance, 94–95
Tristano, Giovanni (architect), 474
Triumphal Arch of Alfonso I of
    Aragona (Naples), 428
Trono Ludovisi (sculpture), 154
Tuscany region. *See also* Siena
    architecture, 19
    Chianti region, 27, 49, 272–283
    Cinque Terre, 27, 261–271
    climate, 28
    cuisine, 21, 206
    Florence, 27, 189
    Lucca, 238–239, 242–249
    overview of, 27, 30, 238, 272–273
    Pisa, 27, 250–261
    San Gimignano, 27, 298–305
Tutti Santi, 33
two-week itinerary, 39–40

• *U* •

Uccello, Paolo (artist), 214, 219
Uffizi Gallery (Florence), 9, 219–220,
    222–224
Umbra (Assisi), 318
Umbria Jazz Festival, 36
Umbria region. *See also* Spoleto
    architecture, 19
    Assisi, 28, 306, 314–321
    cuisine, 21–22
    overview of, 28, 306
    Perugia, 28, 306, 307–314
Universale (Florence), 235
Urna degli Innocenti (jewelry), 408

• *V* •

Valle dei Mulini (Amalfi), 457
Valley of the Temples (Agrigento),
    11, 503, 507–508
value-added tax (IVA), 60
van Dyck, Anthony (artist), 478
Vangi, Giuliano (artist), 389
vaporetto (Venice), 339, 362

Vasari, Giorgio (artist/author),
    219, 226–227, 430
Vatican (Rome), 115–116, 142, 160–165.
    See also St. Peter's Basilica
Vatican Museums (Rome), 9, 163–165
Veanard, Claude (sculptor), 182
Vecchia Pineta (Ostia), 185
Vecchietta, Lorenzo (artist), 295
Venerdì Santo, 34
Venetian Ghetto (Venice), 370
Veneziano, Paolo (artist), 364
Venice
    acqua alta, 339
    architecture of, 20
    as base, 30
    Carnevale, 34, 341, 372
    cuisine, 23–24
    history of, 331–332
    overview of, 28
    for wheelchair-bound traveler, 338
Venice International Film Festival, 36
Vernaccia di San Gimignano, 22
Vernazza, 269
Vernifer (Gaiole), 282
Verona, 28, 381, 392–400
Verona, Giovanni da (artist), 430
Veronese, Paolo (artist), 363, 364, 397
Vertine, 279
Via San Matteo (San Gimignano), 304
Via Veneto (Rome), 115
Viareggio, 34
Villa Adriana (Tivoli), 11, 180–181
Villa Aurora (Florence), 204
Villa Borghese neighborhood
    (Rome), 113, 166–167
Villa Cimbrone (Ravello), 454, 458
Villa dei Quinitili (Rome), 167
Villa d'Este (Tivoli), 27, 181
Villa Diodoro (Taormina), 491
Villa Gregoriana (Tivoli), 182
Villa Jovis (Capri), 447, 449
Villa Kinzica (Pisa), 253–254
Villa Malfitano (Palermo), 479–480
Villa Miranda (Radda), 278–279
Villa Niscemi (Palermo), 484
Villa Rosa di Boscorotondo
    (Panzano), 276–277
Villa Sant'Andrea (Taormina), 491–492

Villaggio Albergo Tenuta di Ricavo (Ricavo), 276
Vinci, Leonardo da (artist)
  background, 515, 516
  Florence, works in, 220
  Milan, works in, 407, 408
  Rome, works in, 163
Vineria (Rome), 177
Vino Vino (Venice), 357, 377
Virtual Pompei, 441
vocabulary, 511–513
Vogalonga, 35
volcanos, 29, 438–440, 495–496
Vomero neighborhood (Naples), 418, 420

• *W* •

walking
  Cinque Terre, 264, 268, 269, 270
  Florence, 195, 228–229
  historic areas, 56
  Milan, 406
  Naples, 420
  Padua, 386
  Palermo, 468
  Pisa, 251
  Positano, 457
  Rome, 116, 117, 169
  Siena, 286
  Spoleto, 322
  Venice, 338–339
wallet, carrying, 60–61
water taxi in Venice, 333, 340–341
weather, 30–33
Web sites
  airlines, 63, 522–523
  apartment, renting, 86
  ATM networks, 58
  bus, 67
  car rental, 77, 78, 523
  cellphone rental, 97
  CIT Tours, 73
  consolidators, 65
  credit-reporting agencies, 61

currency information, 57
cybercafes, 98
ferry, 67
Florence, 236
FS (Ferrovia dello Stato), 72
hotels, 82, 83–85, 523–524
insurance, 95
Italy, 527
magazines, 526–527
Medic Alert Identification Tag, 96
medical issues, 96
package tours, 70
Rail Europe Group, 72
regional airlines, 71
specialty tours, 67
tourist information, 525–526
Transportation Security Administration, 101
travel and air fare, 65–66
U.S. State Department, 92
weather, 522
wi-fi hotspots, 99
Westin Excelsior (Florence), 205
wheelchair-bound visitor to Venice, 338
Wi-fi (wireless fidelity), 99
wine. *See also* enoteche
  Chianti Classico, 21–22, 281
  festivals, 280
  Rome, 22, 174
  Sicily, 23
  Siena, 296–297
  Tears of Christ, 22
woman traveling alone, 521
World War I and II, 18

• *Y* •

Yogobar (Rome), 134

• *Z* •

Zeno of Padua (saint), 396
Zuccari, Frederico (artist), 219

USINESS, CAREERS & PERSONAL FINANCE

Grant Writing

Home Buying

0-7645-5307-0   0-7645-5331-3 *†

Also available:
- Accounting For Dummies †
  0-7645-5314-3
- Business Plans Kit For Dummies †
  0-7645-5365-8
- Cover Letters For Dummies
  0-7645-5224-4
- Frugal Living For Dummies
  0-7645-5403-4
- Leadership For Dummies
  0-7645-5176-0
- Managing For Dummies
  0-7645-1771-6

- Marketing For Dummies
  0-7645-5600-2
- Personal Finance For Dummies *
  0-7645-2590-5
- Project Management
  For Dummies
  0-7645-5283-X
- Resumes For Dummies †
  0-7645-5471-9
- Selling For Dummies
  0-7645-5363-1
- Small Business Kit For Dummies *†
  0-7645-5093-4

OME & BUSINESS COMPUTER BASICS

Windows XP

Excel 2003

0-7645-4074-2   0-7645-3758-X

Also available:
- ACT! 6 For Dummies
  0-7645-2645-6
- iLife '04 All-in-One Desk Reference
  For Dummies
  0-7645-7347-0
- iPAQ For Dummies
  0-7645-6769-1
- Mac OS X Panther Timesaving
  Techniques For Dummies
  0-7645-5812-9
- Macs For Dummies
  0-7645-5656-8
- Microsoft Money 2004 For Dummies
  0-7645-4195-1

- Office 2003 All-in-One Desk
  Reference For Dummies
  0-7645-3883-7
- Outlook 2003 For Dummies
  0-7645-3759-8
- PCs For Dummies
  0-7645-4074-2
- TiVo For Dummies
  0-7645-6923-6
- Upgrading and Fixing PCs
  For Dummies
  0-7645-1665-5
- Windows XP Timesaving
  Techniques For Dummies
  0-7645-3748-2

OOD, HOME, GARDEN, HOBBIES, MUSIC & PETS

Feng Shui

Poker

0-7645-5295-3   0-7645-5232-5

Also available:
- Bass Guitar For Dummies
  0-7645-2487-9
- Diabetes Cookbook For Dummies
  0-7645-5230-9
- Gardening For Dummies *
  0-7645-5130-2
- Guitar For Dummies
  0-7645-5106-X
- Holiday Decorating For Dummies
  0-7645-2570-0
- Home Improvement All-in-One
  For Dummies
  0-7645-5680-0

- Knitting For Dummies
  0-7645-5395-X
- Piano For Dummies
  0-7645-5105-1
- Puppies For Dummies
  0-7645-5255-4
- Scrapbooking For Dummies
  0-7645-7208-3
- Senior Dogs For Dummies
  0-7645-5818-8
- Singing For Dummies
  0-7645-2475-5
- 30-Minute Meals For Dummies
  0-7645-2589-1

TERNET & DIGITAL MEDIA

Digital Photography

Starting an eBay Business

-7645-1664-7   0-7645-6924-4

Also available:
- 2005 Online Shopping Directory
  For Dummies
  0-7645-7495-7
- CD & DVD Recording For Dummies
  0-7645-5956-7
- eBay For Dummies
  0-7645-5654-1
- Fighting Spam For Dummies
  0-7645-5965-6
- Genealogy Online For Dummies
  0-7645-5964-8
- Google For Dummies
  0-7645-4420-9

- Home Recording For Musicians
  For Dummies
  0-7645-1634-5
- The Internet For Dummies
  0-7645-4173-0
- iPod & iTunes For Dummies
  0-7645-7772-7
- Preventing Identity Theft
  For Dummies
  0-7645-7336-5
- Pro Tools All-in-One Desk
  Reference For Dummies
  0-7645-5714-9
- Roxio Easy Media Creator
  For Dummies
  0-7645-7131-1

eparate Canadian edition also available
eparate U.K. edition also available
ailable wherever books are sold. For more information or to order direct: U.S. customers
t www.dummies.com or call 1-877-762-2974.
. customers visit www.wileyeurope.com or call 0800 243407. Canadian customers visit
rw.wiley.ca or call 1-800-567-4797.

SPORTS, FITNESS, PARENTING, RELIGION & SPIRITUALITY

0-7645-5146-9   0-7645-5418-2

Also available:
- Adoption For Dummies
  0-7645-5488-3
- Basketball For Dummies
  0-7645-5248-1
- The Bible For Dummies
  0-7645-5296-1
- Buddhism For Dummies
  0-7645-5359-3
- Catholicism For Dummies
  0-7645-5391-7
- Hockey For Dummies
  0-7645-5228-7

- Judaism For Dummies
  0-7645-5299-6
- Martial Arts For Dummies
  0-7645-5358-5
- Pilates For Dummies
  0-7645-5397-6
- Religion For Dummies
  0-7645-5264-3
- Teaching Kids to Read
  For Dummies
  0-7645-4043-2
- Weight Training For Dummies
  0-7645-5168-X
- Yoga For Dummies
  0-7645-5117-5

TRAVEL

0-7645-5438-7   0-7645-5453-0

Also available:
- Alaska For Dummies
  0-7645-1761-9
- Arizona For Dummies
  0-7645-6938-4
- Cancún and the Yucatán
  For Dummies
  0-7645-2437-2
- Cruise Vacations For Dummies
  0-7645-6941-4
- Europe For Dummies
  0-7645-5456-5
- Ireland For Dummies
  0-7645-5455-7

- Las Vegas For Dummies
  0-7645-5448-4
- London For Dummies
  0-7645-4277-X
- New York City For Dummies
  0-7645-6945-7
- Paris For Dummies
  0-7645-5494-8
- RV Vacations For Dummies
  0-7645-5443-3
- Walt Disney World & Orlando
  For Dummies
  0-7645-6943-0

GRAPHICS, DESIGN & WEB DEVELOPMENT

0-7645-4345-8   0-7645-5589-8

Also available:
- Adobe Acrobat 6 PDF
  For Dummies
  0-7645-3760-1
- Building a Web Site For Dummies
  0-7645-7144-3
- Dreamweaver MX 2004
  For Dummies
  0-7645-4342-3
- FrontPage 2003 For Dummies
  0-7645-3882-9
- HTML 4 For Dummies
  0-7645-1995-6
- Illustrator cs For Dummies
  0-7645-4084-X

- Macromedia Flash MX 2004
  For Dummies
  0-7645-4358-X
- Photoshop 7 All-in-One Desk
  Reference For Dummies
  0-7645-1667-1
- Photoshop cs Timesaving
  Techniques For Dummies
  0-7645-6782-9
- PHP 5 For Dummies
  0-7645-4166-8
- PowerPoint 2003 For Dummies
  0-7645-3908-6
- QuarkXPress 6 For Dummies
  0-7645-2593-X

NETWORKING, SECURITY, PROGRAMMING & DATABASES

0-7645-6852-3   0-7645-5784-X

Also available:
- A+ Certification For Dummies
  0-7645-4187-0
- Access 2003 All-in-One Desk
  Reference For Dummies
  0-7645-3988-4
- Beginning Programming
  For Dummies
  0-7645-4997-9
- C For Dummies
  0-7645-7068-4
- Firewalls For Dummies
  0-7645-4048-3
- Home Networking For Dummies
  0-7645-42796

- Network Security For Dummies
  0-7645-1679-5
- Networking For Dummies
  0-7645-1677-9
- TCP/IP For Dummies
  0-7645-1760-0
- VBA For Dummies
  0-7645-3989-2
- Wireless All In-One Desk Reference
  For Dummies
  0-7645-7496-5
- Wireless Home Networking
  For Dummies
  0-7645-3910-8